Child Development: Learning and Cognition

Child Development: Learning and Cognition

Edited by
Keith Reece

STATES
ACADEMIC PRESS
www.statesacademicpress.com

Published by States Academic Press,
109 South 5th Street,
Brooklyn, NY 11249, USA

ISBN: 978-1-63989-103-0

Cataloging-in-Publication Data

Child development : learning and cognition / edited by Keith Reece.
p. cm.
Includes bibliographical references and index.
ISBN 978-1-63989-103-0
1. Child development. 2. Child psychology. 3. Cognition in children.
4. Learning. I. Reece, Keith.
BF721.C45 2021
155.4--dc23

For information on all States Academic Press publications
visit our website at www.statesacademicpress.com

STATES
ACADEMIC PRESS

Contents

Preface

The sequence of physical, language, thought and emotional changes that occur in a child from birth to the beginning of adulthood is referred to as child development. During this process, a child begins gaining independence of decision making and performing activities. Child development is strongly determined by genetic factors and events during prenatal life. It is also regulated by environmental factors and the learning capacity of the child. Targeted therapeutic intervention and the right home-based practices can actively enhance child development. It covers the full scope of skills that a child masters over their life span including cognitive development, social interaction and emotional regulation, speech and language, physical skills, and sensory awareness. This book explores all the important aspects of child development in the present day scenario. It will also provide interesting topics for research which interested readers can take up. This book is appropriate for students seeking detailed information in this area as well as for experts.

This book has been the outcome of endless efforts put in by authors and researchers on various issues and topics within the field. The book is a comprehensive collection of significant researches that are addressed in a variety of chapters. It will surely enhance the knowledge of the field among readers across the globe.

It gives us an immense pleasure to thank our researchers and authors for their efforts to submit their piece of writing before the deadlines. Finally in the end, I would like to thank my family and colleagues who have been a great source of inspiration and support.

Editor

1

How do Maternal Subclinical Symptoms Influence Infant Motor Development during the First Year of Life?

Giulia Piallini[1], Stefania Brunoro[1], Chiara Fenocchio[1], Costanza Marini[1], Alessandra Simonelli[1], Marina Biancotto[2] and Stefania Zoia[2]*

[1] Department of Developmental Psychology and Socialization, University of Padua, Padua, Italy, [2] Struttura Complessa Tutela Salute Bambini Adolescenti Donne Famiglia, Azienda Sanitaria Universitaria Integrata di Trieste, Trieste, Italy

Edited by:
Petra Hauf,
St. Francis Xavier University, Canada

Reviewed by:
Chris Lange-Küttner,
London Metropolitan University, UK
Vrinda Kalia,
Miami University, USA

***Correspondence:**
Alessandra Simonelli
alessandra.simonelli@unipd.it

An unavoidable reciprocal influence characterizes the mother-child dyad. Within this relationship, the presence of depression, somatization, hostility, paranoid ideation, and interpersonal sensitivity symptoms at a subclinical level and their possible input on infant motor competences has not been yet considered. Bearing in mind that motor abilities represent not only an indicator of the infant's health-status, but also the principal field to infer his/her needs, feelings and intentions, in this study the quality of infants' movements were assessed and analyzed in relationship with the maternal attitudes. The aim of this research was to investigate if/how maternal symptomatology may pilot infant's motor development during his/her first year of life by observing the characteristics of motor development in infants aged 0–11 months. Participants included 123 mothers and their infants (0–11 months-old). Mothers' symptomatology was screened with the Symptom Checklist-90-Revised (SCL-90-R), while infants were tested with the Peabody Developmental Motor Scale-Second Edition. All dyads belonged to a non-clinical population, however, on the basis of SCL-90-R scores, the mothers' sample was divided into two groups: normative and subclinical. Descriptive, *t*-test, correlational analysis between PDMS-2 scores and SCL-90-R results are reported, as well as regression models results. Both positive and negative correlations were found between maternal perceived symptomatology, *Somatization* (SOM), *Interpersonal Sensitivity* (IS), *Depression* (DEP), *Hostility* (HOS), and *Paranoid Ideation* (PAR) and infants' motor abilities. These results were further verified by applying regression models to predict the infant's motor outcomes on the basis of babies' age and maternal status. The presence of positive symptoms in the SCL-90-R questionnaire (subclinical group) predicted good visual-motor integration and stationary competences in the babies. In particular, depressive and hostility feelings in mothers seemed to induce an infant motor behavior characterized by a major control of the environmental space. When mothers perceived a higher level of hostility and somatization, their babies showed difficulties in sharing action space, such as required in the development of stationary positions and grasping abilities. In a completely different way, when infants can rely on a mother with low-perceived symptoms (normative group) his/her motor performances develop with a higher degree of freedom/independence. These findings suggest, for the first time, that even in a non-clinical sample, mother's perceived-symptoms can produce important consequences not in infant motor development as a whole, but in some specific areas, contributing to shape the infant's motor ability and his/her capability to act in the world.

Keywords: maternal depressive symptomatology, infant motor development, PDMS-2, SCL-90-R, fine motor abilities, gross motor abilities

INTRODUCTION

The birth of a child entails a total restructuration of the identity of the new parents, as well as the emergence of the new role of parenthood within the couple. In fact, during pregnancy the process of transition to parenthood emerges exclusively on an imaginative level as the couple begins to compare the idea of becoming parents and co-parents. However, the concrete access to parenthood takes place at the time of baby's birth (Von Klitzing et al., 1999; Carneiro et al., 2006; Simonelli et al., 2012). Given the amount and depth of changes that occur during pregnancy and the postpartum period, it is not surprising that many women find it difficult to deal with this situation. As much as they develop depressive problems, these may have severe effects not just on the mothers, but also on the children and on the family systems themselves. Many studies show that depression can interfere with parenting skills and with the establishment of an attachment bond (Gotlib et al., 1991). Parents play an essential role in the survival and development of the infant and the dyadic relation between parent and infant represents the first, and most important, interaction for the baby. Appropriate interactions with the caregiver are fundamental for the development of the infant and the structure underlying neural mechanisms responsible for the infant's typical or atypical development. Being a parent and adequately responding to the offspring necessities, requires a huge amount of cognitive resources and self-awareness, allowing parents to implement suitable care-giving behaviors (e.g., to consistently respond or to promote baby's actions). In case of parental psychopathology (e.g., depression, post-partum depression, etc.), these abilities may result substantially compromised and the mother may not be able to meet the child's needs functionally, leading to consequences on the infant's development and wellbeing, as well as on the establishment of a healthy and functional parent-infant relationship. During the first months of the newborns' life, many women present the risk of developing a depressive disorder which can affect maternal responsiveness, leading to short and long term consequences on child development (Milgrom et al., 2004), on maternal functioning and on the early mother-child interactions (Parolin and Sudati, 2014).

Postpartum depression negatively affects woman's ability to take on the maternal role and can lead to difficulties in caregiving toward the child, feelings of guilt and poor self-efficacy (Monti and Agostini, 2006). As a consequence, an impoverishment of the dyadic mother-child relationship occurs, since a depressed mother may not be tuned to the child's needs and may be unable to respond appropriately (Parolin and Sudati, 2014). The higher risks facing the child consist in the impairment of cognitive and motor development, poor ability of self-regulation, low self-esteem and behavioral problems (Goodman and Gotlib, 1999; Field, 2010).

In a study conducted in the Barbados Island, Galler et al. (2000) found significant relationships between maternal moods and infant cognitive development; in particular, they found an association between maternal depression and low motor performance in 6 month old infants, without establishing a causal relationship between these factors. Maternal moods at 6 months were associated with lower scores in motor development of the children at the same age; in particular, the children of mothers who reported less confidence, greater hopelessness and lower pleasure in being with the baby, obtained lower scores in the evaluation of motor development (Galler et al., 2000). Although no independent relationships emerged between feeding practices and infant cognitive development, the combination of diminished infant feeding intensity and maternal depression predicted delays in the infant's social development. With their findings, Galler and colleagues demonstrated the need to monitor maternal moods during the postpartum period, in order to relate health programs to infant cognitive development. In the same way, using the Bayley Scales (Bayley, 1969), Lyons-Ruth et al. (1986) found that 12 month old children of depressed mothers were more likely to exhibit unstable, avoidant attachment behaviors and slowed development, in particular lower levels of motor development than children of non-depressed mothers (Lyons-Ruth et al., 1986; Murray and Cooper, 1997).

Moreover, Cornish et al. (2005) examined the impact of brief and chronic depression in a normative sample, finding an association between chronic maternal depression and lower infant cognitive and psychomotor development, with the effects being similar for boys and girls; on the contrary, brief depression did not significantly impact infant performance (Cornish et al., 2005). Nasreen et al. (2013), in a study conducted in Bangladesh, found that postpartum depression was associated with impaired child's growth at 2–3 months and in motor development at 6–8 months. Also, the age of the mother, the child's weight in relation to the mother's age and the maternal anxiety about the infant's care, were directly associated with motor development (Nasreen et al., 2013).

It is important to underline that the relationship between postpartum depression and outcomes on child's development is not linear or direct; indeed different variables might play a role, such as genetic influences, educational level of the mother, child's gender, economic status and involvement of the father or other adults (Sohr-Preston and Scaramella, 2006).

Focusing on the infants, their motor development improves with broad inter-individual variability, not just from the temporary point of view, but also in the strategies with which the infant develops a specific motor skill (Touwen, 1976). Developmental progression is generally divided into a sequence of stages, which are not linear and identical in every child (Thelen, 1995; Camaioni and Di Blasio, 2002; Sheridan, 2009). Considering gross-motor abilities, in the first year of life the child gradually learns posture and balance control and later he/she learns to move around through space, while fine-motor skills rely on the child's ability to use his/her visual-perceptive competences to accomplish eye-hand coordination tasks, for example reaching and grasping objects (Folio and Fewell, 2000). Since the first month of life, newborns are able to stare at a slowly-moving stimulus in his/her field of vision, at 15–25 cm of distance; at 3 months he/she shifts his/her gaze from one side to the other and can keep a rattle in his/her hand for a few seconds. However, the reach-to-grasp action remains strongly linked to vision and partially depending on the environmental prompts, mainly provided by the caregiver.

The fundamental stages of motor development represent a useful instrument to assess the timing and extent of a child's progresses. Nevertheless, even if motor development in the first stages appears biologically determined, afterwards it depends on the combination of practice and learning from a continuous two-way interaction between biological and environmental factors (Zoia et al., 2013).

The newborn's first approach to the world takes place in the relationship with his/her caregiver, usually the mother. The infant takes the first clues to build his/her own environment and experiences from the repertoire of facial expressions, tones, gestures and postures of the mother (Stern, 1977). The transition from reflexes to the ability of reach-to-grasp takes place within this framework, and the infant acquires shared attention for an object, mainly proposed by the caregiver, in a close relational space of interaction with it. In the meantime, the infant also starts to develop actions like rolling, creeping and standing that widen his/her action space.

In the present study, we capitalize on the above-mentioned studies to explore the relation between maternal psychological status and motor development during the first year of life. In particular, when mother-infant dyads are characterized by maternal anxiety or depressive symptoms, even without reaching a clinical level, we raise the issue of possible influences on the development of motor experiences and specific motor skills. The development of reflexes mainly depends on a neurophysiological maturation of the central nervous system, while reaching an object, as well as gross-motor acquisitions (like flexing legs, extending arms, pushing up, rolling, crawling, standing), can be influenced by the differences in environmental stimulations.

Our central question is not just if motor development is general related to maternal psychological status, but whether maternal conditions may differently modulate specific subcomponents of motor development (fine-motor versus gross-motor skills). For example, if the mother perceives somatization or depressive symptoms at a subclinical level, could her status influence her baby's motor experiences? If motor abilities can be influenced by maternal psychic status, is it important what kind of psychopathological symptoms the mother perceives?

MATERIALS AND METHODS

Participants

We recruited 134 mother-infant dyads from the normative population; 5 were excluded for impossibility to complete the infant motor protocol, 4 were excluded due to the age of the infants (≥12 months); 6 were excluded for incompleteness of the maternal protocol. Overall, we conducted the analysis over 119 dyads.

Mothers were 23–43 years old (mean age = 32.87 years). Eighteen mothers (15.1%) had medical problems during pregnancy and 25 mothers (21%) had problems during delivery; 28 mothers (23.5%) had at least one previous experience of abortion. In our sample, 67 mothers (56.3%) had a high educational level and 49 (41.2%) had a medium or low educational level; 100 mothers (84%) had an occupation and 106 mothers (89.1%) were married or lived together with the baby's father. None were socio-economically disadvantaged. All mothers were happy to take part in the research. They were assessed with the Symptom Checklist-90-Revised questionnaires (SCL-90-R; Derogatis, 1983; Italian version by Sarno et al., 2011) to investigate the perception of psychological symptomatology.

Infants were between 0 and 11 months old (mean age = 5.98 months, 55 boys and 64 girls). None of them encountered problems during pregnancy and they were born at term, ranging between 37 and 40 weeks of gestation, with APGAR score between 7/8 and 9/10 and birthweight between 2.3 and 4.4 kg (mean = 3.3 kg, SD = 0.51). Each baby was assessed with Peabody Developmental Motor Scale-Second Edition (PDMS-2; Folio and Fewell, 2000) to evaluate his/her motor development.

Procedures and Instruments

The entire procedure had been submitted to and approved by the Ethic Committee of the University of Padua and each mother agreed to participate with his/her baby to the study by signing the informed consent.

Dyads were recruited from the Babylab Database of the University of Padua and thanks to the collaboration of some Pediatricians. The procedure took place in a laboratory of the Department of Developmental and Social Psychology of the University of Padua. The entire procedure took two sessions, each lasting about 60 min, during which two psychologists administered the PDMS-2 test to the infant, while, in another room, the mother was interviewed and responded to the SCL-90-R questionnaire in presence of another researcher. In this way, data about offspring, marital status, school level, employment and previous problematic pregnancies or experiences of abortion were collected, as well as information about psychic discomfort.

The *SCL-90-R* (Derogatis, 1983; Sarno et al., 2011) was used to evaluate psychological problems and symptoms of psychopathology. This is a relatively brief self-report questionnaire published by the Clinical Assessment division of the Pearson Assessment & Information group. It is designed to evaluate a broad range of psychological problems and symptoms of psychopathology. It consists of 90 items and takes 12–15 min to administer, yielding nine scores relative to primary symptom dimensions and three scores related to global distress indices. The primary symptom dimensions assessed are: somatization, obsessiveness-compulsiveness, interpersonal sensitivity, depression, anxiety, hostility, phobic anxiety, paranoid ideation, psychoticism, and a category of "additional items" useful to evaluate other symptoms. The three indices are: the Global Severity Index (GSI), considered to be a sensitive single quantitative indicator, concerning the respondent's psychological distress status; the Positive Symptom Distress Index (PSDI), considered to be an intensity measure which may also provide information about respondent's distress style; the Positive Symptom Total (PST) which reveals the number of symptoms that the respondent has endorsed to any degree. Particularly, criteria to interpret the GSI score are: with $T < 55$ subjects' general level reported is normative, $55 \leq T < 65$ subject reports from moderate to high level of disease; $T \geq 65$ subject reports a level of disease over the clinical cut-off. Criteria to interpret PST and PSDI are identical: for the PSDI, $T < 55$ indicates that the intensity of the symptoms reported by the subject is normative, $45 \leq T < 65$ underlines a moderate/high level of intensity of the symptoms, and $T \geq 65$ the intensity of the symptoms reported by the subject overcomes the clinical cut-off; regarding the PST, $T < 55$ means that the number of symptoms reported by the subject is normative, $45 \leq T < 65$ subject reports a moderate/high number of symptoms, and $T \geq 65$ the number of symptoms reported by the subject exceeds the clinical cut-off.

The PDMS-2 is a test designed to assess for motor development in children aged from 0 months to 5 years and 11 months. It is composed of 6 subtests: *Reflexes* (administered only from 0 to 11 months), *Stationary*, *Locomotion*, *Object Manipulation* (administered to children aged 12 months and older)—that compose the *Gross Motor Quotient* (GMQ)—*Grasping* and *Visual-Motor Integration*—that compose the Fine *Motor Quotient* (FMQ). The best estimate of child's motor abilities is the *Total Motor Quotient* (TMQ), a combination of the results of Gross and Fine Motor subtests (Folio and Fewell, 2000). According to the Italian standardization of the PDMS-2, all the babies included in this study showed a *TMQ* within the normal range (between 84 and 113).

Descriptive Statistical Analysis

The internal consistence reliability of SCL-90-R questionnaire and PDMS-2 test was evaluated by computing Cronbach's α coefficient. For the SCL-90-R questionnaire, the Cronbach's Alpha coefficients are included between 0.706 (ANX) and 0.831 (DEP). Phobic Anxiety (PHOB) and Psychoticism (PSY) subscales have not been considered in the analysis because they resulted unreliable (Cronbach's Alpha = 0.576 and 0.608 respectively); while for the PDMS-2 sub-scales, the Cronbach's Alpha coefficients are included between 0.877 (Reflexes) and 0.965 (Visual-Motor Integration). In the same way, the coefficients calculated on each Motor Quotient present great levels of reliability (GMQ = 0.978; FMQ = 0.977).

Therefore, descriptive statistics were applied to all variables (see below).

Data Analysis Strategies

Based on the results of the descriptive analysis (reported in the section below) the entire group of mothers was divided into 2 samples according to their perceived psychological symptomatology: we used as a criterion the scores $T \geq 55$ in the global indices of the SCL-90-R (GSI, PST, or PSDI). In this way we obtained two groups:

Normative group ($N = 72$). Mothers of this sample obtained subclinical/clinical score in none of the global indices GSI, PST, and PSDI of the SCL-90-R.

Subclinical group ($N = 47$). Mothers of this sample obtained subclinical/clinical score in at least one of the global indices GSI, PST and PSDI of the SCL-90-R.

This methodological choice allowed to identify those mothers with some kind of psychological symptomatology, remindful that none of these mothers presented a psychopathological diagnosis.

The *t*-test over these groups was calculated. Furthermore, correlations between maternal scores in SCL-90-R questionnaire and children's PDMS-2 scores were analyzed and regression models to predict infant motor outcomes on the basis of babies' age and maternal status were applied.

RESULT

Descriptive Results

In **Table 1** a description of the mothers group examined with the SCL-90-R is reported. With respect to the SCL-90-R subscales, a total of nine mothers scored above $T = 55$ in the Global Severity Index (i.e., 8 mothers reached a GSI score within the subclinical range and 1 mother scored higher than $T = 65$, which represents the cut-off for the clinical range; Gibson and Pick, 2000; Adolph and Berger, 2005, 2006). Twelve mothers topped cut-off $T = 55$ in the Positive Symptom Total (only 1 mother scored PST with $T \geq 65$), while thirty-nine mothers surpassed $T = 55$ in the Positive Symptom Distress Index (13 mothers over 39 scored PSDI with $T \geq 65$). The results of each SCL-90-R scale are detailed in the table below.

Focusing on the PDMS-2 test, the descriptive results of each subscale and quotient split for boys and girls were reported in **Table 2**. The subscales mean scores for the whole sample were: *Reflexes* = 7.29 (*SD* = 4.285), *Stationary* = 24.56 (*SD* = 9.084),

TABLE 1 | Descriptive results: SCL-90-R.

	N	Min	Max	Mean	SD	$T < 55$	$55 \leq T < 65$	$T \geq 65$
SOM	119	37	75	44.76	6.818	109	8	2
OC	119	36	75	46.04	7.508	106	10	3
IS	119	37	70	45.46	6.857	106	11	2
DEP	119	37	73	46.24	6.8	105	12	2
ANX	119	39	64	44.49	4.984	113	6	0
HOS	119	40	75	47.18	7.799	94	22	3
PAR	119	37	68	43.57	7.174	107	11	1
GSI	119	36	65	44.93	5.897	110	8	1
PST	119	28	66	43.09	7.859	107	11	1
PSDI	119	34	75	51.3	9.152	80	26	13

TABLE 2 | Descriptive results divided according to the gender: PDMS-2.

Gender		Min	Max	Mean	SD	Variance
Males $N = 55$	REFLEXES	1	15	7.24	4.36	18.99
	STATIONARY	4	38	23.80	9.51	90.42
	LOCOMOTION	6	71	25.84	18.07	326.47
	GRASPING	2	42	22.18	12.91	166.78
	VISUAL-MOTOR INTEGRATION	4	70	30.53	18.59	345.70
	GMQ	12	122	56.87	30.867	952.78
	FMQ	7	108	52.71	30.924	956.32
	TMQ	19	229	109.58	61.289	3756.40
Females $N = 64$	REFLEXES	1	15	7.34	4.255	18.10
	STATIONARY	8	38	25.22	8.724	76.11
	LOCOMOTION	2	65	25.97	16.179	261.75
	GRASPING	3	49	24.08	13.606	185.12
	VISUAL-MOTOR INTEGRATION	5	69	29.13	17.421	303.48
	GMQ	14	114	58.53	28.080	788.51
	FMQ	8	110	53.20	29.645	878.80
	TMQ	22	224	111.73	57.206	3272.58

Locomotion = 25.91 (*SD* = 17.004), *Grasping* = 23.2 (*SD* = 13.269), *Visual-Motor Integration* = 29.77 (*SD* = 17.909). The quotients for the whole sample were: *GMQ* = 57.76 (*SD* = 29.286), *FMQ* = 52.97 (*SD* = 30.115) and *TMQ* = 110.74 (*SD* = 58.885).

T-Test

The *t*-test analysis on mothers who belonged to the normative and subclinical sample were conducted to investigate if any differences emerged in the motor development of those children whose mothers showed sub-clinical scores in SCL-90-R compared to the normative group. Furthermore, comparisons considering the infants' gender (difference between boys and girls in the entire sample, as well as boys vs. girls in the normative and in the subclinical sample, and finally, normative vs. subclinical sample in the boys' and girls' scores) were also examined. No significant results were found: *t*-test showed no differences regardless of the children's age as the mothers belonged to the normative or subclinical group (**Table 3A**). In the same way, no differences were found in the PDMS-2 scores according to infants' gender (**Table 3B**). This is consistent with the PDMS-2 American and Italian standardizations, which revealed no significant differences in the test performances between boys and girls (Folio and Fewell, 2000; Biancotto et al., 2016).

Correlational Results

The correlations between the scores obtained by the infants at the PDMS-2 subscales and those of the mothers at the SCL-90-R questionnaire were calculated. Due to the PDMS-2 structure, the scores in the test increase with infants' age; for this reason we calculated partial correlations considering the infant's age as a control variable.

All the results found between the maternal scores and the infants' PDMS-2 scores were reported in **Table 4**, divided into the two groups of mothers (normative vs. sub-clinical).

In the group of normative mothers, the Interpersonal Sensitivity (IS) subscale of SCL-90-R questionnaire was positive correlated only with the Locomotion subscale of the PDMS-2 (0.236, $p < 0.05$), therefore locomotion increased with IS. A unique negative correlation was found between the hostility subscale (HOS) of SCL-90-R questionnaire and the Fine Motor Quotient (FMQ; −0.258, $p < 0.05$), which indicated that when mothers perceived low hostility feelings their babies' FMQ score increased.

On the contrary, for the group of subclinical mothers several correlations were found between the maternal psychic status and their babies' motor abilities. More precisely, a unique negative correlation was found between the Somatization (SOM) scale of the SCL-90-R questionnaire and the Reflexes scale of the PDMS-2 (−0.258, $p = 0.03$), that is, a higher presence of somatization symptoms was related with a lower score on baby's reflexes. Diversely, the IS subscale of the SCL-90-R questionnaire positively correlated with the Locomotion, Gross-Motor Quotient (GMQ) and Total Motor Quotient (TMQ) subscale of the PDMS-2 test. The presence of depression symptoms (DEP subscale of SCL-90-R questionnaire) showed positive correlations with the Stationary, Locomotion, Visual-motor integration, GMQ, FMQ, and TMQ of the PDMS-2 (see **Table 3** for values).The HOS scale of the SCL-90-R revealed positive correlations with Locomotion, Visual-motor integration, GMQ, FMQ, TMQ, and Grasping subscale of PDMS-2; similarly the paranoid ideation scale (PAR) correlated with these PDMS-2 subscales, plus the Stationary subscale. Lastly, the Global Severity Index (GSI of the SCL-90-R) showed a positive correlation with Locomotion, GMQ and TMQ scores of the PDMS-2 (see **Table 3** for values).

TABLE 3A | *T*-test: comparison between Subclinical and Normative group.

	Subclinical			Normative			*t*-test		
	Mean	SD	*N*	Mean	SD	*N*	*t*	*df*	*p*
GROUP 0–6 MONTHS									
REFLEXES	4.60	2.697	40	4.00	2.204	29	0.97	67	0.336
STATIONARY	18.55	6.488	40	17.28	5.133	29	0.86	67	0.391
LOCOMOTION	14.98	8.263	40	13.00	6.251	29	1.07	67	0.290
GRASPING	14.20	9.002	40	12.76	7.949	29	0.68	67	0.499
V-M INT.	18.00	8.715	40	16.59	7.149	29	0.71	67	0.483
GMQ	38.13	16.185	40	34.28	12.300	29	1.06	67	0.293
FMQ	32.20	17.350	40	29.34	14.296	29	0.71	67	0.477
TMQ	70.33	32.827	40	63.62	25.873	29	0.90	67	0.371
GROUP 7–11 MONTHS									
REFLEXES	11.44	2.539	32	11.22	2.602	18	0.28	48	0.779
STATIONARY	33.53	2.423	32	33.72	2.492	18	−0.26	48	0.799
LOCOMOTION	40.78	12.130	32	44.56	12.949	18	−1.01	48	0.317
GRASPING	36.78	4.241	32	35.89	2.246	18	0.81	48	0.421
V-M INT.	46.25	14.366	32	47.89	10.493	18	−0.42	48	0.679
GMQ	85.75	15.419	32	89.50	16.745	18	−0.78	48	0.437
FMQ	83.03	15.818	32	83.78	11.755	18	−0.17	48	0.864
TMQ	168.78	29.726	32	173.28	27.729	18	−0.52	48	0.609

TABLE 3B | *T*-test: comparison between Males and Females.

Gender	Males			Females			*t*-test		
	Mean	SD	*N*	Mean	SD	*N*	*t*	*df*	*p*
REFLEXES	7.24	4.36	55	7.34	4.255	64	−0.135	117	0.893
STATIONARY	23.8	9.51	55	25.22	8.724	64	−0.841	117	0.402
LOCOMOTION	25.84	18.07	55	25.97	16.179	64	−0.042	117	0.967
GRASPING	22.18	12.91	55	24.08	13.606	64	−0.769	117	0.443
V-M INT.	30.53	18.59	55	29.13	17.421	64	0.421	117	0.675
GMQ	56.87	30.867	55	58.53	28.08	64	−0.304	117	0.762
FMQ	52.71	30.924	55	53.2	29.645	64	−0.088	117	0.930
TMQ	109.58	61.289	55	111.73	57.206	64	−0.196	117	0.845

Regression Models Results

Regression models analyses were performed for a deeper comprehension of the findings described in the above section. Considering each group of mothers separately (normal and subclinical), the five psychopathological subscales of the SCL-90-R questionnaire that revealed some correlations with the PDMS-2 subscales were considered as predictive factors of the infants' motor abilities. Therefore, somatization, interpersonal sensitivity, depression, hostility and paranoia SCL-90-R subscales, along with the infants' age, were regarded as possible predictors of the motor competence in the different subscales measured by the PDMS-2. Regression analyses were conducted for each dependent motor variable: reflexes, stationary, locomotion, grasping, visual-motor integration subtests and the total motor quotient.

Overall, infants' age had a significant and positive effect on all the PDMS-2 subscales and on the total motor quotient. In particular, for the normative group of mothers the regression models always resulted significant: Total Motor Quotient [$F_{(6, 67)} = 146{,}051$; $p < 0.001$], Reflexes [$F_{(6, 67)} = 30{,}168$; $p < 0.001$]; Stationary [$F_{(6, 67)} = 85{,}614$; $p < 0.001$], Locomotion [$F_{(6, 67)} = 67{,}745$; $p < 0.001$], Grasping [$F_{(6, 67)} = 59{,}495$; $p < 0.001$] and Visual-motor Integration [$F_{(6,67)} = 63{,}103$; $p < 0.001$], with infants' age as the only significant predictor (see **Table 5** for Beta coefficients). Infants' age was a significant predictor also for the subclinical group. However, in this group of mothers some perceived symptoms seem to influence the infants' motor competence and the way in which they act in the environment.

More precisely, the maternal psychic status revealed to have a significant influence on the PDMS-2 total motor competence (TMQ) [$F_{(6, 41)} = 140{,}337$; $p < 0.001$], showing two SCL-90-R symptoms, in addition to age, as predictive factors: somatization and paranoia, with an opposite influence on the TMQ (see **Table 5**). When mothers tend to experience psychological distress

TABLE 4 | Correlational results in Normative and Sub-clinical group.

	SOM	OC	IS	DEP	ANX	HOS	PSR	GSI	PST	PSDI
NORMATIVE GROUP df = 69										
REFLEXES	0.091	0.096	−0.030	0.076	−0.035	0.016	−0.056	0.037	0.055	−0.052
STATIONARY	−0.102	−0.117	−0.033	−0.164	−0.122	−0.148	0.000	−0.162	−0.149	−0.059
LOCOMOTION	0.004	0.051	0.236*	0.101	0.000	0.138	0.217	0.147	0.093	0.126
GRASPING	−0.115	−0.019	−0.072	−0.136	−0.176	−0.168	−0.035	−0.149	−0.166	−0.045
V-M INT.	−0.188	−0.147	0.002	−0.122	−0.134	−0.202	−0.112	−0.142	−0.164	−0.164
GMQ	−0.011	0.020	0.155	0.035	−0.055	0.052	0.146	0.059	0.029	0.058
FMQ	−0.217	−0.128	−0.040	−0.176	−0.209	−0.258*	−0.109	−0.200	−0.227	−0.157
TMQ	−0.134	−0.065	0.059	−0.086	−0.153	−0.125	0.013	−0.087	−0.119	−0.062
SUB-CLINICAL GROUP df = 44										
REFLEXES	−0.315*	0.110	−0.028	0.162	0.081	0.130	0.212	0.056	−0.007	0.050
STATIONARY	−0.086	0.087	0.214	0.387*	0.218	0.088	0.328*	0.215	0.157	0.029
LOCOMOTION	−0.065	0.135	0.403*	0.301*	0.147	0.374*	0.439*	0.321*	0.276	0.069
GRASPING	−0.078	0.198	0.164	0.282	0.122	0.045	0.339*	0.191	0.145	−0.059
V-M INT.	−0.249	0.038	0.169	0.344*	0.142	0.460**	0.253	0.194	0.074	0.090
GMQ	−0.138	0.153	0.372*	0.382*	0.195	0.343*	0.482**	0.325*	0.260	0.072
FMQ	−0.214	0.146	0.212	0.401*	0.169	0.334*	0.375*	0.245	0.138	0.024
TMQ	−0.189	0.163	0.324*	0.426*	0.199	0.370*	0.471**	0.314*	0.221	0.054

$^*p < 0.05$, $^{**}p < 0.001$, $p > 0.06$.

TABLE 5 | Regression models results.

	TMQ		REFLEXES		STATIONARY		LOCOMOTION		GRASPING		V-M INT	
	Subcl.G	(N.G.)	Subcl.G	(N.G.)	Subcl.G	(N.G.)	Subcl.G	(N.G.)	Subcl.G	(N.G.)	Subcl.G	(N.G.)
PREDICTORS												
Age in months	0.96**	(0.97)**	0.88**	(0.86)**	0.95**	0.95**	0.93**	0.88**	0.91**	0.94**	0.95**	0.93**
SOM	−0.08*	(−0.02)	−0.15*	0.06	−0.08	0.02	−0.05	−0.03	−0.08	−0.002	−0.08	−0.06
IS	−0.01	(0.04)	−0.15	−0.03	−0.008	0.005	0.07	0.03	−0.04	−0.009	−0.04	0.12
DEP	0.09	(−0.03)	−0.16	0.05	0.16**	−0.08	0.02	−0.03	0.13	−0.04	0.06	−0.013
HOS	−0.01	(0.02)	−0.05	−0.03	−0.13*	−0.02	0.04	0.06	−0.15*	−0.05	**0.16**	−0.08
PAR	**0.11**	(−0.001)	0.15	−0.04	0.11	0.04	0.10	0.06	0.20	0.023	0.02	−0.08
R2	0.95	(0.93)	0.86	(0.73)	0.94	(0.88)	0.88	(0.86)	0.88	(0.84)	0.93	(0.85)

$^*p < 0.05$, $^{**}p < 0.001$, $p < 0.06$.

in the form of somatic symptoms, their babies showed a more restrained TMQ. On the contrary, when mothers tend to have paranoiac ideas, their infants show better scores on TMQ.

Considering the PDMS-2 subscales, a higher level of maternal somatization seemed to restrict the infants' natural ability to react [Reflexes: $F_{(6, 41)} = 41.607$; $p < 0.001$]. In addition, maternal depression drove infants to develop better stationary competence [Stationary; $F_{(6, 41)} = 102.860$; $p < 0.001$], while feelings of hostility induced an opposite effect, reducing the ability to reach stationary positions (see **Table 5** for Beta values and significance). No influences of psychopathological symptoms arose for infants' locomotion skill, while fine-motor abilities, i.e. grasping and visual-motor integration, were differently affected by maternal hostility thoughts. This mothers' psychological status restricted the grasping actions, which represent activities that require a shared space, not only in physical terms but also from an emotional point of view [Grasping: $F_{(6, 41)} = 51.824$; $p < 0.001$]. Diversely, maternal hostility feelings lead infants to greater visual-motor control [Visual-motor Integration: $F_{(6, 41)} = 94.106$; $p < 0.001$].

DISCUSSION

None of the mothers involved in this study presented a psychopathological diagnosed condition but they were considered as belonging to two different groups according to the presence/absence of psychological difficulties (according to the reliability of the SCL-90-R questionnaire). Their babies belonged to a normative population as well and showed no developmental issues. Infants' performances at the PDMS-2 were within normal range, based on the Italian reference norms (the Italian version of the test revealed good reliability, Biancotto et al., 2016).

Therefore, the aim of this study was not to verify a causal relation between psychopathological maternal conditions and infants' motor development; rather, our goal was to explore how psychological differences in mothers may influence their approach to the baby and therefore the baby's motor development during the first year of life. For this reason, the sample of mothers was divided into two groups according to their perceived symptomatology (GSI, PST, and PSDI scores of the SCL-90-R questionnaire have been considered as discriminants), in order to distinguish a group of mothers who presented psychological discomfort at a subclinical level and a normative one.

As mentioned above, our mother-infant dyads neither had a diagnosed depression condition nor a delay in motor development. Moreover, even the group of mothers who reported a positive symptomatology for depression, somatization, hostility, paranoid ideation and interpersonal sensitivity symptoms did not affect the general motor development of their infant, because no significant differences were found in the motor abilities between infants who belonged to the two groups of mothers (normative vs. sub-clinical one). This result is in accordance with Cornish et al. (2005), who found that only chronic maternal depression was associated with poorer infant psychomotor development (with the effects being similar for boys and girls), while brief maternal depression did not significantly impact the infant's performance (Cornish et al., 2005). The data we collected also showed no differences related to the gender of the infants (males vs. females), in line with the results of Cornish et al. (2005). Several studies have focused on the effect of depression condition on infants' development during the first year of life and showed the detrimental effects of maternal psychological symptomatology—especially Post Partum Depression- on babies' development (Lyons-Ruth et al., 1986; Galler et al., 2000; Nasreen et al., 2013). Conversely it is not surprising at all that, maternal sub-threshold symptomatology did not affect general motor development.

Once again, our intent was to investigate whether, in a non-clinical sample, any particular relationship could be outlined between maternal symptomatology and the quality of infant motor behaviors. Our study focused on a health safeguarding perspective regarding mother-infant dyads. From this point of view, it is worth identifying whether a certain maternal psychological status can contribute to shape infant motor experiences. It would be interesting to understand if different maternal psychological conditions or feelings can influence the quality of motor behaviors; that is, can infants be directed in their motor experiences by perceiving their mothers' dispositions? The results of the correlation analysis drive us to some considerations. First of all, in the normative sample of our population almost no maternal score correlates with the infants' performances at the PDMS-2; on the contrary, evaluating the sample defined as "subclinical," several maternal self-perceived symptomatology positively correlates with the infants' PDMS-2 scores. Secondly, infant motor development resulted similar within the two maternal groups, although mothers who reported a psychological discomfort seemed to influence the way in which their babies had motor experiences. Precisely, in the group of normative mothers, a positive correlation was found between the level of interpersonal sensitivity and the infant locomotion competence, while low hostility related to good experiences in the fine-motor domain (see **Table 3** for the correlation value between hostility and FMQ score). However, the regression analysis revealed that when mothers perceived overall psychological well-being, their babies' motor development was predicted only by the infant's age. This finding is extremely interesting, because it highlights that when an infant can benefit from a mother who has positive feelings regarding herself and others, he/she lives in the most suitable conditions for his/her motor development. When mothers feel self-confident, emotionally supported and adequate in comparison to other people, infants feel free to explore the environment. After all, emerging action capabilities are crucially shaped by an individual's interactions with the environment: one of the most important motives that drive actions and thus development is social interaction (in addition to exploration). The social motive is expressed from birth by the tendency to fixate social stimuli, imitate basic gestures, and engage in social interaction. The social motive is so important that, apparently without it, a person would stop developing entirely (Stern, 1977; Von Hofsten, 2007). On the contrary, when the maternal levels of symptomatology exceeded the range of normality, they correlated and predicted several infants' PDMS-2 scores. In our sample, a negative correlation was found between maternal somatization symptoms and infant's reflexes behavior, which suggest that, in such maternal status, infant's ability to automatically respond to environmental events are restricted. In other words, the outcome of regression analysis showed that, when mothers reported a higher level of somatization, their infant's motor behaviors were non adjusted to future states in a prospective way. Actually, reflexes are not subject to learning, neither adjusted to meet goals or attain other advantages than those for which they originally emerged, but even so, on the basis of our findings, maternal somatization could lead to a reduction of infant's reflexes. Furthermore, maternal hostility thoughts seemed to produce a reduction of stationary positions and grasping behaviors in infants. It is worthy to note that stationary and grasping behaviors always need adult support. The caregiver usually holds the baby up with her hands to help him/her stand up, and in grasping actions the infant reaches an object mainly to share it with the caregiver within a heartfelt inter-subjective space. Therefore, maternal hostility feelings toward others could limit infant's stationary as well as grasping motor behaviors which require abilities to share.

Considering the positive correlations found and the predictive factors that emerged from regression model analysis, symptoms of depression in subclinical mothers seemed to facilitate the development of stationary position abilities in infants, but this could be due to the infants' attempts to stimulate/activate their mothers who feel depressed and engage them into a relationship. In addition, while hostility feelings seemed to limit stationary and grasping behaviors, the same mental status positively influenced the development of visual-motor integration competences (as assessed by items of the PDMS-2). Therefore, maternal hostility condition seemed to drive infants toward improving their abilities to integrate visual and manual movements. The improvement in visual-motor abilities could not be due to better mastery of the reach-to-grasp action but it could be caused by the infant's need to control what is occurring in the shared space with the caregiver. In fact, each of the items included in the PDMS-2 visual-motor integration subscale requires shared action space, as well as engagement with mothers. Therefore, one could speculate that the more the maternal status is characterized by hostile symptoms, the more infants could be pushed toward massive visual-motor control, instead of acquiring knowledge about themselves, others and their environment though actions or enjoyment of interactions.

Considering the discussed results about reflexes and visual-motor abilities, it is important to consider that infants usually explore objects not only for their own benefit, but also to share their newly acquired knowledge with other people. In their study, Karasik et al. (2011) found that in a large majority of cases, infants showed the objects to the parent at hand and they often carried the objects to them. In this way, social motivation places the infant in the broader context of humans that provide information, comfort, and security. Conversely, when mothers feel depressed or hostile, their infants may react by reaching the stationary position earlier and strongly controlling visually guided actions. In our results, the subclinical maternal group reported hostility feeling that positively correlated with the grasping subscale of the PDMS-2 test. This motor behavior has another very important function for babies. When the hand moves toward an object of interest, it enters the infant's visual field and its movements can then be visually perceived and controlled by visual information. The function of these "built-in" skills is to provide activity-dependent input for the sensory-motor and cognitive systems. This allows the infant to explore the relationship between voluntary commands and movements, between vision and proprioception, and to discover the possibilities and the constraints of his/her actions. In addition, even before birth, the reach-to-grasp action seems to have a social cue, such as the possibility to reach another human being (Castiello et al., 2010). In this case, it can be hypothesized that when depressive symptoms are present, even at a subclinical level, infants try to use their grasping ability to engage their mothers and maintain contact with them.

The influence of maternal psychological status is not confined to fine-motor development; when considering the subclinical group, higher scores of the mothers in the SCL-90-R scales (Somatization, Interpersonal Sensitivity, Depression, Hostility and Paranoia) also tend to influence the performance of infants in the PDMS-2 gross-motor abilities, particularly in the stationary scale. At 6 months of age, infants can sit if supported, rotate their head to look around, bear their weight on their legs and skip energetically when helped to stand, while during the second semester they learn how to sit independently, to crawl and to stand up (Sheridan, 2009). Infants also try to control their posture more and more efficiently. In this prospect, motor development, in terms of movement through space and exploration of the surrounding environment, seems to be positively stimulated by maternal perceived depressive symptomatology. It is possible that mothers with depressive non-clinical symptoms induce their own children to autonomously explore the environment, while baby benefits from new neuronal pathways, improvements in perception or biomechanical changes that allow him/her to explore what surrounding objects and events afford in terms of new action modes (Gibson and Pick, 2000; Adolph and Berger, 2006). However, speculation is that in this way the baby can "stimulate" his/her-own mother in terms of movements, displacements, balance, etc. Moreover, it is intriguing to observe that paranoid ideas seemed to produce a similar effect in pushing infant toward the development of good motor skill. On the other hand, when mothers perceive hostility feelings, the effect on motor development seems to change depending on the specific motor ability: stationary, grasping or visual-motor integration skills.

Drawing from these results, a further step in this work could involve the study of the reciprocal influence in the mother-child dyad during the first 3 years of life or beyond, (with a specific set of reach-to-grasp stationary and locomotion actions) to verify if specific psychological conditions influence motor development in specific directions. Certainly, a wider sample and a longitudinal study could provide information about the long term influence of maternal status. It would also be appropriate to investigate whether the relational space and style developed within the dyad may have consequences not only on the quality of movement, but also on behavioral issues such as hyperactivity and impulsive behaviors).

Considering that the relationship between postpartum depression and outcomes on child development is not linear or direct and that different variables such as genetic influences, mother's education level, child's gender, economic status and father's or other adults' involvement might play a role, (Sohr-Preston and Scaramella, 2006), other factors have been considered in this study. Together with the maternal symptomatic condition and infant motor development, previous experiences of abortion, difficult pregnancies, the level of instruction and the employment status of the mother, previous other children and partnership satisfaction have all been controlled.

These results underline the clinical importance of considering both the maternal status and the development of the infant in the perinatal period, Unfortunately, within the national health service, the attention during pregnancy and the infant's early stages of life is mainly focused on the woman; nobody worries about the infant's condition until he/she reaches the age of three, when some behaviors are already set.

AUTHOR CONTRIBUTIONS

GP, SB, CF, and CM collected the data for the research. GP, SB, and AS analyzed and interpreted the data. GP, SB, CF, CM, and AS drafted the work. GP, AS, MB, and SZ critically revised the manuscript for important intellectual content and give the final approval of the version to be published. GP and AS agree to be accountable for all aspects of the work in ensuring that questions related to the accuracy or integrity of any part of the work are appropriately investigated and resolved.

ACKNOWLEDGMENTS

A heart-felt thanks to the families involved in this study for their generous collaboration, without which this study could not have taken place. We are grateful to the referees for their very helpful comments on a previous version of this manuscript.

REFERENCES

Adolph, K. E., and Berger, S. A. (2006). "Motor development," in *Handbook of Child Psychology: Vol. 2, Cognition, Perception, and Language, 6th Edn.*, eds W. Damon, R. Lerner, D. Kuhn, and R. S. Siegler (New York, NY: Wiley), 161–213.

Adolph, K. E., and Berger, S. E. (2005). "Physical and motor development," in *Developmental Science: An Advanced Textbook*, Vol. 5, eds M. H. Bornstein, and M. E. Lamb (Mahwah, NJ: Lawrence Erlbaum Associates), 223–281.

Bayley, N. (1969). *Bayley Scales of Infant Development*. San Antonio: Psychological Corp.

Biancotto, M., Girelli, L., Maggiore, P., Pelamatti, G. M., Rossi, G., Simonelli, A., et al. (2016). *Peabody Developmental Motor Scales, 2nd Edn.* Italian Standardisation. Firenze: Hogrefe.

Camaioni, L., and Di Blasio, P. (2002). *Psicologia dello sviluppo*. Il mulino.

Carneiro, C., Corboz-Warnery, A., and Fivaz-Depeursinge, E. (2006). The prenatal lausanne trilogue play: a new observational assessment tool of the prenatal co-parenting alliance. *Infant Ment. Health J.* 27, 207–228. doi: 10.1002/imhj.20089

Castiello, U., Becchio, C., Zoia, S., Nelini, C., Sartori, L., Blason, L., et al. (2010). Wired to be social: the ontogeny of human interaction. *PLoS ONE* 5:e13199. doi: 10.1371/journal.pone.0013199

Cornish, A. M., McMahon, C. A., Ungerer, J. A., Barnett, B., Kowalenko, N., and Tennant, C. (2005). Postnatal depression and infant cognitive and motor development in the second postnatal year: the impact of depression chronicity and infant gender. *Infant Behav. Dev.* 28, 407–417. doi: 10.1016/j.infbeh.2005.03.004

Derogatis, L. R. (1983). *Manual for the SCL-90-R*. Towson, MD: Clinical Psychometric Research.

Field, T. (2010). Postpartum depression effects on early interactions, parenting, and safety practices: a review. *Infant Behav. Dev.* 33, 1-6. doi: 10.1016/j.infbeh.2009.10.005

Folio, M. R., and Fewell, R. (2000). *Peabody Developmental Motor Scales: Examiner's Manual, 2nd Edn.* Austin: PRO-ED, Inc.

Galler, J. R., Harrison, R. H., Ramsey, F., Forde, V., and Butler, S. C. (2000). Maternal depressive symptoms affect infant cognitive development in Barbados. *J. Child Psychol. Psychiatry* 41, 747–757. doi: 10.1111/1469-7610.00662

Gibson, E. J., and Pick, A. (2000). *An Ecological Approach to Perceptual Learning and Development*. Oxford: Oxford University Press.

Goodman, S. H., and Gotlib, I. H. (1999). Risk for psychopathology in the children of depressed mothers: a developmental model for understanding mechanisms of transmission. *Psychol. Rev.* 106:458. doi: 10.1037/0033-295x.106.3.458

Gotlib, I. H., Whiffen, V. E., Wallace, P. M., and Mount, J. H. (1991). Prospective investigation of postpartum depression: factors involved in onset and recovery. *J. Abnorm. Psychol.* 100:122. doi: 10.1037/0021-843X.100.2.122

Karasik, L. B., Tamis-LeMonda, C. S., and Adolph, K. E. (2011). Transition from crawling to walking and infants' actions with objects and people. *Child Dev.* 82, 1199–1209. doi: 10.1111/j.1467-8624.2011.01595.x

Lyons-Ruth, K., Zoll, D., Connell, D., and Grunebaum, H. U. (1986). The depressed mother and her one year old infant: environment, interaction, attachment, and infant development. *New Dir. Child Adolesc. Dev.* 1986, 61–82. doi: 10.1002/cd.23219863407

Milgrom, J., Westley, D. T., and Gemmill, A. W. (2004). The mediating role of maternal responsiveness in some longer term effects of postnatal depression on infant development. *Infant Behav. Dev.* 27, 443–454. doi: 10.1016/j.infbeh.2004.03.003

Monti, F., and Agostini, F. (2006). *La depressione Postnatale*. Carocci.

Murray, L., and Cooper, P. J. (1997). Editorial: postpartum depression and child development. *Psychol. Med.* 27, 253–260. doi: 10.1017/S00332917960 04564

Nasreen, H. E., Kabir, Z. N., Forsell, Y., and Edhborg, M. (2013). Impact of maternal depressive symptoms and infant temperament on early infant growth and motor development: results from a population based study in Bangladesh. *J. Affect. Disord.* 146, 254–261. doi: 10.1016/j.jad.2012.09.013

Parolin, M., and Sudati, L. (2014). "Il processo di transizioneallagenitorialità," in *La Funzionegenitoriale*, ed A. Simonelli (Milano: Raffaello Cortina Editore), 241–273.

Sarno, I., Preti, E., Prunas, A., and Madeddu, F. (2011). *SCL-90-Rsymptom Checklist-90-R Adattamentoitaliano*. Giunti, Organizzazioni Speciali.

Sheridan, M. D. (2009). *Dallanascitaai Cinque Anni: Le Tappefondamentalidellosviluppo*. Milano: Raffaello Cortina.

Simonelli, A., Bighin, M., and De Palo, F. (2012). Coparenting interactions observed by the prenatal lausanne trilogue play: an Italian replication study. *Infant Ment. Health J.* 33, 609–619. doi: 10.1002/imhj.21350

Sohr-Preston, S. L., and Scaramella, L. V. (2006). Implications of timing of maternal depressive symptoms for early cognitive and language development. *Clin. Child Fam. Psychol. Rev.* 9, 65–83. doi: 10.1007/s10567-006-0004-2

Stern, D. (1977). *The First Relationship: Infant and Mother*. Cambridge: Harvard UP.

Thelen, E. (1995). Motor development: a new synthesis. *Am. Psychol.* 50, 79–95. doi: 10.1037/0003-066X.50.2.79

Touwen, B. (1976). *Neurological Development in Infancy*. London: William Heinemann.

Von Hofsten, C. (2007). Action in development. *Dev. Sci.* 10, 54–60. doi: 10.1111/j.1467-7687.2007.00564.x

Von Klitzing, K., Simoni, H., Amsler, F., and Bürgin, D. (1999).The role of the father in early family interactions. *Infant Ment. Health J.* 20, 222–237. doi: 10.1002/(SICI)1097-0355(199923)20:3<222::AID-IMHJ2>3.0.CO;2-B

Zoia, S., Blason, L., D'Ottavio, G., Biancotto, M., Bulgheroni, M., and Castiello, U. (2013). The development of upper limb movements: from fetal to post-natal life. *PLoS ONE* 8:e80876. doi: 10.1371/journal.pone.0080876

Conflict of Interest Statement: The authors declare that the research was conducted in the absence of any commercial or financial relationships that could be construed as a potential conflict of interest.

2

Infant Hand Preference and the Development of Cognitive Abilities

George F. Michel[1], Julie M. Campbell[1], Emily C. Marcinowski[2], Eliza L. Nelson[3] and Iryna Babik[4]*

[1] Department of Psychology, The University of North Carolina at Greensboro, Greensboro, NC, USA, [2] Department of Physical Therapy, Virginia Commonwealth University, Richmond, VA, USA, [3] Department of Psychology, Florida International University, Miami, FL, USA, [4] Department of Physical Therapy, University of Delaware, Newark, NJ, USA

Hand preference develops in the first two postnatal years with nearly half of infants exhibiting a consistent early preference for acquiring objects. Others exhibit a more variable developmental trajectory but by the end of their second postnatal year, most exhibit a consistent hand preference for role-differentiated bimanual manipulation. According to some forms of embodiment theory, these differences in hand use patterns should influence the way children interact with their environments, which, in turn, should affect the structure and function of brain development. Such early differences in brain development should result in different trajectories of psychological development. We present evidence that children with consistent early hand preferences exhibit advanced patterns of cognitive development as compared to children who develop a hand preference later. Differences in the developmental trajectory of hand preference are predictive of developmental differences in language, object management skills, and tool-use skills. As predicted by Casasanto's body-specificity hypothesis, infants with different hand preferences proceed along different developmental pathways of cognitive functioning.

Keywords: hand preference, infants, embodied cognition, cognitive development

Edited by:
Klaus Libertus,
University of Pittsburgh, USA

Reviewed by:
Amy Needham,
Vanderbilt University, USA
Daniel Casasanto,
The University of Chicago, USA

Correspondence:
George F. Michel
gfmichel@uncg.edu

INTRODUCTION

For the last four decades, one of us (GFM) has been investigating the factors affecting the development of infant hand-use preferences as a means of understanding how infant sensorimotor experiences contribute to the development of hemispheric differences in language processing (cf., Michel, 1988, 1991). The theoretical foundation of this work was derived, in part, from theories of Piaget (1952) and Bruner (1973), which proposed that infant sensorimotor experiences formed the foundation of symbol formation, language skill, concept formation, and reasoning. Also, developmental psychobiological evidence about how nervous system functioning could be shaped by early experience was used to support the notion that infant hand preferences could shape functional lateralization of the hemispheres (Michel, 1998, 2002). Since most neuropsychological research was, and is, conducted within the framework that hemispheric specialization of function derives from gene controlled differences in the structural organization of the two hemispheres, hand preference and related cognitive functions are often considered to be derivative of hemispheric specialization rather than to be contributors to it. However, in the last decade, some forms of embodiment theory (e.g., Barsalou, 2008; Casasanto, 2009) have reopened theoretical consideration that sensorimotor experiences can contribute to the functional organization of the brain.

Certain forms of embodiment theory (e.g., Barsalou, 2008; Casasanto, 2009, 2011) propose that the development of symbolic cognitive and social knowledge depends on the individual's sensorimotor engagement with social companions and physical objects during infancy. Infant vocalizations, facial expressions, and body postures (as sensorimotor actions) elicit actions from social companions, which provide the developing infant with information about the rules of social-relational engagement. This is similar to how the manipulation of objects reveals object properties, their relations, and rules of combination. How infants engage with these aspects of their environment sculpts their brain functioning and structure (Boulenger et al., 2009), which, in turn, affects their cognitive and social development. Thus, if there are group differences in such patterns of engagement, then there ought to be group differences in cognitive and social abilities. One way of testing whether such engagements with objects shape cognitive development would be to compare the cognitive development of groups of individuals who engage the world differently during infancy.

We propose that the development of infant hand preferences creates groups of infants who engage the world differently and hence, they should develop differences in cognitive functioning. This thesis is in accordance with Casasanto's (2011) body-specificity hypothesis and the thesis of this Frontiers' special issue (contributions of sensorimotor experience to cognitive development). We briefly review some of our studies which demonstrate that consistent infant hand preferences predict developmental advances in language development, tool-use, and objects construction skill. We propose that these advances not only contribute to the individual's development of language, concept formation, and reasoning, but also the individual's functional organization of the brain.

THE HAND PREFERENCE PHENOMENON

Hand preferences in adults are related to differences in hemispheric specialization for language skills (e.g., Corballis, 2009; Häberling et al., 2015), word processing differences between hemispheres (e.g., Willems et al., 2010), and a remarkably wide range of performance differences on tasks of cognitive, social, and emotional functioning (Annett, 2002). Moreover, apparently atypical hand preference development seems to be related to nearly every mental and medical health issue (e.g., Michel et al., 2013b, pp. 207–208). Consequently, some investigators have argued that examination of the cognitive and social abilities of different hand preference groups is the perfect test for evaluating embodiment theory (e.g., Casasanto, 2009). Hand preference represents different patterns of hemispheric specialization and such specialization may be relevant for the manifestation of specific aspects of cognitive, social, and emotional functioning. Therefore, the development of hand preference ought to relate to the typical and atypical development of many psychological functions.

However, before we can understand how hand preferences could contribute to variability in embodied cognitive experiences, we first must understand how hand preferences develop. Hand preference is the product of multifaceted developmental processes that begin before birth and expand during early infancy (Michel et al., 2013b). We have found that hand preferences are developing in a cascading fashion with preferences for earlier developing manual skills (e.g., reaching, grasping/acquisition) concatenating into preferences for later developing skills (e.g., unimanual and bimanual manipulation, artifact construction, and tool-use). We observed that a hand preference for acquiring objects starts manifesting before the age of 6 months, becomes prominent during 6–12 month period, and declines thereafter (Michel, 2002; Ferre et al., 2010; Michel et al., 2014). Also, although unimanual manipulation skills develop by 7–8 months, only by 10–11 months of age do infants exhibit a hand preference for unimanual manipulation and that preference matches the preference for acquisition (Campbell et al., 2015a). By 13–14 months of age, there is a significant increase in hand preferences for role-differentiated bimanual manipulation (RDBM, Babik and Michel, 2016). The hand preference for RDBM seems to stabilize by the age of 18 months (Nelson et al., 2013) with 80% of toddlers maintaining the same preference to 24 months. A consistent hand preference for RDBM likely influences the development of hand preference for tool-use, since RDBM is an object manipulation pattern characteristic of most actions involved in tool construction and use throughout the life-span (Vauclair, 1984). Although a right hand preference predominates in all infant manual skills, the hand preferences appear to be distributed continuously across infants (similarly to adult hand preferences, Annett, 2002).

Although approximately 12% of infants have a consistent left hand preference (Michel et al., 2014), the left hand preference does not appear to be as robust as the right preference. In part, this may be a consequence of a maternal influence on the development of infant hand preferences (Harkins and Michel, 1988; Michel, 1992, 1998; Mundale, 1992, unpublished). Right-handed mothers unintentionally engage the use of their infant's right hand during object play (Michel, 1998). In contrast, although left-handed mothers use their left hand more when playing with their infants, the difference in their hand use is small compared to the overwhelming use of the right hand by right-handed mothers. Thus, left preference infants of right-handed mothers (the majority of left preferring infants) are likely to be encouraged (by their mother's actions during socially interactive object play) to use their right hand much more than right preference infants of left-handed mothers (a minority of right preferring infants) are encouraged to use their left hand. Indeed, infants initially manifesting left-hand preference for acquiring objects who had right-hand preferring mothers significantly reduced their left-hand preference by 11 months; whereas infants initially manifesting right-hand preference who had right-hand preferring mothers strengthened their right-hand preference by 11 months (Michel, 1992).

ASSESSING HAND PREFERENCE DEVELOPMENT USING A TRAJECTORY BASED ANALYSIS

The expression of infant hand preferences reflects the consequences of an immature but rapidly developing nervous system and expression can vary according to such factors as circadian rhythm, situational arousal, and the development of other neuromotor abilities, such as postural control and locomotion (Corbetta and Thelen, 2002; Babik et al., 2014). Moreover, the identification of a preference appears to be sensitive to various assessment procedures and conditions (Campbell et al., 2015b). Therefore, assessment of infant hand preferences requires longitudinal designs using tasks that are relatively similar, across age, in the manual challenge that they present for the infant. Object acquisition skills can be used to assess the development of hand preferences during the period from 6 to 14 months of age because this manual skill is prevalent in the infant's repertoire but it is sufficiently challenging to elicit a hand preference across this age period. Moreover, it is incorporated into all other manual skills involving object manipulation (construction of objects and tool use). A hand preference in reaching and object contact predicts the hand preference in object acquisition (Michel and Harkins, 1986) and the hand preference for acquiring objects predicts the hand preference for unimanual object manipulation (Hinojosa et al., 2003; Campbell et al., 2015a) and RDBM (Nelson et al., 2013; Babik and Michel, 2016). Thus, early-developing hand preference for object acquisition is pivotal for the development of hand preference for other more sophisticated manual skills.

We hypothesized that there ought to be consistent developmental trajectories for object acquisition hand preference despite some variation across assessment ages. Nine monthly assessments during the 6–14 month period permitted reliable identification of four latent groups according to their pattern of developmental trajectories using group based trajectory modeling (GBTM, Nagin, 2005; Michel et al., 2013a). GBTM permits identification distinctive patterns in the distribution of a sample's trajectories to define the infant's hand preference We found that 32% of 380 infants have consistent right-hand preferences from 6 to 14 months of age, 12% have consistent left preferences, and 26% have a developmental trajectory trending toward a later developing right preference. The remaining 30% of infants had a consistent trajectory of hand use that showed no differences in hand-use across the ages. Hierarchical Linear Modeling (HLM, Raudenbush et al., 2004), confirmed that the infants assigned to these four latent classes exhibited significantly different trajectories in their development of hand preferences. Infants with a right preference have established that preference by 6 months of age and maintain it for the next 9 months (with a slight decrease in right hand use by 13 and 14 months). Infants with a left preference had not established that preference before 8 months of age, but maintain it thereafter. Infants with a trend toward a right preference start at 6 months without a preference but have established a right preference by 14 months. Those infants without a hand preference maintain that throughout the 6–14 month period. Thus, by the beginning of the second year, hand preferences are exhibiting the common character of a right preference for most and a left preference for about 12% of the infants and about 30% with unclear preferences. Of course, the number of groups identified is less important than the recognition that it is only by the collection of such longitudinal data that consistencies across assessment periods can be identified. It is those consistencies of preference that reflect the operation of neural mechanisms that ought to contribute to the development of other mechanisms associated with cognitive functioning.

HAND PREFERENCE AND LANGUAGE

The development of manual skills dynamically shifts the way infants experience their world, and various changes in motor skills have been linked to changes in language ability (e.g., Iverson, 2010). Here, we highlight our longitudinal studies that have used a trajectory-based approach to characterize hand preference and address how hand preference trajectories may be differentially related to language acquisition.

Nelson et al. (2014) hypothesized that a consistent infant hand preference was a marker for advanced object manipulation skill, whereas an inconsistent preference would be an indicator of a lower skill level and perhaps a different pattern of hemispheric specialization. Nelson et al. (2014) described trajectories in the timing and direction of hand preference among children assessed monthly as infants (6–14 months) and then as toddlers (18–24 months): children with consistent right-hand preference as infants who remained right-handed as toddlers, and children without consistent hand preference as infants who became either right-handed or left-handed as toddlers. Consistency versus inconsistency of hand preference from infancy through toddlerhood explained 25% of the variance in language ability at 2 years of age. Also, consistent right-hand preference from infancy was associated with advanced language skills. Gonzalez et al. (2015) extended this work to include language outcome at 3 years in the same sample and found that children with a consistent hand preference trajectory as toddlers had higher expressive language scores. Thus, early, consistent hand preferences may facilitate the development of language (Nelson et al., 2014; Gonzalez et al., 2015). Although more works needs to be done, Michel et al. (2013a) used Arbib's schema theory (Arbib, 2006) to delineate some of the mechanisms by which the sensorimotor experience associated with a hand preference could contribute to the neural control of expressive language skills.

HAND PREFERENCE AND THE MANUAL CONTROL OF OBJECTS

It is reasonable to assume that infants with a hand preference for engaging with objects would develop greater manual skill and proficiency with the preferred hand and that preference would affect the development of their manual control of objects. Object construction requires manually merging multiple objects into a single, unifying structure, such as stacking blocks into a tower or assembling a puzzle (Marcinowski, 2015). Object construction has recently been related to a variety of cognitive skills at later ages, including mathematical ability (Wolfgang et al., 2003; Nath and Szucs, 2014), language (Marcinowski and Campbell, 2015) and visuospatial skill (Caldera et al., 1999; Levine et al., 2011; Verdine et al., 2014).

Marcinowski (2015) found that infants with a consistent hand preference develop stacking more quickly during 10–14 months period than infants without a hand preference. Consistent left- and right-preferring infants manifested greater stacking skill at 14 months, than infants without a consistent hand preference. Moreover, infants with a trending right preference did not differ in the development of their stacking skill from infants without a preference. Since the trending right group did not exhibit a hand preference for acquisition during the 6–9 months period before stacking began to be assessed, they likely had not developed the manual proficiency needed to stack objects (Chen et al., 2010). Thus, the consistency of a hand preference changes the relation between a hand preference and the cognitive skill of object construction.

Also, Kotwica et al. (2008) reported that infants with consistent hand preferences across four assessment periods (at 7, 9, 11, and 13 months of age) are more effective with the object management skill of object storage than infants without a consistent preference during that period. When infants are given multiple toys (one at a time), they must develop the ability to manipulate and manage these objects so that the latter are available for future interaction. Infants with consistent hand preference demonstrated a greater skill for object storage, such as placing objects in reachable locations and intermanual transfer, than infants without a hand preference (Kotwica et al., 2008). By storing objects more effectively, infants with a hand preference can explore properties of objects, understand relations between objects, and "plan" actions more effectively than infants without a preference (cf., Bruner, 1973). Indeed, Bruner (1973) considered object storage skills to be important for the development of symbolic representation (and hence language development), since an unused, but stored object must be mentally represented by the infant for later retrieval.

Tool use is another important cognitive skill that often involves imitation of complex actions, planning, decision-making, and the ability to account for spatial and temporal characteristics of objects, their properties, and the situation. Many have argued that tool use requires advanced symbolic thinking and representational means-end analysis (Bates et al., 1980), advanced causal understanding (Carpenter et al., 1998; Buttelmann et al., 2008), and an achievement of spatial reasoning that permits coordinating multiple mobile frames of reference (Lockman, 2000). Fraz et al. (2014) tested the development of the tool use skill longitudinally from 10 to14 months in 60 infants with right, left, or no hand preference for acquiring objects. They found that infants with consistent right or left hand preference out-performed those without a hand preference in the number of successfully completed tool-using actions at the ages of 10, 11, and 12 months. However, after 12 months differences between the hand preference groups ceased to be statistically significant. Fraz et al. (2014) concluded that early-development of consistent hand-use preferences for acquiring objects facilitates the onset of the cognitive skill of tool use. Thus, we have shown how longitudinal assessments of the consistency of hand preferences relate to the development of the manipulation of objects that are considered to contribute to the development of symbolic cognitive abilities.

CONCLUSION

We have demonstrated that early-established hand preferences (revealed by their consistency across longitudinal assessments) for object acquisition and manipulation of objects significantly predict developmental advancement of such important elements of cognitive development as expressive language, object construction, object management skills, and tool use. Thus, it is important that longitudinal consistency in infant hand preferences be taken into account while exploring patterns of neurobehavioral functioning and cognitive development. Our results are consistent with the predictions of Casasanto's (2009, 2011) body-specificity hypothesis. Having a more practiced, preferred hand could assist infants in scaffolding their manual proficiency and hence their comprehension of the properties of objects. Such comprehension, in turn, could contribute to the development of other cognitive abilities as revealed in object construction, tool-using, and language development. What remains to be demonstrated is how these differences in hand preference development have influenced the functional organization of the infant's brain.

AUTHOR CONTRIBUTIONS

JC, EM, EN, IB, and GM conceptualized and wrote the paper.

FUNDING

Preparation of this manuscript was supported by NSF grant DLS0716045 awarded to GM and NIH T32HD007376 fellowship awarded to JC and EN.

REFERENCES

Annett, M. (2002). *Handedness and Brain Asymmetry: The Right Shift Theory*. East Sussex: Psychology Press.

Arbib, M. A. (2006). "The mirror-system hypothesis on the linkage of action and language," in *Action to Language via the Mirror Neuron System*, ed. M. A. Arbib (Cambridge: Cambridge University Press), 1–45.

Babik, I., Campbell, J. M., and Michel, G. F. (2014). Postural influences on the development of infant lateralized and symmetrical hand-use. *Child Dev.* 85, 294–307. doi: 10.1111/cdev.12121

Babik, I., and Michel, G. F. (2016). Development of Role-Differentiated Bimanual Manipulation in Infancy: part 2. Hand preferences for object acquisition and RDBM - Continuity or discontinuity? *Dev. Psychobiol.* 58, 257–267. doi: 10.1002/dev.21378

Barsalou, L. (2008). Grounded cognition. *Annu. Rev. Psychol.* 59, 617–645. doi: 10.1146/annurev.psych.59.103006.093639

Bates, E., Carlson-Luden, V., and Bretherton, I. (1980). Perceptual aspects of tool using in infancy. *Infant Behav. Dev.* 3, 127–140. doi: 10.1016/S0163-6383(80)80017-8

Boulenger, V., Hauk, O., and Pulvermüller, F. (2009). Grasping ideas with the motor system: semantic somatotopy in idiom comprehension. *Cereb. Cortex* 19, 1905–1914. doi: 10.1093/cercor/bhn217

Bruner, J. S. (1973). *Beyond the Information Given.* New York, NY: W. W. Norton & Company.

Buttelmann, D., Carpenter, M., Call, J., and Tomasello, M. (2008). Rational tool use and tool choice in humans and great apes. *Child Dev.* 79, 609–626. doi: 10.1111/j.1467-8624.2008.01146.x

Caldera, Y. M., Culp, A. M., O'Brien, M., Truglio, R. T., Alvarez, M., and Huston, A. C. (1999). Children's play preferences, construction play with blocks, and visual-spatial skills: are they related? *Int. J. Behav. Dev.* 23, 855–872. doi: 10.1080/016502599383577

Campbell, J. M., Marcinowski, E. C., Babik, I., and Michel, G. F. (2015a). The influence of a hand preference for acquiring objects on the development of a hand preference for unimanual manipulation from 6 to 14 months. *Infant Behav. Dev.* 39, 107–117. doi: 10.1016/j.infbeh.2015.02.013

Campbell, J. M., Marcinowski, E. C., Latta, J., and Michel, G. F. (2015b). Different assessment tasks produce different estimates of handedness stability during the eight to 14 month age period. *Infant Behav. Dev.* 39, 67–80. doi: 10.1016/j.infbeh.2015.02.003

Carpenter, M., Akhtar, N., and Tomasello, M. (1998). Fourteen-through 18-month-old infants differently imitate intentional and accidental actions. *Infant Behav. Dev.* 21, 315–330. doi: 10.1016/S0163-6383(98)90009-1

Casasanto, D. (2009). Embodiment of abstract concepts: good and bad in right- and left-handers. *J. Exp. Psychol. Gen.* 138, 351–367. doi: 10.1037/a0015854

Casasanto, D. (2011). Different bodies, different minds: the body specificity of language and thought. *Curr. Dir. Psychol. Sci.* 20, 378–383. doi: 10.1177/0963721411422058

Chen, Y.-P., Keen, R., Rosander, K., and von Hofsten, C. (2010). Movement planning reflects skill level and age changes in toddlers. *Child Dev.* 81, 1846–1858. doi: 10.1111/j.1467-8624.2010.01514.x

Corballis, M. C. (2009). The evolution and genetics of cerebral asymmetry. *Philos. Trans. R. Soc. B* 364, 867–879. doi: 10.1098/rstb.2008.0232

Corbetta, D., and Thelen, E. (2002). Behavioral fluctuations and the development of manual asymmetries in infancy: contributions of the dynamic systems approach. *Handb. Neuropsychol.* 8, 311–330.

Ferre, C. L., Babik, I., and Michel, G. F. (2010). Development of infant prehension handedness: a longitudinal analysis during the 6- to 14-month age period. *Infant Behav. Dev.* 33, 492–502. doi: 10.1016/j.infbeh.2010.06.002

Fraz, F., Babik, I., Varholick, J., and Michel, G. F. (2014). Development of hand-use preference for tool-use in infancy. *Dev. Psychobiol.* 57:S13.

Gonzalez, S. L., Nelson, E. L., Campbell, J. M., Marcinowski, E. C., Coxe, S., and Michel, G. F. (2015). 18-24 months handedness predicts 36 months expressive language skills. *Dev. Psychobiol.* 57:S16.

Häberling, I. S., Steinemann, A., and Corballis, M. C. (2015). Cerebral asymmetry for language: comparing production with comprehension. *Neuropsychologia* 80, 17–23. doi: 10.1016/j.neuropsychologia.2015.11.002

Harkins, D. A., and Michel, G. F. (1988). Evidence for a maternal influence on infant hand-use preferences. *Dev. Psychobiol.* 21, 535–542. doi: 10.1002/dev.420210604

Hinojosa, T., Sheu, C.-F., and Michel, G. F. (2003). Infant hand-use preferences for grasping objects contributes to the development of a hand-use preference for manipulating objects. *Dev. Psychobiol.* 43, 328–334. doi: 10.1002/dev.10142

Iverson, J. M. (2010). Developing language in a developing body: the relationship between motor development and language development. *J. Child Lang.* 37, 229–261. doi: 10.1017/S0305000909990432

Kotwica, K. A., Ferre, C. L., and Michel, G. F. (2008). Relation of stable hand-use preferences to the development of skill for managing multiple objects from 7 to 13 months of age. *Dev. Psychobiol.* 50, 519–529. doi: 10.1002/dev.20311

Lockman, J. J. (2000). A perception-action perspective on tool use development. *Child Dev.* 71, 137–144. doi: 10.1111/1467-8624.00127

Levine, S. C., Ratliff, K. R., Huttenlocher, J., and Cannon, J. (2011). Early puzzle play: a predictor of preschoolers' special transformation skill. *Dev. Psychol.* 48, 530–542. doi: 10.1037/a0025913

Marcinowski, E. C. (2015). *How Does Handedness Affect the Development of Construction Skill From 10-24 Months?* doctoral dissertation. University of North Carolina at Greensboro, Greensboro, NC.

Marcinowski, E. C., and Campbell, J. M. (2015). Building on what you have learned object construction skill during infancy predicts the comprehension of spatial relations words. *Int. J. Behav. Dev.* doi: 10.1177/0165025416635283

Michel, G. F. (1988). "A neuropsychological perspective on infant sensorimotor development," in *Advances in Infancy Research*, Vol. 5, eds C. K. Rovee-Collier and L. P. Lipsitt (Norwood, NJ: Ablex Pub. Corp), 1–37.

Michel, G. F. (1991). "Development of infant manual skills: motor programs, schemata, or dynamic systems," in *The Development of Timing Control and Temporal Organization in Coordinated Action*, eds J. Fagard and P. H. Wolff (Melville, NY: Elsevier), 175–199.

Michel, G. F. (1992). Maternal influences on infant hand-use during play with toys. *Behav. Genet.* 22, 163–176. doi: 10.1080/87565649809540723

Michel, G. F. (1998). A lateral bias in the neuropsychological functioning of human infants. *Dev. Neuropsychol.* 14, 445–469.

Michel, G. F. (2002). "Development of infant handedness," in *Conceptions of Development: Lessons from the Laboratory*, eds D. Lewkowicz and R. Lickliter (Philadelphia, PA: Psychology Press), 165–186.

Michel, G. F., Babik, I., Nelson, E. L., Campbell, J. M., and Marcinowski, E. C. (2013a). How the development of handedness could contribute to the development of language. *Dev. Psychobiol.* 55, 608–620. doi: 10.1037/a0033312

Michel, G. F., Babik, I., Sheu, C.-F., and Campbell, J. M. (2014). Latent classes in the developmental trajectories of infant handedness. *Dev. Psychol.* 50, 349–359. doi: 10.1002/dev.420190310

Michel, G. F., and Harkins, D. A. (1986). Postural and lateral asymmetries in the ontogeny of handedness during infancy. *Dev. Psychobiol.* 19, 247–258.

Michel, G. F., Nelson, E. L., Babik, I., Campbell, J. M., and Marcinowski, E. C. (2013b). "Multiple trajectories in the developmental psychobiology of human handedness," in *Embodiment and Epigenesis: Theoretical and Methodological Issues in Understanding the Role of Biology within the Relational Developmental System Part B: Ontogenetic Dimensions*, eds R. M. Lerner and J. B. Benson (Melville, NY: Elsevier Inc), 227–260.

Nagin, D. (2005). *Group-Based Modeling of Development.* Cambridge, MA: Harvard University Press.

Nath, S., and Szucs, D. (2014). Construction play and cognitive skills associated with the development of mathematical abilities in 7-year-old children. *Learn. Instruct.* 32, 73–80. doi: 10.1016/j.infbeh.2013.01.009

Nelson, E. L., Campbell, J. M., and Michel, G. F. (2013). Unimanual to bimanual: tracking the development of handedness from 6 to 24 months. *Infant Behav. Dev.* 36, 181–188. doi: 10.1037/a0033803

Nelson, E. L., Campbell, J. M., and Michel, G. F. (2014). Early handedness in infancy predicts language ability in toddlers. *Dev. Psychol.* 50, 809–814. doi: 10.1037/11494-000

Piaget, J. (1952). *The Origins of Intelligence in Childhood.* New York, NY: International Universities Press.

Raudenbush, S., Bryk, A., Cheong, Y. F., Congdon, R., and du Toit, M. (2004). *HLM 6: Hierarchical Linear & Nonlinear Modeling.* Lincolnwood, IL: Scientific Software International, Inc.

Vauclair, J. (1984). Phylogenetic approach to object manipulation in human and ape infants. *Hum. Dev.* 27, 321–328. doi: 10.1111/cdev.12165

Verdine, B. N., Golinkoff, R. K., Hirsh-Pasek, K., Newcombe, N. S., Filipowicz, A. T., and Change, A. (2014). Deconstructing building blocks: preschoolers' spatial assembly performance relates to early mathematical skills. *Child Dev.* 85, 1062–1076. doi: 10.1177/0956797609354072

Willems, R. M., Hagoort, P., and Casasanto, D. (2010). Body-specific representations of action verbs. *Psychol. Sci.* 21, 67–74. doi: 10.1080/0300443032000088212

Wolfgang, C. H., Stannard, L. L., and Jones, I. (2003). Advanced constructional play with LEGOs among preschoolers as a predictor of later school achievement in mathematics. *Early Child Dev. Care* 173, 467–475. doi: 10.1080/0300443032000088212

Conflict of Interest Statement: The authors declare that the research was conducted in the absence of any commercial or financial relationships that could be construed as a potential conflict of interest.

3

Quantifying Motor Experience in the Infant Brain: EEG Power, Coherence, and Mu Desynchronization

*Sandy L. Gonzalez, Bethany C. Reeb-Sutherland and Eliza L. Nelson**

Department of Psychology, Florida International University, Miami, FL, USA

The emergence of new motor skills, such as reaching and walking, dramatically changes how infants engage with the world socially and cognitively. Several examples of how motor experience can cascade into cognitive and social development have been documented, yet a significant knowledge gap remains in our understanding of whether these observed behavioral changes are accompanied by underlying neural changes. We propose that electroencephalography (EEG) measures such as power, coherence, and mu desynchronization are optimal tools to quantify motor experience in the infant brain. In this mini-review, we will summarize existing infant research that has separately assessed the relation between motor, cognitive, or social development with coherence, power, or mu desynchronization. We will discuss how the reviewed neural changes seen in seemingly separate developmental domains may be linked based on existing behavioral evidence. We will further propose that power, coherence, and mu desynchronization be used in research exploring the links between motor experience and cognitive and social development.

Keywords: infants, EEG power, EEG Coherence, mu desynchronization, motor development, cognitive development, social development

Edited by:
Klaus Libertus,
University of Pittsburgh, USA

Reviewed by:
Martha Ann Bell,
Virginia Polytechnic Institute and State University, USA
April Robyn Levin,
Boston Children's Hospital, USA

***Correspondence:**
Eliza L. Nelson
elnelson@fiu.edu

INTRODUCTION

For infants, learning new motor skills can fundamentally alter their experiences with the world and with others (Campos et al., 2000). Learning a new motor skill may result in a "setting event," where said motor skill increases the likelihood of producing other actions, resulting in a cascade effect in non-motor domains (Bushnell and Boudreau, 1993; Campos et al., 2000; Clearfield, 2011). Experience with sitting, crawling, walking, and motor-exploratory behavior can have cascading effects in object knowledge (Soska et al., 2010), spatial search (Kermoian and Campos, 1988), language (Walle and Campos, 2014), and academic achievement (Bornstein et al., 2013). Moreover, changes in motor development alter the bidirectional relationship between infants and caregivers, as well as infant attention to social stimuli (Campos et al., 1992; Libertus and Needham, 2011; Karasik et al., 2014). However, research on infant development has yet to decipher the neural mechanisms underlying these documented motor cascades into cognitive and social development. Research on the neural underpinnings of these dynamic interactions across domains would allow for better understanding of infant development, complementing behavioral evidence.

Using electroencephalography (EEG), researchers have begun to elucidate links between motor experience and neural plasticity (Bell and Fox, 1996; Corbetta et al., 2014; Cannon et al., 2015). Crucially, infant motor experience has been linked to neural reorganization (Corbetta et al., 2014). Research implementing EEG measures like power, coherence, and mu desynchronization, in conjunction with motor measures, affords unique information on how motor experience may alter infant neural activity and connectivity. Although these studies are useful, most lack data on how observed motor-neural links relate to existing behavioral literature identifying motor experience as relevant for social and cognitive development. The relation between motor development and other domains has been described as one of "reorganization," where motor experience can alter an infant's environment via reorganization of their interactions with social partners and objects (Gustafson, 1984; Biringen et al., 1995; Campos et al., 2000). However, does motor-related *neural reorganization* play a role in subsequent cognitive and social changes? EEG readily provides the tools to answer such questions regarding motor experience in the infant brain.

In this mini-review, we synthesize existing infant EEG literature on motor, cognitive, and social development. We discuss how seemingly isolated EEG findings within each domain may relate to motor development based on behavioral evidence linking motor experience with cognitive and social abilities. First, however, we provide an overview of EEG and optimal EEG measures for quantifying motor experience in the brain: power, coherence and mu desynchronization.

EEG: POWER, COHERENCE, AND MU DESYNCHRONIZATION

Electroencephalography measures real time electrical activity at the scalp via electrodes in a non-invasive and comfortable manner (Bell and Cuevas, 2012). EEG has great tolerance to movement compared to other neuroimaging methods (i.e., MEG, fMRI). During infancy through early childhood, 6–9 Hz is the most commonly examined EEG frequency band (Marshall et al., 2002; Bell and Cuevas, 2012). Using EEG, researchers can study specific attributes or patterns of electrical activity like power, coherence, or mu desynchronization.

Electroencephalography power reflects the electrical activity of a particular group of neurons, providing a measure of activity within a cortical region as projected to the scalp. Power is calculated as voltage squared within a given frequency band. Because it is measured over time, power can identify sustained area specific patterns of electrical activity at baseline or during a task (Bell, 1998). In infants, increases in power may reflect neural maturation within a cortical area (Bell, 2001). Differences in power between regions can provide information on differential patterns of maturation and activation across the cortex. If power is used in combination with behavioral measures of motor development, links between region specific activity and motor experience can be explored.

Coherence is the squared cross-correlation of activity between spatially distinct electrode sites, providing the degree of interconnection between regions (e.g., strength and number of axons; Nunez, 1981; Thatcher et al., 1987)[1]. Bell and Fox (1996) have previously proposed that increased coherence seen when learning a new skill is likely associated with synaptic growth, indicating integration of function across cortical regions. A subsequent decrease in coherence after greater experience with a skill may be associated with synaptic pruning, indicating greater regional differentiation/specialization and neural efficiency. Importantly, if changes in coherence coincide with changes in motor experience or ability, a strong argument can be made regarding the role of motor experience on neural reorganization and plasticity.

Finally, mu desynchronization is largely a motor experience-dependent electrical pattern measured over the sensorimotor cortex, typically at central electrode sites (Cuevas et al., 2014). When infants observe an individual execute a goal-directed action or when the infant executes an action, mu rhythm becomes desynchronized (i.e., decreased power) compared to mu activity during rest (Marshall et al., 2011). To date, the predominant view suggests that mu desynchronization over central regions reflects mirror neuron activity of an extended fronto-parietal network involved in action coordination and execution (Pineda, 2005; Vanderwert et al., 2013; Thorpe et al., 2015), although recent studies suggest that mu desynchronization may be related to a broader neural network which includes the mirror neuron system (Arnstein et al., 2011; Braadbaart et al., 2013). Critically, mu rhythm (and mirror neurons) may bridge action perception and action production, given that the indexed electrical activity responds most to observed goal-directed actions and that mu desynchronization during action observation is dependent on the infant's motor repertoire (Pineda, 2005; van Elk et al., 2008; Marshall et al., 2011; Reid et al., 2011). Recently, mu desynchronization was proposed as a possible measure of early social learning (Cannon et al., 2014).

USE OF POWER, COHERENCE, AND MU DESYNCHRONIZATION

In the following sections we review extant EEG literature on infant motor, cognitive and social development implementing power, coherence, and mu desynchronization. Throughout, we discuss how seemingly disconnected EEG findings across all three domains may be linked based on documented behavioral connections between motor development and cognitive and social abilities.

Motor Development

To our knowledge, Mizuno et al. (1970) and Bell and Fox (1997) have been the only individuals to study motor development and EEG power simultaneously. Although Mizuno et al. (1970) did not explicitly seek to investigate coaction between motor experience and power, their longitudinal study found that infants' ability to hold up their head, sit, stand and walk was accompanied by increased power measured from the occipital region within the 7.17 to 10.30 frequency. Bell and Fox (1997) investigated individual differences at 8 months in crawling, object permanence, and frontal power within the 6–9 Hz band. Eight-month-olds with 1–4 weeks of crawling experience had significantly greater power at medial frontal, lateral frontal, and parietal regions at baseline, compared to pre-locomotor infants

[1] It is important to note that the measured activity between two electrode sites may also be mediated by a third source (i.e., a common input; Bastos and Schoffelen, 2016).

or infants with >4 weeks of crawling (Bell and Fox, 1997; object permanence results discussed in the "Cognitive Development" section). Greater power may indicate increased synchrony or coordination of neural activity within a region, which could reflect increased regional maturation and organization (Nunez, 1981; Bell and Fox, 1992). Increased power in frontal and parietal regions may indicate that onset of crawling is related to a greater need for novice crawlers to recruit these regions for motor planning.

Coherence is an excellent measure of neural changes as infants shift from non-crawling to crawling, and from crawling to walking (Bell and Fox, 1996; Corbetta et al., 2014). Bell and Fox (1996) hypothesized that prior to crawling, infants have an overproduction of synaptic connections, and as crawling experience is gained, "pruning" of unnecessary connections occurs, resulting in an inverted U-shape of coherence. Results found that 8-month-old novice crawlers (1–8 weeks crawling) displayed greater coherence over medial frontal/lateral frontal and medial frontal/occipital regions, compared to same-aged non-crawlers (0 weeks) and experienced crawlers (≥9 weeks). Thus, experience crawling is related to neural reorganization. Recently, Corbetta et al. (2014) explored the relation between walking experience and coherence in 12-month-olds. They also found a motor experience-dependent inverted U-shape of coherence: novice walkers had the highest levels of coherence compared to non-walkers and experienced walkers, specifically between lateral frontal and central electrodes (Corbetta et al., 2014). High coherence in novice walkers and low coherence in experienced walkers may point to synaptic growth as infants begin to walk, and pruning once infants gain experience. Low coherence between lateral frontal and central electrodes may indicate that changes in walking ability relate to greater regional differentiation/specialization between frontal and central regions of the cortex, regions known for their role in motor control (Graziano, 2006), and inhibitory control and working memory (Diamond, 1990).

Mu desynchronization has quickly gained prevalence in investigating motor related neural changes during infancy (Cannon et al., 2014; Cuevas et al., 2014). van Elk et al. (2008) studied mu desynchronization in 14- to 16-month-old crawlers. Infants observed videos of other infants walking or crawling. Mu desynchronization at central electrodes was significantly greater when infants observed crawlers compared to walkers. Recently, Cannon et al. (2015) investigated the relation between motor *ability* and mu desynchronization. Nine-month-olds observed an adult reaching for a toy, and were given the opportunity to reach for the toy themselves. Infant reaching and grasping skill was measured by assessing latency to reach, errors, pre-shaping of the hand, and bimanual reaching. Reach latency was related to mu desynchronization during action observation, with shorter latency correlating with greater desynchronization (Cannon et al., 2015). Marshall et al. (2011) provide additional evidence supporting the role of infant motor experience in mu desynchronization. During observation of an action within their motor repertoire, 14-month-olds displayed mu desynchronization over frontal, central, and parietal regions (Marshall et al., 2011). Findings that mu desynchronization occurs during observation of an action within an infant's motor repertoire suggests a close link between motor experience and mu rhythm activity.

The results reviewed here on motor experience and neural activity lend strong support to the idea of a dynamic motor–neural interaction. Nonetheless, power, coherence, and mu desynchronization have not been used in studies documenting motor development longitudinally. Moreover, it is unknown how these motor-related neural shifts are implicated in behaviorally observed motor cascades. These gaps in the literature must be addressed, as information pertaining to motor-related neural changes over time may help elucidate the role of motor development as a "setting event" in non-motor domains.

Cognitive Development

A common measure of infant cognitive development used in conjunction with EEG measures is performance on the A-not-B task, a behavioral measure of working memory and inhibitory control. A-not-B performance has been implicated in individual differences in power. Measuring power and A-not-B performance from 7 to 12 months, Bell and Fox (1992) found that infants who were tolerant of longer delays prior to A-not-B object retrieval at 12 months displayed a significant decrease in baseline frontal power from 7 to 8 months, and had the greatest monthly increase in frontal power from 9 to 10 months, a different neural trajectory from infants tolerating only short delays. When grouping participants by infants who solved the A-not-B task at 7 or 8 months or infants who solved the A-not-B task at 9 months, infants who solved the A-not-B task by 7–8 months displayed greater power at the right frontal lead, compared to the left frontal lead at 8 months (Bell and Fox, 1992). When measuring power during A-not-B engagement, high performing 8-month-olds displayed an increase in power from baseline to task across frontal pole, medial frontal, parietal, and occipital electrodes, while low performers did not show a significant change in power from baseline to task (Bell, 2001). Measuring power at baseline before A-not-B engagement, 8-month-olds who completed the A-not-B task successfully had greater power at medial frontal and occipital electrodes compared to unsuccessful infants (Bell and Fox, 1997). Overall, research on power and the A-not-B task suggests that neural maturity, particularly in frontal regions, is linked to performance on this cognitive task.

Studies measuring coherence during the A-not-B task find that high A-not-B performers at 8 months display significantly lower right hemisphere coherence between frontal pole-medial frontal regions compared to left frontal pole-medial frontal hemisphere coherence, while low performers show no hemispheric differences in coherence between these regions (Bell, 2001). Longitudinally, behavioral differences on A-not-B performance overlap with neural changes: high and low performers on the A-not-B task diverged in performance around 10 months, coinciding with the age when high performers begin to demonstrate an increase in left hemisphere coherence from 10 to 12 months (based on averaged frontal-parietal and frontal-occipital data), evidence of distinct neural trajectories based on cognitive ability (Bell and Fox, 1992). Frontal coherence was also found to increase when greater inhibitory control was needed by 10-month-olds during the A-not-B task (Cuevas et al., 2012). Focusing on A-not-B performance and coherence at 8 months and at 4.5 years, Bell and Wolfe (2007) found changes in coherence, with all electrode pairs demonstrating decreased coherence from baseline to task at 8 months. By 4.5 years of age, increased coherence (during a different measure of working memory) was found only between medial frontal/posterior temporal pairs and medial frontal/occipital pairs (Bell and Wolfe, 2007). Although both Bell (2001) and Bell and Wolfe (2007) measured coherence in samples of 8-month-olds, one study found changes in coherence only between right frontal pole-medial frontal regions, while the other identified changes in coherence across all electrode pairs measured. The differences in coherence seen in Bell (2001) and Bell and Wolfe (2007) samples likely stems from differential participant grouping between the two studies. Although both studies analyzed baseline-to-task changes in EEG, Bell (2001) grouped infants as high and low performers, while Bell and Wolfe (2007) did not group infants based on performance.

Currently, no study has implicated mu desynchronization with cognitive performance. Perhaps researchers conceptualize mu desynchronization as an index of motor experience only, without considering the behavioral links between motor and cognitive development. We speculate that infants who are successful at tasks like A-not-B may display increased mu desynchronization during observation and execution, but actual research is needed to assess how cognition and mu rhythm relate. We know from Smith et al. (1999) and Smith and Thelen (2003) that errors produced by 8- to 10-month-olds on A-not-B tasks disappear by changing the infant's physical state, like altering posture from sitting to standing between trials. Developmental shifts in posture reorganize infants' experiences with objects, changing multimodal exploration and subsequent object knowledge (Soska and Adolph, 2014; Soska et al., 2010). Moreover, Kermoian and Campos (1988) found that A-not-B performance is correlated to locomotor experience: infants with experience locomoting voluntarily (crawling or in a walker) perform better on the A-not-B task than pre-locomotor infants. Thus, motor experience plays an important role in cognitive development. To date, only Bell and Fox (1997) have attempted to connect motor development (crawling), neural development (power) and cognitive performance (A-not-B task), but no interaction between all three was identified. Future work should investigate how motor experience is linked to observed neural changes concurrent with performance on cognitive tasks.

Social Development

Research on power and infant social development has focused on asymmetrical power between hemispheres. Differential power between left and right frontal regions is considered a marker of individual differences in emotional reactivity to stress with withdrawal-related behaviors being related to greater right versus left frontal activation (Davidson and Fox, 1989). Ten-month-olds who cried during maternal separation in Davidson and Fox (1989) displayed greater right frontal activation during baseline measurement. Similarly, infants identified as behaviorally inhibited at 4 months, who continued to be socially inhibited in early childhood, displayed right hemisphere asymmetry at 9, 14, and 48 months (Fox et al., 2001). Negative reactivity in 9-month-olds with greater right frontal asymmetry was associated with social wariness at 4 years (Henderson et al., 2001). Moreover, 9-month-olds who experienced lower quality maternal caregiving behavior were more likely to have right frontal asymmetry at 3 years (Hane et al., 2010). It is important to note that in studies of temperament, classification regarding inhibition is routinely based on infant *motor activity* in response to novel events (Calkins et al., 1996).

Coherence has also served as a neural tool in relation to infant social development, specifically in research on initiating joint attention (IJA; Mundy et al., 2000, 2003). Mundy et al. (2000) found that lower coherence (i.e., greater differentiation/specialization) between left frontal/central sites at 14 months related to greater IJA at 18 months. Left hemisphere coherence between frontal/central sites at 14 months was also negatively correlated with vocabulary at 24 months, and coherence between left frontal/occipital sites was positively correlated with vocabulary (Mundy et al., 2003). Additionally, greater IJA skill at 14 months was highly associated with greater vocabulary at 24 months (Mundy et al., 2003). Thus, individual differences in infants' IJA and neural development are both related to future vocabulary.

Mu desynchronization has been used as a neural measure in studies of infants' action perception and imitation (Southgate et al., 2010; Saby et al., 2012). When 8-month-olds were presented with videos of goal-directed versus non-goal-directed actions, mu rhythm over central and right frontal regions decreased during observation of goal-directed actions (Nyström et al., 2011). Moreover, when 9-month-olds were presented with stimuli of mimed reaching actions (i.e., non-goal-directed) and stimuli of a grasping hand disappearing behind an occluder (where grasping can only be inferred), mu desynchronization only occurred during occluded grasping, indicating that infants may predict the goal of a social partner (Southgate et al., 2010). Concerning imitation, Saby et al. (2012) found that 14-month-olds displayed greater mu desynchronization over central regions when their actions were imitated. Overall, evidence suggests that mu desynchronization may be implicated in processing of another individual's actions, which is critical for social cognition.

From behavioral work, it is known that motor experience plays an important role in social development (Campos et al., 2000). For example, infant IJA mediates the relation between self-locomotion and anticipatory gaze during means-ends sequences, indicating a close link between locomotion, IJA and social cognition (Brandone, 2015). Perhaps the observed relation between IJA, vocabulary and coherence is a function of motor experience, given that language and motor skills are closely interrelated (Nelson et al., 2014; Walle and Campos, 2014). Moreover, paradigms that alter motor experience prior to the typical onset of a motor skill result in social changes, like increased attention to faces during preferential looking, and dishabituation to "unexpected" goals when observing an individual's goal-directed actions (Sommerville et al., 2005; Libertus and Needham, 2011). Based on the power, coherence, and mu desynchronization literature, it is clear that social development and neural changes interact, but how motor development is implicated in this interaction remains unknown.

CONCLUSION

As reviewed here, research utilizing power, coherence, and mu desynchronization provides great insight on motor, cognitive, and social development as *isolated* domains. Research has yet to gain traction on implementing these EEG tools toward understanding the neural mechanisms underlying documented motor cascades in infant cognitive and social development. Development in one domain is likely not isolated from development in other domains, but instead involves dynamic interactions throughout development (Spencer et al., 2011). Much work is left to be done, as little is known regarding the longitudinal development of measures like mu desynchronization, or how power, coherence, and mu desynchronization relate to our existing knowledge of motor, cognitive and social development. Importantly, while existing behavioral work is supportive of motor to cognitive, and motor to social cascades (e.g., Campos et al., 2000; Libertus and Needham, 2011; Walle and Campos, 2014), inclusion of neural measures in research on these cross-domain relations may further clarify the complex interaction between neural plasticity and behavior. One initial step to help clarify these relations would be to conduct more longitudinal work relating motor, cognitive, and social development to neural changes, as most of the research reviewed here was cross-sectional. New research that finds ways to manipulate motor experience in infancy could also provide an optimal way to disentangle how motor experience is related to reorganization of neural activity and connectivity, and how these possible neural changes manifest concurrently across social and cognitive development. Research with EEG comparing typical and atypical development in motor, cognitive, and social abilities is also needed, as it may shed light on how these domains influence each other, and how neural patterns and connectivity play a role in observed behaviors. The plasticity of the brain in infancy lends itself to prime exploration, and we urge researchers to rely on power, coherence and mu desynchronization as tools to explore it.

AUTHOR CONTRIBUTIONS

Conceived and wrote the paper: SG, BR-S, and EN.

FUNDING

SG was supported by NIH/NIGMS R25 GM061347. Publication of this article was funded by a Florida International University Center for Children and Families Intramural Award to EN.

REFERENCES

Arnstein, D., Cui, F., Keysers, C., Maurits, N. M., and Gazzola, V. (2011). μ-Suppression during action observation and execution correlates with BOLD in dorsal premotor, inferior parietal, and SI cortices. *J. Neurosci.* 31, 14243–14249. doi: 10.1523/JNEUROSCI.0963-11.2011

Bastos, A. M., and Schoffelen, J.-M. (2016). A tutorial review of functional connectivity analysis methods and their interpretational pitfalls. *Front. Syst. Neurosci.* 9:175. doi: 10.3389/fnsys.2015.00175

Bell, M. A. (1998). "The ontogeny of the EEG during infancy and childhood: implications for cognitive development," in *Neuroimaging in Child Neuropsychiatric Disorders*, ed. B. Garreau (Berlin: Springer-Verlag), 97–111. doi: 10.1007/978-3-642-95848-9

Bell, M. A. (2001). Brain electrical activity associated with cognitive processing during a looking version of the A-not-B task. *Infancy* 2, 311–330. doi: 10.1207/S15327078IN0203_2

Bell, M. A., and Cuevas, K. (2012). Using EEG to study cognitive development: issues and practices. *J. Cogn. Dev.* 13, 281–294. doi: 10.1080/15248372.2012.691143

Bell, M. A., and Fox, N. A. (1992). The relations between frontal brain electrical activity and cognitive development during infancy. *Child Dev.* 63, 1142–1163. doi: 10.2307/1131523

Bell, M. A., and Fox, N. A. (1996). Crawling experience is related to changes in cortical organization during infancy: evidence from EEG coherence. *Dev. Psychobiol.* 29, 551–561. doi: 10.1002/(SICI)1098-2302(199611)29:7<551::AID-DEV1>3.0.CO;2-T

Bell, M. A., and Fox, N. A. (1997). Individual differences in object permanence performance at 8 months: locomotor experience and brain electrical activity. *Dev. Psychobiol.* 31, 287–297.

Bell, M. A., and Wolfe, C. D. (2007). Changes in brain functioning from infancy to early childhood: evidence from EEG power and coherence during working memory tasks. *Dev. Neuropsychol.* 31, 21–38. doi: 10.1080/8756564070 9336885

Biringen, Z., Emde, R. N., Campos, J. J., and Appelbaum, M. I. (1995). Affective reorganization in the infant, the mother, and the dyad: the role of upright locomotion and its timing. *Child Dev.* 66, 499–514. doi: 10.2307/1131593

Bornstein, M. H., Hahn, C.-S., and Suwalsky, J. T. D. (2013). Physically developed and exploratory young infants contribute to their own long-term academic achievement. *Psychol. Sci.* 24, 1906–1917. doi: 10.1177/0956797613479974

Braadbaart, L., Williams, J. H. G., and Waiter, G. D. (2013). Do mirror neuron areas mediate mu rhythm suppression during imitation and action observation? *Int. J. Psychophysiol.* 89, 99–105. doi: 10.1016/j.ijpsycho.2013.05.019

Brandone, A. C. (2015). Infants' social and motor experience and the emerging understanding of intentional actions. *Dev. Psychol.* 51, 512–523. doi: 10.1037/a0038844

Bushnell, E. W., and Boudreau, J. P. (1993). Motor development and the mind: the potential role of motor abilities as a determinant of aspects of perceptual development. *Child Dev.* 64, 1005–1021. doi: 10.1111/j.1467-8624.1993.tb04184.x

Calkins, S. D., Fox, N. A., and Marshall, T. R. (1996). Behavioral and physiological antecedents of inhibited and uninhibited behavior. *Child Dev.* 67, 523–540. doi: 10.1111/j.1467-8624.1996.tb01749.x

Campos, J. J., Anderson, D. I., Barbu-Roth, M., Hubbard, E. M., Hertenstein, M. J., and Witherington, D. (2000). Travel broadens the mind. *Infancy* 1, 149–219. doi: 10.1207/S15327078IN0102

Campos, J. J., Kennoian, R., and Zumbahlen, M. R. (1992). Socioemotional transformations in the family system following infant crawling onset. *New Dir. Child Dev.* 1992, 25–40. doi: 10.1002/cd.23219925504

Cannon, E. N., Simpson, E. A., Fox, N. A., Vanderwert, R. E., Woodward, A. L., and Ferrari, P. F. (2015). Relations between infants' emerging reach-grasp competence and event-related desynchronization in EEG. *Dev. Sci.* 19, 50–62. doi: 10.1111/desc.12295

Cannon, E. N., Yoo, K. H., Vanderwert, R. E., Ferrari, P. F., Woodward, A. L., and Fox, N. A. (2014). Action experience, more than observation, influences mu rhythm desynchronization. *PLoS ONE* 9:e92002. doi: 10.1371/journal.pone.0092002

Clearfield, M. W. (2011). Learning to walk changes infants' social interactions. *Infant Behav. Dev.* 34, 15–25. doi: 10.1016/j.infbeh.2010.04.008

Corbetta, D., Friedman, D. R., and Bell, M. A. (2014). Brain reorganization as a function of walking experience in 12-month-old infants: implications for the development of manual laterality. *Front. Psychol.* 5:245. doi: 10.3389/fpsyg.2014.00245

Cuevas, K., Cannon, E. N., Yoo, K., and Fox, N. A. (2014). The infant EEG mu rhythm: methodological considerations and best practices. *Dev. Rev.* 34, 26–43. doi: 10.1016/j.dr.2013.12.001

Cuevas, K., Swingler, M. M., Bell, M. A., Marcovitch, S., and Calkins, S. D. (2012). Measures of frontal functioning and the emergence of inhibitory control processes at 10 months of age. *Dev. Cogn. Neurosci.* 2, 235–243. doi: 10.1016/j.dcn.2012.01.002

Davidson, R. J., and Fox, N. A. (1989). Frontal brain asymmetry predicts infants' response to maternal separation. *J. Abnorm. Psychol.* 98, 127–131. doi: 10.1037/0021-843X.98.2.127

Diamond, A. (1990). The development and neural bases of memory functions as indexed by the AB and delayed response tasks in human infants and infant monkeys. *Ann. N. Y. Acad. Sci.* 608, 267–309; discussion 309–317. doi: 10.1111/j.1749-6632.1990.tb48900.x

Fox, N. A., Henderson, H. A., Rubin, K. H., Calkins, S. D., and Schmidt, L. A. (2001). Continuity and discontinuity of behavioral inhibition and exuberance: psychophysiological and behavioral influences across the first four years of life. *Child Dev.* 72, 1–21. doi: 10.1111/1467-8624.00262

Graziano, M. (2006). The organization of behavioral repertoire in motor cortex. *Annu. Rev. Neurosci.* 29, 105–134. doi: 10.1146/annurev.neuro.29.051605.112924

Gustafson, G. E. (1984). Effects of the ability to locomote on infants' social and exploratory behaviors: an experimental study. *Dev. Psychol.* 20, 397–405. doi: 10.1037//0012-1649.20.3.397

Hane, A. A., Henderson, H. A., Reeb-Sutherland, B. C., and Fox, N. A. (2010). Ordinary variations in human maternal caregiving in infancy and biobehavioral development in early childhood: a follow-up study. *Dev. Psychobiol.* 52, 558–567. doi: 10.1002/dev.20461

Henderson, H. A., Fox, N. A., and Rubin, K. H. (2001). Temperamental contributions to social behavior: the moderating roles of frontal EEG asymmetry and gender. *J. Am. Acad. Child Adolesc. Psychiatry* 40, 68–74. doi: 10.1097/00004583-200101000-00018

Karasik, L. B., Tamis-Lemonda, C. S., and Adolph, K. E. (2014). Crawling and walking infants elicit different verbal responses from mothers. *Dev. Sci.* 3, 1–8. doi: 10.1111/desc.12129

Kermoian, R., and Campos, J. J. (1988). Locomotor experience: a facilitator of spatial cognitive development. *Child Dev.* 59, 908–917. doi: 10.2307/1130258

Libertus, K., and Needham, A. (2011). Reaching experience increases face preference in 3-month-old infants. *Dev. Sci.* 14, 1355–1364. doi: 10.1111/j.1467-7687.2011.01084.x

Marshall, P. J., Bar-Haim, Y., and Fox, N. A. (2002). Development of the EEG from 5 months to 4 years of age. *Clin. Neurophysiol.* 113, 1199–1208. doi: 10.1016/S1388-2457(02)00163-3

Marshall, P. J., Young, T., and Meltzoff, A. N. (2011). Neural correlates of action observation and execution in 14-month-old infants: an event-related EEG desynchronization study. *Dev. Sci.* 14, 474–480. doi: 10.1111/j.1467-7687.2010.00991.x

Mizuno, T., Yamauchi, N., Watanabe, A., Komatsushiro, M., Takagi, T., Iinuma, K., et al. (1970). Maturation patterns of EEG basic waves of healthy infants under twelve-months of age. *Tohoku J. Exp. Med.* 102, 91–98. doi: 10.1620/tjem.102.91

Mundy, P., Card, J., and Fox, N. (2000). EEG correlates of the development of infant joint attention skills. *Dev. Psychobiol.* 36, 325–338. doi: 10.1002/(SICI)1098-2302(200005)36:4<325::AID-DEV7>3.0.CO;2-F

Mundy, P., Fox, N., and Card, J. (2003). EEG coherence, joint attention and language development in the second year. *Dev. Sci.* 6, 48–54. doi: 10.1111/1467-7687.00253

Nelson, E. L., Campbell, J. M., and Michel, G. F. (2014). Early handedness in infancy predicts language ability in toddlers. *Dev. Psychol.* 50, 809–814. doi: 10.1037/a0033803

Nunez, P. L. (1981). *Electric Fields of the Brain: The Neurophysics of EEG.* New York, NY: Oxford University Press.

Nyström, P., Ljunghammar, T., Rosander, K., and Von Hofsten, C. (2011). Using mu rhythm desynchronization to measure mirror neuron activity in infants. *Dev. Sci.* 14, 327–335. doi: 10.1111/j.1467-7687.2010.00979.x

Pineda, J. A. (2005). The functional significance of mu rhythms: translating "seeing" and "hearing" into "doing." *Brain Res. Brain Res. Rev.* 50, 57–68. doi: 10.1016/j.brainresrev.2005.04.005

Reid, V. M., Striano, T., and Iacoboni, M. (2011). Neural correlates of dyadic interaction during infancy. *Dev. Cogn. Neurosci.* 1, 124–130. doi: 10.1016/j.dcn.2011.01.001

Saby, J. N., Marshall, P. J., and Meltzoff, A. N. (2012). Neural correlates of being imitated: an EEG study in preverbal infants. *Soc. Neurosci.* 7, 650–661. doi: 10.1080/17470919.2012.691429

Smith, L. B., and Thelen, E. (2003). Development as a dynamic system. *Trends Cogn. Sci.* 7, 343–348. doi: 10.1016/S1364-6613(03)00156-6

Smith, L. B., Thelen, E., Titzer, R., and McLin, D. (1999). Knowing in the context of acting: the task dynamics of the A-not-B error. *Psychol. Rev.* 106, 235–260. doi: 10.1037/0033-295X.106.2.235

Sommerville, J. A., Woodward, A. L., and Needham, A. (2005). Action experience alters 3-month-old infants' perception of others' actions. *Cognition* 96, 1–11. doi: 10.1016/j.cognition.2004.07.004

Soska, K. C., and Adolph, K. E. (2014). Postural position constrains multimodal object exploration in infants. *Infancy* 19, 138–161. doi: 10.1111/infa.12039

Soska, K. C., Adolph, K. E., and Johnson, S. P. (2010). Systems in development: motor skill acquisition facilitates three-dimensional object completion. *Dev. Psychol.* 46, 129–138. doi: 10.1037/a0014618

Southgate, V., Johnson, M. H., Karoui, I. E., and Csibra, G. (2010). Motor system activation reveals infants' on-line prediction of others' goals. *Psychol. Sci.* 21, 355–359. doi: 10.1177/0956797610362058

Spencer, J. P., Perone, S., and Buss, A. T. (2011). Twenty years and going strong: a dynamic systems revolution in motor and cognitive development. *Child Dev. Perspect.* 5, 260–266. doi: 10.1111/j.1750-8606.2011.00194.x

Thatcher, R. W., Walker, R. A., and Giudice, S. (1987). Human cerebral hemispheres develop at different rates and ages. *Science* 236, 1110–1113. doi: 10.1126/science.3576224

Thorpe, S. G., Cannon, E. N., and Fox, N. A. (2015). Spectral and source structural development of mu and alpha rhythms from infancy through adulthood. *Clin. Neurophysiol.* 127, 254–269. doi: 10.1016/j.clinph.2015.03.004

van Elk, M., van Schie, H. T., Hunnius, S., Vesper, C., and Bekkering, H. (2008). You'll never crawl alone: neurophysiological evidence for experience-dependent motor resonance in infancy. *Neuroimage* 43, 808–814. doi: 10.1016/j.neuroimage.2008.07.057

Vanderwert, R. E., Fox, N. A., and Ferrari, P. F. (2013). The mirror mechanism and mu rhythm in social development. *Neurosci. Lett.* 540, 15–20. doi: 10.1016/j.neulet.2012.10.006

Walle, E., and Campos, J. J. (2014). Infant language development is related to the acquisition of walking. *Dev. Psychol.* 50, 336–348. doi: 10.1037/a0033238

Conflict of Interest Statement: The authors declare that the research was conducted in the absence of any commercial or financial relationships that could be construed as a potential conflict of interest.

4

The General Movement Assessment Helps us to Identify Preterm Infants at Risk for Cognitive Dysfunction

Christa Einspieler[1], Arend F. Bos[2], Melissa E. Libertus[3] and Peter B. Marschik[1,4]*

[1] Research Unit iDN – interdisciplinary Developmental Neuroscience, Institute of Physiology, Center for Physiological Medicine, Medical University of Graz, Graz, Austria, [2] Division of Neonatology, Department of Pediatrics, Beatrix Children's Hospital, University Medical Center, University of Groningen, Groningen, Netherlands, [3] Department of Psychology, Learning Research Development Center, University of Pittsburgh, Pittsburgh, PA, USA, [4] Center of Neurodevelopmental Disorders, Department of Women's Children's Health, Karolinska Institutet, Stockholm, Sweden

Apart from motor and behavioral dysfunctions, deficits in cognitive skills are among the well-documented sequelae of preterm birth. However, early identification of infants at risk for poor cognition is still a challenge, as no clear association between pathological findings based on neuroimaging scans and cognitive functions have been detected as yet. The Prechtl General Movement Assessment (GMA) has shown its merits for the evaluation of the integrity of the young nervous system. It is a reliable tool for identifying infants at risk for neuromotor deficits. Recent studies on preterm infants demonstrate that abnormal general movements (GMs) also reflect impairments of brain areas involved in cognitive development. The aim of this systematic review was to discuss studies that included (i) the Prechtl GMA applied in preterm infants, and (ii) cognitive outcome measures in six data bases. Seven studies met the inclusion criteria and yielded the following results: (a) children born preterm with consistently abnormal GMs up to 8 weeks after term had lower intelligence quotients at school age than children with an early normalization of GMs; (b) from 3 to 5 months after term, several qualitative, and quantitative aspects of the concurrent motor repertoire, including postural patterns, were predictive of intelligence at 7–10 years of age. These findings in 428 individuals born preterm suggest that normal GMs along with a normal motor repertoire during the first months after term are markers for normal cognitive development until at least age 10.

Edited by:
*Petra Hauf,
St. Francis Xavier University, Canada*

Reviewed by:
*Ruth Ford,
Anglia Ruskin University, UK
David Uttal,
Northwestern University, USA*

***Correspondence:**
*Christa Einspieler
christa.einspieler@medunigraz.at*

Keywords: cognition, fidgety movements, general movements, intelligence, motor behavior, posture, preterm

INTRODUCTION

Children born preterm have higher rates of adverse motor, cognitive, behavioral, and psychiatric outcomes than their term-born peers, even in the absence of brain injury (e.g., Johnson, 2007; Doyle and Anderson, 2010; Bos and Roze, 2011; Johnson et al., 2015). Cognitive deficits occur in 25–50% of children born preterm, especially if their birth weight is under 1500 g

---

Abbreviations: DQ, developmental quotient; ELBW, extremely low birth weight; GMs, general movements; GMA, general movement assessment; IQ, intelligence quotient; MDI, mental developmental index; SD, standard deviation.

(Bhutta et al., 2002; Johnson, 2007; Saigal and Doyle, 2008). On average, children born at <32 weeks' gestation score at least 11 points below their term-born peers in a cognitive test (Foulder-Hughes and Cooke, 2003; Larroque et al., 2005). This number increases with inverse proportion to each week of shorter gestation (Bhutta et al., 2002; Johnson, 2007). Although the age of cognitive evaluation had no significant impact on the reported differences (Bhutta et al., 2002), the deficit usually becomes more evident when children enter school and face higher cognitive demands.

The identification of infants at risk for poor cognition is a challenging issue. Clear associations between alterations in the brain structure and cognitive deficits are still scarce, although global white matter damage is common among children born preterm, and gray matter volumes are diminished (Nosarti et al., 2008; Soria-Pastor et al., 2008; Volpe, 2009; Ullman et al., 2015). Recently, de Vries et al. (2015) suggested that subtle white matter injuries and cerebellar lesions may be specifically associated with cognitive problems. Advanced brain imaging techniques such as tract-based special statistics of diffusion tensor imaging are suggested to potentially define early markers for cognitive development in preterm infants if applied at term-equivalent age (van Kooij et al., 2015).

These neuroimaging techniques are not globally available and do not supersede the need to functionally assess the integrity of the young nervous system. One of the most reliable and sensitive non-intrusive techniques, which has been used for more than 25 years, is the assessment of GMs, an early spontaneous movement pattern (Prechtl, 1997, 2001; Prechtl et al., 1997; Einspieler and Prechtl, 2005; Bosanquet et al., 2013).

WHAT ARE GENERAL MOVEMENTS?

Without even being constantly triggered by a specific sensory input, the fetal and neonatal nervous system generates a variety of motor patterns such as simple startles or twitches, but also more complex patterns such as stretching, yawning or GMs (Einspieler et al., 2008, 2012c). The latter involve the entire body in a variable sequence of neck, arm, trunk, and leg movements. They wax and wane, varying in intensity, speed, and range of motion, and have a gradual onset and end. Rotations around the limb axes and slight changes in the direction of movement create the impression of fluency and elegance (Prechtl, 1990; Einspieler and Prechtl, 2005). By and large, GMs have a similar appearance from early fetal life until the end of the second month after term; from term age onward, they are called "writhing movements." At 6–9 weeks postterm age, writhing movements gradually disappear and GMs of a fidgety character gradually emerge (Einspieler and Prechtl, 2005). Observable from 3 to 5 months after term, so-called "fidgety movements" are tiny movements of the neck, trunk, and limbs in all directions and of variable acceleration (Prechtl et al., 1997).

General movements are generated by a neural network, the central pattern generators (CPGs), which are most likely located in the brainstem. In order to lend variability to the motor output, supraspinal projections activate, inhibit and, most importantly, modulate the CPG activity, as does the sensory feedback (Einspieler et al., 2004; Einspieler and Marschik, 2012).

Reduced modulation of the CPGs results in less variable (i.e., abnormal) movements and indicates fetal or neonatal compromise. Abnormal GMs during preterm and term age are classified as (a) poor repertoire GMs, whereby the sequence of movement components is monotonous and the intensity, speed, and range of motion lack the normal variability; (b) cramped-synchronized GMs, which lack the usual smoothness and fluency and appear rigid as the limb and trunk muscles contract almost simultaneously and relax almost simultaneously; (c) chaotic GMs, which are abrupt and tremulous, of large amplitude and high speed; they rarely occur at term age or beyond, but are typically observed in the moderate preterm age (Ferrari et al., 1990; Bos et al., 1997; Einspieler and Prechtl, 2005; Einspieler et al., 2015a). Abnormal fidgety movements are exaggerated in amplitude, speed, and jerkiness (Prechtl et al., 1997). If fidgety movements are only sporadically present or altogether absent at 3–5 months, the infant is likely to develop severe neurological deficits such as cerebral palsy (e.g., Prechtl et al., 1997; Einspieler and Prechtl, 2005; Bruggink et al., 2009; Yang et al., 2012; Bosanquet et al., 2013; Einspieler et al., 2015b).

Apart from incipient yet promising and time-consuming attempts to analyze GMs with the aid of computer-based tools (e.g., Adde et al., 2009; Einspieler and Marschik, 2013; Marcroft et al., 2015), the state-of-the-art GMA applied in research and clinical routine is based on visual Gestalt perception of age-specific normal and abnormal patterns. Experienced observers consistently achieved high inter-scorer agreements ranging from Kappa 0.85 to 0.94 (e.g., Einspieler and Prechtl, 2005; Valentin et al., 2005; Mutlu et al., 2008). For this standardized assessment, the comfortably dressed infant is video-taped in supine position for 3–5 min, provided that the infant is not fussy or crying (Einspieler et al., 1997). In other words, GMA is non-invasive, non-intrusive, cost-effective, and highly reliable.

Since its introduction 26 years ago (Prechtl, 1990), GMA has been increasingly appreciated for predicting motor dysfunctions, especially cerebral palsy (for reviews, see e.g., Spittle et al., 2008; Burger and Louw, 2009; Einspieler et al., 2012b; Noble and Boyd, 2012; Bosanquet et al., 2013). Cramped-synchronized GMs and the absence of fidgety movements are particularly good predictors of cerebral palsy (e.g., Prechtl et al., 1997; Einspieler et al., 2012b), whereas poor repertoire GMs and abnormal fidgety movements tend to be associated with minor neurological dysfunctions (e.g., Nakajima et al., 2006; Einspieler et al., 2007; Bruggink et al., 2008; Yuge et al., 2011). Only recently was the focus put on the question whether or not GMA might also shed light on cognitive and language development (e.g., Butcher et al., 2009; Bruggink et al., 2010; Spittle et al., 2013) or behavioral, mental, and genetic disorders (e.g., Hadders-Algra et al., 2009; Marschik et al., 2009, 2015; Einspieler et al., 2012a, 2014; Zappella et al., 2015).

METHOD

Our aim was to systematically review studies that included cognitive outcome assessments of children born preterm whose

GMs had been examined during infancy. A comprehensive literature search was performed using the following databases: Medline, CINAHL, The Cochrane Library, Science Direct, PsycINFO, and EMBASE. The search strategy included the MeSH terms and search strings ('GM*' OR 'spontaneous motor activity') AND ('cognition' OR 'cognitive' OR 'intelligence'). Requests were limited to human participants. The search strategy additionally included studies published on the website of the General Movement Trust (www.general-movements-trust.info). Furthermore, we searched for alternative studies carried out by the authors of the publications picked for this review, using the same search strategies. The following inclusion criteria were applied: (a) primary research based on the Prechtl assessment of GMs; (b) study samples consisting of preterm infants; (c) the outcome had to be assessed at 12 months postterm age or later. Seven studies met these criteria, comprising a total of 428 individuals; the cognitive outcomes were assessed at ages ranging from 2 to 11 years; details are provided in **Tables 1** and **2**. The studies were conducted in Australia (Spittle et al., 2013), Italy (Beccaria et al., 2012), Norway (Fjørtoft et al., 2013; Grunewaldt et al., 2014), Slovenia (Kodric et al., 2010), and the Netherlands (Butcher et al., 2009; Bruggink et al., 2010). As GMs occur in age-specific patterns we present our results separately for studies involving GMA up to the end of the first month post term (writhing GMs; Section "The Link between Early Normalization of GMs and Cognitive Development") and studies focusing on GMA from 3 to 5 months postterm age (fidgety movements; Section "Fidgety Movements May Not Predict Cognitive Development, But Concurrent Movements and Postures Do").

TABLE 1 | Studies associating writhing GMs with cognitive development, listed according to the age of outcome assessment.

Reference	Cohort	Outcome assessment	Cut-off points	Predictive values
Beccaria et al., 2012	$N = 79$ born ≤ 32 weeks' gestation	**2 years** Griffiths Scales of Mental Development, Italian version	Not given	Not given
Spittle et al., 2013	$N = 94$ born < 30 weeks' gestation	**2 years** Bayley Scales of Infant and Toddler Development, third edition	Abnormal vs. normal writhing GMs related to moderate to severe cognitive impairment	Sensitivity: 80% (95% CI: 44–96%) Specificity: 41% (95% CI: 31–53%) PPV: 14% (95% CI: 7–27%) NPV: 94% (95% CI: 80–99%) Accuracy: 46% (95% CI: 36–56%)
Kodric et al., 2010	$N = 26$ born < 36 weeks' gestation	**2–3 years** (mean = 28.3 months; *SD* = 5.6 months) Bayley Scales of Infant Development, second edition, Slovenian version	Abnormal vs. normal writhing GMs related to *MDI* ≤ 84 vs. *MDI* > 84 (excluding *n* = 3 with cerebral palsy)	Sensitivity: 100% Specificity: 28%
Spittle et al., 2013	$N = 85$ born < 30 weeks' gestation	**4 years** Differential Ability Scale, second edition	Abnormal vs. normal writhing GMs related to moderate to severe impairment in the general cognitive ability	Sensitivity: 89% (95% CI: 64–98%) Specificity: 48% (95% CI: 36–61%) PPV: 33% (95% CI: 20–48%) NPV: 67% (95% CI: 52–80%) Accuracy: 57% (95% CI: 46–68%)
Bruggink et al., 2010	$N = 60$ born < 34 weeks' gestation	**7–11 years** (median = 9 years) Wechsler Intelligence Scale for Children-III, Dutch version	Consistently abnormal GMs to 8 weeks after term vs. normal GMs before 8 weeks after term related to total *IQ* < 85 vs. total *IQ* ≥ 85	Sensitivity: 67% (95% CI: 43–91%) Specificity: 71% (95% CI: 58–84%) PPV: 43% (95% CI: 23–63%) NPV: 86% (95% CI: 75–97%)

CI, confidence interval; IQ, intelligence quotient; MDI, mental developmental index; NPV, negative predictive value; PPV, positive predictive value; SD, standard deviation.

TABLE 2 | Assessment of fidgety movements and the concurrent motor repertoire (at 3–5 months after term) and its predictive value for cognitive development (listed according to the age of outcome assessment).

Reference	Cohort	Outcome assessment	Cut-off points	Predictive values
Spittle et al., 2013	$N = 94$ born < 30 weeks' gestation	**2 years** Bayley Scales of Infant and Toddler Development, third edition	Abnormal/absent fidgety movements vs. normal fidgety movements related to moderate to severe cognitive impairment	Sensitivity: 70% (95% CI: 35–92%) Specificity: 85% (95% CI: 75–91%) PPV: 35% (95% CI: 16–59%) NPV: 96% (95% CI: 88–99%) Accuracy: 83% (95% CI: 75–91%)
Spittle et al., 2013	$N = 85$ born < 30 weeks' gestation	**4 years** Differential Ability Scale, second edition	Abnormal/absent fidgety movements vs. normal fidgety movements related to moderate to severe impairment of the general cognitive ability	Sensitivity: 42% (95% CI: 21–66%) Specificity: 88% (95% CI: 77–94%) PPV: 50% (95% CI: 26–74%) NPV: 84% (95% CI: 72–91%) Accuracy: 77% (95% CI: 68–86%)
Butcher et al., 2009	$N = 65$ born < 34 weeks' gestation	**7–11 years** (median = 9 years) Wechsler Intelligence Scale for Children-III, Dutch version	Not applicable	Not given
Fjørtoft et al., 2013	$N = 40$ $n = 31$ with very low birth weight, mean gestational age = 26.8 weeks ($SD = 1.9$) $n = 9$ born at term (neonatal encephalopathy, intracerebral abscess)	**10 years** Wechsler Intelligence Scale for Children-III, Scandinavian norms	Present fidgety movements plus abnormal[1] concurrent movements related to present fidgety movements plus normal[2] concurrent movements related to total $IQ < 85$ vs. total $IQ \geq 85$	Sensitivity: 90% (95% CI: 60–98%) Specificity: 58% (95% CI: 39–76%) PPV: 53% (95% CI: 31–74%) NPV: 93% (95% CI: 69–99%)
Grunewaldt et al., 2014	$N = 64$ $n = 31$ with ELBW, mean gestational age = 26.1 weeks ($SD = 1.8$) $n = 33$ controls born at term	**10 years** Wechsler Intelligence Scale for Children-III, Scandinavian norms; Stroop Color Word; Tower of London Test; Trail-Making Test	Not given	Not given

[1]*Movements other than fidgety movements appear to be monotonous and/or jerky and/or stiff;* [2]*all movements are carried out smoothly and fluently (according to Einspieler et al., 2004, p. 26). CI, confidence interval; IQ, intelligence quotient; MDI, mental developmental index; NPV, negative predictive value; PPV, positive predictive value; SD, standard deviation.*

THE LINK BETWEEN EARLY NORMALIZATION OF GMs AND COGNITIVE DEVELOPMENT

Many preterm infants – and ELBW infants in particular – show poor repertoire GMs during their first few days of life (de Vries et al., 2008; de Vries and Bos, 2010). Some of them normalize within a few weeks (de Vries and Bos, 2010), whereas others only normalize around term-equivalent age or later (Bruggink et al., 2010; de Vries and Bos, 2011). Some infants exhibit poor repertoire GMs until they reach the age of fidgety movements, i.e., 3–5 months. If fidgety movements are present and normal, the motor outcome will be normal, whereas absent fidgety movements point to a neurodevelopmental dysfunction (Prechtl et al., 1997; Nakajima et al., 2006). Bruggink et al. (2010) were the first to associate the age of GM normalization with later cognition. They longitudinally assessed the GMs of 60 preterm infants from birth to early infancy and compared their findings to the results of the Wechsler Intelligence Scale for Children, third edition, applied at age 7–11 years. IQs – both verbal and performance – were around 100, regardless of whether GMs were normal from the beginning or normalized before term. However, abnormal (i.e., poor repertoire) GMs that persisted until 8 weeks after term were related to IQs almost 1 SD below the mean (median total $IQ = 87$; median verbal $IQ = 88$; median performance $IQ = 88$). School performance was also related to the quality of GMs. The percentage of children who had to repeat a class or attended special education was higher where GMs did not normalize by 8 weeks after term (Bruggink et al., 2010).

Two other studies confirmed the results of Bruggink et al. (2010), although their outcome assessments were carried out at a much lower age. Beccaria et al. (2012) assessed the development of preterm-born children aged 2 years by means of the Griffiths Scales of Mental Development (**Table 1**) and compared the DQs of children who had shown normal writhing GMs with the DQs of children who had exhibited poor repertoire GMs at 1 month after term. Where GMs were still poor repertoire at 1 month after term, the DQ was 11 points lower (mean = 97, *SD* = 12) than in children with normal GMs at 1 month (mean = 108, *SD* = 11; $p < 0.01$). Only the sub-scales "hearing and speech," "eye and hand coordination," and "performance" contributed to these results, whereas the sub-scales "locomotion" and "personal/social" did not. Similar results were found for a smaller sample of Slovenian preterm infants: 15 in 26 preterm infants still had poor repertoire GMs 1 month after term. Their MDI assessed at 2–3 years with the Bayley Scales of Infant Development, second edition, was, on average, eight points lower (mean = 95, *SD* = 11) than that of children with normal writhing GMs (mean = 103, *SD* = 9; $p < 0.05$). Children with cramped-synchronized writhing GMs after term age were more likely to develop motor problems and had MDIs which indicated mental developmental delay (mean = 76, *SD* = 22). Spittle et al. (2013) obtained a slightly different result. In their sample of very preterm-born children (i.e., at <30 weeks' gestation) the cognitive score of the Bayley Scales of Infant and Toddler Development, third edition, assessed at age 2, was only an average of five points lower in children with abnormal GMs at 1 month after term (mean = 96.6, *SD* = 13.2) than that of children who had had normal GMs (mean = 101.4, *SD* = 11.7; $p = 0.06$). Assessed at 4 years, the same children exhibited no difference whatsoever: general reasoning and conceptual abilities bore no relation to the GMs assessed at 1 month after term.

To sum up, the association between writhing GMs and cognitive development is variable, with increasing evidence that abnormal (poor repertoire) GMs – if still present after term – are associated with an MDI/IQ 5–13 points lower than that of children whose writhing GMs were normal. Defining an MDI or *IQ* < 85 as a moderately impaired cognitive outcome, the sensitivity values reached 67–100%, while the specificity values ranged from 28–71% (**Table 1**; Bruggink et al., 2010; Kodric et al., 2010; Spittle et al., 2013).

FIDGETY MOVEMENTS MAY NOT PREDICT COGNITIVE DEVELOPMENT, BUT CONCURRENT MOVEMENTS AND POSTURES DO

Most of the eligible studies reported that fidgety movements were not related to cognitive development (Butcher et al., 2009; Fjørtoft et al., 2013; Grunewaldt et al., 2014). Only Spittle et al. (2013) found in their study on 94 infants born at <30 weeks' gestation that the Bayley-III cognition score assessed at 2 years was, on average, eight points higher in children who had had normal fidgety movements (mean = 100.4, *SD* = 10.8) than in children with absent or abnormal fidgety movements (mean = 92, *SD* = 17.6; $p < 0.05$). The difference between the two groups was even more significant at the 4-year-assessment: the cognitive score of children who had shown normal fidgety movements at 3–5 months was, on average, 14 points higher (mean = 99.8, *SD* = 13.4) than that of children with abnormal or absent fidgety movements (mean = 85.5, *SD* = 18.3; $p < 0.01$; Spittle et al., 2013).

Other authors have related early abnormalities in the posture or the overall movement character to sub-optimal cognition at school age. Butcher et al. (2009) were the first to investigate whether the quality of movements at 3–5 months could predict cognitive performance at school age. They studied 65 children born preterm and found that the number of normal postural patterns displayed between 11 and 16 weeks after term contributed significantly to the prediction of total and verbal IQs, and almost significantly to that of performance IQs. Certain postural patterns such as whether or not infants kept the head in the midline, had a symmetric body posture, or showed various finger postures might reflect the increase of activity levels in several cortical areas as well as in the cerebellum and basal ganglia at 3 months (Chugani et al., 1987). Visual and manual exploration becomes more active and better coordinated by that age (Prechtl, 1986; Einspieler et al., 2004). Independent and variable finger movements facilitate object manipulation and exploration, supplementing visual with extero- and proprioceptive input (Rosenbaum et al., 2012).

Fjørtoft et al. (2013) found that the overall movement character (smooth and fluent vs. monotonous, jerky and/or stiff) at 3–5 months predicted the children's IQ at age 10 years with a sensitivity of 90% and a specificity of 58% (**Table 2**). Similar findings were reported by Grunewaldt et al. (2014) for a group of 31 ELBW infants. Those 20 ELBW infants who did not develop cerebral palsy had normal fidgety movements, but only nine of them had a smooth and fluent movement character. The remaining 11 children with monotonous, jerky, and/or stiff movements in early infancy developed a lower working memory capacity and lower processing speed, but showed no differences with regard to total IQ scores. On magnetic resonance imaging, they had a lower volume of cerebral white matter volume at 3–5 months than children with normal movements. Comparing clinical characteristics, the only difference between the groups was that infants with monotonous, jerky and/or stiff movements were more often small-for-gestational-age singletons than infants with a smooth and fluent movement character. The authors speculated that perhaps fetal growth restriction including the brain had caused the reduced cognitive functioning at school age (Grunewaldt et al., 2014).

LIMITATIONS OF THE STUDIES

Almost none of the authors distinguished between the subcategories of abnormal writhing GMs. Instead, they labeled them as one "abnormal" category, while mentioning that the majority of abnormal GMs were scored as poor repertoire. Spittle et al. (2013) also pooled abnormal and absent/sporadic fidgety movements into "abnormal GMs at 3 months." More details on abnormal GMs at 3 months would substantially add to our understanding of abnormal fidgety movements, whose predictive value is not yet clear (Prechtl et al., 1997; Einspieler et al., 2007; Bruggink et al., 2008; Yuge et al., 2011). None of the studies focused on individual developmental trajectories. The question remains: which abnormal writhing movements lead to which peculiarities at the age of fidgety movements? Do infants with poor repertoire GMs also show a monotonous movement pattern at 3–5 months? Future studies need to shed light on specific individual developmental trajectories of preterm infants and relate them to the children's later cognitive performance.

Another common flaw is that cognitive dysfunction tends to be pooled with motor problems. A considerable number of children studied by Fjørtoft et al. (2013) had both balance problems and a poor cognitive outcome. It is therefore difficult to answer conclusively if there are specific GM markers for cognitive dysfunction.

One final deficiency is the small number of studies on the topic. While only seven studies met the inclusion criteria for our review, we believe that the globally increasing clinical and scientific application of the GMA will bring some remarkable new findings in the very near future. One development that promises to boost activity in the field is the use of smartphone-based applications.

CONCLUSION

The above-mentioned studies on the GMA's predictive value for cognitive development suggest the following: clinicians should be aware that abnormal movements are not only associated with motor impairments but also with potential adverse outcomes in other developmental domains. Abnormal GMs beyond term age and monotonous and jerky movements as well as postural abnormalities at 3–5 months might indicate a high risk for a subsequent cognitive dysfunction. A monotonous motor repertoire during these early months of development might have an adverse effect on the infants' abilities to interact with their environment (Hadders-Algra, 2000). Further and more comprehensive research is needed, although the existing body of literature makes a strong case for early intervention services and follow-up examination to improve the long-term cognitive development of children born preterm.

AUTHOR CONTRIBUTIONS

CE: contributed substantially to the conception of the work, the acquisition, and interpretation; drafted the work and approved the version to be published; agreed to be accountable for all aspects of the work in ensuring that questions related to the accuracy or integrity of any part of the work are appropriately investigated and resolved. AB, ML, and PM: contributed substantially to the design of the work, and interpretation; revised the first draft critically for important intellectual content and approved the version to be published; agreed to be accountable for all aspects of the work in ensuring that questions related to the accuracy or integrity of any part of the work are appropriately investigated and resolved.

FUNDING

General movement assessment studies, especially the development of GMApp – a smartphone-based solution for the GMA – is supported by the Bill and Melinda Gates Foundation (OPP112887) and the Austrian Science Fund, FWF (P25241).

REFERENCES

Adde, L., Helbostadt, J. L., Jensenius, A. R., Taraldsen, G., and Støen, R. (2009). Using computer-based video analysis in the study of fidgety movements. *Early Hum. Dev.* 85, 541–547. doi: 10.1016/j.earlhumdev.2009.05.003

Beccaria, E., Martino, M., Briatore, E., Podesta, B., Pomero, G., Micciolo, R., et al. (2012). Poor repertoire general movements predict some aspects of development outcome at 2 years in very preterm infants. *Early Hum. Dev.* 88, 393–396. doi: 10.1016/j.earlhumdev.2011.10.002

Bhutta, A. T., Cleves, M. A., Casey, P. H., Cradock, M. M., and Anand, K. J. S. (2002). Cognitive and behavioural outcomes of school-aged children who were born preterm: a meta-analysis. *JAMA* 288, 728–737. doi: 10.1001/jama.288.6.728

Bos, A. F., and Roze, E. (2011). Neurodevelopmental outcome in preterm infants. *Dev. Med. Child Neurol.* 53(Suppl. 4), 35–39. doi: 10.1111/j.1469-8749.2011.04062.x

Bos, A. F., van Asperen, R. M., de Leeuw, D. M., and Prechtl, H. F. R. (1997). The influence of septicaemia on spontaneous motility in preterm infants. *Early Hum. Dev.* 50, 61–70. doi: 10.1016/S0378-3782(97)00093-5

Bosanquet, M., Copeland, L., Ware, R., and Boyd, R. (2013). A systematic review of tests to predict cerebral palsy in young children. *Dev. Med. Child Neurol.* 55, 418–426. doi: 10.1111/dmcn.12140

Bruggink, J. L. M., Cioni, G., Einspieler, C., Maathuis, C. G. B., Pascale, R., and Bos, A. F. (2009). Early motor repertoire is related to level of self-mobility in children with cerebral palsy at school age. *Dev. Med. Child Neurol.* 51, 878–885. doi: 10.1111/j.1469-8749.2009.03294.x

Bruggink, J. L. M., Einspieler, C., Butcher, P. R., van Braeckel, K. N. J. A., Prechtl, H. F. R., and Bos, A. F. (2008). The quality of the early motor repertoire in preterm infants predicts minor neurological dysfunction at school age. *J. Pediatr.* 153, 32–39. doi: 10.1016/j.jpeds.2007.12.047

Bruggink, J. L. M., van Braeckel, K. N., and Bos, A. F. (2010). The early motor repertoire of children born preterm is associated with intelligence at school age. *Pediatrics* 125, e1356–e1363. doi: 10.1542/peds.2009-2117

Burger, M., and Louw, Q. A. (2009). The predictive validity of general movements – a systematic review. *Eur. J. Paediatr. Neurol.* 13, 408–420. doi: 10.1016/j.ejpn.2008.09.004

Butcher, P. R., van Braeckel, K., Bouma, A., Einspieler, C., Stremmelaar, E. F., and Bos, A. F. (2009). The quality of preterm infants' spontaneous movements:

an early indicator of intelligence and behavior at school age. *J. Child Psychol. Psychiatr.* 50, 920–930. doi: 10.1111/j.1469-7610.2009.02066.x

Chugani, H. T., Phelps, M. E., and Mazziotti, J. (1987). Positron emission tomography study of human brain functional development. *Ann. Neurol.* 22, 487–497. doi: 10.1002/ana.410220408

de Vries, L. S., Benders, M. J. N. L., and Groenendaal, F. (2015). Progress in neonatal neurology with a focus on neuroimaging in the preterm infant. *Neuropediatrics* 46, 234–241. doi: 10.1055/s-0035-1554102

de Vries, N. K., and Bos, A. F. (2010). The quality of general movements in the first ten days of life in preterm infants. *Early Hum. Dev.* 86, 225–229. doi: 10.1016/j.earlhumdev.2010.03.004

de Vries, N. K., and Bos, A. F. (2011). The motor repertoire of extremely low-birthweight infants at term in relation to their neurological outcome. *Dev. Med. Child Neurol.* 53, 933–937. doi: 10.1111/j.1469-8749.2011.04045.x

de Vries, N. K., Erwich, J. J., and Bos, A. F. (2008). General movements in the first fourteen days of life in extremely low birthweight (ELBW) infants. *Early Hum. Dev.* 84, 763–768. doi: 10.1016/j.earlhumdev.2008.05.003

Doyle, L. W., and Anderson, P. J. (2010). Adult outcome of extremely preterm infants. *Pediatrics* 126, 342–351. doi: 10.1542/peds.2010-0710

Einspieler, C., Hirota, H., Yuge, M., Dejma, S., and Marschik, P. B. (2012a). Early behavioural manifestation of smith-magenis syndrome (del17p11.2) in a 4-month-old boy. *Dev. Neurorehab.* 15, 313–316. doi: 10.3109/17518423.2011.654281

Einspieler, C., and Marschik, P. B. (2012). Central pattern generators and their significance for the foetal motor function. *Klin Neurophysiol* 43, 16–21.

Einspieler, C., and Marschik, P. B. (2013). Complementary thinking: future perspectives on the assessment of general movements. *Dev. Med. Child Neurol.* 55, 682–683.

Einspieler, C., Marschik, P. B., Bos, A. F., Ferrari, F., Cioni, G., and Prechtl, H. F. R. (2012b). Early markers for cerebral palsy: insights from the assessment of general movements. *Future Neurol.* 7, 710–717. doi: 10.2217/fnl.12.60

Einspieler, C., Marschik, P. B., Milioti, S., Nakajima, Y., Bos, A. F., and Prechtl, H. F. R. (2007). Are abnormal fidgety movements an early marker for complex minor neurological dysfunction at puberty? *Early Hum. Dev.* 83, 521–525. doi: 10.1016/j.earlhumdev.2006.10.001

Einspieler, C., Marschik, P. B., Pansy, J., Scheuchenegger, A., Krieber, M., Yang, H., et al. (2015a). The general movement optimality score: a detailed assessment of general movements during preterm and term age. *Dev. Med. Child Neurol.* doi: 10.1111/dmcn.12923 [Epub ahead of print].

Einspieler, C., Marschik, P. B., and Prechtl, H. F. R. (2008). Human motor behaviour – prenatal origin and early postnatal development. *Z. Psychol.* 216, 147–153. doi: 10.1027/0044-3409.216.3.147

Einspieler, C., Prayer, D., and Prechtl, H. F. R. (2012c). *Fetal Behaviour: A Neurodevelopmental Appoach. Clinics in Developmental Medicine, No. 189.* London: Mac Keith Press, 200.

Einspieler, C., and Prechtl, H. F. R. (2005). Prechtl's assessment of general movements: a diagnostic tool for the functional assessment of the young nervous system. *Ment. Retard. Dev. Disabil. Res. Rev.* 11, 61–67. doi: 10.1002/mrdd.20051

Einspieler, C., Prechtl, H. F. R., Bos, A. F., Ferrari, F., and Cioni, G. (2004). Prechtl's method on the qualitative assessment of general movements in preterm, term and young infants. *Clin. Dev. Med.* 167, 1–91.

Einspieler, C., Prechtl, H. F. R., Ferrari, F., Cioni, G., and Bos, A. F. (1997). The qualitative assessment of general movements in preterm, term and young infants – review of the methodology. *Early Hum. Dev.* 50, 47–60. doi: 10.1016/S0378-3782(97)00092-3

Einspieler, C., Sigafoos, J., Bartl-Pokorny, K. D., Landa, R., Marschik, P. B., and Bölte, S. (2014). Highlighting the first 5 months of life: general movements in infants later diagnosed with autism spectrum disorder or Rett syndrome. *Res. Autism Spectr. Dis.* 8, 286–291. doi: 10.1016/j.rasd.2013.12.013

Einspieler, C., Yang, H., Bartl-Pokorny, K. D., Chi, X., Zang, F. F., Marschik, P. M., et al. (2015b). Are sporadic fidgety movements as clinically relevant as is their absence? *Early Hum. Dev.* 91, 247–252. doi: 10.1016/j.earlhumdev.2015.02.003

Ferrari, F., Cioni, G., and Prechtl, H. F. R. (1990). Qualitative changes of general movements in preterm infants with brain lesions. *Early Hum. Dev.* 23, 193–233. doi: 10.1016/0378-3782(90)90013-9

Fjørtoft, T., Grunewaldt, K. H., Løhaugen, G. C., Mørkved, S., Skranes, J., and Evensen, K. A. I. (2013). Assessment of motor behaviour in high-risk-infants at 3 months predicts motor and cognitive outcomes in 10 years old children. *Early Hum. Dev.* 89, 787–793. doi: 10.1016/j.earlhumdev.2013.06.007

Foulder-Hughes, L. A., and Cooke, R. W. I. (2003). Motor, cognitive, and behavioural disorders in children born very preterm. *Dev. Med. Child Neurol.* 45, 97–103. doi: 10.1017/S0012162203000197

Grunewaldt, K. H., Fjørtoft, T., Bjuland, K. J., Brubakk, A. M., Eikenes, L., Håberg, A. K., et al. (2014). Follow-up at age 10 years in ELBW children – functional outcome brain morphology and results from motor assessments in infancy. *Early Hum. Dev.* 90, 571–578. doi: 10.1016/j.earlhumdev.2014.07.005

Hadders-Algra, M. (2000). The neuronal group selection theory: a framework to explain variation in normal motor development. *Dev. Med. Child Neurol.* 42, 566–572. doi: 10.1017/S0012162200001067

Hadders-Algra, M., Bouwstra, H., and Groen, S. E. (2009). Quality of general movements and psychiatric morbidity at 9 to 12 years. *Early Hum. Dev.* 85, 1–6. doi: 10.1016/j.earlhumdev.2008.05.005

Johnson, S. (2007). Cognitive and behavioural outcomes following very preterm birth. *Semin. Fetal Neonatal Med.* 12, 363–373. doi: 10.1016/j.siny.2007.05.004

Johnson, S., Evans, T. A., Draper, E. S., Field, D. J., Manktelow, B. N., Marlow, N., et al. (2015). Neurodevelopmental outcomes following late and moderate prematurity: a population-based cohort study. *Arch. Dis. Child. Fetal Neonatal Ed.* 100, F301–F308. doi: 10.1136/archdischild-2014-307684

Kodric, J., Sustersic, B., and Paro-Panjan, D. (2010). Assessment of general movements and 2.5 year developmental outcomes: pilot results in a diverse preterm group. *Eur. J. Paediatr. Neurol.* 14, 131–137. doi: 10.1016/j.ejpn.2009.04.012

Larroque, B., Marchand, L., and Kaminski, M. (2005). 218 Cognitive status of 5 years old very preterm children: the Epipage study. *Pediatr. Res.* 58, 391. doi: 10.1203/00006450-200508000-00247

Marcroft, C., Khan, A., Embleton, N. D., Trenell, M., and Plötz, T. (2015). Movement recognition technology as a method of assessing spontaneous general movements in high risk infants. *Front. Neurol.* 5:284. doi: 10.3389/fneur.2014.00284

Marschik, P. B., Einspieler, C., Oberle, A., Laccone, F., and Prechtl, H. F. R. (2009). Case report: retracing atypical development: a preserved speech variant of Rett syndrome. *J. Autism Dev. Disord.* 39, 958–961. doi: 10.1007/s10803-009-0703-x

Marschik, P. B., Soloveichick, M., Windpassinger, C., and Einspieler, C. (2015). General movements in genetic disorders: a first look into Cornelia de Lange syndrome. *Dev. Neurorehab.* 18, 280–282. doi: 10.3109/17518423.2013.859180

Mutlu, A., Einspieler, C., Marschik, P. B., and Livanelioglu, A. (2008). Intraindividual consistency in the quality of neonatal general movements. *Neonatology* 93, 213–216. doi: 10.1159/000110870

Nakajima, Y., Einspieler, C., Marschik, P. B., Bos, A. F., and Prechtl, H. F. R. (2006). Does a detailed assessment of poor repertoire general movements help to identify those infants who will develop normally? *Early Hum. Dev.* 82, 53–59. doi: 10.1016/j.earlhumdev.2005.07.010

Noble, Y., and Boyd, R. N. (2012). Neonatal assessments for the preterm infant up to 4 months corrected age: a systematic review. *Dev. Med. Child Neurol.* 54, 129–139. doi: 10.1111/j.1469-8749.2010.03903.x

Nosarti, C., Giouroukou, E., Healy, E., Rifkin, L., Walshe, M., Reichenberg, A., et al. (2008). Grey and white matter distribution in very preterm adolescents mediates neurodevelopmental outcome. *Brain* 131, 205–217.

Prechtl, H. F. R. (1986). New perspectives in early human development. *Eur. J. Obstet. Gynecol. Reprod. Biol.* 21, 347–355. doi: 10.1016/0028-2243(86)90014-6

Prechtl, H. F. R. (1990). Qualitative changes of spontaneous movements in fetus and preterm infants are a marker of neurological dysfunction. *Early Hum. Dev.* 23, 151–158. doi: 10.1016/0378-3782(90)90011-7

Prechtl, H. F. R. (1997). State of the art of a new functional assessment of the young nervous system. An early predictor of cerebral palsy. *Early Hum. Dev.* 50, 1–11.

Prechtl, H. F. R. (2001). General movement assessment as a method of developmental neurology: new paradigms and their consequences. The 1999 Ronnie Mac Keith Lecture. *Dev. Med. Child Neurol.* 43, 836–842.

Prechtl, H. F. R., Einspieler, C., Cioni, G., Bos, A. F., Ferrari, F., and Sontheimer, D. (1997). An early marker for neurological deficits after perinatal brain lesions. *Lancet* 349, 1361–1363. doi: 10.1016/S0140-6736(96)10182-3

Rosenbaum, D. A., Chapman, K. M., Weigelt, M., Weiss, D. J., and van der Wel, R. (2012). Cognition, action, and object manipulation. *Psychol. Bull.* 138, 924–946. doi: 10.1037/a0027839

Saigal, S., and Doyle, L. W. (2008). An overview of mortality and sequelae of preterm birth from infancy to adulthood. *Lancet* 371, 261–269. doi: 10.1016/S0140-6736(08)60136-1

Soria-Pastor, S., Gimenez, M., Narberhaus, A., Falcon, C., Botet, F., Bargallo, N., et al. (2008). Patterns of cerebral white matter damage and cognitive impairment in adolescents born very preterm. *Int. J. Dev. Neurosci.* 26, 647–654. doi: 10.1016/j.ijdevneu.2008.08.001

Spittle, A. J., Doyle, L. W., and Boyd, R. N. (2008). A systematic review of the clinimetric properties of neuromotor assessments for preterm infants during the first year of life. *Dev. Med. Child Neurol.* 50, 254–266. doi: 10.1111/j.1469-8749.2008.02025.x

Spittle, A. J., Spencer-Smith, M. M., Cheong, J. L. Y., Eeles, A. L., Lee, K. J., Anderson, P. J., et al. (2013). General movements in very preterm children and neurodevelopment at 2 and 4 years. *Pediatrics* 132, e452–e458. doi: 10.1542/peds.2013-0177

Ullman, H., Spencer-Smith, M., Thompson, D. K., Doyle, L. W., Inder, T. E., Anderson, P. J., et al. (2015). Neonatal MRI is associated with future cognition and academic achievement in preterm children. *Brain* 138, 3251–3262. doi: 10.1093/brain/awv244

Valentin, T., Uhl, K., and Einspieler, C. (2005). The effectiveness of training in Prechtl's method on the qualitative assessment of general movements. *Early Hum. Dev.* 81, 623–627. doi: 10.1016/j.earlhumdev.2005.04.003

van Kooij, B. J., de Vries, L. S., Ball, G., van Haastert, I. C., Benders, M. J., Groenendaal, F., et al. (2015). Neonatal tract-based spatial statistics findings and outcome in preterm infants. *AJNR Am. J. Neuroradiol.* 33, 188–194. doi: 10.3174/ajnr.A2723

Volpe, J. J. (2009). Brain injury in premature infants: a complex amalgam of destructive and developmental disturbances. *Lancet Neurol.* 8, 110–124. doi: 10.1016/S1474-4422(08)70294-1

Yang, H., Einspieler, C., Shi, W., Marschik, P. B., Wang, Y., Cao, Y., et al. (2012). Cerebral palsy in children: movements and postures during early infancy, dependent on preterm vs. full term birth. *Early Hum. Dev.* 88, 837–843. doi: 10.1016/j.earlhumdev.2012.06.004

Yuge, M., Marschik, P. B., Nakajima, Y., Yamori, Y., Kanda, T., Hirota, H., et al. (2011). Movements and postures of infants aged 3 to 5 months: to what extent is their optimality related to perinatal events and to the neurological outcome? *Early Hum. Dev* 87, 231–237. doi: 10.1016/j.earlhumdev.2010.12.046

Zappella, M., Einspieler, C., Bartl-Pokorny, K. D., Krieber, M., Coleman, M., Bölte, S., et al. (2015). What do home videos tell us about early motor and socio-communicative behaviours in children with autistic features during the second year of life – an exploratory study. *Early Hum. Dev.* 91, 569–575. doi: 10.1016/j.earlhumdev.2015.07.006

Conflict of Interest Statement: The authors declare that the research was conducted in the absence of any commercial or financial relationships that could be construed as a potential conflict of interest.

5

Children's Spatial Representations: 3- and 4-Year-Olds are Affected by Irrelevant Peripheral References

Markus Krüger[1] and Georg Jahn[2]*

[1] *Entwicklungspsychologie und Pädagogische Psychologie, Institut für Psychologie, Ernst-Moritz-Arndt-Universität Greifswald, Greifswald, Germany,* [2] *Institute for Multimedia and Interactive Systems, University of Lübeck, Lübeck, Germany*

Edited by:
Klaus Libertus,
University of Pittsburgh, USA

Reviewed by:
Marko Nardini,
Durham University, UK
Steven M. Weisberg,
University of Pennsylvania, USA
Jamie J. Jirout,
Rhodes College, USA

****Correspondence:***
Markus Krüger
markuskr@uni-greifswald.de

Children as young as 3 years can remember an object's location within an arrangement and can retrieve it from a novel viewpoint (Nardini et al., 2006). However, this ability is impaired if the arrangement is rotated to compensate for the novel viewpoint, or, if the arrangement is rotated and children stand still. There are two dominant explanations for this phenomenon: self-motion induces an automatic spatial updating process which is beneficial if children move around the arrangement, but misleading if the children's movement is matched by the arrangement and not activated if children stand still and only the arrangement is moved (see spatial updating; Simons and Wang, 1998). Another explanation concerns reference frames: spatial representations might depend on peripheral spatial relations concerning the surrounding room instead on proximal relations within the arrangement, even if these proximal relations are sufficient or more informative. To evaluate these possibilities, we rotated children ($N = 120$) aged between 3 and 6 years with an occluded arrangement. When the arrangement was in misalignment to the surrounding room, 3- and 4-year-olds' spatial memory was impaired and 5-year-olds' was lightly impaired suggesting that they relied on peripheral references of the surrounding room for retrieval. In contrast, 6-years-olds' spatial representation seemed robust against misalignment indicating a successful integration of spatial representations.

Keywords: spatial cognition, spatial orientation, spatial updating, spatial representation

INTRODUCTION

Imagine sitting at a desk with several indistinguishable cups turned upside down. A colleague slips a glass bead under one of these cups. You get up, walk around the desk and sit down at the desk again. Of course, you can retrieve the bead. You have remembered the bead's location with respect to your own body and with respect to the array of cups and the boundaries of the desk as local landmarks. In principle, you could have remembered the object's location with respect to boundaries of the room or distal landmarks such as the door, windows, or pictures on the walls. These are all assets even very young children can use for orientation: 16-month-olds can retrieve object locations using dead reckoning or inertial navigation (cf. Newcombe, 1988; Newcombe et al., 1998). And at the age of 21 months or older children successfully include landmarks in egocentric, body-relative representations (Newcombe et al., 1998).

Now imagine again sitting at your desk while your colleague hides the bead. This time, however, your colleague turns the desk by 135° within the room to confuse you. Although the distal landmarks and room boundaries have shifted with respect to the hidden bead, you will be able to retrieve the bead. Interestingly, young children may be impaired by this relative shift of distal landmarks and room boundaries in such a place learning task.

In a previous study Nardini et al. (2006) used a landmark shift task similar to the introductory example to study the development of the ability to rely on local landmarks only. In their study landmark shifts were produced in such a way that participants needed to suppress egocentric coding in addition to devaluing distal information. Nardini et al. (2006) asked children from 3 to 6 years to retrieve a toy that was hidden under one of several cups which were arranged in an irregular array on a board (similar to the array in **Figure 1A**). The study comprised two conditions without landmark shifts (*neither move, child move*) and two conditions with landmark shifts (*both move, array move*): either the array and participant stayed (neither-move) or participants walked around the array about 135° (child-move); and children walked along as the array was rotated about 135° (both-move) or solely the array was rotated about 135° (array-move). During these changes the array was hidden from view.

Children of all age groups were most successful when the array stayed in alignment with the room (neither-move, child-move). This was especially true for the youngest age group: the 3-year-olds' search performance was not even above chance when the alignment changed (both-move, array-move). However, when the alignment changed children were slightly better when their perspective on the array remained the same (both-move).

Nardini et al. (2006) concluded that participants did not solely rely on their perspective on the array, but also encoded hiding places in relation to the surrounding room. This might be seen as an indication for an allocentric representation even in 3-year-olds (cf. Piaget and Inhelder, 1967). An additional factor to bear in mind is the updating of spatial representations by vestibular, proprioceptive, and optic flow information in the course of self-movement (cf. Simons and Wang, 1998; Wang and Simons, 1999; Nardini et al., 2006; Wolbers et al., 2008; Jahn et al., 2012).

This process is called *spatial updating* by Simons and Wang (1998; Wang and Simons, 1999). In their experiments adults were presented with an array of different objects. This array was then hidden from view and the position of one of the objects was changed. Then participants either had to walk a specified path around the array or the array was rotated correspondingly or both. Accuracy in identifying the shifted object was better when participants changed their position. The accuracy decreased when the array was rotated, and when participants moved *and* the array was rotated as well. Simons and Wang (1998; Wang and Simons, 1999) assumed an automatic updating process initiated by self-movement. This process supports spatial orientation – hence participants' advantage when they changed position. Their orientation becomes maladjusted when the spatial-updating process is triggered although the target moves parallel to the subject. Therewith spatial updating is viewpoint-independent and egocentric (in contrast to allocentric), because the subject remains the center of the representations.

The study by Nardini et al. (2006) was not designed to differentiate between effects of spatial updating and effects of the surrounding room. They point out that according to Burgess et al. (2004) at least in adults both factors contribute to the observed results. It could be argued from a theoretical point of view, that spatial updating alone suffices to explain these results: when children walk around the array, spatial updating takes place. This is adaptive when the array stays still

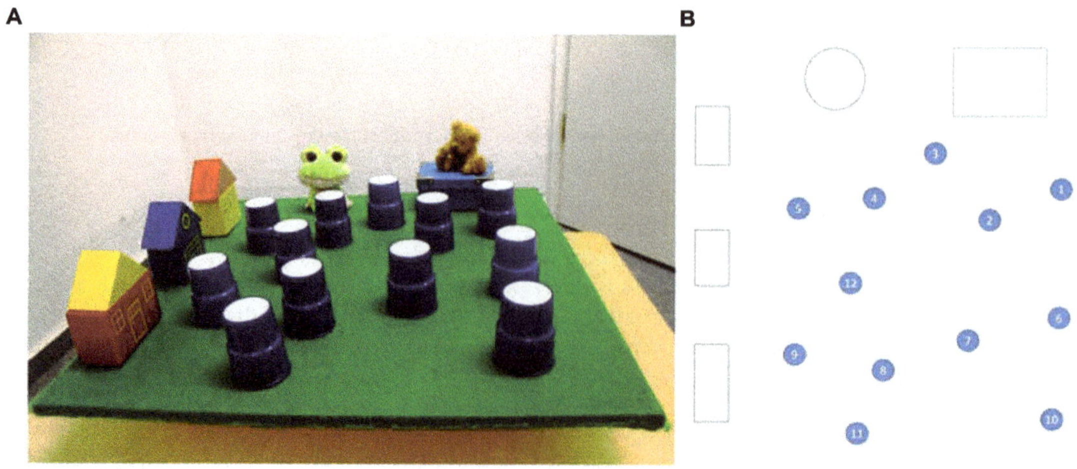

FIGURE 1 | (A) Is a photo of the array seen from the children's perspective. **(B)** Is a schematic overview. The array consisted of a wooden board (70 cm × 70 cm) covered with a green piece of cloth. On the left side of the board a row of three toy houses was placed and on the far side from the children's point of view a toy frog and an on a box sitting teddy bear were placed. All these objects were placed 2.5 cm off the rim. The houses were 5.5 cm in depth and the toy animals were 11 cm in depth. This left an area 62 cm wide and 56.5 cm deep for the hiding spots. The exact coordinates of the hiding spots can be found in Supplementary Table S1.

(child-move) and maladaptive when the array moves with the children (both-move). When the array is rotated the egocentric representation is broken (array-move) and when everything stays the egocentric representation remains intact (neither-move). Encoding the surrounding room is not necessary in this approach.

Therefore, our present reference shift experiment was designed (1) to isolate a possible influence of the surrounding room[1] on young children's object retrieval performance and (2) to test for effects of spatial updating by self-motion:

(1) So, the viewpoints on the array at encoding and at retrieval match in all conditions of the present experiment. But the array's alignment with the surrounding room either differs from encoding at retrieval or is shifted. If participants unnecessarily include information concerning the surrounding room for retrieval in this task, performance should drop if the array is in misalignment.

(2) In one condition we rotated the children together with the array on a platform within the room while in the other condition the children walked along the platform. In the latter case self-motion as a cause for spatial updating of the body-relative location representation is avoided, while other possible sources (e.g., optical flow) that might trigger spatial updating remain intact. On the one hand, this might enhance performance, when the array stays in alignment with the surrounding room, as self-movement supplies additional control and information concerning orientation. It might decrease when the array is rotated out of alignment with the surrounding room, because the spatial updating process becomes dysfunctional in this case. This should result in an interaction between an effect of alignment and an effect of self-motion. On the other hand, self-movement might generally decrease performance, as it constitutes an additional task that might strain resources needed for the retrieval task.

MATERIALS AND METHODS

Participants

In total 120 children participated in this study. They were equally distributed among four age groups: there were 30 three-year-olds (mean age = 3 years 4 months, *SD* = 4 months; 14 boys, 16 girls), 30 four-year-olds (mean age = 4 years 4 months, *SD* = 3 months; 18 boys, 12 girls), 30 five-year-olds (mean age = 5 years 4 months, *SD* = 3 months; 20 boys, 10 girls), and 30 six-year-olds (mean age = 6 years 5 months, *SD* = 3 months; 14 boys, 16 girls).

All children were tested in the same laboratory room at our research center. They participated on a voluntary basis and with the consent of their parents.[2] They were rewarded with a toy after test completion. Parents were reimbursed for their expenses. During the test accompanying parents waited in our lounge.

None of the participants was aware of the purpose of our study or had partaken in a similar study before. All participants were recruited from families registered in Mecklenburg-Vorpommern, Germany.

Materials

An array closely resembling the one used by Nardini et al. (2006) was constructed (see **Figures 1A,B** for details): on two connected sides of a board a number of child-orientated objects were placed for spatial reference. Twelve up-side-down cups were distributed on the board as potential hiding spots. The array was put on a vehicle. This vehicle consisted of a 200 cm long and 100 cm wide platform on four adjustable wheels. The array was firmly fixed on the frontal end of the vehicle's platform with the array's surface 11 cm above it. The spot on which children were supposed to sit down after having mounted the vehicle was marked with a cushion. At the back of the vehicle a handle was attached to allow for the experimenter to maneuver the vehicle. The array could be completely shielded from view with a wooden cover.

All the experiments took place in the same 22.5 m^2 L-shaped room. A 4.1 m × 3.7 m rectangular area was set apart for the experiment while all the furniture was stored in a 2.2 m × 2.8 m wide expanse. There were a door and a curtained off window in two adjoining walls bordering the experimental area.

Procedure

The experiment was introduced to the children as a hide-and-seek game. They were asked to mount the vehicle. While being watched by the children the experimenter hid an item under one of the cups. Children were asked whether they had seen where the toy was hidden. The array was then concealed with the wooden cover. The children were told that in the actual game the experimenter would turn the vehicle or ask them to walk around the vehicle or both (see the four different experimental conditions below). Hereafter the cover was lifted and it was the children's turn to point out the hiding place with a pointer stick. Furthermore children were instructed not to mount, dismount, or walk without being told by the experimenter.

After this short introduction – when children had found the toy and indicated that they had understood the procedure – the actual test started. There were four different experimental conditions that were tested in a within-subjects design. In all these conditions children sat on the vehicle and the experimenter hid a toy under one of the cups, asked the children whether they had seen where the toy was hidden, covered the array,

[1] Here, the surrounding room encompasses distal landmarks and room geometry. While there is some discussion which of these is used for orientation, this is not controlled in the present experiment (cf. Cheng, 1986; Newcombe et al., 1998; Burgess et al., 2004).

[2] This study was not connected to any form of formal education or medical treatment and approval by the ethics committee was not required. Nevertheless, we can guarantee that we consider possible ethical issues for all our studies. Therefore, the used materials were chosen not to pose any undue risk or harm. All participants gave informed consent or consent was given by their respective parents in written form to partake in this study. Even after consent was given, participation was on a voluntary basis and participants could end their cooperation anytime without any consequences. Proceedings were recorded and participants or their parents were allowed to examine protocols at any time. This proceeding is in accordance with ethical directives specified by the Deutsche Gesellschaft für Psychologie (DGPs). Both authors are members of the DGPs.

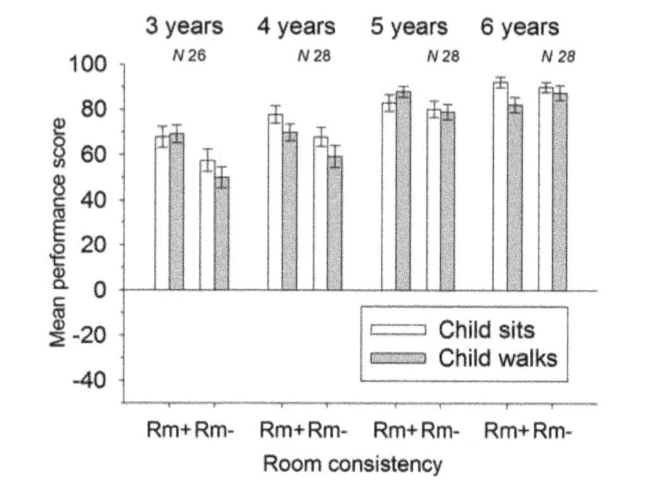

FIGURE 2 | Mean performance scores and standard errors of the different age groups and experimental conditions. Room consistency is given as Room+ for array's ending position consistent with room and Room− for array inconsistent with room (135° rotation).

uncovered the array, and asked the children to indicate the position of the hidden toy. The indicated cup was lifted by the experimenter and if this cup did not reveal the hidden toy the experimenter lifted the right one. However, between the covering and uncovering of the array children either (a) remained seated and the vehicle was turned about 360° (*Room+ Child Sits Condition*), (b) dismounted and were walked around the vehicle and remounted (*Room+ Child Walks Condition*), (c) remained seated and the vehicle was turned about 135° (*Room− Child Sits Condition*), or (d) dismounted, the vehicle was turned about 135° while the children watched, and then the children were walked along the corresponding path and remounted (*Room− Child Walks Condition*). The time needed for self-movement was slightly larger than riding the vehicle, because children had to mount and dismount. Also the time needed for the 135° conditions was slightly shorter than the time needed for the 360° conditions. In all four conditions, the children's view on the array was the same when the toy was hidden and when children were asked to find the toy. Only in the conditions *Room− Child Sits* and *Room− Child Walks* the relation between the surrounding room and the array was disrupted.

Each condition was realized in four trials; this led to 16 trials in total. Trials were presented in a quasi randomized order. Thirty sets of the 16 trials were compiled with the goal (a) to use as many different targets for every individual set as possible without any target being used consecutively and (b) to use each target evenly over all sets. Each of these 30 sets was used once in every age group.

RESULTS

To quantify search performance, a performance score was computed for every trial (cf. Nardini et al., 2006) relating the observed error distance between the center of the target cup and the center of the chosen cup to the chance distance in the respective trial. The chance distance was computed as the mean of the distances between the center of the chosen cup and the centers of all twelve cups including the target cup. The performance score was computed as 100*(chance distance – error distance)/chance distance. Thus, a score around zero can be interpreted as performance at a chance level (i.e., participants are guessing).

For the final analysis 10 children had to be excluded: two 6-year-olds, because they received the wrong test; two 3-year-olds, because the experiment had to be aborted due to non-compliance; one 3-year-old, because the data set was lost due to a technical error; and one 3-year-old, two 4-year-olds, and two 5-year-olds, because their consistent negative performance score implied that they were just guessing or choosing wrong targets on purpose. Of the remaining 110 children, 26 were 3-year-olds (mean age = 36 years 4 months, *SD* = 4 months), 28 were 4-year-olds (mean age = 4 years 5 months, *SD* = 3 months), 28 were 5-year-olds (mean age = 5 years 4 months, *SD* = 3 months), and 28 were 6-year-olds (mean age = 6 years 5 months, *SD* = 3 months). An overview of the remaining children's performance scores can be found in **Figure 2**.

An ANOVA including the within-subjects variables Room (*Room+*, *Room−*), Movement (*Child Sits*, *Child Walks*), and the between-subjects variable Age-group (3, 4, 5, and 6) were computed. There was a significant main effect concerning the factor Room, $F(1,106) = 20$, $p < 0.001$, $\eta^2 = 0.16$, qualified by a significant interaction for the factor Room and Age-group, $F(3,106) = 4.48$, $p = 0.005$, $\eta^2 = 0.11$. Furthermore, there was a significant main effect for the factor Movement, $F(1,106) = 5.49$, $p = 0.021$, $\eta^2 = 0.05$, indicating that children were generally more precise when they remained seated in front

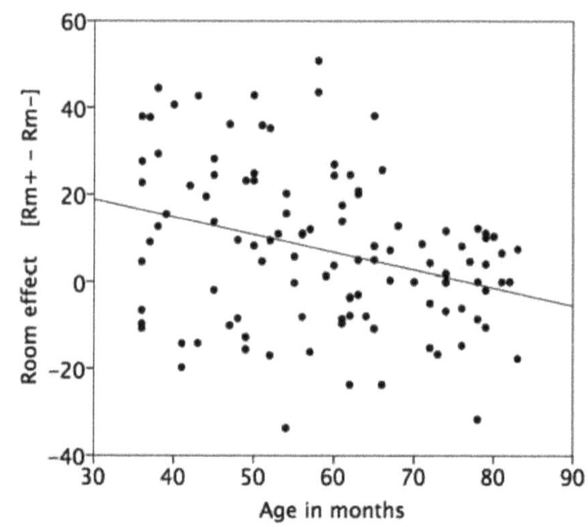

FIGURE 3 | Regression of the difference score reflecting the effect of the landmark shift (difference between the mean performance score in the Room+ and the Room− conditions) on age in months.

of the display (M = 77.3, SD = 18.1) than when they were made to move around (M = 73.3, SD = 18.6). No further significant or marginally significant main effects or interactions were found.

To resolve the interaction between Room and Age-group, four additional ANOVAs for the separate age-groups were computed. There was a significant main effect concerning the factor Room for the 3-year-olds, $F(1,25) = 13.76$, $p = 0.001$, $\eta^2 = 0.36$, for the 4-year-olds, $F(1,27) = 7.08$, $p = 0.013$, $\eta^2 = 0.21$, and a marginally significant effect for the 5-year-olds, $F(1,27) = 3.98$, $p = 0.059$, $\eta^2 = 0.13$, but no such effect was discernable in the 6-year-olds, $F < 1$, $p = 0.45$. Indeed, children were more precise when the display's ending position was consistent with the room (3-year-olds: $M = 68.5$, $SD = 15.8$; 4-year-olds: $M = 73.8$, $SD = 14.0$; and 5-year-olds: $M = 85.4$, $SD = 13.2$) than when the display's ending position was inconsistent with the room (3-year-olds: $M = 53.8$, $SD = 19.3$; 4-year-olds: $M = 63.6$, $SD = 20.0$; and 5-year-olds: $M = 79.6$, $SD = 13.3$).[3]

An additional regression involving age in months and the difference between Room+ and Room– confirmed the age trend concerning the Room effect, standardized coefficient $b^* = -0.32$, $t(108) = -3.47$, $p = 0.001$, adjusted $R^2 = 0.09$ (see **Figure 3**). No reliable difference between the performances of boys and girls was found, $p > 0.10$.

DISCUSSION

The better retrieval performance when the display was consistent with the room clearly confirms the assumption that young children tend to encode the targets including distal references of the surrounding room, even when their perspective on the array is kept stable (cf. Nardini et al., 2006).[4] At the same time the manifest age trend shows children's advancement to more successful retrieval (see **Figure 3**). Performance is not only getting better with age overall, but the effect of room consistency that is evident in the 3-year-olds and 4-year-olds, is barely detectable in the 5-year-olds, and vanished in the 6-year-olds.

The drop in performance when children walked along the vehicle – especially concerning the 4- and 6-year-olds – might be attributed to an automated change in spatial representation that is maladaptive as the perspective on the array is kept stable, because participants' movement is matched by the rotation of the array. However, according to this interpretation one would expect an interaction between the room effect and the movement effect because no such performance loss should occur, when the array is rotated about 360° and the children's movement matches this rotation. Then again, Simons and Wang (1998; Wang and Simons, 1999) make no prediction about what happens, when spatial updating should cancel itself out. Therefore, the apparent difficulties resulting from walking around the vehicle might simply be due to the movement accidentally interfering with children's focus on the task.

Still, this does not answer the question, why there is no interaction discernible between room and movement. One explanation might be that spatial updating is not dependent on active self-movement. At least in adults spatial updating can be triggered by passive movement: Wang and Simons (1999) moved adults seated on an office chair around an array and found the same effect on object identification as described in the Introduction. On the one hand – in hindsight – it does not seem unreasonable to expect that optical flow or the vestibular system is sufficient to detect movement and elicit spatial updating in children, too. Obviously, controlling only one of at least three possible factors triggering spatial updating was not enough. On the other hand, the fact that the vehicle and the array constituted one unit could have helped children – especially when they rode the vehicle – to regard peripheral references as functionally irrelevant.

This was not the case here. Instead in the younger participants we see the strong tendency to encode peripheral references of the surrounding room and use them for retrieval. This use of peripheral references is generally in line with research concerning children's reorientation after being disoriented. In principle, all mechanisms currently discussed for reorientation are applicable here: it is possible that room geometry is used by children (Lee and Spelke, 2008, cf. Cheng, 1986; Gallistel, 1990). As our laboratory room has a unique geometrical shape (see Materials) this might have been a salient and stable feature for the younger children. Children of the tested age-groups should have been able to use distal landmarks (Newcombe, 1988; Newcombe et al., 1998) as our room provided doors, windows, and furniture. Even visual snapshots might have played a role in children's orientation (Piaget and Inhelder, 1967; cf. Diwadkar and McNamara, 1997): when retrieving the object in the Room– conditions the perspective on the array is exactly the same as when the object is hidden. The only change is found in the irrelevant background of the surrounding room. This would amount to younger children paying the same consideration to the relevant center of a visual snapshot as to irrelevant periphery. Anyway, in our experiment no definitive conclusion can be drawn about the exact nature of the distal features used by the younger children and this must be addressed in future experiments by controlling the surrounding room (cf. Burgess et al., 2004).

There is no reason to assume that the older children did not encode peripheral references of the surrounding room or the younger children did not encode the proximal references of the array, but we see a clear trend over age away from erroneously using the surrounding room for retrieval. This empirically clear age trend suggests a more flexible use of spatial information and an underlying shift from the undifferentiated to

[3]This additional analysis suggested that the aforementioned main effect for the factor Movement might only be statistically reliable for the 4-year-olds ($p = 0.026$) and the 6-year-olds ($p = 0.042$), but not for the other age-groups (all $ps > 0.10$).

[4]Although effects of the minimal handling time differences between the 135° trials (Room–) and the 360° trials (Room+) cannot be ruled out, it must be noted that the Room– trials had the shorter duration and therefore should have given participants – if anything – an advantage.

the meaningful or from random to focused in a cognitive adaptive development (see Nardini et al., 2009; Cheng et al., 2013; cf. Siegler, 1996).

ACKNOWLEDGMENTS

We wish to thank Meike Veeser and Mareike Lehmann for assistance in data collection, Heidrun Krüger and Lutz Krüger for technical assistance and proof-reading, and Horst Krist for manifold support and useful comments.

REFERENCES

Burgess, N., Spiers, H. J., and Paleologou, E. (2004). Orientational manoeuvres in the dark: dissociating allocentric and egocentric influences on spatial memory. *Cognition* 94, 149–166. doi: 10.1016/j.cognition.2004.01.001

Cheng, K. (1986). A purely geometric module in the rat's spatial representation. *Cognition* 23, 149–178. doi: 10.1016/0010-0277(86)90041-7

Cheng, K., Huttenlocher, J., and Newcombe, N. S. (2013). 25 years of research on the use of geometry in spatial reorientation: a current theoretical perspective. *Psychon. Bull. Rev.* 20, 1033–1054. doi: 10.3758/s13423-013-0416-1

Diwadkar, V. A., and McNamara, T. P. (1997). Viewpoint dependence in scene recognition. *Psychol. Sci.* 8, 302–307. doi: 10.1111/j.1467-9280.1997.tb00442.x

Gallistel, C. R. (1990). *The Organization of Learning.* Cambridge: MIT Press.

Jahn, G., Wendt, J., Lotze, M., Papenmeier, F., and Huff, M. (2012). Brain activation during spatial updating and attentive tracking of moving targets. *Brain Cogn.* 78, 105–113. doi: 10.1016/j.bandc.2011.12.001

Lee, S. A., and Spelke, E. S. (2008). Children's use of geometry for reorientation. *Dev. Sci.* 11, 743–749. doi: 10.1111/j.1467-7687.2008.00724.x

Nardini, M., Burgess, N., Breckenridge, K., and Atkinson, J. (2006). Differential developmental trajectories for egocentric, environmental and intrinsic frames of reference in spatial memory. *Cognition* 101, 153–172. doi: 10.1016/j.cognition.2005.09.005

Nardini, M., Thomas, R. L., Knowland, V. C. P., Braddick, O. J., and Atkinson, J. (2009). A viewpoint-independent process for spatial reorientation. *Cognition* 102, 241–248. doi: 10.1016/j.cognition.2009.05.003

Newcombe, N. (1988). The paradox of proximity in early spatial representation. *Br. J. Dev. Psychol.* 6, 376–378. doi: 10.1111/j.2044-835X.1988.tb01112.x

Newcombe, N., Huttenlocher, J., Drummey, A. B., and Wiley, J. G. (1998). The development of spatial location coding: place learning and dead reckoning in the second and third years. *Cogn. Dev.* 13, 185–200. doi: 10.1016/S0885-2014(98)90038-7

Piaget, J., and Inhelder, B. (1967). *The Child's Conception of Space*, trans. F. J. Langdon and J. L. Lunzer. New York, NY: W. W. Norton & Company. (Original work published 1948).

Siegler, R. S. (1996). *Emerging Minds: The Process of Change in Children's Thinking.* New York, NY: Oxford University Press.

Simons, D. J., and Wang, R. F. (1998). Perceiving real-world viewpoint changes. *Psychol. Sci.* 9, 315–320. doi: 10.1111/1467-9280.00062

Wang, R. F., and Simons, D. J. (1999). Active and passive scene recognition across views. *Cognition* 70, 191–210. doi: 10.1016/S0010-0277(99)00012-8

Wolbers, T., Hegarty, M., Büchel, C., and Loomis, J. M. (2008). Spatial updating: how the brain keeps track of changing object locations during observer motion. *Nat. Neurosci.* 11, 1223–1230. doi: 10.1038/nn.2189

Conflict of Interest Statement: The authors declare that the research was conducted in the absence of any commercial or financial relationships that could be construed as a potential conflict of interest.

6

Infant Social Development across the Transition from Crawling to Walking

Eric A. Walle *

Psychological Sciences, University of California, Merced, Merced, CA, USA

The onset of walking is a developmental transition that sets in motion a cascade of change across a range of domains, including social interactions and language learning. However, research on the unfolding of such change in the infant across this transition is limited. This investigation utilized a longitudinal design to examine the effect of walking acquisition on infant social development and parent perceptions of the infant to explore how changes in these factors relate with infant language development. Parents reported on infant social behaviors and their perception of the infant, as well as motor and language development, in 2-week intervals from 10.5 to 13 months of age. Mixed linear models revealed infant initiation of joint engagement (e.g., pointing, bringing objects to the parent) and following of the parent's joint engagement cues (e.g., point following, gaze following) increased as a function of infant walking experience, particularly between 2- and 4-weeks after the onset of walking, independent of age. Additionally, the parent's perception of the infant as an individual increased between 2- and 4-weeks after the infant began to walk. Finally, the unique relations of infant walking experience, following of social cues, and the parents' perception of the infant as an individual with infant language development were examined. Infant following of joint engagement behaviors and parent perception of the infant as an individual were related to receptive, but not productive, vocabulary size. Additionally, infant walking experience remained a significant predictor of infant receptive and productive language. These findings provide insight on important factors that change as the infant begins to walk. Future research utilizing more direct assessment of these factors is described, as well as general patterning of developmental change across the transition from crawling to walking.

Edited by:
Klaus Libertus,
University of Pittsburgh, USA

Reviewed by:
Lana Karasik,
College of Staten Island & City University of New York, USA
Ora Oudgenoeg-Paz,
Utrecht University, Netherlands

***Correspondence:**
Eric A. Walle
ewalle@ucmerced.edu

Keywords: social development, language, motor development, walking, joint attention

MOTOR DEVELOPMENT AS A FACILITATOR OF CHANGE

There is a rich, albeit often overlooked, theoretical literature viewing development as a reciprocal and non-linear process of change. Gottlieb's (1983) emphasis on epigenesis highlights the bidirectional and transactional nature of development. Both classic and contemporary theorizing has similarly argued for a bidirectional and dynamic framework of development (e.g., Gibson, 1958; Thelen, 1995; Bernstein, 1996; Thelen and Smith, 1998) in which particular experiences serve as catalysts for developmental cascades (e.g., Spencer et al., 2009; Masten and Cicchetti, 2010). Infant motor development is one particular skill that generates a host of new experiences and is associated with changes in psychological functioning across a broad range of domains (for reviews, see Campos et al., 2000; Iverson, 2010). In particular, a growing body of research indicates that the transition from crawling to walking corresponds with an increase in infant receptive and productive language (Oudgenoeg-Paz et al., 2012; Walle and Campos, 2014; He et al., 2015).

Although this research has demonstrated a clear association between infant motor and linguistic development, it has fallen short in elucidating the mechanisms that account for this developmental change. More concretely, it is unlikely that the acquisition of upright locomotion *per se* causes infants to develop language, just as it is unlikely that infant language causes the onset of walking. Rather, the onset of walking likely corresponds with changes in a broad range of domains, including, but not limited to, language. Research exploring the developmental trajectories of different abilities across the transition from crawling to walking may elucidate the underlying mechanism(s) that account for the relation between walking and language. However, the only longitudinal study to investigate the association between infant walking and language (Walle and Campos, 2014) did not explore potential processes that may account for this link.

The present longitudinal investigation utilized parent report of changes in the infant's following and solicitation of joint engagement, the parent's perceptions of their infant, the infant's language development, and locomotor development. Assessing these abilities in 2-week intervals from 10.5 to 13 months of age permitted the close examination of how each changed across the transition from crawling to walking.

Parent and Infant Joint Engagement

The acquisition of an upright posture increases the infant's visual field (Kretch et al., 2014) and permits greater flexibility with which to view the environment (Frank et al., 2013). These physical changes may promote infant following of adult attentional cues, and thereby facilitate language learning. Engaging in joint attention behavior is essential for the development of language (Tomasello, 1988, 1995). Such episodes of joint engagement occur when one individual directs the attention of another to a shared referent, such as an object or event. Multiple studies have found that infant following of adult attentional cues is related to language development (Tomasello and Todd, 1983; Smith et al., 1988; Mundy et al., 1995; Morales et al., 1998; Brooks and Meltzoff, 2005). Likewise, infant initiation of joint engagement, such as pointing, is also associated with subsequent language development (Brooks and Meltzoff, 2008; LeBarton et al., 2015). Perhaps not surprisingly, infant joint attention, particularly following adult gaze, also develops markedly following the infant's first birthday (Morissette et al., 1995; Morales et al., 2000), when infants typically begin to walk. However, existing longitudinal research of infant following of joint attention cues has not examined how this ability is impacted by the onset of walking.

Furthermore, infant walking also has a significant impact on how the infant engages with the caregiver. Walking infants are reported by parents as more willful (Biringen et al., 1995) and have been observed to be more likely to access objects located further away than crawling infants (Clearfield, 2011; Karasik et al., 2011). Additionally, engaging in mobile bids for the parent's attention, such as carrying an object to the parent, elicits more interactive, and verbally rich responses by the parent and such bids are more frequent by walking than crawling infants (Karasik et al., 2014). Walking infants have also been found to direct the parent's attention to objects using vocalizations and gestures more than crawling infants (Clearfield et al., 2008; Clearfield, 2011; Karasik et al., 2011). These findings indicate that not only may the walking infant be more attuned to follow adult attentional cues, but they also help to generate social contexts in which they themselves elicit parent attention. However, prior longitudinal research has not examined how such changes in infant elicitation of parent attention across this developmental transition is related with infant language development.

The above research indicates that walking infants initiate and engage in richer joint engagement interactions in social contexts than crawling infants. Changes in infants' ability to engage with the environment combined with corresponding changes in parents' responding may help to facilitate infant language acquisition. However, previous research has not examined the developmental trajectories of these skills across the transition from crawling to walking.

Parent Perception of the Infant

The acquisition of walking may also change how parents perceive their infants. How parents perceive their infant has a profound impact on their inferences about infants' behavior (Rubin et al., 1974), interactions with their infants (Will et al., 1976), and expectations of likely actions (Mondschein et al., 2000). Upright locomotion is a uniquely human characteristic. By contrast, a crawling infant is more akin in physical appearance to a quadrupedal animal. Adult attribution of greater intentionality and responsibility to walking infants' than crawling infants may impact infant vocabulary size in two ways.

First, parents may interact differently with their infant if they perceive their infant as more intentional and human-like. Such differences in interactive style may promote specific behaviors and social responses when engaging with the infant, as suggested by parents' differential reinforcement of more speech-like babbling (Warlaumont et al., 2014). Thus, parents who believe that their infant is a more capable interactive partner may provide qualitatively different communication. Second, prior research linking infant walking and language has relied on parent reporting of infant receptive and productive vocabularies. Although the MacAruthur-Bates Communicative Development Inventory (MCDI) is a commonly used and validated measure (see Fenson et al., 1994, 2000; Ring and Fenson, 2000), it is possible that the parents attributing greater linguistic skill to walking infants over crawling infants may inadvertently inflate their vocabulary sizes. For example, a crawling and a walking infant might both utter the same vocalization (e.g., du-ga-ga). The parent's perception of the walking as more human-like may result in the parent attributing greater intentionality to this behavior and conclude that the child was verbalizing (e.g., doggy), whereas the same vocalization by the crawling infant may be dismissed as babbling. Thus, it is possible that previously reported differences in crawling and walking infants' vocabulary sizes is attributable to parents' differential appraisals of their infant's proficiency, not an objective change in language development. Accounting for parents' perception of the infant as an intentional individual when analyzing parent reporting of infant behavior is essential to help rule out this alternative explanation.

THE PRESENT STUDY

No study to the author's knowledge has investigated how the infant joint attention and the parent's perception of the infant relate with language development across the acquisition of upright locomotion. It is essential to examine changes in such skills in order to chart the unfolding trajectory of these domains as function of locomotor experience. Parent report is a useful tool for providing researchers insight on variables warranting closer examination. The present longitudinal study incorporated the use of parent report of the above processes to explore how changes in infant social development across this transition relate with changes in infant language.

The aims of the investigation were two-fold. The first aim was to examine changes in the infant's social context across the transition from crawling to walking. Specifically, parents reported on infant initiating and following of joint attention behaviors, their perception of the infant as an intentional individual, and the infant's receptive and productive language. Use of parent report to measure these behaviors allowed for more frequent assessments across this developmental transition. It was hypothesized that infant initiation and following of joint attention behaviors would increase as a function of locomotor development, independent of age. It was also hypothesized that parents would perceive their infant as more responsible and intentional across the transition from crawling to walking. The second aim examined how changes in infant's social contexts across this motoric transition uniquely predicted language development over time as a function of walking experience. Parent–infant joint engagement, but not the parent's perception of the infant as an individual, was hypothesized to predict infant language controlling for infant age. Additionally, infant walking experience was expected to remain a unique predictor of receptive and productive language in this model.

METHODS

Sample

Forty-three infants (24 female) were included in the present study, beginning when the infant was either 10 months ($n = 17$) or 10.5 months ($n = 26$) old and ending when the infant was 13.5 months of age. This sample was taken from a longitudinal study investigating infant language development and included language data previously reported in Study 1 by Walle and Campos (2014)[1]. This project was approved by the Committee for Protection of Human Subjects, University of California, Berkeley. Infants were predominantly from English-speaking families and heard English for a large proportion of the day. Extensive details regarding the demographics, backgrounds, and language environments of the sample are included in the report by Walle and Campos (2014). Forty infants were crawling at the start of the study (M age of crawling onset = 8.33 months, $SD = 1.44$) and three infants were walking at the start of the study (Age of walk onset = 9.63, 9.86, and 10.49 months, respectively).

[1]Data from 1 infant of the sample from Study 1 of Walle and Campos (2014) was excluded from the present study because the parent did not complete the questionnaire of changes in infant behavior.

Procedure

Parents were emailed instructions for completing an online questionnaire administered using Qualtrics survey software. The email was sent to parents every 2 weeks, beginning when their child was 10- or 10.5-months-old and ending when their infant reached 13.5 months. The parent had 5 days to complete each online questionnaire, after which the link in the email was deactivated.

Measures

The bi-weekly online questionnaire consisted of multiple surveys. The entire questionnaire was completed at each time point. The instructions at the start of the survey stated that the purpose of the study was to "investigate infant language and social development between 10 and 14 months of age." No mentioning of the hypotheses relating to locomotor development was made.

Parents first completed a locomotor survey to indicate when their child had achieved specific locomotor milestones. Crawling onset was operationalized as the date when the infant could self-locomote a distance at least twice his or her body length. Walking onset was operationalized as the date when the infant first bipedally locomoted a distance of 10 feet without falling or needing support (see Adolph, 1997; Adolph et al., 2003). Previous research indicates high validity of parent reporting of infant motor milestones (e.g., Bodnarchuk and Eaton, 2004). No parents reversed their reporting of the onset of a locomotor transition.

Next, the parent completed the MacArthur-Bates Long Form Vocabulary Checklist: Level I (MCDI; Fenson et al., 1994). This survey contains a 396-item checklist in which parents marked words that the infant "understood" (receptive vocabulary) or "understood and says" (productive vocabulary). Parents were permitted to report their child's language development in any language, including signing. Items that the parent marked at previous time points were carried over into subsequent time points. The survey also includes a 12-item section on infant communicative gesturing. Validity and test–retest reliability for the MCDI is reported by Fenson et al. (1994).

Finally, parents completed a series of questions concerning their infants' social development. The questions asked parents to report on: infant pointing, infant bringing an object to the parent, infant point following, infant gaze following, and the parent's perception of the infant as an intentional individual responsible for his/her actions (see Appendix Section). For each question, the parent reported whether the behavior/perception of the infant was demonstrated significantly less, less, about the same, more, or significantly more during the most recent 2-week period in comparison to its frequency in the previous 2-week period. Parent reporting was scored on a scale of −2 (significantly <2 weeks ago) to 2 (significantly >2 weeks ago) to reflect the development of the particular item. Parent ratings at each interval were added cumulatively to reflect infant behavior and parent perception of the infant.

RESULTS

Initial analyses examined correlations between items relating to parent reporting of joint engagement behaviors and perception of their infant. The infant initiated behaviors of joint engagement (i.e., infant pointing, infant bringing object to parent) were highly correlated ($r = 0.83$, $p < 0.001$) and thus were combined into a composite variable named Infant Initiated Joint Engagement. Similarly, infant following of parent-initiated behaviors (i.e., infant following parent point, infant following parent gaze) were also correlated with one another ($r = 0.57$, $p < 0.001$) and were thus combined into a composite variable named Parent Initiated Joint Engagement. Finally, parent reporting of the infant as intentional and responsible for his/her actions were significantly correlated ($r = 0.63$, $p < 0.001$), and thus combined into a single variable named Infant as Individual. No effects of infant gender were observed, thus male and female infants were collapsed in all analyses.

Analytic Strategy

Mixed linear modeling using a first order autoregressive covariance structure was used to analyze change in variables across time. Infant Age and Walking Experience (i.e., number of weeks walking) were included in the models as fixed effects. Of the 296 reports analyzed, 27 contained missing values of parent reporting of infants' social development (9.12%). Visual inspection of the missing observations indicated no pattern of missingness, as the missing values were relatively evenly distributed across time points. Thus, instances of missing data were believed to be completely at random and resolved through imputation of the mean change score for the missing time point, a suitable solution given the circumstances of the present study (see Schafer and Graham, 2002).

Analysis of the skew and kurtosis of parent-reported variables indicated that the data was normally distributed at each time point.

The relation of Infant Age and Walking Experience with each of the three parent reported variables of infant social development (i.e., Infant Initiated Joint Engagement, Parent Initiated Joint Engagement, Infant as an Individual) was analyzed using separate mixed linear models for each social development variable (see **Table 1**). Next, a mixed linear model including Infant Age, Walking Experience, Infant Initiated Joint Engagement, Parent Initiated Joint Engagement, and Infant as an Individual examined the unique relation of these variables with infant (a) Receptive Vocabulary and (b) Productive Vocabulary (see **Table 2**).

Data Transformations

As highlighted in the introduction, development is often non-linear, particularly when examined across a developmental transition. Visual inspection of changes in parent reporting of Infant Initiated Joint Engagement, Parent Initiated Joint Engagement, and Infant as an Individual as a function of Walking Experience suggested the presence of a non-linear, cubic trend (see **Figure 1**). Thus, Walking Experience was transformed using a cubic function (Walking Experience^3) to test for the presence of this non-linear pattern of change (accordingly, a quadratic function, Walking Experience^2, was also computed).

Additionally, in accordance with the previous reporting of the data by Walle and Campos (2014), the natural log of

TABLE 1 | Mixed linear models predicting infant social variables.

Variable	Infant initiated joint engagement		Parent initiated joint engagement		Infant as an individual	
	b	*(SE)*	*b*	*(SE)*	*b*	*(SE)*
Age	0.49**	(0.08)	0.48**	(0.06)	0.57**	(0.06)
Walking Experience	−0.48†	(0.33)	−0.54*	(0.25)	−0.30	(0.26)
Walking Experience^2	0.37*	(0.17)	0.28*	(0.13)	0.15	(0.13)
Walking Experience^3	−0.05*	(0.02)	−0.03*	(0.02)	−0.01	(0.02)

Values represent unstandardized fixed effect estimates and corresponding standard errors. Examination of non-linear trends as follows: Linear, Walking Experience; quadratic, Walking Experince^2; cubic, Walking Experience^3.
*†$p < 0.10$, *$p < 0.05$, **$p < 0.01$.*

TABLE 2 | Full mixed linear model predicting infant MCDI scores.

Variable	Receptive MCDI		Productive MCDI	
	b	*(SE)*	*b*	*(SE)*
Age	12.33**	(1.13)	3.49**	(0.49)
Walking Experience LN	16.53**	(3.57)		
Walking Experience			3.99*	(1.83)
Walking Experience^2			−1.39	(0.93)
Walking Experience^3			0.29*	(0.13)
Parent initiated joint engagement	3.88**	(1.35)	0.18	(0.57)
Infant as an individual	−3.02*	(1.25)	−0.59	(0.53)

Values represent unstandardized fixed effect estimates and corresponding standard errors. Examination of non-linear trends were as follows: logarithmic, Walking Experience LN; linear, Walking Experience; quadratic, Walking Experince^2; cubic, Walking Experience^3.
*†$p < 0.10$, *$p < 0.05$, **$p < 0.01$.*

Walking Experience (Walking Experience LN) was used when predicting Receptive Vocabulary and the cubic function of Walking Experience (Walking Experience^3) was used when predicting Productive Vocabulary. An extensive rationale for selecting these non-linear functions is provided on page 339 of the report by Walle and Campos (2014), specifically that the inclusion of the natural log and cubic functions of walking experience significantly improved the fit of models predicting receptive and productive language, respectively.

Relations between Variables of Infant Social Development

An initial set of analyses examined the relations of Infant Initiated Joint Engagement, Parent Initiated Joint Engagement, and Infant as an Individual. Because each of these variables each assessed an aspect of infants' social development, these variables were expected to be related, yet representative of theoretically distinct constructs. The correlations of the variables were examined at each time point. The correlations of Infant Initiated Joint Engagement and Parent Initiated Joint Engagement were: $r_{T2} = 0.32$, $r_{T3} = 0.64$, $r_{T4} = 0.65$, $r_{T5} = 0.71$, $r_{T6} = 0.79$, $r_{T7} = 0.80$, $r_{T8} = 0.84$. The correlations of Infant Initiated Joint Engagement and Infant as an Individual were: $r_{T2} = 0.32$,

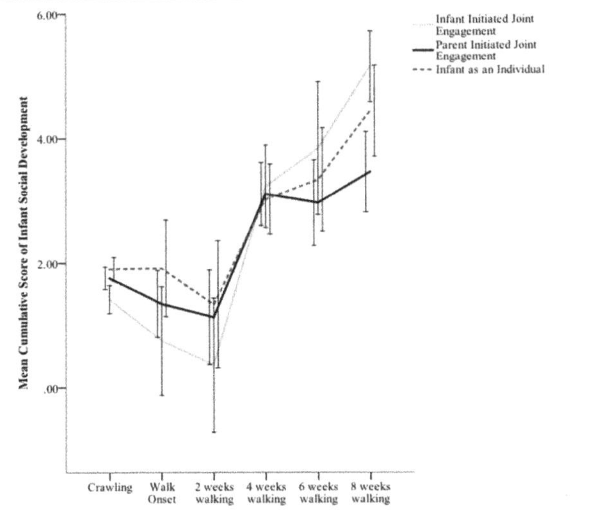

FIGURE 1 | Mean cumulative scores of parent reporting of Infant Initiation of Joint Engagement, Parent Initiation of Joint Engagement, and the parent's perception of the Infant as an Individual as a function of infant walking experience. Error bars represent ± 1 *SE* of the mean.

$r_{T3} = 0.64$, $r_{T4} = 0.65$, $r_{T5} = 0.71$, $r_{T6} = 0.79$, $r_{T7} = 0.80$, $r_{T8} = 0.84$. The correlations of Parent Initiated Joint Engagement and Infant as an Individual were: $r_{T2} = 0.51$, $r_{T3} = 0.66$, $r_{T4} = 0.60$, $r_{T5} = 0.55$, $r_{T6} = 0.59$, $r_{T7} = 0.62$, $r_{T8} = 0.62$. All of the above correlations were significant ($p < 0.05$). Although the variables were correlated with one another, prior theoretical considerations viewed each as a separate construct. Thus, each variable was analyzed separately to examine their relation with infant walking experience. However, analyses examining the unique associations of the variables with infant language included only Parent Initiated Joint Engagement and Infant as an Individual, as these two variables were the least associated (see below).

Infant Initiated Joint Engagement and Infant Walking

Change in Infant Initiated Joint Engagement was examined as a function of Infant Age and Walking Experience. An initial model including only Age and Walking Experience was first tested. A significant effect of Age was present, $t_{(277)} = 6.11, p < 0.001, \beta = 0.29$, but Walking Experience was only trending, $t_{(279)} = 1.84$, $p = 0.067$, $\beta = 0.10$.

Next, a model was tested including the cubic function of Walking Experience. As shown in **Table 1**, significant effects of infant Age, $t_{(275)} = 6.23$, $p < 0.001$, $\beta = 0.29$, the quadratic effect Walking Experience^2, $t_{(229)} = 2.27$, $p = 0.02$, $\beta = 0.64$, and the cubic effect Walking Experience^3, $t_{(229)} = 2.01$, $p = 0.045$, $\beta = 0.35$, were present. The linear effect of Walking Experience did not reach significance, $t_{(237)} = 1.47, p = 0.14, \beta = 0.20$. Although this model seemed to better reflect the pattern of development indicated by the graphing of the data, this model did not demonstrate a significantly better fit than the linear model, $\chi^2(1) = 0.55, p = 0.46$.

Graphing the changes in Infant Initiated Joint Engagement suggested differences between 2- and 4-weeks and 4- and 6-weeks of walking experience (see **Figure 1**). Pairwise comparisons controlling for Infant Age revealed significant differences in Infant Initiated Joint Engagement between 2-weeks ($M = 1.55$, $SE = 0.55$) and 4-weeks ($M = 2.29$, $SE = 0.59$), $t_{(245)} = 2.91, p = 0.004$, 95% CI $[-1.24, -0.24]$, and 4- and 6-weeks ($M = 2.90$, $SE = 0.65$) after the onset of walking, $t_{(244)} = 2.18, p = 0.03$, 95% CI $[-1.17, -0.06]$.

Parent Initiated Joint Engagement and Infant Walking

Change in infant following of Parent Initiated Joint Engagement was examined as a function of Infant Age and Walking Experience. An initial model including only Age and Walking Experience was first tested. A significant effect of Age was present, $t_{(278)} = 8.01$, $p < 0.001$, $\beta = 0.39$, but Walking Experience was not significant, $t_{(279)} = 0.04, p = 0.97, \beta = 0.00$.

Next, a model was tested including the cubic function of Walking Experience. As shown in **Table 1**, significant effects of infant Age, $t_{(276)} = 8.09$, $p < 0.001$, $\beta = 0.39$, the linear effect of Walking Experience, $t_{(237)} = 2.18$, $p = 0.03$, $\beta = 0.30$, the quadratic effect Walking Experience^2, $t_{(228)} = 2.24$, $p = 0.03$, $\beta = 0.65$, and the cubic effect Walking Experience^3, $t_{(228)} = 2.00$, $p = 0.046$, $\beta = 0.36$, were present. Again, although the cubic model appeared to reflect the visual patterning of the data, this model did not demonstrate a significantly better fit than the linear model, $\chi^2(1) = 0.48, p = 0.49$.

Graphing the changes in Parent Initiated Joint Engagement suggested differences between 2- and 4-weeks (see **Figure 1**). Pairwise comparisons controlling for Infant Age confirmed the visual pattern, revealing significant differences between 2-weeks ($M = 1.52$, $SE = 0.40$) and 4-weeks ($M = 1.98$, $SE = 0.43$) after the onset of walking, $t_{(245)} = 2.34$, $p = 0.02$, 95% CI $[-0.84, -0.09]$.

Infant As an Individual and Infant Walking

Change in the Infant as an Individual was examined as a function of Infant Age and Walking Experience. An initial model including only Age and Walking Experience was first tested. A significant effect of Age was present, $t_{(276)} = 8.94, p < 0.001, \beta = 0.40$, but Walking Experience was not significant, $t_{(278)} = 0.84$, $p = 0.40$, $\beta = 0.04$.

Next, a model was tested including the cubic function of Walking Experience. As shown in **Table 1**, a significant effect of infant Age, $t_{(274)} = 9.00$, $p < 0.001$, $\beta = 0.40$, was present. However, neither the linear effect of Walking Experience, $t_{(236)} = 1.16$, $p = 0.25$, $\beta = 0.15$, the quadratic effect Walking Experience^2, $t_{(229)} = 1.14$, $p = 0.26$, $\beta = 0.30$, nor the cubic effect Walking Experience^3, $t_{(229)} = 0.73, p = 0.47, \beta = 0.12$, were significant. Additionally, this model demonstrated worse fit than the linear model, $\chi^2(1) = -1.72, p < 0.001$.

As with the previous two parent-reported variables, graphing of changes of the Infant as an Individual suggested possible differences as a function of infant Walking Experience (see **Figure 1**). Thus, for exploratory purposes, pairwise comparisons controlling for Infant Age examined this interval. Analyses revealed significant differences between 2-weeks (M = 1.80, SE = 0.46) and 4-weeks (M = 2.24, SE = 0.49) after the onset of walking, $t_{(244)} = 2.18$, $p = 0.03$, 95% CI [−0.84, −0.04].

Relations with Language

All of the above variables were included in a single mixed linear model to examine their unique relations with infant receptive and productive vocabulary (see **Table 2**). As with the prior models, infant Age and Walking Experience were also included to determine whether the relations reported by Walle and Campos (2014) would remain significant with inclusion of the variables from the present study. Additionally, although Infant Initiated Joint Engagement and Parent Initiated Joint Engagement were theorized to be unique constructs, they were also highly correlated, $r = 0.79$, $p < 0.001$. Thus, to avoid issues of collinearity, only Parent Initiated Joint Engagement was included in models predicting infant language. The selection for including Parent Initiated Joint Engagement was based on this variable having a smaller correlation with Infant as an Individual than did Infant Initiated Joint Engagement.

Receptive Vocabulary

The effects of Parent Initiated Joint Engagement, $t_{(249)} = 2.87$, $p = 0.004$, $\beta = 0.16$, and parent reporting of the Infant as an Individual, $t_{(251)} = 2.41$, $p = 0.02$, $\beta = 0.14$, each predicted infant receptive vocabulary size. Additionally, infant Age, $t_{(243)} = 10.96$, $p < 0.001$, $\beta = 0.41$, and Walking Experience LN, $t_{(236)} = 4.63$, $p < 0.001$, $\beta = 0.16$, remained significant predictors of receptive vocabulary.

Productive Vocabulary

For infant productive vocabulary, only significant effects for infant Age, $t_{(250)} = 7.10$, $p < 0.001$, $\beta = 0.40$, Walking Experience, $t_{(209)} = 2.18$, $p = 0.03$, $\beta = 0.31$, and the cubic function Walking Experience^3, $t_{(200)} = 2.27$, $p = 0.02$, $\beta = 0.43$, were present. However, Parent Initiated Joint Engagement, $t_{(247)} = 0.32$, $p = 0.75$, $\beta = 0.03$, and the Infant as an Individual, $t_{(243)} = 1.13$, $p = 0.26$, $\beta = 0.10$, were not significant, nor was the quadratic function Walking Experience^2, $t_{(200)} = 1.50$, $p = 0.14$, $\beta = 0.46$.

DISCUSSION

Parent reporting indicated that infant elicitation and following of parent attention increases following the onset of walking, independent of the infant's age. These infant behaviors have not previously been linked with the onset of walking. Interestingly, parents' perception of their infant did not increase as a function of walking experience; only as a function of age. Importantly, the relation of infant walking and language remained significant even after controlling for infant joint attention engagement and the parents' perception of the infant. This suggests that (1) parental bias is unlikely to account for the reported differences in walking and crawling infants' language development, and (2) the study of additional developmental domains, particularly immediately after the transition from crawling to walking, is needed to further explore the association of walking and language. Each of these findings is elaborated upon below and suggestions for further research are described.

Infant and Parent Behaviors across the Transition from Crawling to Walking

Infant and Parent Initiated Joint Engagement

Examination of the longitudinal data revealed that significant increases in infant initiation and following of joint engagement between 2- to 4-weeks and 4- to 6-weeks following the onset of walking. Importantly, these differences were present independent of infant age. Parent reported changes in infants' initiation of joint engagement across the transition from crawling to walking mirrors prior observational findings (e.g., Clearfield et al., 2008; Clearfield, 2011; Karasik et al., 2014). The present results extend previous research by demonstrating the relation of these behaviors with infant concurrent vocabulary size across this transition. Further research is needed to follow up on this finding in two additional contexts. Furthermore, these findings provide support for the possibility that changes in infant following of joint attention cues reported at around 12 months of age may be related to infant walking onset. For example, longitudinal research by Morissette et al. (1995) reported nearly a 70% increase in infants' following of adult gaze to locate a referent between 12 and 15 months of age, likely when most infants had shifted from crawling to experienced walkers.

Parent Perception of Infant As an Individual

Contrary to our hypotheses, the onset of walking did not significantly impact the parent's perception of the infant. Even so, it remains important to examine possible qualitative differences in parent speech to walking infants. Both Walle and Campos (2014) and Walle and Warlaumont (2015) found that parent language input predicted walking, but not crawling, infants' language development, despite walking and crawling infants receiving similar amounts of language input. Additionally, Karasik et al. (2014) found that parents were more likely to respond to infant mobile bids (i.e., carrying an object to the parent) with action directives related to the infants' object of interest. Although mobile bids were more frequent by walking infants, parents demonstrated a similar style of responding when crawling infants engaged in this behavior, suggesting that the parents' perception of the infant in of itself may not impact language input. However, this does not rule out that walking and crawling infants may qualitatively differ in their processing of such input.

Predicting Infant Language Development

Inclusion of the above variables with infant age and walking experience allowed for the examination of the unique relation of the predictors with infant receptive and productive language development.

Receptive Vocabulary

Infant following of parent-initiated episodes of joint engagement was positively related with receptive vocabulary size, independent of infant age and locomotor ability. Interestingly, the relation of infant walking with infant receptive language remained significant, though the coefficient did drop from $b = 35.65$, 95% CI [19.48, 51.82] (as reported by Walle and Campos, 2014, in which the same data was analyzed without the parent-reported social variables) to $b = 16.53$. This suggests that while social engagement behaviors are important for the development of infant language (e.g., Tomasello and Todd, 1983; Iverson and Goldin-Meadow, 2005), their role does not fully account for the relation of infant walking and language. Additionally, the parent's perception of the infant as an individual also significantly predicted receptive language. However, the negative direction of this relation suggests that parents may, in fact, deflate their reporting of infant's receptive language across this transition. Furthermore, parents' perception of the infant as an intentional and responsible individual did not account for the relation of infant walking and language. Though by no means definitive, this finding provides evidence against the possibility that parental bias in reporting infants' language development for crawling and walking infants may account for previous findings reported by He et al. (2015) and Walle and Campos (2014).

Productive Vocabulary

Contrary to the hypotheses, joint engagement behaviors were not related to infant productive vocabulary size. Additionally, parent reporting of infant productive language was not influenced by the parent's perception of the infant as an individual. However, as with receptive language, the relation of infant walking experience was a significant predictor of infant productive vocabulary size. These findings may indicate that productive language development across the transition from crawling to walking is impacted by different mechanisms than those included in the present study. For example, whereas receptive language may be aided by increased adult labeling of objects in the environment during episodes of joint engagement, increases in productive language may be facilitated by other means. For example, physiological changes resulting from an upright posture, such as changes in respiration, positioning of the diaphragm, or length of the vocal tract (Openshaw et al., 1984; Thelen, 1991; see Boliek et al., 1996; Vorperian et al., 2005), may facilitate ease of verbalization and articulation. Additionally, increased motoric coordination more generally, fundamental for both walking and speech production (see Iverson, 2010), may also account for the relation.

Developmental Patterning of Change

The findings from the present investigation also revealed parent reporting of infant initiation and following of joint attention cues significantly increased between 2- and 4-weeks after the infant began to walk. This suggests that changes related to the acquisition of walking may necessitate multiple weeks before manifesting. This finding is similar to the longitudinal findings by Walle and Campos (2014) for infant productive vocabulary. Additionally, similar delays in functional change has been observed across other developmental transitions (e.g., Campos et al., 1992; Eilers et al., 1993; Bertenthal et al., 1994). Future research comparing crawling and walking infants may wish to allow a sufficient amount of walking experience when predicting corresponding developmental change in various domains. Additionally, it is necessary to more closely examine what occurs during the first 4 weeks following the acquisition of infant walking. It has been hypothesized that developmental transitions correspond with a temporary reorganization of various skills as the system adjusts to the new skill and related experiences (see Thelen and Smith, 1994) and empirical research lends some support to this notion (e.g., Clearfield, 2004; Berger, 2010; Parladé and Iverson, 2011). It is possible that infant engagement with the social environment immediately following the onset of walking is hampered due to a need for increased allocation of attention to postural stability. Thus, the benefits afforded by upright locomotion may only be gleaned after sufficient expertise for the new locomotor skill is achieved.

LIMITATIONS FOR CONSIDERATION

Although the present study found associations between parent and infant social behaviors and the infant's language development, there are two notable limitations that warrant acknowledgement.

First and foremost, all data collected relied on parent reporting of infant behavior and development and laboratory and observational assessment of the variables reported in the present study is needed. Laboratory assessments of infant elicitation of adult behavior (e.g., Harding and Golinkoff, 1979; Lempers, 1979; Conrad, 1994) would more precisely examine differences in crawling and walking infants' initiation of joint engagement. Additionally, paradigms similar to those by Butterworth and others (see Butterworth and Cochran, 1980; Butterworth and Jarrett, 1991) in which the adult attempts to direct the infant's attention to novel objects is needed to more carefully observe the parent reported differences found in the present study. In particular, it would be of interest to test infant following of a variety of different communicative cues (Presmanes et al., 2007), particularly adult gaze (Morissette et al., 1995), and infant locating of referents outside of their immediate visual field (Deák et al., 2000). Naturalistic observations in which the parent and child are observed regularly in the home for extensive periods of time would help to corroborate changes in infant initiated joint engagement behaviors, how parents respond to such behaviors, and the relation of the behaviors and interactions with concurrent and subsequent infant language development (Iverson and Goldin-Meadow, 2005; Clearfield et al., 2008; Karasik et al., 2014). Furthermore, research examining the quality of parent language and the reciprocal patterning within the language environment (e.g., parent scaffolding of infant babbling, turn-taking, engagement with joint objects) is vital for furthering understanding the infants' language environments (see Warlaumont et al., 2014).

Second, although the longitudinal design of the study captured developmental change across the transition from crawling to walking, the data collected assessed perceived changes in infant joint engagement and independence, not actual values for these constructs. This more descriptive approach prevented the present study from determining the objective frequency or level of sophistication of infant behaviors. Furthermore, parents may have differed in their operationalization of certain behaviors, such as what they considered indicative of infant following of social cues or independence. What is clearly needed is a multi-method longitudinal investigation incorporating laboratory assessments, direct observation, and parent reporting to examine the developmental trajectories of these variables across the transition from crawling to walking. Such an investigation could feature (1) bi-weekly lab testing of infant joint attention, imitation, representation, receptive and productive language, and lab observation of parent-child interactions, (2) bi-weekly assessment of the home language environment (e.g., Walle and Warlaumont, 2015), and (3) continuous parent reporting of infant development using mobile technology (e.g., Ellis-Davies et al., 2012). Though expensive with regard to time and resources, an investigation of this sort is precisely what is required at this juncture to more precisely examine the relation of infant walking with other psychological skills.

In closing, it is important to highlight the typical fashion that research in developmental psychology often proceeds. First, one identifies a developmental change through observation. Second, one investigates relations of the developmental change and other relevant variables. Third, one engages in more precise testing of the identified variables to establish a causal relation. The present investigation provides important information relevant to the second step that is intended to inform the third. Although a causal association between infant walking and language has not be demonstrated by existing research, the antecedent-consequent nature of the findings supports a view favoring epigenesis over maturational coincidence. Continued research is needed to (1) replicate the relation of walking and language and (2) identify possible mediators or moderators of this relation. Such work would further our understanding of the complex relation of walking with other psychological phenomena.

AUTHOR CONTRIBUTIONS

The author confirms being the sole contributor of this work and approved it for publication.

ACKNOWLEDGMENTS

Work on this article was supported by grants from the Amini Foundation for the Study of Affects and National Institute of Child Health and Human Development Grant HD-62766. I also wish to thank Joseph J. Campos for his support of this research, as well as Alexandra Main for her comments on drafts of this article and Bodo Winter for statistical consultation.

REFERENCES

Adolph, K. E. (1997). Learning in the development of infant locomotion. *Monogr. Soc. Res. Child Dev.* 62, 1–158. doi: 10.2307/1166199

Adolph, K. E., Vereijken, B., and Shrout, P. E. (2003). What changes in infant walking and why. *Child Dev.* 74, 475–497. doi: 10.1111/1467-8624.7402011

Berger, S. E. (2010). Locomotor expertise predicts infants' perseverative errors. *Dev. Psychol.* 46, 326–336. doi: 10.1037/a0018285

Bernstein, N. A. (1996). "On dexterity and its development," in *Dexterity and its Development,* eds M. L. Latash and M. T. Turvey (Hillsdale, NJ: Lawrence Erlbaum Associates), 1–235.

Bertenthal, B. I., Campos, J. J., and Kermoian, R. (1994). An epigenetic perspective on the development of self-produced locomotion and its consequences. *Curr. Dir. Psychol. Sci.* 3, 140–145. doi: 10.1111/1467-8721.ep10770621

Biringen, Z., Emde, R. N., Campos, J. J., and Appelbaum, M. I. (1995). Affective reorganization in the infant, the mother, and the dyad: the role of upright locomotion and its timing. *Child Dev.* 66, 499–514. doi: 10.2307/1131593

Bodnarchuk, J. L., and Eaton, W. O. (2004). Can parent reports be trusted? Validity of daily checklists of gross motor milestone attainment. *Appl. Dev. Psychol.* 25, 481–490. doi: 10.1016/j.appdev.2004.06.005

Boliek, C. A., Hixon, T. J., Watson, P. J., and Morgan, W. J. (1996). Vocalization and breathing during the first year of life. *J. Voice* 10, 1–22. doi: 10.1016/S0892-1997(96)80015-4

Brooks, R., and Meltzoff, A. N. (2005). The development of gaze following and its relation to language. *Dev. Sci.* 8, 535–543. doi: 10.1111/j.1467-7687.2005.00445.x

Brooks, R., and Meltzoff, A. N. (2008). Infant gaze following and pointing predict accelerated vocabulary growth through two years of age: a longitudinal, growth curve modeling study. *J. Child Lang.* 35, 207–220. doi: 10.1017/S030500090700829X

Butterworth, G., and Cochran, E. (1980). Towards a mechanism of joint visual attention in human infancy. *Int. J. Behav. Dev.* 3, 253–272. doi: 10.1177/016502548000300303

Butterworth, G., and Jarrett, N. (1991). What minds have in common is space: spatial mechanisms serving joint visual attention in infancy. *Br. J. Dev. Psychol.* 9, 55–72. doi: 10.1111/j.2044-835X.1991.tb00862.x

Campos, J. J., Anderson, D. I., Barbu-Roth, M. A., Hubbard, E. M., Hertenstein, M. J. J., and Witherington, D. (2000). Travel broadens the mind. *Infancy* 1, 149–219. doi: 10.1207/S15327078IN0102_1

Campos, J. J., Bertenthal, B. I., and Kermoian, R. (1992). Early experience and emotional development: the emergence of wariness of heights. *Psychol. Sci.* 3, 61–64. doi: 10.1111/j.1467-9280.1992.tb00259.x

Clearfield, M. W. (2004). The role of crawling and walking experience in infant spatial memory. *J. Exp. Child Psychol.* 89, 214–241. doi: 10.1016/j.jecp.2004.07.003

Clearfield, M. W. (2011). Learning to walk changes infants' social interactions. *Infant Behav. Dev.* 34, 15–25. doi: 10.1016/j.infbeh.2010.04.008

Clearfield, M. W., Osborne, C. N., and Mullen, M. (2008). Learning by looking: Infants' social looking behavior across the transition from crawling to walking. *J. Exp. Child Psychol.* 100, 297–307. doi: 10.1016/j.jecp.2008.03.005

Conrad, R. M. (1994). *Infant Affect Sharing and its Relation to Maternal Availability.* Unpublished Doctoral Dissertation, University of California, Berkeley.

Deák, G., Flom, R. A., and Pick, A. D. (2000). Effects of gesture and target on 12- and 18-month-olds' joint visual attention to objects in front of or behind them. *Dev. Psychol.* 36, 511–523. doi: 10.1037/0012-1649.36.4.511

Eilers, R. E., Oller, D. K., Levine, S., Basinger, D., Lynch, M. P., and Urbano, R. (1993). The role of prematurity and socioeconomic status in the onset of canonical babbling in infants. *Infant Behav. Dev.* 16, 297–315. doi: 10.1016/0163-6383(93)80037-9

Ellis-Davies, K., Sakkalou, E., Fowler, N. C., Hilbrink, E. E., and Gattis, M. (2012). CUE: the continuous unified electronic diary method. *Behav. Res. Methods* 44, 1063–1078. doi: 10.3758/s13428-012-0205-1

Fenson, L., Bates, E., Dale, P., Goodman, J., Reznick, J. S., and Thal, D. (2000). Measuring variability in early child language: don't shoot the messenger. *Child Dev.* 71, 323–328. doi: 10.1111/1467-8624.00147

Fenson, L., Dale, P. S., Reznick, J. S., Bates, E., Thal, D. J., and Pethick, S. J. (1994). Variability in early communicative development. *Monogr. Soc. Res. Child Dev.* 59, 1–173. doi:10.2307/1166093

Frank, M. C., Simmons, K., Yurovsky, D., and Pusiol, G. (2013). "Developmental and postural changes in children's visual access to faces," in *Proceedings of the*

35th Annual Meeting of the Cognitive Science Society (Austin, TX: Cognitive Science Society), 454–459.

Gibson, J. J. (1958). Visually controlled locomotion and visual orientation in animals. *Br. J. Psychol.* 49, 182–194. doi: 10.1348/000712608X336077

Gottlieb, G. (1983). "The psychobiological approach to developmental issues," in *Handbook of Child Psychology: Vol. II, Infancy and Developmental Psychobiology, 4th Edn.*, ed P. Mussen (New York, NY: Wiley), 1–26.

Harding, C. G., and Golinkoff, R. M. (1979). The origins of intentional vocalizations in prelinguistic infants. *Child Dev.* 50, 33–40. doi: 10.2307/1129038

He, M., Walle, E. A., and Campos, J. J. (2015). A cross-national investigation of the relationship between infant walking and language development. *Infancy* 20, 283–305. doi: 10.1111/infa.12071

Iverson, J. M. (2010). Developing language in a developing body: the relationship between motor development and language development. *J. Child Lang.* 37, 229–261. doi: 10.1017/S0305000909990432

Iverson, J. M., and Goldin-Meadow, S. (2005). Gesture paves the way for language development. *Psychol. Sci.* 16, 367–371. doi: 10.1111/j.0956-7976.2005.01542.x

Karasik, L. B., Tamis-LeMonda, C. S., and Adolph, K. E. (2011). Transition from crawling to walking and infants' actions with objects and people. *Child Dev.* 82, 1199–1209. doi: 10.1111/j.1467-8624.2011.01595.x

Karasik, L. B., Tamis-LeMonda, C. S., and Adolph, K. E. (2014). Crawling and walking infants elicit different verbal responses from mothers. *Dev. Sci.* 17, 388–395. doi: 10.1111/desc.12129

Kretch, K. S., Franchak, J. M., and Adolph, K. E. (2014). Crawling and walking infants see the world differently. *Child Dev.* 85, 1503–1518. doi: 10.1111/cdev.12206

LeBarton, E. S., Goldin-Meadow, S., and Raudenbush, S. (2015). Experimentally induced increases in early gesture lead to increases in spoken vocabulary. *J. Cogn. Dev.* 16, 199–220. doi: 10.1080/15248372.2013.858041

Lempers, J. D. (1979). Young children's production and comprehension of nonverbal deictic behaviors. *J. Genet. Psychol.* 135, 93–102.

Masten, A. S., and Cicchetti, D. (2010). Developmental cascades. *Dev. Psychopathol.* 22, 491–495. doi: 10.1017/S0954579410000222

Mondschein, E. R., Adolph, K. E., and Tamis-Lemonda, C. S. (2000). Gender bias in mothers' expectations about infant crawling. *J. Exp. Child Psychol.* 77, 304–316. doi: 10.1006/jecp.2000.2597

Morales, M., Mundy, P., Delgado, C. E. F., Yale, M., Messinger, D., Neal, R., et al. (2000). Responding to joint attention across the 6- through 24-month age period and early language acquisition. *J. Appl. Dev. Psychol.* 21, 283–298. doi: 10.1016/S0193-3973(99)00040-4

Morales, M., Mundy, P., and Rojas, J. (1998). Following the direction of gaze and language development in 6-month-olds. *Infant Behav. Dev.* 21, 373–377. doi: 10.1016/S0163-6383(98)90014-5

Morissette, P., Ricard, M., and Gouin-Décarie, T. (1995). Joint visual attention and pointing in infancy: a longitudinal study of comprehension. *Br. J. Dev. Psychol.* 13, 163–175. doi: 10.1111/j.2044-835X.1995.tb00671.x

Mundy, P., Kasari, C., Sigman, M., and Ruskin, E. (1995). Nonverbal communication and early language acquisition in children with Down syndrome and in normally developing children. *J. Speech Hear. Res.* 38, 157–167. doi: 10.1044/jshr.3801.157

Openshaw, P., Edwards, S., and Helms, P. (1984). Changes in rib cage geometry during childhood. *Thorax* 39, 624–627. doi: 10.1136/thx.39.8.624

Oudgenoeg-Paz, O., Volman, M. J. M., and Leseman, P. P. M. (2012). Attainment of sitting and walking predicts development of productive vocabulary between ages 16 and 28 months. *Infant Behav. Dev.* 35, 733–736. doi: 10.1016/j.infbeh.2012.07.010

Parladé, M. V., and Iverson, J. M. (2011). The interplay between language, gesture, and affect during communicative transition: a dynamic systems approach. *Dev. Psychol.* 47, 820–833. doi: 10.1037/a0021811

Presmanes, A. G., Walden, T. A., Stone, W. L., and Yoder, P. J. (2007). Effects of different attentional cues on responding to joint attention in younger siblings of children with autism spectrum disorder. *J. Autism Dev. Disord.* 37, 133–144. doi: 10.1007/s10803-006-0338-0

Ring, E. D., and Fenson, L. (2000). The correspondence between parent report and child performance for receptive and expressive vocabulary beyond infancy. *First Lang.* 20, 141–159. doi: 10.1177/014272370002005902

Rubin, J. Z., Provenzano, F. J., and Luria, Z. (1974). The eye of the beholder: parents' views on sex of newborns. *Am. J. Orthopsychiatry* 44, 512–519. doi: 10.1111/j.1939-0025.1974.tb00905.x

Schafer, J. L., and Graham, J. W. (2002). Missing data: our view of the state of the art. *Psychol. Methods* 7, 147–177. doi: 10.1037/1082-989X.7.2.147

Smith, C. B., Adamson, L. B., and Bakeman, R. (1988). Interactional predictors of early language. *First Lang.* 8, 143–156. doi: 10.1177/014272378800802304

Spencer, J. P., Blumberg, M. S., McMurray, B., Robinson, S. R., Samuelson, L. K., and Tomblin, J. B. (2009). Short arms and talking eggs: why we should no longer abide the nativist-empiricist debate. *Child Dev. Perspect.* 3, 79–87. doi: 10.1111/j.1750-8606.2009.00081.x

Thelen, E. (1991). "Motor aspects of emergent speech: a dynamic approach," in *Biological and Behavioral Determinants of Language Development*, eds N. A. Krasnegor, D. M. Rumbaugh, R. L. Schiefelbusch, and M. Studdert-Kennedy (Hilldale, NJ: Erlbaum), 339–362.

Thelen, E. (1995). Motor development: a new synthesis. *Am. Psychol.* 50, 79–95. doi: 10.1037/0003-066X.50.2.79

Thelen, E., and Smith, L. B. (1994). *A Dynamic Systems Approach to the Development of Cognition and Action*. Cambridge, MA: MIT Press.

Thelen, E., and Smith, L. B. (1998). "Dynamic systems theories," in *Handbook of Child Psychology: Vol. 1, Theoretical Models of Human Development, 5th Edn.*, ed W. Damon (New York, NY: Wiley), 563–634.

Tomasello, M. (1988). The role of joint attention in early language development. *Lang. Sci.* 11, 69–88.

Tomasello, M. (1995). "Joint attention as social cognition," in *Joint Attention: Its Origins and Role in Development*, eds C. Moore and P. J. Dunham (Hillsdale, NJ: Erlbaum), 103–130.

Tomasello, M., and Todd, J. (1983). Joint attention and lexical acquisition style. *First Lang.* 4, 197–212. doi: 10.1177/014272378300401202

Vorperian, H. K., Kent, R. D., Lindstrom, M. J., Kalina, C. M., Gentry, L. R., and Yandell, B. S. (2005). Development of vocal tract length during early childhood: a magnetic resonance imaging study. *J. Acoust. Soc. Am.* 117, 338–350. doi: 10.1121/1.1835958

Walle, E. A., and Campos, J. J. (2014). Infant language development is related to the acquisition of walking. *Dev. Psychol.* 50, 336–348. doi: 10.1037/a0033238

Walle, E. A., and Warlaumont, A. S. (2015). "Infant locomotion, the language environment, and language development: a home observation study," in *Proceedings of the 37th Annual Meeting of the Cognitive Science Society* (Santa Barbara, CA: Cognitive Science Society), 2577–2582.

Warlaumont, A. S., Richards, J. A., Gilkerson, J., and Oller, D. K. (2014). A social feedback loop for speech development and its reduction in autism. *Psychol. Sci.* 25, 1314–1324. doi: 10.1177/0956797614531023

Will, J. A., Self, P. A., and Datan, N. (1976). Maternal behavior and perceived sex of infant. *Am. J. Orthopsychiatry* 46, 135–139. doi: 10.1111/j.1939-0025.1976.tb01234.x

Conflict of Interest Statement: The author declares that the research was conducted in the absence of any commercial or financial relationships that could be construed as a potential conflict of interest.

7

The Social Effect of "Being Imitated" in Children with Autism Spectrum Disorder

Annarita Contaldo[1], Costanza Colombi[2], Antonio Narzisi[1] and Filippo Muratori[1]*

[1] Department of Developmental Neuroscience, IRCCS Stella Maris, Calambrone, Italy, [2] Department of Psychiatry, University of Michigan, Ann Arbor, MI, USA

There is evidence that "being imitated" has social effects, and that the imitation of the child's actions may be used as a strategy to promote social engagement in children with autism spectrum disorder (ASD). The observation of someone that imitates us recruits, indeed, neural areas involved in social cognition. We reviewed studies exploring the behavioral consequences of "being imitated" in children with ASD. We aimed at assessing what are the social skills targeted by this strategy, and the factors that may improve the response. The "being imitated" strategy improves social gazes, proximal social behaviors, and play skills, particularly in children with low developmental level, and also when the strategy is implemented by children's mothers. The "being imitated" may be used as a tool in early intervention to improve social skills, helping to assess the effects of intervention at both behavioral and neural level.

Keywords: imitation, being imitated, ASD, early intervention, social brain

Edited by:
Klaus Libertus, University of Pittsburgh, USA

Reviewed by:
Virginia Slaughter, University of Queensland, Australia
Guy Dove, University of Louisville, USA

****Correspondence:***
Annarita Contaldo
annarita.contaldo@fsm.unipi.it

INTRODUCTION

Imitation is a complex ability that plays a crucial role in social interaction, both in adulthood (Chartrand and van Baaren, 2009), and in earliest infancy (Meltzoff and Moore, 1992). The tendency of adults to unconsciously imitate postures and gestures of a partner, the so called "chameleon effect," is thought to be a sort of "social glue" that promotes affiliative behaviors (Uzgiris, 1981; Chartrand and van Baaren, 2009) as well as identification within social groups (Lakin et al., 2003). The social effects of imitation affect both the imitator and the imitated subjects (Uzgiris, 1981). Some experimental studies, indeed, showed that after being imitated, people feel closer to others (Ashton-James et al., 2007) and show an increase in the prosocial orientation toward both the imitator and other people (van Baaren et al., 2004).

Also in infancy, "being imitated" promotes a social orientation toward others. From the age of 9 months, infants recognize when others are imitating them (Agnetta and Rochat, 2004). They pay closer attention, and smile more at an adult who imitates their actions compared with one who responds to their actions without imitating (Meltzoff and Moore, 1999; Carpenter et al., 2013). This increase in social attention has been considered an implicit form of imitation recognition (Nadel, 2002). From 14–18 months of age, infants show a more mature form of imitation recognition. After being imitated, they engage in "testing behaviors" (i.e., repeating or varying actions while watching the imitative partner) to test whether the other is imitating them (Meltzoff, 1995; Asendorpf et al., 1996; Nielsen, 2006).

Therefore, very early in development, infants produce imitation and recognize when others are imitating them; these skills represent the two faces of imitation and are both linked to the development of socio-communicative abilities, such as joint attention, intention understanding, and social reciprocity (Carpenter and Tomasello, 1995; Meltzoff, 1995; Nadel, 2002; Tomasello et al., 2005). Through its two faces (imitating and being imitated), the imitation represents a powerful system of communication (Nadel-Brulfert and Baudonniere, 1982; Meltzoff and Moore, 1992; Nadel, 2002). It has been suggested that reciprocal imitation helps infants to understand that they can act like others and that others can act like them (Meltzoff, 2007). According to the Meltzoff's "Like-me" theory, the recognition of being imitated by others is the starting point for social and cognitive development.

This "like me" recognition of others is thought to be rooted in the same neural system underlying imitation: the mirror neuron system (MNS; Bernier et al., 2007; Marshall and Meltzoff, 2014), which includes the posterior part of the inferior frontal gyrus (IFG), the premotor cortex (PM), and the inferior parietal lobe (IPL; Rizzolatti and Craighero, 2004; Dinstein et al., 2007). MNS is activated by both imitation and action observation (Iacoboni et al., 1999; Buccino et al., 2004; Rizzolatti and Craighero, 2004), and plays a key role in understanding the goal or the meaning of an observed action (Buccino et al., 2004; Gallese et al., 2004; Hamilton and Grafton, 2006; Bernier et al., 2007). Thus, the same mechanisms that allow reproduce the actions of another individual might underlie the ability of recognizing when one is imitated (Decety et al., 2002; Nadel, 2002). In addition, a brain network encompassing the medial orbitofrontal cortex/ventromedial prefrontal cortex (mOFC/vmPFC) and the functionally connected striatum and mid-posterior insula, also involved in the processing of emotional or reward-related stimuli, is activated during the observation of another individual that imitates us (Kühn et al., 2010).

Due to its crucial role for social cognitive development, imitation has been extensively studied in children with autism spectrum disorder (ASD), a neurodevelopmental disorder characterized by impairments in social communication and restricted and stereotyped interests and behaviors (American Psychiatric Association, 2013). Imitation skills or propensity to imitate are significantly impaired in children with ASD from the beginning (Rogers and Pennington, 1991; Williams et al., 2004; Vivanti, 2015). However, some evidence suggests that, like typically developing children and adults, they recognize imitation, and respond positively to "being imitated" by an adult partner (Nadel, 2002; Colombi et al., 2009; Field et al., 2011). Therefore, while their ability to produce imitation is impaired, it is possible that their response to "being imitated" is relatively preserved. Some interventions for children with ASD involve the imitation of the child's actions as a strategy to promote social engagement. These behavioral interventions have been demonstrated to be effective in improving imitation skills (McDuffie et al., 2007; Ingersoll, 2008) as well as social abilities (Dawson et al., 2010; Rogers et al., 2012).

However, there are several key points that need better understanding, to evaluate the usefulness of the "being imitated" in early intervention in ASD. First, what are the social skills more strengthened by this strategy? Indeed, the specific effect of "being imitated" on social abilities in children with ASD is unclear. Second, does a relationship exist between chronological and mental age of the child with ASD and the response to "being imitated?" As previously reported, a more mature explicit form of imitation recognition appears later than the implicit form, in typical development. This explicit form, that subtends the ability to recognize, reproduce, and vary the observed actions, has been linked to the development of more advanced social skills. Third, could the specific characteristics of the setting in which the "being imitated" strategy is implemented (i.e., familiarity of the imitator and repeated session of "being imitated") elicit different responses? Fourth, based on studies exploring the neural basis of "being imitated" in healthy adults and infants, is it possible to hypothesize that this strategy might have a role in promoting the neural reorganization of circuits considered dysfunctional in ASD? The development of social brain is the result of the interaction between the child and the environment, and the engagement with a social partner during reciprocal imitation might promote the cortical specialization of social brain circuitry.

Based on these four questions, this article is organized in three sections (Part 1, Part 2, and Part 3), followed by a brief conclusion section. The first part is an overview on the neural and neurophysiologic correlates of "being imitated" in healthy adults and infants. In the second part, we review the studies exploring the behavioral consequences of "being imitated" in children with ASD and discuss the implications of results for better understanding the link between "being imitated" and social skills in ASD, and the usefulness of the "being imitated" strategy in early intervention. A search was performed in computerized bibliographic databases (PUBMED, WEB of Science) to identify existing literature on the effects of "being imitated" in children with ASD. Search terms included "reciprocal imitation" and/or "being imitated," and/or "mimicry," with either "autism" or "ASD" or "Autism Spectrum Disorder." Additional articles of interest were also located in the reference sections of the articles from the search. Articles included in this review assessed the specific effects of "being imitated" on child's social behaviors. We excluded intervention studies in which the imitation was one of the several naturalistic techniques, such as, for example, studies on the effectiveness of Reciprocal Imitation Training (Ingersoll and Schreibman, 2006; Ingersoll, 2012). In the third part we link behavioral and neuroscientific evidence to discuss the role of "being imitated" in improving both behavior and brain functioning.

PART 1: THE NEURAL BASIS OF BEING IMITATED

Regarding the neural basis of "being imitated" two main questions have been addressed in the literature: how our brain detects that we are imitated, and why should we feel better when someone imitates us? Both the awareness of self-other distinction and the social reward deriving from being imitated have been taken into account to answer these questions.

First studies aimed at exploring the neural basis of "being imitated" employed positron emission tomography (PET) to examine the hemodynamic changes produced when subjects imitated the experimenter's actions or when they were imitated by the experimenter (Chaminade et al., 2002; Decety et al., 2002). They found a different lateralization in the inferior parietal lobule (IPL), related to the "imitate" and "being imitated" condition. The left IPL was activated when subjects imitated another person, whereas the right homologous region was associated with "being imitated" condition. Authors suggest that the IPL might play a fundamental role in the sense of agency, i.e., in attributing the generation of an action to self or to other (Decety and Chaminade, 2003) and in distinguishing self-produced actions from those generated by others (Decety et al., 2002; Chaminade et al., 2002). They postulated that, whereas the left IPL computes the sensory-motor associations necessary to imitate, the right IPL is involved in recognizing that the action performed by the other is similar to that initiated by the self (Decety and Chaminade, 2003). Therefore, when subjects observe their actions imitated by another individual, the right IPL might play a key function for the identification with others and for experience intersubjectivity (Decety and Chaminade, 2003).

Many researchers have demonstrated that the observation of actions engages the same brain areas activated when performing similar actions (Iacoboni et al., 1999; Buccino et al., 2004). These areas include the core components of the MNS, the IPL, and the IFG (Rizzolatti and Craighero, 2004). Indeed, the human MNS is thought to play a key role in imitation, action understanding and social cognition (Gallese et al., 2004; Bernier et al., 2007). The function of the MNS is based on a direct-matching model in which observed actions are directly mapped onto the observers own motor system (Rizzolatti and Sinigaglia, 2010). However, mirror neuron properties may be also based on alternative mechanisms. Indeed, the associative sequence learning (ASL) theory suggests that mirror neurons arise from those sensorimotor experiences, including the being imitated, in which there is a contingent or predictive relationship between observed and performed actions (Heyes, 2010).

It has been proposed that MNS may have evolved, sub serving communication, through firstly the imitation of manual actions, and afterwards the imitation of manual gestures used to communicate, and finally the language (Rizzolatti and Arbib, 1998; Arbib, 2005). This hypothesis is supported by evidence showing that the use of imitation to support communication is more frequent when children are not yet able to use language, and seem to decline after language abilities increases (Nadel, 2002). Nagy et al. (2010), in an fMRI-based study, showed the activation of a lateralized network in the MNS during a communicative paradigm of reciprocal imitation in which the subject both imitated the experimenter's movements and elicited an imitation from the experimenter. Differently from a control condition (non-imitative movement), these imitative conditions recruit a lateralized fronto-parietal network, comprising the right IFG and the left IPL. A strong recruitment of parietofrontal regions in the MNS during reciprocal imitation was also found in the Guionnet et al. fMRI study (2012). In this study, a paradigm of online social interaction was employed to explore the patterns of brain activation developed in a real social interaction where two individuals matched their movements as imitator and model. This experiment was composed of three conditions: free imitation, instructed imitation, and observation. Both free and instructed imitation conditions included two subconditions: imitate and being imitated. Authors found a recruitment of parietofrontal regions in the MNS, regardless of the condition (free or instructed imitation) and of the subcondition (imitate or being imitated). However, they found a greater activation in the dorsal part of the anterior cingulate gyrus (dACC), in the left dorsolateral prefrontal cortex (DLPFC), in the dorsal part of the left anterior insular cortex (dAIC) combined with an increased deactivation in the default mode network (DMN), in the being imitated compared to the imitate subcondition. The authors suggested that these patterns of activation when subjects were imitated might reflect the engagement with others required by social interaction (Guionnet et al., 2012).

However, the role of the MNS in action understanding and social cognition was recently reconsidered based on the assumption that a "mentalizing network," consisting of the temporo-parietal junction (TPJ) and the cortical medial structures (CMS), participates and interacts with the MNS in social understanding (Keysers and Gazzola, 2007; Uddin et al., 2007). Indeed, when "being imitated" has been studied as part of the interaction between two persons, a strong connection between the MNS and the Mentalizing System has been found (Sperduti et al., 2014).

Studies exploring the neural basis of "being imitated" during infancy employed electroencephalographic (EEG) methods during a reciprocal imitation paradigm and focused on the sensorimotor mu rhythm (Reid et al., 2011; Saby et al., 2012). The mu rhythm is considered associated with the activity in the MNS and its desynchronization occurs already in infancy during action execution as well as action observation (Marshall and Meltzoff, 2011). Saby et al. (2012) compared 14-month-old infants' EEG responses during the observation of the same action presented across two different contexts: in one condition, the infants observed the experimenter's action after carrying out the same action, whereas in the other condition they observed the experimenter's action after performing a different action. A greater desynchronization in the mu rhythm was found when infants observed the experimenter imitating their actions than when observing an experimenter's action temporally contingent on the infant's act but non-imitative. The authors stated that the mu rhythm desynchronization during infants' observation of actions is enhanced when there is an imitative connection between the infant's and the observed action (Saby et al., 2012). Moreover, the observation of an experimenter who is attempting to imitate infants' body movements and postures determined greater desynchronization of the 14-month-old infant's mu rhythm compared with a condition in which the experimenter performed a sequence of unfamiliar body movements in a non-interactive fashion (Reid et al., 2011).

All these experimental studies show the activation of multiple brain areas linked to the recognition that the other is imitating us. They do not provide a unified picture and this may be also compatible with the different experimental paradigms employed in these studies. The brain, indeed, processes both the observed action and its social meaning. However, these evidences do not explain fully why "being imitated" promotes prosocial behavior.

To answer this question Kuhn and colleagues explored, in an fMRI study, the positive consequences of "being imitated" by means of an observation paradigm in which participants observed an interaction between two actors (Kühn et al., 2010). They found that the observation of a "being imitated" interaction compared to a "not being imitated" interaction activates brain areas that have been associated with emotion, friendship and reward processing, namely medial orbitofrontal cortex/ ventromedial prefrontal cortex (mOFC/vmPFC) (Bartels and Zeki, 2004; Güroğlu et al., 2008). Sharing the same emotional moods and performing the same movements leads to higher levels of activity in brain areas that have been associated with reward processing, but, interestingly, the content of the behavior that is mimicked (i.e., positive or negative emotions) does not seem to play an important role (Kühn et al., 2011).

PART 2: THE BEHAVIORAL CONSEQUENCES OF "BEING IMITATED" IN CHILDREN WITH ASD

The search identified 14 studies that have analyzed the behavioral consequences of "being imitated" in children with ASD. All the studies reviewed are summarized in **Table 1**. To identify the specific response to "being imitated" we categorized the reviewed articles according to the behavioral measures targeted by the study: social attention (mainly eye gaze behavior), social responsiveness (smiling, verbalizing, vocalizing, approaching, touching toward the experimenter, gestures), motor activities and stereotypies, object manipulation, and play, and imitation skills. As some studies examined multiple measures, the results of a study can be found in different paragraphs. Moreover, to identify the role of both child and experimental setting characteristics in modulating the effect of "being imitated," we reported the response to "being imitated" in function of the developmental level of the participants and the characteristics of the experimental setting (i.e., the familiarity of the imitative partner, the number of imitative sessions and the type of imitative procedure). Both these factors, indeed, have a crucial role in the planning of intervention strategies.

Studies investigating the behavioral consequences of "being imitated" used two different experimental procedures to evaluate the effects on social cognitive abilities. Six studies employed an experimental paradigm in which an unfamiliar experimenter or the child's mother copies the child's object-directed actions, gestures, and vocalizations during a single (Dawson and Adams, 1984; Katagiri et al., 2010; Berger and Ingersoll, 2013) or repeated object play session (Tiegerman and Primavera, 1981, 1984; Dawson and Galpert, 1990).

Another series of studies (Nadel et al., 2000; Field et al., 2001, 2013; Escalona et al., 2002; Heimann et al., 2006; Sanefuji and Ohgami, 2011, 2013; Slaughter and Ong, 2014) investigated the effects of "being imitated" using the Nadel et al. (2000) adapted version of the Still Face (SF) paradigm (Tronick et al., 1978). In the adapted SF paradigm, children with autism interacted with an adult for four phases, each lasting 3 min: First still-face (SF1), Imitation Phase (IP), Second still-face (SF2), and Spontaneous Play (SP). During the SF1, the child walked into a room that was furnished with a sofa, a table, chairs and two sets of identical toys. An unfamiliar adult sat on the sofa with a still face and did not move. During the following IP, the adult imitated everything the child did including the autistic behaviors, such as motor stereotypies and repetitive actions with objects. The SF2 was similar to the first one, and the fourth phase was a spontaneous interaction in which the adult played freely with the child (Nadel et al., 2000). Nadel et al. (2000) hypothesized that, if children looked more at the adult in the SF2 with respect to SF1, after IP, they had developed social expectancies toward the adult. Therefore, to explore the effects of "being imitated" on social responsiveness in children with ASD, three studies compared the child's behavior between the SF1 and SF2 phases (Nadel et al., 2000; Field et al., 2001; Escalona et al., 2002), whereas five studies analyzed the child's behaviors also during the IP and the SP phases (Heimann et al., 2006; Sanefuji and Ohgami, 2011, 2013; Field et al., 2013; Slaughter and Ong, 2014). These latter authors hypothesized that an increase of social behaviors in SP phase after imitation could indicate a generalization of the effects. The results of these studies are, therefore, crucial in order to identify strategies that can be truly effective on social behavior. Children with ASD, indeed, are known to have difficulty in generalizing recently acquired skills to new environments (Ozonoff and Miller, 1995). As for the object-play situation, also in the SF situation the session was single (Nadel et al., 2000; Escalona et al., 2002; Sanefuji and Ohgami, 2011; Slaughter and Ong, 2014) or repeated (Field et al., 2001, 2013; Heimann et al., 2006; Sanefuji and Ohgami, 2013), and was administered by an unfamiliar experimenter (Nadel et al., 2000; Field et al., 2001, 2013; Escalona et al., 2002; Heimann et al., 2006) or by the child's mother (Sanefuji and Ohgami, 2011, 2013; Slaughter and Ong, 2014).

In six studies, the effect of "being imitated" on social behaviors was compared to the effect of a contingent interaction, in which the social partner responds immediately to the child with a similar but not imitative behavior (Field et al., 2001, 2013; Escalona et al., 2002; Heimann et al., 2006; Sanefuji and Ohgami, 2011, 2013). This latter form of interaction, indeed, had been recognized as a useful strategy to promote engagement in ASD.

In the reviewed studies the behavioral measures targeted were: (a) social attention (eye gaze behavior), (b) social responsiveness (distal social behaviors, as smiling, verbalizing; proximal social behaviors as approaching, touching; social gestures as pointing, requesting, offering, and showing), (c) motor activity and stereotypies, (d) object manipulation and play and (e) imitation skills.

Social Attention

One of the core symptoms of ASD is the presence of early deficits in social attention, and in establishing and maintaining eye contact. Some authors hypothesized that the early atypical pattern of attention preclude social input that normally promotes the development of social and linguistic brain circuitry during early sensitive periods (Dawson, 2008). For this reason, understanding what strategies are useful to

TABLE 1 | Summary of studies reviewed.

	Participants	N/Type/Length of session	Type of experimental procedure and familiarity of imitative partner	Target behaviors	Results
Dawson and Adams, 1984	Autism: $N = 15$ Mean Age = 60.6 months IQ = 17–89 (mean: 57.42) Imitation skills (assessed with Uzgiris-Hunt Developmental Scale) = 8 high, 7 low	1 object play session/20 min	Four conditions: A) Free play B) Simultaneous Imitation C) Familiar Scheme D) Novel Scheme Unfamiliar experimenter	Social attention (looking at the examiner's face) Social responsiveness (smiling at, gesturing, touching, and verbalizing to the experimenter) Object manipulation	Social behaviors were more frequent in Condition B than in D only for low imitators. Children with high imitation skills showed similar response to all conditions. The number of object scheme and toy changes was higher in Simultaneous Imitation than in Novel scheme Condition only for low imitators.
Katagiri et al., 2010	Autism: $N = 16$ Two groups = 2 year-old (23.7 months) IQ = 60–100 (mean 78.4) 3 year-old (37.7 months) IQ = 55–135 (mean 92.3)	1 object play session/7 min	Three phases: BL1: 2-min baseline (the experimenter manipulated toys different from those the child manipulated). MP: 3-min mirroring (the experimenter reproduced everything the child did). BL2: a second 2-min baseline (as in BL1). Unfamiliar experimenter	Social attention (gazing at the experimenter's face) Social responsiveness (smiling, verbalizing, vocalizing, approaching, touching, offering toys) Imitation recognition (requesting the experimenter to imitate his/her own action)	Social attention was more frequent in the MP than in the BL1 phase in the 2-year-old group. Social behaviors were more frequent in the MP than in the BL1 phase in the 3-year-old group.
Berger and Ingersoll, 2013	Autism: $N = 30$ Age = 22–93 months (mean 41.45) MA = mean 23.40 months	1 object play session	During an unstructured imitation assessment (UIA, Ingersoll and Meyer, 2011), the experimenter imitated the child's play with a duplicate toy	Less Mature-Imitation recognition (LM-IR): child's looks at the experimenter toy and face. More Mature-Imitation recognition (MM-IR): Testing behavior and looks plus social signal.	The frequency of MM-IR was lower than that of LM-IR. Significant correlation between MM-IR and object and gesture imitation, and social reciprocity. No correlation between MM-IR, LM-IR and developmental level.
Dawson and Galpert, 1990	Autism: $N = 15$ Age = 2–6 years DL = 7 High, 8 Low	14 object play sessions/20 min	Mothers were instructed to imitate child's actions during each session	Social attention (eye gaze behavior) Object manipulation	The duration of eye gaze behavior increased from pre- to post-intervention. The number of object schemes was higher in post-intervention.
Tiegerman and Primavera, 1981	Autism: $N = 6$ Age = 4–6 years Low DL	17 object play sessions/30 min	Three type of play interaction were presented during each session: A) experimenter imitated the child's action with the same object; B) experimenter performed a different action with the same object; C) Experimenter performed a different action with a different object	Object manipulation	The frequency and duration of object manipulation was higher in Condition A than in B and C. The frequency and duration of object manipulation increased significantly over sessions under condition A and this increase was greater than that under condition B and C.
Tiegerman and Primavera, 1984	Autism: $N = 6$ Age = 4–6 years Low DL	17 object play sessions/30 min	As in Tiegerman and Primavera, 1981	Eye gaze behavior	The frequency and mean duration of eye gaze behavior was higher in Condition A than in B and C. The frequency and duration of gaze behavior increased significantly over sessions under condition A and B, and this increase was greater than that under C.

(Continued)

TABLE 1 | Continued

	Participants	N/Type/Length of session	Type of experimental procedure and familiarity of imitative partner	Target behaviors	Results
Nadel et al., 2000	Autism: $N = 8$ Age = preschooler Low DL	1SF session /12 min	*SF modified paradigm:* four phases SF1: First still-face IP: Imitation phase SF2: Second still-face SP: Spontaneous play phase Unfamiliar experimenter	Social attention (looking at a person) Social responsiveness (positive facial expressions, negative facial expressions, social gestures, close proximity, touch).	The frequency of looking at a person, negative facial expressions, social gestures, close proximity, and touch behaviors was significantly higher in SF2 than in SF1 after the imitation phase
Escalona et al., 2002	Autism: $N = 20$ Age = 3–7 years Low DL Two groups: Imitation ($N = 10$) Contingent ($N = 10$)	1 SF session/12 min	*SF modified paradigm*: see above The second phase was different in two groups (imitative or contingently responsive) Unfamiliar experimenter	Social Attention (looking at adult's face) Motor activity and stereotypies Social responsiveness (silence, touching, distance from adult)	The frequency of motor activity was lower and the frequency of touching behavior was higher in SF2 vs. SF1 in the Imitation group. A reduction in distance from the adult was observed in both groups. A decrease in silence (or increase in sounds) was observed in the Contingent group. The frequency of looking at adult was higher in SF2 vs. SF1 only in the Contingent group. No effect on stereotypies.
Field et al., 2001	Autism $N = 20$ Age = 4–6 years Low DL Two groups: Imitation ($N = 10$) Contingent ($N = 10$)	3 SF sessions/12 min	*SF modified paradigm*: see above The second phase was different in two groups (imitative or contingently responsive) Unfamiliar experimenter	Social attention (looking at adult) Social responsiveness (vocalizing/smiling, being close/touching adult, engaging in reciprocal play) Autistic behaviors (stereotypies, playing alone, inactivity) Object play behavior Imitation recognition	The frequency of looking, vocalizing/smiling, touching, and engaging in reciprocal play increased from pre- to post intervention more in the Imitation than in the Contingent group. A reduction in Autistic behaviors (playing alone and inactivity), an increase in Object play behavior and in imitation recognition were observed from pre- to post-intervention more in the Imitation than in Contingent Condition group.
Field et al., 2013	Autism $N = 20$ Age = 4–6 years Low DL Two groups: Imitation ($N = 10$) Contingent ($N = 10$)	3 SF sessions/12 min	*SF modified paradigm*: see above The second phase was different in two groups (imitative or contingently responsive) Unfamiliar experimenter	Social attention (looking at adult) Novel object play behaviors Imitation skill	Children in the Imitation group vs. those in the Contingent group showed higher frequency of looking and novel object play behaviors during the imitation phase. Children in the Imitation group showed higher frequency of looking and imitation behaviors than those in the contingent group in the SP phase.
Heimann et al., 2006	Autism: $N = 20$ Age = 4:4–12:9 years MA: 1:0–4:5 years (mean 2.1) Two groups: Imitation ($N = 10$) Contingent ($N = 10$)	2 SF sessions /12 min	*SF modified paradigm*: see above The second phase was different in two groups (imitative or contingently responsive) Unfamiliar experimenter	Social attention and responsiveness (Touch, Look and Request) Imitation skill	Significant increase in Social behaviors from SF1 to SF2 for children in the Imitation Condition group, but not for children in the Contingent Condition group. A significant increase in Social behaviors was also found in the SP phase after the second session.

(Continued)

TABLE 1 | Continued

	Participants	N/Type/Length of session	Type of experimental procedure and familiarity of imitative partner	Target behaviors	Results
Sanefuji and Ohgami, 2011	Autism: $N = 32$ Age = 54.38 months MA = 27.91 months Two groups: Imitation ($N = 16$) Contingent ($N = 16$) TD: $N = 32$ Age = 27.41 months Two groups: Imitation ($N = 16$) Contingent ($N = 16$)	1 SF session/8 min	*SF modified paradigm*: addition of a spontaneous play phase before SF1 The intervention phase was different in two groups (imitative or contingently responsive) Mother	Social attention (child's looking time directed to the mother)	Children with TD looked at their mothers for a longer duration than did those with ASD. No differences in the frequency of gaze behavior between two groups (imitation and contingent) Children with autism in the Imitation group showed higher frequency of gaze behavior in the SF2 vs. SF1 and in the Imitation phase.
Sanefuji and Ohgami, 2013	Autism: $N = 16$ Age = 53.63 months MA = 52.63 months Two groups: Imitation ($N = 8$) Contingent ($N = 8$)	Five minutes to day for a 2-months period	A SF session (as in Sanefuji and Ohgami, 2011) was conducted before and after the home-based intervention. The intervention was different in two groups (imitative or contingently responsive) Mother	Social attention Object actions imitation	After intervention, children in the Imitation group looked at their mothers for a longer duration and imitated object actions more than did children in the Contingent group.
Slaughter and Ong, 2014	Autism: $N = 10$ Age = 2 years, 8 months to 8 years, 4 months; MA = 5 years, 5 months	2 SF session/9 min	*SF modified paradigm*: addition of a spontaneous play phase before SF1 Children took part in two sessions: one with their mother and the other with the unfamiliar experimenter	Social attention (Looking toward the adult) Social responsiveness (vocalization directed to the adult, approaching, touching, social gestures) Play skills	A significant increase in looking and vocalizing toward the adult was observed in the SP2 phase vs. SP1 with both partners. A significantly greater increase in proximal social behaviors and a greater decrease in playing alone were observed in SP2 when the imitator was the child's mother as opposed to the experimenter. No significant increase in social gestures was found. A significant decrease in playing alone was observed in SP2 after imitation by the mother.

N, number; IQ, intelligence quotient; MA, mental age; TD, typical development. DL, developmental level; SF, still face.

strengthen the visual social attention is crucial for early intervention.

The eye gaze behavior was targeted by most of the reviewed studies. Using the SF paradigm, Nadel et al. (2000) found that children with ASD recognize the adult's imitation, and look more at him/her in the SF2 phase, after being imitated. This effect appears dependent on the imitative interaction with the other and it is not due to a contingently responsive interaction with a partner. Six studies, indeed, compared the effects of an imitative vs. a simply contingently responsive interaction, by employing a SF procedure in which the second phase could be either imitative (Imitation Condition, IC) or contingently responsive (Contingent Condition, CC) (Escalona et al., 2002; Heimann et al., 2006; Field et al., 2011, 2013; Sanefuji and Ohgami, 2011, 2013). All but one studies (Escalona et al., 2002) found that the frequency and duration of eye gaze behavior toward the adult was higher after the imitation than after the contingent condition. Escalona et al. (2002), using the same paradigm, found that the looking time at the adult did not change in the Imitation group but showed an increase only in the Contingent group. In the Heimann et al. study (2006) the percentage of time that the children displayed "looking at a person" behavior was combined with the "touching" and "requesting" behaviors in a Social Interest composite score, so we cannot know the specific increase in eye gaze behavior. However, Social Interest Score increased in SF2 vs. SF1 in the Imitation but not in the Contingent group (Heimann et al., 2006). This effect was evident for both the SF phase following directly the imitation phase and the SP phase at the end of each session. Also other studies (Field et al., 2013; Sanefuji and Ohgami, 2013; Slaughter and Ong, 2014) found an effect on social attention during a spontaneous play phase after being imitated. This could indicate a possible generalizing effect. No study, however, tested whether the increase in social attention after being imitated extends to persons other than the imitator.

A different pattern of response to imitative vs. contingent interaction with the mother was found in typical development (TD) children with respect to children with ASD (Sanefuji and Ohgami, 2011). Children with ASD, indeed, looked at their mothers longer in the Imitative than in the Contingent condition whereas children with TD looked at their mothers longer than those with ASD, but without differences between the two conditions (Sanefuji and Ohgami, 2011). Therefore, the interaction pattern that is able to determine a social effect in children with ASD could be different with respect to children with TD. In children with ASD, indeed, a greater social effect might be determined by those interactions that are characterized by perfect, more than imperfect, contingency; in the "being imitated" strategy, the contingency is perfect because both the temporal and structural aspects of the action are matched. Recent evidence on healthy adult subjects underlines the greater importance of contingency, regardless of similarity, in producing social effects after being imitated (Catmur and Heyes, 2013). These Authors suggested that the ability in detecting and predicting that our own actions cause the action of another person could engender the social behaviors. It could be therefore hypothesized that the impairment in predictive abilities in children with ASD might determine a lower responsivity to simple contingency. This specific research hypothesis would deserve further attention and experimental data. Autism has been in fact also proposed as a disturbance of prediction (Brown and Brüne, 2012; Pellicano and Burr, 2012). So, one of the reason for which the imitation might be more salient than the contingency is that the former is more predictable and familiar for children with ASD, and requires less anticipatory skills.

Employing a different experimental procedure, Tiegerman and Primavera (1984) found an effect of "being imitated" on social attention during the imitative session. These authors, indeed, compared the effects of imitating the child's actions with the same object during repeated object play sessions with two others different non-imitative interaction procedures: performing a different action with the same object or performing a different action with a different object. They found that frequency and duration of eye gaze behavior were higher during the first interaction procedure than others non-imitative interactions. They also found that the frequency and mean duration of gaze behavior increased significantly over repeated sessions for both the first and second interaction procedures, and this increase was greater than that for the third procedure (Tiegerman and Primavera, 1984). A further consideration may arise from these findings. While an imitative interaction, characterized by a strictly contingency (the same action with the same object at the same time) is able to determine an effect immediately, a non-imitative interaction in which the examiner uses the same object (at the same time) is able to determine the same effect but after repeated sessions. Although the Authors do not deal with this hypothesis, it could be possible that also the contingent use of the same object might be able to increase the visual attention in children with ASD. Indeed, children might have been attracted by the same object in the first sessions and then they might have been realized that their own action had caused the other's action. This predictive relationship between the child's actions and those of the examiner could have contributed to social behavior. Unfortunately, following Tiegerman and Primavera's work (1984), no additional studies compared these two different procedures. Further, research would be needed to establish whether the use of a same object during repeated play interactions could be a useful tool in early intervention.

Moreover, social attention increased after repeated sessions of "being imitated," both using the SF paradigm (Field et al., 2001, 2013; Sanefuji and Ohgami, 2011) and an object play experimental procedure (Tiegerman and Primavera, 1984; Dawson and Galpert, 1990). Field et al. (2001) performed three sessions using the SF paradigm and found that the time spent for looking the adult increased from pre- to post-intervention more in the SF2 subsequent to the Imitation than to the Contingent condition. Social attention was also greater during the Imitation phase and in SP phases after Imitative with respect to Contingent condition (Field et al., 2013). A significant correlation was found between the percentage of time during which the adult imitated the child during the imitative phase, and the time during which the child showed social attention in the same phase (Field et al., 2013).

After a parent-based intervention, that was either imitative or contingent, Sanefuji and Ohgami (2013) found a greater increase in social gaze in the imitation group with respect to the contingent group. Therefore, the greater effect of imitation vs. contingency on social attention was evident also when the child's mother was the imitative partner. In their study, Dawson and Galpert (1990) found such effect after a child-mother imitative interaction. They observed a higher duration of children gaze during an imitative vs. free play session, and an increase of this effect after a 2-week period during which children engaged in imitative object play with their mother for 20 min per day. In this study, the increase in social attention after being imitated was not correlated to the developmental level of imitation abilities, play skills, Vineland social age, IQ, or severity of autistic symptoms. Slaughter and Ong (2014) examined whether the familiarity with the social partner might modulate the effect of "being imitated" using a SF procedure (Slaughter and Ong, 2014). The children's social behaviors were coded prior to, and following a 3-min period in which an adult imitated everything they did. In one condition, the partner was the child's mother, and in the other condition, the partner was an unfamiliar experimenter. The results revealed significant increases in social attention (gazes toward the adult) and responsiveness (distal social behaviors) in the SP phase following imitation by both partners. This finding supports the engagement of the family as an important aspect of early intervention in ASD (Rogers et al., 2012; Estes et al., 2013).

Regarding the relationship between the developmental level of children with ASD and the effect of being imitated on social attention, one study found no correlation between the effect of "being imitated" on social attention and child development level (Dawson and Galpert, 1990). Conversely, other two studies seem to suggest that the lower is the developmental or chronological age of the toddler with ASD, the greater is the mirroring effect on social attention (Dawson and Adams, 1984; Katagiri et al., 2010). In the Dawson and Adams study, children with ASD were exposed to four interactive procedures: (1) Free-Play Condition, (2) Simultaneous Imitation Condition (the experimenter simultaneously imitated all children's actions), (3) Familiar Scheme Condition (the experimenter modeled an action that is known to be in the child's behavioral repertoire), and (4) Novel Scheme Condition (the experimenter modeled a novel action). Only in children with low imitative abilities (tested with the Uzgiris-Hunt Scale), the frequency and duration of the eye contact behavior toward the experimenter was higher when he/her modeled an imitative action rather than a familiar or novel action. Conversely, children with more developed imitation skills showed similar responses to all conditions (Dawson and Adams, 1984). An increase in the frequency of social attention (eye gaze behavior) during the imitative vs. the free play phase of an object play session was observed in the Katagiri et al.'s study in a sample of children with ASD. This effect was higher in children aged two with respect to a 3-year-old group, and it correlated negatively with the IQ but not with the severity of autistic symptoms (Katagiri et al., 2010). Some considerations, concerning the link between the effect of "being imitated" and the developmental level of children with ASD, deserve to be further discussed. The finding of a greater effect on social attention in low functioning children could be explained as the manifestation of an implicit form of imitation recognition that is present in children with ASD and determines an increase in the frequency of gaze toward the other but not an increase in more advanced social skills. In support to this hypothesis, findings from Berger and Ingersoll work (2013) demonstrate that a less mature form of imitation recognition is more frequent than a more mature form. Moreover, more advanced social behaviors after "being imitated," as offering toys to the experimenter and requesting the experimenter to imitate his/her own action, correlate positively with the age and the developmental level (Katagiri et al., 2010). Accordingly, children with higher imitation ability and higher developmental and chronological age might show a smaller effect on visual attention because they respond to being imitated with more mature social behaviors. However, the increase in visual attention, showed by low functioning children, could be the demonstration of the capacity to perceive, during highly predictive interactions, the contingency between the own behavior and that of another person.

Taken together, all studies found an increase in social attention, both during and after the imitative session. However, more studies are needed to evaluate the child characteristics and the type of procedure that are able to modulate this effect.

Social Responsiveness

The effects of "being imitated" on other social behaviors than eye gaze were analyzed in eight studies (Dawson and Adams, 1984; Nadel et al., 2000; Field et al., 2001, 2013; Escalona et al., 2002; Heimann et al., 2006; Katagiri et al., 2010; Slaughter and Ong, 2014). These behaviors included smiling and verbalizing to the adult (distal social behaviors), touching and approaching the adult (proximal social behaviors), engaging in reciprocal play, and producing social gestures.

Dawson and Adams (1984) reported that only the children with low imitation abilities showed a frequency of proximal and distal social behaviors that was higher during a Simultaneous imitation, than during a Novel condition. Children with high imitation skills showed similar response to all conditions. Therefore, the "being imitated" strategy might be a useful tool for children with ASD, in particular those with low developmental level. On the other hand, in children with higher imitation and developmental abilities, a less predictive interaction, as a non-imitative but contingent procedure, could result in the same social effect than an imitative procedure.

A significant increase in social responsiveness in children with low functioning was also found in other studies using a SF paradigm (Nadel et al., 2000; Field et al., 2001; Escalona et al., 2002; Heimann et al., 2006). They reported an increase in proximal social behaviors during the SF2 after imitative session. Escalona et al. (2002) reported that social proximal behaviors increased in the Imitation group with respect to the Contingent group. Moreover, a decrease in the distance from the adult was found in both the imitation and contingent groups (Escalona et al., 2002). In the studies of Field et al. (2001, 2013) children showed an increase in both distal and proximal social behaviors, and in engaging in reciprocal play with the experimenter, after repeated imitative sessions.

Katagiri et al. (2010) analyzed the effect of being imitated both on Social attention and Social responsiveness (smiling, verbalizing, vocalizing, approaching, touching, offering toys, and requesting the experimenter to imitate his/her own action). Social behaviors were observed in older children (3-year group) more frequently during the imitative than the free play phase of object play session. This effect was not significantly related to the severity of autistic symptoms, but correlated positively with the IQ. So, differently from the effect on social attention, this study showed that more mature social behaviors were more frequent in older and higher functioning children. The inconsistency of this last result with the previous can be explained by the different type of analyzed behaviors. In this study, in fact, social responsiveness includes more mature social behaviors, namely offering toys and requesting the experimenter to imitate his/her own action. Berger and Ingersoll (2013) found that all children with ASD engaged in less mature recognition behaviors (child's looks at experimenter's face and/or toy) in response to imitation. However, a more mature imitation recognition (child's looks, and testing behaviors) was less frequent and fewer children displayed this behavior. Moreover, the authors found a significant relationships between more mature imitation recognition and other social-cognitive skills (social reciprocity, object imitation, and gesture imitation) (Berger and Ingersoll, 2013).

Slaughter and Ong (2014) explored the role of the familiarity of the imitative partner in modulating the effect of "being imitated" on social behaviors. They found a significant increase in proximal social behaviors and a greater decrease in playing alone during the SP phase when the imitator was the child's mother as opposed to the experimenter. Therefore, differently from the social attention that increased with both social partners, the effect of being imitated on proximal social behaviors was modulated by the familiarity (Slaughter and Ong, 2014). This finding highlights the benefits of asking caretakers to imitate their children during early development, in particular in children with ASD.

Overall, these studies report an increase in social responsiveness both during and after the imitative session. Three studies, which have analyzed separately the social behaviors, found a greater increase in proximal behaviors, compared to distal social behaviors. Conversely, the remaining studies had included the proximal and distal social behaviors in a single category. Such methodological aspects, therefore, limit the possibility to address the issue.

But why should the "being imitated" have a positive effect on social behavior? As suggested by Nadel, the experience of being imitated makes the social situation more salient for children with ASD; this might increase the likelihood that these children will show social responses (Nadel, 2002) and the experience of being imitated could strengthen the circles of reciprocal communication. Such reciprocal communication supporting the first non-verbal interactions between newborns and their mothers plays a constitutive role in the development of an implicit sense of self as social agent (Rochat and Striano, 1999; Nagy and Molnar, 2004). This form of reciprocal mother-infant "protoconversation" could be early impaired in children with ASD and, therefore, interfere with the subsequent maturation of social skills. Through reciprocal imitation (imitating and being imitated), children understand the self-other similarity (Meltzoff, 2007). As hypothesized by Meltzoff (2007), indeed, deficiencies in this "like-me" mechanism, that is the foundation of social cognition, could explain the social impairment observed in ASD.

Motor Activity and Stereotypies

Only two studies analyzed the effect of "being imitated" on motor activity and stereotypies (Field et al., 2001; Escalona et al., 2002). Escalona and colleagues reported that the imitation condition was more effective than the contingent condition in reducing the time spent in motor activity (running, walking, and jumping). The change in motor activity after the imitation condition was attributed to a greater awareness of the adult that diverted the child attention from motor activity (Escalona et al., 2002). Field et al. (2001) found a reduction in autistic behaviors (inactivity and playing alone) from pre- to post-intervention, more in the imitation than in the contingent group. These results fit with the findings that "being imitated" increases proximal social behavior and visual attention toward the adult. No effect on motor stereotypies was found in both studies and further research is needed to explore this area. Also, since some evidence supports the hypothesis that motor stereotypies may be related to poor motor control in people with ASD (Radonovich et al., 2013), future studies should hopefully test also the effect of "being imitated" on motor stereotypies in relation to motor development.

Object Manipulation and Play Skills

Along with a persistent deficit in social communication and social interactions, a restricted and repetitive pattern of behavior, interest or activity is the other core diagnostic domain of ASD (American Psychiatric Association, 2013). Five studies analyzed the effect of "being imitated" in reducing this behavioral pattern. The number of object and toy schemes, the frequency of object manipulation, the play skills, and the ability to initiate new behaviors were taken in consideration (Tiegerman and Primavera, 1981; Dawson and Adams, 1984; Dawson and Galpert, 1990; Field et al., 2001, 2013).

More frequent scheme and toy changes were observed during the imitative than the non-imitative interaction in children with low imitative ability, but not in children with high imitative ability that responded in the same way to both conditions (Dawson and Adams, 1984). The increase in frequency and duration of object manipulation was not correlated to the similarity of the objects, but to the behavioral similarity between the child and adult action. Indeed, it was found a higher increase during a play session in which the experimenter imitated the child's actions with the same object, than when he/she performed a different action to the same object or a different action to a different object (Tiegerman and Primavera, 1981). An increase in the number of action schemes performed with the objects was also found after repeated sessions of imitative intervention by children's mothers (Dawson and Galpert, 1990) or unfamiliar adult (Field et al., 2001, 2013). After repeated sessions, an increase in the time spent in playing with objects and in initiating novel play behaviors was found when children were imitated, with respect to the contingent interaction with an adult (Field et al., 2013).

Two considerations emerge from these studies. First, the increase in object schemes and play skills after the "being imitated" intervention could be indicative of the ability of children with ASD of learning through observation. The greater attention and proximity to the other, due to the "being imitated" intervention, could indeed improve the children's ability in playing and reproducing the observed actions. This fits with the idea that boosting social attention ought to enhance performance in social cognition (Chevallier et al., 2012). A second consideration concerns the role of the familiarity of social partner in modulating the effect of "being imitated" on play skills (Dawson and Galpert, 1990; Slaughter and Ong, 2014). Some naturalistic studies, indeed, had underlined the role of infant-parent interactions in supporting the development of social cognitive skills (Vigotsky, 1978; Arbib et al., 2005; Koterba and Iverson, 2009) and in promoting the functional actions with objects (Contaldo et al., 2013), especially through the enhancement of infants' attention. The attention-focusing quality of infant-directed input offers, indeed, to the developing infant increased opportunity to absorb information from the environment. Moreover, these interactions give children the opportunity to discover the object "affordances" relevant for the action with objects (Von Hofsten, 2004; Arbib et al., 2005). The familiarity of an adult during the "being imitated" interactions could enhance, in children with ASD, the effect on object play abilities.

Imitation Skills

There is evidence that people with ASD have a consistent impairment in imitation (Rogers and Pennington, 1991; Williams et al., 2001; Mostofsky et al., 2006). However, the imitation deficit is not global but some skills, such as the imitation of a goal-directed action on an object, are preserved (Rogers, 1999; Williams et al., 2004). In this paragraph, we report evidences of the ability of children with ASD in recognizing the other's imitation and the effect of being imitated on imitation production.

As proposed by Nadel (2002) there are two levels of imitation recognition: at a low level, it consists of the capacity to recognize structural and temporal contingencies without any attribution of imitative intentionality to the imitator; higher levels imply the recognition of the other's intention to imitate. While the former might lead to increased visual attention, the higher level of imitation recognition might lead to behaviors testing whether the other is imitating. The increase in social attention and in proximal behaviors after being imitated, found in most studies, could indicate a low level form of imitation recognition, as children looked more at an adult imitating them than at one performing a contingent but not imitative behavior. Anyway, the increase in gaze toward the imitator did not imply the children awareness of the real intention of the adult to match their behavior (Nadel et al., 2000). A more mature form of imitation recognition emerges when children perform testing behaviors (i.e. repeating and varying actions while watching the imitative partner) to test whether the other is imitating them, or in the presence of more social signal (Asendorpf et al., 1996; Nielsen, 2006). Three studies reported these behaviors denoting a more mature form of imitation recognition (Field et al., 2001; Katagiri et al., 2010; Berger and Ingersoll, 2013). Katagiri et al. (2010) included "requesting the experimenter to imitate his/her own action" in social behaviors and found that the number of the behaviors included in this category increased after being imitated especially in high functioning children. In this study, however, we cannot assess the role of the development level in modulating the effect of being imitated on imitation recognition because such behavior is not assessed separately but within a broader category of social behaviors. The study by Berger and Ingersoll was aimed at measuring the frequency of two different types of imitation recognition during a naturalistic imitation task: (1) less mature imitation recognition (child's looks at experimenter's face and/or toy), and (2) more mature imitation recognition (child's looks plus testing behaviors). They found that all children showed an increase in less mature imitation recognition, while testing behaviors were less frequent, and fewer children displayed this behavior (Berger and Ingersoll, 2013). The authors found no correlation between imitation recognition and developmental level, but the more mature imitation recognition significantly correlated with imitation production abilities. It is a major achievement that makes us think about the relationship between imitation and motor skills. In fact, the more mature imitation recognition is characterized by the ability to reproduce and vary the observed actions (testing behaviors). Both "testing behaviors" and the spontaneous selection of a movement in order to maintain a reciprocal imitation with a partner require stronger predictive ability and motor skills that appeared affected in autism (Esposito et al., 2011; Gowen and Hamilton, 2013; Trevarthen and Delafield-Butt, 2013; Sacrey et al., 2014). In addition, the selection of a movement to elicit a reciprocal imitation appears to be underpinned by the long-distance connections between frontal cortex and parietal regions (Guionnet et al., 2012) that are thought to be particularly affected by the dysfunctional connectivity characterizing ASD (Belmonte et al., 2004; Hoppenbrouwers et al., 2014). Thus, the early difficulties in initiating and maintaining a communication with the caregiver through reciprocal imitation may be linked to a primary motor impairment that is supposed to characterize early autism. If predictive ability and motor skills are lacking in autism, affected children can recognize the imitation of the others, and can be attracted by it, but they are not able to expand it toward higher levels of imitation recognition.

The findings of these studies suggest that children with ASD are able to recognize imitation by others. However, the imitation recognition ability is not completely preserved and this result may be related to motor impairment. Anyway, even if it is indicative of just a basic imitation recognition, the increase of visual attention is very important, as it is target behavior in many models of treatment for ASD.

Four studies investigated the effect of being imitated on imitation production (Field et al., 2001, 2013; Heimann et al., 2006; Sanefuji and Ohgami, 2013). Field et al. (2001) found an increase in mirror play after three sessions of imitative intervention. Moreover, they found that the percent of time spent by children in imitating the adult in the spontaneous play phase was greater after the imitative than the contingent intervention (Field et al., 2013). An increase in imitation production after an imitative vs. contingent intervention was also found by Sanefuji and Ohgami (2013) during a home-based intervention in which mothers were instructed on how to imitate their child's behaviors, including facial expressions and meaningless utterances. The number of actions reproduced after the experimenter's demonstration was coded pre and after intervention: after intervention, children in the Imitation condition imitated object actions more than did children in the Contingent condition. Another study investigated whether "being imitated" had effects on imitation skills elicited outside the experimental paradigm (Heimann et al., 2006). Therefore, elicited imitation was measured using the PEP-R (Psychoeducative Profile-Revised; Schopler et al., 1990), and scores were compared before and after an intervention session that could be randomly imitative or contingent. There were no statistically significant differences in the PEP-R imitation sub-scale scores between the two groups, either before or after the experiment. However, an analysis of the changes in imitation scores revealed that eight out of ten children in the imitative condition increased their scores at post-assessment, while the same result was found in only two children in the contingent condition (Heimann et al., 2006). Such studies might indicate that being imitated has a greater effect on spontaneous imitation compared to elicited imitation. As previously reported, impaired predictive and motor skills could also reduce the effect of being imitated on elicited imitation. Instead, the spontaneous reproduction of familiar actions could be simpler because it requires lower predictive abilities. Moreover, some neuroscientific studies reported different brain activation pattern during elicited vs. free imitation tasks (Guionnet et al., 2012).

The finding that the basic response to "being imitated" is relatively preserved in children with ASD, while their imitation skills are more impaired, could have different possible explanations. First, even at a neural level, imitating and being imitated seem to have a different lateralization in the brain. Indeed, the left IPL computes the sensory-motor associations necessary to imitate an action demonstrated by the other, and the right IPL is involved in recognizing that the action performed by the other is similar to that initiated by itself (Decety et al., 2002; Decety and Chaminade, 2003). Second, the basic level of imitation recognition is cognitively simpler than the imitation production; it requires the matching between others' and self-produced actions (Nadel, 2002). Differently, the imitation production relies on memory capacities as well as on planning and action selection skills.

PART 3: THE SOCIAL EFFECT OF "BEING IMITATED" IN CHILDREN WITH ASD AND ITS ROLE IN EARLY INTERVENTION

The findings of the behavioral studies previously reported suggest that the imitation of children's actions by therapists or parents, especially at an early age and in children with low developmental and imitation abilities, could be an effective tool to improve social gazes orienting, proximal social behaviors (touching and approaching the adult), and play skills. These effects are evident both during and after the imitative sessions and they increase after repeated imitation sessions. Moreover, these effects are more evident in the "being imitated" condition than in the contingently responsive interaction. Thus, the child's imitation *per se* seems to be responsible for the effect on social behavior. This last finding suggests that the behavioral similarity between the actions of children and the following action of an adult, more than its contingency, should be used as a strategy that would deserve to be systematically included in interventions for children with ASD.

However, the significant interest leading to the design of more effective interventions supposes an effect on neural basis in ASD. Nevertheless, two main theories have been implicated. First, the "broken mirror" theory of autism proposed that a dysfunction of the MNS is responsible for the core social deficits in individuals with ASD (Williams et al., 2001; Dapretto et al., 2006; Oberman and Ramachandran, 2007). However, recent studies suggest that at a neural level, individuals with ASD may not have a global MNS impairment, but they may have impairments within certain nodes of the MNS or in their anatomical connectivity and functional synchronization (Hamilton, 2008; Kana et al., 2011). The evidence that the imitation deficit in autism is not global, but some imitation skills, such as the imitation of a goal directed action on an object, are preserved supports this view (Rogers, 1999; Williams et al., 2004). Such a picture, in which the imitative skills occur with a pattern characterized by peaks and troughs, would seem more compatible with the hypothesis of an alteration in functional connectivity between areas of the nervous system rather than with the hypothesis of a single dysfunction in a "broken" system. Thus, it is supposed that specific training on "being imitated," could improve MNS dysfunctional area and brain connections with other neural network involved in social cognition.

It has been suggested, indeed, that mirror neurons may develop their sensorimotor properties as a result of experience, and that their responses can be modified through experience. As suggested by the ASL theory, these experiences should be characterized by contingent or predictive relationship between observed and performed actions (Heyes, 2010). Based on this theory it could be hypothesized that repeated and highly predictive experience of being imitated could augment the mirror system response. More studies are needed to support this hypothesis. Currently, behavioral studies had demonstrated that "being imitated" is more efficient than "contingency" in promoting visual attention, imitation recognition and imitation production in children with ASD. At a neural level, the observation of an imitative action in typical children is able to determine a greater desynchronization of the mu rhythm with respect to the observation of a contingent action (Saby et al., 2012). In children with ASD, a reduced mu rhythm desynchronization during movement observation has been repetitively found (Bernier et al., 2007; Oberman and Ramachandran, 2007), but the degree of this reduction is sensitive to the level of familiarity (Oberman et al., 2008). In this light, being imitated might also be a useful tool to assess the neural effects of the interventions for ASD.

Second, the "social motivation theory," posits that deficits in the social reward system at the neural level alter the way by which children with ASD orient and engage with social stimuli, and consequently impair the social skill development (Dawson, 2008). Indeed, it has been demonstrated that children with ASD have reward anticipation and processing deficits for social stimuli. While typically developing children find social stimuli more salient than nonsocial stimuli, children with ASD may have the opposite preference (Stavropoulos and Carver, 2014). In this framework, the impairment in social attention is considered the cause of the impaired social cognition: based on this theory, some studies reported abnormal activation in the orbito frontal-striatum-amygdala circuit in response to social stimuli (Zeeland et al., 2010; Dichter et al., 2012). It is, in this light, crucial the identification of those strategies that are able to increase the social attention, in particular for early intervention.

Both the brain areas constituting the MNS (such as the inferior parietal cortex) and the neural circuitry related to social reward (such as the ventromedial prefrontal and orbitofrontal cortex) are activated during the "being imitated" condition (Decety and Chaminade, 2003; Kühn et al., 2011). In the first case, the activation was associated with the process of self-other mapping; in the second case, it has been attributed to the social reward arising from sharing the same emotional state or body movement. Thus, the "being imitated" condition could improve some neural circuits that are impaired in ASD and their activation might be useful in improving the clinical outcome of these children, both at the behavioral and biological level.

CONCLUSIONS AND FUTURE DIRECTIONS

In this review we have discussed findings from behavioral and neuroscientific studies to identify the role of "being imitated" in improving social behavior in children with ASD, one of the most prevalent forms of developmental disability worldwide (Baio, 2012). Some intervention models, indeed, use imitation as a strategy to improve social cognitive skills (Ingersoll, 2008; Rogers et al., 2012).

While the findings of our review show that the imitation of the child's actions could be a tool in early intervention for children with ASD to improve social attention and responsiveness, and play skills, a number of questions remain open. The use of the imitation in improving motor, as well as social abilities in ASD deserves to be tested in future research. Only few studies have investigated whether the positive effect of being imitated on children's social behaviors extends to the imitation skills. They found a slight increase in imitation skills, but more studies are needed given the lack of research on this specific topic.

In addition, the neural basis of being imitated needs to be further investigated both in typically developing children and in those with ASD. Future research could also test the hypothesis that early interventions might result not only in an increase of social skills, but also in a reorganization of neural circuits altered in ASD (Dawson et al., 2002; Dawson, 2008). As the neural bases of imitation have been described, novel electrophysiological or imaging studies could be employed to investigate the neural reorganization of brain networks after intervention, leading to the identification of the most useful strategies for improving brain functioning and behavior.

In conclusion, the "being imitated" in ASD is a key point that could allow to gain new insight into the link between brain, imitation, and social deficits in ASD, and implement more effective intervention strategies, whose effect could be assessed at both behavioral and neural level.

AUTHOR CONTRIBUTIONS

AC, CC, AN, and FM designed the work, revised, and analyzed critically the literature data, wrote the manuscript, approved the final version, and agreed to its publication.

FUNDING

This research was partially supported by grants from the Italian Ministry of Health (Ricerca Corrente to AC and FM).

REFERENCES

Agnetta, B., and Rochat, P. (2004). Imitative games by 9-, 14-, and 18-month-old infants. *Infancy* 6, 1–36. doi: 10.1207/s15327078in0601_1

American Psychiatric Association (2013). *Diagnostic and Statistical Manual of Mental Disorders, 5th Edn.* Arlington, VA, American Psychiatric Association.

Arbib, M. A. (2005). From monkey-like action recognition to human language: an evolutionary framework for neurolinguistics. *Behav. Brain Sci.* 28, 105–167. doi: 10.1017/S0140525X05000038

Arbib, M. A., Oztop, E., and Zukow-Goldring, P. (2005). Language and the mirror system: a perception/action based approach to communicative development. *Cogn. Brain Behav.* 9, 239–272.

Asendorpf, J. B., Warkentin, V., and Baudonnière, P.-M. (1996). Self-awareness and other awareness. II: mirror self-recognition, social contingency awareness, and synchronic imitation. *Dev. Psych.* 32:313. doi: 10.1037/0012-1649.32.2.313

Ashton-James, C., van Baaren, R. B., Chartrand, T. L., Decety, J., and Karremans, J. (2007). Mimicry and me: the impact of mimicry on self-construal. *Soc. Cogn.* 25, 518–535. doi: 10.1521/soco.2007.25.4.518

Baio, J. (2012). *Prevalence of Autism Spectrum Disorders: Autism and Developmental Disabilities Monitoring Network, 14 Sites, United States, 2008.* Morbidity and Mortality Weekly Report, Surveillance Summaries. Volume 61, Number 3. Centers for Disease Control and Prevention.

Bartels, A., and Zeki, S. (2004). The neural correlates of maternal and romantic love. *Neuroimage* 21, 1155–1166. doi: 10.1016/j.neuroimage.2003.11.003

Belmonte, M. K., Allen, G., Beckel-Mitchener, A., Boulanger, L. M., Carper, R. A., and Webb, S. J. (2004). Autism and abnormal development of brain connectivity. *J. Neurosci.* 24, 9228–9231. doi: 10.1523/JNEUROSCI.3340-04.2004

Berger, N. I., and Ingersoll, B. (2013). An exploration of imitation recognition in young children with autism spectrum disorders. *Autism Res.* 6, 411–416. doi: 10.1002/aur.1303

Bernier, R., Dawson, G., Webb, S., and Murias, M. (2007). EEG mu rhythm and imitation impairments in individuals with autism spectrum disorder. *Brain Cogn.* 64, 228–237. doi: 10.1016/j.bandc.2007.03.004

Brown, E. C., and Brüne, M. (2012). The role of prediction in social neuroscience. *Front. Hum. Neurosci.* 6:147. doi: 10.3389/fnhum.2012.00147

Buccino, G., Binkofski, F., and Riggio, L. (2004). The mirror neuron system and action recognition. *Brain Lang.* 89, 370–376. doi: 10.1016/S0093-934X(03)00356-0

Carpenter, M., and Tomasello, M. (1995). Joint attention and imitative learning in children, chimpanzees, and enculturated chimpanzees. *Soc. Dev.* 4, 217–237. doi: 10.1111/j.1467-9507.1995.tb00063.x

Carpenter, M., Uebel, J., and Tomasello, M. (2013). Being mimicked increases prosocial behavior in 18-month-old infants. *Child Dev.* 84, 1511–1518. doi: 10.1111/cdev.12083

Catmur, C., and Heyes, C. (2013). Is it what you do, or when you do it? The roles of contingency and similarity in pro–social effects of imitation. *Cogn. Sci.* 37, 1541–1556. doi: 10.1111/cogs.12071

Chaminade, T., Meltzoff, A. N., and Decety, J. (2002). Does the end justify the means? A PET exploration of the mechanisms involved in human imitation. *Neuroimage* 15, 318–328. doi: 10.1006/nimg.2001.0981

Chartrand, T. L., and van Baaren, R. (2009). Human mimicry. *Adv. Exp. Soc. Psychol.* 4, 219–274. doi: 10.1016/S0065-2601(08)00405-X

Chevallier, C., Kohls, G., Troiani, V., Brodkin, E. S., and Schultz, R. T. (2012). The social motivation theory of autism. *Trends Cogn. Sci.* 16, 231–239. doi: 10.1016/j.tics.2012.02.007

Colombi, C., Liebal, K., Tomasello, M., Young, G., Warneken, F., and Rogers, S. J. (2009). Examining correlates of cooperation in autism: imitation, joint attention, and understanding intentions. *Autism* 13, 143–163. doi: 10.1177/1362361308098514

Contaldo, A., Cola, E., Minichilli, F., Crecchi, A., Carboncini, M. C., Rossi, B., et al. (2013). Object use affects motor planning in infant prehension. *Hum. Mov. Sci.* 32, 498–510. doi: 10.1016/j.humov.2013.02.005

Dapretto, M., Davies, M. S., Pfeifer, J. H., Scott, A. A., Sigman, M., Bookheimer, S. Y., et al. (2006). Understanding emotions in others: mirror neuron dysfunction in children with autism spectrum disorders. *Nat. Neurosci.* 9, 28–30. doi: 10.1038/nn1611

Dawson, G. (2008). Early behavioral intervention, brain plasticity, and the prevention of autism spectrum disorder. *Dev. Psychopathol.* 20, 775–803. doi: 10.1017/S0954579408000370

Dawson, G., and Adams, A. (1984). Imitation and social responsiveness in autistic children. *J. Abnorm. Child Psychol.* 12, 209–226. doi: 10.1007/BF009 10664

Dawson, G., Carver, L., Meltzoff, A. N., Panagiotides, H., McPartland, J., and Webb, S. (2002). Neural correlates of face and object recognition in young children with autism spectrum disorder, developmental delay, and typical development. *Child Dev.* 73, 700–717. doi: 10.1111/1467-8624.00433

Dawson, G., and Galpert, L. (1990). Mothers' use of imitative play for facilitating social responsiveness and toy play in young autistic children. *Dev. Psychopathol.* 2, 151–162. doi: 10.1017/S0954579400000675

Dawson, G., Rogers, S., Munson, J., Smith, M., Winter, J., Greenson, J., et al. (2010). Randomized, controlled trial of an intervention for toddlers with autism: the Early Start Denver Model. *Pediatrics* 125, e17–e23. doi: 10.1542/peds.20 09-0958

Decety, J., and Chaminade, T. (2003). When the self represents the other: a new cognitive neuroscience view on psychological identification. *Conscious. Cogn.* 12, 577–596. doi: 10.1016/S1053-8100(03)00076-X

Decety, J., Chaminade, T., Grèzes, J., and Meltzoff, A. N. (2002). A PET exploration of the neural mechanisms involved in reciprocal imitation. *Neuroimage* 15, 265–272. doi: 10.1006/nimg.2001.0938

Dichter, G. S., Richey, J. A., Rittenberg, A. M., Sabatino, A., and Bodfish, J. W. (2012). Reward circuitry function in autism during face anticipation and outcomes. *J. Autism Dev. Disord.* 42, 147–160. doi: 10.1007/s10803-011-1221-1

Dinstein, I., Hasson, U., Rubin, N., and Heeger, D. J. (2007). Brain areas selective for both observed and executed movements. *J. Neurophysiol.* 98, 1415–1427. doi: 10.1152/jn.00238.2007

Escalona, A., Field, T., Nadel, J., and Lundy, B. (2002). Brief report: imitation effects on children with autism. *J. Autism Dev. Disord.* 32, 141–144. doi: 10.1023/A:1014896707002

Esposito, G., Venuti, P., Apicella, F., and Muratori, F. (2011). Analysis of unsupported gait in toddlers with autism. *Brain Dev.* 33, 367–373. doi: 10.1016/j.braindev.2010.07.006

Estes, A., Olson, E., Sullivan, K., Greenson, J., Winter, J., Dawson, G., et al. (2013). Parenting-related stress and psychological distress in mothers of toddlers with autism spectrum disorders. *Brain Dev.* 35, 133–138. doi: 10.1016/j.braindev.2012.10.004

Field, T., Ezell, S., Nadel, J., Grace, A., Allender, S., and Siddalingappa, V. (2013). Reciprocal imitation following adult imitation by children with autism: reciprocal imitation. *Infant Child Dev.* 22, 642–648. doi: 10.1002/icd.1812

Field, T., Field, T., Sanders, C., and Nadel, J. (2001). Children with autism display more social behaviors after repeated imitation sessions. *Autism* 5, 317–323. doi: 10.1177/1362361301005003008

Field, T., Nadel, J., and Ezell, S. (2011). "Imitation therapy for young children with autism," in *Autism Spectrum Disorders. From Genes to Environment*, ed T. Williams (Rijeka: InTech, Open Acces Publisher), 287–298.

Gallese, V., Keysers, C., and Rizzolatti, G. (2004). A unifying view of the basis of social cognition. *Trends Cogn. Sci.* 8, 396–403. doi: 10.1016/j.tics.2004.07.002

Gowen, E., and Hamilton, A. (2013). Motor abilities in autism: a review using a computational context. *J. Autism Dev. Disord.* 43, 323–344. doi: 10.1007/s10803-012-1574-0

Guionnet, S., Nadel, J., Bertasi, E., Sperduti, M., Delaveau, P., and Fossati, P. (2012). Reciprocal imitation: toward a neural basis of social interaction. *Cerebral Cortex* 22, 971–978. doi: 10.1093/cercor/bhr177

Güroğlu, B., Haselager, G. J., van Lieshout, C. F., Takashima, A., Rijpkema, M., and Fernández, G. (2008). Why are friends special? Implementing a social interaction simulation task to probe the neural correlates of friendship. *Neuroimage* 39, 903–910. doi: 10.1016/j.neuroimage.2007.09.007

Hamilton, A. F. (2008). Emulation and mimicry for social interaction: a theoretical approach to imitation in autism. *Q. J. Exp. Psychol.* 61, 101–115. doi: 10.1080/17470210701508798

Hamilton, A. F. D. C., and Grafton, S. T. (2006). Goal representation in human anterior intraparietal sulcus. *J. Neurosci.* 26, 1133–1137. doi: 10.1523/JNEUROSCI.4551-05.2006

Heimann, M., Laberg, K. E., and Nordoen, B. (2006). Imitative interaction increases social interest and elicited imitation in non-verbal children with autism. *Infant Child Dev.* 15, 297–309. doi: 10.1002/icd.463

Heyes, C. (2010). Where do mirror neurons come from? *Neurosci. Biobehav. Rev.* 34, 575–583. doi: 10.1016/j.neubiorev.2009.11.007

Hoppenbrouwers, M., Vandermosten, M., and Boets, B. (2014). Autism as a disconnection syndrome: a qualitative and quantitative review of diffusion tensor imaging studies. *Res. Autism Spectr. Disord.* 8, 387–412. doi: 10.1016/j.rasd.2013.12.018

Iacoboni, M., Woods, R. P., Brass, M., Bekkering, H., Mazziotta, J. C., and Rizzolatti, G. (1999). Cortical mechanisms of human imitation. *Science* 286, 2526–2528.

Ingersoll, B. (2008). The social role of imitation in autism: implications for the treatment of imitation deficits. *Infants Young Child.* 21, 107–119. doi: 10.1097/01.IYC.0000314482.24087.14

Ingersoll, B. (2012). Brief report: effect of a focused imitation intervention on social functioning in children with autism. *J. Autism Dev. Disord.* 42, 1768–1773. doi: 10.1007/s10803-011-1423-6

Ingersoll, B., and Meyer, K. (2011). Examination of correlates of different imitative functions in young children with autism spectrum disorders. *Res. Autism Spectrum Disord.* 5, 1078–1085. doi: 10.1016/j.rasd.2010.12.001

Ingersoll, B., and Schreibman, L. (2006). Teaching reciprocal imitation skills to young children with autism using a naturalistic behavioral approach: effects on language, pretend play, and joint attention. *J. Autism Dev. Disord.* 36, 487–505. doi: 10.1007/s10803-006-0089-y

Kana, R. K., Wadsworth, H. M., and Travers, B. G. (2011). A systems level analysis of the mirror neuron hypothesis and imitation impairments in autism spectrum disorders. *Neurosci. Biobehav. Rev.* 35, 894–902. doi: 10.1016/j.neubiorev.2010.10.007

Katagiri, M., Inada, N., and Kamio, Y. (2010). Mirroring effect in 2- and 3-year-olds with autism spectrum disorder. *Res. Autism Spectr. Disord.* 4, 474–478. doi: 10.1016/j.rasd.2009.11.004

Keysers, C., and Gazzola, V. (2007). Integrating simulation and theory of mind: from self to social cognition. *Trends Cogn. Sci.* 11, 194–196. doi: 10.1016/j.tics.2007.02.002

Koterba, E. A., and Iverson, J. (2009). Investigating motionese: the effect of infant-directed action on infants' attention and object exploration. *Infant Behav. Dev.* 32, 437–444. doi: 10.1016/j.infbeh.2009.07.003

Kühn, S., Müller, B. C., van Baaren, R. B., Wietzker, A., Dijksterhuis, A., and Brass, M. (2010). Why do I like you when you behave like me? Neural mechanisms mediating positive consequences of observing someone being imitated. *Soc. Neurosci.* 5, 384–392. doi: 10.1080/17470911003633750

Kühn, S., Müller, B. C., van der Leij, A., Dijksterhuis, A., Brass, M., and van Baaren, R. B. (2011). Neural correlates of emotional synchrony. *Soc. Cogn. Affect. Neurosci.* 6, 368–374. doi: 10.1093/scan/nsq044

Lakin, J. L., Jefferis, V. E., Cheng, C. M., and Chartrand, T. L. (2003). The chameleon effect as social glue: evidence for the evolutionary significance of nonconscious mimicry. *J. Nonverbal Behav.* 27, 145–162. doi: 10.1023/A:1025389814290

Marshall, P. J., and Meltzoff, A. N. (2011). Neural mirroring systems: exploring the EEG mu rhythm in human infancy. *Dev. Cogn. Neurosci.* 1, 110–123. doi: 10.1016/j.dcn.2010.09.001

Marshall, P. J., and Meltzoff, A. N. (2014). Neural mirroring mechanisms and imitation in human infants. *Philos. Trans. R. Soc. Lond. B Biol. Sci.* 369:20130620. doi: 10.1098/rstb.2013.0620

McDuffie, A., Turner, L., Stone, W., Yoder, P., Wolery, M., and Ulman, T. (2007). Developmental correlates of different types of motor imitation in young children with autism spectrum disorders. *J. Autism Dev. Disord.* 37, 401–412. doi: 10.1007/s10803-006-0175-1

Meltzoff, A., and Moore, K. (1999). "Persons and representation: why infant imitation is important for theories of human development" in *Imitation in Infancy*, eds J. Nadel and G. Butterworth (Cambridge: Cambridge University Press), 9–35.

Meltzoff, A. N. (1995). Understanding of the intentions of others: re-enactment of intended acts by 18-month-old children. *Dev. Psychol.* 3, 838–850. doi: 10.1037/0012-1649.31.5.838

Meltzoff, A. N. (2007). "Like me": a foundation for social cognition. *Dev. Sci.* 10, 126–134. doi: 10.1111/j.1467-7687.2007.00574.x

Meltzoff, A. N., and Moore, M. K. (1992). Early imitation within a functional framework: the importance of person identity, movement, and development. *Infant Behav. Dev.* 15, 479–505. doi: 10.1016/0163-6383(92)80015-M

Mostofsky, S. H., Dubey, P., Jerath, V. K., Jansiewicz, E. M., Goldberg, M. C., and Denckla, M. B. (2006). Developmental dyspraxia is not limited to imitation in children with autism spectrum disorders. *J. Int. Neuropsychol. Soc.* 12, 314–326. doi: 10.1017/s1355617706060437

Nadel, J. (2002). "Imitation and imitation recognition: functional use in preverbal infants and nonverbal children with autism" in *The Imitative Mind: Development, Evolution, and Brain Bases*, eds A. Meltzoff and T. Prinz (Cambridge: Cambridge University Press), 42–62.

Nadel, J., Croue, S., Matlinger, M.-J., Canet, P., Hudelot, C., Lecuyer, C., and Martini, M. (2000). Do children with autism have expectancies about the social behavior of unfamiliar people? A pilot study using the still face paradigm. *Autism* 4, 133–145. doi: 10.1177/1362361300004002003

Nadel-Brulfert, J., and Baudonniere, P. M. (1982). The social function of reciprocal imitation in 2 year-old peers. *Int. J. Behav. Dev.* 5, 95–109. doi: 10.1177/016502548200500105

Nagy, E., Liotti, M., Brown, S., Waiter, G., Bromiley, A., Trevarthen, C., et al. (2010). The neural mechanisms of reciprocal communication. *Brain Res.* 1353, 159–167. doi: 10.1016/j.brainres.2010.07.066

Nagy, E., and Molnar, P. (2004). Homo imitans or homo provocans? Human imprinting model of neonatal imitation. *Infant Behav. Dev.* 27, 54–63. doi: 10.1016/j.infbeh.2003.06.004

Nielsen, M. (2006). Copying actions and copying outcomes: social learning through the second year. *Dev. Psychol.* 42:555. doi: 10.1037/0012-1649.42.3.555

Oberman, L. M., and Ramachandran, V. S. (2007). The simulating social mind: the role of the mirror neuron system and simulation in the social and communicative deficits of autism spectrum disorders. *Psychol. Bull.* 133:310. doi: 10.1037/0033-2909.133.2.310

Oberman, L. M., Ramachandran, V. S., and Pineda, J. A. (2008). Modulation of mu suppression in children with autism spectrum disorders in response to familiar or unfamiliar stimuli: the mirror neuron hypothesis. *Neuropsychologia* 46, 1558–1565. doi: 10.1016/j.neuropsychologia.2008.01.010

Ozonoff, S., and Miller, J. N. (1995). Teaching theory of mind: a new approach to social skills training for individuals with autism. *J. Autism Dev. Disord.* 25, 415–433. doi: 10.1007/BF02179376

Pellicano, E., and Burr, D. (2012). When the world becomes 'too real': a Bayesian explanation of autistic perception. *Trends Cogn. Sci.* 16, 504–510. doi: 10.1016/j.tics.2012.08.009

Radonovich, K. J., Fournier, K. A., and Hass, C. J. (2013). Relationship between postural control and restricted, repetitive behaviors in autism spectrum disorders. *Front. Integr. Neurosci.* 7:28. doi: 10.3389/fnint.2013.00028

Reid, V. M., Striano, T., and Iacoboni, M. (2011). Neural correlates of dyadic interaction during infancy. *Dev. Cogn. Neurosci.* 1, 124–130 doi: 10.1016/j.dcn.2011.01.001

Rizzolatti, G., and Arbib, M. A. (1998). Language within our grasp. *Trends Neurosci.* 21,188–194. doi: 10.1016/S0166-2236(98)01260-0

Rizzolatti, G., and Craighero, L. (2004). The mirror-neuron system. *Annu. Rev. Neurosci.* 27, 169–192. doi: 10.1146/annurev.neuro.27.070203.144230

Rizzolatti, G., and Sinigaglia, C. (2010). The functional role of the parieto-frontal mirror circuit: interpretations and misinterpretations. *Nat. Rev. Neurosci.* 11, 264–274. doi: 10.1038/nrn2805

Rochat, P., and Striano, T. (1999). Emerging self-exploration by 2-month-old infants. *Dev. Sci.* 2, 206–218. doi: 10.1111/1467-7687.00069

Rogers, S. J. (1999). "An examination of the imitation deficit in autism," in *Imitation in Infancy.* Cambridge Studies in Cognitive Perceptual Development, eds J. Nadel, G. Butterworth (New York, NY: Cambridge University Press), 254–283.

Rogers, S. J., Estes, A., Lord, C., Vismara, L., Winter, J., Fitzpatrick, A., et al. (2012). Effects of a brief Early Start Denver Model (ESDM)–based parent intervention on toddlers at risk for autism spectrum disorders: a randomized controlled trial. *J. Am. Acad. Child Adolesc. Psychiatry* 51, 1052–1065. doi: 10.1016/j.jaac.2012.08.003

Rogers, S. J., and Pennington, B. (1991). A theoretical approach to the deficits in infantile autism. *Dev. Psychopathol.* 3, 137–162. doi: 10.1017/S0954579400000043

Saby, J. N., Marshall, P. J., and Meltzoff, A. N. (2012). Neural correlates of being imitated: an EEG study in preverbal infants. *Soc. Neurosci.* 7, 650–661. doi: 10.1080/17470919.2012.691429

Sacrey, L. A. R., Germani, T., Bryson, S. E., and Zwaigenbaum, L. (2014). Reaching and grasping in autism spectrum disorder: a review of recent literature. *Front. Neurol.* 5:6. doi: 10.3389/fneur.2014.00006

Sanefuji, W., and Ohgami, H. (2011). Imitative behaviors facilitate communicative gaze in children with autism. *Infant Ment. Health J.* 32, 134–142. doi: 10.1002/imhj.20287

Sanefuji, W., and Ohgami, H. (2013). "Being-imitated" strategy at home-based intervention for young children with autism: being-imitated intervention for autism. *Infant Ment. Health J.* 34, 72–79. doi: 10.1002/imhj.21375

Schopler, E., Reichler, R. J., Bashford, A., Lansing, M. D., and Marcus, L. M. (1990). *Individualized Assessment of Autistic and Developmentally Disabled Children: Psychoeducational Profile Revised (PEP-R).* Austin, TX: Pro-Ed.

Slaughter, V., and Ong, S. S. (2014). Social behaviors increase more when children with ASD are imitated by their mother vs. an unfamiliar adult. *Autism Res.* 7, 582–589. doi: 10.1002/aur.1392

Sperduti, M., Guionnet, S., Fossati, P., and Nadel, J. (2014). Mirror neuron system and mentalizing system connect during online social interaction. *Cogn. Process.* 12, 435–476. doi: 10.1007/s10339-014-0600-x

Stavropoulos, K. K., and Carver, L. J. (2014). Reward anticipation and processing of social versus nonsocial stimuli in children with and without autism spectrum disorders. *J. Child Psychol. Psychiatry* 55, 1398–1408. doi: 10.1111/jcpp.12270

Tiegerman, E., and Primavera, L. H. (1981). Object manipulation: an interactional strategy with autistic children. *J. Autism Dev. Disord.* 11, 427–438. doi: 10.1007/BF01531617

Tiegerman, E., and Primavera, L. H. (1984). Imitating the autistic child: facilitating communicative gaze behavior. *J. Autism Dev. Disord.* 14, 27–38. doi: 10.1007/BF02408553

Tomasello, M., Carpenter, M., Call, J., Behne, T., and Moll, H. (2005). Understanding and sharing intentions: the origins of cultural cognition. *Behav. Brain Sci.* 28, 675–691. doi: 10.1017/S0140525X05000129

Trevarthen, C., and Delafield-Butt, J. T. (2013). Autism as a developmental disorder in intentional movement and affective engagement. *Front. Integr. Neurosci.* 7:49. doi: 10.3389/fnint.2013.00049

Tronick, E., Als, H., Adamson, L., Wise, S., and Brazelton, T. B. (1978). The infant's response to entrapment between contradictory messages in face-to-face interaction. *J. Am. Acad. Child Psychiatry* 17, 1–13. doi: 10.1016/S0002-7138(09)62273-1

Uddin, L. Q., Iacoboni, M., Lange, C., and Keenan, J. P. (2007). The self and social cognition: the role of cortical midline structures and mirror neurons. *Trends Cogn. Sci.* 11, 153–157. doi: 10.1016/j.tics.2007.01.001

Uzgiris, I. C. (1981). Two functions of imitation during infancy. *Int. J. Behav. Dev.* 4, 1–12. doi: 10.1177/016502548100400101

van Baaren, R. B., Holland, R. W., Kawakami, K., and van Knippenberg, A. (2004). Mimicry and Prosocial Behavior. *Psychol. Sci.* 15, 71–74. doi: 10.1111/j.0963-7214.2004.01501012.x

Vigotsky, L. (1978). *Mind in Society*. Cambridge, MA: Harvard University Press.

Vivanti, G. (2015). The importance of distinguishing propensity versus ability to imitate in ASD research and early detection. *J. Autism Dev. Disord.* 45, 1119–1120. doi: 10.1007/s10803-014-2254-z

Von Hofsten, C. (2004). An action perspective on motor development. *Trends Cogn. Sci.* 8, 266–272. doi: 10.1016/j.tics.2004.04.002

Williams, J. H., Whiten, A., and Singh, T. (2004). A systematic review of action imitation in autistic spectrum disorder. *J. Autism Dev. Disord.* 34, 285–299. doi: 10.1023/B:JADD.0000029551.56735.3a

Williams, J. H., Whiten, A., Suddendorf, T., and Perrett, D. I. (2001). Imitation, mirror neurons and autism. *Neurosci. Biobehav. Rev.* 25, 287–295. doi: 10.1016/S0149-7634(01)00014-8

Zeeland, S. V., Ashley, A., Dapretto, M., Ghahremani, D. G., Poldrack, R. A., and Bookheimer, S. Y. (2010). Reward processing in autism. *Autism Res.* 3, 53–67. doi: 10.1002/aur.122

Conflict of Interest Statement: The authors declare that the research was conducted in the absence of any commercial or financial relationships that could be construed as a potential conflict of interest.

8

The Elaborated Environmental Stress Hypothesis as a Framework for Understanding the Association Between Motor Skills and Internalizing Problems

Vincent O. Mancini[1], Daniela Rigoli[1], John Cairney[2], Lynne D. Roberts[1] and Jan P. Piek[1]*

[1] School of Psychology and Speech Pathology, Curtin University, Perth, WA, Australia, [2] Department of Family Medicine, McMaster University, Hamilton, ON, Canada

Edited by:
Klaus Libertus,
University of Pittsburgh, USA

Reviewed by:
Thea Ionescu,
Babes-Bolyai University, Romania
Dido Green,
Oxford Brookes University, UK

***Correspondence:**
Vincent O. Mancini
vincent.mancini@curtin.edu.au

Poor motor skills have been shown to be associated with a range of psychosocial issues, including internalizing problems (anxiety and depression). While well-documented empirically, our understanding of why this relationship occurs remains theoretically underdeveloped. The Elaborated Environmental Stress Hypothesis by Cairney et al. (2013) provides a promising framework that seeks to explain the association between motor skills and internalizing problems, specifically in children with developmental coordination disorder (DCD). The framework posits that poor motor skills predispose the development of internalizing problems via interactions with intermediary environmental stressors. At the time the model was proposed, limited direct evidence was available to support or refute the framework. Several studies and developments related to the framework have since been published. This mini-review seeks to provide an up-to-date overview of recent developments related to the Elaborated Environmental Stress Hypothesis. We briefly discuss the past research that led to its development, before moving to studies that have investigated the framework since it was proposed. While originally developed within the context of DCD in childhood, recent developments have found support for the model in community samples. Through the reviewed literature, this article provides support for the Elaborated Environmental Stress Hypothesis as a promising theoretical framework that explains the psychosocial correlates across the broader spectrum of motor ability. However, given its recent conceptualization, ongoing evaluation of the Elaborated Environmental Stress Hypothesis is recommended.

Keywords: motor coordination, motor skills, motor proficiency, environmental stress, internalizing problems, anxiety, depression

There is growing recognition that motor skills have a significant role in psychosocial development. The ability to make accurate and coordinated age-appropriate movements enables opportunities for the optimal development of psychosocial wellbeing. Indeed, studies have shown that poor motor skills are associated with a range of negative psychosocial outcomes. More recently, studies have investigated the psychosocial implications of motor skills in both clinical and non-clinical populations; while early studies often focused on the physical deficits experienced by children diagnosed with developmental coordination disorder (DCD). DCD is a neurodevelopmental disorder characterized by poor motor skills that are unrelated to other physical and/or intellectual impairments (American Psychiatric Association, 2013). The prevalence of DCD is estimated to be between 1.8% and 6% of children, making it one of the most pervasive neurodevelopmental disorders (American Psychiatric Association, 2013).

Literature investigating the psychosocial consequences of poor motor skills has only recently experienced significant empirical development. Skinner and Piek (2001) indicated that children (8–10 years) and adolescents (12–14 years) with DCD reported lower self-worth and higher anxiety when compared to their non-DCD peers. In addition, adolescents with DCD reported higher anxiety than children with DCD, suggesting that these psychosocial consequences become more pronounced with age. In their sample of 47 children with DCD, Green et al. (2006) identified a significant proportion of participants were at risk of psychopathology. Children with both poor motor skills and emotional/behavioral difficulties (EBD) have also been identified as having more depressive symptoms and more problematic behaviors than EBD-only children (Heath et al., 2005). Such findings have stimulated further research in this area of investigation.

Within the literature, the etiology and implications of poor motor skills are often investigated from a diagnostic perspective. Analogous to Skinner and Piek (2001), studies often employ a diagnosis of DCD (or 'probable-DCD') to dichotomize their population into those with or without motor coordination problems, and examine differences between the groups. This approach is not without its limitations, but has proven useful within research seeking to investigate the psychosocial consequences of poor motor skills (when poor motor skills are operationalized within a clinical context). Results have indicated that DCD is associated with a range of psychosocial consequences, including less enjoyment in daily tasks (Bart et al., 2011), low self-esteem (Miyahara and Piek, 2006), less developed social support (Smyth and Anderson, 2000; Skinner and Piek, 2001), poor social skills (Kanioglou et al., 2005), social isolation (Smyth and Anderson, 2000), academic underachievement (Alloway, 2007), peer victimization/bullying (Campbell et al., 2012), decreased quality of life (Hill et al., 2011), and physical inactivity (Cairney et al., 2005). Each of these associated difficulties have important links with internalizing problems (anxiety and depression) in their own right. Furthermore, an individual with DCD could be exposed to any combination of these psychosocial consequences that may contribute to the onset and maintenance of internalizing difficulties, and also complicate intervention strategies.

There is consistent support for an association between DCD and internalizing problems from studies that vary in terms of both population and research design. Skinner and Piek (2001) employed a cross-sectional research design and found that children and adolescents with DCD had higher levels of anxiety than those without. The finding that the association between DCD and internalizing problems becomes more pronounced over time was limited by the cross-sectional design. This has since been supported longitudinally by Lingam et al. (2012). In their community sample of 6,902 children, the authors identified that a diagnosis of probable DCD at 7 years of age was associated with depressive symptoms and mental health difficulties at 10 years of age. Sigurdsson et al. (2002) also identified that poor motor skills in childhood were a risk factor for anxiety in adolescence. These findings provide preliminary suggestion that poor motor skills precede the development of internalizing problems. A monozygotic twin study by Piek et al. (2007) was able to account for genetic effects and shared environmental influences in their sample of 24 pairs of monozygotic twins discordant for probable DCD, whilst also controlling for the confounding influence of ADHD. It was found that twins with DCD demonstrated higher levels of depressive symptoms when compared to the unaffected co-twins. The authors suggested that the higher level of internalizing problems could be attributed to the unique environmental experiences of the twin with DCD, such as more negative peer interactions, academic underachievement, and negative self-perceptions (Piek et al., 2007). Such studies provide examples of the growing evidence to support an association between DCD and internalizing problems, although this area of investigation is currently lacking additional meta-analytic support.

Studies that employ the comparison of DCD (or probable DCD) groups to non-DCD groups have made important contributions to our understanding of the association between poor motor skills and internalizing problems. However, this approach does not take into account that motor skills are distributed dimensionally, rather than dichotomously, throughout the population. Subsequently, there has been an increase in studies that have enlisted community samples which reflect the broader spectrum of motor skills. Cross-sectional and longitudinal studies of community samples have indicated a negative association between motor skills and internalizing symptoms across the full spectrum of motor skills; better motor skills are associated with lower levels of internalizing symptomology (Piek et al., 2010; Rigoli et al., 2012; Wilson et al., 2013; Poole et al., 2015). These findings demonstrate that the psychosocial implications of motor skills are present across the full spectrum of ability, promoting further research in community samples. Therefore, this mini-review focuses on understanding the relationship between the full spectrum of motor skills (including DCD and non-DCD populations) and internalizing problems, and how these intermediary psychosocial issues may mediate this association.

Studies investigating the association between motor skills and internalizing problems have been largely empirical. While the association between motor skills and internalizing problems is well documented, this area is currently limited by a lack of theoretical development underlying the causal nature of this association (Cairney et al., 2013). In this mini-review we discuss the recently proposed Elaborated Environmental Stress Hypothesis by Cairney et al. (2013) that attempts to address this current limitation. A brief overview of the model is provided, before discussing the recent empirical studies evaluating this theoretically driven framework.

THE ELABORATED ENVIRONMENTAL STRESS HYPOTHESIS

The Elaborated Environmental Stress Hypothesis (Cairney et al., 2013) provides a conceptual model (see **Figure 1**) that allows for the testing of causal pathways from motor skills to internalizing problems. This recent framework expanded on the earlier work of Cairney et al. (2010). The Elaborated Environmental Stress Hypothesis illustrates the complex relationship between motor skills and internalizing problems and posits DCD as a primary stressor that exposes the individual to a range of secondary psychosocial stressors (e.g., peer conflict, low social support, poor academic performance, peer victimization, low self-esteem, low self-competence, physical inactivity, and obesity). It is hypothesized that the consistent exposure to these secondary stressors may then give rise to the onset and maintenance of internalizing problems through these potential mediating and moderating variables, whilst also acknowledging that the relationship between motor skills and internalizing problems is likely to be an interaction of both genetic and environmental factors. A more complete description of the model can be found in Cairney et al. (2013).

The Elaborated Environmental Stress Hypothesis was originally developed within the context of children with DCD, and how their poor motor skills may give rise to internalizing problems. However, there is evidence to support the application of the framework across the broader spectrum of motor skills. A negative linear association between motor skills, internalizing problems and other psychosocial variables described in the Elaborated Environmental Stress Hypothesis has been found in community samples (e.g., Wilson et al., 2013; Poole et al., 2015), suggesting that the psychosocial implications of motor skills extend beyond the DCD population. This negative linear association demonstrates that better motor skills are associated with decreased psychosocial problems. This provides important information for prevention and intervention strategies. For example, universal intervention programs that aim to promote motor skills may have psychosocial benefits for the wider population, rather than being limited to only those with DCD (e.g., Piek et al., 2015).

RECENT DEVELOPMENTS

Cairney et al. (2013) provide a comprehensive description of the previous literature that contributed to the development of the Elaborated Environmental Stress Hypothesis. Therefore the present focus is on the recent developments that have occurred since the framework was published. However, where appropriate, some earlier literature is reflected upon in light of these more recent findings. At the time this mini-review was written, the Cairney et al. (2013) framework had been cited 22 times in peer-reviewed literature (*Google Scholar citations, 19 November 2015*). Some of this literature has reflected on the development of the model and its possible use in future studies (e.g., Missiuna and Campbell, 2014), while others have started to provide the empirical evaluation necessary to test this causal framework.

Illustrated in **Figure 1**, the Elaborated Environmental Stress Hypothesis highlights the complex causal network that describes how poor motor skills may lead to internalizing problems. Empirically evaluating this entire framework in a single study presents a range of methodological considerations that make such an approach difficult. These considerations include the response burden for participants, difficulties acquiring a large enough sample size to detect the likely small effects (Wilson et al., 2013), and the complexity of the analyses required to evaluate the full model. Consequently, the Elaborated Environmental Stress Hypothesis is more practically investigated through studies that evaluate a smaller combination of pathways embedded within the broader causal model. This has led to several studies that have since evaluated the various moderating/mediating variables specified by the framework (see **Table 1**).

These studies have used a combination of different samples and research designs, and often provided support for the framework. Wilson et al. (2013) found the relationship between motor skills and internalizing problems in a community sample of 475 young children (4–6 years) to be mediated by social skills. Rigoli et al. (2012) enlisted a community sample of 93 adolescents (12–16 years). Their findings provided further support for the framework; self-perceptions were found to mediate the association between motor skills and internalizing problems. Similar findings have been replicated in a more recent study by Viholainen et al. (2014) with a community sample of 327 female adolescents (12–16 years). Self-concept, specifically related to school-related physical education, was found to mediate the relationship between motor skills and psychosocial wellbeing in this cohort. These results provide further support for this key pathway embedded within the framework.

Recent support for the Elaborated Environmental Stress Hypothesis extends beyond cross-sectional studies. Recent findings by Piek et al. (2015) conducted the first intervention study to evaluate the Elaborated Environmental Stress Hypothesis. The authors use 6 and 18-month follow up data of a 4–6 years old community population who participated in the randomized control trial (RCT) of the *Animal Fun* program (Wilson et al., 2013). The *Animal Fun* program is a 10-week school-based universal intervention program aimed at promoting motor development in 4–6 years old children. Findings from the RCT indicated the intervention group demonstrated significant improvement in prosocial behavior at 6-month follow-up, which remained at 18-month follow up. These results provide support for the pathways in the framework which suggest that interventions to improve motor skills and

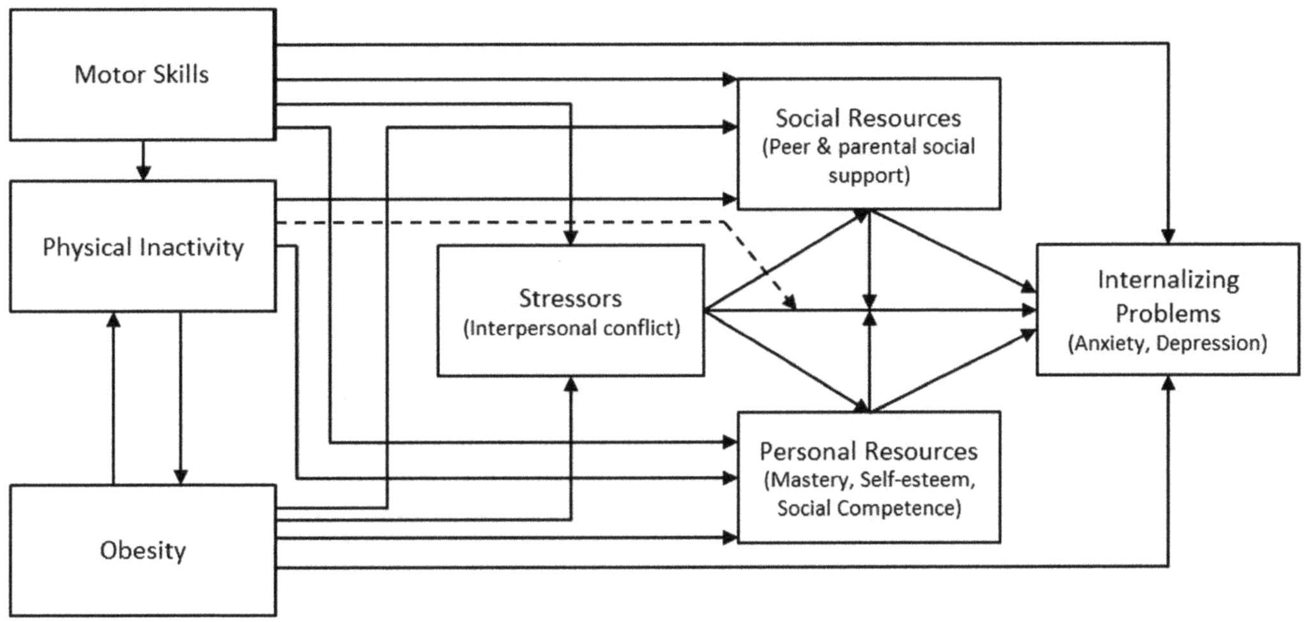

FIGURE 1 | An adapted Elaborated Environmental Stress Hypothesis. This adapted version examines motor skills across the full spectrum of ability; the original Elaborated Environmental Stress Hypothesis described by Cairney et al. (2013) specifically focused on children with developmental coordination disorder (DCD).

TABLE 1 | Summary of recent, peer-reviewed empirical support for the elaborated environmental stress hypothesis by Cairney et al. (2013).

Study	Research design	*N*	Sample type	Key supporting findings
Lingam et al., 2012	Longitudinal	6,902	Community; children (7–10 years)	Motor skills at 7 years of age predict mental health problems at 10 years of age. Poor social skills, peer victimization, self-esteem, and perceived scholastic competence mediate this relationship, in children with probable DCD.
Rigoli et al., 2012	Cross-sectional	93	Community; adolescents (12–16 years)	Self-perceptions mediate the association between motor skills and internalizing problems
Wilson et al., 2013	Cross-sectional	532	Community; children (4–6 years)	Social skills mediate the association between motor skills and internalizing problems
Viholainen et al., 2014	Cross-sectional	327	Community; adolescent females (12–16 years)	Self-concepts mediate the association between motor skills and internalizing problems
McIntyre et al., 2014	Intervention	35	Clinical; adolescents (13–17 years)	Intervention improving exercise in populations with low motor competence also improved their physical self-perceptions
Piek et al., 2015	Intervention	337*	Community; children (4–6 years)	Interventions improving motor skills and participation improve prosocial behavior
Poole et al., 2015	Longitudinal	189*	Community; lifespan (0–40 years)	Childhood motor difficulties predict internalizing problems in adulthood. Limited by retrospective report of childhood motor difficulties at age 29–35 years. Mental health problems measured at 8 years, 22–26 and 29–36 years only.

*N = Total number of participants. *Final sample at final follow-up periods.*

physical engagement will result in secondary improvements in psychosocial areas such as prosocial behavior. Similarly, Bart et al. (2009) found that intervention improving balance reduces anxiety and increased self-esteem in children with comorbid balance and anxiety disorders.

McIntyre et al. (2014) identified that participation in a 13-week physical activity intervention program for adolescents with poor motor skills resulted in an increase in physical self-perceptions, which is congruent with the pathways specified within the framework. A limitation of this study was that no measure of internalizing symptoms was included. However, previous studies have identified that increased physical self perceptions act as a protective factor against internalizing symptoms in similarly aged populations (Rigoli et al., 2012; Wilson et al., 2013; Viholainen et al., 2014).

Longitudinal evaluation of the Elaborated Environmental Stress Hypothesis is currently limited. However, recent longitudinal studies provide support for the causal relationship between motor skills and internalizing problems; this association underpins the entire framework. Lingam et al. (2012) used a community sample of 6,902 children and identified that motor skills difficulties at 7 years of age were associated with mental health difficulties (including internalizing problems) at 10 years of age; however, mental health difficulties were not measured at 7 years of age which limited the ability to conclude a causal relationship. The authors did identify several mediating variables between motor skills and mental health difficulties which were relevant to the Elaborated Environmental Stress Hypothesis, namely poor social skills, peer victimization, self-esteem, and perceived scholastic competence. More recently, Poole et al. (2015) published the results of a longitudinal study which included measures of motor skills and mental health. Their study provided an indication that childhood coordination problems were associated with internalizing problems in adulthood. However, childhood motor difficulties were reported retrospectively at age 29–35 years, relying on a subjective recount of motor skills. Similarly, mental health problems were only measured at age 8 (parent and teacher report) and self-report at age 22–26 and 29–36 years. Consequently, there is a need for more rigorous longitudinal investigation of motor skills and mental health.

These studies provide some indication that poor motor skills do precede the development of internalizing problems. In addition, they also emphasize that motor difficulties in early childhood are associated with psychosocial issues in later life. However, it is important to note that a current lack of longitudinal studies that consider shared risk factors for internalizing problems and motor skills such as infant emotional regulation and maternal stress limits the ability to make conclusions about the causal relationship between motor skills and internalizing problems as specified by the Elaborated Environmental Stress Hypothesis. Research by Hill and Brown (2013) has contributed qualitative support for the psychosocial impacts of DCD in adulthood. Within the recent developments pertaining to the Elaborated Environmental Stress Hypothesis, it was noted that several of these studies used community samples, moving beyond investigating the DCD population only. Each of these studies were able to provide support for different components of the overall framework. These findings promote the efficacy of the Elaborated Environmental Stress Hypothesis as a theoretical framework that is meaningful across the full spectrum of motor skills (and across the lifespan), rather than limited to DCD in childhood only.

While the framework provides a comprehensive description highlighting poor motor skills as a risk factor for internalizing problems, it is important to recognize the other risk factors that may contribute to the onset of anxiety and depression in childhood. Shaw et al. (1997) identified several risk factors during infancy that were related to the development of internalizing problems at pre-school age. Similarly, low socio-economic status and low birth weight/gestational age have also been identified as both risks for DCD and internalizing problems (Lingam et al., 2009). Such evidence provides a suggestion that these pre-disposing risk factors for internalizing problems may have similar repercussions for motor development. While the measurement of infant emotional regulation is notoriously difficult, further longitudinal investigations that consider the risk factors for internalizing factors and poor motor skills (e.g., maternal stress and infant emotional regulation) is necessary in order to achieve a better understanding of the association between internalizing problems and motor skills, and to evaluate the Elaborated Environmental Stress Hypothesis.

CONCLUSION

This mini-review has provided an up-to-date appraisal of the Elaborated Environmental Stress Hypothesis by Cairney et al. (2013). The Elaborated Environmental Stress Hypothesis provides a framework to describe how poor motor skills may lead to the development of internalizing problems through a range of secondary psychosocial consequences. The ability to make accurate, coordinated, age-appropriate movements facilitates the ability to meet developmental milestones and foster opportunities for positive social engagement. Consequently, poor motor skills may increase psychosocial difficulties. It is important to recognize that the Elaborated Environmental Stress Hypothesis does not intend to provide a complete explanation of the etiology of internalizing problems, as psychopathology is multi-factorial. Rather, the purpose of this framework is to highlight motor skills as a potentially important factor to consider when understanding the onset of internalizing problems. There is a growing body of empirical support for the framework, using cross-sectional, intervention, and longitudinal research designs. The key finding from this mini-review is that the Elaborated Environmental Stress Hypothesis has utility beyond the DCD population. Studies enlisting community samples have provided evidence supporting the Elaborated Environmental Stress Hypothesis as a useful framework to understand the psychosocial implications of motor skills across the full spectrum of motor skills. This causal framework also provides a useful tool in the development of intervention strategies. Initiatives that aim to improve motor skills can be complemented by psychosocial components that focus on improving the secondary psychosocial stressors of poor motor skills. This has the capacity to buffer the impact of poor motor skills on internalizing problems. The negative linear association between motor skills and psychosocial issues provides support for universal motor skill interventions such as *Animal Fun*. Preliminary findings have shown that implementation of this movement program in children increased psychosocial wellbeing (Piek et al., 2015). Further empirical investigation of the Elaborated Environmental Stress Hypothesis is recommended, as not all of the causal pathways specified in the framework have been empirically tested, particularly using longitudinal designs. Similarly, there is an alternative argument to suggest that shared predisposing risk factors associated with internalizing problems may have similar implications for motor development (e.g., maternal stress, low socioeconomic status); longitudinal studies are required in order to address this argument. Future evaluations of the framework should identify how key pathways may differ across different contexts (e.g., age/gender), which could facilitate the development of more targeted psychosocial interventions. Future research should consider the model developmentally, in order to identify if these pathways differ across different developmental periods.

AUTHOR CONTRIBUTIONS

VM was the primary author of this study, and wrote the mini-review and received feedback from each of the other supervisors. DR, JC, LR, and JP were all supervisors as part of this PhD research topic. Each of the supervisors provided insight, expertise, and feedback on the paper. They provided several edits and proofreads throughout the refinement of the article.

FUNDING

VM is the recipient of both an Australian Postgraduate Award and Curtin University Postgraduate Scholarship, and would like to acknowledge this.

REFERENCES

Alloway, T. P. (2007). Working memory, reading, and mathematical skills in children with developmental coordination disorder. *J. Exp. Child Psychol.* 96, 20–36. doi: 10.1016/j.jecp.2006.07.002

American Psychiatric Association (2013). *Diagnostic and Statistical Manual of Mental Disorders*, 5th Edn. Arlington, VA: American Psychiatric Publishing.

Bart, O., Bar-Haim, Y., Weizman, E., Levin, M., Sadeh, A., and Mintz, M. (2009). Balance treatment ameliorates anxiety and increases self-esteem in children with comorbid anxiety and balance disorder. *Res. Dev. Disabil.* 30, 486–495. doi: 10.1016/j.ridd.2008.07.008

Bart, O., Jarus, T., Erez, Y., and Rosenberg, L. (2011). How do young children with DCD participate and enjoy daily activities? *Res. Dev. Disabil.* 32, 1317–1322. doi: 10.1016/j.ridd.2011.01.039

Cairney, J., Hay, J. A., Faught, B. E., Wade, T. J., Corna, L., and Flouris, A. (2005). Developmental coordination disorder, generalized self-efficacy toward physical activity, and participation in organized and free play activities. *J. Pediatr.* 147, 515–520. doi: 10.1016/j.jpeds.2005.05.013

Cairney, J., Rigoli, D., and Piek, J. (2013). Developmental coordination disorder and internalizing problems in children: the environmental stress hypothesis elaborated. *Dev. Rev.* 33, 224–238. doi: 10.1016/j.dr.2013.07.002

Cairney, J., Veldhuizen, S., and Szatmari, P. (2010). Motor coordination and emotional-behavioral problems in children. *Curr. Opin. Psychiatry* 23, 324–329.

Campbell, W. N., Missiuna, C., and Vaillancourt, T. (2012). Peer victimization and depression in children with and without motor coordination difficulties. *Psychol. Sch.* 49, 328–341. doi: 10.1002/pits.21600

Green, D., Baird, G., and Sugden, D. (2006). A pilot study of psychopathology in developmental coordination disorder. *Child Care Health Dev.* 32, 741–750.

Heath, N. L., Toste, J. R., and Missiuna, C. (2005). An exploration of the relationship between motor impairment and emotional/behavioural difficulties amongst children suspected of having DCD. *Isr. J. Occup. Ther.* 14, 153–170.

Hill, E. L., and Brown, D. (2013). Mood impairments in adults previously diagnosed with developmental coordination disorder. *J. Ment. Health* 22, 334–340. doi: 10.3109/09638237.2012.745187

Hill, E. L., Brown, D., and Sorgardt, K. (2011). A preliminary investigation of quality of life satisfaction reports in emerging adults with and without developmental coordination disorder. *J. Adult Dev.* 18, 130–134. doi: 10.1007/s10804-011-9122-2

Kanioglou, A., Tsorbatzoudis, H., and Barkoukis, V. (2005). Socialization and behavioral problems of elementary school pupils with developmental coordination disorder. *Percept. Mot. Skills* 101, 163–173. doi: 10.2466/pms.101.1.163-173

Lingam, R., Hunt, L., Golding, J., Jongmans, M., and Emond, A. (2009). Prevalence of developmental coordination disorder using the DSM-IV at 7 years of age: a UK population-based study. *Pediatrics* 123, e693–e700. doi: 10.1542/peds.2008-1770

Lingam, R., Jongmans, M. J., Ellis, M., Hunt, L. P., Golding, J., and Emond, A. (2012). Mental health difficulties in children with developmental coordination disorder. *Pediatrics* 129, e882–e891. doi: 10.1542/peds.2011-1556

McIntyre, F., Chivers, P., Larkin, D., Rose, E., and Hands, B. (2014). Exercise can improve physical self-perceptions in adolescents with low motor competence. *Hum. Mov. Sci.* 42, 333–343. doi: 10.1016/j.humov.2014.12.003

Missiuna, C., and Campbell, W. (2014). Psychological aspects of developmental coordination disorder: can we establish causality? *Curr. Dev. Disord. Rep.* 1, 125–131. doi: 10.1007/s40474-014-0012-8

Miyahara, M., and Piek, J. (2006). Self-esteem of children and adolescents with physical disabilities: quantitative evidence from meta-analysis. *J. Dev. Phys. Disabil.* 18, 219–234. doi: 10.1007/s10882-006-9014-8

Piek, J. P., Barrett, N. C., Smith, L. M., Rigoli, D., and Gasson, N. (2010). Do motor skills in infancy and early childhood predict anxious and depressive symptomatology at school age? *Hum. Mov. Sci.* 29, 777–786. doi: 10.1016/j.humov.2010.03.006

Piek, J. P., Kane, R., Rigoli, D., McLaren, S., Roberts, C. M., Rooney, R., et al. (2015). Does the Animal Fun program improve social-emotional and behavioural outcomes in children aged 4-6 years? *Hum. Mov. Sci.* 43, 155–163. doi: 10.1016/j.humov.2015.08.004

Piek, J. P., Rigoli, D., Pearsall-Jones, J. G., Martin, N. C., Hay, D. A., Bennett, K. S., et al. (2007). Depressive symptomatology in child and adolescent twins with attention-deficit hyperactivity disorder and/or developmental coordination disorder. *Twin Res. Hum. Genet.* 10, 587–596. doi: 10.1375/twin.10.4.587

Poole, K. L., Schmidt, L. A., Missiuna, C., Saigal, S., Boyle, M. H., and Van Lieshout, R. J. (2015). Motor coordination and mental health in extremely low birth weight survivors during the first four decades of life. *Res. Dev. Disabil.* 4, 87–96. doi: 10.1016/j.ridd.2015.06.004

Rigoli, D., Piek, J., and Kane, R. (2012). Motor coordination and psychosocial correlates in a normative adolescent sample. *Pediatrics* 129, e892–e900. doi: 10.1542/peds.2011-1237

Shaw, D. S., Keenan, K., Vondra, J. I., Delliquardi, E., and Giovannelli, J. (1997). Antecedents of preschool children's internalizing problems: a longitudinal study of low-income families. *J. Am. Acad. Child Adolesc. Psychiatry* 36, 1760–1767. doi: 10.1097/00004583-199712000-00025

Sigurdsson, E., Van Os, J., and Fombonne, E. (2002). Are impaired childhood motor skills a risk factor for adolescent anxiety? Results from the 1958 UK birth cohort and the National Child Development Study. *Am. J. Psychiatry* 159, 1044–1046. doi: 10.1176/appi.ajp.159.6.1044

Skinner, R. A., and Piek, J. P. (2001). Psychosocial implications of poor motor coordination in children and adolescents. *Hum. Mov. Sci.* 20, 73–94. doi: 10.1016/S0167-9457(01)00029-X

Smyth, M. M., and Anderson, H. I. (2000). Coping with clumsiness in the school playground: social and physical play in children with coordination impairments. *Br. J. Dev. Psychol.* 18, 389–413. doi: 10.1348/026151000165760

Viholainen, H., Aro, T., Purtsi, J., Tolvanen, A., and Cantell, M. (2014). Adolescents' school-related self-concept mediates motor skills and psychosocial well-being. *Br. J. Educ. Psychol.* 84, 268–280. doi: 10.1111/bjep.12023

Wilson, A., Piek, J. P., and Kane, R. (2013). The mediating role of social skills in the relationship between motor ability and internalizing symptoms in pre-primary children. *Infant Child Dev.* 22, 151–164. doi: 10.1002/icd.1773

Conflict of Interest Statement: The authors declare that the research was conducted in the absence of any commercial or financial relationships that could be construed as a potential conflict of interest.

9

First Steps into Language? Examining the Specific Longitudinal Relations between Walking, Exploration and Linguistic Skills

Ora Oudgenoeg-Paz, M(Chiel). J. M. Volman and Paul P. M. Leseman*

Department of Child, Family and Education Studies, Utrecht University, Utrecht, Netherlands

Edited by:
Klaus Libertus,
University of Pittsburgh, USA

Reviewed by:
Sarah Berger,
College of Staten Island, USA
Jo Van Herwegen,
Kingston University, UK

***Correspondence:**
Ora Oudgenoeg-Paz
O.Oudgenoeg@uu.nl

Recent empirical evidence demonstrates relationships between motor and language development that are partially mediated by exploration. This is in line with the embodied cognition approach to development that views language as grounded in real-life sensorimotor interactions with the environment. This view implies that the relations between motor and linguistic skills should be specific. Moreover, as motor development *initially* changes the possibilities children have to explore the environment, initial relations between motor and linguistic skills should become weaker over time. Empirical evidence pertaining to the duration and specificity of these relations is still lacking. The current study investigated longitudinal relations between attainment of walking and the development of several linguistic skills, and tested whether exploration through self-locomotion mediated these relations. Linguistic skills were measured at age 43 months, which is later than the age used in previous studies. Three hypotheses were tested: (1) the relations between walking and language found at younger ages will decrease over time (2) exploration through self-locomotion will remain an important predictor of spatial language (3) no relation will be found between walking, exploration and the use of grammatical and lexical categories and between exploration and general vocabulary. Thirty-one Dutch children took part in a longitudinal study. Parents reported about age of attainment of walking. Exploration through self-locomotion was measured using observations of play with a standard set of toys at age 20 months. Receptive vocabulary, spatial language and use of grammatical and lexical categories were measured at age 43 months using (standard) tests. Results reveal that age of walking does not directly predict spatial language at age 43 months. Exploration through self-locomotion does significantly and completely mediate the indirect effect of age of walking on spatial language. Moreover, neither age of walking nor exploration predict general vocabulary and the use of grammatical and lexical categories. Results support the idea that the initial relations between motor development and linguistic skills decrease over time and that these relations are specific and intrinsically dependent on the information children pick up through the execution of specific motor activities.

Keywords: motor milestones, independent walking, exploration, spatial language, language development, embodiment

INTRODUCTION

In recent years, an increasing number of theoretical and empirical papers have addressed the link between motor development and development in other domains. One of the central theoretical approaches stressing the role of movement and motor control in cognitive-linguistic development is the embodied cognition approach (e.g., Hockema and Smith, 2009; Iverson, 2010). According to this approach, cognitive skills (including linguistic skills) are softly assembled in real-time from elementary perception-action processes that are rooted in concrete real-life interactions (Thelen and Smith, 1994). Development of new motor skills, such as sitting, crawling and walking opens the door to new ways of interacting with the environment and fundamentally alters children's sensorimotor experiences by bringing new possibilities of exploring the environment (Gibson, 1988; Thelen and Smith, 1994; Soska and Adolph, 2014). The increased possibilities for exploring objects, relations between objects, and spatial layouts provide the cognitive basis for language learning. Therefore, the development of motor skills is expected to predict linguistic advances. The situated nature of cognitive skills (including linguistic skills) suggests highly specific relations between what is explored and the cognitive-linguistic skills that are grounded in these specific sensorimotor interactions. For example, exploring objects that can be stacked is expected to be related to the development of spatial concepts and related prepositions such as '*on*' and '*under*,' but not to the learning of food names or grammatical skills such as verb inflection. While in recent years increasing evidence is reported for a link between the development of motor skills and language development (e.g., Oudgenoeg-Paz et al., 2012; Walle and Campos, 2014; Libertus and Violi, 2016), evidence regarding the *specific* and *meaning-intrinsic* nature of these links, how they influence cognitive-linguistic development over longer periods of time and the role of exploration as a mediating process between motor skill development and cognitive-linguistic outcomes is still scarce. The current study focuses on the specific links between attainment of motor milestones and the development of several linguistic skills. By doing so we aim to study not only which linguistic skills are related to motor development, but also which skills are *not*. The linguistic skills examined in the current study include general and spatial vocabulary and the use of grammatical and lexical categories (e.g., determiners, subjects). In addition, the current study also examines the long-term associations between motor milestone attainment and cognitive-linguistic skills. Previous studies demonstrated mainly relations in the short term, but it is not clear how stable these relations are when examined longitudinally over longer periods of time. Finally, the current study examines the role of exploration behavior as a mediator of the relation between motor milestones attainment and linguistic skills.

In line with the embodied cognition approach, Hockema and Smith (2009) describe linguistic development as composed of recurrent outside-in processes (children perceive information from the environment) and inside-out processes (children act on the environment). For example, when learning semantic categories, children may draw on physical features of objects to categorize them (e.g., all round objects are balls), but children may also actively sort similar objects to the same spatial location, thus making it easier for them to perceive the similarities and construct a semantic category. This model of language learning is also in line with ecological psychology theory stressing the central role of recurrent perception-action processes in development. Children, on the one hand, perceive information to be processed, but on the other hand, they also act in their environment and thus change the information they can perceive (Gibson, 1979; Gibson and Pick, 2000). While the classical ecological approach does not mention cognition at all (Gibson, 1979), the embodied view of cognition as situated in the context of an agent interacting with the environment, is in full agreement with the notion of recurrent perception-action cycles in which increasingly complex affordances are detected and the skill to act upon these affordances is developed. This notion, that is central to the ecological approach, will here be referred to as exploration (Thelen and Smith, 1994; Gibson and Pick, 2000; Smith and Gasser, 2005). The knowledge about the world acquired through exploration forms the basis for the development of advanced cognitive (and linguistic) skills (Gibson and Pick, 2000; Smith and Gasser, 2005).

The attainment of motor milestones dramatically changes children's exploration possibilities and is therefore expected to contribute to further advances in their linguistic development. A major milestone in motor development is the attainment of independent walking. Exploration of the environment through self-locomotion enables children first of all to explore more complex spatial relations that require taking different positions in space or moving objects to different places in space. The exploration of these spatial relations is expected to relate to more complex spatial language (e.g., the prepositions 'behind,' 'between,' 'through'). Moreover, moving around initiates a shift from predominantly egocentric to allocentric view of spatial relations and therefore allows children to learn about different, dynamically changing perspectives of their environment. This shift has been related to advances in spatial cognition (Campos et al., 2000; Newcombe, 2002; Sheya and Smith, 2011). Thus, exploring objects while engaging in self-locomotion enables infants to experience the relationship between their own movement and changing position and the position and view of the object they are exploring (Thelen and Smith, 1994). In addition, walking enables children not only to carry objects from one location to another, but also to draw parents' attention to their exploratory behavior and to the objects they are engaged with. This implies that children that are able to walk independently are more likely to receive linguistic input pertaining to their current focus of attention (Clearfield, 2011; Karasik et al., 2011). Thus, attainment of independent walking is expected to facilitate language acquisition in general, and the acquisition of spatial language in particular, because walking specifically enables children to learn about spatial relationships. We further expect that the relation between the attainment of walking and acquisition of spatial language is mediated by children's exploration behavior as related to self-locomotion. Spatial language, as measured in the current study, includes locative prepositions (e.g., in, on) and verbs describing movement in a specific direction (e.g., push, climb; Landau and Jackendoff, 1993).

Empirical evidence provides support for a link between attainment of walking and advances in general vocabulary. A previous study with the same sample as in the current study has shown that attainment of independent walking predicted a quicker rate of growth in productive vocabulary between ages 16 and 28 months (Oudgenoeg-Paz et al., 2012). Two other studies have shown that the transition from crawling to walking predicted significant increases in both receptive and productive vocabularies in both the US and China (Walle and Campos, 2014; He et al., 2015). In addition, previous work with the current sample has shown that children who attained independent walking earlier than peers engaged more in exploration through self-locomotion at age 20 months. These children also showed better knowledge of spatial vocabulary at age 36 months. Exploration through self-locomotion at age 20 months, largely mediated this effect (Oudgenoeg-Paz et al., 2015).

Thus, previous work has found support for a link between attainment of walking and general and spatial vocabulary. Moreover, exploration through self-locomotion mediated the relation between walking attainment and spatial language at age 36 months. However, whether these early relations endure over longer time is not yet known. According to the embodied cognition approach the importance of motor development is that it facilitates exploration behavior. Therefore, when examined longitudinally, the initial relations between attainment of walking and linguistic skills are expected to decrease as variability in walking skill decreases as well and most children eventually learn to walk (in the current study all but one child before age 20 months). However, the initial individual differences in exploration behavior are expected to remain important for language development, because exploration provides the embodied conceptual basis for language learning. The mediating role of exploration found in previous work provides support for this hypothesis. As the studies regarding general vocabulary tested the relation between walking attainment and language development close to the onset of walking, it is not yet clear whether these relations also remain when language is measured at later ages. To test this hypothesis, the current study investigated the relation between attainment of walking and receptive general vocabulary and spatial vocabulary at age 43 months, that is at a later time and more distant from the actual attainment of independent walking compared to previous studies. Moreover, direct knowledge of the spatial vocabulary included in the current study (i.e., verbs and prepositions) only develops in the 3rd year of life (Pruden et al., 2004). Therefore knowledge of spatial vocabulary at age 43 months is expected to be more advanced and stable than at age 36 months (the age at which spatial vocabulary was measured in our previous study). To summarize, we hypothesize that the link between walking and general and spatial vocabulary seen at younger ages will be much smaller in magnitude and may even disappear when vocabulary is measured at age 43 months.

Previous studies did not examine the role of exploration through self-locomotion in general vocabulary development. We hypothesize that this kind of exploration is especially important for spatial vocabulary, as the kind of information this exploration provides is relevant for this linguistic domain. Therefore, we do not expect any relation between this kind of exploration and general vocabulary. In our previous work (Oudgenoeg-Paz et al., 2015) we have shown that exploration through self-locomotion mediated the relation between attainment of walking and spatial vocabulary. In the current study we expect to replicate this finding and show that while the initial direct effect of attainment of walking might be smaller (or even disappear completely), exploration through self-locomotion will still mediate the (indirect) relations between attainment of independent walking and spatial language at age 43 months.

If the hypotheses derived from the embodied cognition approach to development are taken too generally, they may imply that motor development is related (through exploration and other possible underlying mechanisms) to all areas of cognitive development. This might be taken by some to simply indicate a general maturation process or broad shifts in general developmental stages. However, the grounding of cognition in real-life experiences suggests that the developmental relationships between motor development, exploration and linguistic skills should be *specific* and intrinsically grounded in the information structures present in the environment and the actions these information structures afford (Thelen and Smith, 1994; Wilson, 2002). For example, exploration of nesting cups is expected to be related to the learning of concepts and words such as *'in,' 'out,' 'under,' 'on'* in addition to concepts and words related to colors and textures, but not to learning of concepts and words such as different tools used to work in the garden or grammatical knowledge about the use of determiners. Previous empirical work (e.g., Oudgenoeg-Paz et al., 2012; Walle and Campos, 2014) points to linguistic skills that are related to walking attainment, but fails to show which linguistic skills are *not* related to the attainment of walking. Therefore, in the current study, we attempted to distinguish between linguistic skills that are and are not related to motor development. By doing so, the study will contribute important evidence for the distinction between relations based on processes of general maturation and specific relations based on the nature of real-life experiences as suggested by the embodied cognition approach. More specifically, we hypothesize that attainment of independent walking and exploration through self-locomotion will *not* be related to the development of grammatical knowledge. We focus on the use of lexical and grammatical categories including the subject, determiner, auxiliaries and verbal prefix.

Empirical evidence suggests that the use of such lexical and grammatical categories is usually learned from linguistic input provided by the environment (Saffran, 2001). Types of input that seem to be of particular importance for the acquisition of these categories are infant directed speech (Shi et al., 1998), book reading (Naigles and Hoff-Ginsberg, 1998) and conversation eliciting questions in maternal speech (see Hoff, 2006 for a review). As previously discussed, attainment of walking and exploration through self-locomotion are likely to increase naming of objects by parents or prohibiting sentence (e.g., Gogate and Hollich, 2010; Karasik et al., 2011). However, we do not know of any study or theory linking independent walking and exploration through self-locomotion to linguistic input such as infant directed speech and book reading. Therefore, these types of linguistic input are not likely to be elicited by the attainment of walking and exploration through self-locomotion.

To summarize, in the current study three hypotheses were tested: (1) The relation between walking attainment and general and spatial vocabulary measured at age 43 months, will be weaker than the relations reported at earlier ages and may even completely disappear; (2) Exploration through self-locomotion is expected to mediate the (indirect) relation between attainment of walking and spatial language at age 43 months; (3) No relation is expected between attainment of independent walking and exploration through self-locomotion and the use of grammatical and lexical categories at age 43 months. Moreover, no relation is expected between exploration through self-locomotion and general vocabulary.

The current study included 31 Dutch children who took part in a longitudinal study. For the current analyses data were used from home visits at ages 20 and 43 months. Parental reports were obtained about the age of attainment of independent walking. Exploration through self-locomotion was measured using observations of children playing with a standard set of toys at age 20 months. This age was chosen as at this age (almost) all children are expected to be able to walk independently. Therefore, individual differences in exploration at this age do not merely reflect walking proficiency. In addition, in order to compare the magnitude of the relations with previous work, it is important to maintain the same age used in these studies (e.g., Walle and Campos, 2014; Oudgenoeg-Paz et al., 2015) for the predictors and only shift the outcome measures to a later age. Productive spatial language, receptive vocabulary, and command of grammatical and lexical categories were measured at age 43 months using (standard) tests.

MATERIALS AND METHODS

Participants

The sample is a subgroup of participants from a larger longitudinal study. The sample included 31 Dutch children (58% girls). Data of three additional children were excluded, as these children did not participate in the measurement wave at age 43 months. Participants were recruited through day-care centers in the municipality of Utrecht, The Netherlands, and surroundings and through an address list made available by the municipality. Most parents enjoyed medium to high educational and occupational levels. The children had no known developmental disabilities or delays at the time of recruitment. Informed consent was obtained from the parents for all of the children and the study was conducted in accordance with the ethical guidelines of Utrecht University. For the current study data were used from two measurement waves at the age of 20 months ($M = 20.75$, $SD = 0.61$) and at the age of 43 months ($M = 43.20$, $SD = 0.71$).

Procedure

Exploration behavior and linguistic skills were measured during home visits. Exploration through self-locomotion was measured at age 20 months. The children were filmed while allowed to explore a standard set of objects for 8 min. The set of objects included a hoop (70 cm diameter), a large foam dice (15 cm × 15 cm × 15 cm) and a play tunnel made of polyester (150 cm length and 45 cm diameter). See **Figure 1** for a photo of the objects used. The films of children's interaction with the objects were later edited to remove interruptions (such as stopping to drink). Exploration behavior was then scored based on the first 4 min of uninterrupted play. These 4 min started when the child first made contact with the objects. The duration of 4 min was selected based on pilot coding showing that this duration was both sufficient for most children to interact with all three objects and short enough to prevent children from getting bored and terminating their interaction with the objects. General vocabulary, spatial language and the use of grammatical and lexical categories were measured using playful (standard) tests administered by trained research assistants in a fixed order. The tests of grammatical and lexical categories were administered using a laptop computer. Parental reports were obtained regarding the age of attainment of independent walking. To thank the families for participation, the children were given a small gift at each measurement wave.

Measures

Age of Attaining Independent Walking

At the time of enrolment in the study (between ages 13 and 20 months for the current sample), parents were given the Parental Checklist of Developmental Milestones (Bodnarchuk and Eaton, 2004). Parents were asked to indicate for all milestones in the list at what age their child had attained this milestone. For milestones not yet attained, parents were asked to keep track of their child's development and note when these milestones were attained. A detailed description of each milestone was provided to help parents decide if their child had attained this milestone. For the current study, parental reports regarding age of independent walking were used. The description of this milestone given to the parents was: "The child is walking unsupported across the room; the child uses walking as the main means of moving around." Previous studies have shown that parents' reports using such descriptions are reliable (Bodnarchuk and Eaton, 2004; Berger et al., 2007; Adolph et al., 2011). When the milestone of independent walking was attained prior to enrolment in the study parents were asked to use the records kept by the Child and Infant Health Centre or their own records (such as diaries, blog entries, digital photos, or email communication) to determine the age of onset of independent walking. If parents had no such records, data were considered missing. This was the case for one child in the current sample.

Exploration

Children's exploration behavior was scored by trained observers based on the films of the first 4 min of exploration with the set of objects shown in **Figure 1**. The 4-min recordings were each divided in 24 intervals of 10 s each. Per interval, all the activities of

FIGURE 1 | Objects used in the observations.

the child and the duration of each activity in seconds were noted. In the current study we were interested in spatial exploration and specifically in exploration through self-locomotion. Therefore, the initial detailed scoring at the level of separate explorative activities (such as banging, carrying, and looking) was aggregated and activities were scored as either stationary (i.e., the child was exploring the objects from a stationary position), or engaged in self-locomotion (i.e., the child was changing location by self-movement, such as crawling or walking while exploring the objects). During the 4-min recordings, most children (over 86%) interacted with the objects for more than 96% of the time. The remaining four children interacted with the objects for a minimum of 20 intervals (i.e., 83% of the time), but most of these children interacted with the objects for longer periods. Thus, the coding represents children's posture while exploring the objects.

Examples of exploratory actions observed with the objects while in stationary position are: standing and banging on the tunnel, standing in the hoop, sitting in the tunnel, holding the dice and looking at it, holding and manipulating the dice in sitting position, sitting next to the hoop or dice and lifting it. Examples of exploratory actions observed with the objects while engaged in self-locomotion are: crawling through the tunnel with or without the dice, jumping in and out of the hoop, throwing or rolling the dice and running or crawling after it, walking while dragging the hoop or the tunnel, walking around the tunnel while looking at it, lifting the dice and transferring it toward the hoop and putting it into the hoop.

The objects used were all novel for the children and presented various action possibilities to learn about spatial relations. Therefore, all the actions children performed with the objects could be considered as exploration (Weisler and McCall, 1976; Schuetze et al., 1999; see for example also measurement of exploration used by Needham et al., 2002; Lobo and Galloway, 2013). It should be noted that in the current stud we are not referring to locomotor exploration in the sense of navigation and exploring the space, but rather to exploration of the three objects in a way that requires self-locomotion for exploring the spatial affordances of the objects (either separately or as a combination of objects) or for moving from one object to another (see also Cole et al., 2015). For example, when the infant attempts to crawl through the tunnel he or she explores the spatial affordance of 'moving- through-a-tube' and learns, among other things, about the size relations between aperture of the tunnel and the body and about the spatial relations of *in* the tunnel and *out* of the tunnel. The exploration of these spatial relations is only possible while engaging in self-locomotion. Similarly, when the infant picks the dice, walks with it and transfers it into the hoop it learns about moving objects in space and changing the spatial location of the dice (i.e., the dice can be lifted, carried and transferred to a different location) and it learns about the size relations enabling the hoop to contain the dice and about the relation of *in* and *out* of the hoop. Again, the learning of these complex affordances requires self-locomotion.

A total score was given to each interval based on the longest enduring activity. If both stationary (scored as 0) and engaged in self-locomotion (scored as 1) were present equally long within an interval, a score of 1 was given to the whole interval. Intervals that could not be scored for technical reasons (e.g., child's actions were not visible), were given a missing score. About 9% (three children) of the recordings had more than 50% of the intervals missing and were therefore excluded from the analyses. An additional 48% had less than 50% missing intervals and the majority of these recordings (14 out of the 15 children) had less than 25% missing intervals. Two coders independently scored about 22.6% of the films. The mean Cohen's kappa was 0.81 ($SD = 0.08$) and all kappa values were above 0.70. These values are considered satisfactory (Landis and Koch, 1977).

The total score on exploration through self-locomotion was the proportion of the intervals in which children explored the objects while engaging in self-locomotion at least as much as exploring from a stationary position. This score was preferred to a score based on the total time of self-locomotion, in order to control for the missing intervals.

Spatial Language

Productive knowledge of locative prepositions and verbs containing a direction was measured using two playful tasks. Knowledge of propositions was measured using a hand puppet of Ernie from the TV program Sesame Street and a set of small toys. The toys included furniture for a dollhouse and small objects that fit in and around the furniture. The experimenter and the child used the furniture and objects to build a house for Ernie, according to a photo showing where everything should be located in Ernie's house. The objects were placed so that they represented the entire range of spatial prepositions (e.g., *in* the closet, *between* two chairs). Following this, the child had to explain to Ernie where to find the different objects in the house, by using spatial prepositions to indicate the location of the objects. To prevent the children from pointing to the location, they were asked to talk to Ernie via a toy telephone. The task began with two practice items. During these items the experimenter reminded the children that Ernie cannot see them and that the instruction has to be given in words. When needed, the experimenter modeled the right answer. Children were then encouraged to repeat the right answer. Following the practice items, 10 test items were administered. Each item elicited a different locative preposition. If the child did not answer a question posed by Ernie, the experimenter repeated the question. If the child still did not answer, the experimenter pointed to the location of the object on the photo used to build the house and said: "look there is the [name of object], can you tell Ernie where the [name of object] is?" If the child still did not answer the experimenter provided the right answer. After an answer was given (either correct or wrong, by either the child or the experimenter), Ernie 'found' the object and thanked the child. Children were always given positive feedback for providing an answer, regardless if it was right or wrong.

Productive knowledge of spatial verbs was measured using small dolls of Dora and Boots from the cartoon film 'Dora the Explorer' and two large (A3) pictures. The pictures each depicted a trail leading to either a beach or a treasure chest. Along the trail different locations and objects were drawn. Dora and Boots were moved by the experimenter along the trail and stopped at each location. Whenever Dora and boots stopped the child was asked what they should do at that location. The answer always included a spatial verb. For example, when reaching a slide, Dora says she wants to go down the slide and asks the child how can she get up the slide. The answer should then include the word *climb*. Also in this test if children did not answer the question, the question was repeated. If the child still did not answer, the experimenter prompted the child by saying for example "how can Dora get up the slide? She has to..." If the child still did not answer, the experimenter provided the correct answer. Children were always given positive feedback for every answer they provided either right or wrong. After an answer was given (either correct or wrong, by either the child or the experimenter) Dora and Boots went on to do the activity and then proceeded on the trail. Each child completed the trails on both pictures. The task included 19 test items representing 19 spatial verbs.

The total score on each task (prepositions and verbs) was the number of words produced correctly. Scores on both tasks correlated strongly ($r = 0.70$, $p < 0.001$). A total score was computed by calculating the mean of the scores on the two tasks after Z-transformations were applied. Scores on these tasks correlated moderately ($r = 0.39$, $p = 0.04$ and $r = 0.38$, $p = 0.07$) with scores on a different task measuring receptive and productive knowledge of locative propositions and spatial verbs used at age 36 months (for a description of this task, see Oudgenoeg-Paz et al., 2015).

General Receptive Vocabulary

Receptive vocabulary was measured using the Dutch translation of the normed Peabody Picture Vocabulary Test-III (PPVT-III Dunn and Dunn, 2005). In this test the children are shown sets of four pictures each and are asked to point to the picture representing the word said by the experimenter. Each set contains 12 words. Difficulty level of the test varies with age and standard starting and stopping rules are applied. At age 43 months children always start on the third set and testing is stopped when children make nine or more errors within a specific set. Reliability and validity of this test are reported to be good (Dunn and Dunn, 2005).

Use of Grammatical and Lexical Categories

The use of grammatical and lexical categories was measured using a sentence repetition task developed by Wilsenach (2006). This task is an elicited imitation task following the rationale that in order for children to repeat a sentence containing a specific structure, this structure should be part of the child's grammatical skill. The children saw a robot on a laptop screen. The robot said a sentence and the children were then asked to repeat what the robot said. The test included three training items and 12 test items. During the training phase the children were asked to repeat the training sentences. In this phase the experimenter helped the children if needed by modeling the right answer and coaching them in order to avoid use of strategies such as only repeating the last word. The training items could be repeated as often as needed in order for the children to learn the task. In the test phase no coaching was provided. If, during the test phase, a child did not respond or repeated only one word, the stimulus from the robot was repeated once more. If the child repeated only one word also the second time, this was noted as the answer. If the child provided a response (correct or incorrect) a reward was visible. Rewards were various visual effects that appeal to young children, such as balloons flying across the screen. If the child did not provide a response, the next item was presented directly without first presenting the reward.

We used 12 of the 18 sentences included in the original task. In order to adjust the level of difficulty for the current age group we left out the sentences with distransitive verbs used in the original task. The experimenter noted which words were correctly repeated and which were omitted or incorrectly repeated. Scoring included the number of determiners correctly repeated (range 0–23) and the number of subjects, auxiliaries and verbal prefixes correctly repeated (all with a range of 0–12). A Total score was calculated by computing the mean of the scores on all scales after Z-transformations were applied. Wilsenach (2006) has shown that this task has good reliability. Items in the test with the current sample also showed good reliability with Crobnach's alpha of 0.99.

Statistical Analysis

All three research questions were analyzed using hierarchical regression models, following the steps defined by Baron and Kenny (1986) for testing mediation. First the main effects representing the relation between age of walking attainment and the three dependent variables (i.e., spatial language, general vocabulary and use of grammatical and lexical categories) were tested. Next, the relation between age of walking attainment and the mediator, exploration through self-locomotion, was tested. Third, the mediator was added to the hierarchical regression models. In models where the mediator significantly predicted the dependent variable, the Sobel-Goodman test was applied to test the significance of the mediation. Given the relatively small sample size, bootstrapping was applied in order to obtain more robust parameter estimates.

RESULTS

Descriptive Analysis

In **Table 1** the means and standard deviations of all model variables and their indicators are presented. The variables measuring age of walking and spatial language had each missing data from one child. Exploration through self-locomotion and Lexical and grammatical categories had data missing from three children each. Missing data were estimated, where possible, using single regression-based imputation (Schafer and Graham, 2002; Rubin et al., 2007). This method was chosen, rather than the standard listwise deletion, as it has been shown to be an appropriate method for small samples with a low percentage of missing. Moreover, imputing missing data is important with small samples, in order to prevent reduction in power of the analysis (Rubin et al., 2007). The final analyses were conducted with data of 30 children.

TABLE 1 | Descriptive statistics of model variables and indicators.

Variable	*N* before imputation	(imputed) *N*	*M*	*SD*
Age of independent walking	30	31	15.24	2.34
Exploration through self-locomotion 20 months	28	30	0.46	0.19
Total score productive spatial language 43 months[a]	30	31	−0.08	0.94
Spatial verbs productive 43 months	–	30	10.63	3.34
Spatial prepositions productive 43 months	–	28	5.83	2.14
Receptive vocabulary 43 months[b]	31	31	56.32	10.05
Total score grammatical and lexical categories 43 months[a]	28	31	0.09	0.94
Determiner omission 43 months	–	28	16.57	5.09
Subject omission 43 months	–	28	9.04	2.70
Auxiliary omission 43 months	–	28	9.89	2.62
Verbal prefix omission 43 months	–	28	11.00	1.19

Missing values were imputed at the level of total scores, therefore the total scores presented are after imputation but the raw scores still contain all missing values. [a]*This score is a mean of Z scores* [b]*Raw scores of the PPVT-III were used in the analysis.*

TABLE 2 | Correlations between all model variables ($N = 30$).

	1	2	3	4
(1) Age of independent walking				
(2) Exploration through self-locomotion	−0.46*			
(3) Total score productive spatial language	−0.06	0.42*		
(4) Receptive vocabulary	0.12	0.20	0.71***	
(5) Total score grammatical and lexical categories	−0.04	0.14	0.26	0.34†

†$p \leq 0.10$, *$p \leq 0.05$, ***$p \leq 0.001$.

As can be seen from **Table 1** the variable measuring the use of the verbal prefix in the sentence repetition task showed a ceiling effect as the maximum score on this variable was 12. Therefore, this variable was not used in the total score of grammatical and lexical categories. In addition, it should be noted that at age 20 months (the age at which exploration was measured) all children, but one, could already walk for at least 2 months. The child, who could not walk at age 20 months, was able to walk on her knees. **Table 2** presents the correlations between all the variables included in the analyses. **Table 2** shows that the two vocabulary measures (spatial vocabulary and general vocabulary) correlate strongly as can be expected. In addition, the total score of grammatical and lexical categories correlates moderately (though only marginally significant) with the score on general vocabulary, as can be expected. Finally, the indicators of the total score of spatial language correlated strongly with each other ($r = 0.70$, $p < 0.001$). The same was true for the indicators of the total score of grammatical and lexical categories (r ranges from 0.74 to 0.87, $p < 0.001$).

Factors Predicting Spatial Language

To test whether age of walking predicted spatial language at age 43 months and whether exploration through self-locomotion mediates this effect, a hierarchical regression analysis was conducted. The results are presented in **Table 3**. First, the age of walking was entered as a predictor of spatial language. As can be seen from **Table 3**, age of walking was not a significant predictor of spatial language. Next, the relation between age of walking and the mediator exploration through self-locomotion was examined. As can be seen from their correlation in **Table 2**, age of walking was a significant predictor of exploration through self-locomotion at age 20 months. The negative correlation coefficient indicates that an earlier age of walking predicts a higher level of exploration through self-locomotion at age 20 months. Finally, the mediator exploration through self-locomotion was added to the model (model 2 in the top panel of **Table 3**). The results show that this addition leads to a significant improvement of the model and exploration through self-locomotion significantly and positively predicts spatial language at age 43 months. This effect is medium sized. According to Kenny et al. (1998), there can be complete mediation even if the main effect (in this case the relation between age of walking and spatial language) is not significant. This is because the predictor and independent variable might be too far away in time. To test if this mediation is indeed significant the Sobel-Goodman test was performed. Results revealed that, in line with the hypothesis, exploration through self-locomotion indeed completely and significantly

TABLE 3 | Results of hierarchical regression analyses for factors predicting spatial vocabulary, receptive general vocabulary and grammatical and lexical categories ($N = 30$ for all analyses).

	Model 1			Model 2			
Predictors	***B (SE)***	**β**	R^2	***B (SE)***	**β**	R^2	ΔR^2
Factors predicting spatial vocabulary							
Age of independent walking	−0.02 (0.08)	−0.06	0.004	0.07 (0.08)	0.17	0.20*	0.19*
Exploration through self-locomotion				2.47 (0.97)	0.49*		
Factors predicting receptive general vocabulary							
Age of independent walking	0.52 (0.81)	0.12	0.12	1.15 (0.89)	0.27	0.10	0.08
Exploration through self-locomotion				17.20 (10.94)	0.32		
Factors predicting lexical and grammatical categories							
Age of independent walking	−0.02 (0.06)	−0.04	0.002	0.01 (0.09)	0.03	0.02	0.02
Exploration through self-locomotion				0.74 (1.06)	0.15		

*$p \leq 0.05$.

mediated the effect of age of walking on spatial language ($Z = -2.25, p = 0.03$).

Factors Predicting General Vocabulary and Use of Grammatical and Lexical Categories

To test whether age of walking attainment predicted general vocabulary and grammatical and lexical categories and whether exploration through self-locomotion mediated these effects the same steps were followed as in the previous analysis. Two hierarchical regression analyses were conducted and the results are presented in the bottom part of **Table 3**. From **Table 3** it can be seen that age of walking did not significantly predict general vocabulary or the use of grammatical and lexical categories. Moreover, addition of exploration through self-locomotion to the model did not significantly increase the amount of explained variance as exploration did not significantly predict either outcome variable. Thus, in line with the hypotheses, the present study did not find evidence that age of walking attainment predicts general vocabulary or the use of grammatical and lexical categories. Moreover, also in line with the hypotheses, there was no evidence found that exploration through self-locomotion mediates the relation between walking attainment and these outcome variables.

DISCUSSION

The current study sought to examine whether previously reported relations between age of walking and general and spatial vocabulary are still evident when linguistic skills are measured at age 43 months. In addition, the study aimed to test whether the relations between age of walking and exploration through self-locomotion are specific for certain linguistic skills and not for others. To do so we studied whether age of walking predicts spatial vocabulary, general receptive vocabulary and use of grammatical and lexical categories at age 43 months and whether exploration through self-locomotion, observed at age 20 months, mediates these relations. The results show that the previously reported relations between age of walking and general and spatial vocabulary indeed disappear when linguistic skills are measured at age 43 months. In addition, we have replicated our previous finding (Oudgenoeg-Paz et al., 2015) showing that exploration through self-locomotion mediates the relation between age of walking and spatial vocabulary. However, unlike our previous work, in the current study the direct relation between age of walking and spatial language was no longer significant. Finally, we found no significant relation between age of walking attainment and exploration through self-locomotion and neither general vocabulary nor the use of grammatical and lexical categories. All these findings are in agreement with our hypotheses.

Long Term Effects of Attainment of Walking

Previous work with the current sample (Oudgenoeg-Paz et al., 2012) and work done by others (Walle and Campos, 2014; He et al., 2015) have shown that, early in life, attainment of walking is related to *general* receptive and productive vocabulary development. However, these studies measured language development relatively close to the age of attainment of walking. The current study extends this literature by showing that when vocabulary is measured later in life (at age 43 months) the initial relation found between walking attainment and vocabulary disappears. Similarly we also show that the relation between age of walking and *spatial* vocabulary previously found with this sample at age 36 months (Oudgenoeg-Paz et al., 2015) is no longer present when spatial language is measured at age 43 months. Other studies have shown that at school age there is only a link between motor skills and linguistic skills such as reading and writing in the case of significant motor delays (e.g., Viholainen et al., 2006). Taken together, these results suggest that over longer periods of time the effects of the age of attainment of motor milestones become smaller as most children eventually learn to walk. We do not think, however, that these findings mean that attainment of walking is not important for linguistic skills. At the short term it is clear that attainment of walking propels language development, as is shown by several studies. The decrease in the size of the effect over time is an example of a cascading effect on development. We return to this issue later in this discussion.

Unlike the relation between walking and linguistic skills, we were able to replicate our previous finding regarding the link between exploration through self-locomotion and spatial vocabulary. Exploration through self-locomotion is still significantly related to spatial vocabulary also when it is measured at age 43 months. Moreover, exploration through self-locomotion is also still related to the attainment of walking and thus mediates the initial effect of walking attainment on spatial vocabulary. Our current findings therefore provide additional empirical support for the role of exploration behavior as a mechanism underlying the relation between walking attainment and spatial language. This finding is similar to another study, where infant object exploration, measured using retrospective parental reports, but not the age of attaining motor milestones related to self-locomotion, predicted spatial memory at school age (Oudgenoeg-Paz et al., 2014). These findings suggest that attainment of walking sets in motion a series of processes that in turn contribute to language development. In this case, attainment of walking allows children to explore their environment in new ways and to extend the embodied knowledge basis that underlies language acquisition. Children that walk independently are able to move around and therefore to change their own location and perspective. They are also able to change the spatial arrangement of the environment. These enhanced exploration possibilities are especially related to walking, rather than to other forms of self-locomotion such as crawling, as the visual information acquired through walking is fundamentally different than the information acquired through crawling (Kretch et al., 2012). Exploration through walking enables children's learning about spatial concepts and eventually facilitates advances in spatial language, as shown in the current study.

Taken together, the results support the idea of a developmental cascade. Attainment of walking is important initially, as it facilitates ways of interacting with the environment which are important for linguistic development. The mechanisms through which walking propels the development of general vocabulary have not been studied in the current study. Possible underlying mechanisms discussed in the literature are an increase in gestures following the attainment of walking (for a review see Iverson, 2010) and changes in social interaction patterns which bring along changes in linguistic input (Gogate and Hollich, 2010; Clearfield, 2011; Karasik et al., 2011; Walle and Campos, 2014). Whatever the mechanisms are, the current study suggests that in the longer term, the initial relation between walking and linguistic skills diminishes and it is these underlying mechanisms that remain the important predictors of linguistic skills.

Specific Relations

According to the embodied view of development, the relations between motor skills, exploration and linguistic skills are specific as linguistic skills are grounded in specific sensorimotor interactions with the environment providing specific information. Our findings support this idea. We have shown that attainment of independent walking and exploration through self-locomotion are not related to all areas of linguistic development. Rather, their relation with spatial language (and the relation between walking and general vocabulary found at younger ages) is specific. Information obtained through exploration through self-locomotion, such as information about spatial relations in the larger space, is highly relevant for spatial language, but not for other domains of language.

Traditional approaches to cognitive development view relations between developmental domains as reflecting general maturation or some 'general developmental factor.' This general factor would explain why some children develop quicker than others. Some suggest that this domain general mechanism might involve maturational processes, processing speed, cognitive processes such as statistical learning, executive functions or environmental factors (for a review, see Rhemtulla and Tucker-Drob, 2011). Should such domain general mechanism underlie the relations found in the current study, one would expect a relation between the predictors (age of walking and exploration through self-locomotion) and all linguistic skills measured. However, the results seem to favor a situated model of cognition, as presented by the embodied-cognition approach. In this model, language (and any other cognition) is softly assembled in real-time from concrete real-life sensorimotor experiences (Thelen and Smith, 1994; Hockema and Smith, 2009). Therefore, relations between developmental domains are highly specific and intrinsically related to the specific types of information acquired through interaction with the environment.

An additional alternative explanation might be found in cross-sectional relations between motor and exploration skills and linguistic skills at age 43 months. Some studies indeed report such relations (e.g., Hill, 2001; Alcock and Krawczyk, 2010). The argument might be made that early motor and exploration skills predict current motor and exploration skills and these current skills, in turn, are related to current linguistic skills. In the present study no concurrent measures of exploration and motor skills were included. However, a cross-sectional relation between motor and exploration skills does not preclude a longitudinal relation nor contradicts the idea of a developmental cascade. Moreover, the decrease in the strength of relations between walking and linguistic skills implies that the experiences facilitated by the attainment of walking early in life, are the ones that, in turn, facilitate linguistic development.

Strengths and Limitations

The main limitation of the current study is the small sample size. However, based on previous work (e.g., Oudgenoeg-Paz et al., 2012; Walle and Campos, 2014) we expected to find medium to large effects. The current sample had sufficient power to detect such effects (Kelley and Maxwell, 2003; Tabachnik and Fidell, 2007). Moreover, the use of bootstrapping enabled us to obtain robust estimates despite the small sample size. A second limitation is the measurement of exploration behavior. While this is a good measure of the amount of self-locomotion in general, it does not differentiate between different types of self-locomotion such as crawling and walking. Given recent evidence suggesting that the type of visual information obtained from crawling is essentially different from that obtained through walking (Kretch et al., 2012), it would be interesting to code exploration through self-locomotion also in terms of type of self-locomotion in future studies. The question might also arise whether this measure is not confounded with attainment of walking. It is reasonable to assume that children who attained walking can engage more in exploration through self-locomotion (although crawling children can, of course, also engage in such exploration). However, we measured exploration at the age of 20 months, when all children, but one, were already walking for at least 2 months. Thus, while all children could engage in exploration through self-locomotion, children who attained walking at an earlier age more often chose to explore the objects while engaged in self-locomotion. Furthermore, the correlation between walking attainment and exploration through self-locomotion is medium sized, suggesting that while early walkers do engage more in exploration through self-locomotion at 20 months, other factors also play a role in determining the level of exploration at this age. This measure of exploration also forms a strength of the current study by being relatively context free. That is, while children's exploration was influenced by the specific context of the objects used, the coding is at the level of position and can therefore be also applied to other contexts using different objects. This will enable future studies to examine if the relations reported in the current study are also found in different contexts. An additional strength of the current study is the fact that the measurements were conducted at the children's home. While this offered less opportunity for standardization of the measures, it contributes to the ecological validity of this study, as compared to other work done in a lab setting. Finally, the use of multiple methods (parental reports, tests and observations) and the longitudinal design enabled us to study development over multiple domains and test hypotheses pertaining to developmental relations over time.

Future Directions

Future studies should further explore the specific and intrinsic relations between motor skills, exploration and language development. For example, studies could examine the different aspects of spatial language separately, rather than as a single one-dimensional skill as was done in the current study. An interesting question if whether the same pattern of results is found when verbs and prepositions are studied separately and if the same pattern of results will be found for all spatial words if these are considered individually. Similarly, a more detailed analysis of the general vocabulary data could also be interesting. In the current study, and in most studies in the field, general vocabulary is treated as a single one-dimensional skill. However, if the words in a test such as the PPVT are divided in subgroups representing for example verbs, nouns, prepositions and so forth, hypotheses regarding specific relations between certain linguistic categories and certain motor skills and forms of exploration could be tested. Another interesting direction is the study of the early predictors of grammatical development. Some work suggests that grammatical categories are learned early on through several types of language input such as book reading or asking questions that prompt conversations (Naigles and Hoff-Ginsberg, 1998; Hoff, 2006). The input is, however, not completely independent of the child. Children elicit certain kinds of input through their own actions on the environment (for a discussion of this idea, see Gogate and Hollich, 2010). Therefore future studies should seek for the aspects in children's interaction with the environment that are likely to elicit input that is relevant for the learning of certain grammatical forms.

CONCLUSION

The findings of the current study provide support to several hypotheses derived from an embodied view of development. First, we show that relations between attainment of walking and spatial and general vocabulary that are found at young ages decrease and even disappear with time. We also replicate previous findings showing that exploration through self-locomotion remains an important mediator of the relation between age of walking attainment and spatial language. Thus, results support the idea of cascading effects. While initial differences in motor skills are important for linguistic development early in life, over time individual differences in exploration behavior (which themselves are predicted by differences in the age of walking attainment) seem to be the important predictor of spatial language. Second, the results reveal that the relations between age of independent walking, exploration through self-locomotion and the linguistic skills included in the current study are specific as they were found to be limited to spatial language. This pattern of specific relations supports the embodied-cognition idea of situated language learning in which multiple real-life interactions with the environment provide the semantic basis for learning language.

AUTHOR CONTRIBUTIONS

OO-P took the leading role in conception and design and acquisition of the data. She also fulfilled the leading role in analysis and interpretation of the data. She also took the leading role in drafting and revising the article. MV participated in conception and design of the data and had a large role in analysis and interpretation of the data. He also took part in drafting and revising the article. PL participated in conception and design of the data and had a large role in analysis and interpretation of the data. He also took part in drafting and revising the article.

ACKNOWLEDGMENTS

Work on this article was supported by a grant from The Netherlands Organisation for Scientific Research (NWO).

REFERENCES

Adolph, K. E., Berger, S. E., and Leo, A. J. (2011). Developmental continuity? Crawling, cruising, and walking. *Dev. Sci.* 14, 306–318. doi: 10.1111/j.1467-7687.2010.00981.x

Alcock, K. J., and Krawczyk, K. (2010). Individual differences in language development: relationship with motor skill at 21 months. *Dev. Sci* 13, 677–691. doi: 10.1111/j.1467-7687.2009.00924.x

Baron, R. M., and Kenny, D. A. (1986). The moderator–mediator variable distinction in social psychological research: conceptual, strategic, and statistical considerations. *J. Pers. Soc. Psychol.* 51, 1173–1182. doi: 10.1037/0022-3514.51.6.1173

Berger, S. E., Theuring, C., and Adolph, K. E. (2007). How and when infants learn to climb stairs. *Infant Behav. Dev.* 30, 36–49. doi: 10.1016/j.infbeh.2006.11.002

Bodnarchuk, J. L., and Eaton, W. O. (2004). Can parent reports be trusted?: validity of daily checklists of gross motor milestone attainment. *J. Appl. Dev. Psychol.* 25, 481–490. doi: 10.1016/j.appdev.2004.06.005

Campos, J. J., Anderson, D. I., Barbu-Roth, M. A., Hubbard, E. M., Hertenstein, M. J., and Witherington, D. (2000). Travel broadens the mind. *Infancy* 1, 149–219. doi: 10.1207/S15327078IN0102_1

Clearfield, M. W. (2011). Learning to walk changes infants' social interactions. *Infant Behav. Dev.* 34, 15–25. doi: 10.1016/j.infbeh.2010.04.008

Cole, W. G., Robinson, S. R., and Adolph, K. E. (2015). Bouts of steps: the organization of infant exploration. *Dev. Psychobiol.* 58, 341–354. doi: 10.1002/dev.21374

Dunn, L. M., and Dunn, L. M. (2005). *Peabody Picture Vocabulary Test-III-NL Handleiding (L. Schlichting Trans.).* Amsterdam: Harcourt.

Gibson, E. J. (1988). Exploratory behavior in the development of perceiving, acting and the acquiring of knowledge. *Annu. Rev. Psychol.* 39, 1–42. doi: 10.1146/annurev.ps.39.020188.000245

Gibson, E. J., and Pick, A. D. (2000). *An Ecological Approach to Perceptual Learning and Development.* New York, NY: Oxford University Press.

Gibson, J. J. (1979). *The Ecological Approach to Visual Perception.* Hillsdale, NJ: Lawrence Erlbaum.

Gogate, L. J., and Hollich, G. (2010). Invariance detection within an interactive system: a perceptual gateway to language development. *Psychol. Rev.* 117, 496–516. doi: 10.1037/a0019049

He, M., Walle, E. A., and Campos, J. J. (2015). A cross-national investigation of the relationship between infant walking and language development. *Infancy* 20, 283–305. doi: 10.1111/infa.12071

Hill, E. L. (2001). Non-specific nature of specific language impairment: a review of the literature with regard to concomitant motor impairments. *Int. J. Lang. Commun. Disord.* 36, 149–171. doi: 10.1080/13682820010019874

Hockema, S. A., and Smith, L. B. (2009). Learning your language, outside-in and inside-out. *Linguistics* 47, 453–479. doi: 10.1515/LING.2009.016

Hoff, E. (2006). How social contexts support and shape language development. *Dev. Rev.* 26, 55–88. doi: 10.1016/j.dr.2005.11.002

Iverson, J. M. (2010). Developing language in a developing body: the relationship between motor development and language development. *J. Child Lang.* 37, 229–261. doi: 10.1017/S0305000909990432

Karasik, L. B., Tamis-Lemonda, C. S., and Adolph, K. E. (2011). Transition from crawling to walking and infant's actions with objects and people. *Child Dev.* 82, 1199–1209. doi: 10.1111/j.1467-8624.2011.01595.x

Kelley, K., and Maxwell, S. E. (2003). Sample size for multiple regression: obtaining regression that are accurate, not simply significant. *Psychol. Methods* 8, 305–321. doi: 10.1037/1082-989X.8.3.305

Kenny, D. A., Kashy, D., and Bolger, N. (1998). "Data analysis in social psychology," in *Handbook of Social Psychology*, 4th Edn, eds D. Gilbert, S. Fiske, and G. Lindzey (New York, NY: McGraw-Hill), 233–265.

Kretch, K. S., Franchak, J. M., Brothers, J., and Adolph, K. E. (2012). What infants see depends on locomotor posture. *J. Vis.* 12, 182–182. doi: 10.1167/12.9.182

Landau, B., and Jackendoff, R. (1993). "What" and "where" in spatial language and spatial cognition. *Behav. Brain Sci.* 16, 217–238. doi: 10.1017/S0140525X00029733

Landis, J. R., and Koch, G. G. (1977). The measurement of observer agreement for categorical data. *Biometrics* 33, 159–174. doi: 10.2307/2529310

Libertus, K., and Violi, D. A. (2016). Sit to talk: relation between motor skills and language development in infancy. *Front. Psychol.* 7:475. doi: 10.3389/fpsyg.2016.00475

Lobo, M. A., and Galloway, J. C. (2013). The onset of reaching significantly impacts how infants explore both objects and their bodies. *Infant Behav. Dev.* 36, 14–24. doi: 10.1016/j.infbeh.2012.09.003

Naigles, L. R., and Hoff-Ginsberg, E. (1998). Why are some verbs learned before other verbs? effects of input frequency and structure on children's early verb use. *J. Child Lang.* 25, 95–120. doi: 10.1017/S0305000997003358

Needham, A., Barrett, T., and Peterman, K. (2002). A pick-me-up for infants' exploratory skills: early stimulated experiences reaching for objects using 'sticky mittens' enhances young infrants' object exploration skills. *Infant Behav. Dev.* 25, 279–295. doi: 10.1016/S0163-6383(02)00097-8

Newcombe, N. S. (2002). "Spatial cognition," in *Cognition Volume, Stevens' Handbook of Experimental Psychology*, 3rd Edn, ed. D. Medin (New York, NY: Wiley), 113–163.

Oudgenoeg-Paz, O., Leseman, P. P. M., and Volman, M. J. M. (2014). Can infant self-locomotion and spatial exploration predict spatial memory at school age? *Eur. J. Dev. Psychol.* 11, 36–48. doi: 10.1080/17405629.2013.803470

Oudgenoeg-Paz, O., Leseman, P. P. M., and Volman, M. J. M. (2015). Exploration as a mediator of the relation between the attainment of motor milestones and the development of spatial cognition and language. *Dev. Psychol.* 51, 1241–1253. doi: 10.1037/a0039572

Oudgenoeg-Paz, O., Volman, M. J. M., and Leseman, P. P. M. (2012). Attainment of sitting and walking predicts development of productive vocabulary between ages 16 and 28 months. *Infant Behav. Dev.* 35, 733–736. doi: 10.1016/j.infbeh.2012.07.010

Pruden, S. M., Hirsh-Pasek, K., Maguire, M. J., and Meyer, M. A. (2004). "Foundations of verb learning: Infants form categories of path and manner in motion events," in *Proceedings of the 28th Annual Boston University Conference on Language Development*, (Somerville, MA: Cascadilla press), 461–472.

Rhemtulla, M., and Tucker-Drob, E. M. (2011). Correlated longitudinal changes across linguistic, achievement, and psychomotor domains in early childhood: evidence for a global dimension of development. *Dev. Sci.* 14, 1245–1254. doi: 10.1111/j.1467-7687.2011.01071.x

Rubin, L. H., Witkiewitz, K., St. Andre, J., and Reilly, S. (2007). Methods for handling missing data in the behavioral neurosciences: don't throw the baby rat out with the bath water. *J. Undergrad. Neurosci. Educ.* 5, A71–A77.

Saffran, J. R. (2001). The use of predictive dependencies in language learning. *J. Mem. Lang.* 44, 493–515. doi: 10.1006/jmla.2000.2759

Schafer, J. L., and Graham, J. W. (2002). Missing data: our view of the state of the art. *Psychol. Methods* 7, 147–177. doi: 10.1037//1082-989X.7.2.147

Schuetze, P., Lewis, A., and DiMartino, D. (1999). Relation between time spent in daycare and exploratory behaviors in 9-month-old infants. *Infant Behav. Dev.* 22, 267–276. doi: 10.1016/S0163-6383(99)00006-5

Sheya, A., and Smith, L. B. (2011). "Development through sensorimotor coordination," in *Enaction: Toward a New Paradigm for Cognitive Science*, eds J. Stewart, O. Gapenne, and E. A. Di Paolo (Cambridge, MA: MIT Press), 123–144.

Shi, R., Morgan, J. L., and Allopenna, P. (1998). Phonological and acoustic bases for earliest grammatical category assignment: a cross-linguistic perspective. *J. Child Lang.* 25, 169–201. doi: 10.1017/S0305000997003395

Smith, L. B., and Gasser, M. (2005). The development of embodied cognition: six lessons from babies. *Artif. Life* 11, 13–29. doi: 10.1162/1064546053278973

Soska, K. C., and Adolph, K. E. (2014). Postural position constrains multimodal object exploration in infants. *Infancy* 19, 138–161. doi: 10.1111/infa.12039

Tabachnik, B. G., and Fidell, L. S. (2007). *Using Multivariate Statistics*, 5th Edn. Boston, MA: Allyn and Bacon.

Thelen, E., and Smith, L. B. (1994). *A Dynamic Systems Approach to the Development of Cognition and Action.* Cambridge, MA: MIT Press.

Viholainen, H., Ahonen, T., Lyytinen, P., Cantell, M., Tolvanen, A., and Lyytinen, H. (2006). Early motor development and later language and reading skills in children at risk of familial dyslexia. *Dev. Med. Child Neurol.* 48, 367–373. doi: 10.1017/S001216220600079X

Walle, E., and Campos, J. J. (2014). Infant language development is related to the acquisition of walking. *Dev. Psychol.* 50, 336–348. doi: 10.1037/a0033238

Weisler, A., and McCall, R. R. (1976). Exploration and play: resume and redirection. *Am. Psychol.* 31, 492–508. doi: 10.1037/0003-066X.31.7.492

Wilsenach, A. C. (2006). *Syntactic Processing in Developmental Dyslexia and in Specific Language Impairment: A Study on the Acquisition of the Past Participle Construction in Dutch*. Ph.D. dissertation, NARCIS, The Hague.

Wilson, M. (2002). Six views of embodied cognition. *Psychon. Bull. Rev.* 9, 625–636. doi: 10.3758/BF03196322

Conflict of Interest Statement: The authors declare that the research was conducted in the absence of any commercial or financial relationships that could be construed as a potential conflict of interest.

10

Active Motor Training has Long-term Effects on Infants' Object Exploration

Sarah E. Wiesen[1], Rachel M. Watkins[2] and Amy Work Needham[1]*

[1] Infant Learning Lab, Department of Psychology and Human Development, Peabody College, Vanderbilt University, Nashville, TN, USA, [2] Auditory Development Lab, Department of Hearing and Speech Sciences, Vanderbilt University, Nashville, TN, USA

Long-term changes in infants' behavior as a result of active motor training were studied. Thirty-two infants completed three visits to the laboratory. At the first visit, infants were 3 months old and completed an object exploration assessment. Then the experimenter demonstrated the motor training procedures appropriate for the infant's experimental condition, and parents took home custom infant mittens (either sticky or non-sticky) and a bag of lightweight toys to practice with their infants. Over the course of the following 2 weeks, infants participated in 10 sessions of either active (sticky) or passive (non-sticky) mittens training at home with their parents. Infants who participated in active mittens training wore mittens with the palms covered in Velcro, allowing them to pick up and move around small toys. Infants who participated in passive mittens training wore non-sticky mittens, and their parents moved the toys through their visual fields on their behalf. After completing the training, infants returned to the lab for the second visit. At visit two, infants participated in another object exploration assessment as well as a reaching assessment. Parents returned the training materials to the lab at the second visit, and were told not to continue any specific training regimen from this point forward. Two months later, when infants were about 5.5 months of age, they returned to the lab for a third visit. At the third visit, infants completed the same two assessments as during the second visit. The results of this study indicate that infants who participated in active motor training engaged in more sophisticated object exploration when compared to infants who received passive training. These findings are consistent with others in the literature showing that active motor training at 3 months of age facilitates the processes of object exploration and engagement. The current results and others reveal that the effects of early experience can last long after training ceases.

Keywords: infancy, motor development, early motor intervention, grasping, sticky mittens, object exploration

Edited by:
Petra Hauf,
St. Francis Xavier University, Canada

Reviewed by:
Teresa Mitchell,
University of Massachusetts Medical School, USA
Lana Karasik,
City University of New York, USA

****Correspondence:***
Sarah E. Wiesen
sarah.e.wiesen@vanderbilt.edu

INTRODUCTION

Many years ago, Held and Hein (1963) showed that visually inexperienced kittens learn to guide their actions more effectively after receiving active experience (which they controlled) than they did after receiving passive experience (which they did not control). These classic findings have led many researchers to consider the possibility that visual-motor experience that is controlled and observed by the same individual is critically important for effective learning about moving the body.

One possibility is that infants' learning about how to reach independently is facilitated by observing their own successful actions upon objects. The transition into independent reaching has monumental consequences for infants. Before infants begin reaching, they spend a lot of time on their backs engaging in social interactions (Lobo and Galloway, 2008). Once they begin reaching, infants' opportunities for learning about objects increase dramatically. They begin making purposeful actions on objects and can see the consequences of these action attempts.

Upon successfully contacting objects independently, infants can explore them. Through exploring objects, infants may learn about object properties, such as texture, color, shape, and weight, and about the effects of their own actions on objects (Gibson, 1988; Lederman and Klatzky, 2009). Learning about objects earlier can lead to language learning opportunities as infants learn about objects' similarities, differences, and how objects relate to one another (Lifter and Bloom, 1989; Iverson, 2010; Lobo and Galloway, 2013). Object exploration may also allow infants to learn about object affordances, object categories, and how to use tools to achieve goals. Early object exploration might also influence infants' problem solving abilities. Depth of exploration has been linked with infants' problem solving abilities (Caruso, 1993), so enhancing infants' exploration skills could also boost their problem solving skills.

One question of interest is what motivates infants to attempt to contact and explore objects in their surroundings. A suggested answer to this question, offered many years ago, is that young humans have a drive for competence, which includes understanding the physical objects in their environment (White, 1959; Hunt, 1965). More recently, Von Hofsten (2007) describes two sources of motivation that drive infants' exploration. First, infants find novel objects and events intriguing. Secondly, infants are eager to exercise their new action abilities and find it rewarding to practice their new skills (Berger, 2010; Libertus and Needham, 2014). These factors motivate infants to make repeated efforts to influence their environments. So, manipulating infants' exposure to novel toys or outcomes in response to their actions, or providing early opportunities for infants to practice their action skills may increase infants' motivation to explore.

Prior research has established that 2 weeks of parent-led motor training leads infants to transition into reaching earlier and increases their object exploration skills (Needham et al., 2002; Heathcock et al., 2008; Libertus and Needham, 2010, 2011, 2014). Infants who participated in the active training condition of this early motor intervention began contacting objects and showing increased interest in exploring objects earlier than if they had instead participated in the passive training experience (Libertus and Needham, 2010, 2011, 2014). What features of early motor interventions have led to improvements in infants' early reaching behaviors? Libertus and Needham (2014) examined the role of verbally encouraging infants to contact objects as well as the role of infants' practice physically moving objects. They concluded that both parents' verbal encouragement and practice moving objects themselves are key in promoting the earlier emergence of reaching. Heathcock et al. (2008) found that embedding early motor interventions into infants' and families' daily lives, by showing parents how to facilitate early motor interventions during daily activities with their infants, successfully eliminated the reaching delay that preterm babies are at risk for developing.

The current research utilized sticky mittens training, during which infants wear custom fleece mittens and interact with lightweight toys. In the active training condition, the palms of the mittens are covered in Velcro. Parents present infants with lightweight objects covered in Velcro strips. In the passive training condition, infants' mittens are not covered in Velcro, and parents manipulate the toys on infants' behalf to provide a similar visual experience. Past research found that infants who had 2 weeks of active mittens training showed more visually coordinated swatting motions, alternated between looking and mouthing more frequently, and began reaching earlier (Needham et al., 2002; Libertus and Needham, 2010).

Although prior research has not examined whether there is a lasting impact of mittens training on infants' object exploration, new research has begun to address this question (Libertus et al., in press). In one study, infants who completed 2 weeks of either active or passive mittens training (as described above) at 3 months of age were re-tested 1 year later. The 15-month-old infants who participated in the active mittens training experience a year earlier showed more visual and manual engagement with a toy during a free exploration task than those who had received passive experience a year earlier (Libertus et al., in press).

These results suggest that the sticky mittens training intervention could set in motion a cascade of new learning opportunities; boosting infants' object exploration skills could provide a strong foundation supporting infants' future skills in multiple domains (Bornstein et al., 2013). However, we do not know whether infants' object exploration behaviors show steady improvements throughout the first year of life as a result of active mittens training. Also, the tasks used in the Libertus et al. (in press) study were age appropriate for 15-month-old infants, but they were different from the object exploration tasks used in the original research.

In the current study, we sought to more fully understand the developmental trajectory of this process by probing the effects of active mittens training 2 months after infants concluded mittens training using the same object exploration assessment that has been used in previous research.

MATERIALS AND METHODS

The Institutional Review Board at Vanderbilt University approved all study methods and materials. Parents of all infant participants provided written informed consent prior to their participation in each visit of this study.

Participants

Infants who participated in all three visits of the current study and completed a minimum of 10 sessions of parent-implemented training using either 'sticky mittens' or 'non-sticky mittens' (hereafter referred to as active training or passive training) were included in analyses. Half of the infants were randomly assigned to the active training condition, and the other half was assigned to the passive training condition. Infants completed three visits to the lab when they were approximately 3, 3.5, and 5.5 months of age. Participant characteristics did not differ between the two conditions (see **Table 1**). Data were collected from an additional 14 infants but were excluded from analyses because these infants became fussy during the first visit and were unable to complete the study session.

Training

We designed our training conditions to provide similar experiences in terms of postural experience, exposure to the stimuli, and engaging in social interactions or sharing joint attention with caregivers. Our goal was to determine whether actively moving the toys, in comparison to passively watching a parent move the toys, benefitted infants' object exploration skills. At the first lab visit, all parents were given toys, mittens, and received one-on-one demonstrations and verbal instructions about how to complete either active or passive mittens training with their infants. They also received printed directions describing the training procedure at the conclusion of the first visit. Parents were told that each training session should last approximately 10–12 min, or as long as infants were willing to participate. Parents recorded the dates and durations of training sessions on a log that they returned (along with the toys and mittens) at the second visit to the laboratory

Active Training

Parents first placed mittens on their infants' hands. The palms of the mittens that babies wore in the active training condition were covered in strips of soft Velcro loop. Infants were seated either on adults' laps or in a supported seat (such as a high chair or a well-anchored Bumbo seat) with their arms comfortably resting on a tabletop. Parents were instructed to present one toy at a time to their infants. The toys that infants interacted with in the active training condition were covered in strips of Velcro hook. When infants touched their mittened hands to these toys, the toys stuck to their mittens. Infants were thus able to lift the toys and move them through their visual fields. Each toy was placed within infants' reach. Parents were told to verbally encourage their infants to contact the toys. If infants' contacted the toys, parents removed the toys from the mittens after approximately 10 s.

Passive Training

As in the active training condition, parents first placed mittens on their infants' hands. Unlike in the active training condition, however, the mittens that infants wore in the passive training condition did not have Velcro on them. Instead, the palms of infants' mittens in passive training condition had strips of white ribbons sewn onto them to mimic the appearance of the white strips of Velcro. Likewise, the toys that infants saw in the passive training condition looked very similar to the toys infants interacted with in the active training condition, but the toys used in the passive training condition did not have any Velcro on them. Instead, these toys had strips of electrical tape on them to mimic the appearance of the black strips of Velcro on the toys babies interacted with in the active training condition. The passive training procedure required that parents move the toys to provide a visual experience for their infants that was similar to what infants experienced in active training. Parents were told to move the toys in a semi-circle around their infants' bodies alternating between holding the toy at infants' eye level and on the tabletop, tap the toys on the table to produce sounds, and touch the toys to the palms of their infants' mittened hands. As in the active training condition, infants in the passive training condition only interacted with one toy at a time.

Procedure

All infants included in the final sample completed three visits to our laboratory. The first visit consisted of an object exploration assessment followed by either active or passive mittens training. Between the first and second visits of this study, parents and infants trained at home using the mittens and toys we supplied. Infants returned to the laboratory for their second visit approximately 2 weeks after their first visit. At the second visit, infants participated in the object exploration assessment again, as well as a reaching assessment. The third visit took place approximately 2 months after the second visit. The third visit consisted of the same two measures infants completed at the second visit.

Measures

Object Exploration Assessment

At each of the three visits, infants were presented with a red teether toy (Super Yummy Teether by Discovery Toys) for 30 s. The experimenter attempted to place the teether in infants' hands. If infants dropped the teether before 15 s elapsed the experimenter replaced the teether in the infants' hands. If more than 15 s had elapsed, the experimenter held the teether at the

TABLE 1 | Participant characteristics.

Condition	*N*	Race	Age V1	Age V2	Age V3
Active Training	16 (females = 9)	W = 14 A/W = 1 B = 1	2 m, 20 d (*SD* = 6 d)	3 m, 7 d (*SD* = 10 d)	5 m, 10 d (*SD* = 11 d)
Passive Training	16 (females = 7)	A = 1 W = 14 B = 1	2 m, 21 d (*SD* = 7 d)	3 m, 9 d (*SD* = 5 d)	5 m, 10 d (*SD* = 8 d)

The total number of participants in each group (N) with the number of females per group specified in parentheses is reported in the second column. The number of infants whose parents reported their race as white (W), Asian (A), and black (B) are reported in the third column. Infants' mean ages at visit one (V1), visit two (V2), and visit three (V3) are reported in months (m) and days (d), and the standard deviations are reported in parentheses in columns four through six.

infants' midlines until the conclusion of the assessment. If infants resisted grasping the teether, the experimenter held the teether at infants' midlines throughout the duration of the assessment.

The durations of infants' behaviors were coded by trained observers using frame-by-frame coding software (Libertus, 2008). The following behaviors were assessed: looking (gaze directed toward the teether), touching (manual contact with the teether), reaching (movement of the hand toward the teether), and bimanual exploration (touching the toy with both hands). Two observers coded all of the trials from the three visits using frame-by-frame coding software and overall reliability was high for looking ($ICC = 0.88$), touching ($ICC = 0.99$), reaching ($ICC = 0.86$), and bimanual exploration ($ICC = 0.98$).

Reaching Assessment

At the second and third visits, the experimenter presented infants with a rattle (Sassy Flip and Grip) to assess their reaching skills. During this 2 min assessment, the rattle was moved incrementally closer to infants. In total, the rattle was placed in four positions: out of infants' reach, within infants' reach but far from the infant, within infants' reach and close to them, and in infants' hands. The experimenter placed the rattle in each of these positions for 30 s. Each time she placed the rattle into a new position, the experimenter called the infant's attention to the rattle by looking at it, pointing toward it, and enthusiastically exclaiming "Look! What is this? Do you want this? Can you get it?"

Just as in the assessment of object exploration, the durations of infants' behaviors during the reaching assessment were coded by trained observers using frame-by-frame coding software (Libertus, 2008). Trained research assistants coded for looking, touching, reaching, and bimanual exploration behaviors just like in the assessment of object exploration. Additionally, these research assistants coded infants' grasping (fingers encircling or gripping the toy) during the phase of the reaching assessment when the rattle was placed in the infants' hands. Two observers coded a random sample of trials from each visit using frame-by-frame coding software, and overall reliability was high for looking ($ICC = 0.91$), touching ($ICC = 0.96$), reaching ($ICC = 0.85$), bimanual exploration ($ICC = 0.90$), and grasping ($ICC = 0.99$).

Analysis

Two repeated measures multivariate analyses of variance (MANOVAs) were used to assess changes in infants' behaviors between visits 1 and 2, and visits 1 and 3 during the assessment of object exploration. Visit 1 served as a baseline measure of infants' initial exploration durations, allowing us to measure changes in their behaviors over time. Separate MANOVAS were performed because we hypothesized that bimanual exploration would be minimal at visits 1 and 2 and would increase by visit 3. Thus, our model for testing changes in infants' behaviors from visit 1 to visit 2 measured changes in looking, touching, and reaching, and our model for testing changes in behaviors from visit 1 to visit 3 included looking, touching, reaching, and bimanual exploration.

Repeated measures MANOVAs were also used to assess changes in infants' behaviors between visit 2 and visit 3 during the three phases (out of reach, within reach, and in hand) of the reaching assessment. Since we were testing for changes in different dependent variables during each phase of this assessment, we used three separate repeated measures MANOVAS. Partial eta-squared (η_p^2), a measure of effect size, is reported for all MANOVAs. *T*-tests were performed for follow-up analyses. Difference scores were calculated by subtracting the duration of infants' behaviors at earlier visits from the durations of their behaviors at later visits. Cohen's d (*d*) was calculated for all follow up analyses.

RESULTS

Object Exploration Assessment

We used a repeated measures MANOVA to assess potential differences in infants' exploration behaviors in each condition at visit 1 and visit 2. Visit (first or second) was entered as a within-subject factor, and condition (active or passive) was entered as a between-subject factor. Three dependent variables, all of which were durations of exploration behaviors, were tested: looking, touching, and reaching.

The analysis comparing visits 1 and 2 showed no significant differences.

A second analysis assessed changes from visit 1 to visit 3 in four dependent variables: looking, touching, reaching, and bimanual exploration. Visit (first or third) was entered as a within-subject factor, and condition (active or passive) was entered as a between-subject factor.

This MANOVA revealed a main effect of visit on infant' looking behaviors, $F(1,29) = 6.08$, $p = 0.020$, $\eta_p^2 = 0.173$. Across both groups, on average infants looked less at the teether at visit 3 ($M_{V3} = 14.17$, $SD_{V3} = 8.22$) compared to visit 1 ($M_{V1} = 18.85$, $SD_{V1} = 10.72$). The main effect of condition was non-significant [$F(1,29) = 0.071$, $p = 0.792$, $\eta_p^2 = 0.002$], but there was a significant interaction between visit and condition, $F(1,29) = 9.88$, $p = 0.004$, $\eta_p^2 = 0.254$. Planned comparisons revealed that infants who participated in passive training ($M_{V1} = 21.71$, $SD_{V1} = 8.15$, $M_{V3} = 10.60$, $SD_{V3} = 7.2$), significantly decreased their looking toward the teether from visit 1 to visit 3, $t(14) = -3.69$, $p = 0.002$, 95% CI [-17.57, -4.65], $d = -1.97$. In contrast, infants in the active training condition ($M_{V1} = 16.18$, $SD_{V1} = 12.32$, $M_{V3} = 17.52$, $SD_{V3} = 7.86$) maintained the same amount of looking toward the teether from visit 1 to visit 3, $t(15) = 0.52$, $p = 0.613$, 95 % CI [-4.19, 6.87], $d = 0.27$.

This MANOVA also revealed a significant main effect of visit on the durations of infants' touching behaviors, $F(1,29) = 199.61$, $p < 0.001$, $\eta_p^2 = 0.873$. Across both training conditions, infants tended to touch the teether more at visit 3 ($M_{V3} = 22.54$, $SD_{V3} = 8.15$) than at visit 1 ($M_{V1} = 3.02$, $SD_{V1} = 4.84$). The main effect of condition was non-significant [$F(1,29) = 0.055$, $p = 0.816$, $\eta_p^2 = 0.002$], but again we found a significant interaction between visit and condition, $F(1,29) = 7.96$, $p = 0.009$, $\eta_p^2 = 0.215$. Planned comparisons showed that infants in the active training condition [$M_{V1} = 1.36$, $SD_{V1} = 3.17$, $M_{V3} = 24.63$, $SD_{V3} = 5.92$, $t(15) = 15.04$, $p < 0.001$, 95% CI [19.97, 26.57], $d = 4.82$] as well as the passive training condition [$M_{V1} = 4.78$, $SD_{V1} = 5.75$, $M_{V3} = 20.31$, $SD_{V3} = 9.73$, $t(14) = 6.72, p < 0.001$, 95% CI [10.57, 20.47], $d = 1.85$] increased their durations of touching the teether from visit 1 to visit 3. However, this increase in durations of touching from visit 1 to visit 3 was larger among infants in the active condition compared to the passive condition.

The main effect of visit on infants' reaching behaviors was non-significant, $F(1,29) = 0.031$, $p = 0.861$, $\eta_p^2 = 0.001$. We did find a significant main effect of condition on reaching behaviors, $F(1,29) = 7.39$, $p = 0.011$, $\eta_p^2 = 0.237$. Across both visits, infants in the passive condition ($M = 4.56$, $SD = 4.87$) spent more time reaching for the teether than infants in the active condition ($M = 2.06$, $SD = 2.55$). The interaction between visit and condition was non-significant, $F(1,29) = 1.78$, $p = 0.193$, $\eta_p^2 = 0.058$. In light of our pattern of findings that infants in the active condition increased the amount of time they spent touching the teether from visit 1 to visit 3 more than infants in the passive condition, we interpret these reaching findings to show that infants in the passive condition spent more time struggling to attain the teether at visit 3 whereas infants in the active condition appear to have more successfully maintained manual contact with the teether.

Lastly, we found a significant main effect of visit on infants' bimanual behaviors, $F(1,29) = 49.24$, $p < 0.001$, $\eta_p^2 = 0.629$. Across conditions, infants tended to engage in more bimanual actions at visit 3 ($M_{V3} = 11.35$, $SD_{V3} = 10.07$) as compared to visit 1 ($M_{V1} = 0.03$, $SD_{V1} = 0.14$). We also found a significant main effect of condition on infants' bimanual behaviors [$F(1,29) = 9.00$, $p = 0.005$, $\eta_p^2 = 0.237$], with infants in the active condition engaging in greater durations of bimanual behaviors across visits 1 and 3 ($M = 7.97$, $SD = 10.61$) than infants in the passive training condition ($M = 3.25$, $SD = 6.52$). The interaction between visit and condition was significant as well, $F(1,29) = 9.12, p = 0.005, \eta_p^2 = 0.239$. Planned comparisons showed that infants in the active condition [$M_{V1} = 0.00$, $SD_{V1} = 0.00$, $M_{V3} = 15.94$, $SD_{V3} = 9.85$, $t(15) = 6.47$, $p < 0.001$, 95% CI [10.69, 21.19], $d = 2.29$] as well as the passive condition [$M_{V1} = 0.05$, $SD_{V1} = 0.21$, $M_{V3} = 6.45$, $SD_{V3} = 7.97$, $t(14) = 3.09, p = 0.008$, 95% CI [1.95, 10.83], $d = 1.25$] increased their durations of bimanual engagement from visit 1 to visit 3, but this increase was greater among infants in the active condition. In short, infants engaged in very little bimanual actions at visit 1, but quite a lot at visit 3. At visit 3 the infants in the active training condition outperformed infants in the passive training condition in terms of performing greater durations of bimanual actions.

Reaching Assessment

The reaching assessment was analyzed in three parts: Looking and reaching were assessed when the rattle was out of infants' reach; looking, reaching, grasping, touching, and bimanual exploration were all assessed during the combined portions of the assessment where the rattle was within infants' reach; looking, grasping, touching, and bimanual exploration were assessed during the portion of the assessment when the rattle was placed in infants' hands.

During phase 1, the rattle was purposely placed outside of infants' reach for 30 s. Thus, we did not analyze infants' touching, grasping, or bimanual actions during this phase of the reaching assessment. Rather, we limited our analyses of the first phase to looking and reaching behaviors.

In terms of infants' looking behaviors, the main effect of visit was non-significant, $F(1,30) = 0.03$, $p = 0.873$, $\eta_p^2 = 0.001$. We did find a significant main effect of condition, $F(1,30) = 21.64$, $p < 0.001$, $\eta_p^2 = 0.419$. Across visits 2 and 3, infants in the active condition ($M = 14.73$, $SD = 9.06$) tended to look more at the rattle during phase 1 when the rattle was outside of their reach compared to the passive condition ($M = 7.08$, $SD = 5.90$). The interaction between visit and condition was non-significant, $F(1,30) = 0.25, p = 0.618, \eta_p^2 = 0.008$.

The main effect of visit on infants' durations of reaching was significant, $F(1,30) = 2.98$, $p = 0.095$, $\eta_p^2 = 0.090$. Across both training conditions, infants reaching behaviors increased from visit 2 ($M = 2.57$, $SD = 3.58$) to visit 3 when the rattle was placed out of reach. The main effect of condition [$F(1,30) = 0.048$, $p = 0.828$, $\eta_p^2 = 0.002$], and the interaction between visit and condition were both non-significant, $F(1,30) = 0.04$, $p = 0.836$, $\eta_p^2 = 0.001$.

During the second phase of the reaching assessment, the rattle was placed in two positions within infants' reach. We combined these two 30-s phases of this assessment, and we used another repeated measures MANOVA to analyze the changes in durations of infants' looking, touching, reaching, and grasping behaviors during this portion of the assessment from visit 2 to visit 3.

This MANOVA showed a marginally significant main effect of visit on infants' looking durations, $F(1,30) = 4.03, p = 0.054$, $\eta_p^2 = 0.118$. At visit 2 ($M_{V2} = 31.29$, $SD_{V2} = 15.09$) infants tended to look less at the rattle compared to during visit 3 ($M_{V3} = 38.17$, $SD_{V3} = 13.26$). There was a significant main effect of condition on infants' looking behaviors, $F(1,30) = 10.48$, $p = 0.003$, $\eta_p^2 = 0.259$. Averaged across both visits, infants in the active condition ($M = 39.91$, $SD = 14.99$) tended to look more at the rattle during the second phase of the reaching assessment compared to infants in the passive training condition ($M = 29.5$, $SD = 12.12$). The interaction between visit and condition was non-significant, $F(1,30) = 0.65, p = 0.428, \eta_p^2 = 0.021$.

The main effect of visit on infants' durations of touching was significant, $F(1,30) = 64.43$, $p < 0.001$, $\eta_p^2 = 0.682$. Across both conditions, infants tended to touch the rattle more when it was within reach at visit 3 ($M_{V3} = 30.75$, $SD_{V3} = 15.24$) as compared to visit 2 ($M_{V2} = 8.28$, $SD_{V2} = 7.99$). The main effect of condition was also significant, $F(1,30) = 5.58, p = 0.025$, $\eta_p^2 = 0.157$. Infants in the active training condition ($M = 23.03$, $SD = 19.19$) tended to touch the rattle for greater durations across the two visits compared to infants in the passive training condition ($M = 16.00$, $SD = 12.77$). The interaction between visit and condition was marginally significant, $F(1,30) = 3.08$, $p = 0.089$, $\eta_p^2 = 0.093$. Infants in both the active [$M_{V2} = 9.34$, $SD_{V2} = 7.57, M_{V3} = 36.73, SD_{V3} = 17.35, t(15) = 5.94, p < 0.001$, 95% CI [17.56, 37.22], $d = 2.01$] and passive training conditions [$M_{V2} = 7.23$, $SD_{V2} = 8.34$, $M_{V3} = 24.78$, $SD_{V3} = 10.16$, $t(15) = 5.53, p < 0.001$, 95% CI [10.79, 24.33], $d = 1.89$] increased their durations of touching behaviors from the first to the second visit, with this pattern being more pronounced among the infants with active training.

This MANOVA revealed a significant main effect of visit on infants' durations of reaching, $F(1,30) = 8.45$, $p = 0.007$, $\eta_p^2 = 0.220$. Infants, overall, tended to reach more at the second visit ($M_{V2} = 8.93$, $SD_{V2} = 8.55$) as opposed to the third visit ($M_{V3} = 4.22$, $SD_{V3} = 3.77$). Infants may have experienced greater success in attaining the rattle during this portion of the reaching assessment at visit 3 compared to at visit 2. The main effect of condition [$F(1,30) = 1.10$, $p = 0.303$, $\eta_p^2 = 0.035$] and the interaction between visit and condition were non-significant [$F(1,30) = 1.17$, $p = 0.289$, $\eta_p^2 = 0.037$].

The fourth dependent variable analyzed by this MANOVA was durations of infants' grasping behaviors from visit 2 to visit 3. There was a significant main effect of visit, $F(1,30) = 69.33$, $p < 0.001$, $\eta_p^2 = 0.698$. As a whole, infants grasped the rattle much more at visit 3 ($M_{V3} = 24.81$, $SD_{V3} = 15.39$) than at visit 2 ($M_{V2} = 2.71$, $SD_{V2} = 5.69$). The main effect of condition was also significant, $F(1,30) = 9.57$, $p = 0.004$, $\eta_p^2 = 0.242$. Across the two visits, infants in the active condition ($M = 17.80$, $SD = 19.17$) tended to engage in greater durations of grasping than infants in the passive condition ($M = 9.71$, $SD = 10.95$). Finally, we found a significant interaction between visit and condition, $F(1,30) = 5.56$, $p = 0.025$, $\eta_p^2 = 0.156$. Planned comparisons revealed that infants in the active condition [$M_{V2} = 3.63$, $SD_{V2} = 7.56$, $M_{V3} = 31.98$, $SD_{V3} = 16.53$, $t(15) = 6.14$, $p < 0.001$, 95% *CI* [18.51, 38.21], $d = 2.22$], as well as the passive condition [$M_{V2} = 1.79$, $SD_{V2} = 2.82$, $M_{V3} = 17.63$, $SD_{V3} = 10.30$, $t(15) = 6.07$, $p = < 0.001$, 95% *CI* [10.28, 21.40], $d = 2.04$] increased their durations of grasping from visit 2 to visit 3, but this increase was significantly greater among infants in the active training condition.

A third repeated measures MANOVA analyzed infants' exploration behaviors during the third portion of the reaching assessment, when the rattle was placed in infants' grasp. Looking, touching, grasping, and bimanual actions were entered as dependent variables in this MANOVA. We did not include reaching as a dependent variable because for the most part, the rattle very close to or held in infants' hands.

We found a marginally significant main effect of visit on infants' looking behaviors, $F(1,27) = 3.01$, $p = 0.094$, $\eta_p^2 = 0.100$. Across both conditions, infants looked more at visit 3 ($M_{V3} = 18.63$, $SD_{V3} = 8.50$) than at visit 2 ($M_{V2} = 14.11$, $SD_{V2} = 11.77$). The main effect of condition was non-significant, $F(1,27) = 2.54$, $p = 0.123$, $\eta_p^2 = 0.086$, but the interaction between visit and condition was marginally significant, $F(1,27) = 3.05$, $p = 0.092$, $\eta_p^2 = 0.101$. Infants in the active condition significantly increased their durations of looking from visit 2 ($M_{V2} = 13.87$, $SD_{V2} = 11.04$) to visit 3 [$M_{V3} = 22.64$, $SD_{V3} = 8.09$), $t(14) = 2.99$, $p = 0.010$, 95% *CI* [2.48, 15.06], $d = 0.89$]. In comparison, infants in the passive training condition maintained nearly identical durations of looking from visit 2 ($M_{V2} = 14.36$, $SD_{V2} = 12.92$) to visit 3 [$M_{V3} = 14.34$, $SD_{V3} = 6.84$, $t(13) = -0.01$, $p = 0.994$, 95% *CI* [−9.02,8.96], $d = -0.003$].

The main effects of visit [$F(1,27) = 1.62$, $p = 0.215$, $\eta_p^2 = 0.056$], condition [$F(1,27) = 1.98$, $p = 0.171$, $\eta_p^2 = 0.068$], and the interaction between visit and condition [$F(1,27) = 0.20$, $p = 0.659$, $\eta_p^2 = 0.007$] for touching behaviors were all non-significant. Similarly, the main effects of visit [$F(1,27) = 0.73$, $p = 0.400$, $\eta_p^2 = 0.026$], condition [$F(1,27) = 2.54$, $p = 0.123$, $\eta_p^2 = 0.086$], and the interaction between visit and condition [$F(1,27) = 0.77$, $p = 0.287$, $\eta_p^2 = 0.028$] were non-significant for infants' grasping behaviors.

Finally, we found a main effect of visit on infants' bimanual exploration behaviors, $F(1,27) = 8.12$, $p = 0.008$, $\eta_p^2 = 0.231$. Infants, across the active and passive training conditions, performed longer durations of bimanual exploration at the third visit ($M_{V3} = 12.49$, $SD_{V3} = 9.95$) compared to the second visit ($M_{V2} = 5.19$, $SD_{V2} = 8.19$). The main effect of condition [$F(1,27) = 0.38$, $p = 0.543$, $\eta_p^2 = 0.014$] and the interaction between visit and condition were both non-significant, $F(1,27) = 0.09$, $p = 0.771$, $\eta_p^2 = 0.003$.

DISCUSSION

The current study examined how active and passive mittens training affected infants' exploration behaviors immediately following and 2 months after 2 weeks of parent-led training sessions. Recent findings provide evidence that 2 weeks of active mittens training positively affected infants' visual and manual engagement with a wooden tabletop bead maze toy and parents' ratings of their children's attention spans using the Early Childhood Behavior Questionnaire (ECBQ; Putnam et al., 2006) 12 months after training concluded (Libertus et al., in press). The current study helps to illuminate how mittens training influences infants' motor skills during the interim period, 2 months after the conclusion of training. Because the measures in the current study were designed for 5-month-old infants and the measures in the Libertus et al. (in press) study were designed for 15-month-old infants, these two sets of results cannot be directly compared. Despite this fact, the findings from these two studies are quite consistent with each other. Both studies show evidence of increased visual and manual contact with objects for infants who participated in active mittens experience, compared to those who participated in passive mittens experience. The findings from the current study also indicate that the effect of active mittens training increases between the second and third visits, consistent with a cascading or 'snowballing' effect.

In contrast to our expectations and our prior findings, we did not find differences in infants' exploration patterns between the two training groups immediately after training concluded. We believe this lack of an effect stemmed from a small difference in the procedure we used to conduct the object exploration task in the immediate post-training session. Specifically, the object exploration trial was only 30 s long instead of 60 s long as it was in our prior research. Our attempt to streamline the procedure may have diminished the differences between the training conditions on this measure.

Two months after the end of training, however, we found several differences in infants' exploration behaviors, with longer durations of exploration behaviors among infants who had participated in active as opposed to passive mittens training

(See **Figure 1**). This pattern of findings supports the idea of a developmental cascade because the effects of mittens training became more substantial over time. First, in our object exploration assessment, infants who participated in active mittens training showed significantly larger increases in looking and bimanual exploration, and they showed different patterns of reaching between visits one and three as compared to their peers who participated in passive mittens training.

Second, infants who participated in active mittens training 2 months earlier showed significantly greater increases in grasping (see **Figure 2**) and marginally significant increases in touching and looking behaviors in this assessment. Together, these results indicate that active mittens training positively affected infants' object exploration skills and their motivation to explore. Although these differences between the groups were not noticeable immediately after training, the benefits of active mittens training became more substantial over time.

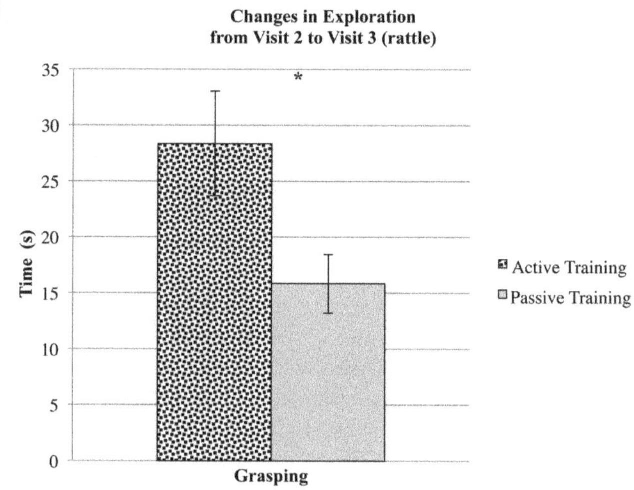

FIGURE 2 | All infants grasped the rattle for significantly longer at visit 3 compared to visit 2, but this increase was larger for infants who participated in active training compared to infants who participated in passive training. Asterisks indicate significant differences ($p < 0.05$).

Object Exploration

These results are consistent with the idea that boosting infants' object exploration skills has cascading effects across development. One reason we make this conclusion is that the differences between our active and passive training groups became more pronounced over time. This pattern of results is consistent with the idea that the infants' abilities continue to build over time. A second reason we consider a developmental cascade a good model for our findings is that the active training procedure did not 'train up' the specific actions we coded in our testing assessments. Because there is not an obvious causal connection between the training procedures and the test measures that improved after training, it suggests to us that there could be some intervening factors that we do not yet know about.

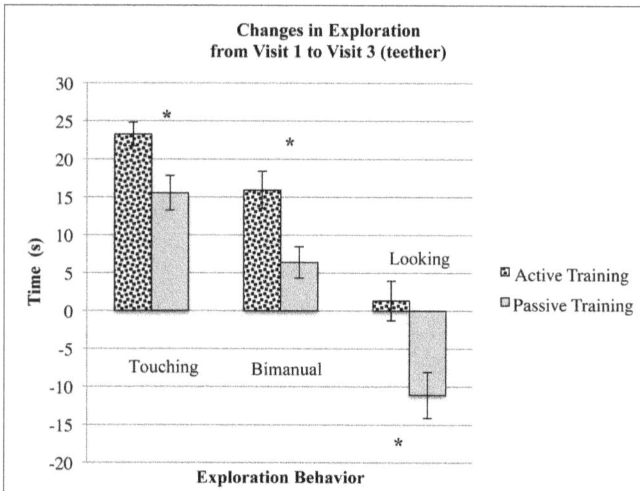

FIGURE 1 | Infants who participated in active mittens training increased their durations of touching and bimanually exploring the teether between visit 1 and visit 3 significantly more than their peers who participated in passive mittens training at 3 months of age. Infants who participated in passive training engaged in similar amounts of looking toward the teether at visits 1 and 3, while infants who participated in passive training looked significantly less at the teether during visit 3. Asterisks indicate significant differences ($p < 0.05$).

For example, our results indicate that active mittens training leads to increases in infants' bimanual object exploration. Bimanual exploration is initially used as infants transport objects to their mouths for oral exploration. Oral exploration can help infants to glean information about object properties such as texture, shape, and affordances (Rochat, 1987). More experience detecting objects' affordances may increase infants' awareness of the properties of objects. Later, bimanual exploration is linked with infants' role differentiated bimanual manipulations in which they use one hand to stabilize the object and their other hand to act on the object (Rochat, 1989; Nelson et al., 2013). Using two hands to explore an object may allow infants to engage in more kinds of actions on the object and garner more information about the object than they can when using only one hand. The development of sophisticated exploration techniques expands learning opportunities available to infants. Object exploration skills may also be linked to infants' perceptions of their surroundings. Baumgartner and Oakes (2013) found that infants who showed more advanced exploratory behaviors were more successful in detecting changes in object properties during a dynamic event. More experience detecting objects' affordances should increase infants' awareness of the properties of objects.

Object exploration skills may serve as a foundation for later skills. Many longitudinal studies have shown that motor development during infancy can be predictive of later outcomes (Bornstein et al., 2013; Bornstein, 2014). Research suggests that babies with more sophisticated motor skills during early infancy might have increased attention spans (Friedman et al., 2005) and engage in more advanced symbolic play as young children (Tamis-LeMonda and Bornstein, 1993).

Motor development at 5 months has been linked to academic outcomes among teenagers (Bornstein et al., 2013). Based on these findings, one might expect that sticky mittens training, by boosting 5-month-old infants' object exploration skills, might have cascading effects across development. Indeed, there are other recently reported findings that provide evidence of differences in 15-month-old infants' object engagement depending upon whether they had received active or passive mittens training 1 year earlier (Libertus et al., in press).

Implications

During active mittens training, parents spent a great deal of time encouraging their infants to make contact with objects and cheering them on when they were successful in doing so. It is likely that this parent–child experience contributed to the benefits in infants' motor skills evidenced in the current study. Interventions that are confined to laboratories or clinics might not have as large of an impact on infants' behaviors because they are not imbedded in infants' daily lives and familial relationships. Research shows that when parents are able to incorporate early motor interventions into daily activities with their infants, outcomes tend to be more positive (Mahoney and Perales, 2006). A review by Hadders-Algra (2013) reiterates this point by recommending that parents need to be involved in offering opportunities for successful reaching among children who are at risk for reaching delays. For example, they suggest that parents ensure their babies have adequate postural support by using cushions or holding their babies' midsections to make reaching easier for them. Parents spend a great deal of time with their infants, and they therefore are capable of (a) implementing interventions in a wider variety of contexts and settings, and (b) scaffolding their infants' experiences in these settings, both of which would be helpful in promoting infants' learning.

Active mittens training may prove to be a successful intervention for infants who are at risk for reaching delays. For example, promising findings suggest that infants who are at risk for developing autism showed increased grasping behaviors after participating in active mittens training (Libertus and Landa, 2014). It is yet to be explored whether infants at risk reaching delays due to factors such as prematurity or Down syndrome might also benefit from this early motor intervention. Fortunately, active mittens training is inexpensive, the training materials can be easily transported, and short training sessions (10–20 min a day) are recommended. For these reasons, the parents of infants who are at risk for reaching delays might find this early motor intervention appealing.

Limitations

Several limitations in the design and interpretation of this study should be acknowledged. The participants in this study are mostly of Caucasian ethnicity and members of a high socio-economic group (as measured by parental education and occupation). Our findings are also based on a small sample size. Additionally, infants whose parents were unable to complete the minimum amount of training and infants who did not return for each of the three laboratory visits were excluded from analyses.

All infants who participated in our study took part in an at-home training regimen. It could therefore be argued that this study does not include a true control condition. However, past research with sticky mittens has compared infants with active training to infants with no training experience (Needham et al., 2002). This study found that infants with active mittens training showed greater object exploration skills compared to their peers without training.

We did not take measures to ensure that parents adhered to training protocol. Parents were responsible for completing a log detailing the frequency and duration of mittens training sessions with their infants. While we are unable to confirm that parents were honest in reporting their training or that they strictly followed the directions we provided, our results indicate that the experiences of infants in the two training conditions led to differing exploration skills. Thus, we feel confident that parents indeed followed training protocol.

While the findings of this study may appear to conflict with prior published research showing immediate benefits of active mittens training once training concludes (Needham et al., 2002; Libertus and Needham, 2010; Libertus and Landa, 2014), we think that this discrepancy is most likely because of subtle differences in our pre- and post-training assessments. Needham et al. (2002) used an identical red teether during pre- and post-training assessments, but infants were given the opportunity to explore the teether for 1 min during four separate trials. In the current study, infants were only permitted to explore the teether for 30 s during pre- and post-training assessments. This shorter duration of measures may have prevented us from detecting significant differences in the exploration behaviors among our training conditions. Similarly, Libertus and Needham (2010) found significant differences among active and passive mittens training conditions, but pre- and post-training assessments were each 2 min long, whereas in the current study infants' pre- and post-training assessments were much shorter. Infants in Libertus and Needham (2010) were also reaching for a rattle that was moved closer to them during four sequential phases of the pre- and post-training assessments rather than exploring a teether that was placed in their grasps. Libertus and Landa (2014) used an abbreviated, 1-min long, version of the pre- and post-training assessments with infants reaching for a rattle used in Libertus and Needham (2010). Procedural differences in pre- and post-training assessments may therefore help to explain this apparent inconsistency in findings between prior studies and the current study.

CONCLUSION

The results of the current study suggest that active mittens training provides an opportunity for pre-reaching infants to actively engage with objects through reaching and grasping, thus facilitating their early motor development. Two months after the conclusion of this early motor intervention, infants who participated in active mittens training showed increased object exploration skills, engaging in complex object engagement patterns such as bilateral exploration, compared to their peers who participated in passive mittens training. We interpret these findings as evidence that early motor experience through active mittens training motivates infants to begin practicing their reaching and grasping, which leads to improvements in their object exploration skills. By drawing parents' attention to their infants' motor achievements, it is likely that parents may encourage their infants' efforts and provide more opportunities for their infants to practice their new motor skills. Future research will examine how such increases in object exploration skills relate to later outcomes, such as language development, tool use, and attention span.

AUTHOR CONTRIBUTIONS

SW analyzed the data and wrote the manuscript. RW completed data collection and did preliminary analyses and helped write the manuscript. AWN designed the study, oversaw data collection, contributed to writing the manuscript, and provided funding for this research.

ACKNOWLEDGMENTS

Grant R01-HD057120 from the NICHD to AWN supported this research. This material is based upon work supported by the National Science Foundation Graduate Research Fellowship under Grant No. (DGE-1445197). Any opinion, findings, and conclusions or recommendations expressed in this material are those of the authors(s) and do not necessarily reflect the views of the National Science Foundation.

REFERENCES

Baumgartner, H. A., and Oakes, L. M. (2013). Investigating the relation between infants' manual activity with objects and their perception of dynamic events. *Infancy* 18, 983–1006. doi: 10.1111/infa.12009

Berger, S. E. (2010). Locomotor expertise predicts infants' perseverative errors. *Dev. Psychol.* 46, 326–336. doi: 10.1037/a0018285

Bornstein, M. H. (2014). Human infancy and the rest of the lifespan. *Annu. Rev. Psychol.* 65, 121–158. doi: 10.1146/annurev-psych-120710-100359

Bornstein, M. H., Hahn, C.-S., and Suwalsky, J. T. D. (2013). Physically developed and exploratory young infants contribute to their own long-term academic achievement. *Psychol. Sci.* 24, 1906–1917. doi: 10.1177/0956797613479974

Caruso, D. (1993). Dimensions of quality in infants' exploratory behavior?: relationships to problem-solving ability. *Infant Behav. Dev.* 16, 441–454. doi: 10.1016/0163-6383(93)80003-Q

Friedman, A. H., Watamura, S. E., and Robertson, S. S. (2005). Movement-attention coupling in infancy and attention problems in childhood. *Dev. Med. Child Neurol* 47, 660–665. doi: 10.1111/j.1469-8749.2005.tb01050.x

Gibson, E. J. (1988). Exploratory behavior in the development of perceiving, acting, and the acquiring of knowledge. *Annu. Rev. Psychol.* 39, 1–41. doi: 10.1146/annurev.ps.39.020188.000245

Hadders-Algra, M. (2013). Typical and atypical development of reaching and postural control in infancy. *Dev. Med. Child Neurol.* 55(Suppl. 4), 5–8. doi: 10.1111/dmcn.12298

Heathcock, J. C., Lobo, M., and Galloway, J. C. C. (2008). Movement training advances the emergence of reaching in infants born at less than 33 weeks of gestational age: a randomized clinical trial. *Phys. Ther.* 88, 310–322. doi: 10.2522/ptj.20070145

Held, R., and Hein, A. (1963). Movement-produced stimulation in the development of visually guided behaviors. *J. Comp. Physiol. Psychol.* 56, 872–876. doi: 10.1037/h0040546

Hunt, J. (1965). "Intrinsic motivation and its role in psychological development," in *Nebraska Symposium on Motivation*, ed. M. Levine (Lincoln: University of Nebraska Press), 189–282.

Iverson, J. M. (2010). Developing language in a developing body: the relationship between motor development and language development. *J. Child Lang.* 37, 229–261. doi: 10.1017/S0305000909990432

Lederman, S. J., and Klatzky, R. L. (2009). Haptic perception: a tutorial. *Attent. Percept. Psychophys.* 71, 1439–1459. doi: 10.3758/APP.71.7.1439

Libertus, K. (2008). *Stop Frame Coding (Version 0.9) [Coding Software]*. Durham, NC.

Libertus, K., Joh, A. S., and Needham, A. (in press). Motor training at 3 months affects object exploration 12 months later. *Dev. Sci.* doi: 10.1111/desc.12370

Libertus, K., and Landa, R. J. (2014). Scaffolded reaching experiences encourage grasping activity in infants at high risk for autism. *Front. Psychol.* 5:1071. doi: 10.3389/fpsyg.2014.01071

Libertus, K., and Needham, A. (2010). Teach to reach: the effects of active vs. passive reaching experiences on action and perception. *Vis. Res.* 50, 2750–2757. doi: 10.1016/j.visres.2010.09.001

Libertus, K., and Needham, A. (2011). Reaching experience increases face preference in 3-month-old infants. *Dev. Sci.* 14, 1355–1364. doi: 10.1111/j.1467-7687.2011.01084.x

Libertus, K., and Needham, A. (2014). Encouragement is nothing without control: factors influencing the development of reaching and face preference. *J. Motor Learn. Dev.* 2, 16–27. doi: 10.1123/jmld.2013-0019

Lifter, K., and Bloom, L. (1989). Object knowledge and the emergence of language. *Infant Behav. Dev.* 12, 395–423. doi: 10.1016/0163-6383(89)90023-4

Lobo, M. A., and Galloway, J. C. (2008). Postural and object-oriented experiences advance early reaching, object exploration, and means-end behavior. *Child Dev.* 79, 1869–1890. doi: 10.1111/j.1467-8624.2008.01231.x

Lobo, M. A., and Galloway, J. C. (2013). The onset of reaching significantly impacts how infants explore both objects and their bodies. *Infant Behav. Dev.* 36, 14–24. doi: 10.1016/j.infbeh.2012.09.003

Mahoney, G., and Perales, F. (2006). The role of parents in early motor intervention. *Down Syndrome Res. Pract.* 10, 67–73. doi: 10.3104/reviews.307

Needham, A., Barrett, T., and Peterman, K. (2002). A pick-me-up for infants' exploratory skills: early stimulated experiences reaching for objects using 'sticky mittens' enhances young infants' object exploration skills. *Infant Behav. Dev.* 25, 279–295. doi: 10.1016/S0163-6383(02)00097-8

Nelson, E. L., Campbell, J. M., and Michel, G. F. (2013). Early handedness in infancy predicts language ability in toddlers. *Dev. Psychol.* 50, 809–814. doi: 10.1037/a0033803

Putnam, S. P., Gartstein, M. A., and Rothbart, M. K. (2006). Measurement of finegrained aspects of toddler temperament: the early childhood behavior questionnaire. *Infant Behav. Dev.* 29, 386–401. doi: 10.1016/j.infbeh.2006.01.004

Rochat, P. (1987). Mouthing and grasping in neonates: evidence for the early detection of what hard or soft substances afford for action. *Infant Behav. Dev.* 10, 435–449. doi: 10.1016/0163-6383(87)90041-5

Rochat, P. (1989). Object manipulation and exploration in 2- to 5-month-old infants. *Dev. Psychol.* 25, 871–884. doi: 10.1037/0012-1649.25.6.871

Tamis-LeMonda, C. S., and Bornstein, M. H. (1993). Antecedents of exploratory competence at one year. *Infant Behav. Dev.* 16, 423–439. doi: 10.1016/0163-6383(93)80002-P

Von Hofsten, C. (2007). Action in development. *Dev. Sci.* 10, 54–60. doi: 10.1111/j.1467-7687.2007.00564.x

White, R. W. (1959). Motivation reconsidered: the concept of competence. *Psychol. Rev.* 66, 297–333. doi: 10.1037/h0040934

Conflict of Interest Statement: The authors declare that the research was conducted in the absence of any commercial or financial relationships that could be construed as a potential conflict of interest.

11

Emerging Executive Functioning and Motor Development in Infants at High and Low Risk for Autism Spectrum Disorder

Tanya St. John[1,2], Annette M. Estes[1,2], Stephen R. Dager[2,3], Penelope Kostopoulos[4], Jason J. Wolff[5], Juhi Pandey[6], Jed T. Elison[7], Sarah J. Paterson[6], Robert T. Schultz[6], Kelly Botteron[8], Heather Hazlett[9,10] and Joseph Piven[9,10]*

[1] Speech and Hearing Sciences, University of Washington, Seattle, WA, USA, [2] UW Autism Center, Center on Human Development and Disability, University of Washington, Seattle, WA, USA, [3] Department of Radiology, University of Washington, Seattle, WA, USA, [4] McConnell Brain Imaging Centre, Montreal Neurological Institute, Montreal, CA, USA, [5] Department of Educational Psychology, University of Minnesota, Minneapolis, MN, USA, [6] Department of Pediatrics, The Center for Autism Research, Children's Hospital of Philadelphia, University of Pennsylvania, Philadelphia, PA, USA, [7] Institute of Child Development, University of Minnesota, Minneapolis, MN, USA, [8] Department of Psychiatry, Washington University School of Medicine, Saint Louis, MO, USA, [9] Carolina Institute for Developmental Disabilities, Chapel Hill, NC, USA, [10] Department of Psychiatry, University of North Carolina, Chapel Hill, NC

Edited by:
Klaus Libertus,
University of Pittsburgh, USA

Reviewed by:
Yoshifumi Ikeda,
Joetsu University of Education, Japan
Meghan Miller,
UC Davis MIND Institute, USA

***Correspondence:**
Tanya St. John
tstjohn@uw.edu

Existing evidence suggests executive functioning (EF) deficits may be present in children with autism spectrum disorder (ASD) by 3 years of age. It is less clear when, prior to 3 years, EF deficits may emerge and how EF unfold over time. The contribution of motor skill difficulties to poorer EF in children with ASD has not been systematically studied. We investigated the developmental trajectory of EF in infants at high and low familial risk for ASD (HR and LR) and the potential associations between motor skills, diagnostic group, and EF performance. Participants included 186 HR and 76 LR infants. EF (A-not-B), motor skills (Fine and Gross Motor), and cognitive ability were directly assessed at 12 months and 24 months of age. Participants were directly evaluated for ASD at 24 months using DSM-IV-TR criteria and categorized as HR-ASD, HR-Negative, and LR-Negative. HR-ASD and HR-Negative siblings demonstrated less improvement in EF over time compared to the LR-Negative group. Motor skills were associated with group and EF performance at 12 months. No group differences were found at 12 months, but at 24 months, the HR-ASD and HR-Negative groups performed worse than the LR-Negative group overall after controlling for visual reception and maternal education. On reversal trials, the HR-ASD group performed worse than the LR-Negative group. Motor skills were associated with group and EF performance on reversal trials at 24 months. Findings suggest that HR siblings demonstrate altered EF development and that motor skills may play an important role in this process.

Keywords: executive functioning, autism, high-risk, motor skills, working memory, inhibition

INTRODUCTION

Autism spectrum disorder (ASD) is a neurodevelopmental disorder characterized by deficits in social communication and repetitive behaviors (DSM-5, American Psychiatric Association, 2013). Core behavioral features of ASD appear to emerge within the first 2 years of life (see Brian et al., 2008; Estes et al., 2015). Atypicalities associated with ASD include executive functioning (EF) deficits and motor impairments. The age at which EF deficits and motor impairments emerge in children who go on to develop ASD and their developmental trajectories are not well understood (Hughes et al., 1994; Hughes, 1996; Happé et al., 2006; Solomon et al., 2008; Corbett et al., 2009; Bhat et al., 2011). Although not considered defining features of ASD, deficits in these domains may be markers for later developmental problems and precede the unfolding of ASD symptoms in the first years of life.

EF refers to a set of cognitive functions that include attention, inhibition of behavior, working memory, cognitive flexibility, planning, and problem solving (Diamond, 2013). EF emerges progressively and increases in complexity with age during typical development (Best and Miller, 2010; Chevalier, 2015). The timing of the emergence of these functions and their developmental progression remains unclear (Diamond, 2002; Best and Miller, 2010; Jones et al., 2014). The ability to inhibit prepotent responses may be among the first functions to emerge (Chevalier, 2015). By 12 months of age infants can effectively inhibit their actions and engage their working memory to find a hidden toy (Diamond and Goldman-Rakic, 1989). There is even evidence of emerging working memory in 6-month old infants (Gilmore and Johnson, 1995). Cognitive flexibility may be the latest EF to emerge (Davidson et al., 2006; Garon et al., 2008). Research is needed to understand whether differences in EF emerge as part of early ASD symptoms and whether EF may be part of a developmental cascade that contributes to later deficits in individuals with ASD.

A broad range of EF impairments have been found in individuals with ASD including impairments in planning, working memory, inhibiting behavior, and cognitive flexibility (Hughes et al., 1994; Hughes, 1996; Hill, 2004a; Happé et al., 2006; Solomon et al., 2008; Corbett et al., 2009). Verbal and Non-verbal IQ is related to performance of EF tasks measuring inhibition, working memory, and cognitive flexibility in children with ASD (Griffith et al., 1999; Dawson et al., 2002; Yerys et al., 2007; Faja et al., 2016). Evidence suggests that deficits in EF may be present in children with ASD by 3 years of age (McEvoy et al., 1993; Adrien et al., 2001; Holmboe et al., 2008), although not all studies support this finding (Griffith et al., 1999; Dawson et al., 2002; Yerys et al., 2007). Griffith et al. (1999), in one of the few longitudinal studies of EF in ASD, found that preschool-aged children with ASD committed the same number of perseverative errors on a spatial reversal task over time while a comparison group of children with developmental delay showed a trend reduction in errors on this task as they grew older. Cross-sectional studies further support the idea of altered EF trajectories of working memory and response inhibition in children with ASD. For example, Luna et al. (2007) found evidence that typically developing individuals improved their performance on a computerized task tapping working memory as age increased whereas the ASD group did not. Similarly, Solomon et al. (2008) found that individuals with ASD did not improve their performance on a task assessing working memory and response inhibition as age increased but rather slightly worsened in their performance over time. All studies to date have focused on EF deficits after symptoms of ASD have manifested and relatively little is known about EF capabilities prior to and during the unfolding of ASD symptoms.

EF and motor development may be interrelated because of underlying neurobiology, as suggested by evidence from behavior-based tasks (Diamond, 2000). Functional neuroimaging studies have found co-activation in the dorsolateral prefrontal cortex and cerebellum on EF tasks such as the Wisconsin card sorting test (Berman et al., 1995) as well as on several working memory tasks not requiring motor-based responses (Awh et al., 1996; Desmond et al., 1997; Hautzel et al., 2009; Durisko and Fiez, 2010). Studies have also found that there are neuronal pathways linking the dorsolateral prefrontal cortex and neocerebellum (see Diamond, 2000 for further discussion). In typically developing infants, the experience of self-locomotion, such as walking, is associated with success on the A-not-B, a task measuring inhibition of prepotent responses and working memory (see Smith et al., 1999). Various motor functions, such as reaching and standing, may also influence performance on the A-not-B (Smith et al., 1999). Furthermore, gross and fine motor skills have been associated with working memory, verbal fluency, and cognitive flexibility (Wassenberg et al., 2005; Livesey et al., 2006; Piek et al., 2008). Older children (12–13 years) with ASD have shown difficulty with tasks requiring simultaneous goal-directed and motor behavior (Hughes, 1996). Interestingly, interventions that improve motor skills in children with ASD may improve certain aspects of EF, such as working memory (Hilton et al., 2014). However, the contribution of early motor skill difficulties to the emergence of EF problems in children who later develop ASD has not been systematically studied.

In this study, we investigated the longitudinal patterns of EF performance in infant siblings at high and low risk for ASD. Siblings of children with ASD are at higher risk for developing ASD compared with siblings of children who do not have an older sibling with ASD. The recurrence rate of risk for ASD in HR siblings is estimated to be between 10 and 18 % (Constantino et al., 2010; Ozonoff et al., 2011) while the population prevalence rate is 1 in 68[1]. High-risk (HR) infants, with older siblings with ASD and low-risk infants (LR), with typically developing older sibling were divided into three outcome groups based on ASD diagnosis at 24 months; HR-ASD, (HR infants who developed ASD) HR-negative (HR infants who did not develop ASD), and LR-Negative (LR infants who did not develop ASD). It was hypothesized that the HR-ASD group would demonstrate less improvement in EF over time and lower EF at 12 and 24 months than the HR-Negative and LR-Negative groups. We further hypothesized that motor skills would be associated with EF performance and group.

[1]Centers for Disease Control Autism and Developmental Disabilities Monitoring Network (2016). Available online at: http://www.cdc.gov/ncbddd/autism/addm.html

METHODS

Participants

Infants at high-familial risk for ASD due to an older sibling with ASD (HR; $n = 186$) and low familial risk for ASD, with typically developing older sibling and no family history of ASD (LR; $n = 76$) were included in this study. HR infants had an older sibling who met criteria for ASD on the Social Communication Questionnaire (SCQ; Rutter et al., 2003) and Autism Diagnostic Interview, Revised (ADI-R; Lord et al., 1994) and had an ASD diagnosis, confirmed by medical records. LR infants had typically developing older siblings who did not meet cut off scores for ASD on the SCQ or Family Interview for Genetics Studies (FIGS; Maxwell, 1992) and had no first-degree relative with ASD or intellectual disability. All participants were screened and excluded based on the following: (1) birth weight <2000 g and/or gestational age < 36 weeks or significant perinatal adversity and/or exposure *in utero* to neurotoxins, (2) medical/neurological conditions affecting growth, development, or cognition (e.g., seizure disorder) or significant sensory impairments (e.g., vision or hearing loss), (3) genetic conditions or syndromes, (4) adopted children or half siblings, (5) twins, (6) first-degree relative with psychosis, schizophrenia, or bipolar disorder (FIGS), (7) contraindication for MRI and, (8) predominant home language other than English.

Procedures

The sample included participants who provided valid A-not-B data at either the 12- or 24-month time point. Participants were recruited through research participant lists, flyers, brochures, email blasts, and community clinics at four clinical sites (Children's Hospital of Philadelphia, University of Washington, University of North Carolina, and Washington University). Following eligibility screening, participants were assessed at 6, 12, and 24 months of age. Written informed consent, approved by each site's Human Subjects Review Board, was obtained for all families.

Cognitive, social development, and EF performance were assessed by a licensed clinical psychologist, doctoral student in clinical psychology, school psychologist, or masters-level psychometrist under supervision of a licensed clinical psychologist or psychiatrist. At 24 months, all participants were assessed using the Mullen Scales of Early Learning (MSEL; Mullen, 1995), the Autism Diagnostic Observation Schedule, Second Edition (ADOS-2; Lord et al., 2012) and ADI-R by research-reliable examiners. Each participant was assigned a clinical best estimate diagnosis made by two clinicians according to the DSM-IV-TR criteria to determine whether the child met the criteria for Autistic Disorder, Pervasive Developmental Disorder-Not Otherwise Specified, or neither. There were 30 high-risk infants meeting DSM-IV criteria for Autistic Disorder or PDD-NOS (HR-ASD), 138 high-risk infants *not* meeting DSM-IV criteria for Autistic Disorder or PDD-NOS (HR-Negative), and 67 low-risk infants *not* meeting DSM-IV-TR criteria for Autistic Disorder or PDD-NOS (LR-Negative).

Table 1 presents demographic and descriptive information including age, gender, race, and maternal education. Groups did not differ in age, race, or sex at either the 12- or 24-month assessment. However there were group differences in maternal education at 24 months, $\chi^2_{(2,N=172)} = 7.37$, $p = 0.025$ but not 12 months, $\chi^2_{(2,N=173)} = 5.64$, $p = 0.059$. Groups differed significantly on MSEL Fine Motor skills at 12 months, $F_{(2,\ 171)} = 3.48$, $p = 0.033$, and at 24 months, $F_{(2,\ 171)} = 9.56$, $p < 0.001$. Groups also differed significantly on MSEL Gross Motor skills at 12 and 24 months $F_{(2,\ 171)} = 3.36$, $p = 0.037$, $F_{(2,\ 171)} = 8.90$, $p < 0.001$, respectively. On the Visual Reception scale of the MSEL, groups differed significantly at 24 months but not at 12 months, $F_{(2,\ 171)} = 4.21$, $p = 0.016$, $F_{(2,\ 171)} = 2.89$, $p = 0.058$, respectively. Floor and ceiling effects were assessed across groups by examining score ranges. Few participants in any group fell at either the floor or ceiling values. Twenty-four participants with A-not-B had missing diagnostic outcome data and 3 LR siblings were diagnosed with ASD and, therefore, were not included in the analysis. In addition, 40 HR-Negative, 13 HR-ASD, and 22 LR-Negative infants at 12 months ($\chi^2 = 0.83$, $p = 0.662$) and 20 HR-Negative, 9 HR-ASD, and 5 LR-Negative infants at 24 months ($\chi^2 = 7.11$, $p = 0.029$) did not provide valid A-not-B data due to training failure, completion of too few trails (<10), or administration errors. Further details about the characteristics of this cohort can be found in Estes et al. (2015).

MEASURES

Executive Function

EF was assessed with the A-not-B task (Piaget, 1954) at 12 and 24 months. The A-not-B has been used as a measure of response inhibition and working memory in children as young as 6 months of age (Diamond, 1985; Diamond and Goldman-Rakic, 1989). The implementation of this task has varied across prior studies. In the current study the infant watched as a toy was hidden to the left or right of midline and was encouraged to find the toy after a delay of 5 s. Once the infant found the hidden toy on two consecutive trials, the side of hiding was reversed. The delay was increased to 12 s if the infant successfully completed two reversal trials. A maximum of 24 trials and 4 reversal trials were administered. Performance was measured by two criteria: (1) proportion of total correct reaches by total trials (working memory) and (2) the proportion of total correct reaches on reversal trials by total reversals trials (inhibition).

Cognitive Ability and Motor Skills

The Mullen Scales of Early Learning (MSEL; Mullen, 1995) is a standardized, normed, developmental assessment for children birth through 68 months. The MSEL yields 5 subscales (Receptive Language, Expressive Language, Visual Reception, Fine Motor, and Gross Motor) and the Early Learning Composite (ELC), an overall index of cognitive ability. The Gross and Fine Motor, and Visual Reception subscale T-score were used in this study. The Visual Reception scale was used as a proxy for overall cognitive ability because the ELC and Non-verbal developmental quotient include the Fine Motor scale, which was used as an independent variable in this study.

TABLE 1 | Study sample characteristics.

	HR-ASD	HR-Negative	LR-Negative	p^a
12 MONTHS				
n	23	101	50	
Age (months)	12.49 (0.52)	12.52 (0.67)	12.55 (0.79)	0.934
Race (%)				
White	78.3	85.0	87.8	0.576
Non-white	21.7	15.0	12.2	
Sex (% male)	73.9	56.4	58.0	0.300
Maternal education (%)				0.059
No College degree	47.8	30.7	20.4	
College degree	52.2	69.3	79.6	
MSEL Visual Reception [b]	50.30 (9.53)	54.14 (9.27)	55.74 (8.07)	0.058
MSEL Fine Motor [b]	54.35 (9.00)	58.18 (8.58)	60.02 (8.23)	0.033
MSEL Gross Motor [b]	44.78 (13.18)	47.77 (11.87)	52.02 (12.19)	0.037
24 MONTHS				
n	19	106	49	
Age (months)	24.26 (0.90)	24.63 (0.90)	24.63 (1.05)	0.270
Race (%)				0.210
White	73.7	87.6	89.4	
Non-white	26.3	12.4	10.6	
Sex (% male)	73.7	59.4	49.0	
Maternal education (%)				0.025
No College degree	42.1	33.3	14.6	
College degree	57.9	66.7	85.4	
MSEL Visual Reception [b]	49.58 (6.96)	52.93 (10.21)	56.80 (10.73)	0.016
MSEL Fine Motor [b]	45.89 (9.47)	49.75 (8.77)	55.14 (8.79)	0.000
MSEL Gross Motor [b]	42.26 (8.63)	49.82 (9.15)	52.04 (7.29)	0.000

[a] *Omnibus ANOVA (Age, MSEL) and Chi-Square (race, maternal education, sex).*
[b] *T-scores.*

ASD Symptoms

The Autism Diagnostic Observation Schedule, second edition (ADOS-2; Lord et al., 2012) is a semi-structured play assessment of communication, social interaction, play skills, and restricted interests/repetitive behavior. Module 1 was administered to all children at 24 months. Empirically derived algorithm scores, based on the severity and number of ASD symptoms demonstrated during the ADOS assessment, yield three classifications, Autism, Autism Spectrum, and Non-Spectrum.

The Autism Diagnostic Interview-Revised (ADI-R; Lord et al., 1994) is a semi-structured parent interview that assesses symptoms of ASD. The ADI-R was administered at 24 months to all parents of HR infants and all LR infants with ASD-related clinical concerns. The ADOS and ADI-R contributed to a clinical best estimate ASD diagnosis.

Statistical Analysis

EF development from ages 12 to 24 months was analyzed using generalized estimating equations (GEE) fit for a binomial distribution and exchangeable correlation matrix using SPSS version 19.0. Dependent variables included the proportion of total correct reaches by total trials (measuring working memory) and total correct reaches on reversal trials by total reversal trials (measuring response inhibition) on the A-not-B. Model predictors included diagnostic group (HR-ASD, HR-Negative, and LR-Negative), maternal education, and the MSEL Visual Reception subscale. Cross-sectional group differences in EF were tested employing logistic regression at 12 and 24 months (see Marcovitch and Zelazo, 1999) using the same dependent variables and model predictors. Separate regression models were run to determine if motor skills were associated with group and EF at 12 and 24 months using the same dependent variables and model predictors, with the addition of the MSEL Fine and Gross Motor subscales.

RESULTS

EF Development

Working Memory

There was a significant main effect of Time ($\chi^2 = 67.73$, $p < 0.001$) but not Group ($\chi^2 = 3.91$, $p = 0.141$) on working memory (proportion of total correct reaches by total trials) after controlling for Visual Reception and maternal education. There was a significant Group x Time interaction for working memory with the LR-Negative group demonstrating improved performance from 12 to 24 months ($\chi^2 = 48.60$, $p < 0.001$) and the HR-ASD ($\chi^2 = 3.98$, $p = 0.046$) and HR-Negative ($\chi^2 = 4.62$, $p = 0.032$) groups demonstrating less improvement than LR-Negative group (see **Figure 1**).

Response Inhibition

There was a significant main effect of Time ($\chi^2 = 6.79$, $p = 0.009$) but not Group ($\chi^2 = 2.15$, $p = 0.342$) on response inhibition (proportion of total correct reaches on reversal trials by total reversal trials) after controlling for Visual Reception and maternal education. The Group x Time interaction was significant for response inhibition with the LR-Negative group improving performance from 12 to 24 months and the HR-Negative group slightly worsening performance over time ($\chi^2 = 5.48$, $p = 0.019$; see **Figure 2**). The HR-ASD group also worsened over time but no interaction effect was detected ($\chi^2 = 2.18$, $p = 0.140$). *Post-hoc* analysis, adding the Fine and Gross Motor subscales as covariates, did not change the pattern or significance of the results reported above.

Group Differences in EF and Motor at 12 Months

Group differences in working memory

There was no significant main effect of group on working memory at 12 months after controlling for maternal education and Visual Reception ($\chi^2 = 0.39$, $p = 0.822$; see Model 1, **Table 2**).

Fine motor and working memory

Lower Fine Motor scores were associated with better working memory at 12 months ($\chi^2 = 10.52$, $p \leq 0.001$, see Model 2, **Table 2**). The Group × Fine Motor interaction at 12 months was not significant ($\chi^2 = 3.09$, $p = 0.213$; see Model 3, **Table 2**).

Gross motor and working memory

There was no main effect of Gross Motor on working memory at 12 months ($\chi^2 = 2.72$, $p = 0.099$, see Model 2, **Table 3**).

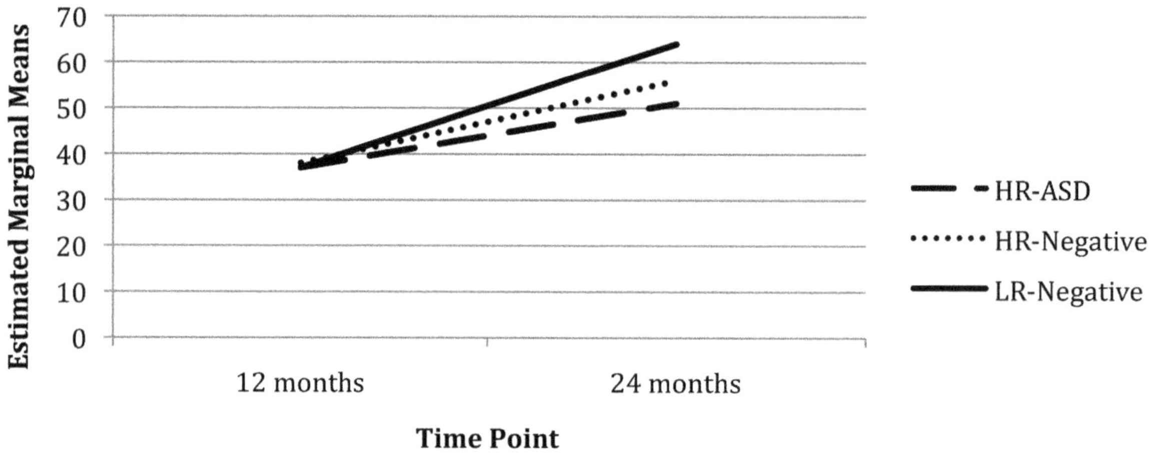

FIGURE 1 | Total correct reaches by total trials over time.

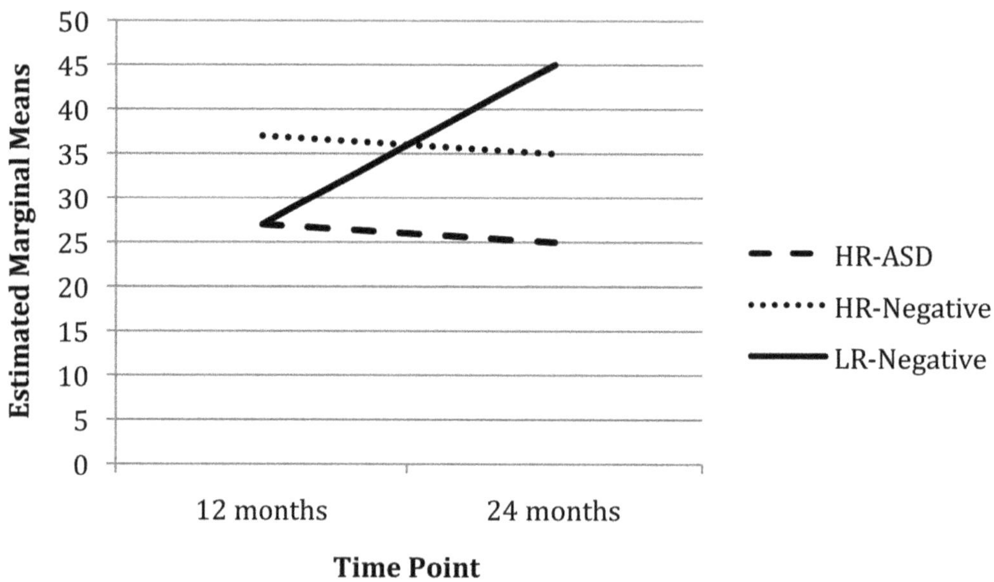

FIGURE 2 | Total correct reaches on reversal trials by total reversal trials over time.

The Group × Gross Motor interaction at 12 months was not significant ($\chi^2 = 0.13$, $p = 0.938$; see Model 3, **Table 3**).

Group differences in response inhibition

There was no significant main effect of group on response inhibition at 12 months after controlling for maternal education and Visual Reception ($\chi^2 = 3.43$, $p = 0.180$, see Model 1, **Table 4**).

Fine motor and response inhibition

Lower Fine Motor scores were associated with better response inhibition at 12 months ($\chi^2 = 4.00$, $p = 0.046$, see Model 2, **Table 4**). The Group × Fine Motor interaction at 12 months was significant. The HR-ASD group demonstrated a negative association between Fine Motor scores and response inhibition and the LR-Negative group demonstrated a positive relationship ($\chi^2 = 5.10$, $p = 0.024$; see Model 3, **Table 4**).

Gross motor and response inhibition

There was no significant main effect of Gross Motor scores on response inhibition at 12 months ($\chi^2 = 1.27$, $p = 0.258$, see Model 2, **Table 5**). The Group × Gross Motor interaction was not significant ($\chi^2 = 1.39$, $p = 0.498$; see Model 3, **Table 5**).

Group Differences in EF and Motor at 24 months

Group differences in working memory

There was a significant main effect of group on working memory at 24 months after controlling for Visual Reception and maternal education with the HR-ASD and HR-Negative groups performing worse than the LR-Negative group (χ^2

TABLE 2 | Summary of model fit for working memory and fine motor at 12 months.

Covariate	Model 1					Model 2					Model 3				
			95% CI					95% CI					95% CI		
	B	SE	LL	UL	P	B	SE	LL	UL	p	B	SE	LL	UL	p
No College Degree[a]	0.07	0.08	−0.10	0.24	0.406	0.05	0.09	−0.12	0.22	0.545	0.05	0.09	−0.12	0.22	0.576
Visual Reception	0.00	0.00	−0.01	0.01	0.853	0.00	0.00	−0.01	0.01	0.422	0.00	0.00	−0.01	0.01	0.545
HR–ASD[b]	0.00	0.13	−0.26	0.25	0.976	−0.06	0.13	−0.32	0.19	0.634	1.35	0.82	−0.27	2.96	0.102
HR-Negative [b]	0.05	0.09	−0.12	0.22	0.598	0.02	0.09	−0.16	0.19	0.854	0.77	0.62	−0.45	1.99	0.214
Fine Motor						−0.01	0.00	−0.02	−0.01	0.001	0.00	0.01	−0.02	0.02	0.745
HR-ASD*Fine Motor [c]											−0.03	0.01	−0.05	0.00	0.086
HR-Negative*Fine Motor [c]											−0.01	0.01	−0.03	0.01	0.223

[a] *Reference group = college degree.*
[b] *Reference group = LR-Negative.*
[c] *Reference group = LR-Negative * Fine Motor.*

TABLE 3 | Summary of model fit for working memory and gross motor at 12 months.

Covariate	Model 1					Model 2					Model 3				
			95% CI					95% CI					95% CI		
	B	SE	LL	UL	p	B	SE	LL	UL	p	B	SE	LL	UL	p
No College Degree[a]	0.07	0.08	−0.10	0.24	0.406	0.07	0.09	−0.10	0.23	0.444	0.06	0.09	−0.10	0.23	0.451
Visual Reception	0.00	0.00	−0.01	0.01	0.853	0.00	0.00	−0.01	0.01	0.625	0.00	0.00	−0.01	0.01	0.624
HR-ASD [b]	0.00	0.13	−0.26	0.25	0.976	0.02	0.13	−0.23	0.27	0.880	0.15	0.53	−0.90	1.19	0.780
HR-Negative[b]	0.05	0.09	−0.12	0.22	0.598	0.07	0.09	−0.11	0.24	0.456	0.20	0.40	−0.57	0.98	0.611
Gross Motor						0.01	0.00	0.00	0.01	0.099	0.01	0.01	−0.01	0.02	0.264
HR-ASD* Gross Motor [c]											0.00	0.01	−0.02	0.02	0.811
HR-Negative* Gross Motor [c]											0.00	0.01	−0.02	0.01	0.726

[a] *Reference group = college degree.*
[b] *Reference group = LR-Negative.*
[c] *Reference group = LR-Negative * Gross Motor.*

TABLE 4 | Summary of model fit for response inhibition and fine motor at 12 months.

Covariate	Model 1					Model 2					Model 3				
			95% CI					95% CI					95% CI		
	B	SE	LL	UL	p	B	SE	LL	UL	p	B	SE	LL	UL	p
No College[a]	0.13	0.26	−0.39	0.64	0.621	0.09	0.26	−0.43	0.61	0.731	0.13	0.27	−0.39	0.66	0.616
Visual Reception	0.02	0.01	−0.01	0.05	0.115	0.03	0.01	0.00	0.06	0.040	0.03	0.01	0.00	0.06	0.062
HR-ASD[b]	−0.01	0.40	−0.80	0.78	0.972	−0.18	0.41	−0.99	0.63	0.660	7.07	3.17	0.86	13.28	0.026
HR-Negative[b]	0.43	0.27	−0.11	0.97	0.116	0.37	0.28	−0.18	0.91	0.185	3.12	2.11	−1.03	7.26	0.140
Fine Motor						−0.03	0.01	−0.06	0.00	0.046	0.02	0.03	−0.04	0.08	0.571
HR-ASD * Fine Motor [c]											−0.13	0.06	−0.25	−0.02	0.024
HR-Negative* Fine Motor[c]											−0.05	0.03	−0.11	0.02	0.191

[a] *Reference group = college degree.*
[b] *Reference group = LR-Negative.*
[c] *Reference group = LR-Negative * Fine Motor.*

= 18.83, $p < 0.001$; see Model 1, **Table 6**). Estimated marginal means and standard errors were generated from this model. Bonferroni corrected pair-wise comparisons further indicated that the HR-ASD and HR-Negative groups did not differ significantly from each other (Omnibus $\chi^2 = 19.67$, $p \leq 0.001$).

TABLE 5 | Summary of model fit for response inhibition and gross motor at 12 months.

Covariate	Model 1 95% CI					Model 2 95% CI					Model 3 95% CI				
	B	SE	LL	UL	*p*	B	SE	LL	UL	*p*	B	SE	LL	UL	*p*
No College[a]	0.13	0.26	−0.39	0.64	0.621	0.16	0.26	−0.36	0.68	0.552	0.17	0.27	−0.35	0.69	0.524
Visual Reception	0.02	0.01	−0.01	0.05	0.115	0.03	0.01	0.00	0.05	0.074	0.03	0.01	0.00	0.06	0.063
HR-ASD[b]	−0.01	0.40	−0.80	0.78	0.972	−0.08	0.41	−0.88	0.72	0.843	−0.53	1.71	−3.88	2.82	0.756
HR-Negative[b]	0.43	0.27	−0.11	0.97	0.116	0.38	0.28	−0.17	0.92	0.176	−1.01	1.32	−3.59	1.57	0.443
Gross Motor						−0.01	0.01	−0.03	0.01	0.258	−0.03	0.02	−0.08	0.01	0.169
HR-ASD* Gross Motor[c]											0.01	0.03	−0.06	0.08	0.833
HR-Negative* Gross Motor [c]											0.03	0.03	−0.02	0.08	0.280

[a]*Reference group = college degree.*
[b]*Reference group = LR-Negative.*
[c]*Reference group = LR-Negative * Gross Motor.*

Fine motor and working memory

Higher Fine Motor scores were associated with better working memory ($\chi^2 = 9.06, p = 0.003$, see Model 2, **Table 6**). The Group × Fine Motor interaction was not significant ($\chi^2 = 0.84$, $p = 0.656$). In the interaction model there was no longer a significant main effect for group (see Model 3, **Table 6**).

Gross motor and working memory

There was no main effect for Gross Motor on working memory ($\chi^2 = 2.73, p = 0.098$; see Model 2, **Table 7**). The Group × Gross Motor interaction was also not significant ($\chi^2 = 5.73, p = 0.057$). However, in the interaction model, there was a significant main effect of Gross Motor skills on working memory ($\chi^2 = 3.95, p = 0.047$) and there was no longer a significant main effect for group (see Model 3, **Table 7**).

Group differences in response inhibition

There was a significant main effect of group on response inhibition at 24 months after controlling for Visual Reception and maternal education with the HR-ASD group and HR-Negative group performing worse than the LR-Negative group ($\chi^2 = 7.39$, $p = 0.025$; see Model 1, **Table 7**). Bonferonni corrected pair-wise comparisons indicated that only the HR-ASD and LR-Negative groups differed (Omnibus $\chi^2 = 7.85, p = 0.020$).

Fine motor and response inhibition

There was no main effect of Fine Motor scores on response inhibition at 24 months ($\chi^2 = 3.56$, $p = 0.059$; see Model 2, **Table 8**). The Group × Fine Motor interaction was also not significant ($\chi^2 = 3.18$, $p = 0.204$; see Model 3, **Table 8**). In the interaction model, Fine Motor significantly predicted response inhibition ($\chi^2 = 5.22, p = 0.022$) with the main effect for group no longer reaching significance.

Gross motor and response inhibition

Higher Gross Motor scores were associated with better response inhibition at 24 months ($\chi^2 = 4.90$, $p = 0.027$; see Model 2, **Table 9**). The Group by Gross Motor interaction was significant at 24 months with the HR-Negative and LR-Negative groups showing a positive relationship between Gross Motor and performance on reversal trials but with the HR-Negative group demonstrating lower scores overall ($\chi^2 = 3.89$, $p = 0.049$; see Model 3, **Table 9**).

DISCUSSION

The current study investigated the early emergence of EF in children at high and low risk for ASD, prior to the onset of the disorder. HR infants who later developed ASD and HR infants who did not develop ASD showed slower growth in working memory from 12 to 24 months of age than LR infants without ASD. The LR-Negative group showed improved response inhibition from 12 to 24 months while the HR-ASD and HR-Negative groups showed little to no improvement in inhibition. At 12 months no group differences in working memory or inhibition were evident. Differences emerged by 24 months with the HR-ASD and HR-Negative groups demonstrating worse working memory and response inhibition than the LR-Negative group. These findings are consistent with prior research suggesting altered trajectories of EF in children with ASD (Griffith et al., 1999; Luna et al., 2007; Solomon et al., 2008). These findings are also consistent with emerging evidence that EF differences may be present in HR-Negative siblings (Hill, 2004b; Holmboe et al., 2010; Warren et al., 2012). This study is unique in providing the earliest evidence to date of EF differences in children with ASD, suggesting that these deficits may emerge in the second year of life, around the same time that the core symptoms of ASD are also emerging and consolidating.

In the current study, evidence was also found that motor skills are associated with EF performance and diagnostic group. At 12 months, worse fine motor skills were associated with better working memory and response inhibition. Interestingly, when looking specifically at differences across groups, the HR-ASD group demonstrated an inverse relationship between fine motor skills and response inhibition, with better fine motor skills related to worse response inhibition. The LR-Negative group demonstrated the expected relationship with better response inhibition related to better fine motor skills. Gross motor skills, however, were not related to EF at 12 months of age. At 24

TABLE 6 | Summary of model fit for working memory and fine motor at 24 months.

Covariate	Model 1 95% CI					Model 2 95% CI					Model 3 95% CI				
	B	SE	LL	UL	p	B	SE	LL	UL	p	B	SE	LL	UL	p
No College Degree[a]	0.32	0.08	0.16	0.49	0.000	0.33	0.08	0.16	0.49	0.000	0.33	0.08	0.17	0.50	0.000
Visual Reception	0.02	0.00	0.01	0.02	0.000	0.01	0.00	0.00	0.02	0.011	0.01	0.00	0.00	0.02	0.011
HR-ASD[b]	−0.52	0.14	−0.79	−0.25	0.000	−0.43	0.14	−0.71	−0.16	0.002	−0.36	0.76	−1.84	1.13	0.639
HR-Negative[b]	−0.34	0.09	−0.51	−0.16	0.000	−0.28	0.09	−0.46	−0.11	0.002	0.15	0.54	−0.90	1.21	0.776
Fine Motor						0.01	0.00	0.01	0.02	0.003	0.02	0.01	0.00	0.04	0.029
HR-ASD* Fine Motor[c]											0.00	0.02	−0.03	0.03	0.965
HR-Negative* Fine Motor [c]											−0.01	0.01	−0.03	0.01	0.408

[a] *Reference group = college degree.*
[b] *Reference group = LR-Negative.*
[c] *Reference group = LR-Negative * Fine Motor.*

TABLE 7 | Summary of model fit for working memory and gross motor at 24 months.

Covariate	Model 1 95% CI					Model 2 95% CI					Model 3 95% CI				
	B	SE	LL	UL	p	B	SE	LL	UL	p	B	SE	LL	UL	p
No College Degree [a]	0.32	0.08	0.16	0.49	0.000	0.32	0.08	0.15	0.482	0.000	0.3	0.1	0.1	0.5	0.000
Visual Reception	0.02	0.00	0.01	0.02	0.000	0.02	0.00	0.01	0.022	0.000	0.0	0.0	0.0	0.0	0.000
HR-ASD [b]	−0.52	0.14	−0.79	−0.25	0.000	−0.47	0.14	−0.75	−0.19	0.001	0.7	0.6	−0.5	1.9	0.244
HR-Negative [b]	−0.34	0.09	−0.51	−0.16	0.000	−0.32	0.09	−0.50	−0.147	0.000	−0.7	0.8	−2.3	0.9	0.403
Gross Motor						0.01	0.00	0.00	0.015	0.098	0.02	0.01	0.00	0.04	0.047
HR-ASD * Gross Motor [c]											0.01	0.02	−0.03	0.04	0.648
HR-Negative * Gross Motor [c]											−0.02	0.01	−0.04	0.00	0.087

[a] *Reference group = college degree.*
[b] *Reference group = LR-Negative.*
[c] *Reference group = LR-Negative * Gross Motor.*

TABLE 8 | Summary of model fit for response inhibition on reversal trials and fine motor at 24 months.

Covariate	Model 1 95% CI					Model 2 95% CI					Model 3 95% CI				
	B	SE	LL	UL	p	B	SE	LL	UL	p	B	SE	LL	UL	p
No College[a]	−0.05	0.20	−0.44	0.34	0.815	−0.03	0.20	−0.42	0.37	0.901	0.02	0.20	−0.38	0.42	0.927
Visual Reception	0.01	0.01	−0.01	0.03	0.227	0.00	0.01	−0.02	0.02	0.734	0.00	0.01	−0.02	0.02	0.727
HR-ASD[b]	−0.88	0.36	−1.59	−0.17	0.016	−0.78	0.37	−1.50	−0.06	0.034	−0.21	1.85	−3.84	3.42	0.909
HR-Negative[b]	−0.40	0.19	−0.78	−0.02	0.038	−0.33	0.20	−0.72	0.06	0.098	1.71	1.23	−0.69	4.11	0.162
Fine Motor						0.02	0.01	0.00	0.04	0.059	0.04	0.02	0.01	0.08	0.022
HR-ASD* Fine Motor[c]											−0.01	0.04	−0.08	0.06	0.816
HR-Negative* Fine Motor [c]											−0.04	0.02	−0.08	0.01	0.090

[a] *Reference group = college degree.*
[b] *Reference group = LR-Negative.*
[c] *Reference group = LR-Negative * Fine Motor.*

months, better fine and gross motor skills were associated with better working memory and response inhibition. Fine motor skills were not associated with group and EF but worse gross motor skills were associated with worse response inhibition. These findings are consistent with prior research reporting an association between motor skills and the A-not-B (see Smith et al., 1999) and add to the growing evidence suggesting a relationship between EF and motor skills in both typically developing children and children with ASD (Hughes, 1996; Diamond, 2000; Hilton et al., 2014).

TABLE 9 | Summary of model fit for response inhibition and gross motor at 24 months.

Covariate	Model 1					Model 2					Model 3				
			95% CI					95% CI					95% CI		
	B	SE	LL	UL	*p*	B	SE	LL	UL	*p*	B	SE	LL	UL	*p*
No College[a]	−0.05	0.20	−0.44	0.34	0.815	−0.05	0.20	−0.44	0.35	0.820	−0.02	0.20	−0.42	0.37	0.917
Visual Reception	0.01	0.01	−0.01	0.03	0.227	0.01	0.01	−0.01	0.03	0.389	0.01	0.01	−0.01	0.03	0.286
HR-ASD[b]	−0.88	0.36	−1.59	−0.17	0.016	−0.74	0.37	−1.46	−0.01	0.047	1.76	2.07	−2.31	5.83	0.396
HR-Negative[b]	−0.40	0.19	−0.78	−0.02	0.038	−0.36	0.20	−0.74	0.03	0.069	2.21	1.31	−0.37	4.78	0.093
Gross Motor						0.02	0.01	0.00	0.04	0.027	0.06	0.02	0.02	0.10	0.005
HR-ASD* Gross Motor[c]											−0.05	0.04	−0.13	0.04	0.261
HR-Negative* Gross Motor [c]											−0.05	0.02	−0.10	0.00	0.049

[a] *Reference group = college degree.*
[b] *Reference group = LR-Negative.*
[c] *Reference group = LR-Negative * Gross Motor.*

Interestingly, HR-Negative siblings demonstrated differences in working memory compared to the LR-Negative group but not compared to the HR-ASD group, suggesting that EF differences may be a manifestation of genetic liability for ASD. Having atypical EF development could reflect a more general genetic vulnerability for developmental problems among HR siblings who do not develop full clinical symptoms of ASD. HR-Negative siblings may demonstrate a range of developmental problems such as lower developmental functioning, language delay, social difficulties, and greater internalizing problems (Landa et al., 2012; Georgiades et al., 2013; Messinger et al., 2013; Pisula and Ziegart-Sadowska, 2015). This is the first study of which we are aware to demonstrate that EF may be impaired in HR siblings who do not develop ASD. Some problems in HR-Negative siblings, such as language impairments and social-emotional problems, may be related to EF deficits, as suggested by the literature in non-ASD populations (Riggs et al., 2006; Henry et al., 2012). Future studies are needed to determine if EF and developmental problems are associated in HR-Negative siblings.

Another notable finding is that HR-ASD siblings had more difficulty inhibiting behavior than LR-Negative siblings at 24 months. The HR-Negative siblings did not differ significantly from either group and performed better than HR-ASD siblings but worse than LR-Negative siblings. It is possible that the working memory demands of the A-not-B were lower than the inhibitory demands which may indicate that children with ASD have more difficulty on tasks that put greater demand on the their EFs but that this may be less of a difficulty for HR siblings that do not go on the develop ASD. Underlying neural differences in HR-ASD siblings could account for differences in response inhibition. For example, decreased activation in the regions associated with inhibition on a behavioral inhibition task in children with ASD has been found (Kana et al., 2007). Another interesting finding was that EF differences in HR-ASD siblings were, in some cases, opposite of what was found in LR-Negative siblings. Again, this could be related to some altered, underlying brain-based process or be the effect of the type of EF that is being engaged. Finally, the impact of motor development on EF performance was noted earlier than overt differences in working memory and response inhibition were observed. This pattern of early emerging, motor-based differences has been found in other studies of HR-ASD siblings (Bolton et al., 2012; Flanagan et al., 2012; Estes et al., 2015). However, the current study, to our knowledge, is the first to tie these differences to EF.

Contrary to expectations, differences in working memory and response inhibition at 12 months of age was not demonstrated. It may be that differences in working memory and response inhibition do not exist as this age. However, Holmboe et al. (2010) found poorer inhibition on a computer-based EF task in 9–10 month old HR infant siblings compared to LR infant siblings, which suggests that EF deficits may exist at young ages but may be hard to detect with motor-based EF tasks. In addition, there may be some specific, developmentally related reason accounting for infant's performance at 12 months of age, such as stage of self-locomotion (e.g., walking) or preference for bi-manual reaching while learning to walk (which is an "incorrect" response on the A-not-B; Smith et al., 1999; Corbetta and Bojczyk, 2002; Karasik et al., 2011). It is also possible that the infants in our study were already fatigued due to unmeasured factors (e.g., time of day, prior cognitive testing, hunger etc.). Moreover, it was unexpected that poorer Fine Motor performance on the Mullen would be associated with better EF performance at 12 months. No prior literature, as far as we are aware, has described a similar finding. Future studies are needed to clarify whether this relationship is due to random variability in our sample, measure fidelity, or reflects a unique relationship between ASD and motor development. If these findings are replicated in independent sample, a possible explanation could be that poorer Fine Motor skills and better A-not-B performance are different sides of the same coin, both related to early ASD symptoms. Specifically, ASD is often related to a preference for objects. Thus, it is possible that the A-not-B, an object-based task, may be inherently rewarding for an infant with emerging ASD symptoms. ASD is also related to difficulties with imitation and motor development, which may lead to lower scores on some of the Fine Motor items. Thus, subtle difficulties with imitation or fine motor skills may impact Mullen performance but not necessarily A-not-B performance and subtle preferences for objects may increase A-not-B performance in the younger ages. However, these considerations are not addressable with the current data set and future studies are needed to replicate and extend this work.

Early findings of EF deficits in school-age children and adults with ASD lead to the theory that EF deficits may be a primary deficit explaining both social and non-social ASD-related symptoms such as rigidity, repetitive behaviors and theory of mind deficits (see Hill, 2004a for review). However, EF deficits in individuals with ASD are not universal (Ozonoff and Strayer, 2001; Yerys et al., 2007) and over time it became clear that the data did not support the primary deficit hypothesis. Although we are looking at early manifestations of EF differences in ASD, we are not proposing that EF differences fully explain all ASD symptoms but instead suggest that they may contribute to some of the deficits observed in individuals with ASD.

Although the A-not-B is one of the most widely used and well-studied measures of EF in infants and young toddlers, it has important limitations. The A-not-B, used to measure EF, is not highly specific and does not simply measure one type of EF. It should also be noted that although working memory and response inhibition were discussed as being separate based on the type of trial administered, these variables are interrelated. Moreover, there are no published norms on the A-not-B and therefore the extent of EF dysfunction compared to same-aged peers is not clear. ASD diagnosis at 24-months demonstrates high classification stability over time among both clinically ascertained samples and HR sibling cohorts (Chawarska et al., 2007; Ozonoff et al., 2011; Rozga et al., 2011; Guthrie et al., 2013). However, there are potential limitations to using 24-month diagnosis or classification. In a recent study, 41% of HR siblings not initially diagnosed at 24-months were later diagnosed at 36 months (Ozonoff et al., 2015). Thus, our finding that the HR-Negative and HR-ASD groups did not differ on working memory and response inhibition could be due to some children in the HR-Negative group who may later meet diagnostic criteria for ASD. Longitudinal follow-up of these children is currently underway to assess whether changes in ASD outcomes occur over time and whether these changes reveal different patterns of early precursors to ASD.

Interestingly, our LR sample included 3 children (3.9%) who developed ASD. This rate is higher than the CDC prevalence estimate of 1.5%. Our study does not provide direct evidence for why this may have occurred. It is possible that there is a higher rate of false positive ASD diagnoses among the LR sample at 24 months. Alternatively, among our LR sample, parents with developmental concerns about other children in the family may be over represented despite screening out families with autism-related developmental concerns in older siblings. However, random sampling variability may also explain the prevalence rate of ASD in our LR sample. Since 1.5% is the point estimate in the general population, a rate of 3.9% would not likely be outside the bounds of what would be expected in random samples taken from the general population.

Studies assessing EF using a broader range of EF measures are needed (Bernier et al., 2010). This study only assessed EF twice, at 12 and 24 months. It appears that the deficits emerged during the time period that was not assessed. Future studies are needed to assess the trajectory of EFs more densely over the second year of life. Further research on EF at 12 months as related to motor development and other functional outcomes such as adaptive functioning, temperament, and emotional regulation could help clarify potential downstream effects of early EF differences in HR infants. In addition, the relationship between 24-month performance on the A-not-B and later development is not measured in this study. Longitudinal follow up through preschool and early school age in infants at risk for autism is needed to elucidate the developmental sequelae of these early group differences. Finally, studies linking early brain and EF differences would elucidate the neurobiological underpinnings of executive dysfunction in ASD.

This study underscores the importance of addressing developmental phenomenon among unaffected high-risk siblings in relation to those who develop ASD. It also highlights the importance of studying EF and motor developmental processes early and over time. Finally, if the findings in this study are replicated, stronger evidence may exist for considering both EF and motor-based interventions for affected and unaffected high-risk siblings.

IBIS NETWORK

The Infant Brain Imaging Study (IBIS) Network is an NIH funded Autism Center of Excellence project and consists of a consortium of 8 universities in the U.S. and Canada. Clinical Sites: University of North Carolina: J. Piven (IBIS Network PI), H.C. Hazlett, C. Chappell; University of Washington: S. Dager, A. Estes, D. Shaw; Washington University: K. Botteron, R. McKinstry, J. Constantino, J. Pruett; Children's Hospital of Philadelphia: R. Schultz, S. Paterson; University of Alberta: L. Zwaigenbaum; University of Minnesota: J. Elison; Data Coordinating Center: Montreal Neurological Institute: A.C. Evans, D.L. Collins, G.B. Pike, V. Fonov, P. Kostopoulos; S. Das; Image Processing Core: University of Utah: G. Gerig; University of North Carolina: M. Styner; Statistical Analysis Core: University of North Carolina: H. Gu

AUTHOR CONTRIBUTIONS

TJ drafted and revised the manuscript and participated in acquisition, analysis, and interpretation of the data. AE participated in manuscript revision, data interpretation, and study conception and design. SD participated in manuscript revision, data interpretation, and study conception and design. PK participated in manuscript revision and data interpretation. JW participated in manuscript revision and data interpretation. Ju P participated in manuscript revision and data acquisition. JE participated in manuscript revision and data interpretation. SP participated in manuscript revision and data acquisition. RS participated in manuscript revision, data interpretation, and study conception and design. KB participated in manuscript revision and study conception and design. HH participated in manuscript revision and study conception and design. JP participated in manuscript revision, data interpretation, and study conception and design.

FUNDING

This work was supported by an NIH Autism Center of Excellence grant (NIMH and NICHD #HD055741 and HD055741), NIH Intellectual and Developmental Disabilities Research Center grant (#U54HD083091), the Simons Foundation (SFARI Grant 140209), and Autism Speaks (6020).

ACKNOWLEDGMENTS

The authors thank the all the IBIS families for their participation in this longitudinal study. A special thank you to Dr. Flaherty who consulted on the statistical methods.

REFERENCES

Adrien, J. L., Rossignol-Deletang, N., Martineau, J., Couturier, G., and Barthelemy, C. (2001). Regulation of cognitive activity and early communication development in young autistic, mentally retarded, and young normal children. *Dev. Psychobiol.* 39, 124–136. doi: 10.1002/dev.1036

American Psychiatric Association (2013). *Diagnostic and Statistical Manual of Mental Disorders*. 5th Edn. Arlington, VA: American Psychiatric Association.

Awh, E., Jonides, J., Smith, E. E., Schumacher, E. H., Koeppe, R. A., and Katz, S. (1996). Association of storage and rehearsal in verbal working memory: evidence from positron emission tomography. *Psychol. Sci.* 7, 25–31. doi: 10.1111/j.1467-9280.1996.tb00662.x

Berman, K. F., Ostrem, J. L., Randolf, C., Gold, J., Goldberg, T., Coppola, R., et al. (1995). Physiological activation of a cortical network during performance of the wisconsin card sorting test: positron emission tomophrahy study. *Neuropsychologia* 33, 1027–1046. doi: 10.1016/0028-3932(95)00035-2

Bernier, A., Carlson, S. M., and Whipple, N. (2010). From external regulation to self-regulation: early parenting precursors of young children's executive functioning. *Child Dev.* 81, 326–339. doi: 10.1111/j.1467-8624.2009.01397.x

Best, J. R., and Miller, P. H. (2010). A developmental perspective on executive function. *Child Dev.* 81, 1641–1660. doi: 10.1111/j.1467-8624.2010.01499.x

Bhat, A., Landa, R., and Galloway, J. (2011). Current perspectives on motor functioning in infants, children, and adults with autism spectrum disorders. *Phys. Ther.* 91, 1116–1129. doi: 10.2522/ptj.20100294

Bolton, P. F., Golding, J., Emond, A., and Steer, C. D. (2012). Autism spectrum disorder and autistic traits in the Avon Longitudinal Study of Parents and Children: precursors and early signs. *J. Am. Acad. Child Adolesc. Psychiatry* 51, 249–260. doi: 10.1016/j.jaac.2011.12.009

Brian, J., Bryson, S. E., Garon, N., Roberts, W., Smith, I. M., Szatmari, P., et al. (2008). Clinical assessment of autism in high-risk 18-month-olds. *Autism* 12, 433–456. doi: 10.1177/1362361308094500

Chawarska, K., Klin, A., Paul, R., and Volkmar, F. (2007). Autism spectrum disorder in the second year: stability and change in syndrome expression. *J. Child Psychol. Psychiatry* 48, 128–138. doi: 10.1111/j.1469-7610.2006.01685.x

Chevalier, N. (2015). The development of executive function: toward more optimal coordination of control with age. *Child Dev. Perspect.* 9, 239–244. doi: 10.1111/cdep.12138

Constantino, J. N., Zhang, Y., Frazier, T., Abbacchi, A., and Law, P. (2010). Sibling recurrence and the genetic epidemiology of autism. *Am. J. Psychiatry* 167, 1349–1356. doi: 10.1176/appi.ajp.2010.09101470

Corbett, B. A., Constantine, L. J., Hendren, R., Rocke, D., and Ozonoff, S. (2009). Examining executive functioning in children with autism spectrum disorder, attention deficit hyperactivity disorder and typical development. *Psychiatry Res.* 166, 210–222. doi: 10.1016/j.psychres.2008.02.005

Corbetta, D., and Bojczyk, K. E. (2002). Infants return to two-handed reaching when they are learning to walk. *J. Mot. Behav.* 34, 83–95. doi: 10.1080/00222890209601933

Davidson, M. C., Amso, A., Anderson, L. C., and Diamond, A. (2006). Development of cognitive control and executive functions from 4 to 13 year: evidence from manipulations of memory, inhibition, and task switching. *Neuropsychologia* 44, 2037–2078. doi: 10.1016/j.neuropsychologia.2006.02.006

Dawson, G., Webb, S., Schellenberg, G. D., Dager, S., Friedman, S., Aylward, E., et al. (2002). Defining the broader phenotype of autism: genetic, brain, and behavioral perspectives. *Dev. Psychopathol.* 14, 581–611. doi: 10.1017/S0954579402003103

Desmond, J. E., Gabrieli, J. D. E., Wagner, A. D., Ginier, B. L., and Glover, G. H. (1997). Lobular patterns of cerebellar activation in verbal working-memory and finger-tapping tasks as revealed by functional MRI. *J. Neurosci.* 17, 9675–9685.

Diamond, A. (1985). Development of the ability to use recall to guide action, as indicated by infants' performance on AB. *Child Dev.* 56, 868–883. doi: 10.2307/1130099

Diamond, A. (2000). Close interrelation of motor development and cognitive development and of the cerebellum and prefrontal cortex. *Child Dev.* 71, 44–56. doi: 10.1111/1467-8624.00117

Diamond, A. (2002). "Normal development of prefrontal cortex from birth to young adulthood: cognitive functions, anatomy, and biochemistry," in *Principles of Frontal Lobe Function*, eds D. T. Stuss and R. T. Knight (New York, NY: Oxford University Press), 466–503.

Diamond, A. (2013). Executive functions. *Annu. Rev. Psychol.* 64, 135–168. doi: 10.1146/annurev-psych-113011-143750

Diamond, A., and Goldman-Rakic, P. S. (1989). Comparison of human infants and rhesus monkeys on Piaget's AB task: evidence for dependence on dorsolateral prefrontal cortex. *Exp. Brain Res.* 74, 24–40. doi: 10.1007/BF002 48277

Durisko, C., and Fiez, J. (2010). Functional activation of the cerebellum during working memory and simple speech tasks. *Cortex* 46, 896–906. doi: 10.1016/j.cortex.2009.09.009

Estes, A., Zwaigenbaum, L., Gu, H., St. John, T., Paterson, S., Elison, J. T., et al. (2015). Behavioral, cognitive, and adaptive development in infants with autism spectrum disorder in the first 2 years of life. *J. Neurodev. Disord.* 7, 1–10. doi: 10.1186/s11689-015-9117-6

Faja, S., Sullivan, K., Meltzoff, A., Estes, A., and Bernier, R. (2016). Executive function predicts the development of play skills for verbal preschoolers with autism spectrum disorders. *Autism Res.* doi: 10.1002/aur.1608. [Epub ahead of print].

Flanagan, J. E., Landa, R., Bhat, A., and Bauman, M. (2012). Head lag in infants at risk for autism: a preliminary study. *Am. J. Occup. Ther.* 66, 577–585. doi: 10.5014/ajot.2012.004192

Garon, N., Bryson, S. E., and Smith, I. M. (2008). Executive function in preschoolers: a review using an integrative framework. *Psychol. Bull.* 134, 31–60. doi: 10.1037/0033-2909.134.1.31

Georgiades, S., Szatmari, P., Zwaigenbaum, L., Bryson, S., Brian, J., Roberts, W., et al. (2013). A prospective study of autistic-like traits in unaffected siblings of probands with autism spectrum disorder. *JAMA Psychiatry* 70, 42–48. doi: 10.1001/2013.jamapsychiatry.1

Gilmore, R., and Johnson, M. (1995). Working memory in infancy: six-month olds' performance on two versions of the oculomotor delayed response task. *J. Exp. Child Psychol.* 59, 397–418. doi: 10.1006/jecp.1995.1019

Griffith, E. M., Pennington, B. F., Wehner, E., and Rogers, S. J. (1999). Executive functions in young children with autism. *Child Dev.* 70, 817–832. doi: 10.1111/1467-8624.00059

Guthrie, W., Swineford, L. B., Nottke, C., and Wetherby, A. M. (2013). Early diagnosis of autism spectrum disorder: stability and change in clinical diagnosis and symptom presentation. *J. Child Psychol. Psychiatry* 54, 582–590. doi: 10.1111/jcpp.12008

Happé, F., Booth, R., Charlton, R., and Hughes, C. (2006). Executive function deficits in autism spectrum disorders and attention-deficit/hyperactivity disorder: examining profiles across domains and ages. *Brain Cogn.* 61, 25–39. doi: 10.1016/j.bandc.2006.03.004

Hautzel, H., Mottaghy,F. M., Specht, K., Müller, H.-W., and Krause, B.J. (2009). Evidence of a modatlity-dependent role of the cerebellum in working memory? An fmri study comparing verbal and abstract n-back tasks. *Neuroimage* 47, 2073–2082. doi: 10.1016/j.neuroimage.2009.06.005

Henry, L., Messer, D. J., and Nash, G. (2012). Executive functioning in children with specific language impairment. *J. Child Psychol. Psychiatry* 53, 37–45. doi: 10.1111/j.1469-7610.2011.02430.x

Hill, E. L. (2004a). Evaluating the theory of executive dysfunction in autism. *Dev. Rev.* 24, 189–233. doi: 10.1016/j.dr.2004.01.001

Hill, E. L. (2004b). Executive dysfunction in autism. *Trends Cogn. Sci.* 8, 26–32. doi: 10.1016/j.tics.2003.11.003

Hilton, C. L., Cumpata, K., Klohr, C., Gaetke, S., Artner, A., Johnson, H., et al. (2014). Effects of exergaming on executive function and motor skills in children with autism spectrum disorder: a pilot study. *Am. J. Occup. Ther.* 68, 57–65. doi: 10.5014/ajot.2014.008664

Holmboe, K., Elsabbagh, M., Volein, A., Tucker, L. A., Baron-Cohen, S., Bolton, P., et al. (2010). Frontal cortex functioning in the infant broader autism phenotype. *Infant Behav. Dev.* 33, 482–491. doi: 10.1016/j.infbeh.2010.05.004

Holmboe, K., Fearon, R. M. P., Csibra, G., Tucker, L. A., and Johnson, M. H. (2008). Freeze-Frame: a new infant inhibition task and its relation to frontal cortex tasks during infancy and early childhood. *J. Exp. Child Psychol.* 100, 89–114. doi: 10.1016/j.jecp.2007.09.004

Hughes, C. (1996). Brief report: planning problems in autism at the level of motor control. *J. Autism Dev. Disord.* 26, 99–107. doi: 10.1007/BF02276237

Hughes, C., Russell, J., and Robbins, T. W. (1994). Evidence for executive dysfunction in autism. *Neuropsychologia* 32, 477–492. doi: 10.1016/0028-3932(94)90092-2

Jones, E., Gliga, T., Bedford, R., Charman, T., and Johnson, M. (2014). Developmental pathways to autism: a review of prospective studies of infants at risk. *Neurosci. Biobehav. Rev.* 39, 1–33. doi: 10.1016/j.neubiorev.2013.12.001

Kana, R., Keller, T., Minshew, N., and Just, M. A. (2007). Inhibitory control in high-functioning autism: decreased activation and underconnectivity in inhibition networks. *Biol. Psychiatry.* 62, 198–206. doi: 10.1016/j.biopsych.2006.08.004

Karasik, L. B., Tamis-LeMonda, C. S., and Adolph, K. E. (2011). Transition from crawling to walking and infants' actions with objects and people. *Child Dev.* 82, 1199–1209. doi: 10.1111/j.1467-8624.2011.01595.x

Landa, R. J., Gross, A. L., Stuart, E. A., and Bauman, M. (2012). Latent class analysis of early developmental trajectory in baby siblings of children with autism. *J. Child Psychol. Psychiatry* 53, 986–996. doi: 10.1111/j.1469-7610.2012.02558.x

Livesey, D., Keen, J., Rouse, J., and White, F. (2006). The relationship between measures of executive function, motor performance and externalising behaviour in 5- and 6-year-old children. *Hum. Mov. Sci.* 25, 50–64. doi: 10.1016/j.humov.2005.10.008

Lord, C., Rutter, M., and Couteur, A. (1994). Autism diagnostic interview-revised: a revised version of a diagnostic interview for caregivers of individuals with possible pervasive developmental disorders. *J. Autism Dev. Disord.* 24, 659–685. doi: 10.1007/BF02172145

Lord, C., Rutter, M., DiLavore, P. C., Risi, S., Gotham, K., and Bishop, S. L. (2012). *Autism Diagnostic Observation Schedule, 2nd Edn. (ADOS-2) Manual (Part I): Modules 1-4.* Torrance, CA: Western Psychological Services.

Luna, B., Doll, S. K., Hegedus, S. J., Minshew, N. J., and Sweeney, J. A. (2007). Maturation of executive function in autism. *Biol. Psychiatry* 61, 474–481. doi: 10.1016/j.biopsych.2006.02.030

Marcovitch, S., and Zelazo, P. D. (1999). The A-not-B error: results from a logistic meta-analysis. *Child Dev.* 70, 1297–1313. doi: 10.1111/1467-8624.00095

Maxwell, M. (1992). *Manual for the Family Interview for Genetic Studies (FIGS).* Bethesda, MD: National Institute of Mental Health.

McEvoy, R., Rogers, S., and Pennington, B. (1993). Executive function and social communication deficits in young autistic children. *J. Child Psychol. Psychiatry* 34, 563–578. doi: 10.1111/j.1469-7610.1993.tb01036.x

Messinger, D., Young, G. S., Ozonoff, S., Dobkins, K., Carter, A., Zwaigenbaum, L., et al. (2013). Beyond autism: a baby siblings research consortium study of high-risk children at three years of age. *J. Am. Acad. Child Adolesc. Psychiatry* 52, 300–308. doi: 10.1016/j.jaac.2012.12.011

Mullen, E. M. (1995). *Mullen Scales of Early Learning: AGS edition.* Circle Pines, MN: American Guidance Service Publishing.

Ozonoff, S., and Strayer, D. L. (2001). Further evidence of intact working memory in autism. *J. Autism Dev. Disord.* 31, 257–263. doi: 10.1023/A:1010794902139

Ozonoff, S., Young, G. S., Carter, A., Messinger, D., Yirmiya, N., Zwaigenbaum, L., et al. (2011). Recurrence risk for autism spectrum disorders: a baby siblings research consortium study. *Pediatrics* 128, e488–e495. doi: 10.1542/peds.2010-2825

Ozonoff, S., Young, G. S., Landa, R. J., Brian, J., Bryson, S., Charman, T., et al. (2015). Diagnostic stability in young children at risk for autism spectrum disorder: a baby siblings research consortium study. *J. Child Psychol. Psychiatry* 56, 988–998. doi: 10.1111/jcpp.12421

Piaget, J. (1954). *The Construction of Reality in the Child.* New York, NY: Basic.

Piek, J., Dawson, L., Smith, L., and Gasson, N. (2008). The role of early fine and gross motor development on later motor and cognitive ability. *Hum. Mov. Sci.* 27, 668–681. doi: 10.1016/j.humov.2007.11.002

Pisula, E., and Ziegart-Sadowska, K. (2015). Broader autism phenotype in siblings of children with ASD—a review. *Int. J. Mol. Sci.* 16, 13217–13258. doi: 10.3390/ijms160613217

Riggs, N. R., Jahromi, L. B., Razza, R. P., Dillworth-Bart, J. E., and Müeller, U. (2006). Executive function and the promotion of social-emotional competence. *J. Appl. Dev. Psychol.* 27, 300–309. doi: 10.1016/j.appdev.2006.04.002

Rozga, A., Huntman, T., Young, G. S., Rogers, S. J., Ozonoff, S., Dapretto, M., et al. (2011). Behavioral profiles of affected and unaffected siblings of children with autism: contribution of measures of mother-infant interaction and nonverbal communication. *J. Autism Dev. Disord.* 41, 287–301. doi: 10.1007/s10803-010-1051-6

Rutter, M., Bailey, A., Lord, C., and Berument, S. (2003). *Social Communication Questionnaire.* Los Angeles, CA: Western Psychological Services.

Smith, L. B., Thelen, E., Titzer, R., and McLin, D. (1999). Knowing in the context of acting: the task dynamics of the A-not-B error. *Psychol. Rev.* 106, 235–260. doi: 10.1037/0033-295X.106.2.235

Solomon, M., Ozonoff, S. J., Cummings, N., and Carter, C. S. (2008). Cognitive control in autism spectrum disorders. *Int. J. Dev. Neurosci.* 26, 239–247. doi: 10.1016/j.ijdevneu.2007.11.001

Warren, Z. E., Foss-Feig, J. H., Malesa, E. E., Lee, E. B., Taylor, J. L., Newsom, C. R., et al. (2012). Neurocognitive and behavioral outcomes of younger siblings of children with autism spectrum disorder at age five. *J. Autism Dev. Disord.* 42, 409–418. doi: 10.1007/s10803-011-1263-4

Wassenberg, R., Kessels, A., Kalff, A., Hurks, P., Jolles, J., Feron, F., et al. (2005). Relation between cognitive and motor performance in 5- to 6-year-old children: results from a large-scale cross-sectional study. *Child Dev.* 76, 1092–1103. doi: 10.1111/j.1467-8624.2005.00899.x

Yerys, B. E., Hepburn, S. L., Pennington, B. F., and Rogers, S. J. (2007). Executive function in preschoolers with autism: evidence consistent with a secondary deficit. *J. Autism Dev. Disord.* 37, 1068–1079. doi: 10.1007/s10803-006-0250-7

Conflict of Interest Statement: The authors declare that the research was conducted in the absence of any commercial or financial relationships that could be construed as a potential conflict of interest.

Walking in School-Aged Children in a Dual-Task Paradigm is Related to Age but not to Cognition, Motor Behavior, Injuries, or Psychosocial Functioning

Priska Hagmann-von Arx[1†], Olivia Manicolo[1†], Sakari Lemola[2] and Alexander Grob[1]*

[1] Department of Psychology, University of Basel, Basel, Switzerland, [2] Department of Psychology, University of Warwick, Coventry, UK

Age-dependent gait characteristics and associations with cognition, motor behavior, injuries, and psychosocial functioning were investigated in 138 typically developing children aged 6.7–13.2 years ($M = 10.0$ years). Gait velocity, normalized velocity, and variability were measured using the walkway system GAITRite without an additional task (single task) and while performing a motor or cognitive task (dual task). Assessment of children's cognition included tests for intelligence and executive functions; parents reported on their child's motor behavior, injuries, and psychosocial functioning. Gait variability (an index of gait regularity) decreased with increasing age in both single- and dual-task walking. Dual-task gait decrements were stronger when children walked in the motor compared to the cognitive dual-task condition and decreased with increasing age in both dual-task conditions. Gait alterations from single- to dual-task conditions were not related to children's cognition, motor behavior, injuries, or psychosocial functioning.

Keywords: gait, dual-task walking, intelligence, executive functions, psychosocial functioning, school-aged children

Edited by:
Petra Hauf,
St. Francis Xavier University, Canada

Reviewed by:
Ruth Ford,
Anglia Ruskin University, UK
Simone V. Gill,
Boston University, USA

***Correspondence:**
Priska Hagmann-von Arx
priska.hagmann@unibas.ch

†Shared first authorship.

INTRODUCTION

Walking is the most important mode of human locomotion (Adolph et al., 2003) and is a remarkably complex motor skill involving neural control systems that produce coordinated limb movements (Hausdorff, 2007). There is evidence that among typically developing children a mature gait pattern is established at about 7 years (Adolph et al., 2003). However, some studies investigating older children have shown that gait variability – subtle stride-to-stride fluctuations reflecting the regularity of a gait pattern – continues to develop across childhood into adolescence (e.g., Hausdorff et al., 1999).

Performing concurrent tasks, like listening to a conversation while walking, is an everyday behavior. Such dual-task situations adversely affect children's walking, indicating that the regulation of gait requires cognitive processes such as executive and attentional functions (e.g., Cherng et al., 2007). Studies investigating children with developmental impairments have shown that children with motor and cognitive deficits are more vulnerable to dual-task gait decrements than typically developing children (e.g., Cherng et al., 2009; Katz-Leurer et al., 2011). Such decrements, in turn, may affect children's motor behavior and psychosocial functioning, as it is known that children with poor motor skills participate in physical activity less frequently than controls (Cairney et al., 2005) and are at higher risk for peer rejection (Bejerot et al., 2013) as well as for social and emotional problems (Zwicker et al., 2012). However, these studies investigated children with developmental impairments, so it is still unclear if the maturity of walking patterns is related to cognition, motor behavior, and psychosocial functioning in typically developing children.

The aim of the present study was to shed light on age-dependent gait characteristics with a focus on gait variability in single- and dual-task walking and for the first time to examine the relation of dual-task effects on gait to cognition, motor behavior, and injuries, as well as psychosocial functioning in typically developing school-aged children.

After typically developing children master independent walking at approximately 12 to 14.5 months of age (Storvold et al., 2013), gait development is characterized by rapid improvements over the subsequent months (Bril and Ledebt, 1998; Adolph et al., 2003) until by the age of 3 years the visually apparent unsteadiness in walking has been replaced by a more stable gait pattern (Sutherland et al., 1988). With increasing age children show more subtle improvements in spatiotemporal gait parameters, including enhanced gait velocity and step length, and reach a mature gait pattern at about 7 years (e.g., Hillman et al., 2009; Holm et al., 2009). However, depending on the assessed gait parameters, there is evidence that gait continues to develop beyond this age (Hausdorff et al., 1999; Hillman et al., 2009; Lythgo et al., 2009, 2011; Froehle et al., 2013; Manicolo et al., 2016). For example, Hausdorff et al. (1999) investigated gait in typically developing children between 3 and 14 years of age. They measured gait velocity – considered a marker of general functional performance (cf. Al-Yahya et al., 2011) – as well as stride-to-stride fluctuations in spatiotemporal parameters (i.e., gait variability), which are sensitive to subtle physiological changes such as neural maturation and are believed to reflect the automaticity and regularity of gait (cf. Hausdorff, 2005). Results revealed that gait velocity was lowest in the youngest age group (aged 3 and 4 years) but did not significantly differ in the middle (aged 6 and 7 years) compared to the oldest (aged 11–14 years) age group, indicating a maturation of gait velocity at approximately 7 years of age. Results regarding gait variability showed a different picture. Gait variability continuously decreased from the youngest to the middle to the oldest age group. Thus, gait further developed after age 7 by becoming more automated and regular during middle and late childhood. In line with Hausdorff et al.'s (1999) findings, results of a recent study conducted by Abbruzzese et al. (2014) showed that when comparing gait variability of typically developing children aged 7–10 years to that of adults, children walked with significantly higher gait variability.

These findings indicate that among typically developing children gait variability decreases with age and that a mature gait pattern involving a high level of automaticity and regularity indicated by low gait variability may not be completely developed in school-aged children. Furthermore, these results highlight the sensitivity of gait variability measures and indicate their relevance when investigating children's development of gait (Hausdorff, 2007).

In everyday life children usually do things concomitantly while walking, for example, listening to someone talk or fastening their jacket buttons. Such concurrent tasks may interfere with walking as less attention can be directed to the regulation of gait. Walking was for many years considered an automatic activity with only little involvement of cognitive processing. However, studies using a dual-task paradigm showed that gait is adversely affected when individuals are asked to walk and perform a concurrent task, indicating that walking requires cognitive resources (Huang and Mercer, 2001; Woollacott and Shumway-Cook, 2002; Huang et al., 2003; Cherng et al., 2007; Gill, 2015). Two theories have been used to explain dual-task effects on gait. The capacity-sharing theory proposes that attentional resources are limited in capacity and have to be shared between two tasks (Kahneman, 1973; Tombu and Jolicoeur, 2003). Researchers have suggested that gait decrements occur when the attentional demands of the concurrent task exceed the attentional resource capacity available (Huang and Mercer, 2001; Woollacott and Shumway-Cook, 2002). In contrast, the bottleneck theory (Pashler, 1994) proposes that two tasks that are performed simultaneously can only be carried out sequentially. This poses high demands on the capacity to switch between tasks, which in turn may lead to diminished performance in one or both of the tasks. However, there is currently no agreement on which theory best explains cognitive processing and dual-task effects (Yogev-Seligmann et al., 2008).

Studies investigating dual-task gait in typically developing children showed that performing a concurrent task while walking caused gait decrements (Huang et al., 2003; Cherng et al., 2007; Boonyong et al., 2012; Hung et al., 2013), indicating that also in children cognitive processes are involved when walking. Most studies on dual-task gait in children investigated spatiotemporal gait parameters such as velocity or stride length (e.g., Cherng et al., 2007; Boonyong et al., 2012; Hung et al., 2013), whereas only a few studies investigated gait variability. These revealed inconsistent results, with some researchers reporting no effect of dual tasking on gait variability (Leitner et al., 2007; Katz-Leurer et al., 2013; Abbruzzese et al., 2014) and others showing an increase in gait variability (Schaefer et al., 2010). However, the sample sizes in these studies were small, limiting the statistical power of these analyses.

Regarding age-dependent differences in dual-task gait, the effects of concurrent tasks on walking are stronger for younger compared to older typically developing children or adults. For example, Boonyong et al. (2012) examined the effect of an auditory concurrent task on spatiotemporal gait parameters in children aged 5 and 6 years, children aged 7–16 years, and healthy adults. Gait decrements such as reduced gait velocity in dual-task conditions were more profound in the younger compared to the older children and were greater in the two groups of children compared to the adults. Further, the study by Abbruzzese et al. (2014) revealed greater dual-task effects on gait variability in typically developing children aged 7–10 years compared to adults when they had to perform concurrent motor tasks such as carrying a tray with a pitcher, indicating that dual-task gait is still developing during childhood.

Furthermore, there is evidence that dual-task gait decrements are apparent for both motor and cognitive concurrent tasks. For instance, Cherng et al. (2007) investigated typically developing children aged 4–6 years while they walked and concurrently performed an easy or a difficult motor (carrying a tray with or without marbles on it) or cognitive (repeating a series of digits forward or backward) task. Results revealed that children showed poorer walking performance in the difficult motor task condition as well as in both cognitive task conditions compared to single-task walking. Comparing gait decrements caused by the different dual-task conditions revealed inconsistent results. The concurrent motor task led to greater decreases in stride length and greater increases in double limb support (i.e., the percentage of a gait cycle when both feet are on the ground) compared to the concurrent cognitive task. In contrast, the concurrent cognitive tasks led to greater increases in base of support (i.e., the area between the feet in contact with the ground), while effects on velocity and cadence (i.e., steps per minute) were not significantly different between task conditions. From a theoretical point of view the multiple-resource model of attention (Wickens, 1991) assumes that two tasks will interfere with each other if they share the same pool of resources. Therefore, one might expect that walking while performing a concurrent cognitive task might not cause the same level of gait decrements as a concurrent motor task that shares resources with walking (Yogev-Seligmann et al., 2008).

Studies investigating children with developmental impairments showed that dual-task effects on gait are stronger in children with poor motor skills (Cherng et al., 2009) and that also children with deficits in executive and attentional functions show more gait alterations while dual tasking than typically developing children. For example, children with severe post-traumatic brain injury showed reduced gait velocity as well as higher gait variability when they had to walk and concomitantly memorize and recall a series of numbers or listen to and identify commonly experienced sounds compared to typically developing children (Katz-Leurer et al., 2011). Further, children born very preterm walked with comparable gait velocity but higher stride velocity variability than their peers born at term when they had to listen to and memorize digits (Hagmann-von Arx et al., 2015). Similarly, studies investigating adults showed that dual-task effects on gait and particularly on gait variability are more profound in older individuals (Beurskens and Bock, 2012) and in patients with neurological impairments (Al-Yahya et al., 2011) who exhibit deficits in executive and attentional functions. Executive functions refer to higher cognitive processes that include the control and allocation of attentional resources necessary for adaptive planning of behaviors (Anderson, 2002). It is assumed that lower executive functions are associated with a reduced capacity to divide attention among multiple tasks and, therefore, go along with higher gait alterations in dual-task situations, as individuals are kept from devoting the appropriate attentional resources to their gait (Springer et al., 2006; Leitner et al., 2007). To our knowledge, however, no study has examined the relation between gait and cognition in typically developing school-aged children.

Motor performance affects other important aspects of children's development (Piek et al., 2006b). Independent walking alters an infant's relation to objects and people and allows the independent approach to new interaction partners (Iverson, 2010). These interactions, in turn, provide context for acquiring psychosocial skills (e.g., Karasik et al., 2011). However, motor skills that are not age-appropriately developed may negatively influence children's behavior and psychosocial functioning. For instance, children with poor motor skills perform more poorly in individual as well as in team games and sports (Cantell et al., 1994; Skinner and Piek, 2001), which may lead them to voluntarily withdraw from situations in which they might demonstrate their motor abilities (Schoemaker and Kalverboer, 1994). In a similar vein, there is evidence that children with impaired motor coordination spend more time alone and participate less often in physical activity such as social play or organized sports than typically developing children (Cairney et al., 2005), which in turn places further motor development at risk (Bouffard et al., 1996). For example, there is evidence that children with low levels of physical activity have an increased risk of injury (Bloemers et al., 2012). Furthermore, children with motor deficits may be perceived by peers as being different or awkward, which may lead to peer rejection (Bejerot et al., 2013). For example, there is evidence that children with poor motor skills are at higher risk of being bullied at school than children with average motor skills (Piek et al., 2006a; Bejerot and Humble, 2013; Bejerot et al., 2013). Withdrawal from or exclusion by the peer group may lead to decreased self-esteem in children with poor motor skills, which in turn may increase emotional and behavioral problems such as symptoms of anxiety and depression (Zwicker et al., 2012).

Taken together, the evidence suggests that (a) in typically developing school-aged children gait is still developing in single and dual tasking, particularly regarding its regularity, (b) children with cognitive deficits show more gait decrements in dual-task conditions, and (c) poor motor skills are related to other aspects of children's development. However, there are important gaps in the research. First, studies investigating age-dependent gait characteristics that include gait variability in single- and dual-task conditions in typically developing school-aged children are rare. Second, studies examining associations between dual-task gait effects and cognition in typically developing children are missing. Finally, to date, no study has examined the relation between dual-task gait effects, motor behavior, injuries, and psychosocial functioning in typically developing children.

In our study, we hypothesized the following: First, for single-task walking, we expected no association between age and gait velocity but hypothesized that age would be negatively related to gait variability, as the latter is sensitive to more subtle changes in gait (Hausdorff, 2005). Second, for dual-task walking, we hypothesized that age would be positively related to gait velocity and negatively related to gait variability, as there is evidence that dual-task gait is still developing (Boonyong et al., 2012; Abbruzzese et al., 2014). Third, we hypothesized that dual-task walking would lead to greater gait decrements (i.e., lower gait velocity and higher gait variability) compared to single-task walking, with greater gait decrements in a motor compared to a cognitive dual-task condition, drawing on the assumption that tasks sharing the same pool of processing resources interfere with each other more strongly (Yogev-Seligmann et al., 2008). Fourth, we hypothesized that cognitive and motor task performance would be decreased in dual- compared to single-task conditions, following the capacity-sharing theory (Kahneman, 1973; Tombu and Jolicoeur, 2003) as well as the bottleneck theory (Pashler, 1994) suggesting that dual-task walking may not only affect gait but also concurrent task performance. Finally, we hypothesized that less dual-task gait effects (i.e., lower change in gait velocity and gait variability from single- to dual-task walking) would be related to better cognitive performance, better motor behavior (i.e., higher sports participation) lower injury risk, and fewer injuries, as well as higher psychosocial functioning (i.e., higher physical and psychological well-being, better moods and emotions, higher self-perception and autonomy, better parent relation, more financial resources, better social support, better school environment, as well as higher social acceptance), as suggested by the notion that motor performance also affects other domains of children's development (Piek et al., 2006b).

MATERIALS AND METHODS

Participants

A total of 141 children (63 girls, 78 boys, M_{age} = 10.0 years, SD = 1.5, age range: 6.7–13.2 years) were recruited from birth announcements in newspapers as well as from local schools in the German-speaking part of Switzerland. All children were screened for developmental coordination disorder using the German version of the Movement Assessment Battery for Children (2nd ed.) with a cut-off below the 16th percentile (Petermann, 2008). Three children were excluded because of significant motor impairment. The final sample for this study consisted of 138 typically developing school-age children aged 6.7–13.2 years (M = 10.0 years, SD = 1.5; 62 girls, 76 boys) enrolled in public primary schools.

The local Ethics Committee approved the study. Parents gave written informed consent for the children to participate and assent was obtained from the children.

Procedure

All children came to the laboratory for a visit that lasted approximately 3 h. Data were collected by trained study personnel. A battery of procedures was given in counterbalanced order to assess single- and dual-task gait and cognitive performance (i.e., intelligence, executive functions). In addition, children's weight was measured with a digital scale, height was measured with a fixed stadiometer, and leg length was measured from greater trochanter to the floor, bisecting the lateral malleolus, with the children wearing their normal clothes and footwear. Parents completed questionnaires to provide information on demographic data, as well as children's participation in sports, injury risk, and psychosocial functioning. Children received a gift voucher of CHF 30 for participating (1 CHF = 1.029 USD; February 2016) and parents received CHF 30 for completing the parental questionnaire.

Measures

Gait Assessment

Gait parameters were measured using a portable GAITRite electronic walkway system (GAITRite Platinum; CIR Systems, USA). This walkway system consists of an electronic mat (length: 7.01 m, width: 0.9 m) with 23,040 integrated pressure sensors. To minimize the effects of acceleration and deceleration, two electronically inactive sections each with a length of 1.25 m were added on each end of the walkway system. Hence, each walk covered a distance of approximately 10 m with an average of eight steps. Children's gait assessment using GAITRite has been established as reliable and valid (Thorpe et al., 2005). Gait analysis was performed according to European guidelines (Kressig and Beauchet, 2006). For each walk, the GAITRite software generates step-to-step values for a range of spatiotemporal gait parameters. The following gait parameters were derived: gait velocity which was measured in centimeters per second. In order to account for differences in children's leg length we additionally normalized gait velocity to a dimensionless quantity using the formula suggested by Hof (1996, p. 223):

$$\text{normalized velocity} = \frac{\textit{gait velocity}}{\sqrt{(g \times l)}}$$

where g is the gravitational constant (9.81 m/s^2) and l is leg length. Further, we assessed gait variability as stride-to-stride variability in stride velocity, stride time, and stride length all expressed as the percentage coefficient of variation (standard deviation/mean × 100).

Prior to gait assessment, children completed just the two tasks that would be used as the concurrent task for 10 s while standing so that their performance in these tasks could be determined. The concurrent tasks were selected according to related dual-task research. First, the children were asked to listen to and recall digits (digits task; Lindenberger et al., 2000; Leitner et al., 2007). For this task, children heard a list of randomized digits presented from a computer over loudspeakers that were installed at the front left and front right corner of the laboratory. Afterward, the children were asked to recall the digits. Second, children were asked to unfasten and fasten a button (button task) at stomach height (Ebersbach et al., 1995; Yang et al., 2007). Performance on this task was measured as the number of times the button could be unfastened and fastened.

Before the gait recordings, children were given one demonstration and one practice trial to familiarize them with the walkway system. Then, children were instructed to walk at their preferred pace without any additional task (single-task condition) with a total of four walking trials. Afterward, the children were instructed to walk at their preferred pace and to simultaneously perform one of the concurrent tasks (dual-task conditions) with two trials each. In the dual-task conditions children were not instructed to prioritize either one of the tasks. After each walk, gait data were analyzed using GAITRite software. For each child, gait parameters were averaged across the corresponding trials for further data analysis. All children successfully completed all walking trials in the first attempt. However, for two children (aged 7.6 and 8.1 years) dual-task gait parameters are not available because of technical error of GAITRite during the testing session.

Cognitive Functions

Intelligence was assessed using the German version of the Wechsler Intelligence Scale for Children (4th ed., WISC-IV; Petermann and Petermann, 2011). The WISC-IV is an individually administered instrument for assessing intellectual abilities in children and adolescents aged 6–16 years with established reliability and validity (e.g., Daseking et al., 2007; Hagmann-von Arx et al., 2012). The WISC-IV comprises 10 core subtests and five supplemental subtests, which were not administered in the current study. The subtests are assigned to four index scores (verbal comprehension, perceptual reasoning, working memory, processing speed) and are combined to form the full-scale IQ with a mean of 100 ($SD = 15$), representing a child's global intellectual functioning. Due to restrictions in testing time intelligence scores are missing for six children.

Executive functions were measured using tasks from the computer-based Cambridge Neuropsychological Test Automated Battery (CANTAB touchscreen tests). CANTAB is suited for children aged from 4 years and provides highly reliable and valid measures for executive functions (e.g., Luciana, 2003). After a motor screening task, which introduced the CANTAB touchscreen to the children, they completed four tasks: The intra-extra dimensional (IED) set shift is a test of rule acquisition. It measures shifting and cognitive flexibility and records the number of errors made during the test. The rapid visual processing (RVP) test is a measure of vigilance or the ability to maintain a certain level of attention while engaged in a repetitive task. The outcome provides a measure of sensitivity to the target regardless of the response tendency. The stockings of Cambridge (SOC) task assesses the planning element of executive functions and records the number of problems solved in the minimum number of moves. Finally, the spatial working memory (SWM) test requires the child to maintain spatial information and to subsequently manipulate the presented items in working memory. The SWM task records the number of search errors. Scores reported in this study are standard scores based on age-corrected norms with $M = 0$ and $SD = 1$. Due to restrictions in testing time measures of executive functions are missing for six children.

Participation in Sports, Injury Risk, and Injuries

Parents reported whether their child was participating in sports. If yes, parents were further asked in which sport their child participated, how many times per week, and for how long. Scores for participation in sports reported in this study are number of minutes per week.

Parents also completed the German adaptation of the Injury Behavior Checklist (IBC; Brandau and Daghofer, 2010). The German IBC consists of 13 items regarding children's risk-taking behaviors that can lead to injury. Parents are asked to rate the statements on a scale of 0 (*never*) to 3 (*very often*). The IBC has high reliability and established validity (Speltz et al., 1990; Brandau and Daghofer, 2010). Reliability in the present study was $\alpha = 0.76$.

To assess injuries, we asked parents to report whether their child had been injured in the past 24 months. If yes, parents were further asked to list all injuries and provide information regarding the location of the accident, the activity being performed while injured, the type of injury, and whether the injury had to be treated. Scores for injuries reported in this study are number of injuries in the past 24 months. These parental reports are available for 129 children.

Psychosocial Functioning

Psychosocial functioning was assessed using the German version of the KIDSCREEN-52, a parental questionnaire with proven reliability and validity (Ravens-Sieberer et al., 2008). KIDSCREEN-52 consists of 52 items assessing the frequency of behavior and feelings or the intensity of an attitude using a 5-point Likert scale with the anchor points 1 (*never*) and 5 (*always*). The items are assigned to 10 dimensions: physical well-being, psychological well-being, moods and emotions, self-perception, autonomy, parent relation and home life, peers and social support, school environment, social acceptance/bullying, and financial resources. Reliability in the present study ranged from $\alpha = 0.67$ (physical well-being) to $\alpha = 0.91$ (psychological well-being). The KIDSCREEN-52 is available for 128 children.

Statistical Procedure

Pearson's correlations were computed to assess the relations between children's demographic variables and all gait parameters in single- and dual-task conditions. Effects of age and dual-task conditions on gait were examined using repeated-measures multivariate analysis of variance (MANOVA) with one within-subject factor (walking condition: single-task vs. dual-task digits vs. dual-task button) and age as a continuous predictor. Significant effects were followed up with Bonferroni corrected *post hoc* pairwise comparisons. To assess effects of age on concurrent task performance, repeated-measures ANOVAs were performed separately for each walking condition with one within-subject factor (task performance: single task vs. dual task) and age as a continuous predictor. Extreme values in gait parameters defined as scores exceeding 3 *SD*s from the mean were truncated to ± 3 *SD*. The level of significance was set to 0.05. The F statistic, p-values (two-tailed), and effect sizes (η^2) as well as regression parameter estimates (standardized beta coefficients) for the relation of age to gait and concurrent task performance for each walking condition are reported.

To examine associations between gait and children's cognition, motor behavior, and injuries, as well as psychosocial functioning we first calculated mean change values which are the mean differences between single-task and dual-task values. Positive signs denote a decrease from single-task to dual-task walking in the respective gait parameter, whereas negative signs denote an increase from single-task to dual-task walking in the respective gait parameter. Afterward, regression analyses with mean change values in gait parameters predicting children's cognition, motor behavior, injuries, and psychosocial functioning were calculated controlling for age. Because of the high number of regressions performed, the level of significance was set to $p < 0.01$ to reduce the probability of alpha error accumulation. To estimate the statistical power given the sample size of the study, *post hoc* power analyses were performed using G*Power (Faul et al., 2007). The chance of detecting medium-sized effects ($r = 0.30$) was 97% at a 0.01 alpha level. All analyses were performed using SPSS Statistics 22 for Apple Mac.

RESULTS

Means, standard deviations, and correlations among children's demographic characteristics and gait parameters in single- and dual-task conditions are provided in **Table 1**.

Age Effects on Gait in Single- and Dual-Task Conditions

Repeated-measures MANOVAs were used to analyze the effects of dual tasking and age on gait. Regarding gait velocity, results revealed a significant within-subject effect of walking condition (Wilks's multivariate test), $F(2,133) = 21.154$, $p < 0.001$, $\eta^2 = 0.241$. Pairwise comparisons revealed higher gait velocity in single-task walking compared to both dual-task conditions ($p < 0.001$) and higher gait velocity in the dual-task condition digits compared to button ($p < 0.001$). There was no significant between-subjects effect of age but a significant Walking Condition × Age interaction (Wilks's multivariate test), $F(2,133) = 3.956$, $p = 0.021$, $\eta^2 = 0.056$: While the effect of age was not significant for single-task walking or the dual-task condition digits, it was significant for the dual-task condition button, such that older children walked with higher gait velocity than younger children when unfastening and fastening a button. The regression parameter estimates for the associations between age and gait velocity in each walking condition are depicted in **Figure 1A**.

Regarding normalized velocity, results revealed a significant within-subject effect of walking condition (Wilks's multivariate test), $F(2,130) = 28.720$, $p < 0.001$, $\eta^2 = 0.306$. Pairwise comparisons revealed higher normalized velocity in single-task walking compared to both dual-task conditions ($p < 0.001$) and higher normalized velocity in the dual-task condition digits compared to button ($p < 0.001$). The between-subjects effect of age was marginally significant, $F(1,131) = 3.141$, $p = 0.079$, $\eta^2 = 0.023$, such that older children walked with lower normalized velocity than younger children. Further, the Walking Condition × Age interaction was significant (Wilks's multivariate test), $F(2,130) = 7.192$, $p < 0.001$, $\eta^2 = 0.100$, indicating that the effect of age on normalized velocity was stronger in the single-task condition compared to the dual-task conditions. The regression parameter estimates for the associations between age and normalized velocity in each walking condition are depicted in **Figure 1B**.

For stride velocity variability, repeated-measures MANOVAs revealed a significant within-subject effect of walking condition (Wilks's multivariate test), $F(2,133) = 8.229$, $p < 0.001$, $\eta^2 = 0.110$. Pairwise comparisons revealed lower variability in single-task walking compared to both dual-task walking conditions ($p < 0.001$) and lower variability in the dual-task condition digits compared to button ($p < 0.001$). Furthermore, there was a significant between-subjects effect of age, $F(1,134) = 22.990$, $p < 0.001$, $\eta^2 = 0.146$, such that older children walked with lower variability than younger children in all walking conditions. The Walking Condition × Age interaction was marginally significant (Wilks's multivariate test), $F(2,133) = 2.800$, $p = 0.064$, $\eta^2 = 0.040$, indicating that the effect of age on gait variability tended to be stronger in the single-task condition and dual-task condition button compared to the dual-task condition digits. The regression parameter estimates for the associations between age and stride velocity variability in each walking condition are depicted in **Figure 1C**.

Regarding stride time variability, results revealed a significant within-subject effect of walking condition (Wilks's multivariate test), $F(2,133) = 4.546$, $p = 0.012$, $\eta^2 = 0.064$. Pairwise comparisons revealed lower variability in single-task walking compared to both dual-task conditions ($p < 0.001$) and lower variability in the dual-task condition digits compared to button ($p < 0.001$). Furthermore, there was a significant between-subjects effect of age, $F(1,134) = 13.328$, $p < 0.001$, $\eta^2 = 0.090$, such that older children walked with lower gait variability than younger children. There was no significant Walking Condition × Age interaction. The regression parameter estimates for the associations between age and stride time variability in each walking condition are shown in **Figure 1D**.

Regarding stride length variability, results revealed a significant within-subject effect of walking condition (Wilks's multivariate test), $F(2,133) = 7.690$, $p = 0.001$, $\eta^2 = 0.104$. Pairwise comparisons revealed lower variability in single-task walking compared to both dual-task conditions ($p < 0.003$) and lower variability in the dual-task condition digits compared to button ($p < 0.001$). Furthermore, there was a significant between-subjects effect of age, $F(1,134) = 16.819$, $p < 0.001$, $\eta^2 = 0.112$, such that older children walked with lower gait variability than younger children. Finally, there was a significant Walking Condition × Age interaction (Wilks's multivariate test), $F(2,133) = 3.114$, $p = 0.048$, $\eta^2 = 0.045$, such that the effect of age on gait variability was stronger in the dual-task condition button compared to single-task walking and the dual-task condition digits. The regression parameter estimates for the associations between age and stride length variability in each walking condition are shown in **Figure 1E**.

Age Effects on Concurrent Task Performance in Single- and Dual-Task Conditions

Children's performances of recalling digits in the single-task ($M = 3.94$, $SD = 0.89$) and dual-task ($M = 4.10$, $SD = 0.91$) conditions were comparable, $F(1,133) = 1.277$, $p = 0.260$, $\eta^2 = 0.010$. However, children's performance

TABLE 1 | Descriptive statistics and correlations for demographics and gait parameters.

	Variable	*M*	*SD*	Correlations																		
				1	2	3	4	5	6	7	8	9	10	11	12	13	14	15	16	17	18	19
Demographics																						
1	Age	10.0	1.5	1																		
2	Sex (% male/female)[a]	(55/45)	–	−0.14	1																	
3	Height (cm)	141.7	10.6	0.79	−0.15	1																
4	Weight (kg)	35.0	8.6	0.68	−0.07	0.82	1															
5	Leg length (cm)	73.4	13.4	0.39	−0.09	0.55	0.47	1														
Single task																						
6	Velocity (cm/s)	132.6	19.0	−0.04	0.00	0.14	0.07	0.04	1													
7	Normalized velocity	4.9	0.7	−0.28	0.04	−0.20	−0.21	−0.27	0.94	1												
8	CV velocity (%)	2.6	0.9	−0.31	0.04	−0.28	−0.18	−0.20	−0.22	−0.12	1											
9	CV stride time (%)	1.9	0.6	−0.29	0.06	−0.30	−0.26	−0.18	−0.11	−0.01	0.57	1										
10	CV stride length (%)	2.1	0.7	−0.23	0.09	−0.28	−0.21	−0.24	−0.33	−0.23	0.71	0.40	1									
Dual task: digits																						
11	Velocity (cm/s)	105.3	16.0	0.08	0.04	0.10	−0.01	0.10	0.59	0.56	−0.23	−0.19	−0.31	1								
12	Normalized velocity	3.9	0.6	−0.14	0.08	−0.20	−0.25	−0.27	0.54	0.62	−0.14	−0.11	0.20	0.95	1							
13	CV velocity (%)	3.4	1.3	−0.18	−0.04	−0.15	−0.10	−0.01	−0.05	0.00	0.20	0.20	0.10	−0.29	−0.23	1						
14	CV stride time (%)	2.4	0.9	−0.21	−0.06	−0.20	−0.18	−0.08	−0.20	−0.13	0.33	0.32	0.25	−0.37	−0.29	0.64	1					
15	CV stride length (%)	2.4	1.0	−0.22	−0.12	−0.13	−0.07	−0.09	−0.08	−0.04	0.17	0.20	0.15	−0.36	−0.30	0.66	0.43	1				
Dual task: button																						
16	Velocity (cm/s)	88.1	16.9	0.23	−0.01	0.17	0.09	0.08	0.36	0.30	−0.19	−0.22	−0.31	0.66	0.59	−0.28	−0.35	−0.30	1			
17	Normalized velocity	3.2	0.6	0.05	0.01	−0.07	−0.09	−0.07	0.36	0.38	−0.12	−0.15	−0.24	0.68	0.68	−0.24	−0.31	−0.26	0.96	1		
18	CV velocity (%)	5.1	2.3	−0.31	0.02	−0.14	0.00	−0.04	0.11	0.14	0.16	0.12	0.13	−0.25	−0.20	0.20	0.22	0.25	−0.59	−0.56	1	
19	CV stride time (%)	3.5	1.6	−0.22	0.00	−0.08	0.02	−0.06	0.03	0.06	0.16	0.13	0.17	−0.31	−0.28	0.14	0.31	0.23	−0.60	−0.59	0.77	1
20	CV stride length (%)	3.7	2.0	−0.28	−0.05	−0.16	−0.07	−0.11	0.00	0.07	0.18	0.12	0.24	−0.29	−0.22	0.12	0.27	0.27	0.55	−0.52	0.78	0.71

CV, coefficient of variation. [a]*0 = male, 1 = female; Significance:* $p < 0.05: r > 0.17; p < 0.01: r > 0.22; p < 0.001: r > 0.27$.

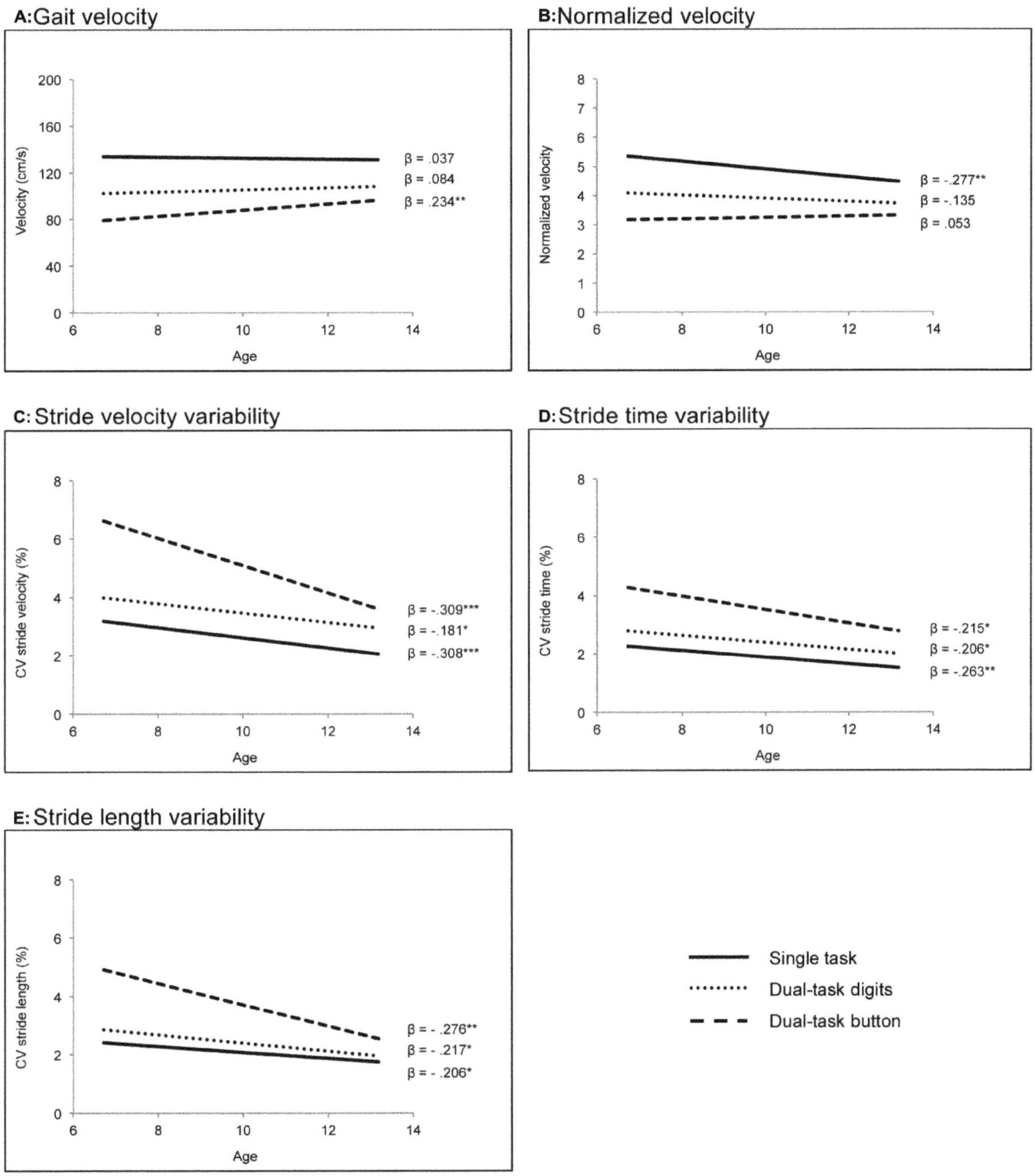

FIGURE 1 | Associations of age (in years) with gait velocity (A), normalized velocity (B), stride velocity variability (C), stride time variability (D), and stride length variability (E) in single-task walking and in the dual-task conditions digits and button. CV, coefficient of variation. $^{*}p < 0.05$, $^{**}p < 0.01$, $^{***}p < 0.001$.

increased with age, $F(1,133) = 12.674$, $p < 0.001$, $\eta^2 = 0.087$; Regression parameter estimates were $\beta = 0.295$, $p < 0.001$ for the single-task condition and $\beta = 0.220$, $p = 0.010$ for the dual-task condition. There was no significant Task Performance × Age interaction, $F(1,133) = 0.702$, $p = 0.403$, $\eta^2 = 0.005$.

Children's performances of unfastening and fastening a button in the single-task ($M = 5.16$, $SD = 1.67$) and dual-task ($M = 6.31$, $SD = 1.90$) conditions were not significantly different, $F(1,132) = 2.509$, $p = 0.116$, $\eta^2 = 0.019$, and were comparable across age [age: $F(1,132) = 3.524$, $p = 0.063$, $\eta^2 = 0.026$; interaction: $F(1,132) = 0.159$, $p = 0.691$, $\eta^2 = 0.001$]; regression parameter estimates were $\beta = 0.171, p = 0.050$ for the single-task condition and $\beta = 0.119, p = 0.172$ for the dual-task condition.

Gait and Associations with Cognition, Motor Behavior, and Injuries, as well as Psychosocial Functioning

Means and standard deviations of children's cognitive performance, motor behavior, and injuries, as well as psychosocial functioning are presented in **Table 2**.

Mean change values between single-task and dual-task gait parameters are presented in **Table 3**. The mean change values were positive for both velocity parameters, indicating a decrease in gait velocity and normalized velocity from single- to dual-task walking, whereas the mean change values were negative for all gait variability parameters, indicating an increase in gait variability from single- to dual-task walking. Regression analyses were calculated to examine the relation between mean change values in gait parameters and children's cognition, motor behavior, and injuries, as well as psychosocial functioning. Results are shown in **Table 3**. Controlling for age, there were no significant associations between mean change values in gait parameters and other aspects of children's development (all $p \geq 0.01$).

TABLE 2 | Means and standard deviations of children's cognition, motor behavior and injuries, as well as psychosocial functioning.

Variable	*n*	*M*	*SD*	Range
Cognition				
Intelligence (WISC-IV FSIQ)	132	105.94	10.48	84–136
Executive functions (CANTAB)				
IED	131	0.24	1.04	–6.64–1.89
RVP	127	– 0.09	1.23	–4.96–1.25
SOC	132	0.01	0.83	–2.61–1.66
SWM	131	0.38	0.89	–2.22–2.75
Motor behavior and injuries				
Participation in sports (minutes/week)	129	214.98	153.51	0–870
Injury risk (IBC)	129	6.20	3.84	0–21
Injuries (number)	127	0.97	1.17	0–5
Psychosocial functioning (KIDSCREEN-52)				
Physical well-being	125	20.91	2.95	12.50–25
Psychological well-being	126	26.01	3.41	14–30
Moods and emotions	126	11.47	3.45	7–23
Self-perception	126	22.30	2.52	12–25
Autonomy	127	20.75	2.61	13–25
Parent relation and home life	127	25.28	3.06	17–30
Financial resources	125	13.30	2.28	3–15
Social support and peers	127	25.16	3.78	8–30
School environment	128	25.91	3.43	12–30
Social acceptance (bullying)	128	4.40	1.68	3–10

CANTAB, Cambridge Neuropsychological Test Automated Battery; IBC, injury behavior checklist; IED, intra-extra dimensional set shift; RVP, rapid visual processing; SOC, stockings of Cambridge; SWM, spatial working memory; WISC-IV FSIQ, Wechsler Intelligence Scales for Children 4th ed., full-scale IQ.

DISCUSSION

The aim of the present study was to investigate age-dependent gait characteristics in single- and dual-task walking and to examine the relation of gait to cognition, motor behavior, and injuries, as well as psychosocial functioning for the first time in typically developing school-aged children. In single-task walking the present study revealed no association between age and gait velocity. This is in accordance with previous research, indicating a maturation of gait velocity at the age of 6–7 years (Hausdorff et al., 1999). However, a negative relation was found between age and normalized velocity. Thus, when accounting for differences in leg length of the children, which were correlated with age and therefore may have confounded our results, older children showed lower velocity than younger children. This finding contradicts previous results where normalized gait velocity was unaffected by age (Dusing and Thorpe, 2007). However, in our study velocity was normalized to leg length (Hof, 1996) whereas Dusing and Thorpe (2007) normalized data to height. Hence, due to the differing methods of normalization, it may not be possible to directly compare the results.

Further, a negative relation was found between age and gait variability what is in line with previous research showing higher gait variability in younger compared to older typically developing school-aged children (Hausdorff et al., 1999). These results provide evidence that gait variability, which is sensitive to more subtle physiological changes such as neural maturation than spatiotemporal gait parameters (Hausdorff, 2005), continues to develop across middle childhood into adolescence. Further, our results highlight the importance of not only assessing spatiotemporal gait parameters but also considering gait variability as an index of gait automaticity and regularity when investigating typically developing children's gait maturation, because these gait measures seem to undergo temporally distinct developmental trajectories.

In dual-task conditions, where children were asked to walk and simultaneously perform a concurrent cognitive task (i.e., listening to and memorizing digits) or motor task (i.e., unfastening and fastening a button), children walked with reduced gait velocity and normalized gait as well as increased gait variability compared to single-task walking. These results are in line with previous research showing that dual-task walking leads to gait decrements in spatiotemporal gait parameters (Cherng et al., 2007; Boonyong et al., 2012; Hung et al., 2013) as well as in gait variability measures (Schaefer et al., 2010), although other studies showed no effect of dual-task walking on gait variability in typically developing children (Leitner et al., 2007; Katz-Leurer et al., 2013; Abbruzzese et al., 2014). Our result that gait was adversely affected when children were asked to walk and perform a concurrent task supports the notion that gait requires cognitive resources (Huang and Mercer, 2001; Woollacott and Shumway-Cook, 2002; Huang et al., 2003; Cherng et al., 2007).

TABLE 3 | Regression analyses with mean changes in gait predicting children's cognition, motor behavior and injuries, as well as psychosocial functioning controlled for age.

Mean changes			Cognition					Motor behavior and injuries			Psychosocial functioning									
	M	*SD*	FSIQ	IED	RVP	SOC	SWM	Sports	IBC	Injuries	PHW	PSW	ME	SP	AUT	PRHL	FR	SSP	SE	SA
Dual task: Digits																				
Velocity	27.3	16.2	0.01	0.04	−0.15	−0.05	0.07	0.03	0.10	0.06	0.09	0.02	−0.01	0.10	−0.03	0.03	−0.06	0.02	0.02	−0.10
Normalized velocity	1.0	0.6	−0.01	0.06	−0.14	−0.06	0.10	0.02	0.11	0.04	0.08	0.01	0.00	0.08	−0.03	0.03	−0.09	0.00	0.00	−0.08
CV velocity	−0.8	1.4	0.03	0.04	−0.03	0.16	−0.10	0.00	−0.13	−0.11	−0.03	0.06	−0.10	−0.01	0.14	0.03	0.09	−0.03	0.12	−0.04
CV stride time	−0.3	1.1	0.02	−0.02	0.05	0.08	−0.08	−0.17	−0.13	−0.05	−0.09	−0.20	0.05	−0.04	0.09	−0.04	−0.01	−0.11	0.13	−0.03
CV stride length	−0.5	0.9	0.05	0.07	−0.11	0.11	−0.04	−0.06	−0.06	0.03	0.13	0.23	−0.13	0.07	0.17	0.21	0.19	0.05	0.19	−0.07
Dual task: Button																				
Velocity	44.5	20.4	0.01	0.00	−0.06	−0.16	0.00	−0.03	−0.13	0.05	−0.01	−0.04	0.07	0.07	−0.05	0.05	−0.03	0.03	0.11	−0.05
Normalized velocity	1.7	0.8	0.01	0.01	−0.06	−0.18	−0.01	−0.05	−0.10	0.05	0.00	−0.11	0.12	−0.02	−0.04	0.02	−0.05	0.01	0.05	−0.03
CV velocity	−2.5	2.3	0.07	0.07	0.06	0.10	0.02	0.08	0.06	0.09	0.10	0.10	0.16	0.05	0.03	0.03	−0.08	−0.07	0.23	−0.09
CV stride time	−1.6	2.0	−0.03	0.00	0.08	0.15	0.05	−0.04	0.03	0.06	0.09	0.13	−0.11	0.03	−0.02	0.02	−0.09	−0.07	0.15	−0.19
CV stride length	−1.6	1.7	0.07	0.04	−0.04	0.14	0.11	−0.02	−0.06	0.11	0.16	0.12	−0.15	0.07	−0.02	0.10	0.00	−0.05	0.17	−0.19

Coefficients are standardized regression coefficients if not otherwise indicated. FSIQ, full-scale IQ; IED, intra-extra dimensional set shift; RVP, rapid visual processing; SOC, stockings of Cambridge; SWM, spatial working memory; IBC, injury behavior checklist; PHW, physical well-being; PSW, psychological well-being; ME, moods and emotions; SP, self-perception; PRHL, parent relation and home life; FR, financial resources; SSP, social support and peers; SE, school environment; SA, social acceptance (bullying); CV, coefficient of variation. All $p \geq 0.01$.

However, the underlying mechanisms for the here reported dual-task interference are not clear (Yogev-Seligmann et al., 2008). In accordance with the capacity-sharing theory (Kahneman, 1973; Tombu and Jolicoeur, 2003), it is possible that having to share limited attentional resources between two attention-demanding tasks lead to decreased task performance in one or both of the tasks. On the other hand, following the bottleneck theory (Pashler, 1994), which claims that two simultaneously performed tasks are cognitively processed sequentially, it may be that switching from one task to the other leads to diminished performance in one or both of the tasks. Therefore, we not only investigated whether gait parameters changed from single- to dual-task walking but also whether the concurrent task performance differed between single- and dual-task conditions. Results showed that, while gait parameters significantly changed from single- to dual-task walking, concurrent task performance (i.e., number of recalled digits and number of times a button could be unfastened and fastened) did not differ between single- and dual-task conditions. Hence, although children were not instructed to prioritize one task over the other, they possibly followed a "posture second" strategy (Bloem et al., 2006) by prioritizing the concurrent task over their walking performance.

Regarding age-dependent dual-task effects on gait, the results revealed that in the motor dual-task condition, age was positively related to gait velocity. This result is in line with previous research on typically developing children showing that younger children walked with lower gait velocity than older children when concurrently performing a second task (Boonyong et al., 2012). However, in our study there were no age-dependent dual-task effects on gait velocity in the cognitive dual-task condition. Normalized velocity showed no age-dependent dual-task effects. Further, in both dual-task conditions, age was negatively related to gait variability such that younger children walked with higher gait variability than older children when concurrently listening to and memorizing digits or unfastening and fastening a button. These results are in line with the study conducted by Abbruzzese et al. (2014) and indicate that gait in dual-task conditions is still developing in middle childhood.

Our results further show that the dual-task effects on walking differed between the two types of concurrent tasks: When walking and concurrently unfastening and fastening a button, children showed greater decrease in gait velocity and normalized velocity, as well as a greater increase in gait variability compared to when walking and concurrently listening to and memorizing digits. This finding indicates that a concurrent motor task may lead to greater dual-task gait decrements than a concurrent cognitive task and can be interpreted from the perspective of the multiple-resource model of attention (Wickens, 1991; Cherng et al., 2007). This model assumes that attentional resources are not unitary but are divided into various pools, which, for example, depend on the modality of input and response. Walking requires visual input and further involves the response of moving and controlling body segments, which Cherng et al. (2007) subsumed under the term somatosensation. The motor concurrent task of unfastening and fastening a button also requires visual input as well as somatosensory response. In contrast, the cognitive concurrent task of listening to and recalling digits requires auditory input and involves vocal response. According to these assumptions, the motor dual-task competes more strongly for processing resources with walking (i.e., visual input and somatosensory response) than the cognitive dual-task, which may have led to greater dual-task gait decrements in the motor compared to the cognitive dual-task condition.

Further, performance in the concurrent cognitive task of listening to and memorizing digits was associated with age such that older children recalled more digits than younger children. This is in accordance with previous research showing that younger children score lower than older children in working memory tests (Gathercole et al., 2004). Performance in the motor task of unfastening and fastening a button, however, was not related to age.

Finally, we investigated whether change in gait from single- to dual-task conditions (i.e., dual-task gait effects) is associated with cognition and other aspects of children's development. Our results revealed no significant relations. Thus, we conclude that contrary to our hypothesis, dual-task gait effects were not meaningfully related to children's cognition, motor behavior, and injuries, or psychosocial functioning. It has to be noted that our hypotheses were derived from studies comparing individuals with cognitive and motor impairments to typically developing controls. For example, regarding cognition, there is evidence that children and adults with deficits in executive and attentional functions show more gait alterations in single- and dual-task conditions compared to controls (e.g., Al-Yahya et al., 2011; Katz-Leurer et al., 2013). Regarding motor behavior and injuries, previous research investigating children with poor motor skills showed that these children participate less often in organized sports (Cairney et al., 2005) and have an increased risk of injury (Bloemers et al., 2012) compared to controls. Regarding psychosocial functioning, such as social acceptance or psychological well-being, previous findings investigating children with poor motor skills showed that these children are at higher risk for being bullied at school (Piek et al., 2006a; Bejerot and Humble, 2013; Bejerot et al., 2013) or for showing symptoms of anxiety and depression (Zwicker et al., 2012). However, we are not aware of studies investigating direct relations between gait and cognition, motor behavior and injuries, and psychosocial functioning in typically developing children. Therefore, our study is the first to provide preliminary evidence that dual-task effects in gait velocity, normalized velocity, and gait variability are not related to these aforementioned aspects of child development during middle childhood. However, the dual-task gait decrements apparent in our study support the notion that also among typically developing children, cognitive processes play an important role in gait. Hence, future studies might investigate whether other cognitive processes that were not investigated in this study, such as inhibition (i.e., inhibiting a prepotent reaction in favor of a less automated response) or cognitive flexibility (i.e., directing the attentional focus from one task to another; Miyake et al., 2000), also contribute to gait performance of typically developing children.

Our study has strengths and limitations. We consider it a strength that gait characteristics were assessed using the GAITRite system, which has proved to be a valid method of measuring gait parameters in children and offers the possibility of reliably identifying subtle changes in gait (Thorpe et al., 2005). During gait assessment children wore their normal clothes and shoes and it was therefore possible to assess gait performance as it is exhibited under everyday circumstances. However, although we investigated age-dependent gait characteristics in single- and dual-task walking of school-aged children, it was not possible to determine at what age gait characteristics, which are still developing during middle childhood, reach maturity, as we did not investigate a comparison sample of adult participants. Furthermore, the children in our study were first asked to perform single-tasks followed by dual-tasks. Therefore, we cannot rule out the possibility that a practice effect benefited the concurrent task performance while dual-tasking. In order to further investigate practice effects, future studies might apply task conditions in counter-balanced order or they might include a control group, which repeats the tasks only in single-task conditions. Additionally, our analyses were performed on cross-sectional data, whereas the testing of developmental trends in single- and dual-task walking should include longitudinal data in future investigations. Future research might also include different types of concurrent tasks when investigating children's gait in dual-task conditions because previous research also showed interference effects on gait for visual and auditory concurrent tasks among typically developing children (Huang et al., 2003). Finally, we investigated gait in straight walking. Future studies might examine age-dependent gait characteristics of walking along curved trajectories (Belmonti et al., 2013), as curvilinear walking may be more common in our everyday life.

CONCLUSION

This study provides important information on age-related changes in gait during middle childhood. Our findings indicate that gait in typically developing children becomes more regular with increasing age in single- and dual-task walking, thereby highlighting the importance of including measures of gait variability when investigating gait development. Since we found dual-task gait decrements to be larger when walking and concurrently performing a motor compared to a cognitive task, our results underscore the importance of taking the type of concurrent task into account when investigating children's gait in a dual-task paradigm. Finally, our study revealed no association of dual-task gait effects with children's cognition, motor behavior and injuries, or psychosocial functioning, indicating that subtle dual-task effects on gait do not go along with other aspects of development in typically developing children during middle childhood.

AUTHOR CONTRIBUTIONS

PH and OM contributed to the study design, acquisition, analysis and interpretation of data. Drafted and revised the manuscript, gave final approval, and agree to be accountable for all aspects of the work in ensuring that questions related to the accuracy or integrity of any part of the work are appropriately investigated and resolved. Both authors contributed the same amount of work to this paper. SL contributed to the analysis and interpretation of data, revised the manuscript, gave final approval, and agrees to be accountable for all aspects of the work in ensuring that questions related to the accuracy or integrity of any part of the work are appropriately investigated and resolved. AG contributed to the study design and interpretation of data, revised the manuscript, gave final approval, and agrees to be accountable for all aspects of the work in ensuring that questions related to the accuracy or integrity of any part of the work are appropriately investigated and resolved.

ACKNOWLEDGMENT

The authors wish to thank Nadine Perkinson-Gloor for support in data collection.

REFERENCES

Abbruzzese, L. D., Ashwini, R. K., Bellows, R., Figueroa, K., Levy, J., Lim, E., et al. (2014). Effects of manual task complexity on gait parameters in school-aged children and adults. *Gait Posture* 40, 658–663. doi: 10.1016/j.gaitpost.2014.07.017

Adolph, K. E., Vereijken, B., and Shrout, P. E. (2003). What changes in infant walking and why. *Child Dev.* 74, 475–497. doi: 10.1111/1467-8624.7402011

Al-Yahya, E., Dawes, H., Smith, L., Dennis, A., Howells, D., and Cockburn, J. (2011). Cognitive motor interference while walking: a systematic review and meta-analysis. *Neurosci. Biobehav. Rev.* 35, 715–728. doi: 10.1016/j.gaitpost.2010.09.017

Anderson, P. (2002). Assessment and development of executive function (EF) during childhood. *Child Neuropsychol.* 8, 71–82. doi: 10.1076/chin.8.2.71.8724

Bejerot, S., and Humble, M. B. (2013). Childhood clumsiness and peer victimization: a case-control study of psychiatric patients. *BMC Psychiatry* 13:68. doi: 10.1186/1471-244X-13-68

Bejerot, S., Plenty, S., Humble, A., and Humble, M. B. (2013). Poor motor skills: a risk marker for bully victimization. *Aggress. Behav.* 39, 453–461. doi: 10.1002/ab.21489

Belmonti, V., Cioni, G., and Berthoz, A. (2013). Development of anticipatory orienting strategies and trajectory formation in goal-oriented locomotion. *Exp. Brain Res.* 227, 131–147. doi: 10.1007/s00221-013-3495-3

Beurskens, R., and Bock, O. (2012). Age-related deficits of dual-task walking: a review. *Neural Plast.* 2012:131608. doi: 10.1155/2012/131608

Bloem, B. R., Grimbergen, Y. A. M., van Dijk, G., and Munneke, M. (2006). The "posture second" strategy: a review of wrong priorities in Parkinson's disease. *J. Neurol. Sci.* 248, 196–204. doi: 10.1016/j.jns.2006.05.010

Bloemers, F., Collard, D., Paw, M. C. A., Van Mechelen, W., Twisk, J., and Verhagen, E. (2012). Physical inactivity is a risk factor for physical activity-related injuries in children. *Br. J. Sport Med.* 46, 669–674. doi: 10.1136/bjsports-2011-090546

Boonyong, S., Siu, K. C., van Donkelaar, P., Chou, L. S., and Woollacott, M. H. (2012). Development of postural control during gait in typically developing children: the effects of dual-task conditions. *Gait Posture* 35, 428–434. doi: 10.1016/j.gaitpost.2011.11.002

Bouffard, M., Watkinson, E. J., Thompson, L. P., Causgrove Dunn, J., and Romanow, S. K. E. (1996). A test of the activity deficit hypothesis with children with movement difficulties. *Adapt. Phys. Act. Q.* 13, 61–73.

Brandau, H., and Daghofer, F. (2010). Elternfragebogen zur erfassung des unfallrisikos von jungen [Parental questionnaire for injury risk assessment of young boys]. *Diagnostica* 56, 33–45. doi: 10.1026/0012-1924/a000007

Bril, B., and Ledebt, A. (1998). Head coordination as a means to assist sensory integration in learning to walk. *Neurosci. Biobehav. Rev.* 22, 555–563. doi: 10.1016/S0149-7634(97)00044-4

Cairney, J., Hay, J. A., Faught, B. E., Wade, T. J., Corna, L., and Flouris, S. (2005). Developmental coordination disorder, generalized self-efficacy toward physical activity, and participation in organized and free play activities. *J. Pediatr.* 147, 515–520. doi: 10.1016/j.jpeds.2005.05.013

Cantell, M., Smyth, M., and Ahonen, T. (1994). Clumsiness in adolescence: educational, motor, and social outcomes of motor delay detected at 5 years. *Adapt. Phys. Act. Q.* 11, 115–129.

Cherng, R. J., Liang, L. Y., Chen, Y. J., and Chen, J. Y. (2009). The effects of a motor and a cognitive concurrent task on walking in children with developmental coordination disorder. *Gait Posture* 29, 204–207. doi: 10.1016/j.gaitpost.2008.08.003

Cherng, R. J., Liang, L. Y., Hwang, I. S., and Chen, J. Y. (2007). The effect of a concurrent task on the walking performance of preschool children. *Gait Posture* 26, 231–237. doi: 10.1016/j.gaitpost.2006.09.004

Daseking, M., Petermann, U., and Petermann, F. (2007). Intelligenzdiagnostik mit dem HAWIK-IV [Assessment of intelligence with the HAWIK-IV]. *Kindh Entwickl.* 16, 250–259. doi: 10.1026/0942-5403.16.4.250

Dusing, S. C., and Thorpe, D. E. (2007). A normative sample of temporal and spatial gait parameters in children using the GAITRite® electronic walkway. *Gait Posture* 25, 135–139. doi: 10.1016/j.gaitpost.2006.06.003

Ebersbach, G., Dimitrijevic, M. R., and Poewe, W. (1995). Influence of concurrent tasks on gait: a dual-task approach. *Percept. Motor Skills* 81, 107–113. doi: 10.2466/pms.1995.81.1.107

Faul, F., Erdfelder, E., Lang, A. G., and Buchner, A. (2007). G*Power 3: a flexible statistical power analysis program for the social, behavioral, and biomedical sciences. *Behav. Res. Methods* 39, 175–191. doi: 10.3758/BF03193146

Froehle, A. W., Nahhas, R. W., Sherwood, R. J., and Duren, D. L. (2013). Age-related changes in spatiotemporal characteristics of gait accompany ongoing lower limb linear growth in late childhood and early adolescence. *Gait Posture* 38, 14–19. doi: 10.1016/j.gaitpost.2012.10.005

Gathercole, S. E., Pickering, S. J., Ambridge, B., and Wearing, H. (2004). The structure of working memory from 4 to 15 years of age. *Dev. Psychol.* 40, 177–190. doi: 10.1037/0012-1649.40.2.177

Gill, S. V. (2015). Walking to the beat of their own drum: how children and adults meet timing constraints. *PLoS ONE* 10:e0127894. doi: 10.1371/journal.pone.0127894

Hagmann-von Arx, P., Grob, A., Petermann, F., and Daseking, M. (2012). Konkurrente validität des HAWIK-IV und der intelligence and development scales (IDS) [Concurrent validity of the HAWIK-IV and the intelligence and development scales (IDS)]. *Z. Kinder Jug. Psych.* 40, 41–50. doi: 10.1024/1422-4917/a000148

Hagmann-von Arx, P., Manicolo, O., Perkinson-Gloor, N., Weber, P., Grob, A., and Lemola, S. (2015). Gait in very preterm school-aged children in dual-task paradigms. *PLoS ONE* 10:e0144363. doi: 10.1371/journal.pone.0144363

Hausdorff, J. M. (2005). Gait variability: methods, modeling and meaning. *J. Neuroeng. Rehabil.* 2:19. doi: 10.1186/1743-0003-2-19

Hausdorff, J. M. (2007). Gait dynamics, fractals and falls: finding meaning in the stride-to-stride fluctuations of human walking. *Hum. Mov. Sci.* 26, 555–589. doi: 10.1016/j.humov.2007.05.003

Hausdorff, J. M., Zemany, L., Peng, C. K., and Goldberger, A. L. (1999). Maturation of gait dynamics: stride-to-stride variability and its temporal organization in children. *J. Appl. Physiol.* 86, 1040–1047.

Hillman, S. J., Stansfield, B. W., Richardson, A. M., and Robb, J. E. (2009). Development of temporal and distance parameters of gait in normal children. *Gait Posture* 29, 81–85. doi: 10.1016/j.gaitpost.2008.06.012

Hof, A. L. (1996). Scaling gait data to body size. *Gait Posture* 4, 222–223. doi: 10.1016/0966-6362(95)01057-2

Holm, I., Tveter, A. T., Frederiksen, P. M., and Vollestad, N. (2009). A normative sample of gait and hopping on one leg parameters in children 7-12 years of age. *Gait Posture* 27, 91–96. doi: 10.1016/j.gaitpost.2008.09.016

Huang, H. J., and Mercer, V. S. (2001). Dual-task methodology: applications in studies of cognitive and motor performance in adults and children. *Pediatr. Phys. Ther.* 13, 133–140. doi: 10.1097/00001577-200113030-00005

Huang, H. J., Mercer, V. S., and Thorpe, D. E. (2003). Effects of different concurrent cognitive tasks on temporal-distance gait variables in children. *Pediatr. Phys. Ther.* 15, 105–113. doi: 10.1097/01.PEP.0000067886.96352.6B

Hung, Y. C., Meredith, G. S., and Gill, S. V. (2013). Influence of dual task constraints during walking for children. *Gait Posture* 38, 450–454. doi: 10.1016/j.gaitpost.2013.01.009

Iverson, J. M. (2010). Developing language in a developing body: the relationship between motor development and language development. *J. Child Lang.* 37, 229–261. doi: 10.1017/S0305000909990432

Kahneman, D. (1973). *Attention and Effort.* Englewood Cliffs, NJ: Prentice Hall.

Karasik, L. B., Tamis-LeMonda, C. S., and Adolph, K. E. (2011). Transition from crawling to walking and infants' actions with objects and people. *Child Dev.* 82, 1199–1209. doi: 10.1111/j.1467-8624.2011.01595.x

Katz-Leurer, M., Rotem, H., Keren, O., and Meyer, S. (2011). Effect of concurrent cognitive tasks on gait features among children post-severe traumatic brain injury and typically-developed controls. *Brain Inj.* 25, 581–586. doi: 10.3109/02699052.2011.572943

Katz-Leurer, M., Rotem, H., and Meyer, S. (2013). Effects of concurrent cognitive tasks on temporo-spatial parameters of gait among children with cerebral palsy and typically developed controls. *Dev. Neurorehabil.* 17, 363–367. doi: 10.3109/17518423.2013.810676

Kressig, R. W., and Beauchet, O. (2006). European GAITRite network group, guidelines for clinical applications of spatio-temporal gait analysis in older adults. *Aging Clin. Exp. Res.* 18, 174–176. doi: 10.1007/BF03327437

Leitner, Y., Barak, R., Giladi, N., Peretz, C., Eshel, R., Gruendlinger, L., et al. (2007). Gait in attention deficit hyperactivity disorder: effects of methylphenidate and dual tasking. *J. Neurol.* 254, 1330–1338. doi: 10.1007/s00415-006-0522-3

Lindenberger, U., Marsiske, M., and Baltes, P. (2000). Memorizing while walking: increase in dual-task costs from young adulthood to old age. *Psychol. Aging* 15, 417–436. doi: 10.1037/0882-7974.15.3.417

Luciana, M. (2003). Practitioner review: computerized assessment of neuropsychological function in children: clinical and research applications of the cambridge neuropsychological testing automated battery (CANTAB). *J. Child Psychol. Psychiirty* 44, 649–663. doi: 10.1111/1469-7610.00152

Lythgo, N., Wilson, C., and Galea, M. (2009). Basic gait and symmetry measures for primary school-aged children and young adults whilst walking barefoot and with shoes. *Gait Posture* 30, 502–506. doi: 10.1016/j.gaitpost.2009.07.119

Lythgo, N., Wilson, C., and Galea, M. (2011). Basic gait and symmetry measures for primary school-aged children and young adults II. Walking at slow, free and fast speed. *Gait Posture* 33, 29–35. doi: 10.1016/j.gaitpost.2010.09.017

Manicolo, O., Grob, A., Lemola, S., and Hagmann-von Arx, P. (2016). Age-related decline of gait variability in children with attention-deficit/hyperactivity disorder: support for the maturational delay hypothesis. *Gait Posture* 44, 245–249. doi: 10.1016/j.gaitpost.2015.12.012

Miyake, A., Friedman, N. P., Emerson, M. J., Witzki, H., Howerter, A., and Wager, T. D. (2000). The unity and diversity of executive functions and their contributions to complex "frontal lope" tasks: a latent variable analysis. *Cogn. Psychol.* 41, 49–100. doi: 10.1006/cogp.1999.0734

Pashler, H. (1994). Dual-task interference in simple tasks: data and theory. *Psychol. Bull.* 116, 220–244. doi: 10.1037/0033-2909.116.2.220

Petermann, F. (2008). *Movement Assessment Battery for Children*, 2nd Edn. Frankfurt: Pearson Assessment.

Petermann, F., and Petermann, U. (2011). *Wechsler Intelligence Scale for Children (WISC-IV).* Frankfurt: Pearson Assessment.

Piek, J. P., Barrett, N. C., Allen, L. S. R., Jones, A., and Louise, M. (2006a). The relationship between bullying and self-worth in children with movement coordination problems. *Br. J. Educ. Psychol.* 75, 453–463. doi: 10.1348/000709904X24573

Piek, J. P., Baynam, G. B., and Barrett, N. C. (2006b). The relationship between fine and gross motor ability, self-perception and self-worth in children and adolescents. *Hum. Mov. Sci.* 25, 65–75. doi: 10.1016/j.humov.2005.10.011

Ravens-Sieberer, U., Gosch, A., Rajmil, L., Erhart, M., Bruil, J., Power, M., et al. (2008). The KIDSCREEN-52 quality of life measure for children and adolescents: psychometric results from a cross-cultural survey in 13 European countries. *Value Health* 4, 645–658. doi: 10.1111/j.1524-4733.2007.00291.x

Schaefer, S., Lövdén, M., Wieckhorst, B., and Lindenberger, U. (2010). Cognitive performance is improved while walking: differences in cognitive-sensorimotor couplings between children and young adults. *Eur. J. Dev. Psychol.* 7, 371–389. doi: 10.1080/17405620802535666

Schoemaker, M. M., and Kalverboer, A. F. (1994). Social and affective problems of children who are clumsy: how early do they begin. *Adapt. Phys. Act. Q.* 11, 130–140.

Skinner, R. A., and Piek, J. P. (2001). Psychosocial implications of poor motor coordination in children and adolescents. *Hum. Mov. Sci.* 20, 73–94. doi: 10.1016/S0167-9457(01)00029-X

Speltz, M. L., Gonzales, N., Sulzbacher, S., and Quan, L. (1990). Assessment of injury risk in young children: a preliminary study of the injury behavior checklist. *J. Pediatr. Psychol.* 15, 373–383. doi: 10.1093/jpepsy/15.3.373

Springer, S., Giladi, N., Peretz, C., Yogev, G., Simon, E. S., and Hausdorff, J. M. (2006). Dual-tasking effects on gait variability: the role of aging, falls, and executive function. *Mov. Disord.* 21, 950–957. doi: 10.1002/mds.20848

Storvold, G. V., Aarethun, K., and Bratberg, G. H. (2013). Age for onset of walking and prewalking strategies. *Early Hum. Dev.* 89, 655–659. doi: 10.1016/j.earlhumdev.2013.04.010

Sutherland, D. H., Olshen, R., Biden, E. N., and Wyatt, M. P. (1988). *The Development of Mature Walking.* Oxford: MacKeith.

Thorpe, D. E., Dusing, S. C., and Moore, C. G. (2005). Repeatability of temporospatial gait measures in children using the GAITRite electronic walkway. *Arch. Phys. Med. Rehabil.* 86, 2342–2346. doi: 10.1016/j.apmr.2005.07.301

Tombu, M., and Jolicoeur, P. (2003). A central capacity sharing model of dual-task performance. *J. Exp. Psychol. Hum.* 29, 3–18. doi: 10.1037/0096-1523.29.1.3

Wickens, C. D. (1991). "Processing resources in attention," in *Multiple-Task Performance*, ed. D. L. Damos (Washington, DC: Taylor & Francis), 3–34.

Woollacott, M., and Shumway-Cook, A. (2002). Attention and the control of posture and gait: a review of an emerging area of research. *Gait Posture* 16, 1–14. doi: 10.1016/S0966-6362(01)00156-4

Yang, Y. R., Chen, Y. C., Lee, C. S., Cheng, S. J., and Wang, R. Y. (2007). Dual-task-related gait changes in individuals with stroke. *Gait Posture* 25, 185–190. doi: 10.1016/j.gaitpost.2006.03.007

Yogev-Seligmann, G., Hausdorff, J. M., and Giladi, N. (2008). The role of executive function and attention in gait. *Mov. Disord.* 23, 329–342. doi: 10.1002/mds.21720

Zwicker, J. G., Missiuna, C., Harris, S. R., and Boyd, L. A. (2012). Developmental coordination disorder: a review and update. *Eur. J. Paediatr. Neurol.* 16, 573–581. doi: 10.1016/j.ejpn.2012.05.005

Conflict of Interest Statement: The authors declare that the research was conducted in the absence of any commercial or financial relationships that could be construed as a potential conflict of interest.

13

Fine Motor Skills Predict Maths Ability Better than they Predict Reading Ability in the Early Primary School Years

Nicola J. Pitchford, Chiara Papini, Laura A. Outhwaite and Anthea Gulliford*

School of Psychology, University of Nottingham, Nottingham, UK

Edited by:
Klaus Libertus,
University of Pittsburgh, USA

Reviewed by:
Bert De Smedt,
Katholieke Universiteit Leuven,
Belgium
Caroline Hornung,
University of Luxembourg,
Luxembourg

***Correspondence:**
Nicola J. Pitchford
nicola.pitchford@nottingham.ac.uk

Fine motor skills have long been recognized as an important foundation for development in other domains. However, more precise insights into the role of fine motor skills, and their relationships to other skills in mediating early educational achievements, are needed to support the development of optimal educational interventions. We explored concurrent relationships between two components of fine motor skills, Fine Motor Precision and Fine Motor Integration, and early reading and maths development in two studies with primary school children of low-to-mid socio-economic status in the UK. Two key findings were revealed. First, despite being in the first 2 years of primary school education, significantly better performance was found in reading compared to maths across both studies. This may reflect the protective effects of recent national-level interventions to promote early literacy skills in young children in the UK that have not been similarly promoted for maths. Second, fine motor skills were a better predictor of early maths ability than they were of early reading ability. Hierarchical multiple regression revealed that fine motor skills did not significantly predict reading ability when verbal short-term memory was taken into account. In contrast, Fine Motor Integration remained a significant predictor of maths ability, even after the influence of non-verbal IQ had been accounted for. These results suggest that fine motor skills should have a pivotal role in educational interventions designed to support the development of early mathematical skills.

Keywords: fine motor skills, literacy, maths, executive functions, socio-economic status, early years education

INTRODUCTION

Converging evidence from neuroimaging studies, brain-lesioned patients, and developmental disorders suggests a fundamental interrelation between motor and cognitive development (see Diamond, 2000, for a review). For example, brain imaging studies have demonstrated a strong functional coupling between brain regions typically thought to underpin exclusively either cognitive or motor processes (Abe and Hanakawa, 2009; Stoodley, 2012). In addition, clinical populations, such as those identified with Attention Deficit Hyperactivity Disorder and Development Coordination Disorder, that were originally associated with a single domain now show notable co-occurrence of both motor and cognitive difficulties (Piek et al., 1999; Pitcher et al., 2003; Alloway, 2007).

Evidence is also accumulating from studies of typically developing children for a close association between motor and cognitive development. When gross measures of motor and cognitive skills are considered, results from across several studies produce inconsistent findings as to the extent and significance of the relationship between motor and cognitive development (e.g., Wassenberg et al., 2005; Roebers and Kauer, 2009; Davis et al., 2011; Jenni et al., 2013). However, when motor and cognitive skills are subdivided into different components, specific correlations emerge. A recent review by van der Fels et al. (2014) systematically investigated findings from typically developing children aged 4–16 years. The authors concluded that the link between motor and cognitive domains could be explained more specifically by relationships between fine motor skills and higher-order cognitive skills. This corroborates the results of Davis et al. (2011), who found that fine motor skills and visual attention underpinned the more generic association between motor and cognitive domains.

Different definitions and operationalizations of fine motor skills are apparent in the literature, but we consider fine motor skills to "encompass control and coordination of the distal musculature of the hands and fingers," as defined by Bruininks and Bruininks (2005, p. 2). Within this definition two different components are distinguished: (1) Fine motor integration is conceptualized as a manual ability which requires synchronized hand–eye movements and the processing of a visual stimulus in order to produce adequate motor output; and (2) fine motor precision is conceptualized as a 'pure' fine manual skill which relies on a minimal visual-perceptual component. Fine motor integration, but not fine motor precision, has been shown to contribute significantly to academic achievement (Carlson et al., 2013), suggesting these are separate components of fine motor skills.

Fine motor skills are thought to be essential for early learning. On average, in regular kindergarten schools in the US 33–66% of daily activities involve fine motor skills, such as coloring, copying, cutting, and drawing (Marr et al., 2003). A similar percentage of time has been recorded in US primary schools as being dedicated to activities that involve fine motor skills (McHale and Cermak, 1992). Fine motor skills have been shown to be a powerful predictor of school readiness (Grissmer et al., 2010) and fine, but not gross, motor skills are sometimes included in assessments of school readiness (Bala et al., 2010). In addition, fine motor skills are related to school adaptation and social behavior during the transition from preschool to primary school (Bart et al., 2007) and classroom engagement at the end of second grade (Pagani et al., 2010). These studies highlight the integral relationship that development of early fine motor skills has with readiness and adaptation to early primary school.

Fine motor skills in the early years have also been shown to predict later academic achievement, especially in reading and mathematics (e.g., Son and Meisels, 2006; Grissmer et al., 2010; Pagani et al., 2010; Cameron et al., 2012; Dinehart and Manfra, 2013) and to predict underachievement in able students at school (Stoeger et al., 2008, 2013). In particular, fine motor integration has received more attention than tasks of fine motor precision and fine motor integration has been identified to be a strong predictor of later achievement (Tramontana et al., 1988; Kulp, 1999; Kurdek and Sinclair, 2001).

Possible mechanisms underpinning the link between fine motor skills and scholastic attainment have recently been put forward. Cameron et al. (2016), for example, highlighted that fine motor skills afford children the opportunity to practice mapping visual representations to emerging literacy and mathematical skills, through practicing writing letters, counting objects, and sorting objects into similar categories based on mathematical concepts, such as number (e.g., groups of three), shape (e.g., squares and circles), and size (e.g., big and small). Likewise, Becker et al. (2014) argued that good fine motor skills enables children to script letters and numbers automatically and this in turn directs cognitive resources toward conceptual processes, such as connecting figures and sounds, understanding mathematical concepts and decoding words.

Accordingly, for maths, fine motor skills may underlie the acquisition of quantitative and spatial concepts and could be supported through early years classroom activities and aids that capitalize on fine motor skills for successful execution, such as Snap Cubes, Numicon, and cutting out shapes. In contrast, the link between fine manual skills and reading acquisition is likely to emerge through writing, when children begin to represent letters and words on a page. The phonics instruction that is taught in UK primary schools as standard (Department for Education, 2010) also makes use of fine motor skills to assist the mapping of sounds through actions (e.g., running fingers up the arm to represent ants whilst saying the sound /a/). However, it seems that precise motor movements are not as critical in supporting early phonological skills through sound-based interventions as they might be for acquiring early mathematical skills, where the motor movement maps directly to the conceptual representation. A specific illustration of this is with finger counting which requires direct linkage between precise finger movements and the corresponding number concept. Whilst there has been much focus on the role of role of finger counting in mathematical ability, the most recent consensus appears to be that fingers can assist but are not necessary in the acquisition of number skills (e.g., Crollen et al., 2011a,b; Lafay et al., 2013). As children learn to write letters and numbers over the first year of school, the relationship between fine motor skills and reading and maths ability may become stronger over this period, when precision in scripting letters and numbers is necessary in supporting the mappings between letters to sounds and words and numbers to numerical concepts.

In addition, a specific role of visuo-spatial skills and fine motor precision has been proposed to underpin some mathematical abilities. For example, Barnhardt et al. (2005) showed that children with poor visual motor integration skills made more errors in spacing letters, words, and number problems on a page relative to their peers with good visual motor integration skills. They argued that difficulties with spatial alignment and organization of letters and numbers on a page can lead to incorrect answers in maths tasks, even when the underlying computation might be accurate. Similarly, in a recent study with UK children aged 8–10 years, Simms et al. (2016) showed that tasks of visuo-motor integration and visuo-spatial skill were significantly related to performance on the number line estimation task, which is purported to measure precise numerical representations (e.g., Siegler and Ramani, 2008) and proportional judgment skills (e.g., Ebersbach et al., 2008). They suggested that the spatial components and need for motor precision in the number line estimation task accounted for the observed association with visuo-motor integration and visuo-spatial skills. This suggests there might be a specific role for fine motor precision in early mathematical attainment, yet to date, no study has attempted to differentiate this from fine motor integration skills.

Fine motor skills have been associated with several other cognitive abilities, including processing speed (Wassenberg et al., 2005), executive functions (Livesey et al., 2006; Rigoli et al., 2012), and scholastic skills (Morales et al., 2011). Recent studies that have investigated how fine motor skills are associated with literacy and maths abilities have also recognized the importance of executive functions in mediating this relationship. For example, in a prospective study spanning the transition into kindergarten, Cameron et al. (2012) found specific effects of fine motor integration (using the design copy task from the Early Screening Inventory-Revised, Meisels et al., 1997) and executive functions on six measures of achievement, including literacy and maths, as assessed with the Woodcock–Johnson III Tests of Achievement (Woodcock et al., 2001). Becker et al. (2014), in a concurrent study with 127 pre-kindergarten and kindergarten children in the US, finding that visual-motor skills and behavioral self-regulation significantly predicted early maths ability and emergent literacy, noted that executive functions were additionally related to early literacy skills, In contrast, in a concurrent study with a sample of 97 pupils spanning 5–18 years, Carlson et al. (2013) reported a specific role for fine motor integration but not fine motor coordination in predicting mathematics ability; but neither components of fine manual control contributed significantly to reading ability when SES, gender and IQ were controlled. Further still, a longitudinal study of children in early primary school by Roebers et al. (2014) failed to find a specific role for fine motor skills and non-verbal IQ in predicting mathematics, reading and spelling ability, once executive functions were accounted for.

These studies imply a complex relationship between the development of fine motor, cognitive and scholastic skills. However, other demographic characteristics, such as gender and socio-economic status (SES), are known to affect these abilities. Gender differences have been reported in the development of fine compared to gross motor skills (e.g., Sigmundsson and Rostoft, 2003). A recent study by Morley et al. (2015) conducted in the UK with 4- to 7-year-old children showed that, after controlling for age, girls outperformed boys on all tasks involving fine motor skill, whereas boys outperformed girls on gross motor tasks involving catching and dribbling a ball. Furthermore, a study by McPhillips and Jordan-Black (2007) compared motor development in two groups of children, aged 4–5 years and 7–8 years, from two schools of low SES and two schools of high SES in Northern Ireland. For both age groups, they found a significant main effect of SES and gender on the overall motor score but no interaction effect. Specifically, on tasks of manual dexterity, they found that girls outperformed boys and children of lower SES performed less well than those of higher SES.

The evidence accrued in the literature thus far implies that underdevelopment of fine motor skills in the early years might be a significant risk factor for later scholastic attainment. Children from low socio-economic backgrounds are vulnerable to poor development of fine motor skills in the early years (Dinehart and Manfra, 2013; Morley et al., 2015) and there has been some consideration of the environmental factors influencing this relationship (Vazir et al., 1998; de Barros et al., 2003), with the lack of opportunities to engage with preschool activities that promote fine motor skills being a prominent explanation. SES is also known to predict early cognitive development (e.g., Duncan et al., 1994), the development of executive functions, i.e., the ability to follow commands, remember sequences of information and inhibit responses, and the development of these underlying skills in early scholastic skills (e.g., Duncan et al., 2007; Mazzocco and Kover, 2007).

Understanding the impact of gender and SES on fine motor skills is particularly relevant in the UK, where children from low SES backgrounds have been identified to be at risk of lower reading and maths skills compared to higher SES populations (Strand, 1997, 2014; Sammons et al., 2004; Anders et al., 2012). More specifically, boys from white working class backgrounds are purported to be of particular risk to underachievement at school (Strand, 2014). This is particularly problematic to Nottinghamshire, the region where this study took place, because pockets of underachievement in children from low SES homes are present across the shire.[1] Achievement in basic skills of literacy and numeracy is a question of significant concern in the UK. These long-held concerns focus upon a proportion of lower attaining students, resistant to overall rises evident in national attainment data sets, a so-called 'stubborn-tail of underachievement' (Tymms and Merrell, 2007). In order to address underachievement in reading attainments, the UK Government has implemented a phonics-based reading intervention across all primary schools (Department for Education, 2010). In contrast, there is currently no specified national intervention for maths.

The inception of this study came through a request from head teachers within this region, who had grown increasingly concerned about the role of fine motor skills in the development of reading and maths skills in the early primary years, perceiving that upon entering the school system at age 4 years, children from low socio-economic backgrounds were apparently showing impoverished manual skills. It was thus important to determine the contributory effects of fine motor skills on early reading and maths performance in boys and girls from low–medium SES backgrounds in the first years of primary school in order to target interventions most appropriately. In this study, we explore the relationship between fine motor skills and scholastic performance in the early primary school years (Study 1) whilst taking into account other potential influences on performance (Study 2).

[1]See http://www.nottinghamshire.gov.uk/care/childrens-social-care/nottinghamshire-childrens-trust/child-poverty and table 3 of the following website http://www.ons.gov.uk/economy/regionalaccounts/grossdisposablehouseholdincome/bulletins/regionalgrossdisposablehouseholdincomegdhi/2015-05-27

Considering educational programs aimed at raising achievement, we additionally viewed these investigations as an opportunity to explore the relative effects of the UK's national literacy intervention, on the one hand, and in contrast, the absence of a national strategy to support numeracy acquisition, on the other. The questions raised by the existing literature coincided with head teacher concerns: both were therefore investigated through an exploration of concurrent associations between fine motor skills and scholastic abilities, in two samples of primary school children.

To date, no study has investigated concurrently the role of fine motor skills on the development of early scholastic skills across genders, in a UK sample of low–medium SES pupils in the early primary school years. Most studies reported in the literature are prospective and investigate the influence of fine motor skills in preschool years on later acquired scholastic skills (Son and Meisels, 2006; Luo et al., 2007; Grissmer et al., 2010; Pagani et al., 2010; Cameron et al., 2012; Dinehart and Manfra, 2013; Roebers et al., 2014). Concurrent investigation of the association between fine motor skills and early scholastic skills, taking into account SES and gender, will provide insight into how these factors are related at a particular age. This is important for informing interventions that may optimally support early years development in literacy and numeracy, where emerging evidence suggests they may require a component of fine motor skill. Studies that have adopted concurrent investigation of fine motor skills and scholastic abilities tend to span a broad age range and do not focus on the early primary years (e.g., Carlson et al., 2013). In addition, they tend to focus on just one aspect of fine motor skill, such as fine motor integration (e.g., Kulp, 1999; Becker et al., 2014; Santi et al., 2015). To understand more precisely the role of fine motor skills in early reading and maths acquisition different components of fine manual control need to be assessed (Grissmer et al., 2010; Cameron et al., 2012; Carlson et al., 2013). In addition, the contribution of reading on early maths ability and vice versa needs to be examined in relation to fine motor skills, as Duncan et al. (2007) found early reading and mathematical skills were the strongest predictors of both reading and mathematics in middle childhood. Likewise, Hooper et al. (2010) found similar results across different ethnic groups and Purpura et al. (2011) found three measures of early literacy to be predictive of both concurrent and subsequent mathematical ability. This association may result from co-dependence of similar skills, so considering the influence of fine motor skills on reading and maths ability, whilst taking into account concurrent maths and reading ability, respectively, controls for the potential impact of additional skills that are related to both reading and maths. To our knowledge, to date, no study has investigated concurrent relationships between early reading and maths ability whilst simultaneously investigating the influence of different components of fine motor skill.

The present study investigated the role of two components of fine manual control in the development of early reading and maths skills. Measures of Fine Motor Integration and Fine Motor Precision were taken from the same assessment battery of motor development (BOT-2, Bruininks and Bruininks, 2005) enabling direct comparison to be made between these two components of fine manual control. Similarly, measures of Word Reading and Mathematical Reasoning were taken from the Weschler Individual Achievement Test second Edition (Wechsler, 2005) enabling direct comparison to be made between these key scholastic skills. Our focus was on pupils from low SES backgrounds to address the high levels of underachievement that is commonly reported in this population. In study 1, we explored concurrent relationships between fine motor skills and reading and maths ability in a group of children aged 5–7 years from low SES backgrounds attending Year 1 of primary school. In study 2, we explored the interrelation of non-verbal IQ and verbal short-term memory with fine motor skills and reading and maths ability in a group of Foundation year children aged 4–5 years from low-to-medium SES backgrounds. Verbal short-term memory was used in the study as a proxy for working memory, which is considered to be a measure of executive functions. Complex span tasks are typically used to assess working memory but are difficult for young children to perform reliably, as working memory starts to develop from about 4 years of age (Gathercole et al., 2004). We used a simple span task as a measure of short-term memory, which young children can perform reliably, as studies show a high degree of overlap between short-term memory and working memory (see Aben et al., 2012). Moreover, short-term memory has been shown to play a pivotal role in explaining the relationship between working memory and higher reasoning abilities (Hornung et al., 2011). In addition, we administered a task of non-verbal IQ to determine if fine motor skills continue to contribute to early reading and maths ability after controlling for non-verbal IQ (see Roebers et al., 2014).

STUDY 1

Methods

Participants

In total, 62 typically developing children attending Year 1 of primary school were recruited from three primary schools located in low SES areas within Nottingham. The sample consisted of 29 males and 33 females that ranged in age between 65 and 80 months (5 years 5 months to 6 years 8 months). None of the children had been identified with special educational needs, indicating the absence of significant motor, intellectual, attentional or behavioral difficulties in this sample.

Ethical approval for the study was granted from the School of Psychology, University of Nottingham, which complies with the ethical guidelines of the British Psychological Society. Informed consent was obtained from parents/guardians for each child who participated in the study.

Measures

Pupils were evaluated on fine motor skills and two measures of early scholastic achievement, namely reading and maths. The standardized tests described below were chosen because they are suitable for the age range of pupils in this study and are considered to be 'gold standard' assessments of motor skill (Gwynne and Blick, 2004) and have UK norms for reading and maths ability. In addition, a UK based measure of SES was obtained for each pupil.

Fine motor skills

The *Bruininks–Oseretsky Test of Motor Proficiency, Second Edition* (BOT-2; Bruininks and Bruininks, 2005) was used to assess fine motor skills. This age-adjusted measure is suitable for children aged 4–21 years and consists of eight subtests. Both subtests of the *Fine Manual Control* composite index were administered. (1) Fine Motor Precision requires children to draw, fold, and cut within a specific boundary, and (2) Fine Motor Integration requires children to reproduce drawings of various geometric shapes that range in complexity from a simple circle to overlapping pencils. Both of these tasks involve activities that require precise control of finger and hand movement. As emphasis is placed on precision of response items are not timed. A composite measure of Fine Manual control was also obtained using the test norms. As reported in the test manual, reliability coefficients (internal consistency) for these two subtests in children aged 5–6 years were high in the normative sample, ranging from 0.75 to 0.84 (Bruininks and Bruininks, 2005, p. 52). For each subtest, items were scored according to the procedure provided in the test manual and standardized scores were generated from raw scores with the gender-specific test norm $\mu = 15$ and $\sigma = 5$.

Scholastic skills

Early scholastic achievement was evaluated using the *Wechsler Individual Achievement Test, Second Edition* (WIAT-II^{UK}; Wechsler, 2005). This age-adjusted measure is suitable for children aged 4–21 years and consists of nine subtests. Two subtests were used in this study. (1) Word Reading which assesses the ability to name single letters, recognize sounds in a word and read whole words, and (2) Mathematical Reasoning which assesses the ability to solve problems about numbers and probability and interpret graphs. As reported in the test manual, reliability coefficients (inter-item comparison) for these two subtests in children aged 5–6 years were high in the normative sample, ranging from 0.92 to 0.99 (Wechsler, 2005, p. 86). For each subtest standardized scores were generated from raw scores with the test norm $\mu = 100$ and $\sigma = 15$.

Socio-economic Status (SES)

The Income Deprivation Affecting Children Index (IDACI) rank 2010 was used to determine a measure of SES for each pupil. This measure is based on residential postcodes in the UK and reflects the proportion of children aged 0–15 years living in low-income families within a particular postcode area (Department for Communities and Local Government, 2011). On a national scale, rank 1 represents the most deprived area and 32482 represents the least deprived. In this study, IDACI ranks ranged from 56 to 24688, with a median value of 4025 ($n = 60$). SES data was missing for two children so the SES index of their school was used as a close estimate for their SES.

Procedure

In each of the three participating schools, Year 1 teaching assistants were trained by the first author to administer the standardized tests described above. A half-day training session was held for the teaching assistants and clear printed guidelines were provided for test administration in addition to the test manuals. Teaching assistants could contact the first author throughout the data collection period with any queries about test administration. Completed response forms were stored securely in each school and were collected by the first author for analysis once data collection was finalized.

Teaching assistants administered each of the four measures described above to individual pupils on a one-to-one basis, in a quiet area of their school, free from distraction. Tests were administered over one or two short sessions, each lasting 10–20 min. Breaks were given in between tests and when necessary in accordance with the child's engagement with the process. The following fixed order was used to administer the tests: (1) Fine Motor Precision, (2) Fine Motor Integration, (3) Word Reading, and (4) Mathematical Reasoning.

Upon completion of data collection by all three schools, one coder (second author) scored all of the data for every participant on each of the four subtests. The coder received specific training from the first author. As scoring for the motor subtests involved some level of subjective interpretation, a second rater scored a random sample of data from 20 pupils and the agreement between the two raters was calculated using a two-way, mixed, absolute agreement, single-measure intra-class correlation (ICC). The resulting ICC was in the excellent range (ICC = 0.996), indicating high degree of agreement between coders. The second author entered all of the data into SPSS version 22.0 (IBM Corp, 2013) for statistical analysis.

Statistical Analysis

For each participant, standard scores were generated for the four subtests and used for all the analyses described below. Normality and equality of variance were explored across the whole sample and across gender and assumptions for parametric statistics were met. Three pupils with relatively high SES were identified as outliers through graphical representation (see Appendix 1) so the same analyses were conducted after removal of these children. As the significance of results did not change following removal of these outliers, results, and figures are reported for the total sample.

Relationships between fine motor, reading, and maths skills were investigated using paired-samples *t*-tests and effect sizes were calculated with Cohen's *d* (Cohen, 1988). Pearson's correlations were conducted to explore associations between tasks and Spearman's rank correlation was used to assess if SES impacted on task performance. For the correlational analyses Bonferroni corrected *p*-values were applied to account for multiple comparisons. The effect of gender on fine motor skills and scholastic attainment was investigated using separate two-way mixed ANOVAs. Finally, the extent to which fine motor skills predicted attainment in reading and maths was explored in two hierarchical multiple regressions. In the final step of each regression analysis, we entered the other scholastic skill to evaluate the unique contribution of fine motor skills whilst controlling for a range of generic skills that contribute to scholastic progression (such as verbal IQ and executive functions). Preliminary analyses ensured no violation of the assumptions of multicollinearity.

Results

A complete dataset was obtained for 60 pupils. All the pupils completed the two subtests of fine motor skill, one pupil was not given the Mathematical Reasoning subtest and the Word Reading scores for two pupils were excluded because of a mistake in the test administration.

Relationships between Fine Motor and Scholastic Skills

Group performance across the four subtests is summarized in **Table 1**. As can be seen, overall group mean scores fall within 1 SD of the test norms for all tasks and the SDs are close to the test norms. Whilst mean performance on the two subtests of fine motor skill was similar overall, there was a noticeable discrepancy in the overall sample between reading and maths of 8.90. This value is below the minimum difference of 9.71 required for statistical significance at 0.05 level of the standardization sample. However, for this sample, a paired-samples t-test demonstrated that the overall group difference in reading and maths ability was statistically significant [$t(59) = 4.71, p < 0.001$] and was captured by a medium effect size (Cohen's $d = 0.58$), showing the relative strength for reading.

A series of Pearson's correlations were conducted to investigate associations between measures. Results are reported in **Table 2** and scatter plots are available in Appendix I. **Table 2** shows that, as expected, the two measures of fine motor skill correlated significantly as did the two measures of scholastic attainment. Medium to strong positive correlations were also found between fine motor and scholastic skills, and these were significant in all cases except for Word Reading and Fine Motor Precision.

Impact of SES on Task Performance

A series of Spearman's rank-order correlations were conducted to explore the relationship between SES and early fine motor and scholastic skills (see **Table 2** and Appendix I). Results revealed no significant correlation between SES and any of the scholastic and motor tasks.

Effects of Gender on Task Performance

To explore the effects of gender on early fine motor skills and scholastic attainment, two separate two-way mixed ANOVAs were conducted with Gender (Boys, Girls) as the between-subjects variable and Task (1: Fine Motor Precision, Fine Motor Integration; 2: Word Reading, Mathematical Reasoning) as the within-groups variable. Results are shown in **Figure 1**. No significant effect of gender on task performance was found for either fine motor skills [$F(1,58) = 1.03, p = 0.314$] or scholastic attainment [$F(1,58) = 0.17$, $p = 0.683$] and no significant interaction was found between gender and task performance for either domain [1: Gender and Fine Motor Skills: $F(1,58) = 0.04$, $p = 0.841$; 2: Gender and Scholastic Attainment: $F(1,58) = 1.75$, $p = 0.192$]. Main effects of task corroborated the findings of the paired-sample t-tests reported above. Whilst both measures of fine motor skill appear to develop side-by-side [$F(1,58) = 0.45$, $p = 0.505$] scholastic attainment was significantly higher for reading than for maths [$F(1,58) = 21.57, p < 0.001$].

Predictors of Scholastic Attainment

Two separate hierarchical multiple regressions were performed to investigate the unique contribution that fine motor skills made to the prediction of early reading and maths performance. Gender and SES were not entered into the regression as no significant effects were found. Thus, the three variables that were significantly related to reading or maths were entered progressively into the model in the following order: Fine Motor Precision, Fine Motor Integration and Mathematical Reasoning (for the reading regression) and Word Reading (for the maths regression). Results are summarized in **Table 3**.

For Word Reading, only models 2 and 3 were statistically significant ($F \geq 4.79$, $p \leq 0.012$) and explained 14–35% of the variance. Significant improvements to the model were found at step 2 when adding in Fine Motor Integration ($\Delta R^2 = 0.10$, $p = 0.011$) and at step 3 when adding in Mathematical Reasoning ($\Delta R^2 = 0.21$, $p < 0.001$). While Fine Motor Integration was a significant predictor in model 2 ($p = 0.011$), its contribution was no longer significant when Mathematical Reasoning was added at step 3 ($p = 0.147$). Mathematical Reasoning was the only significant predictor in model 3 and accounted of 21% of unique variance, although Fine Motor Precision showed a strong tendency toward significance ($p = 0.053$).

For Mathematical Reasoning, all models were statistically significant (all $F \geq 32.06$, $p \leq 0.001$) and explained 36–57% of the variance. Significant improvements to the model were found at every step of the regression analysis ($p \leq 0.012$). Whilst Fine Motor Precision was a significant predictor in each model (all $p \leq 0.003$), the contribution of Fine Motor Integration was no longer significant when Word Reading was added into the model at step 3. Fine Motor Precision accounted of 36% of unique variance, Fine Motor Integration added a further 6% of unique variance, and Word Reading added a further 15% of unique variance.

Discussion

Study 1 examined the nature of concurrent relationships between Fine Motor Precision and Fine Motor Integration, gender, SES and scholastic achievement in children from low SES backgrounds in Year 1 of primary school in the UK.

Across the sample, group performance on the four subtests was close to the test norms. As expected, the two measures of fine motor skill were closely related as were the two measures of scholastic attainment. However, whilst the two motor skills were similarly developed, a significant discrepancy was found between scholastic skills, with performance in reading exceeding that in maths. As the measures of reading and maths were taken from the same battery of scholastic tests direct comparisons in attainment across domains can be drawn as these subtests have been standardized on the same normative sample. Previous research has identified a close relationship between the development of early literacy and numeracy skills (Purpura et al., 2011; Kleemans et al., 2012). In this study, early reading skills were more

TABLE 1 | Study 1.

Group	Fine Motor Skills (BOT-2) Mean (*SD*) Min–Max		Scholastic skills (WIAT-II) Mean (*SD*) Min–Max	
	Fine Motor Precision	**Fine Motor Integration**	**Word Reading**	**Mathematical Reasoning**
Boys ($n = 28$)	14.8 (4.6) 6–23	14.3 (5.2) 5–25	102.5 (17.4) 55–130	96.3 (17.2) 63–133
Girls ($n = 32$)	13.6 (4.3) 5–24	13.3 (4.4) 4–22	106.5 (14.7) 83–141	95.3 (12.5) 63–114
Total ($n = 60$)	14.2 (4.4) 5–24	13.8 (4.8) 4–25	104.6 (16.0) 55–141	95.7 (14.7) 63–133

Group performance (standard score) on each of the four subtests. BOT-2 test norm $\mu = 15$ and $\sigma = 5$. WIAT-II test norm $\mu = 100$ and $\sigma = 15$.

TABLE 2 | Study 1.

	IDACI rank	Word Reading	Mathematical Reasoning	Fine Motor Precision	Fine Motor Integration
IDACI rank	/				
Word Reading	$\rho = 0.098$ $p = 0.458$	/			
Mathematical Reasoning	$\rho = 0.186$ $p = 0.155$	**$r = 0.550$*** **$p < 0.001$**	/		
Fine Motor Precision	$\rho = -0.006$ $p = 0.963$	$r = 0.198$ $p = 0.129$	**$r = 0.597$*** **$p < 0.001$**	/	
Fine Motor Integration	$\rho = -0.074$ $p = 0.576$	**$r = 0.377$*** **$p = 0.003$**	**$r = 0.569$*** **$p < 0.001$**	**$r = 0.609$*** **$p < 0.001$**	/

*Correlations among predictors and outcome variables of Study 1. Spearman's rank (ρ) and Pearson's (r) correlation coefficients are reported as appropriate. Significant correlations with uncorrected p-values highlighted in bold. *Significant correlations which survived Bonferroni correction at $\alpha = 0.05/4 = 0.013$.*

advanced than early maths skills. This result is consistent with UK national statistics that show a similar pattern at the end of Key Stage 1 when children are aged 7–8 years (Department for Education, 2014). This may be indicative of the effectiveness of the current UK literacy intervention program that starts during the Foundation Year of schooling when children are aged 4–5 years. Our results suggest an early protective effect of the national literacy intervention for supporting the acquisition of reading skills. In contrast, a similar national level structured early intervention approach for mathematics is not currently implemented in the UK.

The gender analysis showed no significant interaction between gender across scholastic skills. However, the reading-maths discrepancy was captured by a large effect size for girls (Cohen's $d = 0.82$) and by a small–medium effect-size in boys (Cohen's $d = 0.36$), suggesting that female pupils were more vulnerable to this discrepancy than their male counterparts. Moreover, no gender effect was found for either fine motor task, suggesting that in this sample fine motor skills have developed similarly in boys and girls. Whilst these results are contrary to current literature reviewing gender differences in educational achievement (Cassen and Kingdon, 2007; Strand, 2014) and motor skill development (Morley et al., 2015), the reading-maths discrepancy reported here nevertheless highlights a need to provide additional support for maths education that would benefit all pupils.

The correlational analyses showed no relationship between SES and fine motor skills or scholastic skills, probably due to the narrow range of SES in our sample. However, the purpose of this study was to examine the relationship between fine motor skills and scholastic attainment in pupils from low SES backgrounds so our sample was drawn from low SES areas. Accordingly, we did not expect to find significant relationships between SES and task performance in this study. Future research might explore how SES influences the development of fine motor and scholastic skills and their associations in a sample drawn from a wider range of SES backgrounds.

Interestingly, when investigating the relation between fine motor and scholastic skills, regression analyses showed a stronger influence of fine motor skills in predicting early maths than early reading skills. Specifically, Fine Motor Integration was shown to be a significant predictor for reading but when Mathematical Reasoning was taken into account Fine Motor Integration no longer significantly predicted reading performance. In contrast, both Fine Motor Integration and Fine Motor Precision significantly predicted maths ability, but the contribution of Fine Motor Integration was no longer significant when Word Reading was taken into account. These results suggests some degree of overlap between Fine Motor Integration and Word Reading and Mathematical Reasoning, which might arise from each of these skills drawing to some extent, at least, on visuo-spatial processes. The additional influence of Fine Motor Precision in predicting

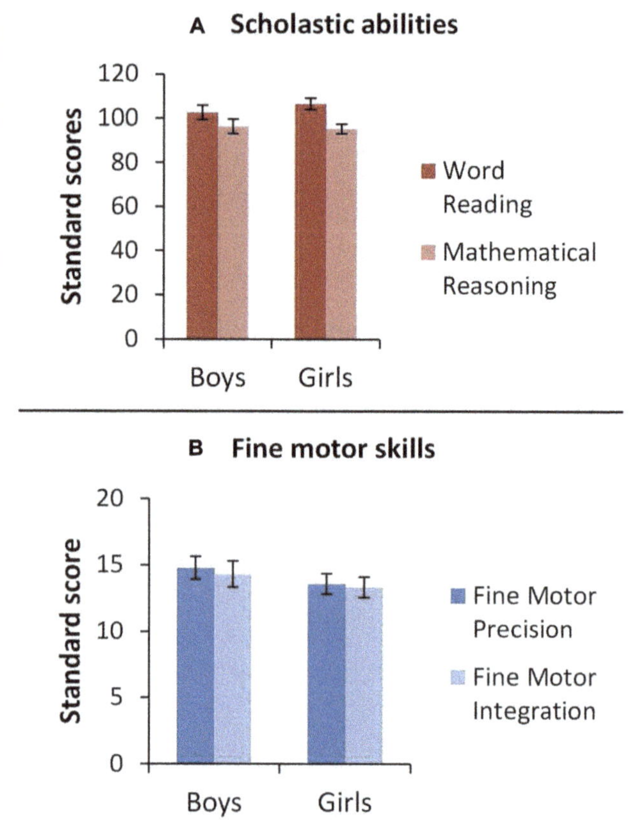

FIGURE 1 | Study 1. Bar graph representing mean performance (standard score, *y*-axis) for boys and girls (*x*-axis) for **(A)** scholastic skills and **(B)** fine motor skills. Error bars represent 1 standard error.

maths ability supports recent studies that have highlighted the need for precise manual movements in a range of mathematical tests (e.g., Barnhardt et al., 2005; Simms et al., 2016). Overall, these results support the notion that fine motor skills are more intimately related to early maths than early reading ability. This has important implications for potential maths interventions.

However, before firm conclusions can be drawn it is important to recognize the main limitation of this study, namely, that additional cognitive skills that are also related to scholastic achievement, such as non-verbal IQ and verbal STM were not included in this study. Previous studies that have investigated the influence of these cognitive abilities and of fine motor skills on reading and maths performance have provided mixed evidence. As previously highlighted, Cameron et al. (2012) found specific effects of Fine Motor Integration and executive functions on literacy and maths. Becker et al. (2014) found Fine Motor Integration and behavioral self-regulation predicted early maths and literacy ability but that executive functions were additionally related to early literacy skills. In contrast, Carlson et al. (2013) reported a specific role for Fine Motor Integration, but not fine motor coordination, in predicting mathematics ability but neither components of fine manual control contributed significantly to reading ability when SES, gender and IQ were controlled. Finally, as previously noted, Roebers et al. (2014) failed to find a specific role for fine motor skills and non-verbal IQ in predicting mathematics, reading and spelling abilities, once executive functions were accounted for.

In order to address the contradictory evidence in the current literature, we replicated Study 1 with a younger group of children in Foundation Stage 2 who were aged 4–5 years in Study 2 and included measures of non-verbal IQ and verbal STM. Foundation Stage 2 pupils were selected for Study 2 for two reasons. Firstly, this is the first year of compulsory schooling in the UK and we aimed to examine whether the effects of the national policy focus upon phonics and literacy development were evident, even in children who had just started school. Secondly, additional research suggests that the correlates of educational underachievement lie, at least in part, in the child's experiences and development during the first year of primary school (Melhuish et al., 2008), leading to a focus upon the interrelationship of variables at that age.

STUDY 2

Methods

Participants

Thirty-four typically developing children in the Foundation Stage 2 of one primary school from an average SES area of Nottinghamshire, UK were recruited to the study. The sample included 17 males and 17 females that ranged in age between 50 and 61 months (4 years 2 months to 5 years 1 month). The overall SES of this sample was higher than in Study 1 as IDACI ranks ranged from 5920 to 31716, with a median value of 22512 ($n = 34$), although the sample included some children from deprived backgrounds. None of the children had been identified with special educational needs, indicating the absence of significant motor, intellectual, attentional, or behavioral difficulties in this sample.

Ethical approval for the study was granted from the School of Psychology, University of Nottingham, in line with the British Psychological Society ethical guidelines. Prior informed consent was obtained from parents/guardians for each child that participated in the study.

Measures

As in Study 1, children were given the Fine Motor Precision and Fine Motor Integration tasks from the BOT-2 (Bruininks and Bruininks, 2005) to assess fine manual control and Word Reading and Mathematical Reasoning from the WIAT-II (Wechsler, 2005) to assess scholastic attainment. Normative scores for the Mathematical Reasoning subtest of the WIAT-II are not available for children of this age range, so to establish the validity of using this subtest with our sample an additional test for maths ability was given that is appropriate for this age range. The additional maths test consisted of 50 items based on the UK national mathematics curriculum for early years. Basic maths skills assessed in this test included counting, understanding and using numbers, simple addition and subtraction and shape, space, and measure recognition

TABLE 3 | Study 1.

Step	Variable(s)	Model		Significance	Change		Unstandardized Coefficients	Standardized Coefficients	Significance
		R	R^2	F (df), p	ΔR^2	Significance ΔF	B, SE	β	t, p
Word Reading (SS)									
1	Fine Motor Precision	0.20	0.04	2.37 (1,58), 0.129	0.04	0.129	0.71, 0.46	0.20	1.54, 0.129
2	Fine Motor Precision +	0.38	0.14	4.79 (2,57), **0.012**	0.10	**0.011**	−0.18, 0.56	−0.05	−0.33, 0.745
	Fine Motor Integration						1.37, 0.52	0.41	2.64, **0.011**
3	*Fine Motor Precision +*	0.60	0.35	10.21 (3,56), **<0.001**	0.21	**<0.001**	−1.05, 0.53	−0.29	−1.98, *0.053*
	Fine Motor Integration +						0.71, 0.48	0.21	1.4 7, 0.147
	Mathematical Reasoning						0.65, 0.15	0.60	4.26, **<0.001**
Mathematical Reasoning (SS)									
1	**Fine Motor Precision**	0.60	0.36	32.06 (1, 58), **<0.001**	0.36	**<0.001**	1.99, 0.35	0.60	5.66, **<0.001**
2	**Fine Motor Precision +**	0.65	0.42	20.94 (2, 57), **<0.001**	0.06	**0.012**	1.32, 0.42	0.40	3.13, **0.003**
	Fine Motor Integration						1.01, 0.39	0.33	2.59, **0.012**
3	**Fine Motor Precision +**	0.75	0.57	24.22 (3,56), **<0.001**	0.15	**<0.001**	1.39, 0.37	0.42	3.75, **<0.001**
	Fine Motor Integration +						0.50, 0.37	0.16	1.38, 0.175
	Word Reading						0.38, 0.09	0.41	4.26, **<0.001**

Model fits for the hierarchical multiple regressions identifying significant predictors of early reading and maths attainment. Significant predictors highlighted in bold.

(Outhwaite and Pitchford, under review). Items increased in difficulty in line with progression. No discontinuity rule was applied so all questions were administered. IDACI rank scores were determined from the child's postcode as an indication of their SES. Additional measures of non-verbal IQ and verbal STM were administered.

Non-verbal IQ

The Block Design and Symbol Search subtests from the *Wechsler Preschool and Primary Scale of Intelligence-Third Edition* (WPPSI-III; Wechsler, 2003) were used as a measure of non-verbal IQ. These age-adjusted tasks are suitable for children aged 2 years 6 months to 7 years 3 months. The Block Design subtest requires children to reproduce block patterns presented as a constructed model or picture using one or two colored blocks within a specified time. The Symbol Search subtest requires children to identify whether or not a target symbol appears within an array of similar symbols. Children are given a specified time to conduct the task. As reported in the test manual, reliability coefficients (internal consistency) for these two subtests in children aged 4–5 years were high in the normative sample, ranging from 0.76 to 0.85 (Wechsler, 2003, p. 52). For each subtest, standardized scores were generated from raw scores with the test norm $\mu = 10$ and $\sigma = 3$. For each child, scores from the two subtests were averaged to produce a composite measure of non-verbal IQ.

Verbal short-term memory (STM)

The Number Recall and Word Order subtests from the *Kaufman Assessment Battery for Children Second Edition* (KABC-II; Kaufman and Kaufman, 2004) were used to measure verbal STM. The KABC-II is an age-adjusted measure that is suitable for children aged 3–18 years. Number Recall requires children to verbally repeat a series of one digit, one syllable numbers, presented to them verbally by the experimenter. Word Order requires children to touch a series of common object silhouettes in the same order as was previously presented verbally by the experimenter. As reported in the test manual, reliability coefficients (internal consistency) for these two subtests in children aged 4–5 years were high in the normative sample, ranging from 0.79 to 0.88 (Kaufman and Kaufman, 2004, p. 88). Raw scores were converted to standardized scores with the test norm $\mu = 10$ and $\sigma = 3$. For each child, scores on the two subtests were then averaged to give a composite measure of verbal STM.

Procedure

Children were assessed individually by the third author on each of the tasks described above in a quiet area, free from distraction, in their familiar school environment. Tests were administered over three short sessions, each lasting 10–20 min. Short breaks were given between tasks to ensure children remained engaged. Tasks were administered in the following order to be consistent with Study 1: Fine Motor Precision, Fine Motor Integration, Word Reading, Mathematical Reasoning, Block Design, Symbol Search, Number Recall, and Word Order. The second author coded performance of the motor tasks, consistent with Study 1. A second coder (the third author) scored the motor tasks from a random sample of six pupils to ensure inter-rater reliability. The ICC analysis revealed a high level of agreement between the coders (ICC = 0.988).

Statistical Analysis

Performance on the Mathematical Reasoning subtest of the WIAT-II was strongly correlated with performance on the early years maths test ($r = 0.69$, $p < 0.001$), demonstrating that the Mathematical Reasoning subtest is a valid measure for this age group. Thus, all subsequent analyses are reported for Mathematical Reasoning. To allow for direct comparisons to be made between Word Reading and Mathematical

Reasoning, raw scores were converted to percentage correct, and percentage correct was used for all statistical analyses. Normality and equality of variance were explored across the whole sample and across gender and assumptions for parametric statistics were met. The same statistical analyses as in Study 1 were conducted. Group performance across the two measures of fine motor skill and scholastic skill were examined using paired-samples t-tests and effect sizes were calculated using Cohen's d (Cohen, 1988). Associations between fine motor skills, non-verbal IQ, verbal STM, and scholastic abilities were explored using Pearson's correlations whereas associations with SES and task performance were investigated using Spearman's rank-order correlations. Bonferroni corrected p-values were applied to account for multiple comparisons. The effects of gender on fine motor skills and scholastic attainment was investigated using separate two-way mixed ANOVAs. Finally, two hierarchical regression analyses were conducted to explore the relative contributions of the two measures of fine motor skill, non-verbal IQ, verbal STM in reading and maths attainment when taking into account maths and reading ability, respectively. Preliminary analyses ensured no violation of the assumptions of multicollinearity.

Results

Relationships between Fine Motor Skills, Non-verbal IQ, Verbal STM, and Scholastic Attainment

Table 4 summarizes group mean performance on the six different ability measures. For the subtests where standardized scores are available, overall group mean performance falls within 1 SD of the test norms for all tasks and the SDs are close to the test norms. Performance on the two subtests of fine motor skill were similar and a paired-sample t-test revealed no significant difference [$t(33) = 0.63$, $p = 0.531$]. In contrast, for scholastic abilities a paired-sample t-test revealed significantly higher performance in reading than for maths, [$t(33) = 2.47$, $p = 0.019$], with a small-medium effect size (Cohen's $d = 0.45$).

A series of Pearson's correlations was conducted to investigate the associations between the fine motor skills, non-verbal IQ, verbal STM, and scholastic ability. Results are reported in **Table 5** and scatter plots are available in Appendix II. Again, as shown in Study 1, the two measures of fine motor skill correlated significantly as did the two measures of scholastic attainment. For Word Reading, significant, medium-to-strong, positive correlations were found with verbal STM and Fine Motor Integration, although the latter did not survive Bonferroni correction. For Mathematical Reasoning, significant, medium-to-strong, positive correlations were found with Fine Motor Integration and non-verbal IQ, although the correlation with non-verbal IQ did not survive Bonferroni correction. Furthermore, Fine Motor Precision was significantly associated with both non-verbal IQ and verbal STM, whereas Fine Motor Integration was significantly associated only with non-verbal IQ and this correlation did not survive Bonferroni correction.

Impact of SES on Fine Motor and Scholastic Skills

A series of Spearman's rank-order correlations were conducted to explore the relationship between SES and early fine motor and scholastic skills (see **Table 5**). Results revealed only a weak positive correlation between SES and Word Reading, which did not survive Bonferroni correction.

Effects of Gender on Task Performance

To explore the effects of gender on early fine motor skills and scholastic attainment, two separate two-way mixed ANOVAs were conducted with Gender (Boys, Girls) as the between-subjects variable and Task (1: Fine Motor Precision, Fine Motor Integration; and 2: Word Reading, Mathematical Reasoning) as the within-groups variable. Results are shown in **Figure 2**. No significant effect of gender on task performance was found for either fine motor skills [$F(1,32) = 0.74$, $p = 0.395$] or scholastic attainment [$F(1,32) = 1.17$, $p = 0.288$] and no significant interaction between gender and task performance was found for either domain [1: Gender and Fine Motor Skills: $F(1,32) = 0.01$, $p = 0.906$; 2: Gender and Scholastic Attainment: $F(1,32) = 2.68$, $p = 0.112$]. Main effects of task corroborated the findings reported in Section "Relationships between Fine Motor Skills, Non-verbal IQ, Verbal STM, and Scholastic Attainment." Whilst there was no significant difference between group performance on the tasks of fine motor skill [$F(1,32) = 0.39$, $p = 0.537$] scholastic attainment was significantly higher for reading than for maths [$F(1,32) = 6.39$, $p = 0.017$].

Predictors of Scholastic Attainment

Two separate hierarchical multiple regressions were conducted to examine the unique contribution of fine motor skills, non-verbal IQ, and verbal STM on early reading and maths ability. Thus, the three variables that were significantly related to reading or maths (prior to Bonferroni correction) were entered progressively into the model in the following order: verbal STM, Fine Motor Integration and Mathematical Reasoning for Word Reading, and non-verbal IQ, Fine Motor Integration and Word Reading for Mathematical Reasoning. Results are summarized in **Table 6**.

For Word Reading, all models were statistically significant ($F \geq 9.19$, $p \leq 0.001$) and explained a total variance ranging from 30 to 53%. Significant improvements to the model were found at steps 1 and 3 but not at step 2 when Fine Motor Integration was added to the model ($\Delta R^2 = 0.08$, $p = 0.060$). Verbal STM was found to be a significant contributor at all steps and accounted for a unique 30% of total variance. On the contrary, Fine Motor Integration was not a significant predictor at either step 2 or 3. Finally, Mathematical Reasoning was found to be significant contributor to Word Reading at step 3 and accounted for 16% of total variance.

For Mathematical Reasoning all models were statistically significant (all $F \geq 6.69$, $p \leq 0.014$) and explained 18–46% of the total variance. Significant improvements were reported at each step of the regression (all $\Delta R^2 \geq 0.13$, $p \leq 0.024$). At each step, the last variable entered became the only significant predictor of the model. Thus, significant predictors were non-verbal IQ only at step 1, Fine Motor Integration only at step 2, and Word Reading only at step 3 (see **Table 6**).

TABLE 4 | Study 2.

Group	Scholastic Skills (WIAT-II) *M* (*SD*) Min–Max		Fine Motor Skills (BOT-2) *M* (*SD*) Min–Max		Non-Verbal IQ (WPPSI-III) *M* (*SD*) Min–Max	Verbal STM (K-ABC) *M* (*SD*) Min–Max
	Word Reading	Mathematical Reasoning	Fine Motor Precision	Fine Motor Integration	Block Design and Processing Speed Composite	Word Order and Number Recall Composite
Boys ($n = 17$)	18.1 (9.5) 3.1–32.1	16.9 (3.9) 11.9–25.4	40.3 (11.8) 14.6–61.0	39.0 (16.6) 17.5–72.5	41.6 (12.4) 13.8–65.0	37.5 (7.7) 22.6–49.1
Girls ($n = 17$)	22.5 (9.0) 7.6–35.1	17.1 (4.7) 10.5–30.0	44.5 (11.9) 22.0–68.3	42.5 (19.2) 7.5–67.5	41.1 (8.0) 26.0–53.0	41.2 (8.8) 28.3–54.7
Total ($n = 34$)	20.3 (9.4) 3.1–35.1	17.0 (4.3) 10.5–29.9	42.4 (11.8) 14.6–68.3	40.7 (17.8) 7.5–72.5	41.3 (10.6) 13.8–65.0	39.3 (8.4) 22.6–54.7

Group performance (% correct) on each of the four subtests.

TABLE 5 | Study 2.

	IDACI rank	Word Reading	Mathematical Reasoning	Fine Motor Precision	Fine Motor Integration	Non-verbal IQ	Verbal STM
IDACI rank	/						
Word Reading	**$\rho = 0.368$ $p = 0.032$**	/					
Mathematical Reasoning	$\rho = 0.073$ $p = 0.682$	**$r = 0.584$* $p < 0.001$**	/				
Fine Motor Precision	$\rho = -0.023$ $p = 0.896$	$r = 0.238$ $p = 0.175$	$r = 0.313$ $p = 0.071$	/			
Fine Motor Integration	$\rho = 0.109$ $p = 0.540$	**$r = 0.420$ $p = 0.013$**	**$r = 0.496$* $p = 0.003$**	**$r = 0.528$* $p = 0.001$**	/		
Non-verbal IQ	$\rho = -0.031$ $p = 0.861$	$r = 0.278$ $p = 0.112$	**$r = 0.426$ $p = 0.012$**	**$r = 0.455$* $p = 0.007$**	**$r = 0.421$ $p = 0.013$**	/	
Verbal STM	$\rho = 0.284$ $p = 0.103$	**$r = 0.538$* $p = 0.001$**	$r = 0.208$ $p = 0.237$	**$r = 0.451$* $p = 0.007$**	$r = 0.272$ $p = 0.119$	$r = 0.287$ $p = 0.100$	/

*Correlations among predictors and outcome variables of Study 2. Spearman's (ρ) and Pearson's (r) correlation coefficients are reported as appropriate. Significant correlations with uncorrected p-values highlighted in bold. *Significant correlations which survived Bonferroni correction at $\alpha = 0.05/6 = 0.008$.*

Discussion

Consistent with Study 1, performance on all tasks was close to the test norms thus this sample can be considered representative of a wider population. Again, whilst no difference was found between the two fine motor tasks, a significant advantage for reading in comparison to maths was revealed (Cohen's $d = 0.45$). It is interesting that the difference between reading and maths was evident with this group of 4- to 5-year-old children, as they had only just started primary school. This replicates the findings from Study 1, where the reading-maths discrepancy was captured by a larger effect size of 0.58. Overall, these results suggest that the discrepancy between early reading and maths ability is present at the start of primary school and tends to increase over the first 12 months.

There are several reasons why this discrepancy in reading and maths ability is shown in children that have just started compulsory schooling in the UK. It could be that the test of Mathematical Reasoning is not as sensitive as the Word Reading subtest for children aged 4–5 years. Although normative data is not available from the WIAT-II for Mathematical Reasoning for children aged 4–5 years, we showed that the performance of pupils in our sample correlated highly with a non-standardized test of maths that is based on the early curriculum in the UK, thus providing validation for its use with this age group. Furthermore, the correlation between percentage correct on Word Reading and Mathematical Reasoning for the 4- to 5-year-old children ($r = 0.584$) was similar to that of the 5- to 6-year-old year children in Study 1 using standard scores ($r = 0.550$), illustrating a similar strength of association between these two measures of scholastic attainment across the first 2 years of primary school. Alternatively, the discrepancy in reading and maths ability that was found in our study might reflect the focus on teaching phonics that is implemented across all UK primary schools in the early years. The relatively higher scores in reading compared to maths suggest that the phonic intervention that is implemented in this age group at a national level has an immediate and sustained positive effect on reading attainment.

Similar to Study 1, the two motor skills were strongly associated, but only Fine Motor Integration correlated significantly with reading and maths ability. This supports our prediction that the influence of fine motor precision on reading and maths ability may become stronger over the first year of schooling, as children practice scripting letters and numbers and linking these symbolic representations to the

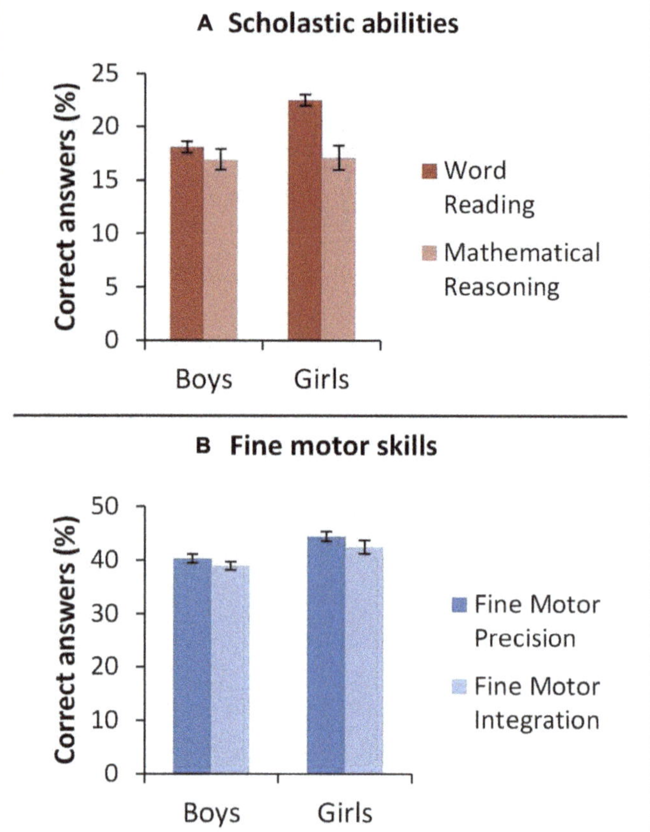

FIGURE 2 | Study 2. Bar graph representing mean performance (percentage of correct answer, *y*-axis) for boys and girls (*x*-axis) on **(A)** scholastic skills and **(B)** fine motor skills. Error bars represent 1 standard error.

underlying phonological and numerical concepts. Furthermore, verbal STM was associated with early reading ability whereas non-verbal IQ was associated with early maths skills. Consistent with Study 1, no gender differences were found, confirming a similar progression for boys and girls in this younger age group.

As with Study 1, the regression analyses showed a different pattern of results for reading and maths. For the prediction of reading performance, verbal STM was identified as a significant predictor at all steps, explaining a unique 30% of the total variance. Fine Motor Integration was no longer a significant predictor of early reading ability once verbal STM and Mathematical Reasoning were accounted for. In contrast, the regression analysis for maths showed that non-verbal IQ, Fine Motor Integration and Word Reading accounted for an equal portion of the total variance explained by the regression model (13–18%). Fine Motor Integration remained a significant predictor of early maths ability once non-verbal IQ was accounted for, but not when Word Reading was added into the model at step 3. The results from step 3 of the regression analyses should be treated with caution, however, due to the likely lack of power in the model when three predictor variables are considered with a relatively small sample size.

Overall, the results from Study 2 corroborate those of Study 1 in that Fine Motor Integration was found to be a significant predictor of early maths ability, but not a significant predictor of early reading ability, even when relevant cognitive abilities were taken into account. Our results are similar to those of Mayes et al. (2009) who found that, above the main contribution of IQ, short-term memory significantly predicted word reading, whereas visuo-spatial integration and grapho-motor ability significantly predicted maths ability in elementary school pupils (kindergarten through fifth grade). Together, these studies indicate an enhanced role for Fine Motor Integration in early maths development compared to early reading development. This has implications for the design of interventions to support the development of early maths skills.

GENERAL DISCUSSION

The role of fine motor skills in early development and subsequent educational achievement has begun to be clarified by recent studies. The two studies reported here present an investigation of these concurrent relationships and of the additional contribution of short-term memory and non-verbal IQ in typically developing, low-mid SES populations. Concurrent relationships were captured between variables at critical points in development leading into early childhood, thereby offering evidence to support the fine-tuning of programs at a pivotal stage for early education. A key finding was that for these groups, attainment was higher in reading than for maths. This contradicts the current national picture and suggests the need for greater consideration of the early years maths curriculum. Furthermore Fine Motor Integration was pinpointed by both studies as a key variable in predicting maths attainment, resilient to effects of cognition. Fine Motor Integration correlated positively with maths performance in both studies, whereas Fine Motor Precision correlated significantly with maths only in Study 1, when children had been in compulsory schooling for one year. Furthermore, in Study 1, Fine Motor Precision remained a significant predictor of maths ability even when the influence of reading acquisition was taken into account. This suggests that the influence of Fine Motor Precision on maths ability emerges over the first year of schooling and might be closely linked with the numeracy skills that children are acquiring over the first year of primary school and the practice children have in writing numbers and carrying out other maths-based activities that require precise motor movements, such as cutting out shapes and using aids such as Snap Cubes® and Numicon.

Several potential mechanisms might underpin the association between fine motor skills and maths ability reported here. For example, Luo et al. (2007) proposed there may be a common window of biological maturation across domains, or that both domains facilitate mental development, or that there might be a common supra-ordinate category of general intelligence, or that the association arises from a stimulating parenting style that cuts across domains. Other authors have given more specific reasons, suggesting that finger counting

TABLE 6 | Study 2.

Step	Variable(s)	Model		Significance	Change		Unstandardized Coefficients	Standardized Coefficients	Significance
		R	R^2	*F* (df), *p*	ΔR^2	Significance ΔF	*B, SE*	β	*t, p*
Word Reading (%)									
1	**Verbal STM**	0.54	0.30	13.40 (1,32), **0.001**	0.30	**0.001**	0.61, 0.17	0.54	3.66, **0.001**
2	**Verbal STM** +	0.61	0.38	9.19 (2,31), **0.001**	0.08	0.060	0.52, 0.17	0.46	3.11, **0.004**
	Fine Motor Integration						0.15, 0.08	0.29	1.95, 0.060
3	**Verbal STM** +	0.73	0.53	11.23 (3,30), **<0.001**	0.16	**0.004**	0.48, 0.15	0.43	3.24, **0.003**
	Fine Motor Integration +						0.04, 0.08	0.07	0.49, 0.627
	Mathematical Reasoning						1.0, 0.32	0.46	3.16, **0.004**
Mathematical Reasoning (%)									
1	**Non-verbal IQ**	0.42	0.18	6.79 (1,32), **0.014**	0.18	**0.014**	0.25, 0.10	0.42	2.61, **0.014**
2	Non-verbal IQ +	0.55	0.30	6.69 (2,31), **0.004**	0.13	**0.024**	0.16, 0.10	0.26	1.57, 0.127
	Fine Motor Integration						0.16, 0.07	0.39	2.37, **0.024**
3	Non-verbal IQ +	0.68	0.46	8.37 (3,30), **<0.001**	0.15	**0.007**	0.13, 0.09	0.21	1.44, 0.159
	Fine Motor Integration +						0.09, 0.06	0.23	1.42, 0.165
	Word Reading						0.10, 0.04	0.44	2.91, **0.007**

Model fits for the hierarchical multiple regressions identifying significant predictors of early reading and maths attainment in Study 2. Significant predictors highlighted in bold.

could be the linking mechanism between fine motor skills and mathematical skills (Di Luca and Pesenti, 2011; Moeller et al., 2011). Finger counting might be closely related to the emergence of Fine Motor Precision becoming a significant predictor of maths ability in Study 1, as children learn to count over the first year of primary school. The absence of a significant correlation between Fine Motor Precision and maths in Study 2, during the first year of compulsory schooling in the UK, suggests an intimate link between the development of fine motor precision and maths skills in response to teaching. Another possibility that could account for the significant correlation between fine motor integration and maths ability found across both age groups (Study 1 and Study 2) is that both fine motor integration and maths ability utilize visuo-spatial processes that are coordinated through a common neural pathway, such as the feed-forward feed-back connections between cerebellum and pre-frontal cortex. When the cerebellum is damaged in early childhood, prior to the onset of formal schooling, strong associations between fine manual control and scholastic abilities, including mathematics, have been found (Davis, unpublished thesis, p. 217). Furthermore, visuo-spatial skills and visuo-motor integration have been recently associated with number line estimation tasks (Simms et al., 2016) which are known to be strong and reliable predictors of mathematical attainment.

The finding that fine motor skills are intimately linked to early maths attainment has implications for educational intervention. Within the UK there are national concerns regarding the persistent low attainment in maths. For example, the UK is currently 26th out of 65 countries for maths attainment by school-leaving age (APPG, 2014). Consequently, concerns are particularly focused upon the educational trajectory of lower SES groups, and upon the importance of early years intervention to reduce the achievement gap as the lower SES groups move through schooling (George et al., 2012). The critical importance of fine-tuning interventions toward appropriate mechanisms to enable progress by the higher risk groups is evident. Key, for example, to the contingency of early years provision in enhancing later outcomes is the quality of provision (Sammons et al., 2004; George et al., 2012), highlighting the need for precision in the nature of the curriculum offered.

Higher educational risk forms through a complex interplay of factors, which require differentiated understanding, at population and community levels (Strand, 2014), and school-level (Sammons et al., 2004; Hargreaves, 2014). School improvement research has included a focus, amongst other features, upon curriculum and pedagogy to explore and mediate the relationships governing scholastic outcomes (Muijs et al., 2004; Strand, 2010). Developmental psychology is well-placed to provide empirically grounded insights into development in informing educational programs, and is arguably underused in the thrust toward school improvement.

The results from our studies challenge previous research (Purpura et al., 2011; Kleemans et al., 2012) and national level data on the relative acquisition of reading and maths (Ofsted, 2015) where both domains in the early years and start of schooling typically appear as commensurate, including for children of lower and average SES households. In accord with the review of educational provision by Ofsted (2015), our results suggests that there may, in contrast to the aggregated picture, be significant local variation in practice and in outcomes within the numeracy curriculum in the early years, undermining the policy drive to overcome factors influencing poorer trajectories for those of lower SES, and the national gap in performance between higher and lower SES groups.

Our results suggest there may be potential risk within the early years curriculum where there is a strong focus on supporting the acquisition of literacy skills through the implementation of a national literacy strategy but no similar strategy for mathematical development. The longer-term consequences of not focussing on early numeracy have been noted (Melhuish et al., 2008) and this concern is reflected at a policy level, in calls for a greater focus upon the teaching of early years maths (APPG, 2014). The greater relative attention paid in the past decade to literacy interventions in the Foundation Stage and Key Stage 1 in the UK has prioritized phonic knowledge and skills in the curriculum (Department for Education, 2014) with comparatively less focus upon the teaching of maths, a phenomenon confirmed by a recent investigation into early years provision and its effects (Ofsted, 2015). Identifying the relatively lower focus upon maths education in early years settings currently, it was noted that this was the view of practitioners themselves, some of whom felt less confidence in the specifics of promoting mathematics in the early years (Ofsted, 2015).

Debate upon the teaching of maths has noted various questions requiring still further empirical evidence, for example: the extent to which mathematical knowledge goals are focused on at the expense of number sense (Dyson et al., 2013); types of instruction (Fuchs et al., 2013); the role of executive functions (Cragg and Gilmore, 2014; Carden and Cline, 2015); the relative role of spatial skills (Nunes et al., 2009; Cheng and Mix, 2014); and more recently, the neural predictors of response to instruction (Supekar et al., 2013). There is, in addition, a long-term debate in early years education on the relative need for discovery or play-based learning versus the role of instruction (Gifford, 2004; Chambers et al., 2010).

Evidence in our studies potentially signals the value of a highly active component of the universal curriculum, in order to promote fine motor skills, with implied gains possible in scholastic achievement. A play-based curriculum could be entirely consonant with one that also holds a focus upon the development of spatial skills such as those employed by Verdine et al. (2014). The need for discrete, although age appropriate instruction, is also underlined through the systematic review evidence of Sharples et al. (2011), which signals the importance of an instructional component in any early years curriculum that seek to reduce the attainment gap for children of lower SES. In addition, the absence of evidence in our studies of significant difference in fine motor skill by gender, in contrast to data elsewhere, consolidates the argument in favor of a universal approach to fine motor skill promotion, as does the report of the current lowering of motor skill norms at a population level (Gaul and Issartel, 2016).

The generic early years curriculum is thought to promote positive motor developments (Marr et al., 2003). Bala et al. (2010), for example, found that a longer period at kindergarten was associated with better grapho-motor skills (fine hand coordination, as well as ability to copy different figures as a whole and their parts) in both females and males. Interestingly, those principalities with higher numeracy outcomes, long term, are generally those where formal education commences later (Jerrim and Choi, 2014). It is likely that, prior to entry into compulsory education, a carefully structured play-based approach in the early years would simultaneously support fine motor skills and the development of number sense, through children's interactions with objects and their environment.

Finally, the rationale for developing fine motor skills in young children is supported by data illustrating the promotion of cognitive or scholastic gains as dependent outcomes from motor skills interventions. Despite low–weak correlations in the studies considered, the systematic review of evidence by van der Fels et al. (2014) led to a conclusion that fine motor skills interventions might support development in other domains. In concordance with the pattern of data here, Westendorp et al. (2014), working with a learning-disabled population, found evidence of positive effects of a ball skill intervention upon problem-solving skills. Other evidence is available in respect of specific populations, such as those with Developmental Co-ordination Disorder (Bond, 2011), where some positive gains have been found possible through targeted educational intervention, and Case-Smith (1996) showed the effectiveness of an occupational therapy service in preschool children, in relation to fine motor skill and self-care, mobility, and social function.

CONCLUSION

The evidence that there can be significant pockets of delay in maths attainment relative to literacy, in low SES groups, and that Fine Motor Integration can be closely related to maths outcomes enhances the argument for a closely focused early years maths curriculum, potentially with a strong enactive and spatial training element, to support visual-motor integration skills.

The extrapolations from this data could be enhanced by further predictive studies, with additional measurement of executive function skills within the population. Because the data here contradicts the national picture upon numeracy attainment, further similar investigations are warranted, to explore whether this finding exists, localized, elsewhere. Intervention studies that offer greater insight into the specific role of Fine Motor Integration and Fine Motor Precision in maths activities, and their contribution to diverse aspects of maths scholastic attainment, would also be welcome. Finally, investigations encompassing older age groups, or longitudinal data, would be valuable, in order to gain insight into how the relationship between Fine Motor Integration and Fine Motor Precision and maths may change with age, together with a greater knowledge of the contribution of other skills, such as executive functions, with the passing of time.

Overall, the results from both of our studies showed relative strengths in reading compared to maths in young pupils from low-to-mid SES backgrounds. Furthermore, both studies showed fine motor skills were not influenced by gender or SES, but were closely related to early maths skills, in particular Fine Motor Integration, even when additional cognitive skills were accounted for. Together, this provides clear evidence for the need for an early intervention approach to maths education, which includes a fine motor skill component, in particular visuo-spatial skills requiring fine motor integration.

AUTHOR CONTRIBUTIONS

NP lead the research. She ran Study 1, wrote the methods, results, and discussion, co-wrote the introduction with CP and edited the overall manuscript. CP scored and analyzed the data for studies 1 and 2, co-wrote the introduction with NP, took responsibility for the references and edited the overall manuscript. LO conducted study 2, wrote the methods and edited the overall manuscript. AG informed on the research programme from an educational psychology perspective. She wrote the general discussion and edited the overall manuscript.

FUNDING

This research was conducted in part, through Ph.D. studentships awarded to CP (University of Nottingham) and LO (ESRC).

REFERENCES

Abe, M., and Hanakawa, T. (2009). Functional coupling underlying motor and cognitive functions of the dorsal premotor cortex. *Behav. Brain Res.* 198, 13–23. doi: 10.1016/j.bbr.2008.10.046

Aben, B., Stapert, S., and Blokland, A. (2012). About the distinction between working memory and short-term memory. *Front. Psychol.* 3:301. doi: 10.3389/fpsyg.2012.00301

Alloway, T. P. (2007). Working memory, reading, and mathematical skills in children with developmental coordination disorder. *J. Exp. Child Psychol.* 96, 20–36. doi: 10.1016/j.jecp.2006.07.002

Anders, Y., Rossbach, H.-G., Weinert, S., Ebert, S., Kuger, S., Lehrl, S., et al. (2012). Home and preschool learning environments and their relations to the development of early numeracy skills. *Early Child. Res. Q.* 27, 231–244. doi: 10.1016/j.ecresq.2011.08.003

APPG (2014). *Maths and Numeracy in the Early Years.* Available at: http://www.nationalnumeracy.org.UK/sites/default/files/media/appg_paper_-_eys.pdf

Bala, G., Krneta, Z., and Katiæ, R. (2010). Effects of kindergarten period on school readiness and motor abilities. *Coll. Antropol.* 34(Suppl. 1), 61–67.

Barnhardt, C., Borsting, E., Deland, P., Pham, N., and Vu, T. (2005). Relationship between visual-motor integration and spatial organization of written language and math. *Optom. Vis. Sci.* 82, E138–E143. doi: 10.1097/01.OPX.0000153266.50875.53

Bart, O., Hajami, D., and Bar-Haim, Y. (2007). Predicting school adjustment from motor abilities in kindergarten. *Infant Child Dev.* 16, 597–615. doi: 10.1002/icd.514

Becker, D. R., Miao, A., Duncan, R., and McClelland, M. M. (2014). Behavioral self-regulation and executive function both predict visuomotor skills and early academic achievement. *Early Child. Res. Q.* 29, 411–424. doi: 10.1016/j.ecresq.2014.04.014

Bond, C. (2011). Supporting children with motor skills difficulties: an initial evaluation of the Manchester Motor Skills Programme. *Educ. Psychol. Pract.* 27, 143–153. doi: 10.1080/02667363.2011.567093

Bruininks, R. H., and Bruininks, B. D. (2005). *Bruininks-Oseretsky Test of Motor Proficiency*, 2nd Edn. Minneapolis, MN: NCS Pearson.

Cameron, C. E., Brock, L. L., Murrah, W. M., Bell, L. H., Worzalla, S. L., Grissmer, D., et al. (2012). Fine motor skills and executive function both contribute to kindergarten achievement. *Child Dev.* 83, 1229–1244. doi: 10.1111/j.1467-8624.2012.01768.x

Cameron, C. E., Cottone, E. A., Murrah, W. M., and Grissmer, D. W. (2016). How are motor skills linked to children's school performance and academic achievement? *Child Dev. Perspect.* 10, 93–98. doi: 10.1111/cdep.12168

Carden, J., and Cline, T. (2015). Problem solving in mathematics: the significance of visualisation and related working memory. *Educ. Psychol. Pract.* 31, 235–246. doi: 10.1080/02667363.2015.1051660

Carlson, A. G., Rowe, E., and Curby, T. W. (2013). Disentangling fine motor skills' relations to academic achievement: the relative contributions of visual-spatial integration and visual-motor coordination. *J. Genet. Psychol.* 174, 514–533. doi: 10.1080/00221325.2012.717122

Case-Smith, J. (1996). Fine motor outcomes in preschool children who receive occupational therapy services. *Am. J. Occup. Ther.* 50, 52–61. doi: 10.5014/ajot.50.1.52

Cassen, R., and Kingdon, G. (2007). *Tackling Low Educational Achievement. Report for Joseph Rowntree Foundation.* Available at: https://www.jrf.org.U.K./sites/default/files/jrf/migrated/files/2063-education-schools-achievement.pdf

Chambers, B., Cheung, A., Slavin, R. E., Smith, D., and Laurenzano, M. (2010). *Effective Early Childhood Education Programs: A Systematic Review. John Hopkins University Center for Research and Reform in Education.* Available at: http://www.bestevidence.org/early/early_child_ed/early_child_ed.htm

Cheng, Y. L., and Mix, K. S. (2014). Spatial training improves children's mathematics ability. *J. Cogn. Dev.* 15, 2–11. doi: 10.1080/15248372.2012.725186

Cohen, J. (1988). *Statistical Power Analysis for the Behavioural Sciences*, 2nd Edn. Mahwah, NJ: Lawrence Erlbaum Associates.

Cragg, L., and Gilmore, C. (2014). Skills underlying mathematics: the role of executive function in the development of mathematics proficiency. *Trends Neurosci. Educ.* 3, 63–68. doi: 10.1016/j.tine.2013.12.001

Crollen, V., Mahe, R., Collignon, O., and Seron, X. (2011a). The role of vision in the development of finger-number interactions: finger-counting and finger-monitoring in blind children. *J. Exp. Child Psychol.* 109, 525–539. doi: 10.1016/j.jecp.2011.03.011

Crollen, V., Seron, X., and Noël, M. P. (2011b). Is finger-counting necessary for the development of arithmetic abilities? *Front. Psychol.* 2:242. doi: 10.3389/fpsyg.2011.00242

Davis, E. E., Pitchford, N. J., and Limback, E. (2011). The interrelation between cognitive and motor development in typically developing children aged 4-11 years is underpinned by visual processing and fine manual control. *Br. J. Psychol.* 102, 569–584. doi: 10.1111/j.2044-8295.2011.02018.x

de Barros, K. M. F. T., Fragoso, A. G. C., de Oliveira, A. L. B., Cabral Filho, J. E., and de Castro, R. M. (2003). Do environmental influences alter motor abilities acquisition? A comparison among children from day-care centers and private schools. *Arq. Neuropsiquiatr.* 61, 170–175. doi: 10.1590/S0004-282X2003000200002

Department for Communities and Local Government (2011). *The English Indices of Deprivation 2010.* Available at: https://www.gov.uk/government/statistics/english-indices-of-deprivation-2010

Department for Education (2010). *Phonics Core Criteria and the Self-assessment Process.* Available at: https://www.gov.uk/government/publications/phonics-teaching-materials-core-criteria-and-self-assessment

Department for Education (2014). *Phonics Screening Check and National Curriculum Assessments at Key Stage 1 in England, 2014.* Available at: https://www.gov.UK/government/uploads/system/uploads/attachment_data/file/356941/SFR34_2014_text.pdf

Di Luca, S., and Pesenti, M. (2011). Finger numeral representations: more than just another symbolic code. *Front. Psychol.* 2:272. doi: 10.3389/fpsyg.2011.00272

Diamond, A. (2000). Close interrelation of motor development and cognitive development and of the cerebellum and prefrontal cortex. *Child Dev.* 71, 44–56. doi: 10.1111/1467-8624.00117

Dinehart, L., and Manfra, L. (2013). Associations between low-income children's fine motor skills in preschool and academic performance in second grade. *Early Educ. Dev.* 24, 138–161. doi: 10.1080/10409289.2011.636729

Duncan, G. J., Brooks-Gunn, J., and Klebanov, P. K. (1994). Economic deprivation and early childhood development. *Child Dev.* 65, 296–318. doi: 10.1111/1467-8624.ep9405315105

Duncan, G. J., Dowsett, C. J., Claessens, A., Magnuson, K., Huston, A. C., Klebanov, P., et al. (2007). School readiness and later achievement. *Dev. Psychol.* 43, 1428–1446. doi: 10.1037/0012-1649.43.6.1428

Dyson, N. I., Jordan, N. C., and Giutting, J. (2013). A number sense intervention for low-income kindergartens at risk for mathematics difficulties. *J. Learn. Disabil.* 46, 166–181. doi: 10.1177/0022219411410233

Ebersbach, M., Luwel, K., Frick, A., Onghena, P., and Verschaffel, L. (2008). The relationship between the shape of the mental number line and familiarity with numbers in 5- to 9-year old children: evidence for a segmented linear model. *J. Exp. Child Psychol.* 99, 1–17. doi: 10.1016/j.jecp.2007.08.006

Fuchs, L. S., Geary, D. C., Compton, D. L., Fuchs, D., Schatschneider, C., Hamlett, C. L., et al. (2013). Effects of first-grade number knowledge tutoring with contrasting forms of practice. *J. Educ. Psychol.* 105, 58–77. doi: 10.1037/a0030127

Gathercole, S. E., Pickering, S. J., Ambridge, B., and Wearing, H. (2004). The structure of working memory from 4 to 15 years of age. *Dev. Psychol.* 40, 177–190. doi: 10.1037/0012-1649.40.2.177

Gaul, D., and Issartel, J. (2016). Fine motor skill proficiency in typically developing children: on or off the maturation track? *Hum. Mov. Sci.* 46, 78–85. doi: 10.1016/j.humov.2015.12.011

George, A., Stokes, L., and Wilkinson, D. (2012). Does early education influence key stage 1 attainment? Evidence for england from the millennium cohort study. *Natl. Inst. Econ. Rev.* 222, R67–R80. doi: 10.1177/0027950112222 00106

Gifford, S. (2004). A new mathematics pedagogy for the early years: in search of principles for practice. *Int. J. Early Years Educ.* 12, 99–115. doi: 10.1080/0966976042000225507

Grissmer, D., Grimm, K. J., Aiyer, S. M., Murrah, W. M., and Steele, J. S. (2010). Fine motor skills and early comprehension of the world: two new school readiness indicators. *Dev. Psychol.* 46, 1008–1017. doi: 10.1037/ a0020104

Gwynne, K., and Blick, B. (2004). Motor performance checklist for 5-year-olds: a tool for identifying children at risk of developmental co-ordination disorder. *J. Paediatr. Child Health* 40, 369–373. doi: 10.1111/j.1440-1754.2004. 00404.x

Hargreaves, D. H. (2014). A self-improving school system and its potential for reducing inequality. *Oxford Rev. Educ.* 40, 696–714. doi: 10.1080/03054985.2014.979014

Hooper, S. R., Roberts, J., Sideris, J., Burchinal, M., and Zeisel, S. (2010). Longitudinal predictors of reading and math trajectories through middle school for african american versus caucasian students across two samples. *Dev. Psychol.* 46, 1018–1029. doi: 10.1037/a0018877

Hornung, C., Brunner, M., Reuter, R. A. P., and Martin, R. (2011). Children's working memory: its structure and relationship to fluid intelligence. *Intelligence* 39, 210–221. doi: 10.1016/j.intell.2011.03.002

IBM Corp (2013). *IBM SPSS Statistics for Windows, Version 22.0.* Armonk, NY: IBM Corp.

Jerrim, J., and Choi, Á (2014). The mathematics skills of school children: how does England compare to the high-performing East Asian jurisdictions? *J. Educ. Policy* 29, 349–376. doi: 10.1080/02680939.2013.831950

Jenni, O. G., Chaouch, A., Caflisch, J., and Rousson, V. (2013). Correlations between motor and intellectual functions in normally developing children between 7 and 18 years. *Dev. Neuropsychol.* 38, 98–113. doi: 10.1080/87565641.2012.733785

Kaufman, A. S., and Kaufman, N. L. (2004). *Kaufman Assessment Battery for Children*, 2nd Edn. Circle Pines, MN: AGS Publishing.

Kleemans, T., Peeters, M., Segers, E., and Verhoeven, L. (2012). Child and home predictors of early numeracy skills in kindergarten. *Early Child. Res. Q.* 27, 471–477. doi: 10.1016/j.ecresq.2011.12.004

Kulp, M. T. (1999). Relationship between visual motor integration skill and academic performance in kindergarten through third grade. *Optom. Vis. Sci.* 76, 159–163. doi: 10.1097/00006324-199903000-00015

Kurdek, L. A., and Sinclair, R. J. (2001). Predicting reading and mathematics achievement in fourth-grade children from kindergarten readiness scores. *J. Educ. Psychol.* 93, 451–455. doi: 10.1037/0022-0663.93.3.451

Lafay, A., Thevenot, C., Castel, C., and Fayol, M. (2013). The role of fingers in number processing in young children. *Front. Psychol.* 4:488. doi: 10.3389/fpsyg.2013.00488

Livesey, D., Keen, J., Rouse, J., and White, F. (2006). The relationship between measures of executive function, motor performance and externalising behaviour in 5- and 6-year-old children. *Hum. Mov. Sci.* 25, 50–64. doi: 10.1016/j.humov.2005.10.008

Luo, Z., Jose, P. E., Huntsinger, C. S., and Pigott, T. D. (2007). Fine motor skills and mathematics achievement in east asian american and european american kindergartners and first graders. *Br. J. Dev. Psychol.* 25, 595–614. doi: 10.1348/026151007X185329

Marr, D., Cermak, S., Cohn, E. S., and Henderson, A. (2003). Fine motor activities in head start and kindergarten classrooms. *Am. J. Occup. Ther.* 57, 550–557. doi: 10.5014/ajot.57.5.550

Mayes, S. D., Calhoun, S. L., Bixler, E. O., and Zimmerman, D. N. (2009). IQ and neuropsychological predictors of academic achievement. *Learn. Individ. Differ.* 19, 238–241. doi: 10.1016/j.lindif.2008.09.001

Mazzocco, M. M. M., and Kover, S. T. (2007). A longitudinal assessment of executive function skills and their association with math performance. *Child Neuropsychol.* 13, 18–45. doi: 10.1080/09297040600611346

McHale, K., and Cermak, S. A. (1992). Fine motor activities in elementary school: preliminary findings and provisional implications for children with fine motor problems. *Am. J. Occup. Ther.* 46, 898–903. doi: 10.5014/ajot.46.10.898

McPhillips, M., and Jordan-Black, J.-A. (2007). The effect of social disadvantage on motor development in young children: a comparative study. *J. Child Psychol. Psychiatry* 48, 1214–1222. doi: 10.1111/j.1469-7610.2007. 01814.x

Meisels, S. J., Marsden, D., Wiske, M., and Henderson, L. (1997). *Early Screening Inventory - Revised.* New York, NY: Pearson Early Learning.

Melhuish, E. C., Phan, M. B., Sylva, K., Sammons, P., Siraj-Blatchford, I., and Taggart, B. (2008). Effects of the home learning environment and preschool center experience upon literacy and numeracy development in early primary school. *J. Soc. Issues* 64, 95–114. doi: 10.1111/j.1540-4560.2008.00550.x

Moeller, K., Martignon, L., Wessolowski, S., Engel, J., and Nuerk, H. C. (2011). Effects of finger counting on numerical development the opposing views of neurocognition and mathematics education. *Front. Psychol.* 2:328. doi: 10.3389/fpsyg.2011.00328

Morales, J., Gonzalez, L.-M., Guerra, M., Virgili, C., and Unnithan, V. (2011). Physical activity, perceptual-motor performance, and academic learning in 9-to-16-years-old school children. *Int. J. Sport Psychol.* 42, 401–415.

Morley, D., Till, K., Ogilvie, P., and Turner, G. (2015). Influences of gender and socioeconomic status on the motor proficiency of children in the U.K. *Hum. Mov. Sci.* 44, 150–156. doi: 10.1016/j.humov.2015. 08.022

Muijs, D., Harris, A., Chapman, C., Stoll, L., and Russ, J. (2004). Improving schools in socio-economically disadvantaged areas - a review of research evidence. *Sch. Eff. Sch. Improv.* 15, 149–175. doi: 10.1076/sesi.15.2.149.30433

Nunes, T., Bryant, P., Sylva, K., and Barros, R. (2009). *Development of Maths Capabilities and Confidence in Primary School.* London: Department for Children, Schools and Families.

Ofsted (2015). *Teaching and Play in the Early Years: A Balancing Act?* Available at: https://www.gov.U.K./government/publications/teaching-and-play-in-the-early-years-a-balancing-act

Pagani, L. S., Fitzpatrick, C., Archambault, I., and Janosz, M. (2010). School readiness and later achievement: a french canadian replication and extension. *Dev. Psychol.* 46, 984–994. doi: 10.1037/a0018881

Piek, J. P., Pitcher, T. M., and Hay, D. A. (1999). Motor coordination and kinaesthesia in boys with attention deficit-hyperactivity disorder. *Dev. Med. Child Neurol.* 41, 159–165. doi: 10.1111/j.1469-8749.1999.tb00575.x

Pitcher, T. M., Piek, J. P., and Hay, D. A. (2003). Fine and gross motor ability in males with ADHD. *Dev. Med. Child Neurol.* 45, 525–535. doi: 10.1111/j.1469-8749.2003.tb00952.x

Purpura, D. J., Hume, L. E., Sims, D. M., and Lonigan, C. J. (2011). Early literacy and early numeracy: the value of including early literacy skills in the prediction of numeracy development. *J. Exp. Child Psychol.* 110, 647–658. doi: 10.1016/j.jecp.2011.07.004

Rigoli, D., Piek, J. P., Kane, R., and Oosterlaan, J. (2012). An examination of the relationship between motor coordination and executive functions in adolescents. *Dev. Med. Child Neurol.* 54, 1025–1031. doi: 10.1111/j.1469-8749.2012.04403.x

Roebers, C. M., and Kauer, M. (2009). Motor and cognitive control in a normative sample of 7-year-olds. *Dev. Sci.* 12, 175–181. doi: 10.1111/j.1467-7687.2008.00755.x

Roebers, C. M., Röthlisberger, M., Neuenschwander, R., Cimeli, P., Michel, E., and Jäger, K. (2014). The relation between cognitive and motor performance and their relevance for children's transition to school: a latent variable approach. *Hum. Mov. Sci.* 33, 284–297. doi: 10.1016/j.humov.2013.08.011

Sammons, P., Elliot, K., Sylva, K., Melhuish, E., Siraj-Blatchford, I., and Taggart, B. (2004). The impact of pre-school on young children's cognitive attainments at entry to reception. *Br. Educ. Res. J.* 30, 691–712. doi: 10.1080/0141192042000234656

Santi, K. L., Francis, D. J., Currie, D., and Wang, Q. (2015). Visual-motor integration skills: accuracy of predicting reading. *Optom. Vis. Sci.* 92, 217–226. doi: 10.1097/OPX.0000000000000473

Sharples, J., Slavin, R., Chambers, B., and Sharp, C. (2011). *Effective Classroom Strategies for Closing the Gap in Educational Achievement for Children and Young People Living in Poverty, Including white Working-Class Boys. The Centre for Excellence and Outcomes in Children and Young People's Services (C4EO).* Available at: https://www.york.ac.uk/media/iee/documents/Closing%20the%20Gap.pdf

Siegler, R. S., and Ramani, G. B. (2008). Playing linear numerical board games promotes low-income children's numerical development. *Dev. Sci.* 11, 655–661. doi: 10.1111/j.1467-7687.2008.00714.x

Sigmundsson, H., and Rostoft, M. S. (2003). Motor development: exploring the motor competence of 4-year-old Norwegian children. *Scand. J. Educ. Res.* 47, 451–459. doi: 10.1080/00313830308588

Simms, V., Clayton, S., Cragg, L., Gilmore, C., and Johnson, S. (2016). Explaining the relationship between number line estimation and mathematical achievement: the role of visuomotor integration and visuospatial skills. *J. Exp. Child Psychol.* 145, 22–33. doi: 10.1016/j.jecp.2015.12.004

Son, S., and Meisels, S. J. (2006). The relationship of young children's motor skills to later reading and math achievement. *Merrill Palmer Q.* 52, 755–778. doi: 10.1353/mpq.2006.0033

Stoeger, H., Suggate, S., and Ziegler, A. (2013). Identifying the causes of underachievement: a plea for the inclusion of fine motor skills. *Psychol. Test Assess. Model.* 55, 274–288.

Stoeger, H., Ziegler, A., and Martzog, P. (2008). Deficits in fine motor skill as an important factor in the identification of gifted underachievers in primary school. *Psychol. Sci. Quat.* 50, 134–146.

Stoodley, C. J. (2012). The cerebellum and cognition: evidence from functional imaging studies. *Cerebellum* 11, 352–365. doi: 10.1007/s12311-011-0260-7

Strand, S. (1997). Pupil progress during Key Stage 1: a value added analysis of school effects. *Br. Educ. Res. J.* 23, 471–487. doi: 10.1080/0141192970230406

Strand, S. (2010). Do some schools narrow the gap? Differential school effectiveness by ethnicity, gender, poverty, and prior achievement. *Sch. Eff. Sch. Improv.* 21, 289–314. doi: 10.1080/09243451003732651

Strand, S. (2014). School effects and ethnic, gender and socio-economic gaps in educational achievement at age 11. *Oxford Rev. Educ.* 40, 223–245. doi: 10.1080/03054985.2014.891980

Supekar, K., Swigart, A. G., Tenison, C., Jolles, D. D., Rosenberg-Lee, M., Fuchs, L., et al. (2013). Neural predictors of individual differences in response to math tutoring in primary-grade school children. *Proc. Natl. Acad. Sci. U.S.A.* 110, 8230–8235. doi: 10.1073/pnas.1222154110

Tramontana, M. G., Hooper, S. R., and Selzer, S. C. (1988). Research on the preschool prediction of later academic achievement: a review. *Dev. Rev.* 8, 89–146. doi: 10.1016/0273-2297(88)90001-9

Tymms, P., and Merrell, C. (2007). *Standards and Quality in English Primary Schools Over Time: The National Evidence (Primary Review Research Survey 4/1).* Cambridge: University of Cambridge Faculty of Education.

van der Fels, I. M. J., te Wierike, S. C. M., Hartman, E., Elferink-Gemser, M. T., Smith, J., and Visscher, C. (2014). The relationship between motor skills and cognitive skills in 4-16 year old typically developing children: a systematic review. *J. Sci. Med. Sport* 18, 697–703. doi: 10.1016/j.jsams.2014.09.007

Vazir, S., Naidu, A. N., and Vidyasagar, P. (1998). Nutritional status, psychosocial development and home environment of Indian rural children. *Indian Pediatr.* 35, 959–966.

Verdine, B. N., Irwin, C. M., Golinkoff, R. M., and Hirsh-Pasek, K. (2014). Contributions of executive function and spatial skills to preschool mathematics achievement. *J. Exp. Child Psychol.* 126, 37–51. doi: 10.1016/j.jecp.2014.02.012

Wassenberg, R., Feron, F. J. M., Kessels, A. G. H., Hendriksen, J. G. M., Kalff, A. C., Kroes, M., et al. (2005). Relation between cognitive and motor performance in 5- to 6-year-old children: results from a large-scale cross-sectional study. *Child Dev.* 76, 1092–1103. doi: 10.1111/j.1467-8624.2005.00899.x

Wechsler, D. (2003). *Wechsler Preschool and Primary Scale of Intelligence*, 3rd Edn. London: Pearson Assessment.

Wechsler, D. (2005). *Wechsler Individual Achievement Test*, 2nd Edn. London: The Psychological Corp.

Westendorp, M., Houwen, S., Hartman, E., Mombarg, R., Smith, J., and Visscher, C. (2014). Effect of a ball skill intervention on children's ball skills and cognitive functions. *Med. Sci. Sport. Exerc.* 46, 414–422. doi: 10.1249/MSS.0b013e3182a532b3

Woodcock, R. W., McGrew, K. S., and Mather, N. (2001). *Woodcock-Johnson III Tests of Achievement.* Itasca, IL: Riverside.

Conflict of Interest Statement: The authors declare that the research was conducted in the absence of any commercial or financial relationships that could be construed as a potential conflict of interest.

14

A Matter of Balance: Motor Control is Related to Children's Spatial and Proportional Reasoning Skills

Andrea Frick[1,2]* *and Wenke Möhring*[2,3]

[1] Department of Psychology, University of Bern, Bern, Switzerland, [2] Department of Psychology, University of Fribourg, Fribourg, Switzerland, [3] Department of Psychology, Temple University, Philadelphia, PA, USA

Recent research has shown close links between spatial and mathematical thinking and between spatial abilities and motor skills. However, longitudinal research examining the relations between motor, spatial, *and* mathematical skills is rare, and the nature of these relations remains unclear. The present study thus investigated the relation between children's motor control and their spatial and proportional reasoning. We measured 6-year-olds' spatial scaling (i.e., the ability to reason about different-sized spaces), their mental transformation skills, and their ability to balance on one leg as an index for motor control. One year later ($N = 126$), we tested the same children's understanding of proportions. We also assessed several control variables (verbal IQ and socio-economic status) as well as inhibitory control, visuo-spatial and verbal working memory. Stepwise hierarchical regressions showed that, after accounting for effects of control variables, children's balance skills significantly increased the explained variance in their spatial performance and proportional reasoning. Our results suggest specific relations between balance skills and spatial as well as proportional reasoning skills that cannot be explained by general differences in executive functioning or intelligence.

Keywords: cognitive development, motor control, balance, proportional reasoning, spatial scaling, inhibitory control, working memory, executive functions

Edited by:
Klaus Libertus,
University of Pittsburgh, USA

Reviewed by:
Nicola Pitchford,
University of Nottingham, UK
Chiara Meneghetti,
University of Padova, Italy

***Correspondence:**
Andrea Frick
depsy@gmx.net

INTRODUCTION

The idea that cognitive and motor development are closely intertwined goes back to early developmental theories (e.g., Gesell and Thompson, 1934; Piaget, 1952). For example, Piaget claimed that the emergence of cognitive skills is based on sensorimotor experience. With increasing motor activity, infants become equipped with new possibilities to discover their environment and understand themselves as active agents, resulting in increasingly differentiated cognitive structures. These early seminal theories laid the basis for later theoretical frameworks (e.g., Gibson, 1988; Bushnell and Boudreau, 1993; Diamond, 2000) and inspired many studies supporting a close relation between motor and cognitive development in general and spatial cognition in particular. Another line of research showed a specific connection between performance on spatial cognitive tasks and mathematical thinking (for a review, see Mix and Cheng, 2012). However, research examining the relations between motor, spatial, *and* mathematical skills is rare, and the nature of these relations remains unclear. The present study thus investigated the relation between children's balance skills and their spatial scaling, mental transformation, as well as proportional reasoning skills, using a longitudinal approach.

Relation Between Motor and Cognitive (Spatial) Skills

Previous research has shown that providing infants with increased experience in a particular motor skill such as reaching enhanced their object segregation skills (Needham, 2000), visual exploration of faces and objects (Libertus and Needham, 2010, 2011), and understanding of intentional movements (Sommerville et al., 2005; for a review, see Hauf, 2007). It has also been shown that the onset of motor milestones such as independent sitting or walking had beneficial effects on infants' perceptual abilities (Campos et al., 1992; Soska et al., 2010) and on their social-emotional development (for a review, see Campos et al., 2000). Moreover, longitudinal studies indicated that early gross-motor skills predicted later cognitive performance, such as executive functions or perceptual processing (Murray et al., 2006; Piek et al., 2008). Even at old age, motor abilities have been found to be associated with cognitive performance (e.g., perceptual speed and executive control, Voelcker-Rehage et al., 2010).

Further evidence for a close link between motor development and cognitive performance comes from a study by Davis et al. (2011). Using standardized tests, the authors found that cognitive and motor skills were closely related in children between 4 and 11 years of age. Interestingly, a principal component analysis revealed that children's visual processing and fine manual control showed considerable cross-loadings on both a cognitive and a motor factor. The authors concluded that the interrelation between cognitive and motor development may be underpinned by these specific skills. However, both of these variables were assessed using tasks that required high-level spatial processing. For example, visual processing was assessed by having participants construct a copy of an abstract design using 3D shapes or find the fastest route across a grid with obstacles. Fine manual control tasks included coloring, drawing, folding, cutting-out forms, and copying geometric shapes. Therefore, it could be argued that spatial skills were in fact responsible for the observed correlations.

Indeed, many studies found specific relations between motor ability and spatial cognition, with a particular focus on mental rotation. They showed that manual experience enhanced infants' mental rotation performance (e.g., Möhring and Frick, 2013; Schwarzer et al., 2013b; Frick and Wang, 2014), and that infants' locomotor experience was associated with a better understanding of rotational movements (Frick and Möhring, 2013; Schwarzer et al., 2013a). Furthermore, correlational evidence indicated that 5- to 6-year-olds' motor control and coordination skills were associated with mental rotation (Jansen and Heil, 2010). More specifically, Jansen and colleagues (Jansen et al., 2011; Jansen and Kaltner, 2014), showed that balance skills were especially important in predicting 10-year-olds' and older adults' mental rotation performance.

Relation Between Spatial and Mathematical Skills

Another body of research has provided mounting evidence suggesting that spatial reasoning is closely related to mathematical understanding (for a review, see Mix and Cheng, 2012). For example, findings have demonstrated connections between mental object rotation and arithmetic skills in adolescents (Reuhkala, 2001; Kyttälä and Lehto, 2008), as well as mental rotation and performance on the math subtest of the Scholastic Aptitude Test (Casey et al., 1995). Longitudinal studies indicated that children's mental transformation skills predicted their accuracy in locating numbers on a line, which in turn was related to their later mathematical proficiency (Gunderson et al., 2012; LeFevre et al., 2013). Furthermore, a training study showed that spatial-numerical training was more beneficial for preschoolers' mental number line performance and mathematical achievement than purely numerical training (Fischer et al., 2011). Considering this evidence for a strong link between spatial and mathematical skills, as well as the literature showing a close connection between spatial abilities and motor processes outlined above, the question emerges whether motor skills are also related to children's mathematical performance.

Relation Between Mathematical and Motor Skills

There actually is some evidence that motor skills may be associated with math performance. For example, Lopes et al. (2013) assessed motor coordination and academic achievement (Language and Math National Exams) in Portuguese 9- to 12-year-olds, and found that children with motor coordination deficits exhibited a higher probability of low academic achievement compared to children with normal motor coordination. This result is all the more alarming considering that 52% of the children were found to exhibit motor coordination deficits and no child showed good motor coordination. Other research (Carlson et al., 2008) found that the number of hours of physical education per week was associated with higher mathematics performance in female (but not male) kindergarteners and first-graders. Furthermore, longitudinal findings (Luo et al., 2007) indicated that fine-motor skills significantly predicted mathematics achievement over time (kindergarten through first grade), and likely explained performance differences between ethnic groups in the United States.

However, many of the previous studies investigating a link between motor skills and academic achievement did not control for general cognitive abilities, which makes the results hard to interpret. For example, it is possible that the correlations were due the children's general developmental status, and that some children were more mature and advanced in all of the variables measured. Such a scenario is not unlikely, as deficits in cognitive and motor development often co-occur (e.g., Piek et al., 2004) and motor skills are considered an important index for brain maturation (Magill, 1996). Another possibility is that a positive association between motor and cognitive skills is due to a specific relation. Consequently, in order to find out more about the specific nature of the relation between motor and cognitive abilities and possible shared processes, it is necessary to control for such general cognitive variables.

Rationale and Aims of the Study

In the present study, we investigated whether motor control is related to 6-year-old children's spatial skills as well as predictive for their understanding of proportions, using a longitudinal design. In contrast to previous studies, we controlled for general cognitive abilities as well as other possible covariates that will be described below. We tested children shortly before and after they transitioned to primary school, because spatial skills can be measured reliably but still develop considerably at this age, and would therefore exhibit large individual variance. Furthermore, we intended to assess basic mathematical skills (proportional reasoning) at an age when it was unlikely that children had received much formal educational input on the specific topic yet.

As an index for motor control, we assessed children's ability to stand on one leg. Balance skills have previously been associated with cognitive ability in 5- to 6-year-old boys (Planinsec, 2002), reading and math skills in 7- to 11-year-olds (Knight and Rizzuto, 1993), spatial skills (Jansen et al., 2011; Jansen and Kaltner, 2014), and executive functioning in adolescents (Rigoli et al., 2012). Furthermore, balance is a prerequisite for many more complex motor skills (such as walking or riding a bicycle). Thus, it is relevant for locomotor abilities, which in turn are related to spatial skills early in life (Frick and Möhring, 2013; Schwarzer et al., 2013a). Yet, unlike many other motor tasks, balance does not require high-level spatial processing, and can therefore be considered a pure measure of motor control.

As measures of spatial skills, we assessed children's mental transformation abilities, using the *Children Mental Transformation Task* (Levine et al., 1999). This test assesses children's ability to mentally combine two shapes (by translation or rotation). Based on previous findings (Jansen et al., 2011), we expected that children's mental transformation skills would be related to motor control. However, in extension to previous research that mainly focused on mental rotation, we also assessed children's spatial scaling abilities using the *Spatial Scaling Test* (Frick and Newcombe, 2012). Spatial scaling refers to the ability to compare different-sized spaces. We expected to find a similar link to motor control, based on recent findings suggesting that spatial scaling is based on similar mental transformation strategies (transforming one space in *size* to match the other) as mental rotation (transforming one object in *orientation* to match the other; Möhring et al., 2014). The relation between spatial scaling and motor abilities has not been investigated to date. This is surprising given that spatial scaling is a foundational skill for understanding and using scaled representations (i.e., maps or models) and plays an important role for many daily and professional activities, such as using a map to navigate or a blueprint to build a skyscraper.

Scaling also has important educational implications and has been defined as an important and overarching theme for science education by the U.S. National Research Council (2012). In fact, previous research has indicated that children's spatial scaling abilities are closely related to the ability to reason about proportions (Boyer and Levine, 2012; Möhring et al., 2015a). Proportional reasoning, in turn, has been associated with children's formal fraction knowledge (Möhring et al., 2015b), raising the possibility that proportional reasoning might be an important precondition for children's understanding of crucial mathematical concepts, such as fractions or divisions. Given these close relations, in the present study we tested the same children's understanding of proportions one year later. Children were given the *Proportional Reasoning Task* (adapted from Möhring et al., 2015a), in which they were asked to rate how much cherry flavor would be tasted in different juice-water mixtures.

We also assessed several possible covariates. Previous studies have revealed that keeping postural control requires high-level cognitive processes such as attention (for a review, see Woollacott and Shumway-Cook, 2002). Motor control was also associated with inhibition and working memory (WM; Piek et al., 2004; Roebers and Kauer, 2009), with visuo-spatial WM being more important than verbal WM (Alloway and Temple, 2007; Rigoli et al., 2012). Moreover, WM was found to be related to mathematical performance in adults, typically developing children, and in children with math difficulties (for a review, see Raghubar et al., 2010). Similar to findings for motor control, visuo-spatial WM in particular was related to mathematical understanding (Kyttälä et al., 2003; Bull et al., 2008), and locating relational quantities on a number line (Vukovic et al., 2014).

Consequently, one potential factor underlying the motor-cognition link might be found in children's executive functions. Indeed, Roebers et al. (2013) found that after accounting for executive functions (inhibition, cognitive flexibility, verbal WM), fine-motor skills no longer predicted children's school achievement. Similarly, Lehmann et al. (2014) showed that after controlling for WM, balance skill was no longer related to children's mental rotation performance. Thus, these studies point to a major contribution of executive functions to the motor-cognition link, which is why we included measures of children's inhibitory control, verbal, and visuo-spatial WM. Finally, to control for general effects of intelligence, we also included a measure of verbal IQ (i.e., an IQ measure that is minimally related to spatial, mathematical, and motor skills). Furthermore, socio-economic status (SES) was assessed to control for general effects of children's social environment.

MATERIALS AND METHODS

Participants

The present research was conducted as part of a larger longitudinal study investigating how spatial skills in kindergarten are related to later school achievement. Children were recruited during their last kindergarten year in 24 different rural and urban kindergartens in Switzerland. Signed parental consent forms and children's verbal assents were obtained prior to the study from 140 children (62 girls, mean age = 6.49 years, SD = 0.27, range = 6.01–6.99; 78 boys, mean age = 6.46, SD = 0.34, range = 5.99–7.01). One year later, the same children were tested again, except for 14 children, who had moved to a different school district (2), were sick on the day of assessment (1), or no longer had parental consent (11). The final sample for which both complete data sets were available comprised 126 children (55 girls, mean age = 7.55 years, SD = 0.28, range = 6.98–8.09; 71 boys, mean age = 7.53, SD = 0.35, range = 6.95–8.13).

Procedures followed ethical guidelines and were approved by the Institutional Review Board of the University of Bern.

Procedure

The first assessment (T1) was administered at the end of children's last kindergarten year, before children transitioned to primary school. The second assessment (T2) took place at the end of first grade. T1 consisted of two test sessions, each lasting about 30 min, with about 1–2 weeks in between ($M = 10.4$ days; $SD = 8.5$ days). Children were tested individually in a separate room in their kindergarten. For most tests, materials were presented on a table, with the experimenter sitting orthogonally to the side of the participants. Children completed the *Spatial Scaling Test* (SST: Frick and Newcombe, 2012), and the *Children's Mental Transformation Task* (CMTT, Levine et al., 1999) among four other tasks examining spatial transformation abilities[1]. Children also completed some tasks that assessed non-spatial skills, such as inhibitory control, verbal IQ, and balance. Furthermore, SES was assessed via parent questionnaires. At T2, visuo-spatial and verbal working memory were assessed along with proportional reasoning skills in one single session. In the following, the tasks that were at the focus of the present paper will be described in more detail; descriptions of the tasks that were not central to the present research question can be found in the respective publications (see Footnote 1). After each session, children were praised regardless of the level of their performance and received a small snack or toy.

Measures

Children's *balance* was measured as an index of gross-motor skills. Children were asked to stand on one leg as long as they could, while the experimenter measured the time (in s) using a stopwatch. If a child was only able to balance for a few seconds, he or she was instructed to relax, take a deep breath, and then allowed a second try. Hopping was not allowed and the test was ended after a maximum of 100 s.

In the *Spatial Scaling Test* (SST, Frick and Newcombe, 2012), children were told a story about a farmer, whose chickens hid their eggs in the fields. They were presented with drawings of green "fields" (see **Figure 1A**). The shapes of the fields were rectangular (22 cm by 14 cm), long narrow strips (26 cm by 4 cm), or circular (20 cm in diameter; with two landmarks). In each trial, a map was placed directly to the right of the field. The map showed the same picture with a target object (egg) in it, and either had the same size or was smaller than the field, such that every distance on the map corresponded to a four times larger distance in the field. Children were asked to help the farmer find the eggs by placing a small rubber peg on the field in the same position where the picture (map) showed the egg. Every combination of scaling factor and field was presented four times, using different target locations, amounting to a total of 24 trials, which took approximately 7–8 min to complete. The experimenter marked the position and scored the responses after the experiment, using a transparency that showed concentric circles of increasing radii (1, 1.5, and 2 cm) around the target locations. Responses within these circles were scored with 1, 2/3, or 1/3 point, respectively, and summed across trials.

The *Children's Mental Transformation Task* (CMTT) was adapted from Levine et al. (1999). Children were presented with two black shapes on white paper. They were asked to imagine what kind of shape the two pieces would form if moved together and choose among four presented alternatives. We used an abbreviated version of the original test, presenting 12 items in which the two pieces had to be translated horizontally and rotated 60° each to form the target shape, and 12 items that required a diagonal translation but no rotation. These 24 items took children approximately 6–9 min to complete.

The *Proportional Reasoning Task* was adapted from Möhring et al. (2015a). Children were told a story about a bear, who likes to drink cherry juice mixed with water. Then, children were presented with combinations of red and blue rectangles representing cherry juice and water that were 2 cm wide and of varying lengths (see **Figure 1B**). Children were asked to estimate the cherry taste of each mixture by drawing a mark on a horizontal line (15 cm). A single cherry to the left of the rating scale indicated a weak cherry taste; a heap of cherries to the right of the rating scale indicated a strong cherry taste. Two instruction trials presented mixtures that were not used in later test trials (first trial: 1 unit juice vs. 10 units water, second trial: 3 units juice vs. 0.3 unit water), and children were given corrective feedback. Children did not receive feedback on subsequent test trials, in which three levels of juice (2, 4, 6 units) and water (3, 6, 9 units) were combined in a full factorial design. These nine combinations were shown twice, amounting to 18 trials that were presented in a quasi-random order that avoided direct repetitions of factor levels. The task took approximately 5–6 min. After the task, the experimenter measured the locations of the marks on the rating scale (in mm).

Inhibitory control was measured using the *Fruit Stroop* task (Archibald and Kerns, 1999), in an adapted version by Röthlisberger et al. (2010). This task is appropriate for preschool or kindergarten children, because as opposed to the classic Stroop task, it does not require reading skills (MacLeod, 1991). Children saw a total of four A4 pages. The first page contained 25 colored squares (blue, yellow, red, green) and children were asked to name the colors of the squares, going through them row by row (baseline). The second page showed 25 colored fruits and vegetables, and children were again asked to name their colors (congruent). Page 3 showed the same fruits and vegetables in black-and-white (neutral), and page 4 in wrong colors (incongruent), and children were asked to name the colors they *should* have (e.g., a banana was shown in blue with the correct response being "yellow"). The task took approximately 6–7 min. An interference score was calculated after a formula suggested by Archibald and Kerns (1999), which calculates costs in response times when seeing incongruent colors, taking into account children's baseline naming speeds. Higher scores indicate stronger interference (and lower inhibitory control).

[1] The other four tests were: *Perspective-Taking Test for Children* (PTT-C, Frick et al., 2014), *Ghost Rotation Test* (Frick et al., 2013), *Diagrammatic Representations Test* (DRT, Frick and Newcombe, 2015), and *Cross-sectioning for Children* (Ratliff et al., 2010).

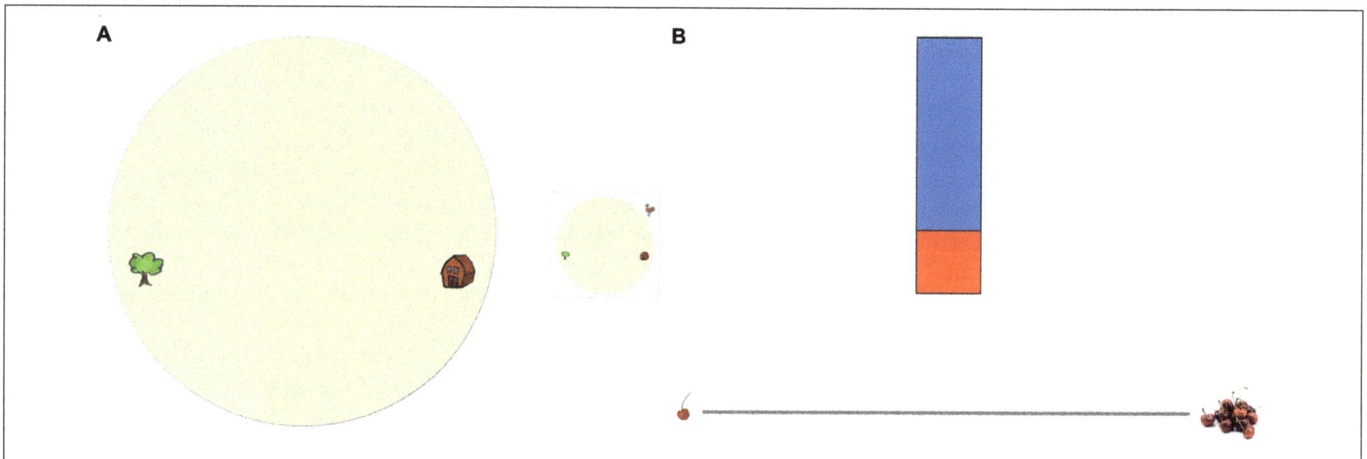

FIGURE 1 | (A) Example for an item of the *Spatial Scaling Test* (circular field, scaling factor 1:4), and **(B)** example for an item of the *Proportional Reasoning Test* (two units of cherry juice vs. six units of water).

Children's *visuo-spatial working memory* was tested using the *Position Span Task* that was newly designed for the present study. The task was based on the Corsi block-tapping task (Corsi, 1972), but the stimuli were made more child-friendly and presented on a computer monitor (19" laptop, presented with Microsoft PowerPoint). Children saw the head of a groundhog pop up (2 s) in different locations on a green 4 by 4 grid (see **Figure 2**). Between the appearances, the empty grid remained visible (0.5 s). After a sequence of targets, the empty grid showed up with a red frame around it, and children were asked to point to where they had seen the animal pop up in backward order. Span length (i.e., number of targets) started at two and was increased by one after every third trial (up to a maximum of seven targets). If on any difficulty level a child made more than two mistakes, the test was terminated. The task took approximately 5–8 min. Responses were scored with one point for every sequence that was reproduced in the correct order.

Children's *verbal working memory* was tested using the *Backward Color Recall Task* (Schmid et al., 2008). Children saw a sequence of colored circles (blue, yellow, red, green, brown, black) showing up (1 s) in the center of the white computer screen. Between the appearances, the screen was completely white (1 s). Children were asked to name the colors in backward order when a visual prompt appeared. Span length (number of circles) started at two and was increased by one after every third trial (up to a maximum of seven circles). The test was terminated if a child made two or more mistakes on one difficulty level. The task took approximately 3–5 min. Responses were scored with one point for every sequence that was reproduced in the correct order.

Verbal IQ was assessed using the active and passive vocabulary subtests of the HAWIVA-III (Ricken et al., 2007). On the passive vocabulary subtest, children saw four pictures and had to point to the one that the experimenter named; on the active vocabulary test, children were shown one picture and asked to name it. The subtests took about 3–4 min each. Scores were summed across active and passive vocabulary subtests to obtain a general vocabulary score, and transformed into a verbal IQ score according to norm tables.

Socio-economic Status was calculated based on parents' occupations, which were classified according to the 'International Standard Classification of Occupation' (ISCO-88, International Labour Office, 1990) and then transformed into an 'International Socio-Economic Index' (ISEI: Ganzeboom et al., 1992). We used the higher ISEI of the mother or father. If no present occupation was indicated for either of them, we used the ISEI of the occupation they were trained for. Using this procedure, we were able to determine the SES of all but three children (2%).

RESULTS

Data of 126 children were available for T1 and T2. In a first step, we scanned each variable for outliers and excluded values that were more than 2.5 standard deviations above or below the mean (1–4 values, 0.8–3% per variable).

The data of the proportional reasoning task were standardized to account for individual response tendencies (cf. Möhring et al., 2015a,b). That is, some children may have used the entire rating scale for their proportional estimations, whereas others may have constrained their responses to only one end of the scale. To account for such individual tendencies to shift responses to one end of the rating scale, we used a within-participant standardization (*ipsatization*; Hicks, 1970). Each child's individual mean was subtracted from his or her responses and these values were divided by the child's individual standard deviation. In order to create an index for children's proportional reasoning performance in terms of their deviation from the normative responses, we calculated the mean absolute difference between these ipsatized responses and the correct (ipsatized) values.

Descriptives

Means, standard deviations, and ranges of the abilities tested are summarized in **Table 1**. In the balance task, 15 children (5 boys and 10 girls) were able to stand on one leg for the maximum of 100 s. To test for possible sex differences, a MANOVA was

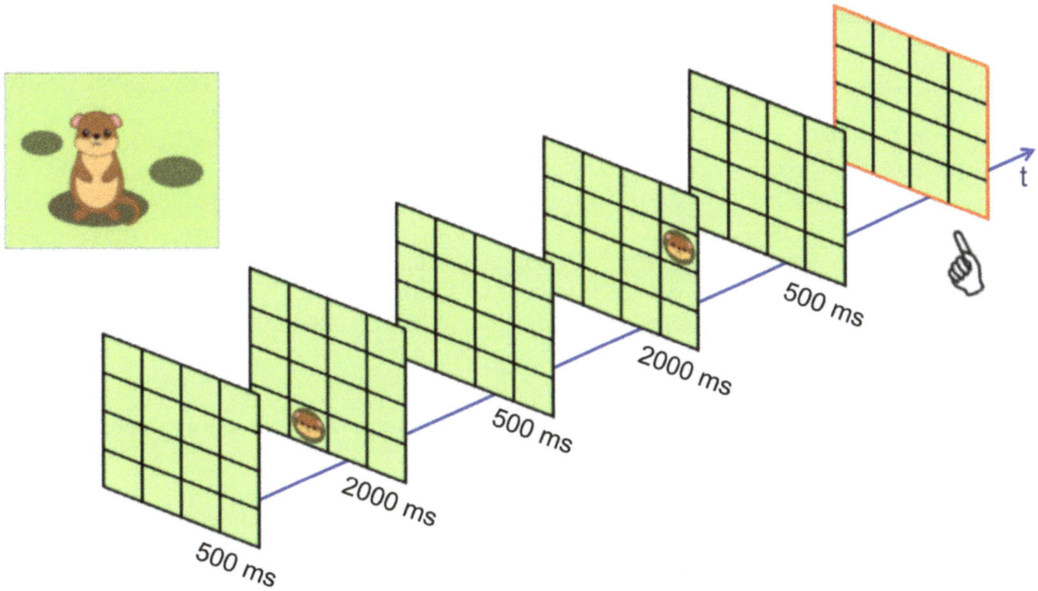

FIGURE 2 | Example for an item of the starting level (span length of 2) of the Position Span Task.

calculated with all variables in **Table 1** and SES as dependent variables and sex as a between-participant variable. The analysis showed a significant effect of sex, $F(9,96) = 1.96$, $p < 0.05$, $\eta^2 = 0.16$. *Post hoc* pairwise comparisons (Sidak corrected) revealed that this was mainly due to a significant sex difference in balance skills, with girls showing better performance ($M = 59.1$, $SD = 31.7$) than boys ($M = 37.6$, $SD = 29.7$). There were no further effects of sex (all $ps > 0.07$).

Correlations

Pearson correlations in **Table 2** show that proportional reasoning, spatial scaling, and mental transformation abilities were significantly related. That is, children with higher spatial scaling and mental transformation scores showed smaller deviations from the normative responses in the proportional reasoning test. More importantly, spatial scaling, mental transformation, and proportional reasoning abilities were also strongly correlated to how long children were able to stand on one leg[2]. Children with better balance skills showed higher scaling and mental transformation scores and smaller deviations in the proportional reasoning task, even after accounting for differences in verbal IQ and sex. Visuo-spatial WM was correlated to balance, spatial scaling, mental transformation, and proportional reasoning (the latter being reduced to a trend when controlled for verbal IQ and sex)[3]. In contrast, verbal WM, inhibitory control, and SES were not significantly correlated to any variables of interest, and were therefore not considered in the following analyses.

TABLE 1 | Means, standard deviations (SD), and ranges of children's performance in the tasks measuring balance, spatial scaling, and proportional reasoning, as well verbal IQ, inhibition, visuo-spatial and verbal working memory (WM).

		Mean (*SD*)	Range
T1	Balance (in s)	44.88 (31.08)	2–100
	Spatial Scaling (score)	14.91 (2.86)	8–21.33
	Children's Mental Transformation Task (score)	19.18 (3.27)	10–24
	Verbal IQ	99.84 (10.44)	61–121
	Inhibition (score)	32.26 (8.97)	15.75–57.18
T2	Proportional Reasoning (non-ipsatized deviation in mm)	18.93 (8.33)	7.42–43.67
	Visuo-spatial WM (correct sequences)	6.51 (2.06)	1–11
	Verbal WM (correct sequences)	6.00 (1.70)	2–10

Relation Between Balance Skills and Spatial Scaling

To investigate whether children's balance skills were related to their ability to scale spatial information even after accounting for effects of control variables and visuo-spatial WM, a hierarchical linear regression analysis was carried out with scaling performance as the predicted variable. As predictor variables, the control variables of sex and verbal IQ were entered in a first

[2]These correlations of main interest were still significant if Bonferroni corrections for multiple comparisons were applied. Bonferroni corrections were not applied on the entire correlation matrix in order not to inflate type II error probability, and not to increase the risk of failing to detect possibly important predictors that should be accounted for in the subsequent regression analyses.

[3]Normal distributions of the responses could not be assumed for all variables. Therefore, we also ran the correlation analyses using the bootstrapping method (cf. Efron and Tibshirani, 1993). In these analyses the same correlations proved to be significant at $p < 0.05$, except that with bootstrapping, the partial correlation between visuo-spatial WM and proportional reasoning was also significant ($r_{partial} = -0.20, p < 0.05$), and the correlation between scaling and proportional reasoning was no longer significant ($r = -0.14, p = 0.15$; $r_{partial} = -0.15, p = 0.14$).

TABLE 2 | Pearson correlations between balance, spatial scaling, mental transformation (CMTT), proportional reasoning, inhibition, visuo-spatial and verbal WM, as well as the control variables of socio-economic status (SES), verbal IQ, and sex.

	1	2	3	4	5	6	7	8	9	10
(1) Balance	–	0.30**	0.29**	−0.26**	−0.08	0.25**	−0.04	0.09	0.08	0.33***
(2) Spatial Scaling	0.33***	–	0.38***	−0.18*	−0.08	0.38***	0.10	0.17^{t}	−0.02	−0.03
(3) CMTT	0.28**	0.40***	–	−0.32***	−0.08	0.33***	0.16	0.09	0.28**	0.08
(4) Proportional Reasoning[1]	−0.25**	−0.20*	−0.25**	–	0.02	−0.20*	−0.04	−0.16	−0.34***	−0.11
(5) Inhibition[1]	−0.06	−0.08	−0.08	0.02	–	−0.07	−0.08	−0.14	−0.01	−0.06
(6) Visuo-spatial WM	0.26**	0.38***	0.32***	−0.18^{t}	−0.07	–	0.17	0.08	0.08	0.03
(7) Verbal WM	−0.02	0.10	0.12	0.01	−0.09	0.16	–	0.04	0.17^{t}	−0.09
(8) SES	0.10	0.18^{t}	0.05	−0.12	−0.15	0.06	0.00	–	0.18^{t}	−0.05
(9) Verbal IQ								–	–	0.15
(10) Sex										–

Above diagonal: zero-order correlations; below diagonal: partial correlations, controlled for sex and verbal IQ. Missing values were excluded pairwise.
[1] Variables with inverse scoring (deviation or interference measures).
****$p < 0.001$, **$p < 0.01$, * $p < 0.05$, $^{t}p < 0.06$.*

step, visuo-spatial WM in a second step, and balance in a third step. Because normal distribution could not be assumed for all residuals, bootstrapped p-values are reported here and in the following analyses (Efron and Tibshirani, 1993). Results showed that the control variables and visuo-spatial WM explained 15% of the variance. Visuo-spatial WM was the only significant predictor ($\beta = 0.39$, $p < 0.01$). However, even after accounting for these effects, balance still explained an additional, significant part of the variance ($\Delta R^2 = 0.06, \beta = 0.27, p < 0.01$).

Relation Between Balance Skills and Mental Transformation

To test whether balance skills were connected to children's mental transformation performance as measured by the CMTT, above and beyond effects of control variables and visuo-spatial WM, we ran a regression analysis similar to the one above, but with the CMTT score as predicted variable. The control variables (sex and verbal IQ) were again entered as predictor variables in a first step, followed by visuo-spatial WM in the second step, and balance in the third step. The analysis revealed that the control variables and visuo-spatial WM accounted for 17% of the variance, with verbal IQ ($\beta = 0.26, p < 0.01$) and visuo-spatial WM ($\beta = 0.30, p < 0.01$) being significant predictors. Again, adding balance increased the explained variance significantly ($\Delta R^2 = 0.04, \beta = 0.23, p < 0.01$).

Relation Between Balance Skills and Proportional Reasoning

To examine whether balance skills were connected to children's ability to reason about proportions above and beyond effects of control variables and visuo-spatial WM, we ran a regression analysis similar to the one above, but with proportional reasoning as predicted variable. The control variables (sex and verbal IQ) were again entered as predictor variables in a first step, followed by visuo-spatial WM in the second step, and balance in the third step. The analysis revealed that the control variables and visuo-spatial WM accounted for 14% of the variance, with verbal IQ being the strongest and only significant predictor among these variables ($\beta = -0.33, p < 0.01$). Again, adding balance increased the explained variance significantly ($\Delta R^2 = 0.04$, $\beta = -0.22$, $p < 0.013$[4]).

DISCUSSION

The results of the present study indicate a tight relation between balance skills and spatial scaling as well as mental transformation performance. Hierarchical linear regression analyses revealed that balance explained a significant proportion of the variance in spatial scaling as well as in mental transformation scores, even after accounting for children's verbal IQ, sex, and visuo-spatial WM. These results extend previous research that investigated the predictive value of balance skills on mental rotation performance (Jansen et al., 2011; Jansen and Kaltner, 2014), and also supports recent research suggesting that spatial scaling is based on similar mechanisms as mental rotation (Möhring et al., 2014).

Regression analyses showed that balance skills in kindergarten explained a significant amount of the variance in proportional reasoning skills at the end of first grade, above and beyond effects of verbal IQ, sex, and visuo-spatial WM. Given that proportional reasoning seems to be closely connected to children's formal fraction knowledge (Möhring et al., 2015b), it might be considered as an index of formal mathematical skills. Therefore, our results not only indicate a strong relation between motor and spatial abilities, but also point to a connection between motor and some mathematical skills. Future research may clarify how scaling abilities relate to broader and more standardized measures of mathematical abilities or to mathematical abilities that do not rely on proportional reasoning.

Contrary to previous findings (Roebers et al., 2013; Lehmann et al., 2014), motor skill was still a significant predictor for cognitive performance after accounting for effects of WM. The differences to Lehmann et al. (2014) results might be explained by differences in age groups and sample sizes. Lehmann et al. (2014) tested much younger children, who showed bottom effects

[4] Even with corrected alpha-level of $p < 0.016$ to account for the fact that three regression analyses were performed, all significant predictors remained significant.

and very little variance on some variables. Furthermore, the regression analyses of the present study presumably had more power due to a larger sample size and fewer predictors. The discrepancies to Roebers et al. (2013) results could be due to the fact that those results were based on fine-motor skills, whereas the present study focused on a gross-motor skill. Indeed, Piek et al. (2008) showed that gross-motor not fine-motor skills predicted later cognitive performance. But also the cognitive skills that were measured in the two studies differed considerably, with the present study focusing on the much more specific skill of proportional reasoning, rather than academic achievement in general. Future research should take a closer look at the specific roles of fine- and gross-motor skills for academic achievement in general, and math performance in particular.

The present study not only showed that balance was still a significant predictor for spatial as well as proportional reasoning skills after accounting for verbal IQ, SES, and visuo-spatial WM, but also no correlations were found with verbal WM and inhibitory control. These findings rule out the possibility that results might have been driven by individual differences in children's *general* intelligence or developmental status and, therefore, suggest very *specific* relations between balance skills and spatial and proportional reasoning. The causal direction of these relations cannot be determined based on the present correlational results. However, it is likely that balance skills are foundational for spatial and proportional reasoning abilities, based on findings obtained with cross-lagged designs (Roebers et al., 2013), which showed that motor skills were more predictive for later cognitive performance than vice-versa. Further evidence for a causal role of motor skills comes from experimental training studies showing beneficial effects of infants' motor experience on cognitive performance (e.g., Needham, 2000; Libertus and Needham, 2010, 2011; Möhring and Frick, 2013; Schwarzer et al., 2013a; Frick and Wang, 2014).

But how may a connection between children's balance and spatial skills as well as their later proportional reasoning be explained, and why is balance especially such a strong predictor? There are at least two possibilities. On the one hand, balance is an important precondition for many other motor tasks, such as independent locomotion. Thus, having good balance skills may facilitate children's opportunities to actively explore their spatial environment. This may boost their spatial cognitive skills, as it allows them to build better spatial mental representations of their surroundings and to gain a deeper understanding of spatial relations between objects and agents. On the other hand, good balance skills may be indicative of an effective coordination of visual, proprioceptive, and vestibular information, which might be a precondition for building a stable representation of our spatial environment. For example, in order to perceive the environment as stable, the brain needs to combine single visual inputs (e.g., from fixations between saccades) with information about body posture, head, and eye-movement. Having good balance skills may ensure reliable information from these senses and provide a solid basis for sensory integration, which may be an important precondition for constructing robust spatial representations. As outlined by Gunderson et al. (2012), such robust spatial representations may also play a crucial role in building meaningful spatial representations of numbers, which leads to an improved mathematical understanding (cf. Siegler and Booth, 2004; see also Walsh, 2003, for a theory on how concepts of space and number may be connected).

CONCLUSION

Results from the present study showed that balance skills in kindergarten were (a) positively associated with spatial scaling and spatial transformation skills, and (b) predictive for proportional reasoning skills at the end of first grade, even after accounting for children's verbal IQ, SES, and visuo-spatial WM. Results further suggested that these relations are very specific and not due to general differences in intelligence or executive functions. Future intervention and training studies are needed to clarify the causal role of motor development and the particular importance of balance skills for children's cognitive development. In our increasingly technological society, and especially in urban environments, children have fewer opportunities to practice gross-motor skills, whereas fine-motor skills may be less restricted. Thus, research on the effects of decreased balance skills on cognitive development is of high relevance, and may have important implications for academic success.

AUTHOR CONTRIBUTIONS

AF: conception and design of the study; data acquisition, analysis, and interpretation; drafting parts of and revising manuscript. WM: data analysis and interpretation; drafting parts of and revising manuscript. Both authors approve of the submitted version.

FUNDING

This research was supported by a research grant from the Swiss National Science Foundation # PZ00P1_131866.

ACKNOWLEDGMENTS

We wish to thank Claudia Roebers, Annik Völke, Salome Pedrett, and Brendan Ryan for helpful comments, and Denise Baumeler, Joël E. Bayard, Leunora Fejza, Ines Holzmann, and Lisa Odermatt for their help with data collection.

REFERENCES

Alloway, T. P., and Temple, K. J. (2007). A comparison of working memory skills and learning in children with developmental coordination disorder and moderate learning difficulties. *Appl. Cogn. Psychol.* 21, 473–487. doi: 10.1002/acp.1284

Archibald, S. J., and Kerns, K. A. (1999). Identification and description of new tests of executive functioning in children. *Child Neuropsychol.* 5, 115–129. doi: 10.1076/chin.5.2.115.3167

Boyer, T. W., and Levine, S. C. (2012). Child proportional scaling: is 1/3=2/6=3/9=4/12? *J. Exp. Child Psychol.* 111, 516–533. doi: 10.1016/j.jecp.2011.11.001

Bull, R., Espy, K. A., and Wiebe, S. A. (2008). Short-term memory, working memory, and executive functioning in preschoolers: longitudinal predictors of mathematical achievement at age 7 years. *Dev. Neuropsychol.* 33, 205–228. doi: 10.1080/87565640801982312

Bushnell, E. W., and Boudreau, J. P. (1993). Motor development and the mind: the potential role of motor abilities as a determinant of aspects of perceptual development. *Child Dev.* 64, 1005–1021.

Campos, J. J., Anderson, D. I., Barbu-Roth, M. A., Hubbard, E. M., Hertenstein, M. J., and Witherington, D. (2000). Travel broadens the mind. *Infancy* 1, 149–219. doi: 10.1207/S15327078IN0102_1

Campos, J. J., Bertenthal, B. I., and Kermoian, R. (1992). Early experience and emotional development. *Psychol. Sci.* 3, 61–64. doi: 10.1111/j.1467-9280.1992.tb00259.x

Carlson, S. A., Fulton, J. E., Lee, S. M., Maynard, L. M., Brown, D. R., Kohl, H. W., III, et al. (2008). Physical education and academic achievement in elementary school: data from the early childhood longitudinal study. *Am. J. Public Health* 98, 721–727. doi: 10.2105/AJPH.2007.117176

Casey, M. B., Nuttall, R. L., Pezaris, E., and Benbow, C. P. (1995). The influence of spatial ability on gender differences in math college entrance test scores across diverse samples. *Dev. Psychol.* 31, 697–705. doi: 10.1037/0012-1649.31.4.697

Corsi, P. M. (1972). Human memory and the medial temporal region of the brain. *Diss. Abstr. Int.* 34:819B.

Davis, E. E., Pitchford, N. J., and Limback, E. (2011). The interrelation of cognitive and motor function in typically developing children aged 4-11 years is underpinned by visual processing and fine manual control. *Br. J. Psychol.* 102, 569–584. doi: 10.1111/j.2044-8295.2011.02018.x

Diamond, A. (2000). Close interrelation of motor development and cognitive development and of the cerebellum and prefrontal cortex. *Child Dev.* 71, 44–56. doi: 10.1111/1467-8624.00117

Efron, B., and Tibshirani, R. J. (1993). *An Introduction to the Bootstrap*. New York, NY: Chapman & Hall.

Fischer, U., Moeller, K., Bientzle, M., Cress, U., and Nuerk, H. C. (2011). Sensori-motor spatial training of number magnitude representation. *Psychon. Bull. Rev.* 18, 177–183. doi: 10.3758/s13423-010-0031-3

Frick, A., Hansen, M. A., and Newcombe, N. S. (2013). Development of mental rotation in 3- to 5-year-old children. *Cogn. Dev.* 28, 386–399. doi: 10.1016/j.cogdev.2013.06.002

Frick, A., and Möhring, W. (2013). Mental object rotation and motor development in 8- and 10-month-old infants. *J. Exp. Child Psychol.* 115, 708–720. doi: 10.1016/j.jecp.2013.04.001

Frick, A., Möhring, W., and Newcombe, N. S. (2014). Picturing perspectives: development of perspective-taking abilities in 4- to 8-year-olds. *Front. Psychol.* 5:386. doi: 10.3389/fpsyg.2014.00386

Frick, A., and Newcombe, N. S. (2012). Getting the big picture: development of spatial scaling abilities. *Cogn. Dev.* 27, 270–282. doi: 10.1016/j.cogdev.2012.05.004

Frick, A., and Newcombe, N. S. (2015). Young children's perception of diagrammatic representations. *Spatial Cogn. Comput. Interdiscip. J.* 15, 227–245. doi: 10.1080/13875868.2015.1046988

Frick, A., and Wang, S. (2014). Mental spatial transformations in 14- and 16-month-old infants: effects of action and observational experience. *Child Dev.* 85, 278–293. doi: 10.1111/cdev.12116

Ganzeboom, H. B. G., De Graaf, P. M., Treiman, D. J., and De Leeuw, J. (1992). A standard international socio-economic index of occupational status. *Soc. Sci. Res.* 21, 1–56. doi: 10.1016/0049-089X(92)90017-B

Gesell, A., and Thompson, H. A. (1934). *Infant Behaviour: Its Genesis and Growth*. New York, NY: McGraw-Hill.

Gibson, E. J. (1988). Exploratory behavior in the development of perceiving, acting, and the acquiring of knowledge. *Annu. Rev. Psychol.* 39, 1–41. doi: 10.1146/annurev.ps.39.020188.000245

Gunderson, E. A., Ramirez, G., Beilock, S. L., and Levine, S. C. (2012). The relation between spatial skill and early number knowledge: the role of the linear number line. *Dev. Psychol.* 48, 1229–1241. doi: 10.1037/a0027433

Hauf, P. (2007). Infants' perception and production of intentional actions. *Prog. Brain Res.* 164, 285–301. doi: 10.1016/S0079-6123(07)64016-3

Hicks, L. E. (1970). Some properties of ipsative, normative, and forced-choice normative measures. *Psychol. Bull.* 74, 167–184. doi: 10.1037/h0029780

International Labour Office (ed.) (1990). *International Standard Classification of Occupations. ISCO-1988*. Geneva: International Labour Office.

Jansen, P., and Heil, M. (2010). The relation between motor development and mental rotation ability in 5-to 6-year-old children. *Eur. J. Dev. Sci.* 4, 66–74.

Jansen, P., and Kaltner, S. (2014). Object based and egocentric mental rotation performance in older adults: the importance of gender differences and motor ability. *Neuropsychol. Dev. Cogn. B Aging Neuropsychol. Cogn.* 21, 296–316. doi: 10.1080/13825585.2013.805725

Jansen, P., Schmelter, A., Kasten, L., and Heil, M. (2011). Impaired mental rotation performance in overweight children. *Appetite* 56, 766–769. doi: 10.1016/j.appet.2011.02.021

Knight, D., and Rizzuto, T. (1993). Relations for children in grades 2, 3, and 4 between balance skills and academic achievement. *Percept. Mot. Skills* 76, 1296–1298. doi: 10.2466/pms.1993.76.3c.1296

Kyttälä, M., Aunio, P., Lehto, J. E., Van Luit, J., and Hautamaki, J. (2003). Visuospatial working memory and early numeracy. *Educ. Child Psychol.* 20, 65–76. doi: 10.1136/jnnp-2012-303309

Kyttälä, M., and Lehto, J. (2008). Some factors underlying mathematical performance: the role of visuospatial working memory and non-verbal intelligence. *Eur. J. Psychol. Educ.* 22, 77–94. doi: 10.1007/BF03173141

LeFevre, J.-A., Jimenez Lira, C., Sowinski, C., Cankaya, O., Kamawar, D., and Skwarchuk, S.-L. (2013). Charting the role of the number line in mathematical development. *Front. Psychol.* 4:641. doi: 10.3389/fpsyg.2013.00641

Lehmann, J., Quaiser-Pohl, C., and Jansen, P. (2014). Correlation of motor skill, mental rotation, and working memory in 3- to 6-year-old children. *Eur. J. Dev. Psychol.* 11, 560–573. doi: 10.1080/17405629.2014.888995

Levine, S. C., Huttenlocher, J., Taylor, A., and Langrock, A. (1999). Early sex differences in spatial skill. *Dev. Psychol.* 35, 940–949. doi: 10.1037/0012-1649.35.4.940

Libertus, K., and Needham, A. (2010). Teach to reach: the effects of active vs. passive reaching experiences on action and perception. *Vis. Res.* 50, 2750–2757. doi: 10.1016/j.visres.2010.09.001

Libertus, K., and Needham, A. (2011). Reaching experience increases face preference in 3-month-old infants. *Dev. Sci.* 14, 1355–1364. doi: 10.1111/j.1467-7687.2011.01084.x

Lopes, L., Santos, R., Pereira, B., and Lopes, V. P. (2013). Associations between gross motor coordination and academic achievement in elementary school children. *Hum. Mov. Sci.* 32, 9–20. doi: 10.1016/j.humov.2012.05.005

Luo, Z., Jose, P. E., Huntsinger, C. S., and Pigott, T. D. (2007). Fine motor skills and mathematics achievement in East Asian American and European American kindergartners and first graders. *Br. J. Dev. Psychol.* 25, 595–614. doi: 10.1348/026151007X185329

MacLeod, C. M. (1991). Half a century of research on the Stroop effect: an integrative review. *Psychol. Bull.* 109, 163–203. doi: 10.1037/0033-2909.109.2.163

Magill, F. N. (1996). *International Encyclopedia of Psychology*. London: Fitzroy Dearborn.

Mix, K. S., and Cheng, Y. L. (2012). The relation between space and math: developmental and educational implications. *Adv. Child Dev. Behav.* 42, 197–243. doi: 10.1016/B978-0-12-394388-0.00006-X

Möhring, W., and Frick, A. (2013). Touching up mental rotation: effects of manual experience on 6-month-old infants' mental object rotation. *Child Dev.* 84, 1554–1565. doi: 10.1111/cdev.12065

Möhring, W., Newcombe, N. S., and Frick, A. (2014). Zooming in on spatial scaling: preschool children and adults use mental transformations to scale spaces. *Dev. Psychol.* 50, 1614–1619. doi: 10.1037/a0035905

Möhring, W., Newcombe, N. S., and Frick, A. (2015a). The relation between spatial thinking and proportional reasoning in preschoolers. *J. Exp. Child Psychol.* 132, 213–220. doi: 10.1016/j.jecp.2015.01.005

Möhring, W., Newcombe, N. S., Levine, S. C., and Frick, A. (2015b). Spatial proportional reasoning is associated with formal knowledge about fractions. *J. Cogn. Dev.* doi: 10.1080/15248372.2014.996289

Murray, G. K., Veijola, J., Moilanen, K., Miettunen, J., Glahn, D. C., Cannon, T. D., et al. (2006). Infant motor development is associated with adult cognitive categorisation in a longitudinal birth cohort study. *J. Child Psychol. Psychiatry* 47, 25–29. doi: 10.1111/j.1469-7610.2005.01450.x

National Research Council (2012). *A Framework for K-12 Science Education: Practices, Crosscutting Concepts, and Core Ideas. Committee on a Conceptual Framework for New K-12 Science Education Standards. Board on Science Education, Division of Behavioral and Social Sciences and Education.* Washington, DC: The National Academies Press.

Needham, A. (2000). Improvements in object exploration skills may facilitate the development of object segregation in early infancy. *J. Cogn. Dev.* 1, 131–156. doi: 10.1207/S15327647JCD010201

Piaget, J. (1952). *The Origins of Intelligence in Children (M. Cook, Trans.).* New York, NY: International Universities Press.

Piek, J. P., Dawson, L., Smith, L. M., and Gasson, N. (2008). The role of early fine and gross motor development on later motor and cognitive ability. *Hum. Mov. Sci.* 27, 668–681. doi: 10.1016/j.humov.2007.11.002

Piek, J. P., Dyck, M. J., Nieman, A., Anderson, M., Hay, D., Smith, L. M., et al. (2004). The relationship between motor coordination, executive functioning and attention in school aged children. *Arch. Clin. Neuropsychol.* 19, 1063–1076. doi: 10.1016/j.acn.2003.12.007

Planinsec, J. (2002). Relations between the motor and cognitive dimensions of preschool girls and boys. *Percept. Mot. Skills* 94, 415–423. doi: 10.2466/pms.2002.94.2.415

Raghubar, K. P., Barnes, M. A., and Hecht, S. A. (2010). Working memory and mathematics: a review of developmental, individual difference, and cognitive approaches. *Learn. Ind. Dif.* 20, 110–122. doi: 10.1016/j.lindif.2009.10.005

Ratliff, K. R., McGinnis, C. R., and Levine, S. C. (2010). "The development and assessment of cross-sectioning ability in young children," in *Proceedings of the 32nd Annual Conference of the Cognitive Science Society*, eds S. Ohlsson and R. Catrambone (Austin, TX: Cognitive Science Society), 2816–2821.

Reuhkala, M. (2001). Mathematical skills in ninth-graders: relationship with visuo-spatial abilities and working memory. *Educ. Psychol.* 21, 387–399. doi: 10.1080/01443410120090786

Ricken, G., Fritz, A., Schuck, K. D., and Preuss, U. (2007). *HAWIVA-III: Hannover-Wechsler-Intelligenztest für das Vorschulalter – III.* Bern: Huber.

Rigoli, D., Piek, J. P., Kane, R., and Oosterlaan, J. (2012). An examination of the relationship between motor coordination and executive functions in adolescents. *Dev. Med. Child Neurol.* 54, 1025–1031. doi: 10.1111/j.1469-8749.2012.04403.x

Roebers, C. M., and Kauer, M. (2009). Motor and cognitive control in a normative sample of 7-year-olds. *Dev. Sci.* 12, 175–181. doi: 10.1111/j.1467-7687.2008.00755.x

Roebers, C. M., Röthlisberger, M., Neuenschwander, R., Cimeli, P., Michel, E., and Jäger, K. (2013). The relation between cognitive and motor performance and their relevance for children's transition to school: a latent variable approach. *Hum. Mov. Sci.* 33, 284–297. doi: 10.1016/j.humov.2013.08.011

Röthlisberger, M., Neuenschwander, R., Michel, E., and Roebers, C. M. (2010). Exekutive funktionen: zugrundeliegende kognitive prozesse und deren korrelate bei kindern im späten vorschulalter. *Z. Entwicklungspsychol. Pädagog. Psychol.* 42, 99–110. doi: 10.1026/0049-8637/a000010

Schmid, C., Zoelch, C., and Roebers, C. (2008). Das Arbeitsgedächtnis von 4- bis 5-jährigen kindern: theoretische und empirische analyse seiner funktionen. *Z. Entwicklungspsychol. Pädagog. Psychol.* 40, 2–12. doi: 10.1026/0049-8637.40.1.2

Schwarzer, G., Freitag, C., Buckel, R., and Lofruthe, A. (2013a). Crawling is associated with mental rotation ability by 9-month-old infants. *Infancy* 18, 432–441. doi: 10.1111/j.1532-7078.2012.00132.x

Schwarzer, G., Freitag, C., and Schum, N. (2013b). How crawling and manual object exploration are related to the mental rotation abilities of 9-month-old infants. *Front. Psychol.* 4:97. doi: 10.3389/fpsyg.2013.00097

Siegler, R. S., and Booth, J. L. (2004). Development of numerical estimation in young children. *Child Dev.* 75, 428–444. doi: 10.1111/j.1467-8624.2004.00684.x

Sommerville, J. A., Woodward, A. L., and Needham, A. N. (2005). Action experience alters 3-month-old infants' perception of other's actions. *Cognition* 96, 1–11. doi: 10.1016/j.cognition.2004.07.004

Soska, K. C., Adolph, K. E., and Johnson, S. P. (2010). Systems in development: motor skill acquisition facilitates three-dimensional object completion. *Dev. Psychol.* 46, 129–138. doi: 10.1037/a0014618

Voelcker-Rehage, C., Godde, B., and Staudinger, U. M. (2010). Physical and motor fitness are both related to cognition in old age. *Euro. J. Neurosci.* 31, 167–176. doi: 10.1111/j.1460-9568.2009.07014.x

Vukovic, R., Fuchs, L. S., Geary, D. C., Jordan, N. C., Gersten, R., and Siegler, R. S. (2014). Sources of individual differences in children's understanding of fractions. *Child Dev.* 85, 1461–1476. doi: 10.1111/cdev.12218

Walsh, V. (2003). A theory of magnitude: common cortical metrics of time, space, and quantity. *Trends Cogn. Sci.* 7, 483–488. doi: 10.1016/j.tics.2003.09.002

Woollacott, M., and Shumway-Cook, A. (2002). Attention and the control of posture and gait: a review of an emerging area of research. *Gait Posture* 16, 1–14. doi: 10.1016/S0966-6362(01)00156-4

Conflict of Interest Statement: The authors declare that the research was conducted in the absence of any commercial or financial relationships that could be construed as a potential conflict of interest.

15

The Relationship between Social and Motor Cognition in Primary School Age-Children

*Lorcan Kenny[1,2], Elisabeth Hill[3] and Antonia F. de C. Hamilton[2,4]**

[1] Centre for Research in Autism and Education (CRAE), University College London, Institute of Education, London, UK, [2] School of Psychology, The University of Nottingham, Nottingham, UK, [3] Department of Psychology, Goldsmiths, University of London, London, UK, [4] Institute of Cognitive Neuroscience, University College London, London, UK

There is increased interest in the relationship between motor skills and social skills in child development, with evidence that the mechanisms underlying these behaviors may be linked. We took a cognitive approach to this problem, and examined the relationship between four specific cognitive domains: theory of mind, motor skill, action understanding, and imitation. Neuroimaging and adult research suggest that action understanding and imitation are closely linked, but are somewhat independent of theory of mind and low-level motor control. Here, we test if a similar pattern is shown in child development. A sample of 101 primary school aged children with a wide ability range completed tests of IQ (Raven's matrices), theory of mind, motor skill, action understanding, and imitation. Parents reported on their children's social, motor and attention performance as well as developmental concerns. The results showed that action understanding and imitation correlate, with the latter having a weak link to motor control. Theory of mind was independent of the other tasks. These results imply that independent cognitive processes for social interaction (theory of mind) and for motor control can be identified in primary school age children, and challenge approaches that link all these domains together.

Keywords: social cognition, motor skill, theory of mind, imitation, action understanding

Edited by:
Petra Hauf,
St. Francis Xavier University, Canada

Reviewed by:
Klaus Libertus,
University of Pittsburgh, USA
Nicola Pitchford,
The University of Nottingham, UK

****Correspondence:***
Antonia F. de C. Hamilton
a.hamilton@ucl.ac.uk

INTRODUCTION

Cognitive psychologists have traditionally studied human development within distinct domains. For example, social cognition (often exemplified by theory of mind tasks) has been studied separately from motor skill or visual skill. However, it is increasingly recognized that there may be links in the brain and cognitive systems underlying these different types of skill. The present paper aimed to examine the claim that motor and social skills develop in concert. To do this, we tested a large sample of primary school age children on a number of cognitive tasks designed to target theory of mind, mirror neuron systems, imitation and motor systems, and examined correlations between performance in these different domains.

Mechanisms Underlying Motor and Social Behavior

In the present paper, we take a cognitive approach to development, meaning that we are interested primarily in the information processing mechanisms underlying different behaviors. We consider the information processing mechanisms of motor behavior, social behavior and all other behaviors including affect, language and perception, to all fall within the realm of cognitive neuroscience (Gazzaniga, 2004). We distinguish specific domains within this realm, and are guided in this classification by our knowledge of adult neuroscience. The present paper focuses on four distinct domains: social cognition, motor cognition, imitation and mirror neuron systems, which contribute in different ways to both motor behavior and social behavior.

Tasks used to assess social cognition in children include mentalizing (thinking about others' thoughts), emotion and face recognition, and many other aspects of social behavior. The current study focuses on mentalizing in order to examine specific claims about the relationship between mentalizing and mirror neuron systems (Gallese et al., 2009; Hamilton, 2009). Tasks commonly used to assess motor cognition include performing hand actions, sequencing actions, whole body movements and balance. The current study focuses on planning and sequencing of hand actions, again because these are most closely linked to mirror neuron systems (Tunik et al., 2007). Tasks used to assess mirror neuron systems, which may contribute to both motor and social behavior, include imitation tasks and action understanding tasks. Developmentally, rapid improvements are seen in all of these tasks over infancy with development continuing in the primary school years (Bushnell and Boudreau, 1993; Jones, 2009).

Hypothesized Links between Cognitive Domains

We can distinguish three different hypotheses for the relationship between different cognitive domains: (1) independent domains, (2) a single domain, and (3) domains interacting over development, and we describe each hypothesis in turn. Other hypotheses such as dynamical systems are also possible, but we return to these in the discussion (McClelland, 2010).

The Independent Domains Hypothesis

Traditional neurocognitive approaches tend to view different domains as independent. For example, different systems such as language, mentalizing, and motor control were considered largely distinct. In particular, mentalizing is considered as a highly specialized skill drawing on abstract abilities such as meta-representation (Perner, 1991) and quite unlike motor skills. If this were the case, we would expect development of mentalizing to be independent of development in motor control. Neuroimaging data also suggest that the different social and motor tasks described above draw on distinct brain networks. Mentalizing tasks reliably activate a brain network including medial prefrontal cortex and temporoparietal junction (Frith and Frith, 2003). Tasks involving understanding of actions or imitation typically activate a different brain network in the inferior parietal and inferior frontal lobe (Caspers et al., 2010). These brain regions are commonly referred to as the mirror neuron system (Rizzolatti and Craighero, 2004) and thus we will describe the tasks that activate these areas as mirroring tasks. Finally, motor tasks may engage mirror neuron systems but also draw on cerebellum and basal ganglia (Middleton and Strick, 2000). Thus, the domains of mentalizing, mirroring and motor control are at least partially distinct in terms of brain systems. The present paper aims to test if they are also distinct in terms of development.

The Single Domain Hypothesis

Even if brain and cognitive systems for mirroring and mentalizing are distinct in adulthood, it is possible that they develop from a single, primary system. For example, it has recently been suggested that 'action cognition' provides a basis for many different social-cognitive skills (Gallese et al., 2009). Building on the discovery of mirror neurons, which respond when a monkey performs an action and also sees another person act, it has been suggested that performing and understanding action is the developmental origin of human social skills. The idea put forth by the action cognition theory is that proficiency in social interactions fundamentally relies on the motor system to decode the movements of others to allow for attributions of intentions and mental states. The logic being employed here is this; when we observe another person's movement our own motor system is activated in a way analogous to if we were performing the same action ourselves. It is this activation that allows us to introspect on what our intentions would be if we were performing that action and this would allow an inference about why the person is performing the action. Some papers have made further claims linking the mirror neuron system to empathy, theory of mind and social skills more broadly (Gallese et al., 2004) including the failure of social skill in autism (Rizzolatti et al., 2009). Under such a framework, adequate development of motor and mirror systems (jointly) is essential for the development of social skill, and there is a direct causal relationship between the development of these cognitive domains.

The Interactive Environment Hypothesis

A third hypothesis concerning the relationship between cognitive domains in development is an environmentally mediated hypothesis. This model sees the child's development as a result of the interaction between the child and the environment, where changes to the environment can have a substantial effect on development. Achievements in one domain could thus have an impact on another domain via the environment. There is growing evidence for such cross-domain interactions at various developmental stages. For example, when a baby learns to sit up, she can see the world differently and adults may address her differently. This change in the environment may then lead to advances in the infant's social skills, compared to her peers who are not yet able to sit. Evidence for this type of interaction can be seen in the finding that babies who have not yet learned to sit independently and those who have mastered the skill are comparable on measures of face processing, while those who are novice sitters perform worse, indicative of a reorganization taking place within the face processing system (Cashon et al., 2013). Another study finds that a baby who is given more opportunities to actively engage with objects shows an increase in orienting to faces relative to a baby given only passive experience with non-social objects (Libertus and Needham, 2011). Furthermore, crawling and walking in infants leads to changes in social interaction from parents (Campos et al.,

2000; Karasik et al., 2011) and improvements in language skills (Iverson, 2010). Overall, the interactionist viewpoint predicts that different cognitive domains may be linked, but the underlying mechanism is external to the child. Such links may thus be weaker than a directly shared brain mechanism, or might only be measurable in longitudinal studies that track the child and her environment over time.

Previous Studies of Social and Motor Development

As this brief review summarizes, the domains of mentalizing, mirroring, imitation and motor cognition could be unlinked, directly linked or linked via the environment. There are few previous studies of the development of motor and social skills in typical children. One large project tested 390 primary school children on fine and gross motor skills, theory of mind, emotion processing, and cognitive control. They found the motor skills correlated highly with IQ, language, social, and attentional skills. Parent ratings of social behavior were related to measured social skills but not motor skills (Dyck et al., 2004). Several studies have examined the relationship between motor and intellectual (not social) skills in children. For example, scores from standardized measures of gross cognitive and gross motor abilities are moderately and significantly correlated (Davis et al., 2011). Further, this study found that this relationship is largely accounted for by variances in visual processing and fine manual control, suggesting that these domains may well be linked via the environment. A number of studies have not found any reliable relationship between tasks tapping motor and social development, or links that are mediated by other higher order cognitive abilities such as memory and visual processing (Wassenberg et al., 2005; van der Fels et al., 2014).

Many more studies have examined motor and social skills in children with developmental disorders including autism and developmental coordination disorder (DCD). Children with autism are diagnosed on the basis of poor social skills, but up to 80% of them also have DCD (Green et al., 2009). Infants at risk of autism (due to having an older sibling with a diagnosis) are reported to have poor postural control (Flanagan et al., 2012) and difficulties with fine motor and grasping skills (Libertus et al., 2014). Motor difficulties such as these have been found to relate to later social and communicative ability (Bhat et al., 2012; Leonard et al., 2014) but although motor impairments are related to social abilities in autistic children, the relationship does not stand in their unaffected siblings (Hilton et al., 2012). In another study, autism severity as measured by scores on the Autism Diagnostic Observation Scale (ADOS), correlated with a measure of praxis that includes imitation tests, but not with more basic motor skills (Dziuk et al., 2007). Similarly, children with DCD differ from their typical peers in their use of social play (Kennedy-Behr et al., 2011). Additionally, autistic children's scores on motor control assessments such as the Movement Assessment Battery for Children (M-ABC) or the Bruininks-Oseretsky Test of Motor Proficiency, Second Edition (BOT-2) predict the social behavior reported by parents (Hilton et al., 2007). A comparison between a group of autistic children and control groups matched for chronological age, motor skill, and developmental age suggests the impairment in motor skill is greater than would be expected based on ability alone (Staples and Reid, 2010). Similarly, a prospective study of children with DCD found that children with higher levels of motor clumsiness at age 5 had fewer social pastimes at age 15 (Cantell et al., 1994). These studies all suggest links between motor and social abilities in developmental disorders. However, many of these studies did not test specific components of motor and social cognition, relying instead on reports of behavior from parents or observations.

When more detailed cognitive assessments are carried out, results seem more mixed. In one intriguing study, children who were better able to adapt to lifting a heavy object also performed better on theory of mind tasks (Sabbagh et al., 2010), an effect that was not explained by age or executive function. Tests of motor cognition in autism suggest poor motor planning (Hughes, 1996) and posture knowledge (Dowell et al., 2009) in some cases but not others (Hamilton et al., 2007; van Swieten et al., 2010). Some studies report difficulties in chaining actions together in sequences (Cattaneo et al., 2007) but others do not (Pascolo and Cattarinussi, 2012). Detailed testing of visuomotor adaptation in children with autism did not find group differences (Mostofsky et al., 2004; Gidley Larson et al., 2008).

Similar variability is found in studies of how children with autism understand other people's actions – a social component of motor cognition. Some studies report difficulties in answering questions about why a person did an action (Boria et al., 2009) or in predicting what will come next in a movie (Zalla et al., 2010) but other studies find no differences in the ability to make sense of hand gestures (Hamilton et al., 2007). Studies of imitation show intact performance on emulation tasks (copying the goal of an action) but poor performance on mimicry tasks (copying precise kinematic features; Hamilton, 2008; Edwards, 2014). For example, when participants with autism performed a motor task on a touch-screen computer that allowed careful matching of the motor, attentional and memory demands between the conditions, they still had poorer accuracy in the imitation condition compared to the emulation condition (Stewart et al., 2013). There is also a debate about how much imitation difficulties in autism relate to a motor or a cognitive deficit (Vanvuchelen et al., 2007). Overall, there is no single aspect of motor cognition that can be directly linked to poor social cognition – more research is needed to understand how motor and social developmental processes mesh together.

The present paper aims to measure motor abilities and social abilities in a large sample of children, using well-defined cognitive tasks. We aim to go beyond assessments of a child's everyday behavior as measured in parent report or clinical measures. By tracking specific cognitive processes, we will be able to make much stronger links between the development of motor and social skills, and the neurocognitive theories of their origins. The present study uses a cross-sectional design, and thus cannot provide a causal account of how strengths in one domain might contribute to strengths in a different domain. However, it can provide an initial measure of the strength of inter-domain links, with a view to future longitudinal studies. In the following section, we set out and justify the tasks used in the present study.

Testing Cognitive Development

To test for links between the motor, mirror and mentalizing domains, we needed a set of cognitive tasks that could measure children's performance in each area. For the mentalizing domain, we used theory of mind tasks, which have been well-studied over the last 30 years. Performance on explicit tests of theory of mind becomes reliable from about age 4 (for review see, Wellman et al., 2001). Using a variety of tests with differing complexity, developmental improvements can be traced from the age of 3 years up to 8 years or even into adolescence (Dumontheil et al., 2010; Calero et al., 2013). In the present paper, we used a battery of theory of mind tasks drawn from past work (Wellman and Liu, 2004) as our measure of mentalizing ability.

To measure the intersection of social and motor processes, we used two types of task which, in adults, engage mirror neuron systems in the brain, namely action understanding tasks and imitation tasks (Buccino et al., 2004; Iacoboni et al., 2005). To assess action understanding, we used a gesture recognition task derived from studies of patients with apraxia (Mozaz et al., 2002) in which a child must choose which photograph of a hand gesture would best fill the gap in a cartoon action. We also used a grasp-intention task in which a child must use a photograph of how an object is grasped to decide 'why' the actor is holding the object – to move it or to use it (Boria et al., 2009). To assess imitation abilities, we instructed children to imitate a series of hand/arm actions and measured accuracy. Instructed imitation is likely to be a better measure of mirror system function than the propensity to spontaneously imitate (Vivanti, 2015).

Cognitive tests of motor systems are also not easy to find. Studies have traditionally focused on the performance of tasks relevant to daily life, such as walking or writing (Sugden, 2007). Here we aimed to retain a cognitive focus and use tasks that can be linked to specific motor processes, including motor planning, sequencing and prediction. Thus, we used a bar task which requires the child to consider the end posture in an action sequence before beginning to move – a measure of motor planning (Cohen and Rosenbaum, 2004; Rosenbaum et al., 2006). Motor planning skills improve over 3–10 years-old age range (Stöckel et al., 2012; Weigelt and Schack, 2015). We also used a sequencing task (Harrington and Haaland, 1992) which assessed how long it took to switch between different actions rather than performing the same action repeatedly.

The Present Study

The present study aimed to measure specific cognitive processes underlying motor and social skill in primary school age children, and to determine how they develop together. We used several tasks to measures performance in four different cognitive domains - of theory of mind, action understanding, imitation and motor control, as detailed above. The present paper focuses only on the domain-level of analysis because the theories that motivated this study are specified at that level. Analysis of performance on individual tasks within each domain will be presented in a different paper. We tested a large sample of children (n = 101) to obtain good statistical power. A power analysis shows that obtaining a medium effect size with 95% power in a multiple regression with seven predictors requires a sample size of 89 participants. If motor and cognitive skills develop from distinct cognitive systems, then performance on the theory of mind tasks will not be related to performance on the mirroring or motor tasks. In contrast, if the engagement of a single cognitive system (such as the mirror neuron system) drives both motor and social development, then the different cognitive domains will correlate tightly across participants. If motor and social skills are linked only via environmental effects, then weak correlations between domains may be observed as well as with IQ.

MATERIALS AND METHODS

Participants

We invited children aged between 4 and 12 years-old to participate in the project. Families were contacted through local primary schools and a database of people interested in research. All parents completed an informed consent form before their children took part, and the study was approved by the University of Nottingham School of Psychology ethics board.

For the first phase of the project, parents of 188 children completed four questionnaires – the Developmental Coordination Disorder Questionnaire (DCDQ; Wilson and Crawford, 2010), The Social Responsiveness Scale (SRS; Constantino and Gruber, 2005) and the Conners 3 ADHD index (Conners 3AI; Conners, 2008), as well as a family background questionnaire collecting data on child's age, languages spoken, socioeconomic status (based on parents' jobs) and any developmental concerns about their child. A more detailed analysis of this phase of the project will be reported elsewhere.

Of the 188 children, 101 participated in the second phase of this project which involved detailed cognitive testing. Data from all 101 is reported here. This sample was not selected entirely at random. First, the availability of children and schools for testing constrained the choice of participants. Second, children whose scores on either the SRS or the DCDQ were toward either end of the distribution of scores obtained from the phase one sample were deliberately oversampled. This is because a fully random sample would include many children with mid-range scores. By oversampling children with extreme scores, we maximized the variance in abilities among the children tested and increased our power to detect associations between the different measures in our study. None of the children tested had a formal diagnosis of developmental delay, but some were receiving additional support from their school or undergoing assessments for difficulties.

Cognitive Testing

The 101 children who completed cognitive testing were assessed by a trained researcher in a quiet room at their school or at the University of Nottingham. They completed the following tasks spread over 2–4 sessions.

Mentalizing Assessment

This included widely used theory of mind tasks – the diverse desires task, diverse beliefs task, knowledge access task, explicit false-belief task, implicit false-belief task, and contents false-belief task were used as in Hamilton et al. (2007). A child was given 1 point for each task where they passed control questions and demonstrated theory of mind. Children completed six sequences of a picture-sequencing task (Baron-Cohen et al., 1986) and were given 1 point for each fully correct answer and a score of 0.5 was given if the final picture of a sequence was correct but the second and third were in the wrong order. Children completed six trials of a penny-hiding task (Gratch, 1964) which is an interactive measure of strategic mentalizing. The child was given one point for each appropriate attempt to hide a coin from the experimenter. Scores for all the theory of mind tasks (six classic tasks, six picture sequencing trials, and six penny hiding trials) were totaled for each child. The data were then linearly scaled so that the sample mean was 0 and standard deviation was 1. Inspection of the quantile plots in R showed no substantial deviation from normality so no further data transformations were applied.

Mirror System Assessment

This included tests of imitation, intention understanding and posture knowledge. In the imitation task, the experimenter sat opposite the child and asked the child to watch the action and then to copy as closely as possible as if looking in a mirror. The experimenter demonstrated with the hand mirroring the child's dominant hand, and the child used his/her dominant hand to respond. One practice trial was given to ensure the instructions were understood. Children performed six trials with meaningful actions and six with meaningless actions (blocked, with block order counterbalanced) and performance was scored from video. Two trained raters coded all videos for overall imitation quality (0, 1, or 2) and specific error types, but only the former are reported here. Reasonable inter-rater reliability was achieved (Cohen's weighted kappa was 0.75). Quality scores were summed for each child and averaged across raters, giving a score out of 24. As before, data were linearly scaled to have a mean of 0 and standard deviation of 1. Inspection of the quantile plots in R showed deviation from normality that was best corrected with by squaring the values, so this transformation was applied.

The intention understanding task was based on Boria et al. (2009). New picture stimuli were generated showing a hand touching, lifting or using a variety of everyday objects. Stimuli were piloted with typical adults to ensure that the objects and actions could be clearly identified. On each trial, the child first saw a card with a picture of an everyday object and was asked – what is it? Responses were 99.7% correct. Then the child was asked if the hand was holding or touching the object. For the holding images, the child was asked – why is he holding it? To use it or to move it? 10 different objects were photographed, resulting in 10 hold-to-use photos and 10 hold-to-move photos. Responses to the 'why' question for each of these 20 photos were scored with 1 point for each correct answer, giving a score out of 20. The posture knowledge task was identical to that used by Hamilton et al. (2007). On each trial, the children saw a cartoon of a person performing an action with the hands missing, together with three photos of hands in different postures and were asked 'which hands fill the gap?' Correct responses were given 1 point with a total score out of 16. Scores on the intention understanding task and the posture knowledge task were summed for each child. As before, data were linearly scaled to have a mean of 0 and standard deviation of 1. Inspection of the quantile plots in R showed no substantial deviation from normality so no further data transformation was applied.

Motor Assessment

This included two tasks – a test of motor planning and a test of motor sequencing. The motor planning task was based on Rosenbaum et al. (1990), and previously used in autism research (Hughes, 1996; Hamilton et al., 2007). On each trial, the child saw a bar with two ends of different colors resting horizontally on a rest 10 cm above the table, and two targets (paper disks on the table) of different colors. They were asked to place one end of the bar on one of the targets (e.g., place the red end on the black target). On four trials, this could be comfortably achieved by grasping the bar at the start of the trial with an overhand grip, while on four trials the less-common underhand grip was more appropriate. Typical adults are able to plan their movements to end in a comfortable posture by adopting a less-common posture at the start of the action (Rosenbaum et al., 2006) and this ability develops over childhood (Adalbjornsson et al., 2008). Thus, this task assesses motor planning. Children received a score out of 8 with one point for each trial where the appropriate grip was used. Motor planning scores were linearly scaled to have a mean of 0 and standard deviation of 1.

The motor sequencing task was based on Harrington and Haaland (1992), and aimed to assess motor speed and the ability to switch between actions. The apparatus was a set of black boxes each with one movable part – a switch to flick, a button to push or a dial to twist. On each trial, the experimenter prepared an array of five of these boxes in a specific order (e.g., flick, twist, twist, flick, flick). When the child was ready with his/her hand on the start location on the left of the desk, the experimenter revealed the array of boxes and the child moved his/her hand along the array performing each action in turn. Trials were videoed and the time from moving away from the start-location to moving away from the last action was coded. 40% of videos were second scored and the correlation between the two scorers was $r = 0.93$. Some box sequences contained no transitions (e.g., push-push-push-push) while others contained one, two, three or four transitions (e.g., push-twist-push-twist-push). Data were analyzed by fitting each child's movement time on each trial to a linear model with five predictors: one for each action (flick/push/twist), one for transition time (coded 1 for switch and 0 for a stay) and one for learning (a linear decrease over the 15 trials). Outliers in these parameter estimates were identified as values 3 standard deviation above/below the mean ($n = 8$ out of 404 data points) and replaced with the group mean.

To combine the motor task scores into a single score for each child, the following transformations were applied. First, values for each score (motor planning; flick-time; push-time; twist-time; transition time; learning) were linearly scaled so that each full set of scores had a mean of 0 and standard deviation of 1. The combined motor score was then defined as: – (*flick-time* + *push-time* + *twist-time*)/3 + *motor planning* – *transition time* using the linearly scaled scores for each. Timing values were negative to ensure that larger values reflect better performance, consistent with other data in this analysis. Inspection of quantile plots showed no substantial deviation from normality so no further data transformation was applied.

IQ Assessment

Raven's colored progressive matrices (Raven et al., 1998) were used to measure each child's non-verbal IQ (nvIQ). Raw scores (not normed scored) were then linearly scaled to have a mean of 0 and standard deviation of 1, in line with other data in this analysis. Inspection of the quantile plots in R showed no substantial deviation from normality so no further data transformation was applied.

Parent Report Scores

Parents completed the SRS, the DCDQ and Conners 3 AI scale. Scores on these scales correlated highly, and a detailed analysis of these data will be reported elsewhere. Descriptive statistics on the raw scores are presented in **Table 1** to illustrate the sample of children tested here. The present study focused on cognitive performance, so we combined the parent report scores into a single factor reflecting parent concerns. To create the factor, we first inspected the raw scores on each of the three parent-report instruments (SRS, DCDQ and Conners) using quantile plots in R. DCD-Q scores were then squared to reduce the deviation from normality. SRS scores and Conners scores were inverted so that a larger value indicates better performance (to be consistent with all other measures). Each transformed score was then linearly scaled to have a mean of 0 and standard deviation of 1, and the scores were summed for each child. This gives a combined parent-report measure that weights social, motor and attentional concerns equally, and which gives higher values to children showing better performance across these domains. Each child's primary caregiver was asked for their current occupation and responses were coded using the International Standard Classification of Occupations (ILO, 2012) where higher values indicate lower socioeconomic status.

TABLE 1 | Characteristics of 101 participants.

	Mean	*SD*	Minimum	Maximum
Age (years)	7.88	1.69	4.88	11.55
SES	3.13	1.5	1	9
Attention (Conners)	5.4	6.0	0	20
Motor skill (DCDQ)	56.6	14.2	16	75
Social development (SRS)	40.9	31.8	0	145
nvIQ (Raven's raw score)	25.4	6.6	11	36
Handedness	10 left	3 ambidextrous		88 right
Gender	60 male	41 female		
Any parental concern about possible developmental issues	76 no	35 yes		

Statistical Analysis

Data for 101 children were available. As described above, scores on each individual task were transformed to ensure that the data were normally distributed and linearly scaled to ensure that higher values reflect better performance. This gave summary scores for each of the following domains: theory of mind; imitation; mirroring; motor skill; non-verbal IQ; parent report; together with age and gender data for each child. The correlations between each of these sets of summary scores were calculated. Then four general linear models (GLMs) were set up to test which factors predicted each of the four cognitive domains of interest. For example, the Theory of Mind model tested how their imitation score, mirroring score, motor score, nvIQ, parent score, age and gender, predicted a child's Theory of Mind score. The imitation model tested how their ToM score, mirroring score, motor score, nvIQ, parent score, age and gender, predicted a child's imitation score. Effectively, these models tested whether performance in each cognitive domain was accounted for by general effects (e.g., nvIQ) or if performance was closely linked to another cognitive domain.

To further probe the data, we conducted a number of exploratory analyses. First, we excluded all children for whom parents had indicated a developmental concern, that is, all children who are receiving additional help at school or undergoing assessments for a developmental disorder. Then we re-ran the GLM models on the remaining sample of typical children. This checks if our results are driven only by the atypical children in the sample. Second, we split the sample into 3 age bands with equal numbers of children in each band. We then re-ran the GLM models on these three samples. This checks if links between different domains might be apparent in only some age ranges. However, both these analyses are conducted on smaller samples and have reduced statistical power.

To explore cross-domain links in the full sample without confounds of age, we examined correlations between the residuals of each domain after removing effects of age, non-verbal IQ and gender. Specifically, we set up a GLM predicting theory of mind performance as a function of age, non-verbal IQ and gender. We took the residuals from this model as a measure of each child's theory of mind performance after age, gender and IQ effects are removed. In the same way, we set up three separate GLMs of mirroring performance; motor performance and imitation each as functions of age, non-verbal IQ and gender. We took the residuals of all four models and examine the pattern of correlations between them. This gives insight into the relationship between different cognitive domains across the full sample of 101 children but without any confounding effects of age or IQ.

RESULTS

Correlations

The correlations between all the scores in the complete dataset are illustrated in **Figure 1**. Note that correction for multiple comparisons has not been applied, but an appropriate Bonferroni threshold for 21 comparisons would be $p < 0.002$. Correlations between almost all measures were high; with the exception that parent questionnaire scores did not correlate with motor scores, theory of mind scores or age, using the corrected significance threshold.

General Linear Models

Four GLM analyses were performed, to test the relationship between performance on the cognitive tasks and parent report in different domains. Results of these analyses are presented in **Table 2**. Model 1 found that theory of mind scores could be predicted based on age and non-verbal IQ but were not related to motor, imitation or mirror system performance. Model 2 found that motor scores could be predicted from gender and non-verbal IQ, with imitation skill as a marginal predictor. Note that this model had a weaker overall fit (adjusted $R^2 = 0.28$) than any of the other models. Model 3 found that mirror system scores could be predicted from imitation scores and non-verbal IQ, but motor and theory of mind scores did not contribute. Model 4 showed that imitation scores could be predicted from age, parent questionnaires and mirror system scores, with motor scores as a marginal predictor.

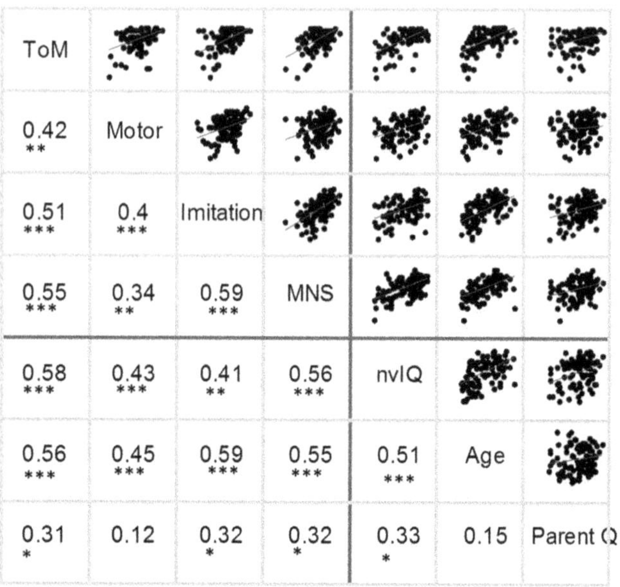

FIGURE 1 | Correlations between all variables. In the upper triangle, each dot represents one participant and the line-of-best-fit is shown in red. In the lower triangle, values are Pearson's *r*. * indicates correlations meeting the $p < 0.002$. Bonferroni corrected threshold. ** indicates correlations at $p < 0.00001$. *** indicates correlations at $p < 0.0000001$.

TABLE 2 | Results of the GLM analyses performed to test the relationship between performance on the cognitive tasks and parent report measures.

	b	*SE*	*t*	ß	*p*
Model 1: Theory of Mind					
Overall model	$F = 12.69$, df = 7,93, $p < 0.0001$, adj $r^2 = 0.45$				
Intercept	−0.96	0.50	−1.92	−0.96	0.058
Gender	−0.09	0.16	−0.54	−0.09	0.592
Age	0.13	0.06	2.09	0.13	**0.039***
Parent Questionnaires	0.03	0.03	0.99	0.03	0.325
Motor	0.05	0.05	0.94	0.05	0.350
Imitation	0.12	0.11	1.19	0.13	0.237
MNS	0.10	0.07	1.50	0.10	0.137
Non-verbal IQ	0.26	0.10	2.63	0.26	**0.010***
Model 2: Motor					
Overall model	$F = 6.53$, df = 7,93, $p < 0.0001$, adj $r^2 = 0.28$				
Intercept	−1.01	1.06	−0.95	−1.01	0.343
Gender	−0.79	0.32	−2.48	−0.79	**0.015***
Age	0.19	0.13	1.45	0.19	0.150
Parent Questionnaires	−0.07	0.07	−1.01	−0.07	0.313
ToM	0.20	0.22	0.94	0.20	0.350
Imitation	0.37	0.22	1.72	0.37	0.089
MNS	−0.06	0.14	−0.41	−0.06	0.682
Non-verbal IQ	0.41	0.21	1.99	0.42	**0.049***
Model 3: Mirroring					
Overall model	$F = 13.76$, df = 7,93, $p < 0.0001$, adj $r^2 = 0.47$				
Intercept	−1.21	0.79	−1.52	−1.21	0.132
Gender	0.01	0.25	0.05	0.01	0.961
Age	0.15	0.10	1.56	0.15	0.122
Parent Questionnaires	0.05	0.05	0.94	0.05	0.352
ToM	0.24	0.16	1.50	0.24	0.137
Motor	−0.03	0.08	−0.41	−0.03	0.682
Imitation	0.48	0.16	3.02	0.48	**0.003****
Non-verbal IQ	0.41	0.16	2.62	0.41	**0.010***
Model 4: Imitation					
Overall model	$F = 13.49$, df = 7,93, $p < 0.0001$, adj $r^2 = 0.47$				
Intercept	−1.67	0.47	−3.56	−1.67	0.001
Gender	0.24	0.15	1.55	0.24	0.125
Age	0.19	0.06	3.34	0.19	**0.001****
Parent Questionnaires	0.07	0.03	2.18	0.07	**0.032***
ToM	0.12	0.10	1.19	0.12	0.237
Motor	0.08	0.05	1.72	0.08	0.089
MNS	0.19	0.06	3.02	0.19	**0.003****
Non-verbal IQ	−0.10	0.10	−1.00	−0.10	0.318

*$p < 0.05$, **$p < 0.01$.

Overall, the correlation analysis and the GLM models provide a consistent picture. Imitation and mirror system performance are related to each other, and are weakly linked to motor skill. Theory of mind scores are linked to nvIQ but not to any of the motor scores. To summarize these results, we illustrate the factors which reliably predict performance in each of the four cognitive domains in **Figure 2**.

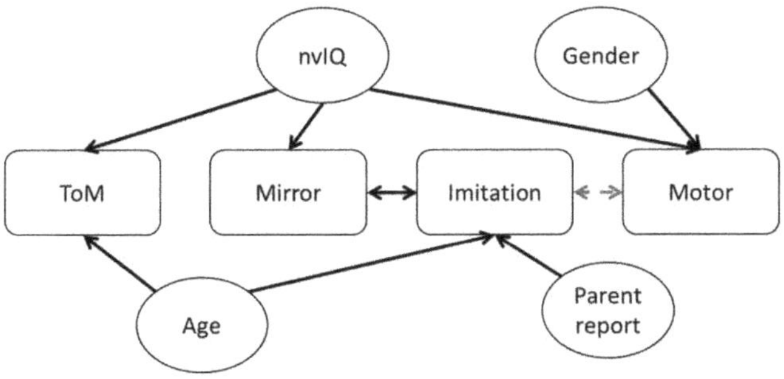

FIGURE 2 | Summary of significant effects found. The four cognitive domains are listed across the centre. Each solid arrow indicates a factor which predicted performance in that cognitive domain. Each dashed arrow indicates a marginally significant predictor.

Further Exploratory Analyses

We performed several exploratory analyses to check the robustness of our results. First, we implemented the four GLM models on the data from the 76 children for whom there was no parental report of any developmental concerns. Results for the ToM model showed that parent report scores were a reliable predictor of performance ($p = 0.039$) but no other predictors were significant. Results for the Motor model showed that gender ($p = 0.034$) and nvIQ ($p = 0.026$) were reliable predictors, replicating the pattern found in the full sample. Results for the mirroring model showed that imitation ($p = 0.0049$) and nvIQ ($p = 0.027$) were reliable predictors, replicating the pattern found in the full sample. Results for the Imitation model showed that age ($p = 0.034$), parent reports ($p = 0.028$) and Mirroring ($p = 0.0049$) were reliable predictors, replicating the pattern found in the full sample. Thus, the analysis of data from only children with no developmental concerns gave a very similar pattern to the full data sample, with no indication of stronger relationships between cognitive domains in this more homogenous sample.

Second, we split the data into three sub-samples by age: a young group of 33 children aged 4.8–6.7 years; a mid-aged group of 33 children aged 6.8–9 years and an old group of 34 children aged 9–11.5 years. We implemented the GLM models on data from each sub-sample separately. In these 12 GLMs, the only predictors meeting the $p < 0.05$ threshold were: in the young group, nvIQ predicts mirroring performance; in the mid-aged group, Mirroring, Imitation, and Motor performance were all reliable predictors of each other; in the old group, Ravens predicted motor performance and age predicted mirroring performance. There were no indications of strong relationships between the specific cognitive domains that differ from our main report in these subsamples, though we note that these analyses are likely to be underpowered.

Third, we aimed to examine each cognitive domain without confounding effects of age and IQ. To do this, we modeled performance in each of the four cognitive domains separately as a function of age, non-verbal IQ, and gender. We took the residuals from each model as measures of each child's domain performance without any age, gender or IQ effects. We took the residuals of all four models and examined the pattern of correlations between them. This gives insight into the relationship between different cognitive domains across the full sample of 101 children but without any confounding effects of age or IQ. Correlations in this model were given in **Table 3**. The only correlation which survives an appropriate correction for multiple comparisons ($p < 0.005$) is the correlation between imitation and mirroring, a result also found in our primary analysis.

TABLE 3 | Results of the residuals correlation.

	ToM	Motor	Imitation	MNS	Parent report
ToM		0.12	0.23	0.23	0.16
Motor	0.248		0.17	0.03	−0.04
Imitation	0.019	0.089		0.36	0.26
MNS	0.020	0.802	0.000		0.19
Parent report	0.117	0.661	0.009	0.054	

Upper triangle indicates correlation coefficient, lower triangle indicates p-values.

DISCUSSION

In this study of 101 children, we examined cognitive performance across the motor and social domains. We found that performance on theory of mind tasks was independent of action understanding, imitation, and motor skill. However, action understanding and imitation were closely related, and somewhat linked to motor skill. These results have important implications for theories of how different cognitive domains develop and are related to one another.

In the introduction, we set out three possible models for the relationship between social and motor skills. These skills could develop independently, they could be fully integrated or they could be linked via the environment. The present data do not give support to a wholly integrated model (hypothesis 2) such as the action cognition framework set out by Gallese et al. (2009). With that theory comes the testable hypothesis that performance on tasks tapping motor cognition, the mirror neuron system and social cognition will all be necessarily related. In our data, imitation and action understanding were closely linked, and weakly correlated to motor cognition. This supports the claim that the process of understanding another agent's action involves the recruitment of a perception-action network. However, the social abilities measured with theory of mind tasks were independent of mirror and motor skills. This argues against the hypothesis that difficulties in social cognition cascade downstream from impaired motor cognition, or that shared understanding of perception and action contributes to mentalizing. It remains possible that social and motor cognition could be more integrated at earlier stages of development than was considered by the present study and it may be that it becomes increasingly modularized across development or the relationship may differ when different components of motor cognition are considered (e.g., Sabbagh et al., 2010).

In contrast, our data align well with the cognitive task distinctions suggested by adult neuroimaging data and by traditional cognitive theories. In neuroimaging studies, action understanding and imitation engage the same brain systems; partially overlapping with other motor skills, while theory of mind engages different systems. Similarly, in our developmental data, action understanding and imitation are mutually predictive, and have a weak relationship to motor skill.

Our data cannot rule out the possibility that different cognitive domains interact over developmental time, linked by the environment. There is evidence for this in some longitudinal studies. For example, questionnaire data from over 62,000 children as part of a cohort study revealed that motor skill at 18 months predicted communication skills at 3 years (Wang et al., 2014). Bart et al. (2007) found that motor skills in kindergarten predicted study skills and disruptive behavior (but barely predicted social behavior) a year later. Ommundsen et al. (2010) found that motor skill in 1st grade predicted social status in 4th grade, measured in 80 children. Note that all these studies used self-report or teacher report measures of social behavior, rather than cognitive tests. Thus, it remains unclear if motor cognition can be directly linked to social cognition in a longitudinal fashion.

Our data also cannot rule out the possibility that there are links between performance on specific tasks within different cognitive domains, which does not emerge when performance in each domain is combined as we have done here. For example, Davis et al. (2011) found that subscores in tests of visual processing and fine manual control were correlated in a group of 4–11 years-old children and that this task-level effect drove the link between motor and intelligence domains. It is possible that there are similar relationships between specific tasks in our study, but unfortunately there are too many tasks and not enough participants to implement the PCA or task-level analysis used by Davis et al. (2011). It would be interesting to test if specific tasks or specific cognitive sub-components are linked across domains in future work.

Clinical Relevance

The results of the present study have implications for how we understand disorders of both social and motor cognition. For instance, if motor and social skills develop independently of each other, as the data presented here suggest, then it is not clear why there is such a high degree of co-morbidity of autism and DCD. The present study did not test children with a diagnosis of autism or DCD, but some children were undergoing assessments for a variety of developmental concerns. This enabled us to test a larger and more variable sample. However, without participants diagnosed with disorders, it is not possible to know if the same relationships between motor and social skills hold on that sample. It is possible, for example, that motor cognition and theory of mind are closely linked in autism even if they are not linked in a typical sample. It is possible that the relationship is qualitatively different in atypical populations and that cognitive systems may be more interdependent and have increasing cascade effects on each other. Alternatively, it may be that an underlying neurological susceptibility to cognitive delay or deficit may similarly affect abilities that are reasonably unrelated in typical development.

The independence between mentalizing ability and motor cognition in this study has implications for the design of interventions for those who are at a social or motoric disadvantage. For example, there have been studies exploring the effects of interventions targeting imitation skill in autism to improve social emotional functioning (Ingersoll, 2012). While Ingersoll found improvements in social emotional functioning when children were followed-up were related to treatment it was not clear that improvements in imitation was the mechanism through which these improvements were manifest.

Strengths and Weaknesses

This study is limited in some ways. Most of our experimental measures were based on previously published work, to ensure robustness. However, our measure of motor sequencing was novel and has not previously been used with children. The sequencing task requires children to complete a series of actions, where the number of switches from one action type to another can vary. Reaction time was measured from video coding which may also have introduced an element of error. Furthermore, the novelty of this task makes it difficult to determine what optimal performance should look like. Some of the measures used produced some ceiling effects and so were not capturing the full variance that exists in the population for these measures. This was particularly the case for the Theory of Mind tasks and despite normalizing the distribution it may be that the distribution of scores would have had greater variance in a younger sample or if more implicit measures of mentalizing were used. Furthermore, the questionnaires used to measure parental reports of a child's behaviors are designed to be used as screening measures for differentiating children who potentially have a clinical diagnosis from those who do not and as such they were not designed to measure ability equally across the entire range of typical social, motor and attentional ability.

There are also several statistical and analysis issues which could affect our conclusions. First, our sampling strategy involved selecting children for cognitive testing who had extreme scores on the parent report measures, in order to maximize the variance in our sample. While none of the children in our sample have a clinically diagnosed developmental disorder, it is possible that this sampling method could bias our results if there are discontinuities between typical and atypical development. The fact that we find similar results when we analyze data only from children with no developmental concerns argues that our sampling method did not introduce strong biases into our analysis. Second, it is possible that performance in different cognitive domains changes non-linearly with age. Our analysis uses only linear models and cannot capture this. Substantially larger sample sizes would be needed to examine non-linear age effects. Finally, we tested children across a wide age range but did not have enough participants to break down the dataset into smaller, more homogenous groups to test if the relationship between cognitive domains changes over development.

This study did, however, have some areas of strength. First, the large sample offered good statistical power to detect relationships between multiple variables. The results we found are consistent in both our primary GLM analysis, which takes a conservative approach to testing for strong relationships between cognitive domains, and in three further exploratory analyses which tested for these relationships in sub-samples of the data. Second, the present study employed cognitive tasks that were measuring children's abilities in certain domains rather than their parent's perception of their ability relative to normative performance. This is a very important distinction as it allows for a more fine-grained exploration of the component aspects of cognition that would be too difficult to elicit in questionnaires. The relationship between parent measures in these domains with children's performance on related tasks from the current sample will be explored in more detail elsewhere.

CONCLUSION

The data presented in the current study suggest that different domains of social and motor skill, specifically the theory of mind domain and the mirroring domain, are relatively independent in this sample. This argues against a 'single domain hypothesis,' but is compatible with an 'independent domains' hypothesis or an 'interactive environment' hypothesis. Longitudinal data will be needed to discriminate and further test these hypotheses, and thus to better understand the ways in which different cognitive processes interact across motor and social development. This is especially the case in developmental disorders when the development of these cognitive capacities may be incommensurate with each other and in turn with the requirements of the environment, leading to functional impairment. Intervention studies should be used to not only address questions of efficacy and effectiveness at improving motor and social proficiency but also in order to test the mechanisms through which social and motor skill develop in concert or autonomously. We suggest that future research should adopt a cognitive approach to the measurement of motor skill, mirror neuron system functioning, and social cognition in clinical and non-clinical control groups in order to test and develop our understanding of the mechanisms of development.

AUTHOR CONTRIBUTIONS

AH, LK and EH designed the study. LK collected the data. AH & LK analysed the data. AH, LK and EH wrote the paper and have approved it for publication.

ACKNOWLEDGMENTS

The Waterloo Foundation funded the research presented in this paper. The authors are grateful to the schools and families who participated without whom this research would not have been possible.

REFERENCES

Adalbjornsson, C. F., Fischman, M. G., and Rudisill, M. E. (2008). The end-state comfort effect in young children. *Res. Q. Exe. Sport* 79, 36–41. doi: 10.1080/02701367.2008.10599458

Baron-Cohen, S., Leslie, A. M., and Frith, U. (1986). Mechanical, behavioural and intentional understanding of picture stories in autistic children. *Br. J. Dev. Psychol.* 4, 113–125. doi: 10.1111/j.2044-835X.1986.tb01003.x

Bart, O., Hajami, D., and Bar-Haim, Y. (2007). Predicting school adjustment from motor abilities in kindergarten. *Infant Child Dev.* 16, 597–615. doi: 10.1002/icd.514

Bhat, A. N., Galloway, J. C., and Landa, R. J. (2012). Relation between early motor delay and later communication delay in infants at risk for autism. *Infant Behav. Dev.* 35, 838–846. doi: 10.1016/j.infbeh.2012.07.019

Boria, S., Fabbri-Destro, M., Cattaneo, L., Sparaci, L., Sinigaglia, C., Santelli, E., et al. (2009). Intention understanding in autism. *PLoS ONE* 4:e5596. doi: 10.1371/journal.pone.0005596

Buccino, G., Vogt, S., Ritzl, A., Fink, G. R., Zilles, K., Freund, H.-J., et al. (2004). Neural circuits underlying imitation learning of hand actions: an event-related fMRI study. *Neuron* 42, 323–334. doi: 10.1016/S0896-6273(04)00181-3

Bushnell, E. W., and Boudreau, J. P. (1993). Motor development and the mind: the potential role of motor abilities as a determinant of aspects of perceptual development. *Child Dev.* 64, 1005–1021. doi: 10.2307/1131323

Calero, C. I., Salles, A., Semelman, M., and Sigman, M. (2013). Age and gender dependent development of theory of mind in 6- to 8-years old children. *Front. Hum. Neurosci.* 7:281. doi: 10.3389/fnhum.2013.00281

Campos, J. J., Anderson, D. I., Barbu-Roth, M. A., Hubbard, E. M., Hertenstein, M. J., and Witherington, D. (2000). Travel broadens the mind. *Infancy* 1, 149–219. doi: 10.1207/S15327078IN0102_1

Cantell, M. H., Smyth, M. M., and Ahonen, T. P. (1994). Clumsiness in adolescence: educational, motor, and social outcomes of motor delay detected at 5 years. *Adapt. Phys. Activ. Q.* 11, 115–129.

Cashon, C. H., Ha, O.-R., Allen, C. L., and Barna, A. C. (2013). A U-shaped relation between sitting ability and upright face processing in infants. *Child Dev.* 84, 802–809. doi: 10.1111/cdev.12024

Caspers, S., Zilles, K., Laird, A. R., and Eickhoff, S. B. (2010). ALE meta-analysis of action observation and imitation in the human brain. *Neuroimage* 50, 1148–1167. doi: 10.1016/j.neuroimage.2009.12.112

Cattaneo, L., Fabbri-Destro, M., Boria, S., Pieraccini, C., Rizzolatti, G., Monti, A., et al. (2007). Impairment of actions chains in autism and its possible role in intention understanding. *Proc. Natl. Acad. Sci. U.S.A.* 104, 17825–17830. doi: 10.1073/pnas.0706273104

Cohen, R. G., and Rosenbaum, D. A. (2004). Where grasps are made reveals how grasps are planned: generation and recall of motor plans. *Exp. Brain Res.* 157, 486–495. doi: 10.1007/s00221-004-1862-9

Constantino, J. N., and Gruber, P. C. (2005). *Social Responsiveness Scale (SRS).* Los Angeles, CA: Western Psychological Services.

Conners, C. K. (2008). *Conners*, 3rd Edn. Toronto, ON: Multi-Health Systems.

Davis, E. E., Pitchford, N. J., and Limback, E. (2011). The interrelation between cognitive and motor development in typically developing children aged 4-11 years is underpinned by visual processing and fine manual control. *Br. J. Psychol.* 102, 569–584. doi: 10.1111/j.2044-8295.2011.02018.x

Dowell, L. R., Mahone, E. M., and Mostofsky, S. H. (2009). Associations of postural knowledge and basic motor skill with dyspraxia in autism: implication for abnormalities in distributed connectivity and motor learning. *Neuropsychology* 23, 563–570. doi: 10.1037/a0015640

Dumontheil, I., Apperly, I. A., and Blakemore, S. (2010). Online usage of theory of mind continues to develop in late adolescence. *Dev. Sci.* 13, 331–338. doi: 10.1111/j.1467-7687.2009.00888.x

Dyck, M. J., Hay, D., Anderson, M., Smith, L. M., Piek, J., and Hallmayer, J. (2004). Is the discrepancy criterion for defining developmental disorders valid? *J. Child Psychol. Psychiatry* 5, 979–995. doi: 10.1111/j.1469-7610.2004.t01-1-00290.x

Dziuk, M. A., Gidley Larson, J. C., Apostu, A., Mahone, E. M., Denckla, M. B., and Mostofsky, S. H. (2007). Dyspraxia in autism: association with motor, social, and communicative deficits. *Dev. Med. Child Neurol.* 49, 734–739. doi: 10.1111/j.1469-8749.2007.00734.x

Edwards, L. A. (2014). A meta-analysis of imitation abilities in individuals with autism spectrum disorders. *Autism Res.* 7, 363–380. doi: 10.1002/aur.1379

Flanagan, J. E., Landa, R., Bhat, A., and Bauman, M. (2012). Head lag in infants at risk for autism: a preliminary study. *Am. J. Occupat. Ther.* 66, 577–585. doi: 10.5014/ajot.2012.004192

Frith, U., and Frith, C. D. (2003). Development and neurophysiology of mentalizing. *Philos. Trans. R. Soc. Lon. Ser. B Biol. Sci.* 358, 459–473. doi: 10.1098/rstb.2002.1218

Gallese, V., Keysers, C., and Rizzolatti, G. (2004). A unifying view of the basis of social cognition. *Trends Cogn. Sci.* 8, 396–403. doi: 10.1016/j.tics.2004.07.002

Gallese, V., Rochat, M., Cossu, G., and Sinigaglia, C. (2009). Motor cognition and its role in the phylogeny and ontogeny of action understanding. *Dev. Psychol.* 45, 103–113. doi: 10.1037/a0014436

Gazzaniga, M. S. (2004). *The Cognitive Neurosciences.* Cambridge, MA: MIT press.

Gidley Larson, J. C., Bastian, A. J., Donchin, O., Shadmehr, R., Mostofsky, S. H., Larson, J. C. G., et al. (2008). Acquisition of internal models of motor tasks in children with autism. *Brain J. Neurol.* 131(Pt 11), 2894–2903. doi: 10.1093/brain/awn226

Gratch, G. (1964). Response alternation in children: a developmental study of orientations to uncertainty. *Hum. Dev.* 7, 49–60. doi: 10.1159/000270053

Green, D., Charman, T., Pickles, A., Chandler, S., Loucas, T., Simonoff, E., et al. (2009). Impairment in movement skills of children with autistic spectrum disorders. *Dev. Med. Child Neurol.* 51, 311–316. doi: 10.1111/j.1469-8749.2008.03242.x

Hamilton, A. F. (2008). Emulation and mimicry for social interaction: a theoretical approach to imitation in autism. *Q. J. Exp. Psychol.* 61, 101–115. doi: 10.1080/17470210701508798

Hamilton, A. F. (2009). Research review: goals, intentions and mental states: challenges for theories of autism. *J. Child Psychol. Psychiatry* 50, 881–892. doi: 10.1111/j.1469-7610.2009.02098.x

Hamilton, A. F., Brindley, R. M., and Frith, U. (2007). Imitation and action understanding in autistic spectrum disorders: how valid is the hypothesis of a deficit in the mirror neuron system? *Neuropsychologia* 45, 1859–1868. doi: 10.1016/j.neuropsychologia.2006.11.022

Harrington, D. L., and Haaland, K. Y. (1992). Motor sequencing with left hemisphere damage. *Brain* 115, 857–874. doi: 10.1093/brain/115.3.857

Hilton, C., Wente, L., LaVesser, P., Ito, M., Reed, C., and Herzberg, G. (2007). Relationship between motor skill impairment and severity in children with Asperger syndrome. *Res. Autism Spect. Disord.* 1, 339–349. doi: 10.1016/j.rasd.2006.12.003

Hilton, C. L., Zhang, Y., Whilte, M. R., Klohr, C. L., and Constantino, J. (2012). Motor impairment in sibling pairs concordant and discordant for autism spectrum disorders. *Autism* 16, 430–441. doi: 10.1177/1362361311423018

Hughes, C. (1996). Control of action and thought: normal development and dysfunction in autism: a research note. *J. Child Psychol. Psychiatry* 37, 229–236. doi: 10.1111/j.1469-7610.1996.tb01396.x

Iacoboni, M., Molnar-Szakacs, I., Gallese, V., Buccino, G., Mazziotta, J. C., and Rizzolatti, G. (2005). Grasping the intentions of others with one's own mirror neuron system. *PLoS Biol.* 3:e79. doi: 10.1371/journal.pbio.0030079

ILO (2012). *International Standard Classification of Occupations 2008 (ISCO-08): Structure, Group Definitions and Correspondence Tables.* Geneva: ILO.

Ingersoll, B. (2012). Brief report: effect of a focused imitation intervention on social functioning in children with autism. *J. Autism Dev. Disord.* 42, 1768–1773. doi: 10.1007/s10803-011-1423-6

Iverson, J. M. (2010). Developing language in a developing body: the relationship between motor development and language development. *J. Child Lang.* 37, 229–261. doi: 10.1017/S0305000909990432

Jones, S. S. (2009). The development of imitation in infancy. *Philos. Trans. R. Soc. Lon. B Biol. Sci.* 364, 2325–2335. doi: 10.1098/rstb.2009.0045

Karasik, L. B., Tamis-LeMonda, C. S., and Adolph, K. E. (2011). Transition from crawling to walking and infants' actions with objects and people. *Child Dev.* 82, 1199–1209. doi: 10.1111/j.1467-8624.2011.01595.x

Kennedy-Behr, A., Rodger, S., and Mickan, S. (2011). Physical and social play of preschool children with and without coordination difficulties: preliminary findings. *Br. J. Occupat. Ther.* 74, 348–354. doi: 10.4276/030802211X13099513661199

Leonard, H. C., Elsabbagh, M., Hill, E. L., and The Basis team. (2014). Early and persistent motor difficulties in infants at-risk of developing autism spectrum disorder: a prospective study. *Eur. J. Dev. Psychol.* 11, 18–35. doi: 10.1080/17405629.2013.801626

Libertus, K., and Needham, A. (2011). Reaching experience increases face preference in 3-month-old infants. *Dev. Sci.* 14, 1355–1364. doi: 10.1111/j.1467-7687.2011.01084.x

Libertus, K., Sheperd, K. A., Ross, S. W., and Landa, R. J. (2014). Limited fine motor and grasping skills in 6-month-old infants at high risk for autism. *Child Dev.* 85, 2218–2231. doi: 10.1111/cdev.12262

McClelland, J. L. (2010). Emergence in cognitive science. *Topics Cogn. Sci.* 2, 751–770. doi: 10.1111/j.1756-8765.2010.01116.x

Middleton, F. A., and Strick, P. L. (2000). Basal ganglia and cerebellar loops: motor and cognitive circuits. *Brain Res. Rev.* 31, 236–250. doi: 10.1016/S0165-0173(99)00040-5

Mostofsky, S. H., Bunoski, R., Morton, S. M., Goldberg, M. C., and Bastian, A. J. (2004). Children with autism adapt normally during a catching task requiring the cerebellum. *Neurocase* 10, 60–64. doi: 10.1080/13554790490960503

Mozaz, M., Gonzalez Rothi, L. J., Anderson, J. M., Crucian, G. P., and Heilman, K. M. (2002). Postural knowledge of transitive pantomimes and intransitive gestures. *J. Int. Neuropsychol. Soc.* 8, 958–962. doi: 10.1017/S1355617702870114

Ommundsen, Y., Gundersen, K. A., and Mjaavatn, P. E. (2010). Fourth graders' social standing with peers: a prospective study on the role of first grade physical activity, weight status, and motor proficiency. *Scand. J. Educ. Res.* 54, 377–394. doi: 10.1080/00313831.2010.493344

Pascolo, P. B., and Cattarinussi, A. (2012). On the relationship between mouth opening and "broken mirror neurons" in autistic individuals. *J. Electromyogr. Kinesiol.* 22, 98–102. doi: 10.1016/j.jelekin.2011.07.009

Perner, J. (1991). *Understanding the Representational Mind. Learning, Development, and Conceptual Changes Series.* Cambridge, MA: MIT Press.

Raven, J., Raven, J., and Court, J. (1998). *Coloured Progressive Matrices.* Oxford: Oxford University Press.

Rizzolatti, G., and Craighero, L. (2004). The mirror-neuron system. *Ann. Rev. Neurosci.* 27, 169–192. doi: 10.1146/annurev.neuro.27.070203.144230

Rizzolatti, G., Fabbri-destro, M., and Cattaneo, L. (2009). Mirror neurons and their clinical relevance. *Nat. Clin. Pract. Neurol.* 5, 24–34. doi: 10.1038/ncpneuro0990

Rosenbaum, D., Cohen, R., Meulenbroek, R. J., and Vaughan, J. (2006). "Plans for grasping objects," in *Motor Control and Learning SE - 2,* eds M. Latash and F. Lestienne (New York, NY: Springer), 9–25.

Rosenbaum, D. A., Marchak, F., Barnes, H. J., Vaughan, J., Slotta, J. D., and Jorgensen, M. J. (1990). "Constraints for action selection: overhand versus underhand grips," in *Attention and Performance 13: Motor Representation and Control,* ed. M. Jeannerod (Mahwah, NJ: Lawrence Erlbaum Associates, Inc.), 321–342.

Sabbagh, M. A., Hopkins, S. F. R., Benson, J. E., and Flanagan, J. R. (2010). Conceptual change and preschoolers' theory of mind: evidence from load-force adaptation. *Neural Netw.* 23, 1043–1050. doi: 10.1016/j.neunet.2010.08.007

Staples, K., and Reid, G. (2010). Fundamental movement skills and autism spectrum disorders. *J. Autism Dev. Disord.* 40, 209–217. doi: 10.1007/s10803-009-0854-9

Stewart, H. J., McIntosh, R. D., and Williams, J. H. G. (2013). A specific deficit of imitation in autism spectrum disorder. *Autism Res.* 6, 522–530. doi: 10.1002/aur.1312

Stöckel, T., Hughes, C. M. L., and Schack, T. (2012). Representation of grasp postures and anticipatory motor planning in children. *Psychol. Res.* 76, 768–776. doi: 10.1007/s00426-011-0387-7

Sugden, D. A. (2007). *Ecological Intervention for Children with Movement Difficulties: Movement ABC-2. Harcourt Assessment/Pearson Assessment.* Available at: https://books.google.co.uk/books?id=TRubXwAACAAJ

Tunik, E., Rice, N. J., Hamilton, A., and Grafton, S. T. (2007). Beyond grasping: representation of action in human anterior intraparietal sulcus. *Neuroimage* 36, T77–T86. doi: 10.1016/j.neuroimage.2007.03.026

van der Fels, I. M. J., Te Wierike, S. C. M., Hartman, E., Elferink-Gemser, M. T., Smith, J., and Visscher, C. (2014). The relationship between motor skills and cognitive skills in 4-16 year old typically developing children: a systematic review. *J. Sci. Med. Sport* 18, 697–703. doi: 10.1016/j.jsams.2014.09.007

van Swieten, L. M., van Bergen, E., Williams, J. H. G., Wilson, A. D., Plumb, M. S., Kent, S. W., et al. (2010). A test of motor (not executive) planning in developmental coordination disorder and autism. *J. Exp. Psychol. Hum. Percept. Perform.* 36, 493–499. doi: 10.1037/a0017177

Vanvuchelen, M., Roeyers, H., and De Weerdt, W. (2007). Nature of motor imitation problems in school-aged boys with autism: a motor or a cognitive problem? *Autism* 11, 225–240. doi: 10.1177/1362361307076846

Vivanti, G. (2015). The importance of distinguishing propensity versus ability to imitate in ASD research and early detection. *J. Autism Dev. Disord.* 45, 1119–1120. doi: 10.1007/s10803-014-2254-z

Wang, M. V., Lekhal, R., Aarø, L. E., and Schjølberg, S. (2014). Co-occurring development of early childhood communication and motor skills: results from a population-based longitudinal study. *Child Care Health Dev.* 40, 77–84. doi: 10.1111/cch.12003

Wassenberg, R., Feron, F. J. M., Kessels, A. G. H., Hendriksen, J. G. M., Kalff, A. C., Kroes, M., et al. (2005). Relation between cognitive and motor performance in 5- to 6-year-old children: results from a large-scale cross-sectional study. *Child Dev.* 76, 1092–1103. doi: 10.1111/j.1467-8624.2005.00899.x

Weigelt, M., and Schack, T. (2015). The development of end-state comfort planning in preschool children. *Exp. Psychol.* 57, 476–782. doi: 10.1027/1618-3169/a000059

Wellman, H. M., Cross, D., and Watson, J. (2001). Meta-analysis of theory-of-mind development: the truth about false belief. *Child Dev.* 72, 655–684. doi: 10.2307/1132444

Wellman, H. M., and Liu, D. (2004). Scaling of theory-of-mind tasks. *Child Dev.* 75, 523–541. doi: 10.1111/j.1467-8624.2004.00691.x

Wilson, B. N., and Crawford, S. G. (2010). *The Developmental Coordination Disorder Questionnaire 2007 (DCDQ'07). Administrative Manual for the DCDQ'07 with Psychometric Properties.* Calgary, AB: Alberta Health Services.

Zalla, T., Labruyère, N., Clément, A., and Georgieff, N. (2010). Predicting ensuing actions in children and adolescents with autism spectrum disorders. *Exp. Brain Res.* 201, 809–819. doi: 10.1007/s00221-009-2096-7

Conflict of Interest Statement: The authors declare that the research was conducted in the absence of any commercial or financial relationships that could be construed as a potential conflict of interest.

The reviewer KL and handling Editor declared a current collaboration and the handling Editor states that the process nevertheless met the standards of a fair and objective review.

16

Asymmetric Dynamic Attunement of Speech and Gestures in the Construction of Children's Understanding

Lisette De Jonge-Hoekstra[1], Steffie Van der Steen[2]*, Paul Van Geert[1] and Ralf F. A. Cox[1]*

[1] Department of Developmental Psychology, Behavioural and Social Sciences, University of Groningen, Groningen, Netherlands, [2] Department of Special Needs Education and Youth Care, Behavioural and Social Sciences, University of Groningen, Groningen, Netherlands

Edited by:
Klaus Libertus,
University of Pittsburgh, USA

Reviewed by:
Sarah Berger,
University of New York, USA
Caitlin Fausey,
University of Oregon, USA
Drew Hamilton Abney,
University of California, Merced, USA

***Correspondence:**
Lisette De Jonge-Hoekstra
lisette.hoekstra@rug.nl;
Steffie Van der Steen
s.van.der.steen@rug.nl

As children learn they use their speech to express words and their hands to gesture. This study investigates the interplay between real-time gestures and speech as children construct cognitive understanding during a hands-on science task. 12 children ($M = 6$, $F = 6$) from Kindergarten ($n = 5$) and first grade ($n = 7$) participated in this study. Each verbal utterance and gesture during the task were coded, on a complexity scale derived from dynamic skill theory. To explore the interplay between speech and gestures, we applied a cross recurrence quantification analysis (CRQA) to the two coupled time series of the skill levels of verbalizations and gestures. The analysis focused on (1) the temporal relation between gestures and speech, (2) the relative strength and direction of the interaction between gestures and speech, (3) the relative strength and direction between gestures and speech for different levels of understanding, and (4) relations between CRQA measures and other child characteristics. The results show that older and younger children differ in the (temporal) asymmetry in the gestures–speech interaction. For younger children, the balance leans more toward gestures leading speech in time, while the balance leans more toward speech leading gestures for older children. Secondly, at the group level, speech attracts gestures in a more dynamically stable fashion than vice versa, and this asymmetry in gestures and speech extends to lower and higher understanding levels. Yet, for older children, the mutual coupling between gestures and speech is more dynamically stable regarding the higher understanding levels. Gestures and speech are more synchronized in time as children are older. A higher score on schools' language tests is related to speech attracting gestures more rigidly and more asymmetry between gestures and speech, only for the less difficult understanding levels. A higher score on math or past science tasks is related to less asymmetry between gestures and speech. The picture that emerges from our analyses suggests that the relation between gestures, speech and cognition is more complex than previously thought. We suggest that temporal differences and asymmetry in influence between gestures and speech arise from simultaneous coordination of synergies.

Keywords: recurrence analysis, synergies, children's learning, microdevelopment, cognitive development, dynamic skill theory

INTRODUCTION

How do children learn and develop understanding? How does cognitive change arise? In developmental psychology, this is one of the most intriguing questions, as evidenced by the considerable literature on the topic (see for instance, Piaget and Cook, 1952; Sternberg, 1984; Perry et al., 1988; Siegler, 1989; Carey and Spelke, 1994; Vygotsky, 1994; Thelen, 2000; Gelman, 2004; Anderson et al., 2012; Van der Steen et al., 2014). In search for the mechanisms behind cognitive development, the hands of children have come up as a vital ingredient. As children learn new things, or when they communicate or explain things, they use both their speech for verbal utterances and their hands to gesture (Goldin-Meadow et al., 1992; Anastas et al., 2011; Alibali and Nathan, 2012).

Gestures and speech are coupled, and mostly they are well-aligned, such that meaning expressed in gestures matches that expressed in speech. However, sometimes gestures and speech do not overlap, and a so-called gesture–speech mismatch occurs (Church and Goldin-Meadow, 1986; Perry et al., 1992; Goldin-Meadow, 2003). It has been demonstrated that during such gesture–speech mismatches, people (children and adults) express their cognitive understanding in gestures before they are able to put them into words (Crowder and Newman, 1993; Gershkoff-Stowe and Smith, 1997; Garber and Goldin-Meadow, 2002). Gesture–speech mismatches are especially likely to occur when a person is on the verge of learning something new. This makes them a hallmark of cognitive development (Perry et al., 1992; Goldin-Meadow, 2003), and shows that gestures and cognition are coupled as well. In the literature the explanation for this link has been attributed to gestures being a medium to express arising cognitive strategies (Goldin-Meadow et al., 1993), to highlight cognitively relevant aspects (Goldin-Meadow et al., 2012), to add action information to existing mental representations (Beilock and Goldin-Meadow, 2010), to simulate actions (Hostetter and Alibali, 2010), to decrease cognitive load during tasks (Goldin-Meadow et al., 2001) and to construct cognitive insight (Trudeau and Dixon, 2007; Stephen et al., 2009a,b; Boncoddo et al., 2010).

A conceptual framework which has been largely ignored in the research on gestures, and which follows from the work by Iverson and Thelen (1999), is that of synergetics and self-organization dynamics introduced by Haken (1977/1983), Kugler and Turvey (1987), and Kelso (1995). First of all, at the behavioral level, gestures and speech are considered to be action systems (Reed, 1982) That is, they are functional units organized to perform a specific task, like a hands-on science task in the present study. In addition, at the coordination level, we argue that gestures and speech form two coupled synergies. Within the context of action control, a synergy is a temporarily stable task-specific collective organization (Kelso, 1995), which emerges through self-organization out of a large set of underlying components distributed across body, brain, and environment.

To elaborate, gestures and speech require the precise coordination of many different muscles, joints, neurons, as well as related perceptual subsystems. Speech articulation, even for the simplest utterances, involves well over 70 muscles in the respiratory, laryngeal ('voice box') and pharyngeal (throat) systems as well as of the mouth, the tongue, etcetera (Galantucci et al., 2006; Turvey, 2007). Moreover, speech is highly attuned, for instance, to auditory information, but also to vision (needed for, e.g., interpersonal communication). Gesturing results from the coordinated contractions of 10s of muscles in the shoulder, upper arm, forearm, hand, and fingers of both upper limbs (Weiss and Flanders, 2004), and involves a tight informational link to proprioceptive as well as visual subsystems to stay attuned to the environment. Synergies for speech and gestures consist of several (overlapping) neural structures involved in information-motor couplings, across the central nervous system. Cognitive subsystems loosely associated with attention, memory and the planning of movements will play a role in gestures as well as in speech. Importantly, the gesture and speech synergies share several of these underlying components, and their recruitment will temporally overlap in any given task (cf. Wijnants et al., 2012a).

During communication or the expression of thoughts and ideas, the gesture and speech synergies synchronize to a high degree (McNeill, 1992). This synchronization reflects that the self-organizing process underlying the creation of both synergies is able to recruit the underlying components in the service of both gestures and speech adequately and synchronously. In fact, because of the tight coupling of the gesture and speech synergies, trying not to use either gestures or speech while communicating, or to desynchronize them, proves to be detrimental for the other (Goldin-Meadow et al., 2009). Moreover, Goldin-Meadow et al. (2001) found that if children or adults do not gesture -either by instruction or by choice- while they explain how they solved a mathematical problem, they perform worse on recalling a list of words or letters that they had to remember while they explained the mathematical problem. Goldin-Meadow et al. (2001, p. 521) conclude that "...gestures and speech form an integrated and, indeed, synergistic system in which effort expended in one modality can lighten the load on the system as a whole."

From the perspective of synergetics and self-organization dynamics, the decline in performance if one only speaks but does not gesture should be related to suboptimal coordination of the gesture and speech synergies. More generally, when demands on the action systems increase, such as, for instance, in a novel or challenging task, the synergies become relatively less stable and less synchronized as compared to less challenging tasks. Novel and challenging tasks often have several new and (seemingly) conflicting task constraints. Since synergies are task specific, different task constraints lead to different collective organizations, competing for existence and the recruitment of (shared) components. Following Wijnants et al. (2012a), who studied synergetic control under conflicting task constraints in the context of a Fitts task, we reason that the gesture–speech mismatch in a novel task (Goldin-Meadow, 2003) resides in a less optimal simultaneous organization and coordination of the gesture and speech synergies. As a result, the usually tightly coupled synergies of gestures and speech dissociate, due to overlapping recruitment of the underlying components involved, resulting in the observable gesture–speech mismatch. Consequently, a gesture–speech mismatch can take different forms, such as instances in which gestures convey different content than speech, in which there are only gestures but no speech, and in which there is only speech but no gestures, similar to what Goldin-Meadow et al. (2001) found.

Most studies examining the gesture–speech mismatch have thus far focused on series of problem solving events in which, across different trials with some time in between, children are asked to solve a certain problem and explain their solution. These studies have focused on children's solutions to, for instance, a series of mathematical equivalence problems (Alibali and Goldin-Meadow, 1993), Tower of Hanoi-problems (Garber and Goldin-Meadow, 2002), conservation tasks (Goldin-Meadow et al., 1993), and gear solving tasks (Boncoddo et al., 2010). From these studies, it appears that children show new problem solving strategies by means of gestures in earlier trials, to be followed by speech one or multiple trials later. A more detailed understanding of how such patterns of gestures and speech arise, and how this relates to our proposal of suboptimal coordination of synergies and cognitive development, requires a study of children's verbal and non-verbal behaviors as they occur in real time (Pine et al., 2007), that is, during a task, considering their temporal order and coupling. The current study investigates the non-linear, dynamic interplay of children's gestures and speech as they construct their cognitive understanding during a hands-on science task. Analysis tools will be employed which allow us to quantify the process of dynamic attunement between speech and gestures across all possible time scales during the task.

The current focus on the coupled dynamics of gestures and speech as it occurs in the moment and across time scales resonates with the relatively recent call for microgenetic studies to investigate the process (rather than just the outcome) of cognitive development (e.g., Grannot and Parziale, 2002; Siegler, 2006; Flynn et al., 2007; Van der Steen et al., 2012; Cox and Van Dijk, 2013). These microdevelopmental studies are exponents of the complex dynamical systems approach to behavior, cognition, and development (Van Geert, 1998, 2003, 2011; Smith and Thelen, 2003). This approach aims to infer the "why" and "how" of development (Thelen and Corbetta, 2002), using the language of complex dynamical systems: multi-causality, self-organization, variability, stability, non-linearity and so on, and the accompanying data-analytical tools.

To explain these terms in short, multi-causality pertains to the notion that development cannot be ascribed to one component or level of the developing system, but instead emerges from the continuous interaction of all the levels of the developing system (Thelen and Smith, 2007). Self-organization means that patterns and order emerge from the continuous interaction of all levels of the developing system, without external interference. Variability and stability follow from self-organization, as both variable and stable behavior occur within a developing system. For new stable behavior, i.e., new patterns, to emerge, a system typically displays variable behavior before settling in a new, more stable, pattern. Variability is thus a hallmark of developmental change. Moreover, this indicates that development is inherently non-linear, with periods of stable and variable behavior (Van Geert, 2008). Multicausality, self-organization and variability are also mechanisms that are apparent in our proposal that diverse components coordinate to form the synergies of gestures and speech, and that the dynamics within and between the synergies, under certain conditions, result in gesture–speech mismatches.

Dynamic skill theory is a theory of cognitive development encompassing dynamical system principles (Van Geert and Fischer, 2009). It provides a model that allows researchers to structurally investigate processes of cognitive development (Fischer, 1980; Fischer and Bidell, 2006). Dynamic skill theory states that the development of cognitive skills — defined as actions and thinking abilities, which includes verbalizations and gestures — proceeds through a series of hierarchically, ordered levels. That is, the development of cognitive skills follows a structure in which higher-order skills are constructed of a combination of skills at lower levels. According to dynamic skill theory, skills develop through a series of 10 levels, divided over three tiers, although not in a simple linear fashion (see below). The first tier is the sensorimotor tier, which consists of perceptions, actions and observable relations between these perceptions and actions. The second representational tier goes beyond the observable relations between actions and perceptions, although still restrained to concrete situations. The last tier, abstractions, includes non-concrete rules that apply in general (Schwartz and Fischer, 2004). Each tier consists of three levels, single sets, mappings (relations between single sets), and systems (relations between mappings).

In accordance with the notion of nested timescales, which implies that development occurs at different, though tightly interconnected timescales, the levels as distinguished by dynamic skill theory are applicable to both macro (long term) and micro (short term) development (Schwartz and Fischer, 2004; Fischer and Bidell, 2006). This means that people also go through these levels on the short-term time scale, for example during a new task, in a non-linear fashion, so that drops, spurts and stable periods in understanding occur (Van der Steen et al., 2012). This makes this theory particularly suitable for detailed, within-task dynamical analyses. Furthermore, dynamic skill theory provides a structure in which the concepts expressed in and constructed by gestures and speech can be compared, as it can be applied to both actions and verbalizations (Granott et al., 2002; Hoekstra, 2012). Lastly, dynamic skill theory's model can grasp meaningful intra-individual variability on the short term timescale, by allowing for fluctuations in cognitive understanding during a single task, as well as the (sometimes differing) levels displayed by gestures and speech. This intra-individual variability has been linked to learning and transitioning to a higher (cognitive) level (Van Geert and Van Dijk, 2002; Yan and Fischer, 2002; Goldin-Meadow, 2003; Schwartz and Fischer, 2004; Van Geert and Steenbeek, 2005; Siegler, 2007). Although it has never been studied explicitly, understanding at the level of the sensorimotor tier might lead to a different interplay of gestures and speech, compared to understanding at the level of the representational tier.

As learning is an inherently non-linear process (Van Geert, 2008), and intra-individual variability in cognitive understanding and strategies is a hallmark of transitioning to more advanced levels, non-linear time-series methods are needed to investigate these processes. One such method is recurrence quantification analysis (RQA; Webber and Zbilut, 2005; Marwan et al., 2007).

RQA originates from the study of natural systems, and has recently been applied to the study of human behavior and development (e.g., Shockley et al., 2002; Aßmann et al., 2007; Wijnants et al., 2009, 2012b). RQA is based on the detection and quantification of recurrent (i.e., repeatedly occurring) behavioral states, one of the most fundamental and important properties of dynamic systems. By using RQA and the notion of recurrence, measures of interest in a dynamic analysis of the behavior of a system, such as stability, regularity, and complexity can be retrieved from the time series. For a full overview of the RQA method, see the paper by Marwan et al. (2007), and for a useful guide to applying it see the chapter by Webber and Zbilut (2005).

A methodological advancement of RQA, cross-recurrence quantification analysis (CRQA; Zbilut et al., 1998; Shockley et al., 2002; Marwan et al., 2007) will be used in this paper to study the interplay of gestures and speech. With CRQA, the shared dynamics of two coupled systems, such as, for instance, parent-child dyads (Dale and Spivey, 2006; De Graag et al., 2012; Lichtwarck-Aschoff et al., 2012; Cox and Van Dijk, 2013), staff-client dyads (Reuzel et al., 2013, 2014) and adult dyads (Shockley et al., 2003; Richardson and Dale, 2005; Richardson D.C. et al., 2007; Richardson M.J. et al., 2007; Louwerse et al., 2012) can be studied. In CRQA, recurrence is generally defined as some match of behavioral state in the two systems under study. In RQA and CRQA alike, recurrence is not confined to states at exactly the same moment, but it is also noted when these particular matching states occur in the systems at either an earlier or later point in time, in fact across all possible time scales. These time scales range from the smallest time scale of the sample rate (seconds), to the duration of the entire observation. Linear tools fall short to fully capture the underlying dynamics of the cognitive system, which is fundamentally non-stationary and non-linear, as well as continuously attuning to a changing environment. Recurrences of system trajectories, on the other hand, can provide important clues as to the system from which they derive, in this case, the cognitive system (cf. Marwan and Webber, 2014).

To summarize, children's use of gestures and speech is known to be informative about their cognitive capabilities, which change on a developmental time scale (Goldin-Meadow, 1998). As we have argued above, synergetic control and synergetic competition form a valuable explanatory framework for this research topic, which might lead to novel insights. As synergies are reflected in the dynamic organization of behavior (cf. Stephen et al., 2009b), we will analyze children's gestures and speech as they construct understanding in real time. To this end, CRQA will be applied to the two time series of skill levels (based on dynamic skill theory) displayed in children's gestures and speech, while they are working on an educational science task. The main research question of this study is: how is the leading role of gestures over speech in children's cognitive change, as reported in previous studies, related to and reflective of an underlying dynamic interplay between gestures and speech during task performance? Research outcomes will pertain to the dynamic attunement of gestures and speech, focusing, for instance, on their temporal relation, leader-follower hierarchy, and asymmetric coupling. Furthermore, the dynamic interplay between gestures and speech during task performance will be related to age and more general measures of performance outside the task. Specific research questions, hypotheses, and their rationale will be given after a more detailed introduction of recurrence procedures and the derived measures of dynamic organization in the Section "Materials and Methods."

MATERIALS AND METHODS

Participants

For this study, the data of 12 Dutch children, six boys and six girls, were analyzed. The participants took part in a larger longitudinal project (see Van der Steen, 2014), and were on average 39.1 months old ($SD = 3.8$) at the start of the longitudinal data collection. In this larger study, children individually worked on scientific tasks about air pressure and gravity, under guided supervision of a researcher, in 4-months intervals. All children were recruited at their daycare centers or (pre)schools by asking their parents for a written consent. Parents were told about the nature of the study (children's longitudinal development of scientific understanding), but not about the specific tasks that were administered. The study was approved by the ethical committee of the Psychology Department of the University of Groningen.

For the current study, we chose to analyze children's (non)verbal behavior during an air pressure task administered at the sixth measurement (see below). We chose this task because the task protocol gradually builds up to a wrap-up question in which children are able to show their understanding of the task at that point. Our sample included five children from kindergarten ($M = 57.2$ months, $SD = 2.2$ months), and seven children from first grade ($M = 69.4$ months, $SD = 4.4$ months). **Table 1** gives an overview of characteristics of each child, including children's early math- and language-scores on standardized tests from a national pupil-monitoring system that the children performed in kindergarten. These tests are administered twice a year to keep track of primary school children's progress on the subjects math and (Dutch) language. For the Kindergarten tests, children are asked to count, classify objects and phrase words. Scores can range from 1 to 5, with 1 as the lowest and 5 as the highest attainable score. In addition, **Table 1** provides children's average skill level score during the past five measurements, as measured in their verbalizations.

Procedure

During the task, researcher and child were involved in a natural hands-on teaching–learning interaction. An adaptive protocol was constructed, which guaranteed that all children were asked the basic questions reflecting the core building blocks of the task and the incorporated scientific concepts (see Van der Steen et al., 2012 for an excerpt of an interaction). At the same time, the protocol left enough space for children to take initiative and manipulate the material. The researcher started by showing the task material to the child, asking about its purpose and functioning. The child was then encouraged to explore the material, while the researcher asked questions, such as "What do

TABLE 1 | Overview of characteristics of the 12 participating children.

Child	Grade	Age (months)	Math-score	Language-score	Average score past tasks
1	KG	58	5	–	2.65
2	KG	55	5	5	2.27
3	KG	60	2	3	0.77
4	KG	58	5	5	2.55
5	KG	55	5	4	2.45
6	1	64	4	5	2.31
7	1	64	5	5	2.56
8	1	69	4	4	2.42
9	1	76	4	4	2.27
10	1	69	3	3	1.98
11	1	73	4	4	2.75
12	1	71	5	5	2.79
Mean	–	*64.3*	*4.25*	*4.27*	*2.32*

you think we should use this for?" Furthermore, the researcher was allowed to provide guidance by asking follow-up questions, encouraging the child to try out his/her ideas using the material, and by summarizing the child's findings or previous answers. The guidance never included statements indicating whether the child was right or wrong. We analyzed the interaction until the child answered a 'wrap-up' question ("After investigating all of this, can you now explain how this device works?"), after which the protocol prescribed the researcher to start with another topic. This part of the interaction (from the first question until the 'wrap-up' question) took 5–12 min (on average a little over 8 min). All interactions took place within children's schools, always guided by the same researcher, and were recorded on video.

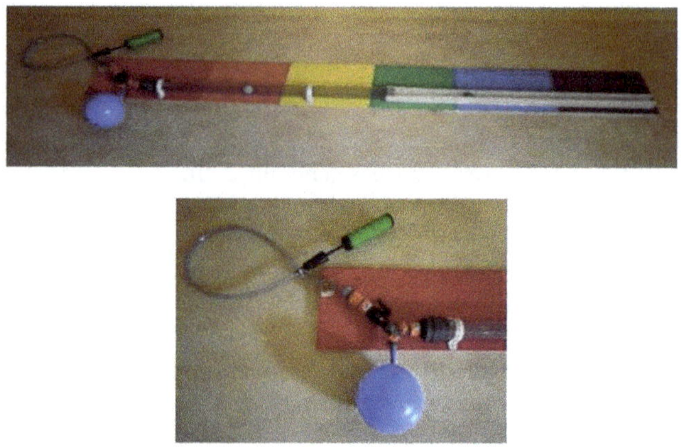

FIGURE 1 | The "air canon" and a close-up of the pump mechanism of this task.

Materials

The task explored was called the "air canon," specifically designed for this study. It was designed to let children explore how air pressure can be used to set materials in motion, and how air can be temporary stored in a balloon and released to have an even bigger impact on objects. The task consisted of wood, garden sprinkler parts, a transparent drainage tube, a gutter made from part of a room divider, a ball pump, balloon, and ping-pong balls (see **Figure 1**). There are three (sprinkler) taps on this device, one to (dis)connect the air pump, one to (dis)connect the balloon, and one to (dis)connect the drainage tube. Through questioning and exploring, children realize they have to open some taps (and close others) to make the canon work. There are two ways to shoot a ping-pong ball down the tube: (1) simply opening the taps connected to the pump and tube (closing the tap to the balloon), and repeatedly pumping, and (2) by inflating the balloon first (closing the tap to the tube), and then releasing the air into the tube. The colors on the wood serve as a measuring device to see how far the ball goes.

Analysis

Coding Procedure

The interactions were first coded for children's verbal utterances, and then for gestures/task manipulations. Both coding systems are described in more detail in the Appendix. The verbal utterances were coded in four steps using the computer program MediaCoder (Bos and Steenbeek, 2006). We started with the determination of the exact points in time when children's utterances started and ended. The second step involved the classification of these verbal utterances into categories (e.g., description, prediction, explanation). As a third step, meaningful units of the child's coherent task-related utterances were formed, so that utterances (sentences) about the same topic with only a short break in between were joined together for the fourth step. In this fourth and final step, the complexity of the child's verbalized understanding within a unit was determined, using a scale based on Dynamic skill theory. The dynamic skill levels ranged from the levels of the sensorimotor tier to single abstractions, with levels of the representational tier in between. For example, at the first level of the sensorimotor tier (level 1), the child states a single characteristic of the task, such as "This tube is long." At the first level of the abstract tier (level 7), the child mentions an abstraction that goes beyond the material, for example a statement about air pressure in general. This range of levels

(1–7) approximately corresponds to the attainable levels for the children's age (see Fischer and Bidell, 2006). Only utterances that displayed correct characteristics or possible task operations or mechanisms were coded as a skill level. This verbal coding procedure is explained in more detail elsewhere (Van der Steen et al., 2012, 2014).

In order to make sure that the codes of verbal utterances were reliable, a standardized codebook was used. For each step of coding, three raters went through a training of coding three video fragments of 15 min and compared their codes with those of an expert-rater (who constructed the codebook and training). The codes of the third fragment were compared to the codes of the expert-rater and a percentage of agreement was calculated. The reliability of the percentage of agreement is based on Monte Carlo permutation testing. The codes of one of the raters were shuffled 1000 times, so that the order of the codes became random. The p-value is the amount of times that the percentage of agreement of the shuffled codes was the same (or higher) as the empirical percentage of agreement, divided by the times that the codes were shuffled (1000). On average, the empirical percentage of agreement was: categories: 87% (range: 81–93; $p < 0.01$), combining verbalizations into units: 93% (range: 89–96; $p < 0.01$), and level of understanding: 90% (range: 83–95; $p < 0.01$).

The child's gestures and task manipulations (hereafter: gestures) were coded independently from the verbal utterances. The coding procedure for gestures also involved multiple steps. During the first step, the exact point in time when a gesture started and ended was determined, along with a broad categorization of the gesture into the categories *short answers*, *representations/manipulations*, and *emblems* (such as "thumbs up"). For the second step, the broad categories of the first step were refined to more specific categories. For example, *short answers* were allocated to *nodding yes*, *shaking no*, etc., *representations/manipulations* were split into *characteristic* (such as representing 'hard'), *movement* (such as representing 'fast,' or the course of a ball), *representation* (such as representing relations among different objects), while *emblems* were kept undifferentiated. The third and last step involved assigning levels of complexity, based on Dynamic skill theory (similar to how the verbal utterances were coded), to all *representations/manipulations*. For more details about the gesture codebook, see the Appendix, and Hoekstra (2012).

To ensure reliable coding of children's gestures, two raters coded four training video fragments of 10 min independently, while following the standardized codebook, and their percentages of agreement were calculated for each step of coding. The reliability of the percentages of agreement was based on Monte Carlo permutation testing, like for the coding procedure for verbal utterances. On average, the percentages of agreement was: 97% (range: 94–100; $p < 0.01$) for the first step (broad categorization), 86% (range: 78–91; $p < 0.01$) for the second step (refined categories), and 92% (range: 88–98; $p < 0.01$) for the third step (level of complexity).

Time Series

Before performing CRQA on the data, the codes of the video fragments were transformed into a time series of the skill levels of speech, and a time series of the skill levels of gestures, with a sample rate of 1 s. If there was no event (i.e., no skill level), this was indicated with a 0 in the time series. In **Figure 2**, the time series of skill levels of gestures and skill levels of speech of one of the children in our sample is depicted. In order to be able to distinguish the lines in **Figure 2** clearly, only the first 300 s of the 392 s in total are displayed.

Cross Recurrence Quantification Analysis

For categorical data, CRQA starts by plotting in a plane (called the cross recurrence plot, CRP, see **Figure 3**) all congruent appearances of some pre-specified matching values within a pair of time series, by putting one of the time series along the horizontal axis and the other along the vertical axis. Specifically, the CRP represents all those instances when the behavioral state of one subsystem (e.g., skill level in verbalization) at some moment in time is matched by the behavioral state of another subsystem (e.g., skill level in gesture) at the same or any other moment in time during the observation. These instances are depicted as colored dots in the CRP, which are canonically referred to as 'recurrent points.' From the spatial layout of these colored dots, several recurrence measures can be derived (see below). These CRQA-measures reveal hidden structure concealed in the shared dynamics of the two interaction subsystems (speech and gestures) across all possible time scales, which is informative about the dynamic organization of the cognitive system. **Figure 3** illustrates the CRP of gestures and speech for the same child as the time series in **Figure 2**. The CRPs

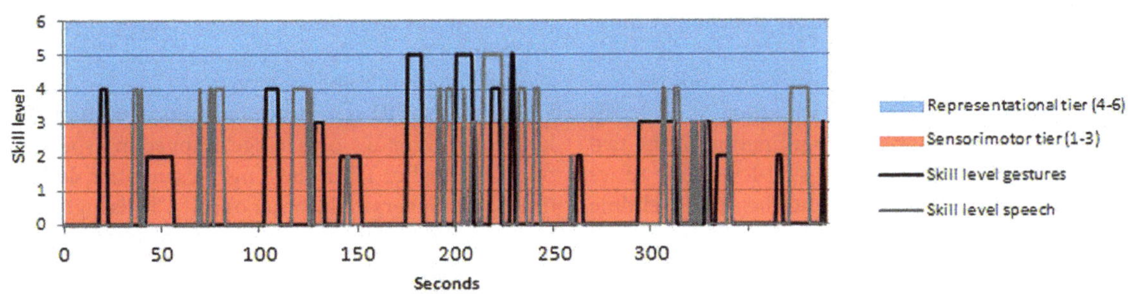

FIGURE 2 | Time series of skill levels of gestures and speech of one child (boy, 55 months).

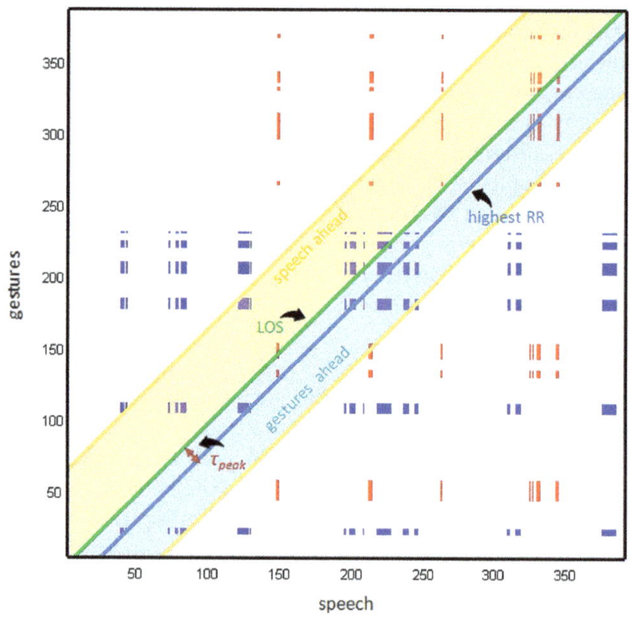

FIGURE 3 | Cross recurrence plot (CRP) of one child (boy, 55 months).

of the other children are available as supplementary materials. In this study, matching states (i.e., recurrent points) are defined as same-tier skill levels, and are color-coded in the CRP as follows: blue dots represent instances in which gestures and speech both display a skill level from the sensorimotor tier (i.e., skill levels 1, 2, or 3). Red dots represent instances in which the skill levels as displayed by gestures and speech are both from the representational tier (i.e., skill levels 4, 5, or 6). Finally, yellow dots in the CRP represent a gesture–speech recurrence of the highest, abstract tier (i.e., skill level 7). The latter did not occur in our sample and these recurrences will therefore not appear in the analysis.

In **Figure 3**, the green diagonal line is the LOS, on which recurrent points have a delay of 0 s. These represent instances when both speech and gestures display a skill level from the same tier at the *exact* same time. The percentage of recurrent points on this line is called the percentage of synchrony (%Sync), which is a measure of linear static synchrony of the two subsystems. The recurrence rate (RR) is a measure depicting the proportion of recurrent points in the entire CRP. Hence, RR reflects the extent to which behaviors of one subsystem are matched by those of the other subsystem across all possible time scales, from the high end determined by the sample rate of 1 s, up until the low end determined by the duration of the observation. As such, RR is a basic measure of the coupling and coordination of the two subsystems. In the CRP of **Figure 3**, the skill-level time series of gestures is plotted on the vertical axis and the skill-level time series of verbalizations on the horizontal axis. This means that all colored dots above the LOS represent instances in which a skill level expressed in speech earlier in time is matched by same-tier skill level expressed in gestures at a later moment. Congruously, colored dots below the LOS represent instances in which skill levels from the same tier are displayed by gestures at an earlier moment and matched by speech later.

As can be seen in **Figure 3**, most colored dots in the CRP align to form block and line structures. Generally, such structures indicate instances where behaviors which are briefly expressed by one subsystem are accompanied by episodes of lingering in the matching behavior by the other subsystem. This provides information about the shared dynamics of the gesture–speech interaction, and specifically about the strength and direction of the coupling between the two subsystems, as we shall demonstrate (see Cox et al., 2016). Thus far, research using CRQA has focused on diagonal and vertical lines. However, notice how the line structures in the CRP stretch into the horizontal and vertical direction (and not diagonal), which is quite common for categorical time series. Analysis of the diagonal lines and the associated measures will therefore not be discussed here.

The different directions of the line structures (vertical and horizontal) provide differential and complementary information about the coupling between the two subsystems represented by the time series along the axes. For instance, a vertical line structure in the CRP (**Figure 3**) means that a brief skill-level expression in speech is followed (above LOS) or preceded (below LOS), with some delay, by a much longer same-tier skill level expression in gestures. Similarly, horizontal line structures represent instances in which a skill level that is expressed briefly in gestures, is followed (below LOS) or preceded (above LOS) by a much longer same-tier skill level in speech. More generally, line structures represent instances in which shortly expressed skill levels from a certain tier in one subsystem 'trapped' the other subsystem in a lingering same-tier expression for some time. In this study we will relate them to the relative strength and direction of the gesture–speech coupling, such that vertical line structures reflect the extent to which speech subsystems influence gestures, whereas horizontal line structures reflect the extent to which gestures subsystems influence speech.

To capture the asymmetric dynamic attunement between gestures and speech, we performed *anisotropic* CRQA (Cox et al., 2016), by calculating recurrence measures for the horizontal and vertical line structures separately and comparing them. The first measure derived from the line structures is 'Laminarity,' defined as the proportion of recurrent points that are part of a vertical (LAM_V) or horizontal (LAM_H) line structure. Laminarity reflects the degree to which subsystems are trapped into expressing a same-tier skill level for some period of time. LAM_V depicts how much gestures constitute larger structures of points in the CRP, whereas LAM_H does so for speech. Second, 'Trapping Time' is the average length of either the vertical (TT_V) or horizontal (TT_H) line structures. TT is measured in units of time and estimates how long subsystems are, on average, trapped in a specific state. In our study, the higher TT is, the longer a same-tier skill level from one time series lingers in the other one. If TT_V is high, gestures tend to be trapped in relatively long periods of same-tier skill levels that are also expressed by speech at some point, and for high TT_H speech tends to be trapped in relatively long periods of same-tier skill levels that are also expressed by gestures at some point. Finally, 'Maximum Line' also gives information about duration of line structures, with $MaxL_V$ the length of the longest vertical line and $MaxL_H$ the length of the longest horizontal line. In other words, MaxL measures the duration of the longest same-tier skill-level expression for speech and gestures. High $MaxL_V$ means that gestures are trapped in a single tier of skill levels, and $MaxL_H$ means that speech is trapped strongly in a single tier.

These three measures have been related to behavioral rigidity and regularity in previous studies (De Graag et al., 2012; Cox and Van Dijk, 2013). Accordingly, in the present study, we will interpret the CRQA-measures of horizontal and vertical line structures as 'differential' rigidity of speech and gestures, respectively. In addition, the relative size of these measures informs about the relative strength and direction of the coupling between speech and gestures.

LOS-Profile Analysis

Besides analyzing the global structure of the recurrence plot, we will also look in more detail at several recurrence measures within a smaller time window around the LOS (see, e.g., Richardson and Dale, 2005; Reuzel et al., 2013, 2014). **Figure 4** depicts the so-called LOS profile of an interval of 60 s on each side of the LOS, derived from the CRP in **Figure 3**. The LOS profiles of the other children are available as supplementary materials. The interval of 60 s above and below the LOS is chosen intuitively, so as speech and gestures can either lead or follow each other with a maximum delay of 1 min. In **Figure 4**, the position of the LOS, corresponding to a delay of 0 s, is indicated with a green line. The LOS profile is drawn 'from the perspective' of gestures, in that a positive delay indicates instances of recurrence in which gestures are ahead of speech in time (blue area), whereas a negative delay indicates instances in which speech is ahead of gestures (yellow area). The orange envelope curve represents the RR at each delay; this delay is called τ (RR_τ ; see, e.g., Marwan et al., 2007).

Several measures can be derived from this LOS profile, which inform about the coordination of the two subsystems within the chosen interval of 2 min around the LOS. Firstly, in **Figure 4** the RR shows a clear peak of around 0.09 at a delay of 16 s. This maximum recurrence rate, defined as the highest proportion of recurrent points within the LOS profile, is called RR_{peak}, and is indicated with the blue line in **Figure 4**. The distance of this peak from the LOS (in seconds), or in other words, the delay of RR_{peak}, is called τ_{peak}, and is indicated with the red arrows. Please note that τ_{peak}, with a value of 16 s, is also visible in **Figure 2**, as the skill levels displayed in gestures are clearly ahead in time of the skill levels displayed in speech. An example of what a match between gestures and speech with a delay of 16 s could be is: with his hands, a boy depicts that if you turn a switch, the ball will roll down the tube (level 3, tier 1). Around 16 s later, he says: "It [the ball] rolls, because it is round" (level 3, tier 1). The final measure that we can derive from the LOS profile is Q_{LOS}. Q_{LOS} is the total proportion of recurrent points at the left side of the LOS (yellow area), divided by the total proportion of recurrent points at the right side of the LOS (blue area). If Q_{LOS} is lower than 1, this indicates that gestures are generally leading speech in time, whereas a Q_{LOS} with a value higher than 1 indicates the opposite.

Research Questions and Hypotheses

The research question of the current study is: does the leading role of gestures over speech in children's cognitive change, as reported in previous studies, arise from and reflect an underlying dynamic interplay between gestures and speech during task performance? To answer this general question, four specific research CRQA questions and corresponding hypotheses were formulated, which will be introduced below.

Research Question 1

The first research question is: what is the temporal relation between gestures and speech, with regard to the displayed (skill) level of understanding? Studies thus far demonstrated that, across tasks, children express their cognitive insights in gestures before they are able to put them into words (Crowder and Newman, 1993; Gershkoff-Stowe and Smith, 1997; Garber and Goldin-Meadow, 2002). Here we will investigate whether these results can be extrapolated to a smaller (i.e., within-task) time scale, and whether theoretical claims of previous studies can be corroborated and possibly extended to the perspective of gesture–speech mismatches as originating from the suboptimal simultaneous coordination of the gestures- and speech synergies. To this end we performed LOS-profile analysis on the gesture–speech interaction. The associated measures should display a significant asymmetry in the amount of recurrence around the LOS (Q_{LOS}) and display a recurrence peak (RR_{peak}) at some delay

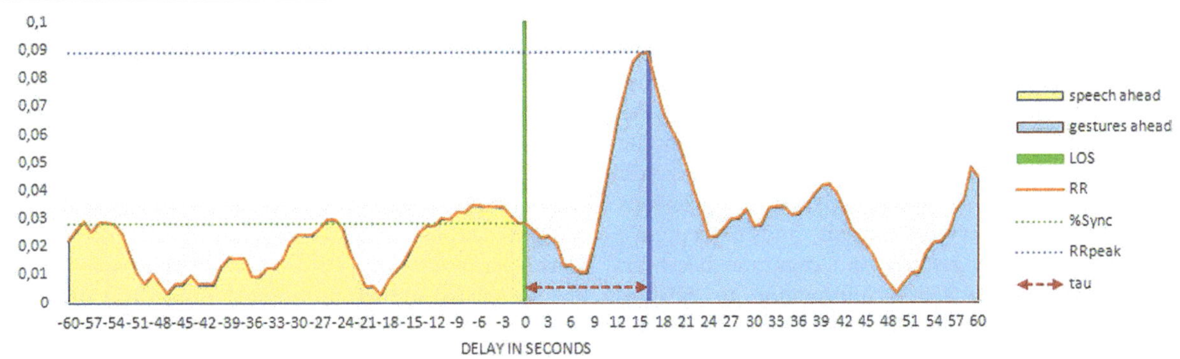

FIGURE 4 | LOS (line of synchrony) profile plot of one child (boy, 55 months).

(τ_{peak}) in the blue area of children's LOS profile (see **Figure 4**), indicating a leading role of gestures on speech.

Research Question 2

The second research question is: what is the relative strength and direction of the interaction coupling between the gesture and speech subsystems? For this we looked at LAM, TT, and MaxL for both vertical and horizontal line structures, across the entire CRP. The mutual, ongoing, possibly asymmetric influence between gestures and speech will be visible in the CRP by the isentropic patterns of colored line structures representing same-tier skill levels. Accordingly, we expect vertical and horizontal LAM, TT and MaxL, and especially their differences, to inform us about the coupled dynamics of gestures and speech, and its potential asymmetry with regard to strength and direction.

Research Question 3

The third research question is closely related to the second, but focused on the specific skill-level tiers: what is the relative strength and direction of the interaction between gestures and speech *for the different levels of understanding* (i.e., skill-level tiers)? To investigate this, two CRPs were analyzed and compared for each child. The first CRP *only* displayed matches of gestures and speech of a skill level from the sensorimotor (S-)tier (i.e., levels 1, 2, or 3), while the second CRP *only* displayed matches of a skill level from the representational (R-)tier (i.e., levels 4, 5, or 6). Subsequently, vertical and horizontal LAM, TT, and MaxL were calculated from these CRPs, and compared on the group level. Furthermore, to capture the relative strength and direction of the coupling, that is, the asymmetry between gestures and speech within a child, we calculated a relative difference score for each measure, for each child. This relative difference score is defined as the standardized difference between the measures derived from the vertical lines minus the measures derived from the horizontal line, as follows: V-H_{LAM} was calculated as $LAM_V - LAM_H$ (LAM is a proportion and can readily be compared), V-H_{TT} as $(TT_V - TT_H)/(TT_V + TT_H)$, and V-$H_{MaxL}$ as $(MaxL_V - MaxL_H)/(MaxL_V + MaxL_H)$. A model simulation by Cox et al. (2016) of the relation between relative difference in coupling strength and relative difference in horizontal and vertical line measures showed a strong association between relative coupling strength and the difference between LAM and TT, but not for MaxL. The relative difference scores of the S- and R-tier scores were also compared on a group level.

There are two reasons to expect dynamic differences in the gesture–speech interaction for different levels of understanding. First, as explained, skill levels from the sensorimotor tier include expressions about perceptions, action, and observable relations between these perceptions and actions, whereas skill levels from the representational tier are assigned to expressions that go beyond these observable actions and perceptions. Previously, the link between gestures and cognition has been assigned to gestures adding action information to existing mental representations (Beilock and Goldin-Meadow, 2010) and gestures simulating actions (Hostetter and Alibali, 2010). This presumed close relation between actions and gestures might culminate in a different interplay between gestures and speech at the sensorimotor tier compared to the representational tier. Also, more complicated levels of understanding are likely to arise when the task is complicated, that is to say, when children perceive the task to be more challenging. A challenging task might trigger learning, and previously it has been shown that gesture–speech mismatches tend to occur when a child is on the verge of learning something new (Goldin-Meadow, 2003). As described earlier, we suggest that gesture–speech mismatches in a difficult, new and/or challenging task, arise from suboptimal simultaneous coordination of the gesture and speech synergies. When this suboptimal simultaneous coordination happens, the tight coupling between the action systems breaks down and becomes less dynamically stable and strong than for a less challenging task. Together we are inclined to expect that vertical and horizontal LAM, TT, and MaxL will show different patterns of values at different levels of understanding.

Research Question 4

The final research question is: how are the measures of coordination between gestures and speech subsystems related to more stable child characteristics and school outcome measures, such as age and general level of cognitive performance? Children's use of speech and gestures is known to change over time (Goldin-Meadow, 1998). These changes are necessarily reflected in the dynamic organization of gestures and speech. Furthermore, as there is a link between gestures and cognition (Perry et al., 1988), children's general level of cognitive performance is also expected to be related to this dynamic organization. We investigate these possible relations by calculating correlations between Age, Math score, Language score, and Average skill level across the previous five interactions with the researcher and the LOS-profile measures (%Sync, RR_{peak}, Q_{LOS}, and τ_{peak}), the CRQA-measures (RR, LAM_V, LAM_H, TT_V, TT_H, $MaxL_V$, and $MaxL_H$) derived from the sensorimotor and representational tier, and the relative difference scores (V-H_{LAM}, V-H_{TT}, and V-H_{MaxL}) for each of the tiers.

Monte Carlo Analysis

Throughout the Section Results, *p*-values for differences between two measures were calculated by using Monte Carlo permutation tests (Todman and Dugard, 2001), which enabled us to reliably obtain significance levels with this relatively small sample (Ninness et al., 2002). Using this procedure, the probability that an empirically observed difference can be found was repeatedly calculated, in this case 1000 times, each time using a random distribution of the original data. If the average probability that the difference occurs in these random samples was small (i.e., <0.05), we concluded that there is an actual difference present in the empirical data, which cannot be simulated using random samples, and hence, was not caused by chance. When a Monte Carlo permutation test was used to compare two values, we also calculated the effect size in the form of Cohen's *d*, that is, the observed difference divided by the pooled SD. A value of *d* between 0.2 and 0.3 is generally considered to be small, a value around 0.5 as medium, and a value of 0.8 and higher as large (Cohen, 1988).

RESULTS

Research Question 1: What is the Temporal Relation between Gestures and Speech, in Terms of their Displayed Skill Level?

For the first research question we expected that the LOS-profile analysis measures would display a significant asymmetry in the amount of recurrence around the LOS (Q_{LOS}) and display a peak in the recurrence (RR_{peak}) at some delay (τ_{peak}), indicating a leading role of gestures on speech. An overview of the values for Q_{LOS}, RR_{peak}, and τ_{peak} in our sample can be found in **Table 2**. As described in the Section "Materials and Methods," if Q_{LOS} is lower than 1, this suggests that gestures are leading speech in time. In our sample, Q_{LOS} ranged from 0.48 to 1.78, with an average of 1.08 which was not significantly higher than 1 ($p = 0.72$). The average Q_{LOS} ($M = 0.86$) of the children in Kindergarten was lower than the average Q_{LOS} ($M = 1.24$) of the children in first grade ($p = 0.04$, $d = 0.90$). This suggests that the gesture–speech dynamics had an opposite temporal pattern in the two age groups, with a leading role for speech for the first graders.

The observed RR_{peak} should exceed chance level, that is, there should be a real peak in the profile, for the observed τ_{peak} to make any sense. To verify this, a Monte Carlo procedure was performed to assess whether children's observed RR_{peak} significantly differed from chance. This was the case for all children in our sample (all p-values < 0.01), except for child 3 ($p = 0.63$). Therefore τ_{peak} of child 3 was not included in the subsequent analyses of this research question. On average τ_{peak} was 6.09 within the group, which was significantly higher than 0 ($p = 0.03$), indicating that gestures were ahead of speech in time. The average τ_{peak} of children in Kindergarten ($M = 18$) differed from that of the first graders ($M = -0.71$; $p < 0.01$, $d = 2.22$). In addition, the average τ_{peak} of children in Kindergarten was significantly higher than 0 ($p < 0.01$) and the average τ_{peak} of children in the first grade was significantly lower than 0 ($p < 0.01$). This is conform the earlier result (above), meaning that for the younger children in our sample gestures were ahead in time of speech (18 s on average), whereas, oppositely, gestures were behind in time of speech (0.71 s on average) for the older children.

Research Question 2: What is the Relative Strength and Direction of the Interaction between the Gesture and Speech Subsystems?

See **Table 2** for an overview of LAM, TT, and MaxL for both vertical and horizontal line structures. LAM_V ranged from 0.893 to 1.000 ($M = 0.975$), which means that 89.3–100% of the recurrent points comprised vertical line structures. TT_V ranged from 3.2 to 8.3 ($M = 5.8$), indicating that the average vertical lines in the recurrence plot consisted of 3.2–8.3 recurrent points. This reflects that gestures were trapped into same-tier skill-level episodes with average durations between 3 and 8 s for the different children. $MaxL_V$ ranged from 5 to 26 ($M = 17.6$), which means that the maximum length of a vertical line in an individual recurrence plot ranged from 5 to 26 recurrent points. In other words, the maximum episode of gestures being trapped into a same-tier skill level lasted between 5 and 26 s. Calculations of the horizontal line structures revealed that the extent to which speech is trapped into displaying the same-tier skill level was somewhat less, with LAM_H ranging from 0.624 to 0.924 ($M = 0.805$), TT_H ranging from 2.3 to 5.5 ($M = 3.7$), and $MaxL_H$ ranging from 3 to 27 ($M = 9.2$). At the group level, LAM_V, TT_V, and $MaxL_V$ were higher than LAM_H, TT_H, and $MaxL_H$, respectively (all p-values < 0.01; $d_{LAMV > LAMH} = 2.01$; $d_{TTV > TTH} = 1.72$; $d_{MaxLV > MaxLH} = 1.31$). Interestingly, this is true for all children for LAM and TT, and for 9 out of 12 children also for MaxL. This finding clearly suggests an asymmetric dynamic attunement of gestures and speech, with gestures relatively more regularly and more rigidly displaying the same-tier skill level compared to speech.

TABLE 2 | Overview of LOS-profile measures and CRQA-measures of all 12 childrens.

		LOS profile analysis measures			CRQA-measures over entire CRP						
Child	**Grade**	Q_{LOS}	RR_{peak}	τ_{peak}	**RR**	LAM_V	LAM_H	TT_V	TT_H	$MaxL_V$	$MaxL_H$
1	KG	0.46	0.056	18	0.013	0.986	0.910	5.2	3.4	21	7
2	KG	0.58	0.089	16	0.019	0.996	0.885	6.4	3.8	19	10
3	KG	0.91	0.015	–	0.004	0.968	0.687	4.3	2.6	12	3
4	KG	0.98	0.076	2	0.011	1.000	0.885	7.4	5.1	26	11
5	KG	1.31	0.012	36	0.002	0.893	0.901	3.2	3.1	5	6
6	1	1.28	0.034	−1	0.010	0.957	0.701	6.6	2.6	16	5
7	1	0.48	0.039	−1	0.009	0.979	0.922	5.8	4.0	18	12
8	1	1.65	0.034	0	0.006	0.973	0.624	4.8	2.8	12	5
9	1	0.90	0.140	0	0.025	0.992	0.924	6.3	5.1	15	15
10	1	0.92	0.053	−1	0.016	1.000	0.789	6.0	5.5	25	27
11	1	1.78	0.021	−1	0.002	0.959	0.632	5.4	2.7	18	3
12	1	1.66	0.073	−1	0.018	1.000	0.793	8.3	3.6	24	6
Mean	–	*1.08*	*0.053*	*6.09*	*0.011*	*0.975*	*0.805*	*5.8*	*3.7*	*17.6*	*9.2*

Research Question 3: What is the Relative Strength and Direction of the Gesture–Speech Interaction for Different Skill-Levels Tiers?

We expected RR and vertical and horizontal LAM, TT, and MaxL to be different for different levels of understanding. To analyze this, we first compared the averages of RR, LAM_V, LAM_H, TT_V, TT_H, $MaxL_V$, and $MaxL_H$ on the sensorimotor (S-)tier with those on the representational (R-)tier. An overview of these CRQA-measures can be found in **Table 3** (S-tier) and **Table 4** (R-tier). The differences between the CRQA-measures of the S-tier or R-tier are weak to absent ($p_{RR} = 0.19$, $d = 0.31$; $p_{LAM-V} = 0.45$, $d = 0.05$; $p_{TT-V} = 0.45$, $d = 0.03$; $p_{MaxL-V} = 0.45$, $d = 0.05$; $p_{\text{LAM-H}} = 0.42$, $d = 0.08$; $p_{TT-H} = 0.91$, $d = 0.54$; $p_{MaxL-H} = 0.36$, $d = 0.12$). This means that there were no group-level differences in the relative strength and direction of the interaction between gestures and speech for lower (S-tier) levels nor for higher (R-tier) levels of understanding.

Next, we analyzed whether the measures derived from the vertical and horizontal line structures showed the same pattern of differences for the S-tier and R-tier. LAM_V was not higher than LAM_H for both the S-tier ($M_{LAM-V} = 0.496$, $M_{LAM-H} = 0.391$, $p = 0.14$, $d = 0.38$) and the R-tier ($M_{LAM-V} = 0.479$, $M_{LAM-H} = 0.413$, $p = 0.30$, $d = 0.22$). However, the analysis revealed TT_V to be higher than TT_H for both the S-tier ($M_{TT-V} = 5.81$, $M_{TT-H} = 3.19$, $p < 0.01$, $d = 2.06$) and R-tier ($M_{TT-V} = 5.75$, $M_{TT-H} = 3.88$, $p = 0.01$, $d = 0.99$). In addition, $MaxL_V$ was higher than $MaxL_H$ for both the S-tier ($M_{MaxL-V} = 12.42$, $M_{MaxL-H} = 7.50$, $p = 0.03$, $d = 0.80$) and R-tier ($M_{MaxL-V} = 12.75$, $M_{MaxL-H} = 6.83$, $p = 0.02$, $d = 0.92$).

TABLE 3 | Overview of the CRQA-measures, calculated over skill levels 1–3 (sensorimotor tier).

	Child	Grade	% RR*	LAM_V	LAM_H	$V\text{-}H_{LAM}$	TT_V	TT_H	$V\text{-}H_{TT}$	$MaxL_V$	$MaxL_H$	$V\text{-}H_{MaxL}$
	1	KG	66.9	0.669	0.595	0.074	7.6	3.2	0.41	21	7	0.50
	2	KG	29.3	0.289	0.226	0.063	8.3	2.5	0.53	19	3	0.73
	3	KG	99.3	0.961	0.687	0.273	4.3	2.3	0.31	12	3	0.60
	4	KG	7.2	0.072	0.048	0.024	6.0	3.2	0.30	6	7	−0.08
	5	KG	73.3	0.733	0.672	0.061	3.2	3.1	0.01	5	6	−0.09
	6	1	95.6	0.915	0.672	0.243	6.7	2.6	0.44	16	5	0.52
	7	1	31.5	0.308	0.248	0.059	7.0	3.3	0.37	18	5	0.57
	8	1	73.9	0.721	0.480	0.241	4.3	2.7	0.24	8	4	0.33
	9	1	29.8	0.290	0.267	0.023	7.6	3.9	0.32	15	15	0.00
	10	1	60.3	0.603	0.539	0.064	5.1	5.4	−0.03	10	27	−0.46
	11	1	20.5	0.192	0.103	0.089	4.7	3.0	0.22	10	3	0.54
	12	1	19.8	0.198	0.161	0.037	5.0	3.3	0.21	9	5	0.29
M	–	*KG*	*55.2*	*0.545*	*0.446*	*0.10*	*5.9*	*2.9*	*0.31*	*12.6*	*5.2*	*0.33*
M	–	*1*	*47.3*	*0.461*	*0.353*	*0.11*	*5.8*	*3.4*	*0.25*	*12.3*	*9.1*	*0.26*
M		*Overall*	*50.6*	*0.496*	*0.391*	*0.104*	*5.8*	*3.2*	*0.28*	*12.4*	*7.5*	*0.29*

% RR reflects the percentage of recurrence found on the S-tier, as compared to the overall recurrence rate on both the S- and R-tier, displayed in **Table 2.*

TABLE 4 | Overview of the CRQA-measures, over skill levels 4–6 (representational tier).

	Child	Grade	% RR*	LAM_V	LAM_H	$V\text{-}H_{LAM}$	TT_V	TT_H	$V\text{-}H_{TT}$	$MaxL_V$	$MaxL_H$	$V\text{-}H_{MaxL}$
	1	KG	33.1	0.316	0.315	0.002	3.1	3.9	−0.11	5	7	−0.17
	2	KG	70.7	0.707	0.660	0.047	5.8	4.7	0.11	9	10	−0.05
	3	KG	0.7	0.007	0.000	0.007	3.0	0.0	1.00	3	1	0.50
	4	KG	92.8	0.928	0.837	0.090	7.5	5.3	0.17	26	11	0.41
	5	KG	26.7	0.160	0.229	−0.069	3.0	3.0	0.00	3	5	−0.25
	6	1	4.4	0.042	0.030	0.013	4.8	4.0	0.09	7	4	0.27
	7	1	68.5	0.671	0.674	−0.003	5.3	4.4	0.09	11	12	−0.04
	8	1	26.1	0.252	0.145	0.107	7.0	3.3	0.35	12	5	0.41
	9	1	70.2	0.702	0.657	0.045	5.8	5.9	−0.01	10	10	0.00
	10	1	39.7	0.397	0.250	0.147	8.2	5.7	0.18	25	8	0.52
	11	1	79.5	0.767	0.530	0.237	5.6	2.7	0.35	18	3	0.71
	12	1	80.2	0.802	0.632	0.170	9.8	3.7	0.45	24	6	0.60
M		*KG*	*44.8*	*0.424*	*0.408*	*0.02*	*4.5*	*3.4*	*0.23*	*9.2*	*6.8*	*0.09*
M	–	*1*	*52.7*	*0.519*	*0.417*	*0.10*	*6.7*	*4.2*	*0.21*	*15.3*	*6.9*	*0.35*
M	*Overall*	*Overall*	*49.4*	*0.479*	*0.413*	*0.066*	*5.8*	*3.9*	*0.22*	*12.8*	*6.8*	*0.24*

% RR reflects the percentage of recurrence found on the S-tier, as compared to the overall recurrence rate on both the S- and R-tier, displayed in **Table 2.*

Lastly, the relative difference scores between the S-tier and R-tier did not differ ($p_{V-H-LAM} = 0.15$, $d = 0.43$; $p_{V-H-TT} = 0.28$, $d = 0.22$; $p_{V-H-MaxL} = 0.38$, $d = 0.13$).

To summarize, the average differences between the CRQA-measures of vertical and horizontal lines showed the same pattern for the S-tier and R-tier. This means that the relative strength and direction of the coupling between gestures and speech did not differ between the levels of understanding. At the group level, they were similarly asymmetric for both tiers. Also, laminarity (LAM) did not show the same asymmetry at the individual levels of understanding, as it did when the tiers were joined together for Research Question 2.

Does Age Play a Role?

Prompted by the differences between younger and older children found for Research Question 1, we investigated whether similar age-group differences were present in the strength and direction of the interaction between gestures and speech for different levels of understanding. To this end, we compared the children in Kindergarten and first grade with regard to their CRQA-measures and relative difference scores on the S-tier and R-tier. These measures are displayed in **Tables 3** and **4**.

For the S-tier, no clear differences between the CRQA-measures of younger and older children were found ($p_{RR} = 0.26$, $d = 0.34$; $p_{LAM-V} = 0.30$, $d = 0.26$; $p_{LAM-H} = 0.25$, $d = 0.37$; $p_{TT-V} = 0.46$, $d = 0.05$; $p_{TT-H} = 0.07$, $d = 0.73$; $p_{MaxL-V} = 0.50$, $d = 0.06$; $p_{MaxL-H} = 0.12$, $d = 0.57$). There were also no differences between the younger and older children with regard to the average relative difference scores on the S-tier ($p_{V-HLAM} = 0.41$, $d = 0.09$; $p_{V-HTT} = 0.24$, $d = 0.36$; $p_{V-HMaxL} = 0.35$, $d = 0.20$). For the R-tier, only TT_V of the older children was higher than TT_V of the younger children ($p_{TT-V} = 0.04$, $d = 1.12$). Even though the other CRQA measures on the R-tier might appear to be higher for the older children, no meaningful differences were found ($p_{RR} = 0.40$, $d = 0.17$; $p_{LAM-V} = 0.31$, $d = 0.29$; $p_{LAM-H} = 0.48$, $d = 0.03$; $p_{TT-H} = 0.17$, $d = 0.54$; $p_{MaxL-V} = 0.12$, $d = 0.73$; $p_{MaxL-H} = 0.51$, $d = 0.02$). Considering the relative difference scores, only V-H_{LAM} was higher for older than for younger children ($p_{V-HLAM} = 0.02$, $d = 1.11$). There were no clear difference for V-H_{TT} ($p_{V-HTT} = 0.46$, $d = 0.06$) and only slightly for V-H_{MaxL} ($p_{V-HMaxL} = 0.07$, $d = 0.85$).

In conclusion, for the less difficult levels of understanding on the S-tier, older and younger children did not differ in the strength and direction of the interaction between gestures and speech. However, for the more difficult levels of understanding there were age-differences in the asymmetry of the gesture–speech interaction: gestures displayed longer average periods of lingering in the R-tier (TT_V) and were more regular (V-H_{LAM}) for the older children than for the younger children.

Research Question 4: How are the Measures of Coordination between Gestures and Speech Subsystems Related to More Stable Child Characteristics and School Outcome Measures?

An overview of the significant correlations between child characteristics and school outcome measures, and the LOS-profile measures, CRQA -measures and relative difference scores can be found in **Table 5**. The entire correlation table is available in the supplementary materials. First we will describe the findings for the LOS-profile measures across both tiers, followed by the CRQA-measures and relative difference scores separately for each tier.

When recurrences on the sensorimotor and representational tier are combined, the correlation of %Sync and age had a value of 0.57. This means that relatively older children tended to show the same-tier skill level at the same time in gestures and

TABLE 5 | Significant correlations between child characteristics and CRQA-measures.

		Age (months)	Math score	Language score	Average score past tasks
Both tiers	%Sync	0.57*			
	τ_{peak}	−0.73**			
S-tier	LAM_V		−0.54*		−0.58**
	LAM_H				−0.52*
	V-H_{LAM}		−0.62**		−0.58**
	TT_V			0.53*	
	V-H_{TT}			0.59*	
R-tier	LAM_V		0.51*		0.56*
	LAM_H		0.57*		0.54*
	V-H_{LAM}	0.65**			
	TT_V	0.51*			
	TT_H	0.61**			0.61**
	V-H_{TT}		−0.68**		−0.67**
	$MaxL_H$	0.65**			
	V-H_{MaxL}	0.52*	−0.50*		

*Values marked with * are significant at $p < 0.1$, values marked with ** are significant at $p < 0.05$. The complete correlation matrix can be found in the supplementary materials.*

speech. The correlation of −0.73 between τ_{peak} and age in months corroborates to this finding, as it implies that younger children tended to show a more extensive delay between gestures and speech in displaying the same-tier skill level, with gestures being ahead of speech in time.

For the S-tier separately, LAM_V and V-H_{LAM} were both negatively correlated with children's Math score and Average score on past tasks ($r = -0.54$ and $r = -0.58$, respectively). This means that for children who performed better on math and past tasks, gestures were being trapped into S-tier episodes less prominently. Moreover, for these children the asymmetry between gestures and speech was smaller. LAM_H was also negatively correlated with the average score on past tasks ($r = -0.52$), which suggests that for children with a higher score on past tasks, speech was less prone to be trapped into S-tier episodes as well. Language score was correlated with TT_V ($r = 0.53$) and V-H_{TT} ($r = 0.59$) on the S-tier, which shows that for children with a higher Language score, gestures were trapped into longer average S-tier episodes, and that the associated asymmetry between gestures and speech tends to be bigger.

For the more difficult skill-levels on the R-tier, it turns out that all CRQA and LOS profile measures are significantly correlated with age or measures of general performance. Both LAM_V and LAM_H are correlated with Math score ($r = 0.51$ and $r = 0.57$, respectively) and the average score on past tasks ($r = 0.56$ and $r = 0.54$, respectively). This suggests that for children with a higher score on math or past tasks, both speech and gestures were trapped into R-tier episodes more often. Age correlates with V-H_{LAM}, which means that the asymmetry between gestures and speech tended to be bigger for older children. TT_V was related to Age ($r = 0.51$), suggesting that older children were trapped into longer average R-tier gesturing episodes. Both Age and Average score on past tasks were correlated with TT_H ($r = 0.61$ and $r = 0.61$, respectively), which means that children who are older or who performed better on past tasks were trapped into longer average R-tier speech episodes. As V-H_{TT} is negatively correlated with both Math score and Average score on past tasks ($r = -0.68$ and $r = -0.67$, respectively), children who performed well on math or past tasks tended to display a smaller asymmetry in the average duration of gestures and speech R-tier lingering. $MaxL_H$ and V-H_{MaxL} were related to age ($r = 0.65$ and $r = 0.52$, respectively), which suggests that older children had a longer maximum episode of speech being trapped at the R-tier, but at the same time, the asymmetry between gestures and speech tended to be larger for this. Finally, V-H_{MaxL} was negatively correlated with Math score ($r = -0.50$). So children with a higher score on math had a smaller asymmetry in the longest gestures and speech R-tier lingering episode.

DISCUSSION

Summary of Results

The present study concentrated on how the earlier reported leading role of gestures over speech in children's cognitive change arises from the asymmetries in the dynamic attunement of gestures and speech during task performance. Appreciating the dynamic nature of this issue naturally implied using of the language and methods of complex dynamical systems. Accordingly, we used CRQA, a novel non-linear time series method, to analyze the two skill-level time series as coded from children's gestures and speech while they were working on an educational science task. To be able to address this rather broad issue intelligibly we proposed four specific research questions, focusing on: (1) the temporal relation between gestures and speech, (2) the relative strength and direction of the interaction between gestures and speech, (3) the relative strength and direction between gestures and speech for different levels of understanding, and (4) the relations between measures of dynamic organization and more stable child characteristics and school outcome measures.

Firstly, regarding the temporal relation, older and younger children differed in the (temporal) asymmetry in the gestures–speech interaction. In the 2 min window of the LOS-profile analysis, in younger, i.e., Kindergarten, children, the balance leant more toward gestures leading speech in time, whereas the balance leant more toward speech leading gestures in time for the older first-grade students. This difference between older and younger children is even more pronounced when we look at the actual temporal delay in seconds. While gestures are, on average, ahead of speech for 18 s for the younger children, speech only slightly precedes gestures for just under a second for the older children.

Secondly, we investigated the relative strength and direction of the interaction between gestures and speech as it plays out on all possible timescales, ranging from the sample rate (1 s) to the entire interaction (~489 s). As described earlier, calculating and comparing recurrence measures of vertical and horizontal line structures is informative about the coordinative structures in the gesturing–speech interaction. At the group level, we found LAM, TT, and MaxL to point toward speech influencing gestures more regularly and rigidly into displaying the same-tier skill level than vice versa. Moreover, when comparing the strength and direction for different levels of understanding (Research Question 3), this asymmetry in gestures and speech extended to both the sensorimotor and representational tier. The relative difference scores did not differ for the S-tier and R-tier. In other words, there are no differences in the coupling between gestures and speech for different levels of understanding at the group level.

However, when we compared the CRQA measures for different levels of understanding of children from first grade and Kindergarten, an interesting pattern of differences appeared. Although no differences were present at the S-tier, at the more difficult R-tier level of understanding, older and younger children did differ in the coupling between gestures and speech. All CRQA measures were higher for the older children at the R-tier, suggesting that the coupling between gestures and speech was more rigid at higher levels of understanding.

The relation of age with the coupling between gestures and speech is also apparent when we relate the CRQA measures to individual child characteristics. The correlations between age and %Sync, and between age and τ_{peak} support the results from the LOS-profile analysis. This again shows that gestures are more ahead of speech in time when children are younger, and that they are more temporally aligned when children are older. The results reveal a larger asymmetry in the gesture–speech attunement for older children. A higher score on schools' standardized language tests is also related to more asymmetry between gestures and speech, but only for the less difficult levels of understanding (S-tier).

However, children's average score on past tasks and their scores on math seem to be related to speech attracting gestures less, and also to less asymmetry between gestures and speech for the less difficult levels of understanding. For the more difficult levels of understanding (R-tier), both speech and gestures tend to attract each other more for children with a higher score on math or past tasks, which points to more symmetry between speech and gestures. Moreover, a higher score on math or past tasks is also related to less asymmetry between gestures and speech at the R-tier.

Dynamic, Entangled Development of Gestures, Speech, and Cognitive Skills

Earlier studies have shown that children express new cognitive insights by means of gestures before they are able to put them into words. An important nuance following from the present study is that although gestures might appear to be ahead in time of speech during children's learning, this does not imply that gestures influence speech to a larger extent. Learning is a process that occurs at multiple, nested time scales, by means of entangled processes of action, perception and cognition. In studies thus far, such a process approach has not been considered with respect to the interplay of gestures and speech in children's learning. At the very least our study shows that the relation between gestures, speech, and cognition in our sample is much more dynamic and bidirectional than previously thought, with a high degree of inter-individual variability. In addition, children differ in how speech and gestures are coupled, whereby gestures are not always ahead of speech, or leading speech, as cognitive understanding unfolds. Moreover, the gestures-speech coupling is related to age and measures of scholastic and cognitive performance that exceed the time-span of a single task.

Age, Language Score, and the Dynamic Emergence of Speech and Gestures

One particularly prominent result is that, with increasing age, speech and gestures become more synchronized and tightly coupled. Within this tight coupling for older children, speech attracts gestures more than vice versa in displaying the same-tier skill level. A possible explanation for this finding can be found in Iverson and Thelen's (1999) account of the dynamic emergence of speech and gestures. They suggest that the link between speech and gestures starts with the hand-mouth linkage that is already apparent in newborns. Coordination between oral and manual actions is very common in newborn's spontaneous actions, such as bringing their hands to the facial area or sucking their fingers. These connections between oral and manual actions are characterized by a low threshold—as they are so easily and spontaneously performed—and high activation, because of their frequency. Around the age of 6–8 months, both rhythmical arm movement and rhythmical babbling emerge, through which coinciding vocal and manual activities are entrained.

The linkages between the hands and mouth become more controlled as children develop, with the emergence of the first gestures and words around 9–14 months of age. Typically, children's gestures precede and outnumber their spoken words tremendously during this period. To be more specific, children's pointing gestures precede the word for an object by, on average, 3 months, and gesture-plus-word combinations precede two-word combinations by an average of 4.7 months (Iverson and Goldin-Meadow, 2005). According to Iverson and Thelen (1999), the reason for this is that, in comparison to the vocal articulators, the control of the hands is more advanced and therefore it is easier for children to communicate by means of gestures. In other words, for gestures the threshold is low and activation is high, while for speech the threshold is high and activation is low. However, as children practice their vocal skills, the threshold of speech becomes lower and activation higher. The activation of speech eventually becomes so high, that it captures and concurrently activates gestures. Stated differently, as children's language skills become more advanced, their speech system activates their gesture system, and thereby the two motor systems become more synchronized.

Returning to our finding that older children in our sample show higher levels of synchronization and coupling between speech and gestures. It is safe to assume that older children have more developed speech and gesture synergetic control. The reason for this is that both action systems have been explored and practiced more, and under more different and variable task conditions, than in the younger children (cf. Iverson and Thelen, 1999). Because of this, the speech and gesture synergies are more entrained, which means that older children can coordinate the two synergies more optimally and simultaneously. This reasoning and the finding that speech influences gestures more than vice versa in older children, is in line with Iverson and Thelen's (1999) notion of speech capturing gestures when vocal skills become more practiced. A final noteworthy observation in this respect is that the older children in our sample just entered first grade, in which they learn to read and write. Although speculative at this point, it is not farfetched to expect that this emphasis on language in the first grade increases how much speech is able to influence gestures (cf. Shanahan and Roof, 2013).

As already implied in the previous section, the explanation that gestures are ahead of speech in time for the younger children, with an average delay of 18 s, might also be found in the simultaneous coordination of the synergies of speech and gestures. For the younger children the task might be more difficult than for the older children, and pose considerably more conflicting task constraints. These conflicting task constraints may cause the two synergies to be unable to simultaneously exist in an optimal way. This makes the tightly coupled synergies dissociate, with the gesture synergy being created first and the speech-synergy later. The average lag of 18 s between speech and gestures might intuitively seem hard to understand, but such contingencies over relatively large timescales have been found before in the context of communication, albeit with younger children. For example, Jaffe et al. (2001) report a 20–30 s lag between contingencies in the vocal patterns of 4-months-old infants and their mothers or strangers. Moreover, Jaffe et al. (2001) point to other studies, which found a 20–30 s cycle in infant attention (Brazelton et al., 1974), a 10–45 s cycle in coordination of facial engagement (Lester et al., 1985), and a 20 s lag in facial engagement correlation (Cohn and Tronick, 1988). Although this concerns interpersonal coordination, these studies demonstrate that latencies of this magnitude are not extreme.

Jaffe et al. (2001) propose that the 20–30 s lag between contingencies in the vocal patterns of the infants and their mother or a stranger is an indication for a slow rhythm in the interaction. This slow rhythm can only be found by analyzing the data in much detail, as opposed to rhythms such as vocalization-pause or turn taking, which are detectable for untrained observers. To return to our study: both speech and gestures are suggested to originate from coinciding rhythmical activities (Iverson and Thelen, 1999; Abney et al., 2014), and in fact, speech and gestures are rhythmical activities in itself (Loehr, 2007). The average delay between speech and gestures of 18 s that we found for the younger children might be a slow rhythm in the gesture–speech interaction. This slow rhythm may reside in a process on a larger timescale, in which both the synergies of gestures and speech are nested. Which specific process this would be remains a question for future research.

The relation we found between a higher language score and more asymmetry in the speech-gesture coupling fits with the dynamic emergence account of speech and gestures as outlined above. With an explained variance of 25%, better language skills are associated with a stronger influence of speech on gestures. Interestingly, the relation between a higher language score and more asymmetry is not apparent for the higher levels of understanding on the R-tier. An explanation for this might be that the levels of understanding on the R-tier go beyond the skill of naming observable task characteristics, but rather involve relations among task elements, and relations among relations (cf. Fischer and Bidell, 2006; see below). A second explanation might be that understanding on the R-tier is more difficult, which causes a different interplay between the synergies of speech and gestures than on the S-tier - in this case less asymmetry in influence.

Average Score on Past Tasks, Math-Score, and Higher-Order Understanding Emerging from Actions

Contrary to age and language score, a higher average score on past tasks is not related to a leading role of speech over gestures, but instead to a more symmetric interaction between speech and gestures. In order to grasp this finding, consider how higher-order understanding emerges from actions. In a previous study, participants were asked to perform a gear task and predict the turning direction of a target gear (Trudeau and Dixon, 2007). At first, all participants simulated the motions of the gears with their hands, i.e., force tracing, to predict in which direction the target gear would turn. After a certain number of these problems, participants discovered a higher-order relation, alternation, which is concealed in the task. Alternation, like all higher-order relations, is a relation among relations and requires coordinating two or more lower-order relations and integrating multiple actions over time. Participants varied considerably in how many simulations they performed before discovering alternation, and Trudeau and Dixon (2007) found that the number of alternating actions performed before discovering the higher-order rule predicted the likelihood of generalization of this rule to new problem types. Trudeau and Dixon (2007) explained this finding by stating that for participants who made more correct alternating actions before discovering the higher order rule, the representation of alternation stems from a larger corpus of actions. This larger corpus of relevant (i.e., task-related) actions increases the chance of discovering and being able to generalize the higher-order relation. Extrapolating on this thought, children for whom speech is less leading over gestures might be more open to gesturing, that is, they might gesture more. This provides them with the larger corpus of actions, which increases their chance of discovering higher-order relations by means of actions, resulting in a higher score on (past) tasks.

Even more so, the gestures of children may also elicit discovering these higher-order relations in other tasks. Indeed, Smith (2010) has emphasized the essence of the motor system in learning higher-order regularities. She states that "It is action that creates a task, that couples component systems in the moment, and that selects and creates the momentary dynamic input on which learning must depend" (p. 264). In the context of action, component systems become coupled and coordinated within diverse tasks, which makes action essential for learning higher-order relations and generalizing learning such relations to other tasks. With respect to our findings, gesturing may also elicit the discovery of higher-order relations in other tasks, which might explain why children for whom speech was less leading over gestures performed better on past tasks.

Next to a higher average score on past tasks, a higher math score is also related to a more symmetric interaction between gestures and speech, whereby speech is less leading over gestures. Note that these two scores were highly correlated ($r = 0.84$), meaning that children who scored high on math were also likely to have done well on previous tasks. It is well-known that gestures are beneficial for math learning (e.g., Cook and Goldin-Meadow, 2006; Ehrlich et al., 2006; Broaders et al., 2007; Alibali and Nathan, 2012; Cook et al., 2012, 2013; Novack et al., 2014). The reason why gestures are related to math might be the same as why gestures are related to a higher average score on past tasks: from gestures, higher-order (mathematical) understanding can emerge and generalize. Indeed, Cook et al. (2013) and Novack et al. (2014) found that gestures are related to the generalization and transfer of mathematical knowledge to new problem types.

To summarize this subsection, children within our study for whom speech is less leading over gestures may perform better on both math and past tasks because they are more open to gesturing, from which higher-order understanding is thought to emerge and generalize. A reason for this might lie in the importance of variability in learning (e.g., Van Geert and Van Dijk, 2002). If the first system influences the second system to a lesser degree, that second system is obviously less constrained by the first, and can adhere more adaptively to task requirements. In other words, the coupling of the two systems can be characterized as more flexible, which allows for different types of coordination between them and with the environment.

Following the framework introduced earlier, we interpret the finding that speech is less leading over gestures in terms of synergetic competition. Accordingly, a decreasing leading role of speech over gestures indicates a more optimal and efficient (simultaneous) coordination of both synergies. However this optimal coordination of both synergies does not necessarily have to be simultaneous since we found that more temporal synchrony of speech and gestures is not related to a better score on past tasks or a better math performance in our study. Future studies could focus more specifically on how improved understanding of concepts and/or performance on a task is related to a more optimal (possibly but not necessarily simultaneous) coordination of both the speech and gestures synergies. This could become visible, for instance, by a decrease in the temporal delay between gesture and speech behaviors (Goldin-Meadow et al., 1993), a phase-transition like change from a period of suboptimal coordination of one or both synergies to state of simultaneous optimal coordination (cf. Haken et al., 1985), or perhaps by a change in the temporal structure of gestures and speech (Wijnants et al., 2009, 2012a; cf. Den Hartigh et al., 2015).

CONCLUSION

Our results suggest that speech and gestures may be more *tightly coupled* for the older children in first grade and children with a high language score, because their speech and gesture systems are more developed. The reason that speech *leads* over gestures for these children may as well stem from this developmental process, and might be enhanced by the emphasis on language in first grade. For children with a higher average score on past tasks and math score, speech is leading less over gestures, possibly leaving more room for higher-order understanding to emerge from their action experiences through gesturing. Because of the time-intensive coding procedures and the in-debt nature of our analyses, this study used a small *N*. Note that we used Monte Carlo permutation tests, which are particularly strong in the case of small sample sizes. The credibility of our results is further strengthened by the relatively large effect sizes we found (Cohen, 1988). Nonetheless, this study deserves replication to check whether the findings can be verified and eventually also further refined and strengthened.

It is important to note that speech leading less over gestures is not the same as *less speech* or *less coupling between gestures and speech*. In fact, higher-order understanding, and more broadly speaking, cognition itself, resides in and emerges from the coupling between a multitude of perception-action subsystems, such as those related to speech and gestures (Goldin-Meadow, 1998). Congruously, within our study, the child for whom there was no RR_{peak}, that is, for whom coupling between gestures and speech was weaker, had low scores on all the other variables of cognitive performance. To elaborate, it is not the mere presence or absence of coupling between subsystems that is important, but rather the nature of their coupling, in the sense of interaction-dominant dynamics (Van Orden et al., 2003, 2005). How the subsystems are coupled determines how development will progress, and whether and how higher-order understanding will occur. Our findings suggest that a coupling in which the influence of gestures and speech is more balanced (i.e., where speech is less leading), seems to be beneficial for higher-order understanding to develop in this respect, in a hands-on science and technology task.

As cognition resides in and emerges from the dynamic coupling between perception-action subsystems, and learning is a non-linear process with variability as its hallmark, methods that capture this coupling over time are necessary to understand how development comes about. The complex dynamical systems approach provides a framework for asking question and interpreting answers pertaining to how higher-order relations can emerge from perception-action couplings. In our study, we investigated how the speech and gesture subsystems of children are coupled during a hands-on educational science task. Among other things, we found this coupling to be related to other measures of cognitive performance. Instead of gestures expressing or adding to a rather disembodied cognitive insight before speech is able to express it, we outlined how higher-order understanding might emerge from the changing coupling between gestures and speech over time. Moreover, we proposed a new mechanism, of competing and suboptimal coordinated synergies resulting in gestures-speech mismatches, that builds a bridge between the existing research on gestures and recent views on cognition as fundamentally embedded and embodied. Future studies should investigate if the dynamic organization of gestures and speech indeed points to gesture–speech mismatches as originating from competing synergies of gestures and speech.

AUTHOR CONTRIBUTIONS

LDJ-H: draft of manuscript, coding of videos, design coding system gestures, design figures and tables, interpretation of analyses. SVdS: draft of manuscript, task administration with children, coding of videos, design coding system speech, correlation analyses. PVG: editing of manuscript, general advice on research procedure and writing, suggestions for references, calculation effect sizes. RC: draft and editing of manuscript, recurrence quantification analyses (ideas and execution), interpretation of analyses.

FUNDING

Part of this study was funded by the program "Platform Betatechniek," supported by the Dutch ministry of Education, Culture and Science (Ministerie van Onderwijs, Cultuur en Wetenschap).

REFERENCES

Abney, D. H., Warlaumont, A. S., Haussman, A., Ross, J. M., and Wallot, S. (2014). Using nonlinear methods to quantify changes in infant limb movements and vocalizations. *Front. Psychol.* 5:771. doi: 10.3389/fpsyg.2014.00771

Aßmann, B., Romano, M. C., Thiel, M., and Niemitz, C. (2007). Hierarchical organization of a reference system in newborn spontaneous movements. *Infant Behav. Dev.* 30, 568–586. doi: 10.1016/j.infbeh.2007.04.004

Alibali, M. W., and Goldin-Meadow, S. (1993). "Modeling learning using evidence from speech and gesture," in *Proceedings of the Fifteenth Annual Conference of the Cognitive Science Society* (Hillsdale, NJ: Erlbaum), 203–208.

Alibali, M. W., and Nathan, M. J. (2012). Embodiment in mathematics teaching and learning: evidence from learners' and teachers" gestures. *J. Learn. Sci.* 21, 247–286. doi: 10.1080/10508406.2011.611446

Anastas, J. R., Stephen, D. G., and Dixon, J. A. (2011). The scaling behavior of hand motions reveals self-organization during an executive function task. *Physica A* 390, 1539–1545. doi: 10.1016/j.physa.2010.11.038

Anderson, M. L., Richardson, M. J., and Chemero, A. (2012). Eroding the boundaries of cognition: implications of embodiment. *Top. Cogn. Sci.* 4, 717–730. doi: 10.1111/j.1756-8765.2012.01211.x

Beilock, S. L., and Goldin-Meadow, S. (2010). Gesture changes thought by grounding it in action. *Psychol. Sci.* 21, 1605–1610. doi: 10.1177/09567976 10385353

Boncoddo, R., Dixon, J. A., and Kelley, E. (2010). The emergence of a novel representation from action: evidence from preschoolers. *Dev. Sci.* 13, 370–377. doi: 10.1111/j.1467-7687.2009.00905.x

Bos, J., and Steenbeek, H. (2006). *MediaCoder: A Simple Application for Coding Behavior Within Media Files*. Groningen: University of Groningen.

Brazelton, T. B., Kozlowski, B., and Main, M. (1974). "The origins of reciprocity," in *The Effect of the Infant On Its Caregiver*, eds M. Lewis and L. Rosenblum (New York: Elsevier).

Broaders, S. C., Cook, S. W., Mitchell, Z., and Goldin-Meadow, S. (2007). Making children gesture brings out implicit knowledge and leads to learning. *J. Exp. Psychol. Gen.* 136, 539–550. doi: 10.1037/0096-3445.136.4.539

Carey, S., and Spelke, E. (1994). "Domain-specific knowledge and conceptual change," in *Mapping the Mind: Domain Specificity in Cognition and Culture*, eds L. A. Hirshfeld and S. A. Gelman (Cambridge: Cambridge University Press), 169–200.

Church, R. B., and Goldin-Meadow, S. (1986). The mismatch between gesture and speech as an index of transitional knowledge. *Cognition* 23, 43–71. doi: 10.1016/0010-0277(86)90053-3

Cohen, J. (1988). *Statistical Power Analysis for the Behavioral Sciences*. Hillsdale, NJ: Lawrence Erlbaum Associates, 590.

Cohn, J., and Tronick, E. (1988). Mother-infant face-to-face interaction: influence is bidirectional and unrelated to periodic cycles in either partner's behavior. *Dev. Psychol.* 24, 386–392. doi: 10.1037/0012-1649.24.3.386

Cook, S. W., Duffy, R. G., and Fenn, K. M. (2013). Consolidation and transfer of learning after observing hand gesture. *Child Dev.* 84, 1863–1871. doi: 10.1111/cdev.12097

Cook, S. W., and Goldin-Meadow, S. (2006). The role of gesture in learning: do children use their hands to change their minds? *J. Cogn. Dev.* 7, 211–232. doi: 10.1207/s15327647jcd0702_4

Cook, S. W., Yip, T. K., and Goldin-Meadow, S. (2012). Gestures, but not meaningless movements, lighten working memory load when explaining math. *Lang. Cogn. Proc.* 27, 594–610. doi: 10.1080/01690965.2011.567074

Cox, R. F. A., Van der Steen, S., Guevara, M., De Jonge-Hoekstra, L., and Van Dijk, M. (2016). "Chromatic and anisotropic cross-recurrence quantification analysis of interpersonal behaviour," in *Proceedings in Mathematics & Statistics: Recurrence Plots and Their Quantifications: Expanding Horizons*, eds C. Webber, C. Ioana, and N. Marwan (New York, NY: Springer Verlag).

Cox, R. F. A., and Van Dijk, M. (2013). Micro-development in parent-child conversations: from global changes to flexibility. *Ecol. Psychol.* 25, 304–315. doi: 10.1080/10407413.2013.810095

Crowder, E. M., and Newman, D. (1993). Telling what they know: the role of gesture and language in children's science explanations. *Pragmat. Cong.* 1, 341–376. doi: 10.1075/pc.1.2.06cro

Dale, R., and Spivey, M. (2006). Unraveling the dyad: using recurrence analysis to explore patterns of syntactic coordination between children and caregivers in conversation. *Lang. Learn.* 56, 391–430. doi: 10.1111/j.1467-9922.2006.00372.x

De Graag, J. A., Cox, R. F. A., Hasselman, F., Jansen, J., and De Weerth, C. (2012). Functioning within a relationship: mother-infant synchrony and infant sleep. *Infant Behav. Dev.* 35, 252–263. doi: 10.1016/j.infbeh.2011.12.006

Den Hartigh, R. J. R., Cox, R. F. A., Gernigon, C., Van Yperen, N. W., and Van Geert, P. L. C. (2015). Pink noise in rowing ergometer performance and the role of skill level. *Motor Control* 19, 355–369. doi: 10.1123/mc.2014-0071

Ehrlich, S. B., Levine, S. C., and Goldin-Meadow, S. (2006). The importance of gesture in children's spatial reasoning. *Dev. Psychol.* 42, 1259–1268. doi: 10.1037/0012-1649.42.6.1259

Fischer, K. W. (1980). A theory of cognitive development: the control and construction of hierarchies of skills. *Psychol. Rev.* 87, 477–531. doi: 10.1037/0033-295X.87.6.477

Fischer, K. W., and Bidell, T. R. (2006). "Dynamic development of action, thought and emotion," in *Theoretical Models of Human Development. Handbook of Child Psychology*, 6th Edn, eds W. Damon and R. M. Lerner (New York, NY: Wiley), 86.

Flynn, E., Pine, K., and Lewis, C. (2007). Using the microgenetic method to investigate cognitive development: an introduction. *Infant Child Dev.* 16, 1–6. doi: 10.1002/icd.503

Galantucci, B., Fowler, C. A., and Turvey, M. T. (2006). The motor theory of speech perception reviewed. *Psychon. Bull. Rev.* 13, 361–377. doi: 10.3758/BF03193857

Garber, P., and Goldin-Meadow, S. (2002). Gesture offers insight into problem-solving in adults and children. *Cogn. Sci.* 26, 817–831. doi: 10.1207/s15516709cog2606_5

Gelman, R. (2004). *Cognitive Development: Stevens' Handbook of Experimental Psychology*. Hoboken, NJ: John Wiley and Sons, Inc. doi: 10.1002/0471214426.pas0212

Gershkoff-Stowe, L., and Smith, L. B. (1997). A curvilinear trend in naming errors as a function of early vocabulary growth. *Cogn. Psychol.* 34, 37–71. doi: 10.1006/cogp.1997.0664

Goldin-Meadow, S. (1998). The development of gesture and speech as an integrated system. *New Dir. Child Adolesc. Dev.* 79, 29–42. doi: 10.1002/cd.23219 987903

Goldin-Meadow, S. (2003). *Hearing Gesture: How Our Hands Help us Think*. Cambridge, MA: Harvard University Press, 304.

Goldin-Meadow, S., Alibali, M. W., and Church, R. B. (1993). Transitions in concept acquisition: using the hand to read the mind. *Psychol. Rev.* 100, 279–297. doi: 10.1037/0033-295X.100.2.279

Goldin-Meadow, S., Cook, S. W., and Mitchell, Z. A. (2009). Gesturing gives children new ideas about math. *Psychol. Sci.* 20, 267–272. doi: 10.1111/j.1467-9280.2009.02297.x

Goldin-Meadow, S., Levine, S. C., Zinchenko, E., Yip, T. K., Hemani, N., and Factor, L. (2012). Doing gesture promotes learning a mental transformation task better than seeing gesture. *Dev. Sci.* 15, 876–884. doi: 10.1111/j.1467-7687.2012.01185.x

Goldin-Meadow, S., Nusbaum, H., Kelly, S. D., and Wagner, S. (2001). Explaining math: gesturing lightens the load. *Psychol. Sci.* 12, 516–522. doi: 10.1111/1467-9280.00395

Goldin-Meadow, S., Wein, D., and Chang, C. (1992). Assessing knowledge through gesture: using children's hands to read their minds. *Cogn. Instr.* 9, 201–219. doi: 10.1207/s1532690xci0903_2

Granott, N., Fischer, K. W., and Parziale, J. (2002). "Bridging to the unknown: a transition mechanism in learning and development," in *Microdevelopment: Transition Processes in Development and Learning*, eds N. Granott and J. Parziale (Cambridge: Cambridge University Press), 25.

Grannot, N., and Parziale, J. (eds) (2002). *Microdevelopment: Transition Processes in Development and Learning*. Cambridge: Cambridge University Press, 368.

Haken, H. (1977/1983). *Synergetics, An Introduction: Nonequilibrium Phase Transitions and Self-Organization in Physics, Chemistry and Biology*. Berlin: Springer.

Haken, H., Kelso, J. A. S., and Bunz, H. (1985). A theoretical model of phase transitions in human hand movements. *Biol. Cybern.* 51, 347–356. doi: 10.1007/BF00336922

Hoekstra, L. (2012). *Curious Minds: Children's Hands and their Scientific Understanding: The Construction of a Coding System for Gestures and Acting on*

Material, and an Exploratory Case Study. Ph.D. thesis, University of Groningen, Groningen.

Hostetter, A. B., and Alibali, M. W. (2010). Language, gesture, action! A test of the Gesture as Simulated Action framework. *J. Mem. Lang.* 63, 245–257. doi: 10.1016/j.jml.2010.04.003

Iverson, J. M., and Goldin-Meadow, S. (2005). Gesture paves the way for language development. *Psychol. Sci.* 16, 367–371. doi: 10.1111/j.0956-7976.2005.01542.x

Iverson, J. M., and Thelen, E. (1999). Hand, mouth and brain: the dynamic emergence of speech and gesture. *J. Conscious. Stud.* 6, 19–40.

Jacoby, W. G. (2000). Loess: a nonparametric, graphical tool for depicting relationships between variables. *Elect. Stud.* 19, 577–613. doi: 10.1016/S0261-3794(99)00028-1

Jaffe, J., Beebe, B., Feldstein, S., Crown, C. L., and Jasnow, M. D. (2001). Rhythms of dialogue in infancy: coordinated timing in development. *Monogr. Soc. Res. Child Dev.* 66, 1–132.

Kelso, J. A. S. (1995). *Dynamic Patterns: The Self-Organization of Brain and Behavior*. Cambridge, MA: The MIT Press.

Kugler, P. N., and Turvey, M. T. (1987). *Information, Natural Law, and the Self-Assembly of Rhythmic Movement*. Hillsdale, NJ: Lawrence Erlbaum Associates, Inc.

Lester, B. M., Hoffman, J., and Brazelton, T. B. (1985). The rhythmic structure of mother-infant interaction in term and preterm infants. *Child Dev.* 56, 15–27. doi: 10.2307/1130169

Lichtwarck-Aschoff, A., Hasselman, F., Cox, R. F. A., Pepler, D., and Granic, I. (2012). A characteristic destabilization profile in parent-child interactions associated with treatment efficacy for aggressive children. *Nonlinear Dynamics Psychol. Life Sci.* 16, 353–379.

Loehr, D. (2007). Aspects of rhythm in gesture and speech. *Gesture* 7, 179–214. doi: 10.1075/gest.7.2.04loe

Louwerse, M. M., Dale, R., Bard, E. G., and Jeuniaux, P. (2012). Behavior matching in multimodal communication is synchronized. *Cogn. Sci.* 36, 1404–1426. doi: 10.1111/j.1551-6709.2012.01269.x

Marwan, N., Carmen Romano, M., Thiel, M., and Kurths, J. (2007). Recurrence plots for the analysis of complex systems. *Phys. Rep.* 438, 237–329. doi: 10.1016/j.physrep.2006.11.001

Marwan, N., and Webber, C. L. Jr. (2014). "Mathematical and computational foundations of recurrence quantifications," in *Recurrence Quantification Analysis: Theory and Best Practices*, eds C. L. Webber Jr. and N. Marwan (New York, NY: Springer), 41.

McNeill, D. (1992). *Hand and Mind: What Gestures Reveal about Thought*. Chicago, IL: University of Chicago Press.

Ninness, C., Newton, R., Saxon, J., Rumph, R., Bradfield, A., Harrison, C., et al. (2002). Small group statistics: a Monte Carlo comparison of parametric and randomization tests. *Behav. Soc. Issues* 12, 53–63. doi: 10.5210/bsi.v12i1.79

Novack, M. A., Congdon, E. L., Hemani-Lopez, N., and Goldin-Meadow, S. (2014). From action to abstraction: using the hands to learn math. *Psychol. Sci.* 25, 903–910. doi: 10.1177/0956797613518351

Perry, M., Church, R. B., and Goldin-Meadow, S. (1988). Transitional knowledge in the acquisition of concepts. *Cogn. Dev.* 3, 359–400. doi: 10.1016/0885-2014(88)90021-4

Perry, M., Church, R. B., and Goldin-Meadow, S. (1992). Is gesture-speech mismatch a general index of transitional knowledge? *Cogn. Dev.* 7, 109–122. doi: 10.1016/0885-2014(92)90007-E

Piaget, J., and Cook, M. (Trans.) (1952). *The Origins of Intelligence in Children*, 2nd Edn. New York, NY: W. W. Norton and Company, 418.

Pine, K. J., Lufkin, N., Kirk, E., and Messer, D. (2007). A microgenetic analysis of the relationship between speech and gesture in children: evidence for semantic and temporal asynchrony. *Lang. Cogn. Proc.* 22, 234–246. doi: 10.1080/01690960600630881

Reed, E. S. (1982). An outline of a theory of action systems. *J. Mot. Behav.* 14, 98–134. doi: 10.1080/00222895.1982.10735267

Reuzel, E., Embregts, P. J. C. M., Bosman, A. M. T., Cox, R., Van Nieuwenhuijzen, M., and Jahoda, A. (2013). Conversational synchronization in naturally occurring settings: a recurrence-based analysis of gaze directions and speech rhythms of staff and clients with intellectual disability. *J. Nonverbal Behav.* 37, 281–305. doi: 10.1007/s10919-013-0158-9

Reuzel, E., Embregts, P. J. C. M., Bosman, A. M. T., Cox, R. F. A., Van Nieuwenhuijzen, M., and Jahoda, A. (2014). Verbal interactional dominance and coordinative structure of speech rhythms of staff and clients with an intellectual disability. *Nonlinear Dynamics Psychol. Life Sci.* 18, 371–396.

Richardson, D. C., and Dale, R. (2005). Looking to understand: the coupling between speakers' and listeners' eye movements and its relationship to discourse comprehension. *Cogn. Sci.* 29, 39–54. doi: 10.1207/s15516709cog0000_29

Richardson, D. C., Dale, R., and Kirkham, N. Z. (2007). The art of conversation is coordination: common ground and the coupling of eye movements during dialogue. *Psychol. Sci.* 18, 407–413. doi: 10.1111/j.1467-9280.2007.01914.x

Richardson, M. J., Schmidt, R. C., and Kay, B. A. (2007). Distinguishing the noise and attractor strength of coordinated limb movements using recurrence analysis. *Biol. Cybern.* 96, 59–78. doi: 10.1007/s00422-006-0104-6

Schwartz, M. S., and Fischer, K. W. (2004). "Building general knowledge and skill: cognition and microdevelopment in science learning," in *Cognitive Developmental Change: Theories, Models, and Measurement*, eds A. Demetriou and A. Raftopoulos (Cambridge: Cambridge University Press), 28.

Shanahan, L. E., and Roof, L. M. (2013). Developing strategic readers: a multimodal analysis of a primary school teacher's use of speech, gesture and artefacts. *Literacy* 47, 157–164. doi: 10.1111/lit.12002

Shockley, K., Butwill, M., Zbilut, J. P., and Webber, C. L. Jr. (2002). Cross recurrence quantification of coupled oscillators. *Phys. Lett. A* 305, 59–69. doi: 10.1016/S0375-9601(02)01411-1

Shockley, K., Santana, M. V., and Fowler, C. A. (2003). Mutual interpersonal postural constraints are involved in cooperative conversation. *J. Exp. Psychol. Hum. Percept. Perform.* 29, 326–332. doi: 10.1037/0096-1523.29.2.326

Siegler, R. S. (1989). Mechanisms of cognitive development. *Annu. Rev. Psychol.* 40, 353–379. doi: 10.1146/annurev.ps.40.020189.002033

Siegler, R. S. (2006). "Microgenetic analyses of learning," in *Handbook of Child Psychology*, 6th Edn, eds D. Kuhn and R. Siegler (Hoboken, NJ: John Wiley and Sons, Inc.), 46.

Siegler, R. S. (2007). Cognitive variability. *Dev. Sci.* 10, 104–109. doi: 10.1111/j.1467-7687.2007.00571.x

Smith, L. B. (2010). Action as developmental process – a commentary on Iverson's "Developing language in a developing body: the relationship between motor development and language development". *J. Child Lang.* 37, 263–267. doi: 10.1017/S0305000909990535

Smith, L. B., and Thelen, E. (2003). Development as a dynamic system. *Trends Cogn. Sci.* 7, 343–348. doi: 10.1016/S1364-6613(03)00156-6

Stephen, D. G., Boncoddo, R. A., Magnuson, J. S., and Dixon, J. A. (2009a). The dynamics of insight: mathematical discovery as a phase transition. *Mem. Cogn.* 37, 1132–1149. doi: 10.3758/MC.37.8.1132

Stephen, D. G., Dixon, J. A., and Isenhower, R. W. (2009b). Dynamics of representational change: entropy, action, and cognition. *J. Exp. Psychol. Hum. Percept. Perform.* 35, 1811–1832. doi: 10.1037/a0014510

Sternberg, R. J. (1984). *Mechanisms of Cognitive Development*. New York, NY: Freeman, 218.

Thelen, E. (2000). Grounded in the world: developmental origins of the embodied mind. *Infancy* 1, 3–28. doi: 10.1207/S15327078IN0101_02

Thelen, E., and Corbetta, D. (2002). "Microdevelopment and dynamic systems: applications to infant motor development," in *Microdevelopment: Transition Processes in Development and Learning*, eds N. Granott and J. Parziale (Cambridge: Cambridge University Press), 20.

Thelen, E., and Smith, L. B. (2007). "Dynamic systems theories," in *The Child: An Encyclopedic Companion*, eds Shweder and A. Richard (Chicago, IL: The University Of Chicago Press), 264–265. doi: 10.1002/9780470147658.chpsy0106

Todman, J. B., and Dugard, P. (2001). *Single-Case and Small-n Experimental Designs: A Practical Guide to Randomization Tests*. Mahwah, NJ: Lawrence Erlbaum Associates Publishers, 304.

Trudeau, J. J., and Dixon, J. A. (2007). Embodiment and abstraction: actions create relational representations. *Psychon. Bull. Rev.* 14, 994–1000. doi: 10.3758/BF03194134

Turvey, M. T. (2007). Action and perception at the level of synergies. *Hum. Mov. Sci.* 26, 657–697. doi: 10.1016/j.humov.2007.04.002

Van der Steen, S. (2014). *"How Does It Work?" A Longitudinal Microgenetic Study On The Development Of Young Children's Understanding Of Scientific Concepts*. Doctoral dissertation, University of Groningen, Groningen.

Van der Steen, S., Steenbeek, H., Van Dijk, M., and Van Geert, P. (2014). A process approach to children's understanding of scientific concepts: a longitudinal case study. *Learn. Individ. Diff.* 30, 84–91. doi: 10.1016/j.lindif.2013.12.004

Van der Steen, S., Steenbeek, H., and Van Geert, P. (2012). "Using the dynamics of a person-context system to describe children's understanding of air pressure," in *Current Topics in Children's Learning and Cognition*, eds H. Kloos, B. J. Morris, and J. L. Amaral (Rijeka: InTech), 21–44.

Van Geert, P. (1998). A dynamic systems model of basic developmental mechanisms: Piaget, Vygotsky, and beyond. *Psychol. Rev.* 105, 634–677. doi: 10.1037//0033-295X.105.4.634-677

Van Geert, P. (2003). "Dynamic systems approaches and modeling of developmental processes," in *Handbook of Developmental Psychology*, eds J. Valsiner and K. J. Conolly (London: Sage), 32.

Van Geert, P. (2008). "Nonlinear complex dynamic systems in developmental psychology," in *Chaos and Complexity in Psychology - The Theory of Nonlinear Dynamical Systems*, eds S. Guastello, M. Koopmans, and D. Pincus (Cambridge: Cambridge University Press), 39.

Van Geert, P. (2011). The contribution of complex dynamic systems to development. *Child Dev. Perspect.* 5, 273–278. doi: 10.1111/j.1750-8606.2011.00197.x

Van Geert, P., and Steenbeek, H. (2005). Explaining after by before: basic aspects of a dynamic systems approach to the study of development. *Dev. Rev.* 25, 408–442. doi: 10.1016/j.dr.2005.10.003

Van Geert, P., and Van Dijk, M. (2002). Focus on variability: new tools to study intra-individual variability in developmental data. *Infant Behav. Dev.* 25, 340–374. doi: 10.1016/S0163-6383(02)00140-6

Van Geert, P. L. C., and Fischer, K. W. (2009). "Dynamic systems and the quest for individual based models of change and development," in *Toward a New Grand Theory of Development? Connectionism and Dynamic Systems Theory Reconsidered*, eds J. P. Spencer, M. S. C. Thomas, and J. McClelland (Oxford: Oxford University Press), 22.

Van Orden, G. C., Holden, J. G., and Turvey, M. T. (2003). Self-organization of cognitive performance. *J. Exp. Psychol. Gen.* 132, 331–350. doi: 10.1037/0096-3445.132.3.331

Van Orden, G. C., Holden, J. G., and Turvey, M. T. (2005). Human cognition and 1/f scaling. *J. Exp. Psychol. Gen.* 134, 117–123. doi: 10.1037/0096-3445.134.1.117

Vygotsky, L. S. (1994). "The development of academic concepts in school aged children," in *The Vygotsky Reader*, eds R. Van der Veer and J. Valsiner (Oxford: Wiley-Blackwell), 15.

Webber, C. L. Jr., and Zbilut, J. P. (2005). "Recurrence quantification analysis of nonlinear dynamical systems," in *Tutorials in Contemporary Nonlinear Methods for the Behavioral Sciences*, eds M. A. Riley and G. C. Van Orden (Arlington, VA: National Science Foundation), 68.

Weiss, E. J., and Flanders, M. (2004). Muscular and postural synergies of the human hand. *J. Neurophysiol.* 92, 523–535. doi: 10.1152/jn.01265.2003

Wijnants, M. L., Bosman, A. M. T., Hasselman, F., Cox, R. F. A., and Van Orden, G. C. (2009). 1/f scaling fluctuation in movement time: temporal structure changes with massed practice. *Nonlinear Dynamics Psychol. Life Sci.* 13, 79–98.

Wijnants, M. L., Cox, R. F. A., Hasselman, F., Bosman, A. M. T., and Van Orden, G. C. (2012a). A trade-off study revealing nested timescales of constraint. *Front. Physiol.* 3:116. doi: 10.3389/fphys.2012.00116

Wijnants, M. L., Hasselman, F., Cox, R. F. A., Bosman, A. M. T., and Van Orden, G. (2012b). An interaction-dominant perspective on reading fluency and dyslexia. *Ann. Dyslexia* 62, 100–119. doi: 10.1007/s11881-012-0067-3

Yan, Z., and Fischer, K. (2002). Always under construction: dynamic variations in adult cognitive microdevelopment. *Hum. Dev.* 45, 141–160. doi: 10.1159/000057070

Zbilut, J. P., Giuliani, A., and Webber, C. L. Jr. (1998). Detecting deterministic signals in exceptionally noisy environments using cross-recurrence quantification. *Phys. Lett. A* 246, 122–128. doi: 10.1016/S0375-9601(98)00457-5

Conflict of Interest Statement: The authors declare that the research was conducted in the absence of any commercial or financial relationships that could be construed as a potential conflict of interest.

17

Performance of Motor Sequences in Children at Heightened vs. Low Risk for ASD: A Longitudinal Study from 18 to 36 Months of Age

Valentina Focaroli[1], Fabrizio Taffoni[2], Shelby M. Parsons[3], Flavio Keller[1] and Jana M. Iverson[3]*

[1] Laboratory of Developmental Neuroscience, Università Campus Biomedico di Roma, Rome, Italy, [2] Laboratory of Biomedical Robotics and Biomicrosystems, Università Campus Biomedico di Roma, Rome, Italy, [3] Department of Psychology, University of Pittsburgh, Pittsburgh, PA, USA

Recent research shows that motor difficulties are a prominent component of the behavioral profile of autism spectrum disorder (ASD) and are also apparent from early in development in infants who have an older sibling with ASD (High Risk; HR). Delays have been reported for HR infants who do and who do not receive an eventual diagnosis of ASD. A growing body of prospective studies has focused on the emergence of early motor skills primarily during the first year of life. To date, however, relatively little work has examined motor skills in the second and third years. Thus, the present research was designed to investigate motor performance in object transport tasks longitudinally in HR and LR (Low Risk) children between the ages of 18 and 36 months. Participants (15 HR children and 14 LR children) were observed at 18, 24, and 36 months. Children completed two motor tasks, the Ball Task and the Block Task, each of which included two conditions that varied in terms of the precision demands of the goal action. Kinematic data were acquired via two magneto inertial sensors worn on each wrist. In the Block Task, HR children reached more slowly (i.e., mean acceleration was lower) compared to LR children. This finding is in line with growing evidence of early delays in fine motor skills in HR children and suggests that vulnerabilities in motor performance may persist into the preschool years in children at risk for ASD.

Keywords: motor development, autism spectrum disorder, fine motor skills, reaching, kinematic data

Edited by:
Petra Hauf,
St. Francis Xavier University, Canada

Reviewed by:
Chris Lange-Küttner,
London Metropolitan University, UK
Fabia Franco,
Middlesex University, UK

****Correspondence:***
Valentina Focaroli
v.focaroli@unicampus.it

INTRODUCTION

Children who have an older sibling with a diagnosis of autism spectrum disorder (ASD) are at heightened risk (HR) for developing ASD and other developmental delays than are children with a typically-developing older sibling and no family history of ASD (Low Risk; LR; Ozonoff et al., 2011; Messinger et al., 2013). Due to the importance of early identification and intervention in achieving positive outcomes for individuals with ASD, there has been a surge of interest in conducting prospective studies of HR infants (see Gliga et al., 2014; Jones et al., 2014, for reviews). One of the most robust findings in this literature is that as a group, HR children, and even those who do not receive an ASD diagnosis, display high inter-individual variability in multiple developmental domains (Zwaigenbaum et al., 2005, 2009). Of importance for the present study is the now widely reported finding of motor delays in HR infants from the first months of life (e.g., Flanagan et al., 2012; Nickel et al., 2013; Libertus et al., 2014). Specifically, at 6 months, HR infants with no subsequent ASD diagnosis have been shown to exhibit less grasping of objects (Kaur et al., 2015) and less bimanual coordination while playing with objects (Bhat et al., 2009) and to spend less time in object mouthing (Koterba and Iverson, 2009; Koterba et al., 2014; Kaur et al., 2015) than their LR peers. They also appear to be delayed in reaching early motor milestones, such as sitting independently (Iverson and Wozniak, 2007; Nickel et al., 2013).

The progressive acquisition of motor skills provides opportunities to acquire and to refine abilities that are relevant in domains beyond motor abilities, such as language and social interaction (Iverson and Goldin-Meadow, 2005; Iverson, 2010). For example, the ability to reach and grasp for an object and to extend it to an interlocutor supports the development of shared attention between infant and caregiver. Karasik et al. (2011) showed that the onset of independent walking influences the quality of infants' social bids. In addition, the ability to manipulate and mouth an object may influence the phonetic characteristics of vocalizations by introducing vocal tract closure and variation in consonant production (Fagan and Iverson, 2007).

A crucial aspect of object manipulation is motor planning. It refers to the capacity to plan the necessary steps to achieve goal directed actions (Gentilucci et al., 1997). Studies of motor planning abilities in children with ASD have suggested some difficulties with planning goal-directed actions globally (i.e., Fabbri-Destro et al., 2009). More generally, deficits or delays in action planning may affect aspects of everyday life. They may also impact social and communicative functioning since the motor system plays a fundamental role in social exchanges. Thus, for example, the ability to plan and produce movements within an appropriate time frame may be crucial for reciprocal social interaction (Zampella and Bennetto, 2013).

To date, the growing literature on motor concerns in HR infants has mainly focused on the first year of life and has examined the attainment of motor milestones, object exploration, and the development of fine and gross motor skills using standardized assessment tools such as the Vineland Adaptive Behavior Scales (Sparrow et al., 2005) and the Mullen Scales of Early Learning (Mullen, 1995). In the present study, we extend this line of research by examining the development of the ability to coordinate the motor action sequences needed to transport an object from a starting location to a final target (object transport task) in the second and third years of life. From a neurophysiogical perspective, an action sequence can be defined as a chain of elementary motor acts (e.g., reaching and grasping) that are connected to one another and depend on movement intentions or goals (Fogassi et al., 2005). When an action is performed (e.g., reaching for a block to build a tower), motor acts need to be connected. For instance, when building a tower, children need to lift the hand and reach for a block, shape the fingers to grasp the block, and then place it on top of the target (Sacrey et al., 2014). The final goal of an action sequence guides the relative precision of the actions necessary to accomplish the task (Wilmut et al., 2013). Here we varied the degree of precision required by the final action in order to study potential differences in the performance of goal-directed action sequences.

The present study investigated the development of the ability to execute connected motor acts in HR children who do not go on to receive a diagnosis of ASD and in comparison LR children from 18 to 36 months of age using two different object transport tasks. While previous research on motor development in HR infants has relied on observational methods or administration of standardized assessments, a unique feature of our approach is the combination of behavioral observation with sensor technology specifically developed for use in naturalistic settings that permitted the collection of kinematic data as children performed the tasks. Our aim was to acquire a deeper understanding of the developmental trajectory of motor performance in object transport tasks in HR children and to compare their performance to that of LR peers. Analyses of behavioral and kinematic data allowed us to test for potential differences in task performance as a function of age, condition, and group.

MATERIALS AND METHODS

Participants

Fifteen children (8 male) with an older full biological sibling with ASD participated in this research. Children in the HR group were drawn from a larger longitudinal study of the early development of HR infants (e.g., LeBarton and Iverson, 2013). Their families were recruited through a university-based Autism Research Program, parent support organizations, and local agencies and schools serving families of children with ASD. Prior to infant enrollment in the larger study, the Autism Diagnostic Observation Schedule (ADOS; Lord et al., 2000) was administered to all older siblings by a trained clinician to confirm their diagnosis. At 36 months, HR children were seen for final diagnostic assessment and classification by an experienced clinician blind to all previous study data using the ADOS and DSM-IV criteria. All of the HR children scored below the threshold for ASD and did not receive an ASD diagnosis.

The data presented below were collected as part of an ancillary study of motor planning in HR and LR toddlers from 12 to 36 months of age. For purposes of the ancillary study, we recruited a comparison group of 14 LR children (8 male) with an older typically-developing sibling and no family history of ASD (i.e., no first- or second-degree relatives diagnosed with ASD). LR children were recruited via advertisements in local parent magazines, newsletters, neighborhood circulars, pediatricians' offices, daycare and preschool centers, neighborhood email distribution lists, and word of mouth.

All children in both groups were born full-term, from uncomplicated pregnancies and deliveries, and came from English-speaking homes. Although information on family income was unavailable, parental occupations were identified for the purpose of providing a general index of social class. Because many of the mothers were home raising their children, Nakao-Treas occupational prestige scores (Nakao and Treas, 1994) were calculated for fathers' occupations. Groups did not differ statistically in race/ethnicity, maternal or paternal education, or paternal occupational prestige score. Demographic data for the sample are presented in **Table 1**.

Procedure

Prior to the first ancillary study visit, parents of HR and LR children signed an informed consent form giving permission for their child's participation in the study. All study procedures were approved by the University of Pittsburgh Institutional Review Board. As part of the larger longitudinal study, all HR participants were visited monthly at home between the ages of 5 and 14 months with follow up visits at 18, 24, and 36 months (for further description of the procedures employed in the larger study, see Parladé and Iverson, 2015). For HR children, ancillary study visits generally occurred at a time different from the regularly scheduled visit for the larger study. LR children were seen on or within a few days of the monthly anniversary of their birthday.

All children were seen at home with a primary caregiver for a session lasting ~1 h. Children sat opposite an experimenter, who administered two object transport tasks that increased in level of difficulty. For this reason, tasks were presented in fixed order. Task objects were presented within reaching distance and at the child's midline. Each task involved two conditions differing in the degree of precision required by the goal action. In the Ball Task (adapted from Claxton et al., 2003), children were first administered three trials in which they were asked to throw a small ball (5 cm in diameter) into a transparent plastic tray (30 × 15 × 5 cm). In these *Throw* trials, the goal action (throwing the ball in the tray) does not require precise movement. These were followed by three *Fit* trials, in which children were asked to insert the same ball into a clear plastic tube (6.5 cm in diameter, see **Figure 1**). In this case, greater precision is required because the center of the ball must be aligned with the axis of the tube for insertion to be successful.

The second task, the Block Task (adapted from Chen et al., 2010), immediately followed the Ball Task. On the first set of three trials (*Throw* condition), children were asked to throw a block (side 5.5 cm) into a large open container (30 × 15 × 5 cm; see **Figure 2**). On the next five trials (*Stack* condition), children were asked to place each of five blocks, one at a time, on a target block to build a tower. In these trials, children had to transport the block to the target and then carefully adjust the block to place it successfully on the target block. A schematic representation of the tasks is presented in **Figure 3**. Sessions were video recorded for later coding.

TABLE 1 | Demographic data for HR and LR groups.

	HR ($n = 15$)	LR ($n = 14$)
GENDER		
Female (%)	7 (47%)	6 (43%)
Male (%)	8 (53%)	8 (57%)
Racial or ethnic minority (%)	0 (0%)	0 (%)
MATERNAL EDUCATION		
Graduate or professional school (%)	6 (40%)	5 (36%)
Some college or college degree (%)	7 (47%)	8 (57%)
High school (%)	2 (13%)	1 (7%)
PATERNAL EDUCATION		
Graduate or professional schools (%)	6 (40%)	6 (43%)
Some college or college degree (%)	7 (47%)	8 (57%)
High school (%)	2 (13%)	0 (0%)
Mean paternal occupational prestige (SD)	52.91 (15.93)	61.47 (14.71)

Kinematic Data Collection

Kinematic data were collected from the wrists via a magneto-inertial platform consisting of two wrist bracelets (WAMS, **Figure 4**) instrumented by a 9 axis magneto-inertial sensor (Taffoni et al., 2012). Data were sent to a remote laptop through a Serial-Bluetooth converter (Parani-ESD200, Sena Technologies Inc.). The module allows for a range of 30 m, enabling the monitoring of children in unstructured environments such as the home.

Developmental Assessments

As part of the larger longitudinal study, the Mullen Scales of Early Learning (MSEL; Mullen, 1995) were administered to all HR infants at 18, 24, and 36 months by a trained researcher. The MSEL provides a measure of general cognitive functioning from 0 to 68 months. It consists of five subscales: Visual Reception, Receptive Language, Expressive Language, Fine Motor, and Gross Motor. Internal consistency ranges from 0.83 to 0.95. The Visual Reception, Fine Motor, Expressive Language, and Receptive Language scores can be used to calculate an overall Early Learning Composite (ELC) *T* score. The MSEL was not administered to LR infants in the ancillary study. MSEL scores for the HR group at 18, 24, and 36 months are presented in **Table 2**. As is apparent, in general, performance across all five domains fell within the range for the normative sample at each age.

Coding and Variable Creation

Videos were coded by a team of coders naive to children's risk status (HR or LR) using ELAN software.[1] Prior to commencing coding, all coders were trained to a criterion of 80% agreement on three consecutive training videos. Coding focused specifically on two motor acts: *reaching* and *placement*. *Reaching* began at the first frame in which the child moved the hand from the work surface and ended at the first frame in which the hand contacted the object. *Placement* began from the first frame in which the child lifted the object from the table and ended when the child released it into or on the target. We then calculated the durations of each reach and placement action using these onset and offset times. Interrater reliability was assessed by having a second trained observer independently code a randomly selected 51% of the videos for each task, with the constraint that both groups and all three ages were approximately equally represented in the videos. A tolerance window of 0.1 s was utilized. For the Ball Task, mean intercoder agreement was 0.84 for reach duration and 0.93 for place duration; those for the Block Task were highly comparable (reach duration = 0.83; placement duration = 0.91).

[1] https://tla.mpi.nl/tools/tla-tools/elan/elan-description/

FIGURE 1 | Stimuli used in the Ball Task: in the Throw condition, the child had to reach for the ball and throw it into the tray; in the Fit condition, the child had to insert the ball into the cylinder.

FIGURE 2 | Stimuli used in the Block Task: in the Throw condition, the child had to reach for the block and throw it into the tray; in the Stack condition, the child had to reach for the block and stack it on a target block to build a tower.

Kinematic data from the WAMS sensors were low pass filtered with a cut-off frequency of 20 Hz to cut noise due to higher frequencies. Filtered data were used to calculate the mean acceleration during reaching movement (Taffoni et al., 2014). The mean acceleration of reaching is a scalar value defined as:

$$\bar{a} = \frac{1}{T} \int_0^T \left| \vec{a}(t) - R(t) g_0 \right| dt$$

T is the duration of reaching, $\vec{a}(t)$ is the accelerometer output at time t, $R(t)$ is the orientation matrix describing sensor orientation at time t with respect to a fixed reference frame (see Murray et al., 1994), and g_0 is the gravitational acceleration expressed in the same reference frame. The vector difference in the norm operator ($|\ldots|$) allows subtraction of the gravitational acceleration from the overall acceleration measurement to consider only the acceleration of children's reaching movements. Finally, the integral allowed us to assess the temporal average of the measured acceleration obtaining a scalar metric measuring the performed reaching.

Statistical Analysis

Prior to conducting statistical analyses, we computed a series of t-tests to determine whether there were gender differences on any variables. No significant differences emerged, so the analyses reported below were conducted without including gender in the analyses. We utilized random effects regression (STATA 12.1) for our primary analyses. According to Snijders and Bosker (1999), this method accounts for interdependency and structuring of the data and allows the use of multiple data points from the same participant (rather than aggregating all measurements from the same individual and making these values the unit of analysis) while avoiding the problem of pseudoreplication. In addition, the analysis is particularly well suited for analyzing behavioral data that typically have one or more levels of aggregations (Snijders and Bosker, 1999; van de Pol and Wright, 2009). Random effects regression models were computed separately for each task on each of the dependent variables (reaching duration, placement duration, mean acceleration of reaching), with Age (18, 24, 36 months), Condition (*Throw* vs. *Fit*; *Throw* vs. *Stack*), and Group (HR vs. LR) as predictors and with participants as a random factor. The distributions of each dependent variable were checked for normality prior to conducting analyses. Where necessary, appropriate transformations were applied.

RESULTS

Ball Task

Descriptive statistics for each of the variables from the Ball Task are presented in **Table 3**. As is apparent, reaching and placement durations varied by age and by condition. Statistical analyses revealed that durations of both actions decreased significantly (reaching duration $z = 3.23$; $p < 0.01$; placement duration $z = 4.47$; $p < 0.01$), while mean acceleration of reaching tended to increase over time ($z = 4.19$; $p < 0.01$). With regard to Condition, placement duration was significantly longer ($z = -4.66$; $p < 0.01$) in the Fit compared to the Throw condition. There was no significant effect of Group on any of the variables examined. Thus, children (regardless of risk status) demonstrated increasing efficiency in executing action sequences over time: reaching movements showed greater acceleration (i.e., higher rate of change in wrist velocity) and were thus shorter in duration, as were placement actions. However, the precision demands of fitting the ball in the tube resulted in longer placement durations compared to the Throw condition.

Block Task

Descriptive statistics from the Block Task are presented in **Table 4**. These data suggest that overall, as in the Ball Task, there were developmental decreases in reaching and placement durations, while mean reaching acceleration tended to increase. Placement durations were longer in the Stack than in the Throw

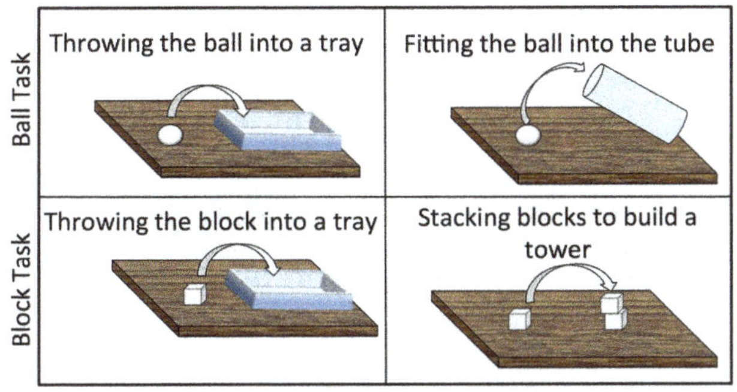

FIGURE 3 | Schematic representation of the Ball and Block Tasks. The arrows represent what was to be done with the ball or the block: throw the ball or the block into the tray; fit the ball into the cylinder; stack the block to build a tower.

FIGURE 4 | Sensorized bracelet worn by the children. We use two identical bracelets, one for the right arm, and one for the left arm, in order to measure children's movement during the execution of the tasks. We used two bracelets since we did not know which arm the child will use to carry out the task.

condition. In addition, mean acceleration of reaching values were higher in the LR compared to the HR group at all three ages. Statistical analyses confirmed these differences. Reaching and placement durations decreased significantly (reaching $z = 5.38$; $p < 0.01$; placement $z = -5.24$; $p < 0.01$) and mean reaching acceleration increased significantly with age ($z = 2.57$; $p < 0.01$). Placement duration was also affected by the precision demands of the goal action, such that durations were longer in the Stack than in the Throw condition ($z = 7.69$; $p < 0.01$). The group difference in mean acceleration of reaching was also significant ($z = -2.16$; $p = 0.03$). Thus, while children in both groups became more efficient in producing action sequences over time, HR children exhibited reduced acceleration in their reaching movements (i.e., rate of change in wrist velocity was slower compared to LR children).

Table 5 reports a summary of the statistical effects found in both tasks.

DISCUSSION

General Remarks

In the present study, we investigated the development of the ability to coordinate different action sequences in an object transport task in children at heightened risk for ASD from 18 and to 36 months of age. Our goals were to describe the development of this skill in HR and LR children and to determine whether their performance differed in motor tasks of varying levels of difficulty. Because most previous research on the development of motor abilities in HR children has focused mainly on the first year of life, the present study enhances our understanding of developmental trajectories by examining behavior from 18 months of age. In light of previous findings indicating that the end goal of an action affects how children organize their motor acts (e.g., Claxton et al., 2003), we utilized two object transport tasks that involved conditions differing in the level of precision required by the goal action.

In both tasks, we observed developmental change in the nature of reaching and placement actions, with both becoming temporally shorter. The decrease in reach durations was likely due to the accompanying increase in mean acceleration of the reaching movement, such that with age, children showed more efficient control of the reaching movement. In addition, children's placement actions at all ages were affected by precision manipulations in both tasks. Compared to the imprecise (Throw) condition, placement actions in the precise (Fit; Stack) goal action conditions were longer in duration.

TABLE 2 | Mean Standard (T)[a] Scores (and standard deviations) on the Mullen Scales of Early Learning for HR Toddlers at 18, 24, and 36 months.

	18 Months [Mean (SD)]	24 Months [Mean (SD)]	36 Months [Mean (SD)]
MSEL SUBSCALES			
Gross motor	47.80 (8.91)	42.44 (8.16)	–[b]
Visual reception	49.60 (10.11)	46.38 (6.98)	59.14 (10.15)
Fine motor	53.40 (5.83)	47.23 (7.64)	48.50 (9.51)
Receptive language	36.53 (13.85)	47.69 (12.63)	49.29 (8.21)
Expressive language	42.40 (10.85)	47.85 (8.87)	54.07 (11.39)
Early learning composite[c]	91.47 (13.96)	99.85 (14.12)	105.86 (15.69)

[a]*MSEL subscale T score mean = 50, SD = 10.*
[b]*Because the Gross Motor subscale covers ages birth to 33 months and is not part of the Early Learning Composite, it was not administered at 36 months.*
[c]*Early Learning Composite T score mean = 100, SD = 15.*

Group Motor Differences

Interestingly, differences between the LR and HR groups were only observed in the Block Task, and only in mean acceleration of reaching, with values significantly lower for HR than for LR children. This difference suggests that the Block Task may be more challenging for HR than for LR children. Why might this be the case? One possibility is that the two tasks differ in the degree of difficulty in the precision conditions (Fit vs. Stack). Previous work suggests that when children stack cubes to build a tower, they are guided by internal models of balancing blocks at the geometric center (Karmiloff-Smith and Inhelder, 1975; Krist et al., 2005; Bonawitz et al., 2007). Although the presence of such internal models may guide children's performance, stacking cubes one on top of another to build a tower places additional demands that are not present when fitting a ball in a tube. When

TABLE 3 | Descriptive statistics from the ball task.

	18			24			36		
	Full sample Mean (SD)	LR Mean (SD)	HR Mean (SD)	Full sample Mean (SD)	LR Mean (SD)	HR Mean (SD)	Full sample Mean (SD)	LR Mean (SD)	HR Mean (SD)
THROW									
Reach duration (s)	0.68 (0.19)	0.72 (0.17)	0.63 (0.19)	0.68 (0.30)	0.71 (0.30)	0.56 (0.30)	0.57 (0.23)	0.51 (0.18)	0.63 (0.26)
Place duration (s)	1.32 (1.52)	1.32 (1.38)	1.31 (1.65)	1.04 (0.56)	0.89 (0.54)	1.16 (0.56)	0.52 (0.19)	0.53 (0.23)	0.50 (0.14)
Mean acc. reaching (m/s^2)	2.34 (0.79)	2.30 (0.42)	2.38 (1.03)	2.16 (1.33)	2.60 (1.35)	1.61 (1.06)	3.27 (1.50)	3.17 (1.69)	3.38 (1.26)
FIT									
Reach duration (s)	0.61 (0.21)	0.62 (0.19)	0.60 (0.23)	0.59 (0.17)	0.60 (0.16)	0.58 (0.17)	0.49 (0.12)	0.47 (0.13)	0.51 (0.12)
Place duration (s)	1.53 (1.07)	1.80 (1.32)	1.30 (0.72)	1.08 (0.82)	0.77 (0.23)	1.35 (1.02)	0.83 (0.34)	0.83 (0.40)	0.82 (0.26)
Mean acc. reaching (m/s^2)	2.22 (0.71)	2.30 (0.64)	2.11 (0.78)	2.99 (1.41)	2.88 (1.58)	3.17 (1.06)	3.57 (1.62)	3.07 (1.57)	4.10 (1.50)

TABLE 4 | Descriptive statistics from the block task.

	18			24			36		
	Full sample Mean (SD)	LR Mean (SD)	HR Mean (SD)	Full sample Mean (SD)	LR Mean (SD)	HR Mean (SD)	Full sample Mean (SD)	LR Mean (SD)	HR Mean (SD)
THROW									
Reach duration (s)	0.60 (0.15)	0.59 (0.13)	0.61 (0.17)	0.55 (0.16)	0.53 (0.14)	0.57 (0.16)	0.45 (0.11)	0.42 (0.11)	0.61 (0.17)
Place duration (s)	1.99 (1.52)	2.13 (1.91)	1.86 (0.98)	1.51 (1.37)	1.46 (1.40)	1.55 (1.34)	0.81 (0.95)	2.13 (1.91)	1.86 (0.98)
Mean acc. reaching (m/s^2)	3.10 (2.20)	3.84 (2.47)	2.36 (1.57)	2.83 (1.35)	3.03 (1.52)	2.46 (0.88)	3.33 (1.34)	3.84 (2.47)	2.36 (1.57)
STACK									
Reach duration (s)	0.61 (0.17)	0.65 (0.20)	0.57 (0.11)	0.58 (0.15)	0.64 (0.13)	0.52 (0.14)	0.49 (0.13)	0.48 (0.12)	0.50 (0.14)
Place duration (s)	2.78 (1.34)	2.68 (1.06)	2.87 (1.54)	2.33 (0.80)	2.50 (0.73)	2.16 (0.83)	1.88 (0.73)	2.10(0.67)	1.62 (0.71)
Mean acc. reaching (m/s^2)	2.58 (1.20)	3.12 (1.12)	1.98 (0.96)	2.56 (0.75)	2.47 (0.75)	2.79 (0.71)	3.55 (1.87)	3.75 (1.78)	3.31 (1.95)

building a tower, children must reach for a cube at a fixed location and transport it to the target position, which changes from one cube to the next due to the increasing height of the tower. By contrast, in the Ball Task, the target position is identical from trial to trial.

A second possibility stems from the fact that the two tasks differ in the affordances of the objects on which children acted. In the Ball Task, children manipulated a sphere, which has no privileged affordances. By contrast, in the Block Task children reached for and grasped a cube, which requires more refined manipulation skills. A large body of research has demonstrated that from relatively young ages, infants adjust the aperture and shape of the hand in ways that match characteristics of the target object (e.g., shape, size) during the reaching movement (Lockman et al., 1984; von Hofsten and Fazel-Zandy, 1984; von Hofsten and Rönnqvist, 1988; Ornkloo and von Hofsten, 2007). The lower mean acceleration observed during reaching among HR children may be indicative of difficulty coordinating the approach toward the cube with alterations in hand shape when a target object must be grasped in a particular way in order to be moved from a surface, transported to a new location, and positioned precisely. Such a difficulty may be indicative of vulnerabilities in the prospective control of movement. Some support for this possibility comes from a recent study of reaching in 10-month-old HR and LR infants (Ekberg et al., 2016). In this research, LR and HR infants reached for a ball that was moving down a curvilinear path off an inclined tabletop, and experimenters measured reach latency, or the time between the ball's entry into reaching space and the onset of infants' reaches. Compared to LR infants, who began their reaches about 200 ms *before* the ball entered their reaching space (i.e., they reached predictively), HR infants initiated reaching movements just as the ball entered reaching space.

This interpretation is further supported by studies that have reported grasping delays and difficulties in younger HR infants (e.g., Libertus et al., 2014). Our findings provide a window into the subsequent developmental trajectory of these abilities and suggest that there may be persistent, subtle alterations in fine motor control in HR children. Along these lines, Leonard et al. (2014a) recently reported that HR children who had poor motor skills at 9 months performed poorly on a standardized motor assessment at ages 5–7 years. While these differences may be relatively small and subtle, they may have cascading effects on development in other developmental domains (e.g., language, social; Iverson, 2010; Leonard et al., 2014b). Taken together, our findings and those of prior studies indicate a real need for additional research on grasping in older HR children, and in particular, ways in which modulation of hand aperture and shape for grasping may vary in these children in relation to LR peers. While these are relatively basic components of skilled action,

TABLE 5 | Results of the random effects regressions.

Dependent variables	Independent variables		
	Age	Condition	Group
BALL TASK			
Reach duration	$z = 3.23^{**}$	$z = 2.12$	$z = 0.04$
Place duration	$z = 4.47^{**}$	$z = -4.66^{**}$	$z = -1.20$
Mean acc. reach	$z = 4.19^{**}$	$z = 1.51$	$z = 0.43$
BLOCK TASK			
Reach duration	$z = 5.38^{**}$	$z = -1.13$	$z = 0.13$
Place duration	$z = -5.24^{**}$	$z = 7.69^{**}$	$z = -0.23$
Mean acc. reach	$z = 2.57^{**}$	$z = -0.27$	$z = -2.16^{*}$

Asterisks Mark Significant Effects. $^{*}p < 0.05$; $^{**}p < 0.01$.

disruptions in any of them may also have significant cascading effects on the organization and planning of movement in daily life.

Considerations on Related Cascading Effects

There is some evidence that motor skills are related to social, emotional, and communicative functioning. For example, Cummins et al. (2005) showed that children with motor problems demonstrate less skill in emotion recognition. This may impact social interaction abilities since because emotion recognition is foundational for social behaviors such as empathy. There is also some indication of a relation between motor coordination and anxious and depressed behavior in preschoolers. Parents of children with motor difficulties reported higher levels of internalizing behavior problems than did parents of children with typical motor skills (Piek et al., 2008). While these correlational data do not allow us to make inferences about the direction of these relationships, it is clear that motor difficulties can negatively impact children's school performance (e.g., writing, drawing) and participation in games and activities with peers, leaving them at risk for social exclusion and lower self-esteem.

Limitations and Future Work

In sum, the data from the present study point to the potential existence of subtle difficulties with fine motor skills in HR children in the second and third years of life. Experimental research has consistently found that children at risk for ASD (i.e., Landa et al., 2013) and children with an ASD diagnosis (i.e., Vernazza-Martin et al., 2005; Ozonoff et al., 2008) experience motor delays that are apparent from early in life. Motor difficulties could be related to neuronal organization and cortical connectivity; they may in fact suggest disrupted fronto-striatal pathways and basal ganglia as well as alterations in cerebellar and brain stem functions (Fournier et al., 2010).

Although these findings add to our understanding of the development of motor skills in HR and LR children in an age range that has received little empirical attention, a note of caution regarding their interpretation is in order. The sample sizes were relatively small, and results clearly merit replication with larger groups of children. In addition, data were collected in a naturalistic setting (children's homes), which precluded the possibility of controlling some aspects of task presentation. Nevertheless, our data highlight the promise of collecting kinematic data in such settings and their potential value in revealing subtle variations in movement organization and quality that cannot be readily observed in video recordings. They also underscore the utility of studying motor behavior in the context of everyday actions that children frequently perform.

AUTHOR CONTRIBUTIONS

VF provided data coding and elaboration and data analysis. She prepared the manuscript and submitted it after receiving and approving both revisions and comments of all co-authors; FT provided technical support and elaboration of all kinematic data. He also contributed to the manuscript preparation before giving his approval of the present version of the manuscript; SMP provided fundamental support during data acquisition and video coding, she gave precious comments and revisions which were integrated in the last version of the manuscript, that was finally approved. FK contributed to design the experimental protocols and he suggested ideas for the interpretation of specific aspects of results. He also made useful comments for the final discussion of the paper. He then agreed that the present version was ready for the submission. He supervised the Italian group of researchers. JMI gave her fundamental contribute to design the work and the experimental protocols, to the interpretation of data and results. She also provided significant revisions and comments during the different phases of the manuscript elaboration before giving her approval of the final manuscript version. She supervised the US group of researchers and coordinated the whole team.

ACKNOWLEDGMENTS

This research was supported by grants from the National Institutes of Health (R01 HD054979 and R21 HD068584) to JI. Additional support was provided by HD35469 and HD055748 to N.J. Minshew. We thank members of the Infant Communication Lab at the University of Pittsburgh for help with data collection and coding, Francesco Motolese for assistance with processing of kinematic data, and Elsa Addessi, Gabriele Schino, and Diane Williams for valuable contributions at various stages of the project. Special thanks to the children and their families, without whose enthusiastic and dedicated participation the study could not have been completed. Portions of these data were presented at the 2013 International Conference on Infant studies, Berlin, Germany, and the 2014 36th Annual International IEEE EMBS Conference, Chicago, IL.

REFERENCES

Bhat, A. N., Downing, K., Galloway, J. C., and Landa, R. J. (2009). "A comparison of object exploration strategies between infant siblings of children with autism and typically developing infants at 6 months of age," in *Poster Presented at the Annual International Meeting for Autism* Research (Chicago, IL).

Bonawitz, E. B., Lim, S., and Schulz, L. E. (2007). "Weighing the evidence: children's naïve theories of balance affect their exploratory play," in *28th Annual Proceedings of the Cognitive Science Society* (Nashville).

Chen, Y., Keen, R., Rosander, K., and von Hofsten, C. (2010). Movement planning reflects skill level and age changes in toddlers. *Child Dev.* 81, 1846–1858. doi: 10.1111/j.1467-8624.2010.01514.x

Claxton, L. J., Keen, R., and McCarty, M. E. (2003). Evidence of motor planning in infant reaching behavior. *Psychol. Sci.* 14, 354-356. doi: 10.1111/1467-9280.24421

Cummins, A., Piek, J. P., and Dyck, M. J. (2005). Motor coordination, empathy and social behaviour in school-aged children. *Dev. Med. Child Neurol.* 47, 437–442. doi: 10.1017/S001216220500085X

Ekberg, T. L., Falck-Ytter, T., Bölte, S., Gredebäck, G., and EASE Team. (2016). Reduced prospective motor control in 10-month-olds at risk for autism spectrum disorder. *Clin. Psychol. Sci.* 4, 129–135.doi: 10.1177/2167702615576697

Fabbri-Destro, M., Cattaneo, L., Boria, S., and Rizzolatti, G. (2009). Planning actions in autism. *Exp. Brain Res.* 192, 521-525. doi: 10.1007/s00221-008-1578-3

Fagan, M. K., and Iverson, J. M. (2007). The influence of mouthing on infant vocalization. *Infancy* 11, 191–202. doi: 10.1111/j.1532-7078.2007.tb00222.x

Flanagan, J. E., Landa, R., Bhat, A., and Bauman, M. (2012). Head lag in infants at risk for autism: a preliminary study. *Am. J. Occup. Ther.* 66, 577–585. doi: 10.5014/ajot.2012.004192

Fogassi, L., Ferrari, P. F., Gesierich, B., Rozzi, S., Chersi, F., and Rizzlatti, G. (2005). Parietal lobe: from action organization to intention understanding. *Science* 308, 662–667. doi: 10.1126/science.1106138

Fournier, K. A., Hass, C. J., Naik, S. K., Lodha, N., and Cauraugh, J. H. (2010). Motor coordination in autism spectrum disorders: a synthesis and meta-analysis. *J. Autism Dev. Disord.* 40, 1227–1240. doi: 10.1007/s10803-010-0981-3

Gentilucci, M., Negrotti, A., and Gangitano, M. (1997). Planning an action. *Exp. Brain Res.* 115, 116–128. doi: 10.1007/PL00005671

Gliga, T., Jones, E. J., Bedford, R., Charman, T., and Johnson, M. H. (2014). From early markers to neuro-developmental mechanisms of autism. *Dev. Rev.* 34, 189–207. doi: 10.1016/j.dr.2014.05.003

Iverson, J. M. (2010). Developing language in a developing body: the relationship between motor development and language development. *J. Child Lang.* 37, 229–261. doi: 10.1017/S0305000909990432

Iverson, J. M., and Goldin-Meadow, S. (2005). Gesture paves the way for language development. *Psychol. Sci.* 16, 367–371. doi: 10.1111/j.0956-7976.2005.01542.x

Iverson, J. M., and Wozniak, R. H. (2007). Variation in vocal-motor development in infant siblings of children with autism. *J. Autism Dev. Disord.* 37, 158–170. doi: 10.1007/s10803-006-0339-z

Jones, E. J., Gliga, T., Bedford, R., Charman, T., and Johnson, M. H. (2014). Developmental pathways to autism: a review of prospective studies of infants at risk. *Neurosci. Biobehav. Rev.* 39, 1–33. doi: 10.1016/j.neubiorev.2013.12.001

Karasik, L. B., Tamis–LeMonda, C. S., and Adolph, K. E. (2011). Transition from crawling to walking and infants' actions with objects and people. *Child Dev.* 82, 1199–1209. doi: 10.1111/j.1467-8624.2011.01595.x

Karmiloff-Smith, A., and Inhelder, B. (1975). If you want to get ahead, get a theory. *Cognition* 3, 195–212. doi: 10.1016/0010-0277(74)90008-0

Kaur, M., Srinivasan, S., and Bhat, A. (2015). Atypical object exploration skills in infants at-risk for autism between 6 to 15 months of age. *Front. Psychol.* 6:798. doi: 10.3389/fpsyg.2015.00798

Koterba, E. A., and Iverson, J. M. (2009). Investigating motionese: the effect of infant-directed action on infants' attention and object exploration. *Infant Behav. Dev.* 32, 437–444. doi: 10.1016/j.infbeh.2009.07.003

Koterba, E. A., Leezenbaum, N. B., and Iverson, J. M. (2014). Object exploration at 6 and 9 months in infants with and without risk for autism. *Autism* 18, 97–105. doi: 10.1177/1362361312464826

Krist, H., Horz, H., and Schönfeld, T. (2005). Children's block balancing revisited: no evidence for representational redescription. *Swiss J. Psychol.* 64, 183–193. doi: 10.1024/1421-0185.64.3.183

Landa, R. J., Stuart, E. A., Gross, A. L., and Faherty, A. (2013). Developmental trajectories in children with and without autism spectrum disorders: the first 3 years. *Child Dev.* 84, 429–442. doi: 10.1111/j.1467-8624.2012.01870.x

LeBarton, E. S., and Iverson, J. M. (2013). Fine motor skill predicts expressive language in infant siblings of children with autism. *Dev. Sci.* 16, 815–827. doi: 10.1111/desc.12069

Leonard, H. C., Bedford, R., Charman, T., Elsabbagh, M., Johnson, M. H., Hill, E. L., et al. (2014a). Motor development in children at risk of autism: a follow-up study of infant siblings. *Autism* 18, 281–291. doi: 10.1177/1362361312470037

Leonard, H. C., Elsabbagh, M., and Hill, E. L. (2014b). Early and persistent motor difficulties in infants at-risk of developing autism spectrum disorder: a prospective study. *Eur. J. Dev. Psychol.* 11, 18–35. doi: 10.1080/17405629.2013.801626

Libertus, K., Sheperd, K. A., Ross, S. W., and Landa, R. J. (2014). Limited fine motor and grasping skills in 6 month old infants at high risk for Autism. *Child Dev.* 85, 2218–2231. doi: 10.1111/cdev.12262

Lockman, J. J., Ashmead, D. H., and Bushnell, E. W. (1984). The development of anticipatory hand orientation during infancy. *J. Exp. Child Psychol.* 37, 176–186. doi: 10.1016/0022-0965(84)90065-1

Lord, C., Risi, S., Lambrecht, L., Cook, E. H. Jr., Leventhal, B. L., Di Lavore, et al. (2000). The autism diagnostic observation schedule—generic: a standard measure of social and communication deficits associated with the spectrum of autism. *J. Autism Dev. Disord.* 30, 205–223. doi: 10.1023/A:1005592401947

Messinger, D., Young, G. S., Ozonoff, S., Dobkins, K., Carter, A., Zwaigenbaum, L., et al. (2013). Beyond autism: a baby siblings research consortium study of high-risk children at three years of age. *J. Am. Acad. Child Adolesc. Psychiatry* 52, 300–308. doi: 10.1016/j.jaac.2012.12.011

Mullen, E. M. (1995). *Mullen Scales of Early Learning.* Circle Pines, MN: American Guidance Service.

Murray, R. M., Li, Z., Sastry, S. S., and Sastry, S. S. (1994). *A Mathematical Introduction to Robotic Manipulation.* Boca Raton, FL: CRC Press.

Nakao, K., and Treas, J. (1994). Updating occupational prestige and socioeconomic scores: how the new measures measure up. *Sociol. Methodol.* 24, 1–72. doi: 10.2307/270978

Nickel, L. R., Thatcher, A. R., Keller, F., Wozniak, R., and Iverson, J. M. (2013). Posture development in infants at heightened versus low risk for autism spectrum disorders. *Infancy* 18, 639–661. doi: 10.1111/infa.12025

Ornkloo, H., and von Hofsten, C. (2007). Fitting objects into holes: on the development of spatial cognition skills. *Dev. Psychol.* 43:404. doi: 10.1037/0012-1649.43.2.404

Ozonoff, S., Young, G. S., Carter, A., Messinger, D., Yirmiya, N., Zwaigenbaum, L., et al. (2011). Recurrence risk for autism spectrum disorders: a baby siblings research consortium study. *Pediatrics* 128, 1–8. doi: 10.1542/peds.2010-2825

Ozonoff, S., Young, G. S., Goldring, S., Greiss-Hess, L., Herrera, A. M., Steele, J., et al. (2008). Gross motor development, movement abnormalities, and early identification of autism. *J. Autism Dev. Disord.* 38, 644–656. doi: 10.1007/s10803-007-0430-0

Parladé, M. V., and Iverson, J. M. (2015). The development of coordinated communication in infants at heightened risk for Autism Spectrum Disorder. *J. Autism Dev. Disord.* 45, 2218–2234. doi: 10.1007/s10803-015-2391-z

Piek, J. P., Bradbury, G. S., Elsley, S. C., and Tate, L. (2008). Motor coordination and social–emotional behaviour in preschool–aged children. *Int. J. Disabil. Dev. Educ.* 55, 143–151. doi: 10.1080/10349120802033592

Sacrey, L. A. R., Germani, T., Bryson, S. E., and Zwaigenbaum, L. (2014). Reaching and grasping in autism spectrum disorder: a review of recent literature. *Front. Neurol.* 5:6. doi: 10.3389/fneur.2014.00006

Snijders, T., and Bosker, R. (1999). *Multilevel Modeling: An Introduction to Basic and Advanced Multilevel Modeling.* London: Sage.

Sparrow, S. S., Cicchetti, D. V., and Balla, D. A. (2005). *Vineland Adaptive Behavior Scales. 2nd Edn.* Oxford: NCS Pearson, Inc.

Taffoni, F., Focaroli, V., Formica, D., Gugliemelli, E., Keller, F., and Iverson, J. M. (2012). "Sensor-based technology in the study of motor skills in infants at risk for ASD," in *2012 4th IEEE RAS & EMBS International Conference on Biomedical Robotics and Biomechatronics (BioRob),* Rome: IEEE. 1879–1883.

Taffoni, F., Focaroli, V., Keller, F., and Iverson, J. M. (2014). "A technological approach to studying motor planning ability in children at high risk for ASD," in *2014 36th Annual International Conference of the IEEE Engineering in Medicine and Biology Society (EMBC)*, Chicago, IL: IEEE. 3638–3641.

van de Pol, M., and Wright, J. (2009). A simple method for distinguishing within- versus between subject effects using mixed models. *Anim. Behav.* 77, 753–758. doi: 10.1016/j.anbehav.2008.11.006

Vernazza-Martin, S., Martin, N., Vernazza, A., Lepellec-Muller, A., Rufo, M., Massion, J., et al. (2005). Goal directed locomotion and balance control in autistic children. *J. Autism Dev. Disord.* 35, 91–102 doi: 10.1007/s10803-004-1037-3

von Hofsten, C., and Fazel-Zandy, S. (1984). Development of visually guided hand orientation in reaching. *J. Exp. Child Psychol.* 38, 208–219. doi: 10.1016/0022-0965(84)90122-X

von Hofsten, C., and Rönnqvist, L. (1988). Preparation for grasping an object: a developmental study. *J. Exp. Psychol.* 14:610. doi: 10.1037/0096-1523.14.4.610

Wilmut, K., Byrne, M., and Barnett, A. L. (2013). To throw or to place: does onward intention affect how a child reaches for an object? *Exp. Brain Res.* 226, 421–429. doi: 10.1007/s00221-013-3453-0

Zampella, C., and Bennetto, L. (2013). "Motor planning," in *Encyclopedia of Autism Spectrum Disorders*, ed R. F. Volkmar (New York, NY: Springer), 1920–1925.

Zwaigenbaum, L., Bryson, S., Lord, C., Rogers, S., Carter, A., Carver, L., et al. (2009). Clinical assessment and management of toddlers with suspected autism spectrum disorder: insights from studies of high-risk infants. *Pediatrics* 123, 1383–1391. doi: 10.1542/peds.2008-1606

Zwaigenbaum, L., Bryson, S., Rogers, T., Roberts, W., Brian, J., and Szatmari, P. (2005). Behavioral manifestations of autism in the first year of life. *Int. J. Dev. Neurosci.* 23, 143–152. doi: 10.1016/j.ijdevneu.2004.05.001

Conflict of Interest Statement: The authors declare that the research was conducted in the absence of any commercial or financial relationships that could be construed as a potential conflict of interest.

18

Ready, Set, Go! Low Anticipatory Response during a Dyadic Task in Infants at High Familial Risk for Autism

Rebecca J. Landa[1,2], Joshua L. Haworth[1,2] and Mary Beth Nebel[3,4]*

[1] Center for Autism and Related Disorders, Kennedy Krieger Institute, Baltimore, MD, USA, [2] Department of Psychiatry and Behavioral Sciences, Johns Hopkins University School of Medicine, Baltimore, MD, USA, [3] Center for Neurodevelopmental and Imaging Research, Kennedy Krieger Institute, Baltimore, MD, USA, [4] Department of Neurology, Johns Hopkins University School of Medicine, Baltimore, MD, USA

Edited by:
Petra Hauf,
St. Francis Xavier University, Canada

Reviewed by:
Caspar Addyman,
Goldsmiths, University of London, UK
Natalia Arias-Trejo,
Universidad Nacional Autónoma de México, Mexico
Jennifer L. Mayer,
University of Roehampton, UK

****Correspondence:***
Rebecca J. Landa
landa@kennedykrieger.org

Children with autism spectrum disorder (ASD) demonstrate a host of motor impairments that may share a common developmental basis with ASD core symptoms. School-age children with ASD exhibit particular difficulty with hand-eye coordination and appear to be less sensitive to visual feedback during motor learning. Sensorimotor deficits are observable as early as 6 months of age in children who later develop ASD; yet the interplay of early motor, visual and social skill development in ASD is not well understood. Integration of visual input with motor output is vital for the formation of internal models of action. Such integration is necessary not only to master a wide range of motor skills, but also to imitate and interpret the actions of others. Thus, closer examination of the early development of visual-motor deficits is of critical importance to ASD. In the present study of infants at high risk (HR) and low risk (LR) for ASD, we examined visual-motor coupling, or action anticipation, during a dynamic, interactive ball-rolling activity. We hypothesized that, compared to LR infants, HR infants would display decreased anticipatory response (perception-guided predictive action) to the approaching ball. We also examined visual attention before and during ball rolling to determine whether attention engagement contributed to differences in anticipation. Results showed that LR and HR infants demonstrated context appropriate looking behavior, both before and during the ball's trajectory toward them. However, HR infants were less likely to exhibit context appropriate anticipatory motor response to the approaching ball (moving their arm/hand to intercept the ball) than LR infants. This finding did not appear to be driven by differences in motor skill between risk groups at 6 months of age and was extended to show an atypical predictive relationship between anticipatory behavior at 6 months and preference for looking at faces compared to objects at age 14 months in the HR group.

Keywords: autism, infant, anticipation, social, motor

INTRODUCTION

Autism spectrum disorders (ASD) are defined by social communication impairment along with repetitive and restricted patterns of behavior and interests (RRBI) (American Psychiatric Association [APA], 2013). However, motor impairments, beyond repetitive motor mannerisms, are prevalent in ASD, and school age children with ASD demonstrate abnormal patterns of motor learning. When learning novel movements, children with ASD show a bias against visual feedback from the external world in favor of proprioceptive feedback from their own bodies (Haswell et al., 2009). This sensory bias has been replicated several times, appears to be specific to ASD (Izawa et al., 2012) and is a robust predictor of motor, imitation and social skill deficits (Haswell et al., 2009; Izawa et al., 2012; Marko et al., 2015). This reduced sensitivity to visual feedback also is consistent with reports that children with ASD exhibit patterns of motor deficits that reflect impairments in visual-motor integration. Children with ASD perform worse on clinical assessments of visual-motor integration (Mayes and Calhoun, 2007) and struggle to incorporate visual input into movement planning (Glazebrook et al., 2009; Dowd et al., 2012). Children with ASD also display particular difficulty with motor tasks that rely heavily on hand-eye coordination, including ball skills (Siaperas et al., 2012; Whyatt and Craig, 2012; Ament et al., 2015) and gesture imitation (Edwards, 2014). Indeed, in ball catching, for example, children must integrate visual and motor systems, using visual information to anticipate the timing of the ball's arrival at their body and mount the motor act of preparing to catch the ball before the ball's actual arrival (Ament et al., 2015). Furthermore, recent neuroimaging evidence suggests that altered connectivity, within and between visual and motor networks, may contribute to motor and social impairments in children with ASD (Fishman et al., 2014; Nebel et al., 2014, 2016).

The combined results of these prior behavioral and imaging studies implicate a connection between visual-motor integration and the severity of core ASD symptoms. However, it is unclear both when these visual-motor integration deficits emerge in the developmental cascade of behavioral and neural abnormalities leading to ASD and when their association with ASD symptomatology can be detected. During the prodromal period of ASD (Landa et al., 2007; Yirmiya and Charman, 2010; Landa et al., 2013), non-specific (to ASD) differences in motor development have been observed in infants at high risk (HR) for ASD (i.e., children who have at least one older sibling with an ASD diagnosis) (Landa and Garrett-Mayer, 2006; Flanagan et al., 2012; Leonard et al., 2014; Libertus et al., 2014). Early motor delays also appear to have predictive value for the later development of social and communication impairments (Bhat et al., 2012; Leonard et al., 2014), including ASD (Sutera et al., 2007; Bolton et al., 2012; Flanagan et al., 2012). Such social deficits are detectable not only during interaction with others, but also in eye tracking paradigms such as those demonstrating atypical attention to faces (Chawarska et al., 2010). Compelling evidence also suggests that atypical visual attention is observable by mid infancy in infants at high familial risk (HR) for ASD (Ibanez et al., 2008; Elsabbagh et al., 2009), including reduced attention to faces in children that are later diagnosed with ASD (Osterling and Dawson, 1994; Maestro et al., 2001).

While promising, these studies have focused on body movements or visual attention in isolation. Focused investigation of the development of visual-motor integration offers unique potential to provide a window into ASD pathophysiology for several reasons. Many of the early behaviors used to identify children with ASD (e.g., joint attention and the manipulation and sharing of objects) require efficient coordination between visual and motor systems. In addition, alterations in early motor and visual attention development could perturb the typical coupling of visual perception and reaching. Such coupling is important for infants to develop an understanding of event sequences (Hauf and Prinz, 2007) and for infants to learn how to plan action in order to influence the outcome of an event (Cattaneo et al., 2007). In infants later diagnosed with ASD, anticipatory abnormality has been reported (Bryson et al., 2007; Brisson et al., 2012). For example, a recent retrospective study provides evidence of reduced anticipatory responses in young children with ASD during feeding (Brisson et al., 2012). Integration of visual input with motor output is vital for the formation of internal models of action necessary to develop a wide range of motor skills and also to imitate (Wolpert et al., 2003) and interpret the actions of others (Falck-Ytter et al., 2006), which could play an important role in interpreting the intentions of others and generating socially appropriate behavior during social interaction (Pfister et al., 2013; Angus et al., 2014). Thus, closer examination of motor, and specifically visual-motor, deficits in infants at HR for ASD is of critical importance.

Examining visual-motor integration in infants at HR for ASD also may reveal important information about the cohering of brain systems. As an infant learns a new action, the brain purportedly constructs an association between motor commands and sensory feedback. These internal models of the action allow the brain to predict the sensory consequences of self-generated motor commands and to produce motor commands that maximize expected reward while minimizing effort (Shadmehr and Krakauer, 2008). The emergence of reaching in infancy offers a unique developmental window within which to investigate trajectories of visual-motor integration in children at HR for ASD. When infants begin to reach, they swat at toys (Thelen et al., 1993) and struggle to adjust their reaching response to anticipate the size, texture or orientation of objects prior to contact (Corbetta et al., 2000). Around the age that motor delays have been observed in HR infants, infants with typical development begin to incorporate visually available information into reaching movements. Typically, 5-month-old infants rely on haptic feedback and align their hands only after making contact with an object; however, by age 8 months, infants begin to use visual feedback to anticipate contact while still reaching (McCarty et al., 2001; Witherington, 2005). Reaching toward a moving object is particularly taxing on visual-motor integration and the perception-action coupling system. To successfully complete the task, a child must attend to and use visual information regarding the speed of the moving object as well as its size and shape to appropriately time and control the catching action (van der Meer et al., 1994, 1995).

In the present study of infants at high and low familial risk for ASD, possible behavioral markers of visual-motor coupling during a naturalistic, interactive dyadic ball rolling activity were investigated. A hypothesis was that, compared to LR infants, HR infants would display decreased anticipatory response (perception-guided predictive action) to a ball rolling toward them. Anticipatory responses require, among other things, visual-motor integration (perception-action coupling) and motor planning, the development of which are hypothesized to be delayed in HR infants based on reported delays in motor and visual attention. Also examined was visual attention before and during ball-rolling, hypothesized to contribute to differences in anticipatory behavior. Given the strong association between visual-motor coupling and the severity of social deficits in school age children with ASD (Haswell et al., 2009; Izawa et al., 2012; Marko et al., 2015), we examined whether maturity of anticipatory response at age 6 months would show an association with maturity in sensorimotor and social (ASD symptomatology and attention to social stimuli – faces) functioning during transition from the prodromal period into the full manifestation of ASD (Landa et al., 2013), age 14 months, in HR and LR groups.

MATERIALS AND METHODS

Participants

The Johns Hopkins Medical Institutional Review Board approved all aspects of this study. Written informed consent was obtained from the legal guardians of all participants prior to enrollment.

Participants included 66 infant siblings of children with ASD (HR) and 43 infants at low risk (LR) for ASD, defined as having no familial history of ASD, who were enrolled in a prospective, longitudinal study focusing on early patterns of development in ASD (Landa and Garrett-Mayer, 2006) and early markers of ASD. The infants in this report represent all those who completed the experimental ball rolling task described below (except for five who completed the task but data were uncodable due to infant fussiness or parent intervention during the task). Demographic information about the sample is provided in **Table 1**. Children in the study are tested at age 6 and 14 months.

Out of 109 infants who completed the ball-rolling experiment at age 6 months, 21 did not complete a 14-month visit. Nine of the 21 attrited from the study and 12 missed their 14-month study visit. Fifty-four of the 66 HR infants and 34 of the 43 LR infants who completed the ball-rolling task at age 6 months also completed the Autism Diagnostic Observation Schedule (ADOS; Lord et al., 1999, 2012), the Mullen Scales of Early Learning (MSEL; Mullen, 1995), and an eye tracking task at age 14 months. Two children (one in each group) who received the ADOS-Generic (Lord et al., 1999) Module 1 were removed from further analyses. At age 14 months, the ADOS-Toddler (ADOS-T; Lord et al., 2012) was administered to the remaining 86 children, enabling us to examine the relationship between infants' anticipatory behavior at age 6 months and social functioning at age 14 months.

Participants were recruited through local Infants and Toddlers programs, ASD advocacy groups, Kennedy Krieger outpatient clinics, pediatricians' offices, community events and parent self-referral. Inclusion criteria were (1) being 5 months, 0 day to 8 months 30 days and (2) having English as the primary language of the infants' parents. Infants were excluded if they had any of the following, per review of medical and developmental history: (1) <34 weeks or >42 weeks gestational age; (2) <2300 g birth weight; (3) severe birth trauma; (4) head injury sustained before or during the study; (5) illicit drug or excessive alcohol exposure; (6) major hearing or visual impairment; (7) non-febrile seizures; (8) any known genetic syndrome; or (9) severe birth defects. All infants in the HR group had an older sibling with idiopathic ASD, confirmed by the ADOS, meeting DSM-IV autism or Pervasive Developmental Disorder-Not Otherwise Specified or DSM-5

TABLE 1 | Participant demographics at ages 6 and 14 months.

Measure	Group at age 6 months				Group at age 14 months			
	LR $n = 43$		HR $n = 66$		LR $n = 33$		HR $n = 53$	
Male/*female*	24/*19*		36/*30*		18/*15*		29/*24*	
Has (a) Sibling(s)	26		66		20		53	
	$\bar{X}$	*SD*	$\bar{X}$	*SD*	$\bar{X}$	*SD*	$\bar{X}$	*SD*
Age	6.7	0.51	6.7	0.56	14.8	0.77	14.8	0.78
AOSI Total	5.4	3.0	7.5*	3.5				
MSEL Gross Motor	6.5	1.0	6.3	1.4	15.7	2.2	14.9	1.8
MSEL Fine Motor	7.1	1.2	6.5*	1.3	17.1	1.4	16.5	1.7
MSEL Visual Reception	7.0	1.0	6.7	0.97	17.2	1.8	15.6*	1.9
ADOS-T overall					3.5	2.2	8.2*	5.6
ADOS-T SA total					2.2	2.0	6.3*	4.8

*Out of 109 infants who completed the ball-rolling experiment at age 6 months, 21 did not complete a 14-month visit. Nine of the 21 attrited from the study and 12 missed their 14-month study visit. AOSI, Autism Observation Scale for Infants; ADOS-T, Autism Diagnostic Observation Schedule-Toddler Module; SA, Social Affect. * indicates significant difference between LR and HR groups, $p < 0.05$.*

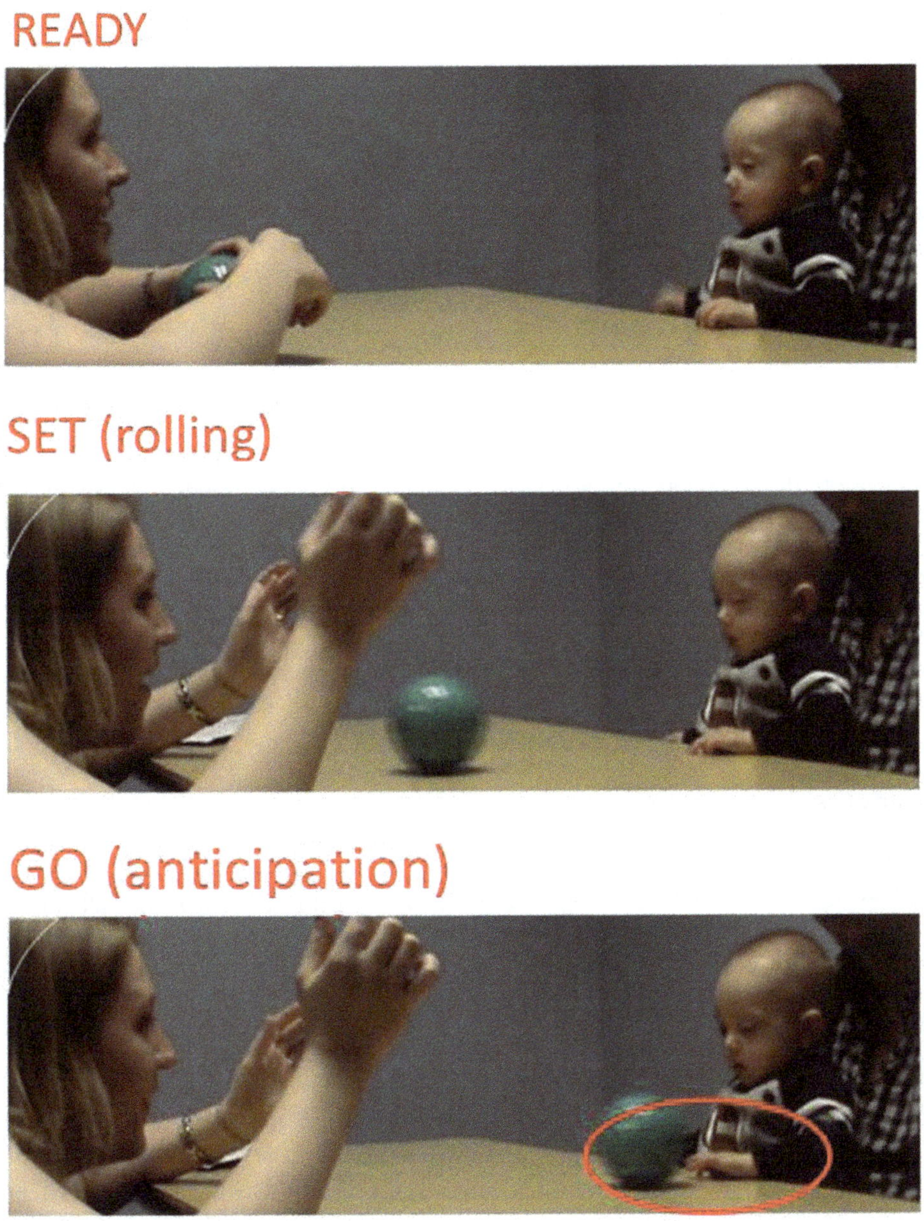

FIGURE 1 | Ready, Set, Go phases of the ball-rolling task.

criteria for ASD (American Psychiatric Association [APA], 1994, 2013), and having a clinical best estimate of ASD established by a trained clinician. Twenty-six of the 43 infants in the LR group had a typically developing older sibling.

Experimental Ball Rolling Task

We coded archived videos of infants' behavior during an experimental ball-rolling task initiated by an examiner. Infants were seated at a table on a caregiver's lap opposite the examiner. Caregivers provided non-restrictive postural support at the hips, mid-trunk, or upper trunk, enabling infants to move their arms, hands, and trunk freely during the task. The task involved the use of a smooth-surface ball, approximately 5′ in diameter and easily clutched. Dependent variables were obtained across three phases (Ready, Set, Go; see **Figure 1**). The coding rubric is presented in **Table 2**. In the "Ready" phase, the examiner bounced the ball three times while smiling and looking at the child. During the "Set" phase, the examiner gently rolled the ball toward the child. The "Go" phase involved the child's response to the approaching ball. At no time did the examiner provide verbal instructions to the infant.

In the "Ready" and "Set" phases, coding focused on maturity of children's attention engagement to relevant stimuli (examiner and ball). During the "Go" phase, maturity of children's

TABLE 2 | Coding schema for maturity of infant attention engagement and anticipatory response.

	Ready phase	Set phase	Go phase
Coder's prompt for scoring	Just before the ball rolls to child, where is the child looking?	As the ball approaches, before contacting child's body, where is the child looking?	Does the child move an arm or hand in anticipation of the approaching ball?
0	Child did not look at the ball or examiner	Child did not look at the ball during roll	No arm/hand movement toward the ball in anticipation
1	Delayed onset of gaze to the ball or examiner	As the ball approaches, child looks at least once to the examiner but not at the ball	Moves arm/hand in anticipation but no contact before ball hits body
2	Immediate gaze to ball **or** examiner	As ball approaches, child looks at the ball fleetingly (ball halfway across table before looking)	Moves arm/hand in anticipation, makes contact before ball hits body, but has to readjust hand position after contact to grasp the ball
3	Immediate gaze to ball **and** examiner	Child watches most of the ball's trajectory toward him/herself (beginning when examiner releases the ball)	Moves arm/hand in anticipation with *open* hand, makes contact before ball hits body, and does not have to readjust hand position to grasp the ball

anticipatory motor response to the ball's approach was coded, as indicated by whether and how children moved their hands toward the ball before it contacted their trunk. Videos were scored by two trained raters, who were blinded to risk status and achieved and maintained ≥90% inter-rater reliability using Cronbach's Alpha measure for the Ready, Set and Go phases.

Descriptive Measures

We used the Mullen Scales of Early Learning (MSEL; Mullen, 1995) Visual Reception, Gross Motor, and Fine Motor scales to assess non-verbal cognitive (visual pattern recognition, memory, and sequencing) and gross and fine motor skill, respectively, at ages 6 and 14 months. The MSEL is a standardized developmental test for children between ages 0–68 months. To investigate whether anticipation behavior at age 6 months was related to sensorimotor behavior at 14 months, a sensorimotor composite score was generated by summing age equivalency scores across the three afore-mentioned MSEL scales. Higher composite scores indicate more mature sensorimotor behavior.

The ADOS was administered at age 14 months to directly assess ASD symptoms, with all children receiving the Toddle Module (Lord et al., 2012) except for two children (1 HR) who received the ADOS-G Module 1 (Lord et al., 1999). The ADOS is a play-based standardized, gold standard assessment of ASD; higher ADOS Total scores represent greater impairment and greater concern for ASD in terms of social deficits.

As another measure of social engagement, we used an eye tracking paradigm to investigate infants' attention to socially relevant stimuli (faces) at age 14 months (Libertus and Needham, 2011, 2014a,b). Pairs of faces and toys were presented side-by-side while infant eye gaze was recorded. A preference for faces was defined as the difference between the proportions of time spent looking at faces versus objects. Face preference values range from −100 to +100, with negative values indicating a visual preference for objects, 0 indicating no preference, and positive values indicating a visual preference for faces.

Statistical Analyses

A logistic regression model was used to explore whether HR and LR infants could be distinguished based on their initiation of anticipatory action response during the ball-rolling activity. The primary independent variable (anticipation) was ordinal, but a number of continuous covariates were included in our model to account for potentially confounding sources of variability between the groups, including age and MSEL Gross Motor and Fine Motor performance at the time of examination. For the regression model, the dependent variable, ASD risk (HR, LR), was labeled according to the rule that $Y_i = 0$ if the ith participant belonged to the LR group and $Y_i = 1$ if the ith participant belonged to the HR group. Then,

$$\text{logit}[P(Y_i = 1)] = \beta_0 + X_i\beta_1$$

where β_0 is the intercept showing the average log odds of having high familial risk of ASD when all covariates are equal to zero, for each subject i; X_i is the vector of ball-rolling behavior scores and covariates added to account for potential confounders on the relationship between familial risk and ball-rolling task response. The exponentiated form of the log odds coefficients (e^{β}) is reported for variables that were significant predictors of risk status along with the corresponding p-value.

Next to be examined was whether familial risk and early anticipation behavior are prognostic of later sensorimotor and ASD-related social functioning. In this analysis, familial risk for ASD and anticipation score at age 6 months served as independent variables. Stratifying subjects by risk (high/low) and anticipation at age 6 months (four levels: 0,1,2,3), two-way analyses of variance were used to test for between-group differences in ASD-related behaviors and sensorimotor skills observed at age 14 months. Additionally, *post hoc* simple main effect analyses and t-tests were performed to further investigate the influence of risk/anticipation combinations on outcome measures, with p-values adjusted for multiple comparisons using Bonferroni correction.

Finally, a logistic regression model was used to investigate whether early anticipation behavior was prognostic of later concern for ASD within the HR group. For this analysis, we grouped together all HR children who received an ADOS total scores indicating at least mild concern for ASD and compared them to HR infants whose ADOS total score indicated no concern for ASD.

RESULTS

Association between Anticipation at Age 6 Months and Familial Risk for ASD

Descriptive information about participants in each group (age, sex, MSEL Gross and Fine Motor scores, and total scores on the AOSI and ADOS) for HR and LR groups are presented in **Table 1**. Conditional distributions of the ball-rolling behavioral variables are presented in **Figure 2**. To explore whether HR and LR infants could be distinguished based on their anticipatory action response during the ball-rolling activity, we constructed a logistic regression model, which included a number of covariates to account for potentially confounding sources of variability between familial risk groups. After plotting the conditional distributions of the ball-rolling behavioral variables, Ready and Set phase data were excluded as covariates because nearly all children performed at ceiling during these phases by (a) immediately directing their attention to the ball and/or examiner prior to the roll and (b) visually tracking the ball for most of its trajectory toward them. The proportion of infants who failed to immediately direct their attention to the ball and/or examiner and visually track the ball for most of its trajectory did not differ significantly between familial risk groups (ready: X2 = 0.19, p = 0.66; roll: X2 = 0.10, p = 0.75). Including age on the day of the ball-rolling experiment, MSEL Gross and Fine Motor scores, and anticipation score as predictors of familial risk, our model as a whole fit significantly better than the intercept only model (X2 = 17.97, df = 6, p = 0.006, McFadden pseudo-R^2 = 0.212). **Table 3** lists odds ratios, z-statistics, and the associated p-value for each predictor. As can be seen from **Table 3**, we detected a marginal between-group age difference. On average, HR infants were slightly older than LR infants at the time of the targeted age 6-month examination, and a 1-month increase in age at the time of examination was associated with decreased odds of belonging to the LR group by a factor of 0.40 (p = 0.076). This age difference could have afforded the HR group a slight performance advantage.

TABLE 3 | Predictors of familial risk for ASD at age 6 months.

Predictor	Odds ratio	z-Statistic	p-Value
Age	0.40	−1.78	0.076
MSEL Gross Motor	1.18	0.83	0.407
MSEL Fine Motor	1.62	2.32	0.020
Anticipation 0–1	5.78	2.68	0.007
Anticipation 0–2	3.32	1.93	0.053
Anticipation 0–3	4.57	2.28	0.023

Positive odds indicate that an increase in the predictor variable (e.g., going from an anticipation score of 0–1) results in an increase in the odds of a participant belonging to the low risk group (versus belonging to the high risk group). The most common score was used as the reference level (0).

The logistic regression model revealed a significant effect of MSEL Fine Motor score on familial risk (HR vs. LR group). Analysis of MSEL motor scales revealed that, on average, HR infants displayed less mature fine motor skills; a one unit increase in MSEL Fine Motor score increased the odds of belonging to the LR group by a factor of 1.62 (p = 0.020). In contrast, 6-month-old MSEL Gross Motor scores were not predictive of familial risk (p = 0.407).

After controlling for age and fine and gross motor skills (based on MSEL Fine and Gross Motor scores), a main effect of anticipation on familial risk group (X2 = 8.4, df = 3, p = 0.039) was identified during the "Go" phase of the task. Regardless of the maturity of the movement, moving a hand/arm in anticipation of the approaching ball (score of 1–3; see **Table 2**) was associated with decreased odds of belonging to the HR group. Displaying no movement in anticipation of catching the ball increased the odds of belonging to the HR group by a factor of 5.78 (p = 0.007) compared to displaying a delayed hand/arm movement (score of 1), by a factor of 3.32 compared to successfully anticipating the ball but having to readjust hand position after making initial contact (score of 2) (p = 0.053), and by a factor of 4.57 compared to successfully anticipating the ball with the proper hand orientation to grab the ball (score of 3) (p = 0.023). In other words, HR infants were less likely than LR infants to initiate action in anticipation of the approaching ball (**Figure 2C**).

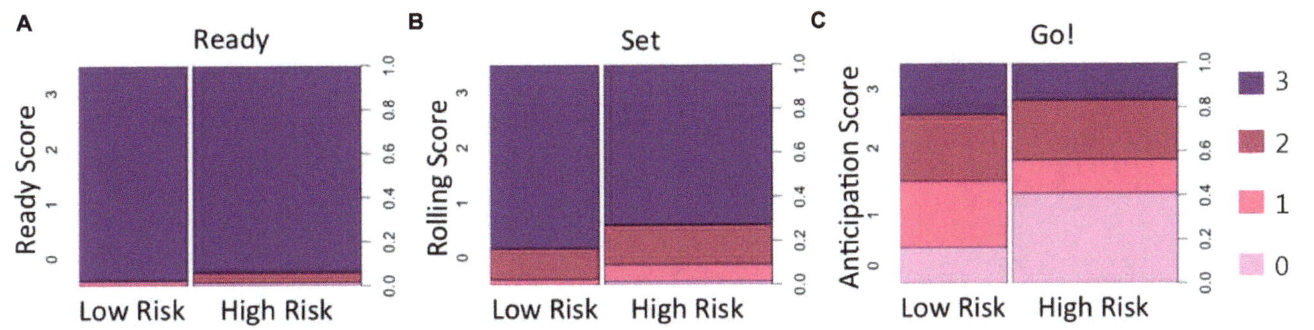

FIGURE 2 | Spine plots of behavioral responses during the three phases of the ball-rolling task. The majority of children in HR and LR groups demonstrated context appropriate looking behavior by **(A)** looking immediately at the ball and/or examiner during the Ready phase (just prior to the examiner releasing the ball) and by **(B)** visually tracking the trajectory of the ball as it slowly rolled across the table toward them during the Set phase. However, the larger light purple area for the HR group in **(C)** indicates that HR infants were less likely to show a context appropriate motor response; they were more likely to fail to move in anticipation of catching the ball before the ball hit their bodies compared to LR infants.

Association between Anticipation at Age 6 Months and Social and Sensorimotor Functioning at Age 14 Months

A two-way ANOVA was conducted to examine relationships among familial risk for ASD (two levels), anticipation behavior at age 6 months (four levels) and total ADOS score at age 14 months. There was a statistically significant main effect of familial risk on total ADOS score [$F_{(3,78)} = 18.656$, $p < 0.001$], with the HR group, on average, exhibiting a higher total score on the ADOS (mean [SD]: 8.15 [5.6]) and more behaviors consistent with ASD than the LR group (3.52 [2.2]). However, there was no significant interaction between familial risk for ASD and anticipation at age 6 months on 14-month total ADOS score [$F_{(3,78)} = 1.40$, $p = 0.25$] (**Figure 3A**). **Table 4** displays 6-month-old anticipatory score counts for the HR group stratified by ASD concern at 14 months of age. Excluding the one HR subject who received the ADOS-G from our logistic regression model of 14-month concern for ASD, 17 children in the HR group scored high enough on the ADOS-T to warrant at least mild concern for ASD. After controlling for age and fine and gross motor skills at age 6 months within the HR group, we did not observe a main effect of 6-month anticipation on 14-month concern for ASD ($X2 = 0.79$, $df = 3$, $p = 0.85$).

Figure 3B displays age 14-month preference for looking at faces stratified by ASD risk group and age 6 month anticipation. We observed a significant interaction between familial risk for ASD and anticipation at age 6 months on our outcome of interest at age 14 months [$F_{(3,78)} = 4.375$, $p = 0.007$]. Simple main effects analysis revealed no significant difference between 14-month preference for faces in HR and LR children who did not move in anticipation of catching the ball at age 6 months

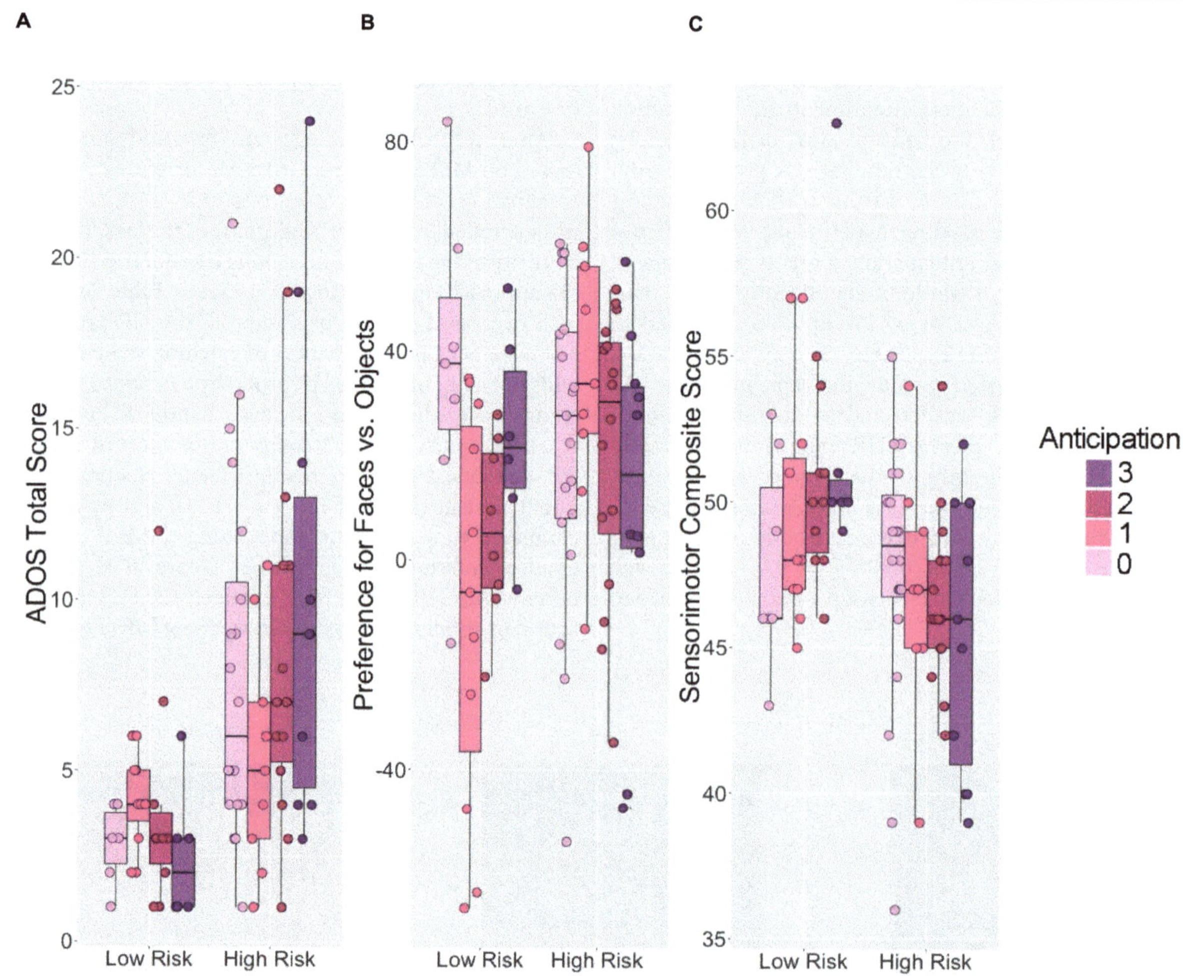

FIGURE 3 | Six-month anticipation behavior versus 14-month social and sensorimotor outcomes for children at low and high familial risk for autism. Boxplots displaying **(A)** ADOS Total Score, **(B)** preference for faces compared to objects, and **(C)** MSEL sensorimotor composite scores. Within each panel, scores for LR children are on the left; scores for HR children are on the right. The upper and lower "hinges" correspond to the first and third quartiles of the distribution for each risk group at each level of 6-month anticipation. Higher **ADOS Total scores** represent worse performance. Face preference values range from −100 to 100, with negative values indicating a visual preference for objects, 0 indicating no preference, and positive values indicating a visual preference for faces. Sensorimotor composite scores were calculated by summing three relevant age-equivalent subscale scores from the Mullen Scales of Early Learning (MSEL): Visual Reception, Gross and Fine Motor. Higher sensorimotor composite scores represent better performance.

TABLE 4 | Six-month anticipatory behavior in the High Risk group stratified by concern for ASD at 14-month-old.

6-month Anticipation	HR at 14-month-old	
	No ASD Concern $n = 36$	At least Mild ASD Concern $n = 17$
0	14 (38.8%)	6 (35.2%)
1	7 (19.4%)	2 (11.7%)
2	9 (25%)	5 (29.4%)
3	6 (16.7%)	4 (23.6%)

The one HR subject who received the ADOS-G instead of the ADOS-T at the 14-month-old time point was excluded from this analysis.

($t = 1.00$, df $= 3$, $p = 0.34$). However, comparison of 14-month face preference behavior of HR and LR children with 6-month anticipation scores of 1 (delayed onset of anticipatory movement) revealed that the HR children exhibited a stronger preference for faces than LR children ($t = 3.099$, df $= 17.8$, $p = 0.006$); on average, HR children who exhibited a delayed anticipatory response to the ball spent 36.6% more time looking at faces than at objects, while LR children who exhibited a delayed onset of anticipatory response to the ball actually spent 8.9% more time looking at objects than at faces. In addition, we observed a simple main effect of anticipation on preference for faces within the LR group [$F_{(3,28)} = 3.373, p = 0.02$]. Follow-up t-tests suggested that LR children who did not move in anticipation of catching the ball exhibited much stronger preference for faces than LR children who exhibited a late (delayed) anticipatory response ($p = 0.009$). Such relationships between anticipation and preference for faces were not observed in the HR group [$F_{(3,50)} = 1.14 = 39$, $p = 0.342$], likely because of the high level of face-looking in the HR infants who showed delayed activation of anticipatory response.

Figure 3C displays 14-month sensorimotor composite scores stratified by ASD risk group and 6-month-old anticipation. We observed a statistically significant main effect of familial risk for ASD on the study-defined sensorimotor composite score at age 14 months [$F_{(3,78)} = 12.4$, $p < 0.001$]; on average, LR children demonstrated higher sensorimotor composite scores (49.9 [4.00]) than HR children (46.7 [4.03]). However, the interaction between familial risk for ASD and anticipation at age 6 months on sensorimotor behavior at age 14 months was not statistically significant [$F_{(3,78)} = 1.67$, $p = 0.18$].

DISCUSSION

Overview of Findings

The aim of this study was to examine whether early ASD risk indicators are detectable in mid infancy, particularly perception-guided predictive action, or initiating anticipatory hand/arm action in response to a visibly approaching object during dyadic interpersonal engagement. To our knowledge, this is the first such study in infants at heightened familial risk for ASD. Six-month-old infants at HR and LR for ASD engaged in a dynamic, interactive dyadic ball-rolling activity with an examiner. No group differences were observed in the infants' visual attention before ('Ready' phase) or during ('Set' phase) ball rolling; both groups demonstrated context appropriate looking behavior, indicating engagement in the activity. However, as hypothesized, HR infants displayed decreased perception-guided predictive action in response to the approaching ball compared to LR infants. This finding did not appear to be driven by differences in motor ability between risk groups at 6 months of age. No relationship was identified in the HR group between 6-month anticipatory action response and 14-month sensorimotor functioning or degree of autism symptomatology, an age window within which many children who will later be diagnosed with ASD remain within the ASD prodromal phase. Surprisingly, HR infants with emerging anticipatory response (score of 1) at age 6 months exhibited greater face preference performance at age 14 months compared to LR infants at the same level of anticipatory response maturity at age 6 months.

Anticipatory Action Responses at Age 6 Months

To successfully anticipate catching a moving object, infants must rapidly incorporate visual information about the size and speed of the ball into their motor plan. Despite their attention to the approaching ball, a subgroup of HR infants completely failed to translate visual information into a successful motor response. Our finding of lower anticipatory action response to the approaching ball in the HR group indicates that the deficit in visual-motor coupling and anticipatory responses previously identified in older children with ASD, even those without intellectual developmental delay, have roots in infancy (Mostofsky et al., 2000; Schmitz et al., 2003; Martineau et al., 2004; Cattaneo et al., 2007; Whyatt and Craig, 2013; Ament et al., 2015; Sharer et al., 2015). Our finding extends that reported by Brisson et al. (2012) whose retrospective study identified a deficit in anticipatory mouth opening in 4- to 6-month-olds later diagnosed with ASD when a spoon approached during feeding. Similarly, Cattaneo et al. (2007) found that children with ASD, unlike those with typical development, failed to show anticipatory mylohyoid activation during observation or execution of grasping an object to eat. A diminished capacity to move in an anticipatory manner at such an early age could reflect a deficit in the brain's ability to construct an internal model relating visual feedback with motor output. Such internal action models are thought to be critical not only to predict the sensory consequences of self-generated motor commands but also to interpret the actions of others.

In our study, the failure of the HR infants' initiation of hand movement to 'catch' the ball rolled toward them by a social partner could be due to lack of attention, lack of motivation to stop and explore the ball, motor impairment (Bhat et al., 2011), diminished motion detection or direction capabilities, failure to comprehend the social contingency of the dyadic game (Nadel, 2002), impaired coupling of visual and temporal information to guide and adapt movement (Ament et al., 2015), or a motor planning deficit resulting in poor timing of movement execution (Forti et al., 2011). In the present study, less mature fine motor skills were identified in the HR than LR infants. However, this immaturity cannot fully account for our finding of anticipatory deficit in HR infants as motor skill level was controlled for in the analyses. Attention and motivation are not viable explanations either, as all infants in both groups were highly attentive to the task and explored the ball after it had been rolled to them (whether or not they demonstrated anticipatory action response). Existing literature suggests that basic motion detection and direction perception thresholds are largely unimpaired in ASD (Mottron et al., 2006) and are not likely to blame for the reduction in anticipatory responses in the HR group. Regardless of the specific underlying mechanism, a lack of anticipatory response during infancy could contribute to a short- or longer-term developmental cascade in which infants' anticipatory failure thwarts the unfolding dynamic exchange with the social partner and diminishes the quality or quantity of social input, which could thereby attenuate social outcomes (Hofer et al., 2008). Early failure of anticipatory action response also could impede infants' learning about action contingencies, which plays a role in the development of action control (Hauf et al., 2004) and could impact a host of later-emerging motor-related social functions such as imitation and joint attention.

Relationship between 6-Month Anticipatory Responses and 14-Month Sensorimotor and Social Behavior

Although a subgroup of HR infants completely failed to translate visual information into a successful motor response at age 6 months, this failure was not associated with an increased likelihood of showing more signs of ASD at age 14 months, as measured by total score on the ADOS. This finding was surprising given others' findings that visual-motor integration deficits are associated with social deficits (Haswell et al., 2009). Perhaps our negative finding is related to the fact that ASD symptoms are just emerging in most children with ASD during the second year of life (Ozonoff et al., 2010; Landa et al., 2013), and about half of children later diagnosed with ASD remain prodromal at age 14 months (Landa et al., 2007, 2013). Perhaps anticipatory behavior at age 6 months will predict ASD at a slightly older age, subsequent to the ASD prodromal phase. Reduced anticipatory response at age 6 months also was not associated with worse sensorimotor performance at age 14 months, as measured by our study-defined sensorimotor composite score. However, we did observe a significant interaction between 6-month anticipation and familial risk for ASD on 14-month attention to faces.

We found that, in the HR group only, emerging anticipatory response (as opposed to absent or acquired) at age 6 months was associated with increased levels of face-looking at age 14 months. High levels of face looking actually may not be typical at age 14 months. In a recent study of face looking in infants from 3 to 11 months of age and adults using an eye tracking task identical to the one used herein, Libertus and Needham (2014a) identified an inverted U shaped curve over time such that lowest levels of face-looking occurred at 3 and 11 months of age; no face preference was identified in the adults. Indeed, our finding of stronger face preference at age 14 months in LR infants who failed to move in anticipation of catching the ball than in those with emerging anticipatory response may indicate a relationship between early observable immaturity in anticipatory behavior and a later atypicality in proportion of time spent looking at faces. This is echoed by the LR infants who exhibited no anticipatory response, as they demonstrated more preference for faces compared to anticipating LR infants. The relationship between early anticipatory behavior and later face preference requires further investigation in children at low and HR for ASD.

The findings discussed above extend our (Landa and Garrett-Mayer, 2006; Bhat et al., 2012; Flanagan et al., 2012; Libertus and Landa, 2013; Libertus et al., 2014) and others' (e.g., Iverson and Wozniak, 2007) reports of motor-related delays in HR infants, others' reports of anticipatory deficits in ASD (e.g., Cattaneo et al., 2007; Brisson et al., 2012), and of visuo-motor abnormalities in ASD (e.g., Sharer et al., 2015), even a report of ASD-specific abnormality in ball catching in high-functioning children with ASD (Ament et al., 2015). Also, these findings are consistent with the hypothesis of predictive impairment in autism which attempts to explain autism as a general impairment in information processing (Sinha et al., 2014) and predicts that motor anticipation will be reduced in individuals with ASD.

Limitations

The greatest limitations of the present study include sample size and the absence of information regarding diagnostic outcomes. Although the sample size was sufficient to detect group differences at age 6 months and moderately distal (8 months later) relationships between infant action anticipation and attention to faces in toddlerhood, ideally we would like to probe whether infant action anticipation is associated with concern for ASD at a developmental stage that is more commonly used for diagnosis (24- or 36 months of age). We are not yet able to discern the implications of deficits in perception-guided predictive action at age 6 months for the emergence of the autism phenotype.

Future Directions

Increasingly, emerging evidence highlights the importance of early action experiences for short and longer-term motor, cognitive, and social outcomes. Yet there is much to learn, particularly with regard to when and how developmental processes are altered in infants at HR for ASD. Research is needed to define the relationship between action control, visual attention, motor skill, action anticipation, contingency learning, imitation and joint attention concurrently and over time during the first 3 years of life. In particular, mechanisms that support action anticipation in HR infants and how these may differ from those in LR infants require definition. The decoupling of early execution of anticipatory action and social functioning 8 months later in HR infants should be further investigated and requires replication. In addition, research focused on the impact of early dyadic, reciprocal action routines and self-generated action experiences in HR infants is needed to determine potential for improving later social functioning; promise of such effects are emerging (Libertus and Landa, 2014; Libertus and Needham, 2014b). Such research is important because the abilities that afford execution of anticipatory action involve the integration of visual information with motor performance, which is needed in the development of internal action models. Such action models likely are relevant to development of motor skills central to social development such as imitation, production of interpretable and well-timed interpersonally synchronous actions, as well as for the understanding of others' action intentions. Ultimately, the goal is to detect developmental vulnerabilities as early in life as possible in infants at HR for ASD and to optimize their outcomes.

AUTHOR CONTRIBUTIONS

RL: study design, task development, coding schema development, conceptualizing the study, writing the manuscript. JH and MBN: coding schema refinement, coding the data, conducting analyses, writing the manuscript.

FUNDING

This study was funded by the National Institute of Mental Health Award Number R01 MH059630 (Landa, PI) and ROAR (Landa PI).

ACKNOWLEDGMENTS

The authors wish to thank the families and children for their generous commitment to this research, to the dedicated staff in the Center for Autism and Related Disorders' research laboratory.

REFERENCES

Ament, K., Mejia, A., Buhlman, R., Erklin, S., Caffo, B., Mostofsky, S., et al. (2015). Evidence for specificity of motor impairments in catching and balance in children with autism. *J. Autism Dev. Disord.* 45, 742–751. doi: 10.1007/s10803-014-2229-0

American Psychiatric Association [APA] (1994). *Diagnostic and Statistical Manual of Mental Disorders (DSM-4).* Washington, DC: American Psychiatric Association.

American Psychiatric Association [APA] (2013). *Diagnostic and Statistical Manual of Mental Disorders (DSM-5).* Washington, DC: American Psychiatric Association.

Angus, D. J., de Rosnay, M., Lunenburg, P., Terwogt, M. M., and Begeer, S. (2014). Limitations in social anticipation are independent of imaginative and Theory of Mind abilities in children with autism but not in typically developing children. *Autism* 19, 604–612. doi: 10.1177/1362361314537911

Bhat, A. N., Galloway, J. C., and Landa, R. J. (2012). Relation between early motor delay and later communication delay in infants at risk for autism. *Infant Behav. Dev.* 35, 838–846. doi: 10.1016/j.infbeh.2012.07.019

Bhat, A. N., Landa, R. J., and Galloway, J. C. C. (2011). Current perspectives on motor functioning in infants, children, and adults with autism spectrum disorders. *Phys. Ther.* 91, 1116–1129. doi: 10.2522/ptj.20100294

Bolton, P. F., Golding, J., Emond, A., and Steer, C. D. (2012). Autism spectrum disorder and autistic traits in the Avon Longitudinal Study of Parents and Children: precursors and early signs. *J. Am. Acad. Child Adolesc. Psychiatry* 51, 249–260. doi: 10.1016/j.jaac.2011.12.009

Brisson, J., Warreyn, P., Serres, J., Foussier, S., and Adrien, J. L. (2012). Motor anticipation failure in infants with autism: a retrospective analysis of feeding situations. *Autism* 16, 420–429. doi: 10.1177/1362361311423385

Bryson, S. E., Zwaigenbaum, L., Brian, J., Roberts, W., Szatmari, P., Rombough, V., et al. (2007). A prospective case series of high-risk infants who developed autism. *J. Autism Dev. Disord.* 37, 12–24. doi: 10.1007/s10803-006-0328-2

Cattaneo, L., Fabbri-Destro, M., Boria, S., Pieraccini, C., Monti, A., Cossu, G., et al. (2007). Impairment of actions chains in autism and its possible role in intention understanding. *Proc. Natl. Acad. Sci. U.S.A.* 104, 17825–17830. doi: 10.1073/pnas.0706273104

Chawarska, K., Volkmar, F., and Klin, A. (2010). Limited attentional bias for faces in toddlers with autism spectrum disorders. *Arch. Gen. Psychiatry* 67, 178–185. doi: 10.1001/archgenpsychiatry.2009.194

Corbetta, D., Thelen, E., and Johnson, K. (2000). Motor constraints on the development of perception-action matching in infant reaching. *Infant Behav. Dev.* 23, 351–374. doi: 10.1016/S0163-6383(01)00049-2

Dowd, A. M., McGinley, J. L., Taffe, J. R., and Rinehart, N. J. (2012). Do Planning and visual integration difficulties underpin motor dysfunction in autism? A kinematic study of young children with autism. *J. Autism Dev. Disord.* 42, 1539–1548. doi: 10.1007/s10803-011-1385-8

Edwards, L. A. (2014). A meta-analysis of imitation abilities in individuals with autism spectrum disorders. *Autism Res.* 7, 363–380. doi: 10.1002/aur.1379

Elsabbagh, M., Volein, A., Holmboe, K., Tucker, L., Csibra, G., Baron-Cohen, S., et al. (2009). Visual orienting in the early broader autism phenotype: disengagement and facilitation. *J. Child Psychol. Psychiatry* 50, 637–642. doi: 10.1111/j.1469-7610.2008.02051.x

Falck-Ytter, T., Gredebäck, G., and von Hofsten, C. (2006). Infants predict other people's action goals. *Nat. Neurosci.* 9, 878–879. doi: 10.1038/nn1729

Fishman, I., Keown, C. L., Lincoln, A. J., Pineda, J. A., and Müller, R. A. (2014). A typical cross talk between mentalizing and mirror neuron networks in autism spectrum disorder. *JAMA Psychiatry* 71, 751–760. doi: 10.1001/jamapsychiatry.2014.83

Flanagan, J. E., Landa, R., Bhat, A., and Bauman, M. (2012). Head lag in infants at risk for autism: a preliminary study. *Am. J. Occup. Ther.* 66, 577–585. doi: 10.5014/ajot.2012.004192

Forti, S., Valli, A., Perego, P., Nobile, M., Crippa, A., and Molteni, M. (2011). Motor planning and control in autism. A kinematic analysis of preschool children. *Res. Autism Spectr. Disord.* 5, 834–842. doi: 10.1016/j.rasd.2010.09.013

Glazebrook, C., Gonzalez, D., Hansen, S., and Elliott, D. (2009). The role of vision for online control of manual aiming movements in persons with autism spectrum disorders. *Autism* 13, 411–433 doi: 10.1177/1362361309105659

Haswell, C. C., Izawa, J., Dowell, L. R., Mostofsky, S. H., and Shadmehr, R. (2009). Representation of internal models of action in the autistic brain. *Nat. Neurosci.* 12, 970–972. doi: 10.1038/nn.2356

Hauf, P., Elsner, B., and Aschersleben, G. (2004). The role of action effects in infants' action control. *Psychol. Res.* 68, 115–125. doi: 10.1007/s00426-003-0149-2

Hauf, P., and Prinz, W. (2007). "The understanding of own and others' actions during infancy," in *Making Minds: The Shaping of Human Minds through Social Context*, eds P. Hauf and F. Forsterling (Amsterdam: John Benjamins), 211–226.

Hofer, T., Hohenberger, A., Hauf, P., and Aschersleben, G. (2008). The link between maternal interaction style and infant action understanding. *Infant Behav. Dev.* 31, 115–126. doi: 10.1016/j.infbeh.2007.07.003

Ibanez, L. V., Messinger, D. S., Newell, L., Lambert, B., and Sheskin, M. (2008). Visual disengagement in the infant siblings of children with an autism spectrum disorder (ASD). *Autism* 12, 473–485. doi: 10.1177/13623613 08094504

Iverson, J. M., and Wozniak, R. H. (2007). Variation in vocal-motor development in infant siblings of children with autism. *J. Autism Dev. Disord.* 37, 158–170. doi: 10.1007/s10803-006-0339-z

Izawa, J., Pekny, S. E., Marko, M. K., Haswell, C. C., Shadmehr, R., and Mostofsky, S. H. (2012). Motor learning relies on integrated sensory inputs in ADHD, but over-selectively on proprioception in autism spectrum conditions. *Autism Res.* 5, 124–136. doi: 10.1002/aur.1222

Landa, R., and Garrett-Mayer, E. (2006). Development in infants with autism spectrum disorders: a prospective study. *J. Child Psychol. Psychiatry* 47, 629–638. doi: 10.1111/j.1469-7610.2006.01531.x

Landa, R. J., Gross, A. L., Stuart, E. A., and Faherty, A. (2013). Developmental trajectories in children with and without autism spectrum disorders: the first three years. *Child Dev.* 84, 429–442. doi: 10.1111/j.1467-8624.2012.01870.x

Landa, R. J., Holman, K. C., and Garrett-Mayer, E. (2007). Social communication development in toddlers with early and later diagnosis of autism spectrum disorders. *Arch. Gen. Psychiatry* 64, 853–864. doi: 10.1001/archpsyc.64.7.853

Leonard, H. C., Bedford, R., Charman, T., Elsabbagh, M., Johnson, M. H., Hill, E. L., et al. (2014). Motor development in children at risk of autism: a follow-up study of infant siblings. *Autism* 18, 281–291. doi: 10.1177/1362361312470037

Libertus, K., and Landa, R. J. (2013). The Early Motor Questionnaire (EMQ): a parental report measure of early motor development. *Infant Behav. Dev.* 36, 833–842. doi: 10.1016/j.infbeh.2013.09.007

Libertus, K., and Landa, R. J. (2014). Scaffolded reaching experiences encourage grasping activity in infants at high risk for autism. *Front. Psychol.* 5:1071. doi: 10.3389/fpsyg.2014.01071

Libertus, K., and Needham, A. (2011). Reaching experience increases face preference in 3-month-old infants. *Dev. Sci.* 14, 1355–1364. doi: 10.1111/j.1467-7687.2011.01084.x

Libertus, K., and Needham, A. (2014a). Face preference in infancy and its relation to motor activity. *Int. J. Behav. Dev.* 38, 529–538. doi: 10.1177/0165025414535122

Libertus, K., and Needham, A. (2014b). Encouragement is nothing without control: factors influencing the development of reaching and face preference. *J. Motor Learn. Dev.* 2, 16–27. doi: 10.1123/jmld.2013-0019

Libertus, K., Sheperd, K. A., Ross, S. W., and Landa, R. J. (2014). Limited fine motor and grasping skills in 6-month-old infants at high risk for autism. *Child Dev.* 85, 2218–2231. doi: 10.1111/cdev.12262

Lord, C., Luyster, R., Gotham, K., Guthrie, W., Risi, S., and Rutter, M. (2012). *Autism Diagnostic Observation Schedule – Toddler Module Manual.* Los Angeles, CA: Western Psychological Services.

Lord, C., Rutter, M., DiLavore, P. S., and Risi, S. (1999). *The ADOS-G (Autism Diagnostic Observation Schedule-Generic).* Santa Monica, CA: Western Psychological Services.

Maestro, S., Muratori, F., Barbieri, F., Casella, C., Cattaneo, V., Cavallaro, M. C., et al. (2001). Early behavioral development in autistic children: the first 2 years of life through home movies. *Psychopathology* 34, 147–152. doi: 10.1159/000049298

Marko, M. K., Crocetti, D., Hulst, T., Donchin, O., Shadmehr, R., and Mostofsky, S. H. (2015). Behavioural and neural basis of anomalous motor learning in children with autism. *Brain* 138(Pt 3), 784–797. doi: 10.1093/brain/awu394

Martineau, J., Schmitz, C., Assaiante, C., Blanc, R., and Barthélémy, C. (2004). Impairment of a cortical event-related desynchronisation during a bimanual load-lifting task in children with autistic disorder. *Neurosci. Lett.* 367, 298–303. doi: 10.1016/j.neulet.2004.06.018

Mayes, S. D., and Calhoun, S. L. (2007). Learning, attention, writing, and processing speed in typical children and children with ADHD, autism, anxiety, depression, and oppositional-defiant disorder. *Child Neuropsychol.* 13, 469–493. doi: 10.1080/09297040601112773

McCarty, M. E., Clifton, R. K., Ashmead, D. H., Lee, P., and Goubet, N. (2001). How infants use vision for grasping objects. *Child Dev.* 72, 973–987. doi: 10.1111/1467-8624.00329

Mostofsky, S. H., Goldberg, M. C., Landa, R. J., and Denckla, M. B. (2000). Evidence for a deficit in procedural learning in children and adolescents with autism: implications for cerebellar contribution. *J. Int. Neuropsychol. Soc.* 6, 752–759. doi: 10.1017/S1355617700677020

Mottron, L., Dawson, M., Soulières, I., Hubert, B., and Burack, J. (2006). Enhanced perceptual functioning in autism: an update, and eight principles of autistic perception. *J. Autism Dev. Disord.* 36, 27–43. doi: 10.1007/s10803-005-0040-7

Mullen, E. M. (1995). *Mullen Scales of Early Learning.* Circle Pines, MN: American Guidance Service.

Nadel, J. (2002). "Imitation and imitation recognition: functional use in preverbal infants and nonverbal children with autism," in *The Imitative Mind: Development, Evolution and Brain Bases*, eds A. N. Meltzoff and W. Prinz (New York, NY: Cambridge University Press), 42–62.

Nebel, M. B., Eloyan, A., Barber, D., and Mostofsky, S. H. (2014). Precentral gyrus functional connectivity signatures of autism. *Front. Syst. Neurosci.* 8:80. doi: 10.3389/fnsys.2014.00080

Nebel, M. B., Eloyan, A., Nettles, C. A., Sweeney, K. L., Ament, K., Ward, R. E., et al. (2016). Intrinsic visual-motor synchrony correlates with social deficits in autism. *Biol. Psychiatry* 79, 633–641. doi: 10.1016/j.biopsych.2015.08.029

Osterling, J., and Dawson, G. (1994). Early recognition of children with autism: a study of first birthday home videotapes. *J. Autism Dev. Disord.* 24, 247–257. doi: 10.1007/BF02172225

Ozonoff, S., Losif, A. M., Baguio, F., Cook, I. C., Hill, M. M., Hutman, T., et al. (2010). A prospective study of the emergence of early behavioral signs of autism. *J. Am. Acad. Child Adolesc. Psychiatry* 49, 256–266. doi: 10.1097/00004583-201003000-00009

Pfister, R., Dignath, D., Hommel, B., and Kunde, W. (2013). It takes two to imitate anticipation and imitation in social interaction. *Psychol. Sci.* 24, 2117–2121. doi: 10.1177/0956797613489139

Schmitz, C., Martineau, J., Barthélémy, C., and Assaiante, C. (2003). Motor control and children with autism: deficit of anticipatory function? *Neurosci. Lett.* 348, 17–20. doi: 10.1016/S0304-3940(03)00644-X

Shadmehr, R., and Krakauer, J. W. (2008). A computational neuroanatomy for motor control. *Exp. Brain Res.* 185, 359–381. doi: 10.1007/s00221-008-1280-5

Sharer, E., Crocetti, D., Muschelli, J., Barber, A. D., Nebel, M. B., Caffo, B. S., et al. (2015). Neural correlates of visuomotor learning in autism. *J. Child Neurol.* 30, 1877–1886. doi: 10.1177/0883073815600869

Siaperas, P., Ring, H. A., McAllister, C. J., Henderson, S., Barnett, A., Watson, P., et al. (2012). Atypical movement performance and sensory integration in Asperger's syndrome. *J. Autism Dev. Disord.* 42, 718–725. doi: 10.1007/s10803-011-1301-2

Sinha, P., Kjelgaard, M. M., Gandhi, T. K., Tsourides, K., Cardinaux, A. L., Pantazis, D., et al. (2014). Autism as a disorder of prediction. *Proc. Natl. Acad. Sci. U.S.A.* 111, 15220–15225. doi: 10.1073/pnas.1416797111

Sutera, S., Pandey, J., Esser, E. L., Rosenthal, M. A., Wilson, L. B., Barton, M., et al. (2007). Predictors of optimal outcome in toddlers diagnosed with autism spectrum disorders. *J. Autism Dev. Disord.* 37, 98–107. doi: 10.1007/s10803-006-0340-6

Thelen, E., Corbetta, D., Kamm, K., Spencer, J. P., Schneider, K., and Zernicke, R. F. (1993). The transition to reaching: mapping intention and intrinsic dynamics. *Child Dev.* 64, 1058–1098. doi: 10.2307/1131327

van der Meer, A., Wee, F. R., Lee, D. N., Laing, L. A., and Lin, J. P. (1995). Development of prospective control of catching moving objects in preterm at-risk infants. *Dev. Med. Child Neurol.* 37, 145–158. doi: 10.1111/j.1469-8749.1995.tb11984.x

van der Meer, A. L., van der Weel, F. R., and Lee, D. N. (1994). Prospective control in catching by infants. *Perception* 23, 287–302. doi: 10.1068/p230287

Whyatt, C., and Craig, C. M. (2013). Interceptive skills in children aged 9–11 years, diagnosed with Autism Spectrum Disorder. *Res. Autism Spectr. Disord.* 7, 613–623. doi: 10.1016/j.rasd.2013.01.003

Whyatt, C. P., and Craig, C. M. (2012). Motor skills in children aged 7–10 years, diagnosed with autism spectrum disorder. *J. Autism Dev. Disord.* 42, 1799–1809. doi: 10.1007/s10803-011-1421-8

Witherington, D. C. (2005). The development of prospective grasping control between 5 and 7 months: a longitudinal study. *Infancy* 7, 143–161. doi: 10.1016/j.infbeh.2007.12.006

Wolpert, D. M., Doya, K., and Kawato, M. (2003). A unifying computational framework for motor control and social interaction. *Philos. Trans. R. Soc. Lond. B Biol. Sci.* 358, 593–602. doi: 10.1098/rstb.2002.1238

Yirmiya, N., and Charman, T. (2010). The prodrome of autism: early behavioral and biological signs, regression, peri- and post-natal development and genetics. *J. Child Psychol. Psychiatry* 51, 432–458. doi: 10.1111/j.1469-7610.2010.02214.x

Conflict of Interest Statement: The authors declare that the research was conducted in the absence of any commercial or financial relationships that could be construed as a potential conflict of interest.

19

The Relationship between Sitting and the use of Symmetry as a Cue to Figure-Ground Assignment in 6.5-Month-Old Infants

Shannon Ross-Sheehy[1], Sammy Perone[2], Shaun P. Vecera[3] and Lisa M. Oakes[4]*

[1] Department of Psychology, University of Tennessee, Knoxville, TN, USA, [2] Institute of Child Development, University of Minnesota, Minneapolis, MN, USA, [3] Department of Psychology, The University of Iowa, Iowa City, IA, USA, [4] Department of Psychology, University of California, Davis, Davis, CA, USA

Two experiments examined the relationship between emerging sitting ability and sensitivity to symmetry as a cue to figure-ground (FG) assignment in 6.5-month-old infants ($N = 80$). In each experiment, infants who could sit unassisted (as indicated by parental report in Experiment 1 and by an in-lab assessment in Experiment 2) exhibited sensitivity to symmetry as a cue to FG assignment, whereas non-sitting infants did not. Experiment 2 further revealed that sensitivity to this cue is not related to general cognitive abilities as indexed using a non-related visual habituation task. Results demonstrate an important relationship between motor development and visual perception and further suggest that the achievement of important motor milestones such as stable sitting may be related to qualitative changes in sensitivity to monocular depth assignment cues such as symmetry.

Keywords: infant perception, figure-ground segregation, sitting ability, symmetry, motor development, perception for action

Edited by:
Klaus Libertus,
University of Pittsburgh, USA

Reviewed by:
Michael Kavsek,
University of Bonn, Germany
Regina Tambellini Harbourne,
Duquesne University, USA

****Correspondence:***
Shannon Ross-Sheehy
rosssheehy@utk.edu

INTRODUCTION

Since the 1960s, we have made considerable advances in our understanding of perceptual development. Research has documented the timing of developmental milestones in infants' perception of color (Dannemiller and Hanko, 1987; Mercer et al., 2014) and depth (Yonas et al., 2002; Hirshkowitz and Wilcox, 2013; Adolph et al., 2014), their ability to segregate objects and detect object boundaries (Cohen and Cashon, 2001; Needham, 2001; Hayden et al., 2011), discriminate between symmetrical and asymmetrical figures (Fisher et al., 1981) as well as factors that influence perceptual and information processing (e.g., Banks and Ginsburg, 1985). This research has led to new insights regarding the interaction between the developmental state of the motor system, and opportunities to detect and learn about the features of objects (e.g., Gibson, 1988; Bushnell and Boudreau, 1993). For example, infants' activity with objects is related to their ability to attend to the appearance of objects embedded in dynamic events (Perone et al., 2008), 3-D object completion is related to infants' manual exploration of objects (Soska et al., 2010), perception of self-propelled motion is related to crawling (Cicchino and Rakison, 2008), and object exploration—including the level of visual attention to objects—is related to infants' experiences picking up objects (Needham et al., 2002). The goal of the present investigation is to extend this literature by examining the relation between independent sitting and figure-ground (FG) segregation in 6.5-month-old infants.

Figure-ground (FG) assignment is vital to visual perception—it allows us to extract the meaningful objects (i.e., figures) from the less meaningful spaces between objects (i.e., grounds). Consequently, faulty coding of figural status could have a catastrophic effect on which items were tagged for further visual and cognitive processing. Because foreground figures occlude other objects, figures are likely to be perceived as close objects in the visual environment. Therefore, FG assignment is intimately tied to depth perception (Palmer, 1999; Vecera et al., 2002). Understanding FG assignment has been of interest to psychologists for decades, and a large body of research has shown that adults use a variety of Gestalt cues, such as symmetry (e.g., Baylis and Driver, 1995), convexity (Kaniza and Gerbino, 1976), and lower region (Vecera et al., 2002) in FG assignment.

Perhaps even more than adults, it is critical that infants solve the problem of FG segregation to guide visual attention, eye movements, and learning. At present, however, we know relatively little about infants' developing sensitivity to Gestalt cues to FG assignment. Segregating visual displays into figure and ground is related to the assignment of visual regions to different depth planes, or *near* vs. *distant* objects (see Palmer, 1999). These depth assignments are important, as they directly influence both infant attention, and perception-for-action cognitions such as when planning a reach. Research has shown that in both looking and reaching tasks, infants prefer the nearer of two objects (Granrud et al., 1984; Craton and Yonas, 1988). During the first postnatal 6 months, infants appear to rely on motion cues to determine what objects are close. For example, von Hofsten and Spelke (1985) observed that when shown a display in which a smaller, closer object occluded a larger, more distant object, 5-month-old infants reached for the closer of two objects in the display, only when the near object moved independently in front of the distant object. Infants did not reach more for the near object when the two objects remained static or when they moved in unison. Similarly, Craton and Yonas (1988) reported that 5-month-old infants reached to a field of dots that moved as if they occluded another field of dots, suggesting they used apparent "boundary flow" to assign depth. Such findings demonstrate that the ability to use motion as a cue to FG assignment develops relatively early, and may rely on the development of visual abilities such as smooth pursuit eye movements and the ocular following response (Nawrot and Nawrot, 2013).

Between 5 and 7 months of age, infants become increasingly sensitive to monocular (pictorial) depth cues (e.g., texture, interposition, and size) in static displays (Walk and Dodge, 1962; Sen et al., 2001; Yonas et al., 2002; Kavsek et al., 2009). For example, 7-month-old infants, but not 5-month-old infants, consistently reach for the "closer" region as specified by pictorial depth cues (Yonas et al., 2002), though a more recent meta-analysis of 16 preferential reaching studies suggests even 5-month-old infants may use pictorial depth cues for depth assignment when viewing the displays monocularly, though the effects are smaller (Kavsek et al., 2009). These findings suggest that infants are able to use pictorial depth cues such as shape, size, and interposition to make judgments about which objects are in front of other objects, a fundamental component of FG assignment, and that this ability develops sometime between 5 and 7 months.

In the present investigation we asked whether sensitivity to the Gestalt cue of symmetry, a robust FG segregation cue in adults (Bahnsen, 1928; see also Palmer, 1999; 2002), also emerges during this age range. By 4 months of age, vertical symmetry enhances encoding and memory (Bornstein et al., 1981; Fisher et al., 1981), however, it is unclear if this early processing advantage is sufficient to drive FG segregation when the symmetrical region is presented as part of a complex object. Given previous findings of relations between motor development and visual perception of objects in this age range (Perone et al., 2008; Soska et al., 2010; Baumgartner and Oakes, 2013), we hypothesized a relation between motor development and sensitivity to symmetry as a cue to FG segregation.

A major motor achievement during this time is the ability to sit upright, without support from the arms. This is a critically important motor achievement that has a cascading effect on infants' perception of many aspects of the visual world. For example, self-sitting creates new opportunities for reaching and manual exploration, which in turn can shape how infants' visually perceive objects. When infants sit independently, both arms are free to extend away from the body, facilitating reaching, and haptic exploration (Adolph and Berger, 2005), and stable reaching has been shown to be preceded by the ability to sit unsupported (Spencer et al., 2000). Therefore, infants who can sit without support should demonstrate increased visual attention toward displays that contain "reachable" targets, or targets that invoke a strong percept of *objectness.* Two findings in the literature support this idea. First, Corbetta et al. (2014) demonstrated infants with more reaching experience devoted more pre-reach visual attention to the *graspable* portion of the target (e.g., the handle), suggesting that reaching experience shaped how infants visually regarded objects prior to and during the act of reaching. In a very different context, Soska et al. (2010) found that the amount of time infants spent looking at objects while they manipulated them was associated with their 3-D completion of a completely different set of visually presented objects. Because looking while manipulating objects is made possible by self-sitting, Soska et al.'s finding further supported our hypothesis of the cascading effect of self-sitting on infants' visual perception of objects; specifically, sitting independently allows infants to explore more with their hands and reach for objects in their environment, thus providing opportunities to learn new properties of objects and visual statistical regularities that indicate object properties.

Another possible cascading effect of sitting is that infants who self-sit spend a greater proportion of their time in a vertical position. This new visual perspective may heighten infants' attention to the statistical regularity of vertical symmetry that defines faces and numerous objects in their environment. Consistent with this possibility, work with sighted, and early blind adults (blind at or near birth) suggests that sensitivity to vertical symmetry is learned though visual experience. Specifically, sighted but blindfolded adults were able to haptically reconstruct configurations that were vertically symmetrical significantly better than both horizontal and asymmetrical configurations. In contrast, early blind subjects showed no special benefit of vertical symmetry (Cattaneo et al., 2010). Moreover, late blind subjects (blind 5 years of age or older) performed no differently than sighted subjects, further supporting the link between early visual experience and sensitivity to the special properties of vertical symmetry (Cattaneo et al., 2013). These results suggest that visual, rather than haptic experience drives sensitivity to vertical symmetry (Cattaneo et al., 2010, 2013).

Here we provide a further test of our hypothesis that self-sitting supports increasing sensitivity to objects defined by vertical symmetry, by asking whether infants who sit independently are more sensitive to *symmetry* for FG assignment. In displays that contain both a symmetrical region and an asymmetrical region, adults tend to perceive the symmetric region as figure and assign the shared edge to that region (Bahnsen, 1928; Baylis and Driver, 1995), presumably reflecting the recognition that the likelihood of any two edges accidentally forming a symmetrical shape is exceedingly rare. We know from previous work that infants are sensitive to symmetry in visual displays (Bornstein et al., 1981; Fisher et al., 1981). We do not yet know when they recognize symmetry as a cue to figure-ground assignment.

We examined FG segregation using a version of the preferential looking technique (e.g., Fantz, 1958; Ross-Sheehy et al., 2003). On each trial, we presented infants with two identical visual events, each of which was composed of a abutting symmetrical and asymmetrical regions (see **Figure 1**). After a 2 s delay, one of the regions in each composite moved, producing a percept of either the symmetrical region as figure, or the asymmetrical region a figure. Thus, there are two possible cues for FG assignment, the shape of each region (symmetrical or asymmetrical) and the motion-defined figure, and these cues could either be consistent (both reveal symmetrical region to be figure) or inconsistent (motion reveals asymmetrical region to be figure). To control for the possibility that infants may simply attend to the moving segment, we created two different types of moving events, move in front events (either symmetrical or asymmetrical) or move behind events (either symmetrical or asymmetrical). Events in which that symmetrical region moves in front of the asymmetrical region (e.g., occluding and unoccluding the asymmetrical region) or in which the asymmetrical region moves behind the symmetrical region (e.g., becoming occluded and unoccluded by the symmetrical regions) contain *consistent* FG assignment cues. Events in which the symmetrical region moves behind the asymmetrical region or in which the asymmetrical region moves in front of the symmetrical region are *inconsistent* FG assignment cues.

A significant preference for consistent events would indicate that infants perceive the shared contour as belonging to the symmetric region. This edge assignment is a necessary requirement for perceiving the symmetric region as figure, as a shared contour is assigned to the nearer, occluding object (i.e., the figure) (Driver and Baylis, 1996) and may be critically involved in object based attention (von der Heydt, 2015). Given that infants as young as 5 months use motion as a cue to depth (Craton and Yonas, 1988), we expected that infants who are not sensitive to symmetry as a cue to FG assignment should see a motion-defined figure on each display and show no systematic preference—that is, these infants would use motion alone to assign the shared contour, and would not find it inconsistent if the object in front (the figure) was asymmetrical. In Experiment 1, we assessed the ability to sit unsupported via parental report. In Experiment 2, we assessed the ability to sit unsupported via an in-laboratory sitting assessment, and we assessed infants' habituation in an unrelated task to address the possibility that sitting and non-sitting infants differed in other ways aside from their perception of symmetry as a figure-ground cue.

FIGURE 1 | Examples of the 4 shape composites and 4 color pairs used in Experiments 1 and 2 .

EXPERIMENT 1

Method

Participants

The final sample included 36 6.5-month-old infants. We divided infants into *sitters* and *non-sitters* based on parental report. Specifically, an experimenter verbally asked parents "Can your infant sit unsupported." Although this is a coarse measurement of sitting, any differences we observe between these two groups of infants provides a first insight into whether sitting ability is related to FG segregation (Note: Experiment 2 included an in-lab assessment of sitting to validate parental report). In Experiment 1, 18 infants (M = 27.54 weeks, SD = 0.99 weeks, range = 26.0–29.57 weeks, 11 girls and 7 boys) were reported to be sitters, and 18 infants (M = 28.4 weeks, SD = 1.34 weeks, range = 25.14–30 weeks, 9 girls and 9 boys) were reported to be non-sitters. We tested an additional 9 infants, but excluded their data from the final analyses due to fussiness (n = 4), equipment failure (n = 3), experimenter error (n = 1), or parental interference (n = 1).

Infants were from predominantly middle-class families and were reported to be Caucasian (n = 30), African American (n = 2), Asian (n = 2), or Hispanic (no race reported) (n = 2). All infants were healthy and full-term, with no birth complications or vision problems. All mothers had graduated from high school, and 80.48% had completed at least a bachelor's degree. In each experiment reported here, infants' names were obtained from county birth records. When infants approached 6 months of age, parents were contacted by letter, and received a follow-up phone call to schedule an appointment. Parents were reimbursed for parking and infants received a small toy for their participation.

Stimuli

Stimuli were computer-generated events that involved a composite composed of adjacent symmetrical and asymmetrical regions (see **Figure 1**). There were four composites in which the symmetrical and asymmetrical region differed in shape but were matched on overall area ranging in size from 11.2 cm (w) by 10.6 cm (h) to 14.2 cm (w) by 10.6 cm (h), and subtending a visual angle of 6.39° by 6.05° to 8.08° by 6.05° at a viewing distance of 100 cm. In addition, for half of the events involving each composite, the symmetrical region was on the left of the display and for the other half of the events the symmetrical region was on the right of the display. An example of each composite shape is presented in **Figure 2**.

We used these composites to create several stimulus events. In each stimulus event, the composite was presented as a static image for a period of 2 s, allowing the infant to make an initial FG judgment. Next, either the symmetrical or the asymmetrical segment slid laterally away from the other segment (duration of 1 s and a distance of 1.2–2.2 cm depending on composite shape), then returned to its original position (duration 1 s). The entire sequence took 4 s, and was repeated 5 times to create each 20 s trial. The events involved either *move-in-front* or *move-behind* movement. When one segment moved *in front of* another region it partially occluded the other segment; as a result, the shared contour is assigned to the *moving* region (i.e., the nonmoving segment appeared to be unoccluded and occluded as the moving segment moved back and forth). When one segment *moved behind* the other segment, it became partially occluded by the other region; as a result, the shared contour is assigned to the *nonmoving* segment (i.e., the moving segment appeared to be unoccluded and occluded as it moved back and forth). Importantly, this edge assignment happens automatically, producing a robust perception of the front occluding region as figure in both cases (see **Figure 2**; Supplementary Videos 1–4).

Five factors (composite shape, color pair, left/right location of symmetrical region, symmetry of moving region, and movement type) were crossed to create 128 stimulus events. Half of the resulting events were *consistent* with respect to symmetry and motion cues—both shape and motion revealed the symmetrical region to be the figure, the other have were *inconsistent* with respect to symmetry and motion cues (see **Figure 2** for examples of the consistent and inconsistent events).

We created 12 pseudo-random orders each consisting of 8 paired-comparison trials (each including a consistent and an inconsistent event), with the following constraints: First, within each order, there were trials with every possible color pair counterbalanced for left/right position—i.e., all infants saw blue/orange, orange/blue, yellow/purple, purple/yellow, pink/brown, brown/pink, green/red, red/green. The order in which these color pairs were presented was determined randomly in each order. Second, within each order, there were trials with every possible composite shape, also counterbalanced for left/right presentation, again presented in a random order. Each of the 8 paired comparison trials was created by combining two identical composites (shape and color), one whose segment motion and motion type produced an inconsistent event, and the other whose segment motion and motion type produced a consistent event. Thus, across the 8 trials, each infant saw each composite shape, each color pair, and every possible combination of movement type, and segment motion, with the constraint that one always be consistent, and the other inconsistent. Left/right location of the consistent event was random.

Apparatus

Infants were tested in a dimly lit room. A black curtain hung from the ceiling to the floor to divide the room. There were four openings in the curtain. Two of the openings revealed two 17″ (43.2 cm) ViewSonic CRT monitors, one opening in between the computer monitors revealed a small, black box that blinked and produced a beeping sound at a rate of 3 Hz to orient infant attention toward the computer monitors, and one opening revealed a small, low light TV camera lens. Stimuli were presented via a Macintosh G4 computer using software developed for the Macintosh (Cohen et al., 2000–2002).

Design

On each trial, infants were shown two events, side-by-side. The same composite (i.e., same shape and color) was presented in each event, but one event was a *consistent event* and the other was an *inconsistent event*. Thus, during the initial 2 s period when the composites were stationary, the two events were identical. Only

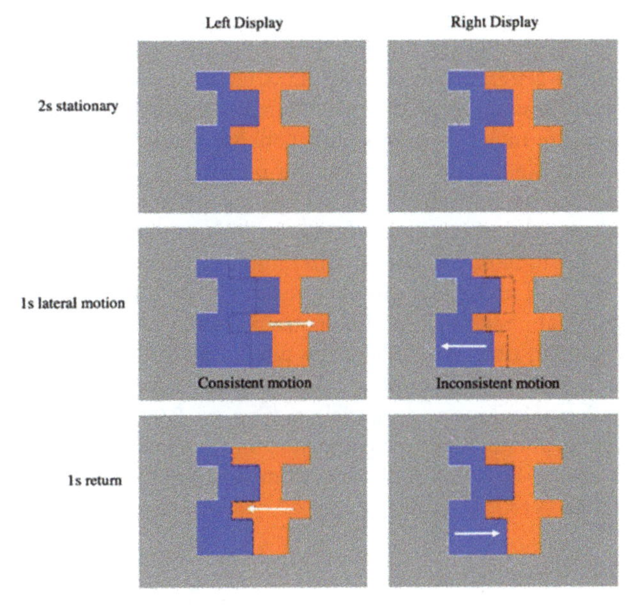

FIGURE 2 | Depicts a single matched motion trial. The left display depicts a move in front stimulus event with consistent symmetry and motion cues. The right display depicts a move in front stimulus event with inconsistent symmetry and motion cues. White arrows indicate the direction of segment motion.

when the regions began to move did it become apparent which event was consistent, and which was inconsistent.

The 8 trials were divided based on *motion alignability*. Specifically, we reasoned that infants would be better able to compare the two types of events if the motion was aligned, or both involved the same type of motion (Gentner et al., 2007). Therefore, for each infant, half of the trials involved *matched* motion, such that both events involved the same kind of movement (e.g., both contained move behind events or move in front events, see for example **Figure 2**). The other trials involved *unmatched* motion, such that each event incorporated a different type of movement (e.g., *one* event contained a move behind event, while the other contained a move in front event). Because we reasoned that it would be easier to process the differences between the events when the motion was aligned, we included this factor in our analyses.

Procedure

A paired-comparison procedure was used to assess infants' sensitivity to symmetry as a cue to FG segregation. To accomplish this, infants were seated on their parent's lap 100 cm in front of the two monitors. Parents wore opaque glasses to prevent bias. Infants received 8 20-s trials. On each trial, a consistent event was presented on one monitor and an inconsistent event was presented on the other monitor, left and right position of the consistent event counterbalanced across trials. As mentioned above, half of the trials were matched motion trials and half were unmatched motion trials

A trained observer sat out of sight and watched the infant on a video monitor connected to a low-light video camera. At the beginning of the experiment and between each subsequent trial, a beeping, flashing light was used to attract the infant's attention to a location between the two monitors. When the observer determined that the infant was looking at this attention-getter, he or she pressed a computer key, simultaneously ending the attention-getter, and beginning the stimulus presentation. The observer was unaware of which stimulus was being presented, and of the infant's sitting status. Looking to the right and left monitors was recorded on-line by pressing and holding one computer key when the infant was looking to the left and another computer key when the infant was looking to the right. Infants were free to look at either or both monitors during each trial for up to 20 s. If no looking was observed in the first 10 s the trial was stopped, and repeated. A different trained observer also recorded the looking times for 25% of the infants off-line from a video record of the session. Mean inter-observer correlation for the duration of looking on each trial was high, $r = 0.98$, and the mean absolute difference between observers for the duration of looking was low, $M = 0.46$ s. Only data from the primary observer are reported here.

Results

Infants' preferences for the consistent event were calculated by dividing the duration of their looking to the consistent event by the total amount of looking to both events combined. These preferences are presented in **Figure 3**. Looking first at results from sitting infants (right half of the figure), it can be

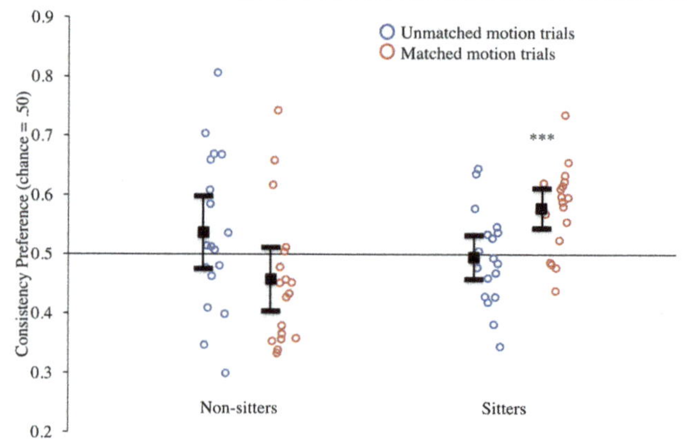

FIGURE 3 | Experiment 1 consistency preference scores for non-matched and matched motion trials by sitting status. Circles represent individual infants, solid black square represents mean responding. (Note: ***denotes $p < 0.001$, error bars represent 95% confidence intervals).

seen that the majority of infants who could sit independently showed a preference for the consistent event that was greater than chance (0.50) on *matched* motion trials (red circles) but not on *unmatched* motion trials (blue circles). This impression was confirmed by a series of *t*-tests comparing these preference scores to chance (0.50). Infants whose parents reported they could sit unsupported had a strong and significant preference for the consistent event in on matched motion trials, $t_{(17)} = 4.50$, $p < 0.001$, $d = 2.18$, but not on unmatched motion trials, $t_{(17)} = -0.28$, $p = 0.79$, $d = -0.13$ (see **Figure 3**). One possible reason that infants exhibit a preference in the matched motion trials is because the motion is alignable, which may facilitate comparison.

Infants whose parents reported that they could not yet sit unsupported are presented in the left half of the figure. In contrast to the independent sitters, these non-sitters showed no systematic preferences in either type of event, and showed increased variability for both matched and unmatched motion trials (see **Figure 3**). Comparisons to chance again confirmed our initial impressions. These infants' mean preference for the consistent event was not significantly different from chance for either the matched motion trials, $t_{(17)} = -1.55$, $p = 0.14$, $d = -0.75$, or unmatched motion trials, $t_{(17)} = 1.16$, $p = 0.26$, $d = 0.56$. Therefore, we have no evidence that 6.5-month-old infants whose parents report that they do not yet sit unsupported are sensitive to symmetry as a cue to FG assignment.

Further, the graph suggests that sitters and non-sitters responded differently to these two types of trials, a conclusion that was confirmed with an ANOVA conducted on the mean consistency preference scores with sitting status (sitters vs. non-sitters) as the between-subjects variable and condition (matched vs. unmatched motion) as the within-subjects variable. This analysis revealed only a significant sitting status by condition interaction, $F_{(1, 34)} = 10.76$, $p = 0.002$, $\eta^2 = 0.240$. We conducted *post-hoc* analyses using two tailed *t*-tests with a Bonferroni's correction for multiple comparisons (and thus only comparisons with $p \leq 0.0125$ were considered significant).

These comparisons revealed that the preference scores of sitters and non-sitters did not differ significantly for the unmatched motion trials, $t_{(34)} = 1.14$, $p = 0.26$, $d = 0.39$, but the preference scores for the sitters were significantly greater than the non-sitters for the matched motion trials, $t_{(34)} = -3.72$, $p = 0.001$, $d = 1.28$. Similarly, when comparing within each sitting group, we found that sitters showed significantly greater consistency preference scores for matched motion trials than non-matched motion trials, $t_{(17)} = -2.86$, $p = 0.01$, $d = -1.39$, whereas the difference between matched and non-matched motion trials for non-sitters was not significant, $t_{(17)} = 1.98$, $p = 0.06$, $d = 0.96$ [1].

Discussion

These results show that infants whose parents reported that they could sit unsupported can use symmetry as a cue to FG segregation. One limitation of this study was that we relied on parental report to determine sitting status, we are dependent on parental impression of their infants' sitting ability. Although Rochat and Goubet (1995) reported 100% agreement between sitting status obtained via an in-laboratory sitting assessment and parental report, parents may not accurately report their own infant's sitting ability, either due to differences in willingness to call sitting "stable" or some other factor. To address this limitation, in Experiment 2 we conducted an independent in-laboratory sitting assessment, allowing us an unbiased assessment of both overall sitting status as well as stable sitting.

A second potential limitation of Experiment 1 is that although we observed a connection between independent sitting and FG segregation, it is impossible to know whether this relation is unique, or whether independent sitting is correlated with cognitive development more generally. To rule out the possibility that sitting infants are simply more developmentally mature, compliant or visually attentive than non-sitting infants, in Experiment 2 we additionally assessed infants' ability on a separate task of processing speed and memory.

EXPERIMENT 2

Method

Participants

The final sample consisted of 44 6.5-month-old infants divided into sitters and non-sitters based on a laboratory sitting assessment (see Procedure Section below): the final sample comprised 23 sitters ($M = 29.29$ weeks, $SD = 0.77$ weeks, range = 27.86–30.29 weeks, 13 boys and 10 girls) and 21 non-sitters ($M = 28.34$ weeks, $SD = 1.17$ weeks, range = 26.43–30 weeks, 9 boys and 12 girls). Infants were from predominantly middle-class families and were reported to be Caucasian ($n = 38$), African American ($n = 1$), Asian ($n = 2$), Multiracial ($n = 1$), or chose not to answer ($n = 2$). All infants were healthy and full-term, with no birth complications or vision problems. All mothers had graduated from high school, and 56.81% had completed at least a bachelor's degree. Four additional infants were tested but their data were not included in the final analyses due to experimenter error ($n = 3$) or parental interference ($n = 1$).

Procedure

Infants participated in three tasks. Infants first participated in the preferential looking task to assess sensitivity to symmetry as a cue to FG assignment. Immediately following the preferential looking task, infants participated in an in-laboratory sitting assessment. Finally, after a short break, infants were tested in a standard habituation task with unrelated stimuli.

Preferential Looking

The stimuli, apparatus, and procedure for the test of infants' sensitivity to symmetry were the same as Experiment 1 with one exception: Experiment 2 contained only matched-motion trials. Infants were presented with 4 20-s, matched motion trials, the same number of matched motion trials as in Experiment 1. A second trained observer re-coded 25% of the infants off-line from a video record of the session. Mean inter-observer correlation for the duration of looking on each trial was high, $r = 0.97$, and the mean absolute difference between observers for the duration of looking was low, $M = 0.45$ s. Only data from the primary observer are reported here.

Sitting Assessment

One of our main goals in Experiment 2 was to assess sitting in a more systematic way, and to validate the parent report measure used in Experiment 1. We assessed sitting using an adaptation of a sitting assessment developed by (Rochat, 1989). Infants were placed on a blanket on the ground in a sitting posture for 30 s. From the video records of this assessment, we classified infants as *sitters* only if they remained in a sitting posture the entire 30 s duration of the session and required no support from their arms or the experimenter. Note that although infants who are learning to sit may be able to sit unsupported for some period of time, *continuous* sitting frequently requires arm support (e.g., leaning on one or both arms) or support from the experimenter. Our interest is in *stable* sitting, and for this reason, infants who required support from their arms or the experimenter, as well as infants whose trunk folded onto their lap, or began to topple over, were classified as non-sitters. Two trained coders classified every session using frame-by-frame analysis. The agreement between these two coders was very high, 90%, and the remaining 10% were resolved between the two coders and constitute the final classifications. Importantly, agreement between the laboratory classification and parental report for sitters was 100%, thus parental report was used as a proxy for the lab assessment if infants were too fussy to complete the sitting assessment ($n = 3$), or in the case of experimenter error ($n = 1$).

It must be pointed out that although this sitting assessment is an improvement over the parental report used in Experiment 1, it is possible that we did not capture sitting differences as completely as we would have had we used a more standardized

[1] Although this comparison appears to be marginal ($p = 0.06$), recall that we used a Bonferroni's correction to adjust for multiple comparisons, and our more conservative criterion for significance was $p \leq 0.0125$. Moreover, any difference between non-sitters for the two types of trials is due to many infants in this group exhibiting a preference that was *less* than chance. However, it is clear from the distribution of individual scores presented in **Figure 3** that these infants did not exhibit a robust and systematic preference for the inconsistent event. The replication in Experiment 2 will address the possibility that non-sitting infants actually prefer the inconsistent event.

measure such as the Alberta Infant Motor Scale (AIMS). Our results may have been stronger if we had used such a measure, and therefore this is a consideration for future research.

Habituation

Infants were habituated (using a sliding-trial-block habituation criterion of 50% decrease in looking) to a single event in which a colorful novel object was manipulated and made some sound (e.g., it was rolled and it clicked). Trial durations were infant controlled; the stimulus remained visible for up to 35 s, or until the infant looked away for 1 s. The habituation phase ended when the infant habituated, or when they had completed 18 trials. Immediately following habituation, infants were tested on 3 novel stimuli, two that shared a single feature with the habituation stimulus (e.g., familiar sound or familiar action), and one that was completely novel. Our dependent measures from the habituation task were of processing speed (total looking time on the initial block of habituation trials, trials to habituation) and response to novelty (dishabituation to the completely novel event).

Results

Our primary analyses were those that evaluated the consistency preference scores for the sitters and non-sitters. The data are presented in **Figure 4**. Once again, the mean responding for the sitters (presented on the right) to these matched motion trials was >0.50, and most infants in this group had scores above this level. Comparing infants' responding to chance indeed confirmed that as in Experiment 1, sitters had a significant preference for the consistent event, $t_{(22)} = 2.20$, $p = 0.04$, $d = 0.94$. The non-sitters showed no clear preference; their mean responding was near 0.50, and individual infants' scores were divided above and below 0.50, $t_{(20)} = 0.25$, $p = 0.81$, $d = 0.11$. It is interesting to point out that this replication of the matched motion trials did not yield a tendency for non-sitters to exhibit a preference for the inconsistent events. Because of this, consistency preference scores between sitters and non-sitters did not differ significantly, $t_{(42)} = -1.33$, $p = 0.19$, $d = -0.41$.

Figure/Ground Segregation and Habituation

A second goal of Experiment 2 was to determine whether sitters and non-sitters differ generally in other cognitive measures, as a possible explanation or the difference in FG segregation. First, to determine whether sitting infants were more cognitively advanced than non-sitting infants, we compared the performance of sitters and non-sitters on the habituation task. Thirty-nine of the 44 infants (21 sitters and 18 non-sitters) also contributed data to the habituation task. Sitters and non-sitters did not differ in duration of looking during the first habituation block, $t_{(37)} = -1.88$, $p = 0.07$, $d = -0.62$, the number of trials required to habituate, $t_{(37)} = 0.81$, $p = 0.42$ $d = 0.27$, or dishabituation to the completely novel event, $t_{(37)} = 0.12$, $p = 0.91$, $d = 0.04$. Of the 5 infants who failed to complete this task, 2 were sitters and 3 were non-sitters. Thus, sitting and non-sitting infants perform equivalently on a completely unrelated cognitive task suggesting that the two groups did not differ in general cognitive ability, at least as assessed by this habituation task.

We also conducted t-tests comparing infants' consistency preference scores as a function of performance on the habituation task. To accomplish this, we created median splits based on looking during the first habituation block, trials to criterion, and novelty preference (split at 0.5). These comparisons did not yield significant differences, all $ps \geq 0.15$. In addition, comparisons of the average visual preference scores for each group to chance revealed that none of these groups (e.g., long lookers, short, lookers, fast habituators, slow habituators, high novelty preference, low novelty preference) had preference scores that differed from chance, all $ps \geq 0.07$.

Discussion

Experiment 2 replicated and extended the results of Experiment 1, by making use of an in-laboratory sitting assessment to provide increased precision and confidence in our classification of infant sitting ability. Importantly, the percent agreement between the in-laboratory sitting assessment used in Experiment 2 and parental report measure used in both Experiments 1 and 2 was 100%. In addition, Experiment 2 confirmed that sitters and non-sitters did not differ in an unrelated cognitive task, indicating that sitting infants are not simply more developmentally advanced than non-sitting infants. Rather, stable sitting appears to be related to emerging sensitivity to the FG assignment cue of symmetry, suggesting the importance of motor development to the development of selective attention, object perception, and FG segregation.

GENERAL DISCUSSION

In two experiments, we demonstrated that at 6.5 months of age, infants' sensitivity to the cue of symmetry for FG segregation was related to self-sitting abilities. In each experiment, infants who could sit independently showed sensitivity to symmetry as a cue to FG segregation whereas infants who could not yet sit independently did not show such sensitivity. These

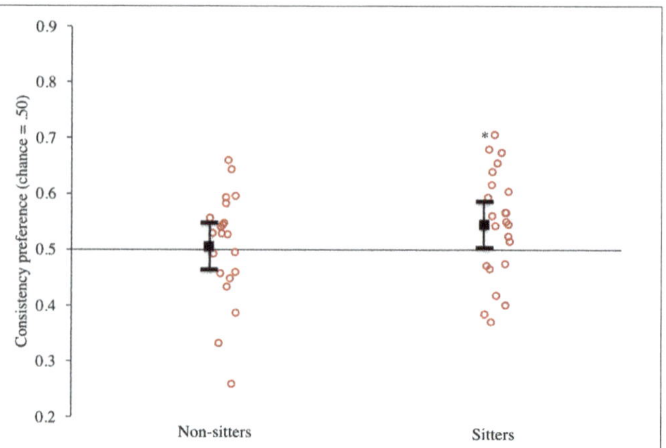

FIGURE 4 | Experiment 2 consistency preference scores by sitting status. Circles represent individual infants, solid black square represents mean responding. (Note: *denotes $p < 0.05$, error bars represent 95% confidence intervals).

results contribute to our understanding of the development of infant visual perception in three important ways. First, although previous research reveals some of infants' developing abilities to segregate objects in complex visual arrays (von Hofsten and Spelke, 1985; Craton and Yonas, 1988; Needham, 2001; Yonas et al., 2002; Kavsek et al., 2009), this study is the first to demonstrate infants' sensitivity to the Gestalt cue of symmetry for FG assignment.

Second, these findings provide insight into how this sensitivity develops. Like pictorial depth cues, FG cues such as size, convexity, and symmetry reflect the environmental regularities and non-accidental properties of objects. For example, a symmetric region is more likely to arise from a symmetric foreground object than from a symmetric background region formed by two foreground objects that happen to have the same contour. Infants may learn such regularities with experience. Indeed, infants are particularly good at detecting and using statistical regularities such as these to learn about the auditory and visual world (e.g., Aslin et al., 1998; Kirkham et al., 2002), and use of these learned regularities persist into adulthood (see Aslin and Newport, 2012), including regularities that organize or group visual information (Vickery and Jiang, 2009; Zhao et al., 2014). We observed that sensitivity to the regularities that facilitate FG assignment emerges between 6 and 7 months, the same age range infants become sensitive to several pictorial depth cues (Yonas et al., 2002). Therefore, between 5 and 7 months infants appear to become sensitive to some of the regularities that help them arrange in depth the objects in complex visual arrays.

Finally, these findings suggest that the ability to sit unsupported is a potential mechanism for the emergence of sensitivity to symmetry as a cue to FG assignment. Research has established that sensitivity to the unique properties of vertical symmetry emerges around 4 months of age (Bornstein et al., 1981; Fisher et al., 1981), however the use of symmetry as a reliable FG assignment cue may not develop until substantially later. We propose that once infants begin to sit independently, infants learn that symmetry is a regular characteristic of *objects*, not backgrounds. Experiments 1 and 2 constitute the first steps toward testing this hypothesis, and the results clearly show that sitting infants, and not those infants that cannot yet sit, preferred to look at the stimulus events consistent with the symmetrical figure.

It should be noted that it is impossible to know exactly why infants demonstrate a preference for the consistent displays. One possibility is that infants simply prefer to look at displays that contain non-deforming symmetry, and that they are not necessarily using symmetry as a FG segregation cue. This is unlikely for three reasons. First, we know displays that contain occlusion and motion like ours produce a robust and likely automatic percept of figure and ground (Kellman and Spelke, 1983; Craton and Yonas, 1988; Cohen and Cashon, 2001; Johnson et al., 2003; Bremner et al., 2015)—each composite contains a single motion-defined figure, and a ground. Thus, it is impossible to interpret a preference for consistent displays independent of the motion-defined FG segregation. Second, despite early sensitivity and even preference for vertical symmetry (Bornstein et al., 1981; Fisher et al., 1981; Bornstein and Krinsky, 1985) sensitivity to symmetry embedded in moving occlusion displays emerges only after infants learn to sit. We and others (Soska et al., 2010; Baumgartner and Oakes, 2013; Corbetta et al., 2014) have suggested that visual and/or motor experiences, such as those that accompany independent sitting, result in increased attention toward plausible objects, and infants have learned that symmetry is a reliable indicator of objectness. Finally, even if infants were able to ignore the motion-defined FG segregation cues and simply preferred to look at non-deforming symmetry, we would expect to find a preference for the consistent displays for both matched and unmatched motion conditions—but we do not.

Why is sitting related to sensitivity to symmetry as a FG assignment cue? One possibility is that the postural control that accompanies stable sitting may allow the infant to demonstrate visual preferences in the task used here. That is, because sitting infants have better postural control, they may be better able to look back and forth between two visually presented stimuli and show a systematic preference for one type of stimulus over another. However, because visual preferences for both static (Fantz, 1958) and dynamic (Ross-Sheehy et al., 2003) stimuli have been revealed in the preferential looking procedure in infants 4 months and younger, this is an unlikely reason for the observed differences between sitters and non-sitters.

A second, more likely, possibility is that stable sitting has consequences for infants' manual and visual exploration of the world, and that this new means of exploration provides the opportunity to discover the regularities that define object boundaries. Infants who can sit unsupported have acquired the postural control required to extend the arms away from the body and reach for the objects that surround them. Clearly the ability to obtain objects from a cluttered visual array provides infants access to information about the regularities that specify object boundaries. In addition, this increased motor experience may help tune their developing perception/action system, allowing them to interact with objects more efficiently. For example, 7-month-old infants have been shown to orient their grasp prior to grasping an object, whereas 5-month-old infants do not, suggesting the important role of prior reaching experience in motor planning and perception for action (McCarty et al., 2001; Witherington, 2005). In addition, selective visual attention to the graspable part of an object has been shown to increase with increased reaching experience (Corbetta et al., 2014). It is possible that infants learn to use object information specified visually through the process of visually identifying to-be-grasped objects, grasping objects, haptically exploring objects, and using tactile feedback to readjust their grasp. Similarly, as the child acquires experience reaching for and successfully grasping objects such as a rattle or a teddy bear, the more the child will learn that graspable objects share some perceptual commonalities, such as symmetry.

Finally, sitting infants likely spend more time each day looking *vertically* at the world; a perspective that may increase infants' detection of symmetry in everyday objects such as faces, bottles, and furniture (Zhao et al., 2014), and early visual experience appears to be critical (Cattaneo et al., 2010, 2013). Recent work suggests that vertical symmetry perception happens early in visual processing, may lead to enhanced or automatic "object-based attention," and results in qualitatively different patterns of neural activation than other forms of object perception (Apthorp and Bell, 2015; Bertamini et al., 2015; Bona et al., 2015; see also Hecht et al., 2016). Thus, it is possible that stable sitting enhances sensitivity to the FG cue of symmetry either through increased visual experience (i.e., statistical learning), increased haptic and motor experience, by providing a more ideal visual perspective to automatically detect vertical symmetry in the environment, or some combination of all three. Future work should be aimed at further refining the relationship between stable sitting and the use of symmetry in FG assignment.

The relationship we propose between unsupported sitting and sensitivity to symmetry as a cue to FG assignment is similar to that observed between self-produced locomotion and the emergence of heights wariness. That is, despite early perceptual sensitivity to visual features such as depth, only increased locomotor experience results in categorically different perception/action plans—avoiding rather than plunging in to unsafe gaps and drop-offs (Campos et al., 1992; Adolph et al., 2014). Here too we suggest that despite early perceptual sensitivity to the statistical redundancies of vertical symmetry (Bornstein et al., 1981; Fisher et al., 1981), only with sitting and subsequent changes in reaching and/or visual experience do infants come to rely on the use of symmetry as a FG assignment cue. Though future work could benefit from a more precise assessment of both of sitting and reaching, these results represent a significant first step toward understanding the complex relations between sitting, motor and visual experience, and visual perception.

In summary, these findings add to our understanding of the development of visual perception in infancy. We have demonstrated that young infants are sensitive to Gestalt cues to FG assignment and that this sensitivity emerges at approximately the same time as sensitivity to pictorial depth cues. These results are compatible with the view that infants' acquisition of these FG cues is a function of their ability to detect and learn statistical regularities and that motor achievements create new opportunities to learn those regularities.

AUTHOR CONTRIBUTIONS

SR, SP, SV, and LO worked together to develop the experiments and techniques presented in this manuscript. SR and SP created and animated the figure-ground stimuli, SP, and LO developed the habituation procedures, and SP, developed the sitting assessments and coding schemes. Data were collected by SR and SP. SR, SP, and LO worked together on the analyses and interpretation of the results, and SR wrote the manuscript with help from SP, SV, and LO Funds, resources, and oversight were provided by LO and SV, with some addition funding provided by SR.

ACKNOWLEDGMENTS

This research was made possible by NIH grants MH64020 and EY022525 awarded to LO, and NIH grant 1F31MH068934-01A1 awarded to SR. These data were reported at the Biennial meeting of the Cognitive Development Society, Park City UT, October 2003. We thank Kristine Kovack-Lesh, Shaena McGivern and the undergraduates at the University of Iowa Infant Cognition lab for help with data collection.

REFERENCES

Adolph, K. E., and Berger, S. E. (2005). "Physical and motor develoment," in *Developmental science: An advanced textbook, 5th Edn.* eds M. H. Bornstein and M. E. Lamb (Hillsdale, NJ: Erlbaum), 223–281.

Adolph, K. E., Kretch, K. S., and LoBue, V. (2014). Fear of heights in infants? *Curr. Dir. Psychol. Sci.* 23, 60–66. doi: 10.1177/0963721413498895

Apthorp, D., and Bell, J. (2015). Symmetry is less than meets the eye. *Curr. Biol.* 25, R267–R268. doi: 10.1016/j.cub.2015.02.017

Aslin, R. N., and Newport, E. L. (2012). Statistical learning: from acquiring specific items to forming general rules. *Curr. Dir. Psychol. Sci.* 21, 170–176. doi: 10.1177/0963721412436806

Aslin, R. N., Saffran, J. R., and Newport, E. L. (1998). Computation of conditional probability statistics by 8-month-old infants. *Psychol. Sci.* 9, 321–324.

Bahnsen, P. (1928). Eine Untersuchung über Symmetrie und Asymmetrie bei visuellen Wahrnehmungen. *Z. Psychol.* 108, 129–154.

Banks, M. S., and Ginsburg, A. P. (1985). Infant visual preferences: a review and new theoretical treatment. *Adv. Child Dev. Behav.* 19, 207–246.

Baumgartner, H. A., and Oakes, L. M. (2013). Investigating the relation between infants' manual activity with objects and their perception of dynamic events. *Infancy* 18, 983–1006. doi: 10.1111/infa.12009

Baylis, G. C., and Driver, J. (1995). Obligatory edge assignment in vision: the role of figure and part segmentation in symmetry detection. *J.Exp. Psychol. Hum. Percept. Perform.* 21, 1323–1342.

Bertamini, M., Makin, A., Palumbo, L., Rampone, G., and Wright, D. (2015). Brain activity in response to visual symmetry. *J. Vis.* 15:578. doi: 10.1167/15.12.578

Bona, S., Cattaneo, Z., and Silvanto, J. (2015). The causal role of the occipital face area (OFA) and lateral occipital (LO) cortex in symmetry perception. *J. Neurosci.* 35, 731–738. doi: 10.1523/jneurosci.3733-14.2015

Bornstein, M. H., Ferdinandsen, K., and Gross, C. G. (1981). Perception of symmetry in infancy. *Dev. Psychol.* 17, 82–86. doi: 10.1037/0012-1649.17.1.82

Bornstein, M. H., and Krinsky, S. J. (1985). Perception of symmetry in infancy: the salience of vertical symmetry and the perception of pattern wholes. *J. Exp. Child Psychol.* 39, 1–19. doi: 10.1016/0022-0965(85)90026-8

Bremner, J. G., Slater, A. M., and Johnson, S. P. (2015). Perception of object persistence: the origins of object permanence in infancy. *Child Dev. Perspect.* 9, 7–13. doi: 10.1111/cdep.12098

Bushnell, E. W., and Boudreau, J. (1993). Motor development and the mind: the potential role of motor abilities as a determinant of aspects of perceptual development. *Child Dev.* 64, 1005–1021.

Campos, J. J., Bertenthal, B. I., and Kermoian, R. (1992). Early experience and emotional development: the emergence of wariness of heights. *Psychol. Sci.* 3, 61–64.

Cattaneo, Z., Fantino, M., Silvanto, J., Tinti, C., Pascual-Leone, A., and Vecchi, T. (2010). Symmetry perception in the blind. *Acta Psychol.* 134, 398–402. doi: 10.1016/j.actpsy.2010.04.002

Cattaneo, Z., Vecchi, T., Fantino, M., Herbert, A. M., and Merabet, L. B. (2013). The effect of vertical and horizontal symmetry on memory for tactile patterns in late blind individuals. *Attent. Percept. Psychophys.* 75, 375–382. doi: 10.3758/s13414-012-0393-x

Cicchino, J. B., and Rakison, D. H. (2008). Producing and processing self-propelled motion in infancy. *Dev. Psychol.* 44, 1232–1241. doi: 10.1037/a0012619

Cohen, L. B., Atkinson, D. J., and Chaput, H. H. (2000–2002). *Habit 2000: A New Program for Obtaining and Organizing Data in Infant Perception and Cognition Studies.* (Version 1.0) [Computer Software]. Austin, TX: The University of Texas.

Cohen, L. B., and Cashon, C. H. (2001). Infant object segregation implies information integration. *J Exp Child Psychol. 78*, 75–83, discussion: 98–106. doi: 10.1006/jecp.2000.2602

Corbetta, D., Thurman, S. L., Wiener, R. F., Guan, Y., and Williams, J. L. (2014). Mapping the feel of the arm with the sight of the object: on the embodied origins of infant reaching. *Front. Psychol.* 5:576. doi: 10.3389/fpsyg.2014.00576

Craton, L. G., and Yonas, A. (1988). Infants' sensitivity to boundary flow information for depth at an edge. *Child Dev.* 59, 1522–1529.

Dannemiller, J. L., and Hanko, S. A. (1987). A test of color constancy in 4-month-old human infants. *J. Exp. Psychol.* 44, 255–267.

Driver, J., and Baylis, G. C. (1996). Edge-assignment and figure-ground segmentation in short-term visual matching. *Cogn. Psychol.* 31, 248–306.

Fantz, R. L. (1958). Pattern vision in young infants. *Psychol. Record* 8, 43–47.

Fisher, C. B., Ferdinandsen, K., and Bornstein, M. H. (1981). The role of symmetry in infant form discrimination. *Child Dev.* 52, 457–462.

Gentner, D., Loewenstein, J., and Hung, B. (2007). Comparison facilitates children's learning of names for parts. *J. Cogn. Dev.* 8, 285–307. doi: 10.1080/15248370701446434

Gibson, E. J. (1988). Exploratory behavior in the development of perceiving, acting, and the acquiring of knowledge. *Annu. Rev. Psychol.* 39, 1–41.

Granrud, C. E., Yonas, A., Smith, I. M., Arterberry, M. E., Glicksman, M. L., and Sorknes, A. C. (1984). Infants' sensitivity to accretion and deletion of texture as information for depth at an edge. *Child Dev.* 55, 1630–1636. doi: 10.2307/1130032

Hayden, A., Bhatt, R. S., Kangas, A., and Zieber, N. (2011). Parts, cavities, and object representation in infancy. *J. Exp. Psychol. Hum. Percept. Perform.* 37, 314–317. doi: 10.1037/a0020987

Hecht, L. N., Cosman, J. D., and Vecera, S. P. (2016). Enhanced spatial resolution on figures versus grounds. *Atten. Percept. Psychophys.* doi: 10.3758/s13414-016-1099-2. [Epub ahead of print].

Hirshkowitz, A., and Wilcox, T. (2013). Infants' ability to extract three-dimensional shape from coherent motion. *Infant Behav. Dev.* 36, 863–872. doi: 10.1016/j.infbeh.2013.09.003

Johnson, S. P., Bremner, J. G., Slater, A., Mason, U., Foster, K., and Cheshire, A. (2003). Infants' perception of object trajectories. *Child Dev.* 74, 94–108. doi: 10.1111/1467-8624.00523

Kaniza, G., and Gerbino, W. (1976). "Convexity and symmetry in figure-ground organization," in *Vision and Atrifact,* ed M. Henle (New York, NY: Springer).

Kavsek, M., Granrud, C. E., and Yonas, A. (2009). Infants' responsiveness to pictorial depth cues in preferential-reaching studies: a meta-analysis. *Infant Behav. Dev.* 32, 245–253. doi: 10.1016/j.infbeh.2009.02.001

Kellman, P. J., and Spelke, E. S. (1983). Perception of partly occluded objects in infancy. *Cogn. Psychol.* 15, 483–524. doi: 10.1016/0010-0285(83)90017-8

Kirkham, N. Z., Slemmer, J. A., and Johnson, S. P. (2002). Visual statistical learning in infancy: evidence for a domain general learning mechanism. *Cognition* 83, B35–B42. doi: 10.1016/S0010-0277(02)00004-5

McCarty, M. E., Clifton, R. K., Ashmead, D. H., Lee, P., and Goubet, N. (2001). How infants use vision for grasping objects. *Child Dev.* 71, 973–987. doi: 10.1111/1467-8624.00329

Mercer, M. E., Drodge, S. C., Courage, M. L., and Adams, R. J. (2014). A pseudoisochromatic test of color vision for human infants. *Vis. Res.* 100, 72–77. doi: 10.1016/j.visres.2014.04.006

Nawrot, E., and Nawrot, M. (2013). The role of eye movements in depth from motion parallax during infancy. *J. Vis.* 13:15. doi: 10.1167/13.14.15

Needham, A. (2001). Object recognition and object segregation in 4.5-month-old infants. *J. Exp. Child Psychol.* 78, 3–22. doi: 10.1006/jecp.2000.2598

Needham, A., Barrett, T., and Peterman, K. (2002). A pick me up for infants' exploratory skills: early simulated experiences reaching for objects using 'sticky' mittens enhances young infants' object exploration skills. *Infant Behav. Dev.* 25, 279–295. doi: 10.1016/S0163-6383(02)00097-8

Palmer, S. E. (1999). *Vision Science: from Hotons to Phenomenology.* Cambridge, MA: MIT Press.

Palmer, S. E. (2002). "Perceptual organization," in *Vision Steven's Handbook of Experimental Psychology, 3rd Edn. Vol. 1: Sensation and Perception,* eds H. Pashler and S. Yantis (Hoboken, NJ: John Wiley and Sons Inc.), 177–234.

Perone, S., Madole, K. L., Ross-Sheehy, S., Carey, M., and Oakes, L. M. (2008). The relation between infants' activity with objects and attention to object appearance. *Dev. Psychol.* 44, 1242–1248. doi: 10.1037/0012-1649.44.5.1242

Rochat, P. (1989). Object manipulation and exploration in 2- to 5-month-old infants. *Dev. Psychol.* 25, 871–884.

Rochat, P., and Goubet, N. (1995). Development of sitting and reaching in 5- to 6-month-old infants. *Infant Behav. Dev.* 18, 53–68.

Ross-Sheehy, S., Oakes, L. M., and Luck, S. J. (2003). The development of visual short-term memory capacity in infants. *Child Dev.* 74, 1807–1822. doi: 10.1046/j.1467-8624.2003.00639.x

Sen, M. G., Yonas, A., and Knill, D. C. (2001). Development of infants' sensitivity to surface contour information for spatial layout. *Perception* 30, 167–176. doi: 10.1068/p2789

Soska, K. C., Adolph, K. E., and Johnson, S. P. (2010). Systems in development: motor skill acquisition facilitates three-dimensional object completion. *Dev. Psychol.* 46, 129–138. doi: 10.1037/a0014618

Spencer, J. P., Vereijken, B., Frederick, J. D., and Thelen, E. (2000). Posture and the emergence of manual skills. *Dev. Sci.* 3, 216–233. doi: 10.1111/1467-7687.00115

Vecera, S. P., Vogel, E. K., and Woodman, G. F. (2002). Lower region: a new cue for figure-ground assignment. *J. Exp. Psychol. Gen.* 131, 194–205. doi: 10.1037/0096-3445.131.2.194

Vickery, T. J., and Jiang, Y. V. (2009). Associative grouping: perceptual grouping of shapes by association. *Attent. Percept. Psychophys.* 71, 896–909. doi: 10.3758/APP.71.4.896

von der Heydt, R. (2015). Figure-ground organization and the emergence of proto-objects in the visual cortex. *Front. Psychol.* 6:1695. doi: 10.3389/fpsyg.2015.01695

von Hofsten, C., and Spelke, E. S. (1985). Object perception and object-directed reaching in infancy. *J. Exp. Psychol. Gen.* 114, 198–212.

Walk, R. D., and Dodge, S. H. (1962). Visual depth perception of a 10-month-old monocular human infant. *Science* 137, 529–530.

Witherington, D. C. (2005). The development of prospective grasping control between 5 and 7 months: a longitudinal study. *Infancy* 7, 143–161. doi: 10.1207/s15327078in0702_2

Yonas, A., Elieff, C. A., and Arterberry, M. E. (2002). Emergence of sensitivity to pictorial depth cues: charting development in individual infants. *Infant Behav. Dev.* 25, 495–514. doi: 10.1016/S0163-6383(02)00147-9

Zhao, L., Cosman, J. D., Vatterott, D. B., Gupta, P., and Vecera, S. P. (2014). Visual statistical learning can drive object-based attentional selection. *Atten. Percept. Psychophys.* 76, 2240–2248. doi: 10.3758/s13414-014-0708-1

Conflict of Interest Statement: The authors declare that the research was conducted in the absence of any commercial or financial relationships that could be construed as a potential conflict of interest.

20

The Relationship between Motor Skills, Perceived Social Support, and Internalizing Problems in a Community Adolescent Sample

Vincent O. Mancini[1], Daniela Rigoli[1], Brody Heritage[2], Lynne D. Roberts[1] and Jan P. Piek[1]*

[1] School of Psychology and Speech Pathology, Curtin University, Perth, WA, Australia, [2] School of Psychology and Exercise Science, Murdoch University, Perth, WA, Australia

Objectives: Poor motor skills are associated with a range of psychosocial consequences, including internalizing (anxious and depressive) symptoms. The Elaborated Environmental Stress Hypothesis provides a causal framework to explain this association. The framework posits that motor skills impact internalizing problems through an indirect effect via perceived social support. However, empirical evaluation is required. We examined whether motor skills had an indirect effect on anxious and depressive symptoms via perceived family support domains.

Methods: This study used a community sample of 93 adolescents (12–16 years). Participants completed measures of motor skills, perceived social support across three dimensions (family, friend, and significant other), depressive symptoms, and anxious symptoms. Age, gender, verbal IQ, and ADHD symptoms were included as control variables.

Results: Regression analysis using PROCESS revealed that motor skills had an indirect effect on depressive symptoms via perceived family support, but not by perceived friend support or significant other support. The negative association between motor skills and anxious symptoms was not mediated by any perceived social support domain.

Conclusions: Findings are consistent with previous literature indicating an association between motor skills and internalizing problems. However, we identified a different pattern of relationships across anxious and depressive symptoms. While anxiety and depressive symptoms were highly correlated, motor skills had an indirect effect on depressive symptoms via perceived family support only. Our findings highlight the importance of family support as a potential protective factor in the onset of depressive symptoms. This study provides partial support for the Elaborated Environmental Stress Hypothesis, however further research is required.

Keywords: motor skills, adolescents, motor development, internalizing problems, anxiety, depression, movement

Edited by:
Petra Hauf,
St. Francis Xavier University, Canada

Reviewed by:
Yoshifumi Ikeda,
Joetsu University of Education, Japan
Simone V. Gill,
Boston University, USA

****Correspondence:***
Vincent O. Mancini
vincent.mancini@curtin.edu.au

BACKGROUND

Motor skills have an important connection with psychosocial wellbeing. Studies have demonstrated that children who have clinical motor impairments, such as developmental coordination disorder (DCD), are at greater risk of experiencing poor psychosocial outcomes, compared to their non-DCD peers. This includes less enjoyment in daily tasks (Bart et al., 2011), low self-esteem (Miyahara and Piek, 2006), less developed social support and friendships (Smyth and Anderson, 2000; Skinner and Piek, 2001), poor social skills (Kanioglou et al., 2005), social isolation and social problems (Smyth and Anderson, 2000; Chen et al., 2009), academic underachievement (Alloway, 2007), peer victimization/bullying (Campbell et al., 2012), decreased quality of life (Hill et al., 2011), withdrawal (Chen et al., 2009), physical inactivity, and obesity (Cairney et al., 2005). In addition, poor motor skills are also associated with symptoms of internalizing disorders such as depression and anxiety (Skinner and Piek, 2001; Francis and Piek, 2003; Lingam et al., 2012; Cairney et al., 2013). This association between poor motor skills and internalizing symptoms could be attributed to common neurodevelopmental etiology between motor skills and emotional regulation (Nicolson et al., 2001; Ekornas et al., 2010). However, each of the previously identified psychosocial consequences of poor motor skills are well-established risk factors for the development of internalizing problems in their own right. Cairney et al. (2013) posited that poor motor skills give rise to these various psychosocial consequences, which in turn results in increased internalizing problems, and these relationships form the basis of their recently proposed Elaborated Environmental Stress Hypothesis. This theoretical framework proposes that the relationship between motor skills and internalizing symptoms is predominantly indirect; poor motor skills may lead to various psychosocial consequences in the individual's surrounding environment (e.g., lower social support, low self-competence, peer victimization, etc.) which subsequently gives rise to increased internalizing symptoms (see Cairney et al., 2013). The model places emphasis on environmental, rather than biological, factors linking motor skills to internalizing problems. In a monozygotic twin study by Piek et al. (2007), twins with DCD were compared to their unaffected co-twin, granting the ability to control for shared genetic factors as well as shared environment. Results demonstrated higher levels of depressive symptoms in the DCD twin compared to their unaffected co-twin. These findings provide support for the Elaborated Environmental Stress Hypothesis; the authors concluded that the differences in depressive symptoms are due to unique environmental stressors associated with DCD.

The Elaborated Environmental Stress Hypothesis (see Cairney et al., 2013, p. 233 for a visual representation) is comprised of multiple direct, mediating, and moderating pathways between motor skills and internalizing symptoms. The complexity of this model has resulted in studies evaluating parts of the model, rather than the model in its entirety. These recent studies have provided support for various pathways embedded within the broader Elaborated Environmental Stress Hypothesis. For example, Wilson et al. (2013) found that the relationship between motor skills and internalizing symptoms in a community sample of young children (4–6 years of age) was mediated by social skills. The authors identified that higher levels of motor skills were associated with higher levels of social skills, which in turn related to a decrease in internalizing symptoms. Rigoli et al. (2012) found the relationship between motor skills and internalizing problems was mediated by levels of self-concept in a normative adolescent sample, another key pathway embedded within the broader Elaborated Environmental Stress Hypothesis. The results of a recent randomized control trial (RCT) by Piek et al. (2015) provided the first intervention study to empirically evaluate the Elaborated Environmental Stress Hypothesis. The authors evaluated the efficacy of the *Animal Fun* universal intervention program aimed at promoting motor and social development in young children (aged 4–6 years). Results demonstrated a lasting increase in prosocial behavior in the intervention group, but not the control group; this increase remained at 6-month and 18-month follow up. The relationships between observed variables were consistent with the pattern of relationships posited by the Elaborated Environmental Stress Hypothesis. These recent empirical developments provide preliminary support for the various pathways specified in the broader causal framework. However, given the recent conceptualization of the model, not all of the pathways contained in the model have yet been empirically evaluated. Therefore, it is important to continue to provide ongoing evaluation of the model.

Early research in the area of poor motor skills often used clinical samples of children with DCD to identify the associated psychosocial consequences (Skinner and Piek, 2001). While studies employing this comparative approach continue to provide important findings, motor skills are best understood as a continuous, rather than dichotomous construct (Wassenberg et al., 2005). More recent developments in the literature have highlighted that the psychosocial implications of motor skills are not limited to children with DCD, but are present across the broader continuum of motor skills (Rigoli et al., 2012; Wilson et al., 2013; Piek et al., 2015). There is a negative linear relationship between internalizing symptoms and motor skills, across the full continuum of movement. In other words, poorer motor skills are associated with increased internalizing symptoms and better movement ability is associated with lower internalizing symptoms. Studies that have utilized broader community samples are able to address the methodological problems that exist when attempting to dichotomize motor skills into clinical (DCD) and non-clinical (not DCD) categories (Hattori et al., 2006). Furthermore, focussing on the extreme end of the motor skill continuum may overestimate the relationship between constructs in the wider population (Rigoli et al., 2012).

Motor skills are considered to be a relatively stable construct, with a predictable pattern of development, stability, and decline over the lifespan (Leversen et al., 2012). The majority of motor coordination literature focuses on motor development in childhood. Childhood represents a critical period for motor development, and often the period in which atypical motor skills are noticed. However, poor motor skills in childhood can persist into adolescence and later life; therefore it is important to consider older populations. Recent literature has identified that the psychosocial implications of poor motor skills extend beyond childhood, into adolescence (Skinner and Piek, 2001; Sigurdsson et al., 2002; Rigoli et al., 2012; Viholainen et al., 2014) and adulthood (Hill and Brown, 2013; Poole et al., 2015). Longitudinal studies have also identified that childhood motor problems can predict psychosocial problems (including internalizing disorders) in later life (Sigurdsson et al., 2002; Lingam et al., 2012; Poole et al., 2015). Skinner and Piek (2001) suggested that the psychosocial consequences of poor motor skills may become more pronounced with age; adolescents with DCD reported higher levels of anxious symptoms than children with DCD. The adolescent DCD group also reported higher levels of anxiety compared to the adolescents without DCD. A secondary finding was that participants with DCD reported lower levels of perceived social support when compared to their non-DCD peers. A limitation of this study was that participants were dichotomized into DCD and non-DCD groups, therefore a linear relationship between motor skills, perceived social support, and internalizing problems could not be tested.

The role of social support in the etiology of internalizing problems in adolescence is well-established. High levels of perceived social support may also act as a protective factor in the onset of internalizing symptoms. Inversely, lower levels of perceived social support are associated with increased internalizing symptoms. In their community sample of 390 students aged 10–15 years, Stewart and Suldo (2011) identified perceived social support from parents, peers, and teachers each uniquely predicted variance in internalizing symptoms. However, perceived parent support emerged as the strongest predictor of all indicators, accounting for 6% of unique variance in their regression model. Similarly, the authors also identified parental support to be the largest unique predictor of externalizing behavior, and also life satisfaction. Rueger et al. (2010) also investigated the impact of perceived social support from various sources (parents, teachers, classmates, close friends, and school) on levels of anxiety and depression in middle school students. Perceived parental support was the most important predictor of all outcomes. As individuals receive support from multiple sources, it is important to consider perceived social support as a multi-factorial construct (Uchino et al., 1996). This approach can also help to identify the most important types of perceived social support.

Anxious and depressive symptoms are often considered concomitantly within the literature. This reflects their shared etiology, similar presentation of symptoms, and high levels of comorbidity (Brady and Kendall, 1992; Kessler and Walters, 1998; Seligman and Ollendick, 1998). The Elaborated Environmental Stress Hypothesis as described by Cairney et al. (2013) conceptualizes internalizing problems as an umbrella term comprised of both anxious and depressive symptoms. Consequently, some studies in the motor coordination literature measure internalizing problems as a single variable (Wilson et al., 2013), or as a latent factor driven by two observed constructs: anxious symptoms and depressive symptoms (Rigoli et al., 2012). However, within the social support literature, studies have identified different relationships between perceived social support and anxious and depressive symptoms. Perceived social support is often found to be associated with depressive symptoms, but less consistently associated with anxious symptoms (Haeffel and Mathew, 2010; Rueger et al., 2010; Väänänen et al., 2014). Consequently, research investigating the relationship between perceived social support and internalizing symptoms should consider anxious and depressive symptoms as separate outcome variables.

Through the reviewed evidence, a relationship between motor skills, perceived social support, and both anxious and depressive symptoms in adolescence has been identified. The Elaborated Environmental Stress Hypothesis provides a model in which these relationships may be framed. It posits perceived social support as a key intermediary factor between motor skills and internalizing symptoms. Lower levels of motor skills are associated with lower perceived social support, which then gives rise to increased levels of internalizing symptoms. In other words, this particular section of the Elaborated Environmental Stress Hypothesis suggests that motor skills has an indirect effect on internalizing problems via perceived social support. However, this is yet to be empirically tested.

STUDY AIMS

The aim of the present study was to empirically evaluate a portion of the Elaborated Environmental Stress Hypothesis by Cairney et al. (2013). Specifically, we tested the proposed indirect pathway from motor skills to internalizing symptoms via perceived social support, in a community sample of adolescents. We also controlled for potential confounding variables of attention deficit/hyperactivity disorder (ADHD), verbal IQ (VIQ), age and gender. ADHD has demonstrated similar psychosocial consequences as DCD (Piek et al., 2007) and has high rates of comorbidity with DCD (Goulardins et al., 2015). We included a parent-report measure that allowed us to statistically account for ADHD symptoms. Verbal IQ (VIQ) was first included as a screening tool to exclude participants with general delayed development (Lingam et al., 2012; Rigoli et al., 2012). Excluding these participants is also important for the present study which utilizes self-report measures. Previous literature has also identified a negative association between VIQ and internalizing symptoms (Rajput et al., 2011). Therefore, we also included VIQ as a control variable. Age and gender were also included as control variables based on previous findings (Sigurdsson et al., 2002; Lingam et al., 2010, 2012).

Based on the reviewed literature, we propose two hypotheses. Hypothesis one states that after controlling for age, gender, VIQ, and ADHD symptoms, motor skills will have an indirect effect on depressive symptoms, via perceived social support from friends, family, and a significant other. Hypothesis two states that after controlling for these same control variables, motor skills will have an indirect effect on anxious symptoms via each of the three domains of perceived social support.

METHODS

Participants

A community sample of 93 adolescents aged 12–16 years (M = 14.21 years, SD = 1.09) took part in the present study. Participants completed a battery of cognitive, psychosocial, and motor skills assessments as part of a larger research project (Rigoli et al., 2012). There were 55 males and 38 females. Participants were recruited through a combination of public advertisements and through 5 randomly selected secondary schools located in metropolitan Perth, Western Australia. Participants were required to have a Verbal Comprehension Index (VCI) score of 70 or above on the Wechsler Intelligence Scale for Children-IV (WISC-IV; Wechsler, 2003). This was to exclude any adolescents whose difficulties may be attributed to general delayed development (Geuze et al., 2001). All included participants had no diagnosis of physical disability, chronic illness, or medical conditions that impact development.

The a-priori power analysis for a linear multiple regression analysis to test for mediation indicated that a sample size of 109 participants was required in order to detect a medium effect size in a model with 8 predictors (four control variables, motor skills, and the 3 domains of perceived social support). The present sample of 93 participants falls slightly short of this recommended value. However, the robustness of the bootstrapped estimation methods used in the analysis would assist in addressing this potential limitation.

Measures

The Movement Assessment Battery for Children Second Edition (MABC-2)

The MABC-2 (Henderson et al., 2007) is a standardized instrument used to measure and describe movement difficulties in children between 3 and 16 years of age across three age bands (3–6 years; 7–10 years; 11–16 years). Motor coordination is measured across three domains; manual dexterity, aiming and catching ability, and balance, which are combined to provide an indication of overall motor ability. The assessment is independently administered by a trained professional, and takes approximately 30 min to complete the eight tasks. Age-based standardized scores are derived for each of the domains and an overall total test score. A child is deemed to be "at risk" of having a movement difficulty if their total test score places them between the 5th and 15th percentile; scores below the 5th percentile suggest a severe movement difficulty. The present study used the standardized total test score of the MABC-2. Previous validation studies of the MABC-2 have reported the measure to demonstrate good test retest reliability for each domain and total standardized scores, inter-rater reliability, criterion-related and discriminant validity (Henderson et al., 2007).

The Multidimensional Scale of Perceived Social Support (MSPSS)

The MSPSS (Zimet et al., 1988) is a widely used, 12 item self-report measure of perceived social support adequacy. The measure provides a subjective assessment of social support from three subscales: family, friends, and a significant other. Participants are asked to report the extent to which they agree with each statement using a 7-point scale (1 = *very strongly disagree*, to 7 = *very strongly agree*). An example item is "*I get the emotional help and support I need from my family.*" Subscale scores are calculated by averaging all responses, with higher scores indicating a higher degree of perceived social support from that particular source. Each of the three subscales of the MSPSS demonstrates good internal reliability, and the three factor structure has been validated with adolescent populations (Canty-Mitchell and Zimet, 2000; Walker et al., 2002). Cronbach's alpha for the present sample is 0.88 for the family subscale, 0.88 for the friend subscale, and 0.88 for the significant other subscale.

The Mood and Feelings Questionnaire—Child Version (MFQ)

The MFQ (Costello and Angold, 1988) is a 33-item self-report questionnaire designed for children and adolescents to report depressive symptoms experienced over the two weeks prior to completing the questionnaire. Responses are recorded by using a 3-point scale (0 = *not true*, 1 = *sometimes true*, 2 = *true*). Total scores range from 0 to 66 with higher scores indicating higher depressive symptoms. The MFQ was designed for use with both clinical and non-clinical populations of children and adolescents, and has been widely validated (Costello and Angold, 1988; Wood et al., 1995; Kuo et al., 2005). Consistent with previous reports of high internal reliability (Costello and Angold, 1988), Cronbach's alpha for the MFQ in the present study was 0.92, indicating good internal reliability.

The Spence Children's Anxiety Scale (SCAS)

The SCAS comprises 38 items designed to measure symptoms of anxiety across 6 subscales: panic attack, agoraphobia, separation anxiety, social phobia, physical injury fears, obsessive compulsive disorder, and generalized anxiety. Responses are recorded by using a 4-point scale (0 = *never*, to 3 = *always*). A total SCAS score is calculated by summing the responses to all 38 items. This total score of the child self-report version was used in the present study. The SCAS has been used in samples of adolescents up to 19 years of age and demonstrates good levels of internal reliability (Spence, 1997), test-retest reliability, convergent and discriminant validity (Spence, 1998; Muris et al., 2000; Essau et al., 2002). Cronbach's alpha for the SCAS in the present study was 0.89, indicating good internal reliability.

Wechsler Intelligence Scale for Children- Fourth Edition (WISC-IV)

The WISC-IV (Wechsler, 2003) is a standardized assessment of cognitive ability for children aged 6–16 years 11 months. The WISC-IV provides an indication of cognitive ability across 4 domains: verbal comprehension, perceptual reasoning, working memory, and processing speed. The WISC-IV is widely used, and considered to be the gold-standard in cognitive assessment for children. It has excellent psychometric properties (Wechsler, 2003). We used the VCI subscale of the WISC-IV in the present study.

Strengths and Weaknesses of ADHD Symptoms and Normal Behavior (SWAN)

The SWAN (Swanson et al., 2006) is a parent-rated assessment of ADHD symptoms. This 18-item measure involves observations based on the last month, asking the parent to rate their child's behavior compared to similarly aged children. A 7-point scale is used, with scores ranging from 3 (*far below average*) to −3 (*far above average*). An overall score is calculated by averaging the total of all 18 items, with higher scores indicating higher ADHD symptoms. The SWAN has been previously supported as an accurate measure of ADHD symptoms in the general population (Martin et al., 2006; Polderman et al., 2007). Cronbach's alpha for the SWAN in the present study was 0.96, indicating excellent internal reliability.

Demographic Variables

Single item measures of age and gender were also collected.

Procedure

The study followed the National Health and Medical Research Council of Australia ethical guidelines. Prior to commencing the study, ethics approval was granted by the relevant University Human Research Ethics Committee and the relevant bodies of the participating schools. Informed consent was obtained from both the adolescent participants and their parents. Participants were then independently assessed by a trained assessor over a period of two sessions (approximately 4.5 h in total). The self-report psychosocial questionnaires were completed by participants, and the parent-report questionnaires by parents. Assessments were conducted at either the family home or at university facilities, selected at the discretion of the families.

RESULTS

Means, standard deviations, ranges, and bivariate correlations for the observed variables in this study are provided in **Table 1**. Five adolescents (5.4% of the total sample) were identified as having significant movement difficulty on the MABC-2 (at or below the 5th percentile). This is comparable to population estimates of 5–6% (American Psychiatric Association, 2013). Two adolescents were identified as at-risk for movement difficulty (between the 6th and 15th percentile). Ten adolescents scored in the clinical range for depression on the MFQ (a score of 29 and above). Seven participants scored in the subclinical range for anxiety on the SCAS (1 standard deviation above the normative mean), and an additional five participants scored in the clinical range (more than 1.5 standard deviations above the normative mean). Two of the five adolescents identified as having significant movement difficulty scored in the clinical range for both the MFQ and the SCAS. One of the two adolescents identified as at-risk for movement difficulty scored in the subclinical range for the SCAS.

Mediation Analysis

Tests of mediation using the PROCESS macro (Hayes, 2013) were conducted in SPSS. The direct and indirect effect of each model were estimated with 10,000 bootstrapped 95% bias-corrected and accelerated (BcA) confidence intervals to assess for statistical significance, as this method is robust to non-normality for the indirect path estimation. Two models were tested, one predicting depressive symptoms and the other predicting anxious symptoms. In each model motor skills scores were specified as the independent variable, and social support from family, friends, and a significant other as the mediator variables, with, gender, age, and ADHD symptoms as covariates.

Depressive Symptoms

In combination, the predictors included in the total model account for approximately 26.36% of the variance in depressive symptoms, Model R^2=0.26 $F_{(8, 84)} = 3.76$, $p < 0.001$, and a large effect (Cohen, 1992). Motor skills did not have an indirect effect on depressive symptoms via perceived friend support, or perceived significant other support, as the confidence intervals of both indirect pathways included zero. There was a significant indirect effect of motor skills on depressive symptoms via perceived family support; $ab = -0.34$, 95% BcA $CI = -0.90$ to -0.024. The association between motor skills and depressive symptoms was lessened but remained significant after the inclusion of the covariates and mediator variables, $c' = -0.86$, 95% BcA $CI = -1.67$ to -0.05. The direct effect, after controlling for the effect of the mediator variables and covariates, was therefore a significant predictor of depressive symptoms. In summary, we identified a direct effect from motor skills to depressive symptoms, and also an indirect effect via perceived family support. These relationships are presented in **Figure 1**.

Anxious Symptoms

For the mediation model with anxious symptoms as the outcome variable, motor skills, the three domains of perceived social support, and the covariates accounted for approximately 19.77% of the variance in anxious symptoms, Model R^2=0.20, $F_{(8, 84)} = 2.59$, $p = 0.014$, and a moderate to large effect (Cohen, 1992). There was no significant indirect effect of motor skills on anxious symptoms via any domain of perceived social support, as all confidence intervals for the ab path estimates included zero within their boundaries. The direct effect of motor skills was significant after accounting for the effect of the mediator variables and the covariates, $c' = -1.45$, 95% BcA $CI = -2.44$ to -0.46. These relationships are presented in **Figure 2**.

DISCUSSION

The aim of the current study was to empirically evaluate a key part of the recently proposed Elaborated Environmental Stress Hypothesis by Cairney et al. (2013). This causal framework posits that poor motor skills give rise to internalizing problems via the intermediary effect of various personal and social factors. Few studies have empirically examined this framework since it was conceptualized. Therefore, the current study is important in adding to existing research. We specifically sought to evaluate whether the relationship between motor skills and internalizing symptoms was mediated by perceived social support in a community adolescent sample. Hypothesis one stated that the relationship between motor skills and depressive symptoms would be mediated by perceived social support from friends, family, and a significant other, after controlling for age, gender, VIQ, and ADHD symptoms. This hypothesis was partially supported. Motor skills had a direct effect on depressive symptoms, and an indirect effect via perceived family support. Hypothesis two stated that the relationship between motor skills and anxious symptoms would be mediated by perceived social support from friends, family, and a significant other, after controlling for age, gender, VIQ, and ADHD symptoms. This

TABLE 1 | Means, standard deviations (*SD*), observed range of scores, and bivariate correlations between variables (*N* = 93).

Variable	Descriptives			Bivariate correlations (Pearson's *r*)													
	Mean	*SD*	Range	1	2	3	4	5	6	7	8	9	10	11	12	13	14
1. MABC-2 Total Test Score[a]	10.63	2.57	3–16	–													
2. MABC-2 Manual Dexterity[a]	9.57	2.47	3–15	0.657**	–												
3. MABC-2 Aiming and Catching[a]	11.03	2.73	4–16	0.656**	0.071	–											
4. MABC-2 Balance[a]	11.42	2.98	4–14	0.780**	0.264*	0.423**	–										
5. MSPSS Total[bc]	5.72	0.88	2–7	0.242*	0.195	0.058	0.302**	–									
6. MSPSS Family Support[bd]	5.78	1.15	1–7	0.223*	0.088	0.180	−0.247*	0.753**	–								
7. MSPSS Friend Support[bd]	5.69	1.05	2–7	0.226*	0.223*	0.006	0.263*	0.758**	0.260*	–							
8. MSPSS Significant Other Support[bd]	5.68	1.11	2–7	0.129	0.160	−0.055	0.213*	0.873**	0.500**	0.585**	–						
9. MFQ Total[be]	13.48	10.43	1–48	−0.329**	−0.108	−0.319**	−0.307**	−0.215*	−0.347**	−0.138	−0.020	–					
10. SCAS Total[be]	21.77	12.49	1–67	−0.324**	0.003	−0.371**	−0.314**	−0.018	−0.106	−0.054	0.119	0.720**	–				
11. WISC-IV VCI[a]	106.63	11.25	81–132	0.152	0.075	0.048	0.155	0.055	−0.004	0.117	0.023	−0.155	−0.185	–			
12. Age (Years)	14.21	1.09	12–17	−0.114	−0.069	−0.066	−0.095	−0.054	−0.101	−0.063	0.036	0.161	0.187	−0.167	–		
13. Gender	–	–	–	−0.069	0.235*	−0.397**	−0.007	0.261*	−0.038	0.359**	0.319**	0.079	0.179	−0.018	0.021	–	
14. ADHD Symptoms[bc]	-1.00	1.02	-3.0–1.22	−0.040	−0.143	0.058	0.011	0.051	−0.030	0.120	0.043	0.170	0.029	−0.284*	0.093	−0.212	–

MABC-2, Movement Assessment Battery for Children, Second-Edition; MSPSS, Multidimensional Scale for Perceived Social Support; MFQ, Mood and Feelings Questionnaire; SCAS, Spence Children's Anxiety Scale; WISC-IV, Wechsler Intelligence Scale for Children; VCI, Verbal Comprehension Index; ADHD, Attention Deficity Hyperactivity Disorder. *$p < 0.05$ (two-tailed). **$p < 0.001$ (two-tailed).

[a] *Standard Score.*

[b] *Raw Score.*

[c] *Scores are calculated by averaging the total of all items in the measure.*

[d] *Scores are calculated by averaging the relevant subscale items in the measure.*

[e] *Scores are calculated by summing all items in the measure.*

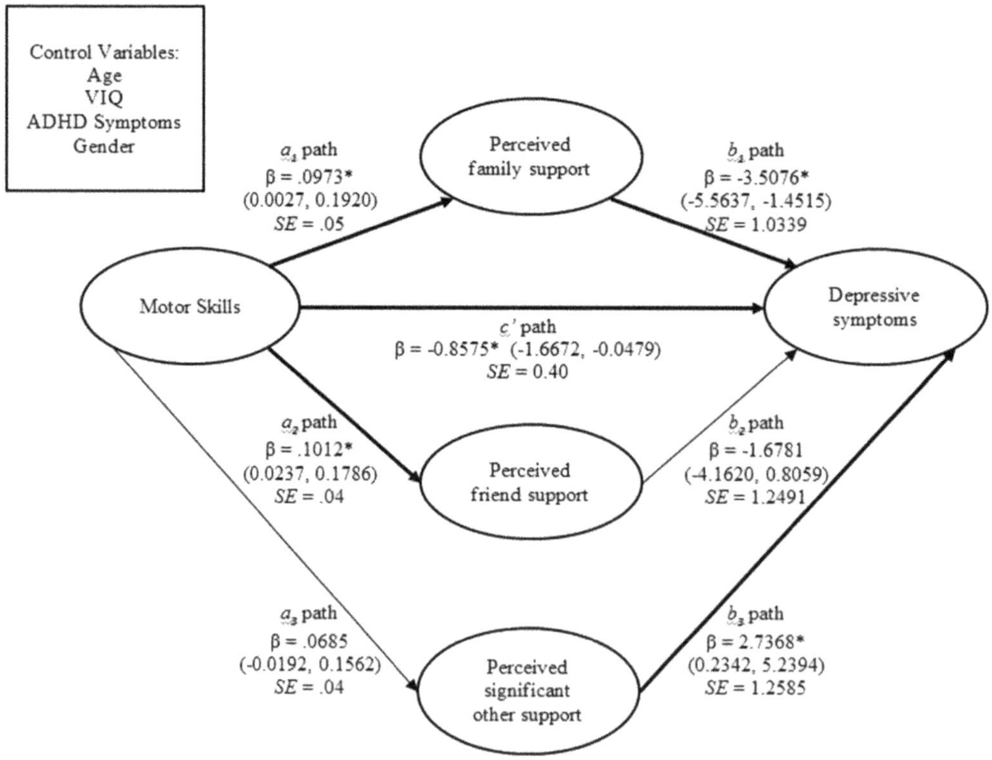

FIGURE 1 | Mediation model in which perceived family support partially has an indirect effect on the association between motor skills and depressive symptoms. Significant pathways are depicted in bold. $^*P < 0.05$. Note: 95% bias-corrected confidence intervals provided in parentheses. β, Standardized coefficient; SE, standard error.

hypothesis was not supported. Motor skills had a direct effect on anxious symptoms, but did not have an indirect effect on anxious symptoms via any domain of perceived social support.

Similar studies that have used measures of internalizing symptoms have found comparable results to the present study. For example, Wilson et al. (2013) found social skills mediated the relationship between motor skills and internalizing symptoms in young children. The authors measured internalizing symptoms as a single construct. Other studies have considered measures of anxious and depressive symptoms as observed variables which are driven by the latent construct of internalizing symptoms (Rigoli et al., 2012). The use of internalizing symptoms as an umbrella term for anxious and depressive symptoms is widely supported (Brady and Kendall, 1992; Kessler and Walters, 1998; Seligman and Ollendick, 1998), though there are several distinctions in the etiology and impact of anxious and depressive symptoms. Our findings highlight the need to examine the importance of perceived social support for adolescents on anxious and depressive symptoms separately. Previous studies in adolescent populations have also noted stronger and more consistent negative linear associations between perceived social support and depressive symptoms, compared to anxious symptoms (Haeffel and Mathew, 2010; Rueger et al., 2010; Väänänen et al., 2014). Analyses that unify anxious and depressive symptoms into internalizing symptoms may risk attenuating the relationship between variables. Furthermore, the Elaborated Environmental Stress Hypothesis includes a range of secondary psychosocial consequences that give rise to internalizing problems; it may be important to consider the differential impacts of these other factors on anxious and depressive symptoms.

While both mediation models accounted for significant variance, a substantial proportion of variance in anxious and depressive symptoms was unaccounted for. This suggests that there are additional factors that contribute to the formation of anxious and depressive symptoms in adolescents. We only investigated a portion of the Elaborated Environmental Stress Hypothesis. Multiple factors posited to mediate and/or moderate the association between motor skills and internalizing symptoms were untested in the present study. It is likely that future studies that look at several factors embedded within the Elaborated Environmental Stress Hypothesis will account for additional variance in internalizing symptoms. This is consistent with the understanding that the etiology of internalizing symptoms across the life span is influenced by multiple factors (Koplewicz and Klass, 1993).

Consistent with previous literature, the current study identified a direct association between motor skills and both anxious and depressive symptoms. This relationship is fundamental to the Elaborated Environmental Stress Hypothesis.

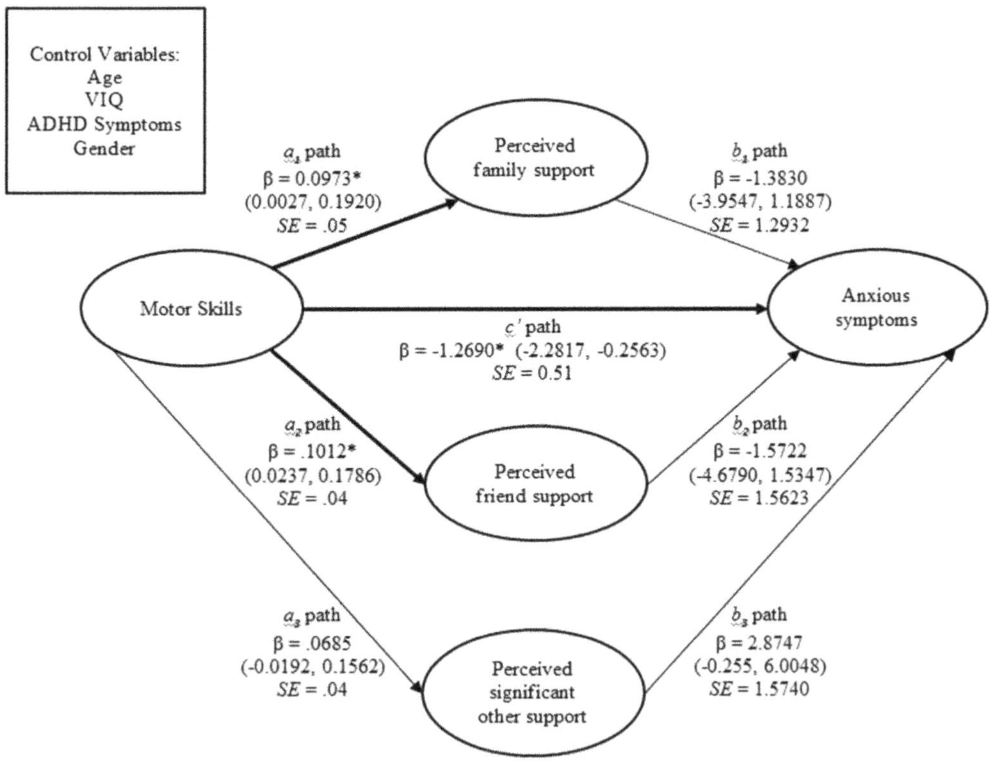

FIGURE 2 | Mediation model in which there is no indirect relationship between motor skills and anxious symptoms. Significant pathways are depicted in bold. $^*P < 0.05$. Note: 95% bias-corrected confidence intervals provided in parentheses. β, Standardized coefficient; SE, standard error.

Cairney et al. (2013) originally developed this framework for use in the child DCD population. However, more recent studies have also provided support for its use in broader community populations (Rigoli et al., 2012; Wilson et al., 2013; Viholainen et al., 2014; Piek et al., 2015). The present study adds to this literature, enlisting a community sample of adolescents and providing partial support for this framework.

In the present study, we specifically focused on perceived social support as a possible secondary consequence. It has been suggested that higher levels of motor skills are associated with higher levels of perceived social support, as it increases the chances for positive peer interactions and formation of friendships (Cairney et al., 2013). Similarly, the presence of poor motor skills may lead to frustration from family members and teachers, who may incorrectly attribute the individual's difficulties as inattention, task avoidance, or laziness (Missiuna et al., 2006). The individual may then perceive a decrease in perceived social support from these sources. Our current findings are congruent with previous research, as we identified a positive linear association between motor skills and perceived social support (from friends and family).

The association between perceived social support and internalizing symptoms in adolescence is well-researched. Higher levels of perceived social support are associated with lower internalizing symptoms (Rueger et al., 2010; Stewart and Suldo, 2011; Väänänen et al., 2014). This has been attributed to high levels of perceived social support providing a protective factor that allows an individual to more effectively handle potentially stressful events (Dumont and Provost, 1999). Perceived social support has been found to be more strongly associated with depressive symptoms compared to anxious symptoms (Haeffel and Mathew, 2010; Rueger et al., 2010; Väänänen et al., 2014). Consistent with these findings, the present results indicate a negative linear association between perceived social support (from family and a significant other) and depressive symptoms; no measure of perceived social support was significantly associated with anxious symptoms.

Perceived social support is multi-factorial (Rueger et al., 2010); therefore we measured perceived social support across three domains relevant to adolescents (friends, family, and a significant other). This allowed us to identify any differences between types of perceived social support and their relationship with motor skills and internalizing symptoms. For the mediation model predicting depressive symptoms, motor skills had an indirect effect on depressive symptoms via perceived family support only. Similarly, perceived family support had the strongest association with depressive symptoms, compared to perceived support from friends and a significant other. The results of the present study indicate that while there is a positive association between motor skills and perceived family support and perceived friend support, only perceived family support was significantly negatively associated with depressive symptoms. The present findings are consistent with previous literature, which has identified family (particularly parents) as the strongest predictor of depressive symptoms and mental health in adolescents (Rueger et al., 2010; Stewart and Suldo, 2011).

This study enlisted a sample of adolescents between 12 and 16 years of age. Consequently, perceived family support may have been the strongest predictor of depressive symptoms due to the central role that family has during early adolescence (Morris et al., 2007). Previous studies have identified a transition in attachment patterns during adolescence, where individuals begin to draw on peers for social support (Noller et al., 2013). The participants in this study were in the early-to-mid stages of adolescent development and the transition from family support to other types of social support may still be underway. It is also equally plausible that perceived family support may be important in an adolescent sample as the family structure (particularly parents) may serve as a "secure base" for individuals to draw support from while they continue to explore and develop peer relationships throughout adolescence (Noller et al., 2013). An awareness of the shifting changes in attachment styles throughout the lifespan provides an important consideration for future studies seeking to explore the relationship between motor skills, perceived social support, and mental health outcomes in different age groups. For example, we may posit that perceived social support from friends, rather than family, may be a stronger predictor of mental health in older adolescent/adult samples. However, other studies have found that perceived family support was a stronger protective factor in depressive symptoms when compared to perceived friend support in adults aged 21–30 years (Pettit et al., 2011). Further empirical investigation is required, specifically within the context of motor skills.

An interesting observation to note was the significant positive association between perceived social support from a significant other and depressive symptoms (see **Figure 1**), suggesting that higher levels of perceived social support from a significant other is related to higher levels of depressive symptoms, which is inconsistent with previous literature. Additional investigation of this relationship is required in order to determine if these findings can be replicated.

This present study employed a cross-sectional, correlational research design to test a recently proposed causal framework. While the associations between motor skills, perceived family support, and depressive symptoms are congruent with the Elaborated Environmental Stress Hypothesis, the present research design was unable to identify temporal precedence between variables, as data was collected at a single point in time. While changes in perceived social support are generally considered to predispose changes in depressive symptoms, it is important to note that there is some research suggesting that depressive symptoms may influence perceived social support (Leskelä et al., 2008). Consequently, further longitudinal and experimental research is required in order to permit causal conclusions. While we employed robust bootstrapping procedures to address the potential limitation of a sample of 93 participants, enlisting a larger sample of adolescents in future studies is advised, particularly as it will allow for the testing of multiple variables and more rigorous analyses.

CONCLUSION

This study evaluated a key pathway specified by the recently proposed Elaborated Environmental Stress Hypothesis, the potential indirect effect of perceived social support between motor skills and internalizing symptoms. We identified an important, direct relationship between motor skills and both depressive and anxious symptoms in a community adolescent sample. There were no indirect effects between motor skills and anxious symptoms via perceived social support from friends, family, or a significant other. However, there was an indirect effect between motor skills and depressive symptoms, via perceived family support only. This study provides partial support for the Elaborated Environmental Stress Hypothesis. The present findings increase our understanding of how motor skills, perceived social support, and internalizing symptoms interact in a community adolescent sample. This has particular implications for the prevention of psychosocial problems in young people with poor motor skills. For example, improving perceived family support may serve as a protective factor that mitigates increased depressive symptoms. Programs aimed at improving the psychosocial outcomes of young people with motor difficulties could potentially include components that seek to improve support from family.

AUTHOR CONTRIBUTIONS

VM was the primary author of the article, who wrote the majority of the manuscript/conducted analysis. DR was responsible for the larger study of which the current data is part of, and also provided feedback on the manuscript. BH provided supervision and assisted in the methodological procedures of the research. LR and JP provided supervision and feedback regarding the process of the research and the subsequent manuscript.

REFERENCES

Alloway, T. P. (2007). Working memory, reading, and mathematical skills in children with developmental coordination disorder. *J. Exp. Child Psychol.* 96, 20–36. doi: 10.1016/j.jecp.2006.07.002

American Psychiatric Association (2013). *Diagnostic and Statistical Manual of Mental Disorders, 5th Edn.* Arlington, VA: American Psychiatric Publishing.

Bart, O., Jarus, T., Erez, Y., and Rosenberg, L. (2011). How do young children with DCD participate and enjoy daily activities? *Res. Dev. Disabil.* 32, 1317–1322. doi: 10.1016/j.ridd.2011.01.039

Brady, E. U., and Kendall, P. C. (1992). Comorbidity of anxiety and depression in children and adolescents. *Psychol. Bull.* 111, 244. doi: 10.1037/0033-2909.111.2.244

Cairney, J., Hay, J. A., Faught, B. E., Wade, T. J., Corna, L., and Flouris, A. (2005). Developmental coordination disorder, generalized self-efficacy toward physical activity, and participation in organized and free play activities. *J. Pediatrics* 147, 515–520. doi: 10.1016/j.jpeds.2005.05.013

Cairney, J., Rigoli, D., and Piek, J. (2013). Developmental coordination disorder and internalizing problems in children: the environmental stress hypothesis elaborated. *Dev. Rev.* 33, 224–238. doi: 10.1016/j.dr.2013.07.002

Campbell, W. N., Missiuna, C., and Vaillancourt, T. (2012). Peer victimization and depression in children with and without motor coordination difficulties. *Psychol. Sch.* 49, 328–341. doi: 10.1002/pits.21600

Canty-Mitchell, J., and Zimet, G. (2000). Psychometric properties of the multidimensional scale of perceived social support in urban adolescents. *Am. J. Commun. Psychol.* 28, 391–400. doi: 10.1023/A:1005109522457

Chen, Y.-W., Tseng, M.-H., Hu, F.-C., and Cermak, S. A. (2009). Psychosocial adjustment and attention in children with developmental coordination disorder using different motor tests. *Res. Dev. Disabil.* 30, 1367–1377. doi: 10.1016/j.ridd.2009.06.004

Cohen, J. (1992). A power primer. *Psychol. Bull.* 112:155. doi: 10.1037/0033-2909.112.1.155

Costello, E. J., and Angold, A. (1988). Scales to assess child and adolescent depression: checklists, screens, and nets. *J. Am. Acad. Child Adolesc. Psychiatry* 27, 726–737. doi: 10.1097/00004583-198811000-00011

Dumont, M., and Provost, M. A. (1999). Resilience in adolescents: protective role of social support, coping strategies, self-esteem, and social activities on experience of stress and depression. *J. Youth Adolesc.* 28, 343–363. doi: 10.1023/A:1021637011732

Ekornas, B., Lundervold, A. J., Tjus, T., and Heimann, M. (2010). Anxiety disorders in 8–11-year-old children: motor skill performance and self-perception of competence. *Scand. J. Psychol.* 51, 271–277. doi: 10.1111/j.1467-9450.2009.00763.x

Essau, C. A., Muris, P., and Ederer, E. M. (2002). Reliability and validity of the spence children's anxiety scale and the screen for child anxiety related emotional disorders in german children. *J. Behav. Ther. Exp. Psychiatry* 33, 1–18. doi: 10.1016/S0005-7916(02)00005-8

Francis, M., and Piek, J. (2003). "The effects of perceived social support and self-worth on depressive symptomatology in children with and without developmental coordination disorder (DCD)," in *Paper Presented at the 38th APS Annual Conference* (Melbourne).

Geuze, R. H., Jongmans, M. J., Schoemaker, M. M., and Smits-Engelsman, B. C. (2001). Clinical and research diagnostic criteria for developmental coordination disorder: a review and discussion. *Hum. Mov. Sci.* 20, 7–47. doi: 10.1016/S0167-9457(01)00027-6

Goulardins, J. B., Rigoli, D., Loh, P. R., Kane, R., Licari, M., Hands, B., et al. (2015). The relationship between motor skills, social problems, and ADHD symptomatology does it vary according to parent and teacher report? *J. Atten. Disord.* 19, 1–10. doi: 10.1177/1087054715580394

Haeffel, G. J., and Mathew, A. R. (2010). Inside thoughts and outside influences: cognitive vulnerability moderates the effect of decreases in perceived social support on depressive symptoms. *J. Soc. Clin. Psychol.* 29, 281–300. doi: 10.1521/jscp.2010.29.3.281

Hattori, J., Ogino, T., Abiru, K., Nakano, K., Oka, M., and Ohtsuka, Y. (2006). Are pervasive developmental disorders and attention-deficit/hyperactivity disorder distinct disorders? *Brain Dev.* 28, 371–374. doi: 10.1016/j.braindev.2005.11.009

Hayes, A. F. (2013). *Introduction to Mediation, Moderation, and Conditional Process Analysis: A Regression-Based Approach.* Guilford, NY: Guilford.

Henderson, S. E., Sugden, D. A., and Barnett, A. L. (2007). *Movement Assessment Battery for Children, 2nd Edn.* London: Psychological Corporation.

Hill, E. L., and Brown, D. (2013). Mood impairments in adults previously diagnosed with developmental coordination disorder. *J. Ment. Health* 22, 334–340. doi: 10.3109/09638237.2012.745187

Hill, E. L., Brown, D., and Sorgardt, K. (2011). A preliminary investigation of quality of life satisfaction reports in emerging adults with and without developmental coordination disorder. *J. Adult Dev.* 18, 130–134. doi: 10.1007/s10804-011-9122-2

Kanioglou, A., Tsorbatzoudis, H., and Barkoukis, V. (2005). Socialization and behavioral problems of elementary school pupils with developmental coordination disorder. *Percept. Motor Skills* 101, 163–173. doi: 10.2466/pms.101.5.163-173

Kessler, R. C., and Walters, E. E. (1998). Epidemiology of DSM–III–R major depression and minor depression among adolescents and young adults in the national comorbidity survey. *Depress. Anxiety* 7, 3–14.

Koplewicz, H. S., and Klass, E. (1993). *Depression in Children and Adolescents.* Chur: Harwood Academic Publishers.

Kuo, E. S., Vander Stoep, A., and Stewart, D. G. (2005). Using the Short Mood and Feelings Questionnaire to detect depression in detained adolescents. *Assessment* 12, 374–383. doi: 10.1177/1073191105279984

Leskelä, U., Melartin, T., Rytsälä, H., Sokero, P., Lestelä-Mielonen, P., and Isometsä, E. (2008). The influence of major depressive disorder on objective and subjective social support: a prospective study. *J. Nerv. Ment. Dis.* 196, 876–883. doi: 10.1097/NMD.0b013e31818ec6cf

Leversen, J. S., Haga, M., and Sigmundsson, H. (2012). From children to adults: motor performance across the life-span. *PLoS ONE* 7:e38830. doi: 10.1371/journal.pone.0038830

Lingam, R., Golding, J., Jongmans, M. J., Hunt, L. P., Ellis, M., and Emond, A. (2010). The association between developmental coordination disorder and other developmental traits. *Pediatrics* 126, 2009–2789. doi: 10.1542/peds.2009-2789

Lingam, R., Jongmans, M. J., Ellis, M., Hunt, L. P., Golding, J., and Emond, A. (2012). Mental health difficulties in children with developmental coordination disorder. *Pediatrics* 129, e882–e891. doi: 10.1542/peds.2011-1556

Martin, N. C., Piek, J. P., and Hay, D. (2006). DCD and ADHD: a genetic study of their shared aetiology. *Hum. Mov. Sci.* 25, 110–124. doi: 10.1016/j.humov.2005.10.006

Missiuna, C., Moll, S., King, G., Law, M., and King, G. (2006). Missed and misunderstood: children with coordination difficulties in the school system. *Int. J. Spec. Educ.* 21, 53–67. Available online at: http://www.internationaljournalofspecialeducation.com/

Miyahara, M., and Piek, J. (2006). Self-esteem of children and adolescents with physical disabilities: quantitative evidence from meta-analysis. *J. Dev. Phys. Disabil.* 18, 219–234. doi: 10.1007/s10882-006-9014-8

Morris, A. S., Silk, J. S., Steinberg, L., Myers, S. S., and Robinson, L. R. (2007). The role of the family context in the development of emotion regulation. *Soc. Dev.* 16, 361–388. doi: 10.1111/j.1467-9507.2007.00389.x

Muris, P., Schmidt, H., and Merckelbach, H. (2000). Correlations among two self-report questionnaires for measuring DSM-defined anxiety disorder symptoms in children: the screen for child anxiety related emotional disorders and the spence children's anxiety scale. *Pers. Individ. Dif.* 28, 333–346. doi: 10.1016/S0191-8869(99)00102-6

Nicolson, R. I., Fawcett, A. J., and Dean, P. (2001). Developmental dyslexia: the cerebellar deficit hypothesis. *Trends Neurosci.* 24, 508–511. doi: 10.1016/S0166-2236(00)01896-8

Noller, P., Feeney, J., and Petersen, C. (2013). *Personal Relationships across the Lifespan.* London: Psychology Press.

Pettit, J. W., Roberts, R. E., Lewinsohn, P. M., Seeley, J. R., and Yaroslavsky, I. (2011). Developmental relations between perceived social support and depressive symptoms through emerging adulthood: blood is thicker than water. *J. Fam. Psychol.* 25, 127. doi: 10.1037/a0022320

Piek, J. P., Kane, R., Rigoli, D., McLaren, S., Roberts, C. M., Rooney, R., et al. (2015). Does the Animal Fun program improve social-emotional and behavioural outcomes in children aged 4–6 years? *Hum. Mov. Sci.* 43, 155–163. doi: 10.1016/j.humov.2015.08.004

Piek, J. P., Rigoli, D., Pearsall-Jones, J. G., Martin, N. C., Hay, D. A., Bennett, K. S., et al. (2007). Depressive symptomatology in child and adolescent twins with attention-deficit hyperactivity disorder and/or developmental coordination disorder. *Twin Res. Hum. Genet.* 10, 587–596. doi: 10.1375/twin.10.4.587

Polderman, T. J., Derks, E. M., Hudziak, J. J., Verhulst, F. C., Posthuma, D., and Boomsma, D. I. (2007). Across the continuum of attention skills: a twin study of the SWAN ADHD rating scale. *J. Child Psychol. Psychiatry* 48, 1080–1087. doi: 10.1111/j.1469-7610.2007.01783.x

Poole, K. L., Schmidt, L. A., Missiuna, C., Saigal, S., Boyle, M. H., and Van Lieshout, R. J. (2015). Motor coordination and mental health in extremely low birth weight survivors during the first four decades of life. *Res. Dev. Disabil.* 43–44, 87–96. doi: 10.1016/j.ridd.2015.06.004

Rajput, S., Hassiotis, A., Richards, M., Hatch, S., and Stewart, R. (2011). Associations between IQ and common mental disorders: the 2000 British

National Survey of Psychiatric Morbidity. *Eur. Psychiatry* 26, 390–395. doi: 10.1016/j.eurpsy.2010.07.002

Rigoli, D., Piek, J., and Kane, R. (2012). Motor coordination and psychosocial correlates in a normative adolescent sample. *Pediatrics* 129, e892–e900. doi: 10.1542/peds.2011-1237

Rueger, S. Y., Malecki, C. K., and Demaray, M. K. (2010). Relationship between multiple sources of perceived social support and psychological and academic adjustment in early adolescence: comparisons across gender. *J. Youth Adolesc.* 39, 47–61. doi: 10.1007/s10964-008-9368-6

Seligman, L., and Ollendick, T. (1998). Comorbidity of anxiety and depression in children and adolescents: an integrative review. *Clin. Child Fam. Psychol. Rev.* 1, 125–144. doi: 10.1023/A:1021887712873

Sigurdsson, E., Van Os, J., and Fombonne, E. (2002). Are impaired childhood motor skills a risk factor for adolescent anxiety? Results from the 1958 UK birth cohort and the National Child Development Study. *Am. J. Psychiatry* 159, 1044–1046. doi: 10.1176/appi.ajp.159.6.1044

Skinner, R. A., and Piek, J. P. (2001). Psychosocial implications of poor motor coordination in children and adolescents. *Hum. Mov. Sci.* 20, 73–94. doi: 10.1016/S0167-9457(01)00029-X

Smyth, M. M., and Anderson, H. I. (2000). Coping with clumsiness in the school playground: social and physical play in children with coordination impairments. *Br. J. Dev. Psychol.* 18, 389–413. doi: 10.1348/026151000165760

Spence, S. H. (1997). Structure of anxiety symptoms among children: a confirmatory factor-analytic study. *J. Abnorm. Psychol.* 106:280. doi: 10.1037/0021-843X.106.2.280

Spence, S. H. (1998). A measure of anxiety symptoms among children. *Behav. Res. Ther.* 36, 545–566. doi: 10.1016/S0005-7967(98)00034-5

Stewart, T., and Suldo, S. (2011). Relationships between social support sources and early adolescents' mental health: the moderating effect of student achievement level. *Psychol. Sch.* 48, 1016–1033. doi: 10.1002/pits.20607

Swanson, J., Schuck, S., Mann, M., Carlson, C., Hartman, K., Sergeant, J., et al. (2006). *Categorical and Dimensional Definitions and Evaluations of Symptoms of ADHD: The SNAP and SWAN Rating Scales*. Irvine: University of California.

Uchino, B. N., Cacioppo, J. T., and Kiecolt-Glaser, J. K. (1996). The relationship between social support and physiological processes: a review with emphasis on underlying mechanisms and implications for health. *Psychol. Bull.* 119:488. doi: 10.1037/0033-2909.119.3.488

Väänänen, J.-M., Marttunen, M., Helminen, M., and Kaltiala-Heino, R. (2014). Low perceived social support predicts later depression but not social phobia in middle adolescence. *Health Psychol. Behav. Med.* 2, 1023–1037. doi: 10.1080/21642850.2014.966716

Viholainen, H., Aro, T., Purtsi, J., Tolvanen, A., and Cantell, M. (2014). Adolescents' school—related self—concept mediates motor skills and psychosocial well—being. *Br. J. Educ. Psychol.* 84, 268–280. doi: 10.1111/bjep.12023

Walker, L. S., Claar, R. L., and Garber, J. (2002). Social consequences of children's pain: when do they encourage symptom maintenance? *J. Pediatr. Psychol.* 27, 689–698. doi: 10.1093/jpepsy/27.8.689

Wassenberg, R., Feron, F. J., Kessels, A. G., Hendriksen, J. G., Kalff, A. C., Kroes, M., et al. (2005). Relation between cognitive and motor performance in 5—to 6—year—old children: results from a large—scale cross—sectional study. *Child Dev.* 76, 1092–1103. doi: 10.1111/j.1467-8624.2005.00899.x

Wechsler, D. (2003). *Wechsler Intelligence Scale for Children-WISC-IV*. San Antonio, TX: Psychological Corporation.

Wilson, A., Piek, J. P., and Kane, R. (2013). The mediating role of social skills in the relationship between motor ability and internalizing symptoms in pre-primary children. *Infant Child Dev.* 22, 151–164. doi: 10.1002/icd.1773

Wood, A., Kroll, L., Moore, A., and Harrington, R. (1995). Properties of the mood and feelings questionnaire in adolescent psychiatric outpatients: a research note. *J. Child Psychol. Psychiatry* 36, 327–334. doi: 10.1111/j.1469-7610.1995.tb01828.x

Zimet, G. D., Dahlem, N. W., Zimet, S. G., and Farley, G. K. (1988). The multidimensional scale of perceived social support. *J. Pers. Assess.* 52, 30–41. doi: 10.1207/s15327752jpa5201_2

Conflict of Interest Statement: The authors declare that the research was conducted in the absence of any commercial or financial relationships that could be construed as a potential conflict of interest.

21

Deliberate Play and Preparation Jointly Benefit Motor and Cognitive Development: Mediated and Moderated Effects

Caterina Pesce[1], Ilaria Masci[1], Rosalba Marchetti[1], Spyridoula Vazou[2], Arja Sääkslahti[3] and Phillip D. Tomporowski[4]*

[1] Department of Movement, Human and Health Sciences, Italian University Sport and Movement "Foro Italico", Rome, Italy, [2] Department of Kinesiology, Iowa State University, Ames, IA, USA, [3] Department of Sport Sciences, University of Jyväskylä, Jyväskylä, Finland, [4] Department of Kinesiology, University of Georgia, Athens, GA, USA

Edited by:
Klaus Libertus,
University of Pittsburgh, USA

Reviewed by:
Mirko Schmidt,
University of Bern, Switzerland
Jan Patricia Piek,
Curtin University, Australia

***Correspondence:**
Caterina Pesce
caterina.pesce@uniroma4.it

In light of the interrelation between motor and cognitive development and the predictive value of the former for the latter, the secular decline observed in motor coordination ability as early as preschool urges identification of interventions that may jointly impact motor and cognitive efficiency. The aim of this study was twofold. It (1) explored the outcomes of enriched physical education (PE), centered on deliberate play and cognitively challenging variability of practice, on motor coordination and cognitive processing; (2) examined whether motor coordination outcomes mediate intervention effects on children's cognition, while controlling for moderation by lifestyle factors as outdoor play habits and weight status. Four hundred and sixty children aged 5–10 years participated in a 6-month group randomized intervention in PE, with or without playful coordinative and cognitive enrichment. The weight status and spontaneous outdoor play habits of children (parental report of outdoor play) were evaluated at baseline. Before and after the intervention, motor developmental level (Movement Assessment Battery for Children) was evaluated in all children, who were then assessed either with a test of working memory (Random Number Generation task), or with a test of attention (from the Cognitive Assessment System). Children assigned to the 'enriched' intervention showed more pronounced improvements in all motor coordination assessments (manual dexterity, ball skills, static/dynamic balance). The beneficial effect on ball skills was amplified by the level of spontaneous outdoor play and weight status. Among indices of executive function and attention, only that of inhibition showed a differential effect of intervention type. Moderated mediation showed that the better outcome of the enriched PE on ball skills mediated the better inhibition outcome, but only when the enrichment intervention was paralleled by a medium-to-high level of outdoor play. Results suggest that specifically tailored physical activity (PA) games provide a unique form of enrichment that impacts children's cognitive development through motor coordination improvement, particularly object control skills, which are linked to children's PA habits later in life. Outdoor play appears to offer the natural ground for the stimulation by designed PA games to take root in children's mind.

Keywords: executive function, variability, enrichment, physical activity, spontaneous play, body weight, children

INTRODUCTION

There is a widespread belief that being physically active is intrinsic to children's behavior. Nevertheless, tracking studies show that trends of inactivity have an early onset at pediatric age (Telama, 2009), with children not meeting the recommended physical activity (PA) guidelines already at preschool age (Tucker, 2008). Secular trends of PA decline are accompanied by a noteworthy decline in physical fitness (Tomkinson and Olds, 2007; Runhaar et al., 2010) and, as early as preschool age, also in motor fitness measured in terms of motor coordination and fundamental motor skills (Roth et al., 2010; Vandorpe et al., 2011). While apparently less relevant for health, motor skill competence is considered critical for meeting PA recommendations later in life (Barnett et al., 2008; Stodden et al., 2008), since persons who have not mastered fundamental motor skills in childhood are more likely to refrain from participating in organized sports and PA. Therefore, motor coordination is emerging as a relevant public health factor (Iivonen and Sääkslahti, 2014; Robinson et al., 2015).

The relationship between PA and motor skill competence has been proposed to be reciprocal. That is, children with higher levels of perceived and actual competence are more likely to engage in PAs, which, in turn, may lead to further skill development and increased perceived and actual competence (Robinson et al., 2015). On the other hand, children with motor difficulties are less inclined to participate in PA, thus limiting their opportunities for practice and further development (Skinner and Piek, 2001). This virtuous or vicious circle has an impact not only on motor development, but also on social, emotional, and cognitive development.

Indeed, longitudinal non-interventional evidence has shown that the development of fundamental motor skills at preschool age predicts social and emotional development (Bart et al., 2007; Piek et al., 2008a), cognitive efficiency and academic achievement (Piek et al., 2008b; Niederer et al., 2011; Roebers et al., 2014) in the subsequent phase of transition to school. This intriguing line of research (van der Fels et al., 2015 for a review) provides evidence on the linkage of motor coordination and skill competence to cognitive efficiency and academic achievement in children (Lopes et al., 2013; Haapala et al., 2014) and adolescents (Rigoli et al., 2012a,b; Marchetti et al., 2015). This interrelation between motor and cognitive developmental trajectories at behavioral level is consistent with neuroscientific evidence on the close parallelism and interaction of the neural substrates of motor coordination and cognitive executive function (Diamond, 2000; Koziol et al., 2011). However, to establish causality, needed is interventional research that assesses how motor and cognitive developmental outcomes are jointly influenced by PA. To this end, particular interest has been devoted to the effects of exercise on children's executive cognitive functions (Tomporowski et al., 2011) that are responsible for goal-oriented behaviors, cognitive flexibility and behavioral adaptability (Etnier and Chang, 2009).

In extensive reviews of interventions aiding executive functions, Diamond and Lee (2011) and Diamond and Ling (2015) stated that structured PA programs focusing on both motor skill development and cognitive engagement have a stronger impact on children's cognitive function than computerized programs without physical effort or physical (aerobic or resistance) training without a cognitive component. The authors also highlighted that to obtain improvements executive functions must not just be used, but continually challenged. Consistent to this, the link between coordinated actions and cognition and the brain substrate that acts as an interface between these domains emerges particularly evident in the study of complex and therefore challenging motor coordination tasks (Serrien et al., 2007).

Coordinative and cognitive complexity of movement tasks have been proposed as potential mechanisms through which PA impacts executive function efficiency beyond the more commonly studied role of exercise-related metabolic and physiological changes (Best, 2010). The idea of cognitive stimulation by coordinatively and cognitively engaging movement tasks has been further developed in terms of 'gross-motor cognitive training' (Pesce, 2012), designed PA and sports characterized by novelty and diversification (Moreau and Conway, 2014) and tailored to aid cognition and metacognition (Tomporowski et al., 2015a), sensorimotor training or physically active mindfulness practices that require 'thoughtful moving' (Ben-Soussan et al., 2015b; Diamond, 2015).

Interventional exercise and cognition studies performed with preadolescent children have a large variety of qualitative PA characteristics (Vazou et al., in press). In some studies, the effect of the coordinative and cognitive challenges of the movement tasks was not disentangled from that of the aerobic exercise intensity, either because the study focused on exercise quantity and dose-response relations (Davis et al., 2011; Hillman et al., 2014), or because coordinative/cognitive engagement was deliberately combined with aerobic exercise or with enhanced PA time to reap largest cognitive benefits (Chang et al., 2013; Reed et al., 2013; Crova et al., 2014; van der Niet et al., 2016). In other studies, the comparison was between aerobic exercise, which is usually performed with movement tasks requiring low coordinative and cognitive engagement (e.g., running), and traditional PE, which is usually centered on motor skill development and learning through lower-intensity exercise tasks (e.g., object control skills, Fisher et al., 2011).

The notion that adding coordinative/cognitive complexity to PA or adding PA to cognitive tasks is beneficial to cognitive performance is supported by few recent studies. They employed more than two intervention arms or held exercise intensity constant between cognitively more or less challenging PA conditions to disentangle spurious effects (Pesce et al., 2013b; Mavilidi et al., 2015; Schmidt et al., 2015). However, none of them has searched for mechanisms that can explain if there is a causal linkage between motor and cognitive outcomes of 'enriched' movement tasks. The present study was aimed at addressing this issue. Cognitive executive functions and motor skills are fundamentally interrelated at both the levels of behavior and brain substrate (Koziol et al., 2011) and this relationship especially emerges when complex motor coordination comes into play (Serrien et al., 2007). Thus, we hypothesized that an enriched PA intervention with coordinative and cognitive challenges embedded in playful activities would have positive outcomes on executive function linked to motor coordination outcomes.

A second aim of the present study was to evaluate whether eventual benefits of the enriched PA intervention are affected by lifestyle factors such as spontaneous outdoor play habits and weight status. The studies on enriched PA effects on children's cognition have been mainly performed in physical education (PE). However, PA experiences in a structured context as PE are only one side of the coin. Play that occurs in natural outdoor environments stimulates variation in children's movements and at the same time effectively acts as physical training (Fjortoft, 2004). An actual issue of debate is whether the dichotomy of spontaneous play vs. deliberate practice may be reconciled either proposing a common framework (Côté and Hancock, 2016), or identifying intermediate forms of play and practice that bridge the two extremes (MacNamara et al., 2015). We hypothesize that structuring PE in form of deliberate play and deliberate preparation, that emphasize enjoyment and participation in a variety of play activities (Côté et al., 2007) and focus on fundamental motor skills acquisition by means of developmentally appropriate tasks (Giblin et al., 2014), respectively, may promote a reciprocal influence and transfer effects between PE and spontaneous play. According to transfer taxonomy (Barnett and Ceci, 2002), while the physical and functional contexts are different (school vs. playground), the modality of learning and learned procedural skills are similar (hands-on discovery and problem-solving heuristic). Thus, it was hypothesized that spontaneous play might amplify the effectiveness of our PE program centered on deliberate play and preparation. This effect was hypothesized to occur not only in the motor skills domain, but also in the cognitive domain, since executive function may benefit from the enjoyable and physical nature of the activities (Pellegrini and Smith, 1998; Diamond and Ling, 2015).

As regards weight status, evidence shows both motor and cognitive disadvantages of overweight children as compared to their lean peers (Krombholz, 2013; Reinert et al., 2013). Longitudinal non-interventional research shows that in the absence of targeted intervention, the evolution of motor coordination over time is closely related to children's weight status, with an increasingly wider gap between overweight and lean children's coordination along development (D'Hondt et al., 2013). Thus, we evaluated whether the enriched PA environment may represent a means to support the development of children who are at risk of poor coordination and cognition.

MATERIALS AND METHODS

The research program, developed as a part of a Corporate Social Responsibility commitment for PA promotion for children, was approved by the Ethics Committee of the "Umberto I" hospital of the First Rome University and authorized by the provincial and regional PE School Offices, the Committees of the school involved and children's parents, who gave written informed consent. Bilateral agreements were signed between the regional School Office, the University and the corporate.

Participants

Nine hundred and twenty preschool and primary school children aged 5–10 years (480 boys and 440 girls) belonging to eight schools of the municipality of Alba (Italy) volunteered. In the ecological school setting schools and classes, but not individuals could be recruited. Thus, the present study design was group (cluster) randomized, with children in the same school and class sharing the same environment. The progress through the phases of enrollment, intervention allocation, follow-up, and data analysis is represented in **Figure 1**.

As local community stakeholders (e.g., provincial School Office, corporate) supported the research project, the rate of declining by school principals, personnel and parents was 0%. Within schools, 36 classes were stratified random sampled, with six classes for each school grade (last preschool year and primary school grades) to be randomly assigned to the enriched or traditional PE (three classes each). The final sample was composed of 460 children, aged 5–6 (163), 7–8 (144), and 9–10 years (153), with 232 (115 males and 117 females) belonging to the classes assigned to the enriched PE and 228 (115 males and 113 females) belonging to the traditional PE classes.

Reduction of participants from those assessed as eligible was due to school logistics (e.g., adapting testing time constraints; 17% random sampled and excluded) and to a data loss (e.g., children's absence at one or more baseline and/or post-intervention testing days; 39%). Since those children were balanced across intervention and control classes, no intent-to-treat analysis was performed. As concerns missing data, we evaluated (1) the number of cases missing per variable and (2) the number of variables missing per case. (1) No individual variables were missing data for more than half the cases and percentage missing cases were balanced among variables (M-ABC variables: 20% at baseline plus 3% at post-test; weight status and outdoor play at weekend: 21% each). (2) 15% of the cases were missing data for more than half of the variables. The likelihood of children being absent on testing days was probably not influenced by differences in basic demographic characteristics or socio-economic status, which, though not assessed because considered sensitive information, are presumed limited in a small-size town. Furthermore to limit data loss at post-test to children who changed school/residence or were absent from school for prolonged periods, two possible testing days were planned for each test 1 week apart.

Intervention Characteristics

All children assigned to the intervention or control group participated in PE for 1 h once a week. The teacher–child ratio was about 1:25 in the control classes, as prescribed by Italian legislation, but was altered in the experimental classes due to the additional presence of the external specialist teacher. The intervention lasted 6 months, from November to April, preceded and followed by testing in October and May, respectively. Neither teachers, nor children could be blinded after assignment to the intervention or control group. In fact, only the classroom generalist teachers of the intervention classes took actively part to teacher training together with PE specialist teachers to realize

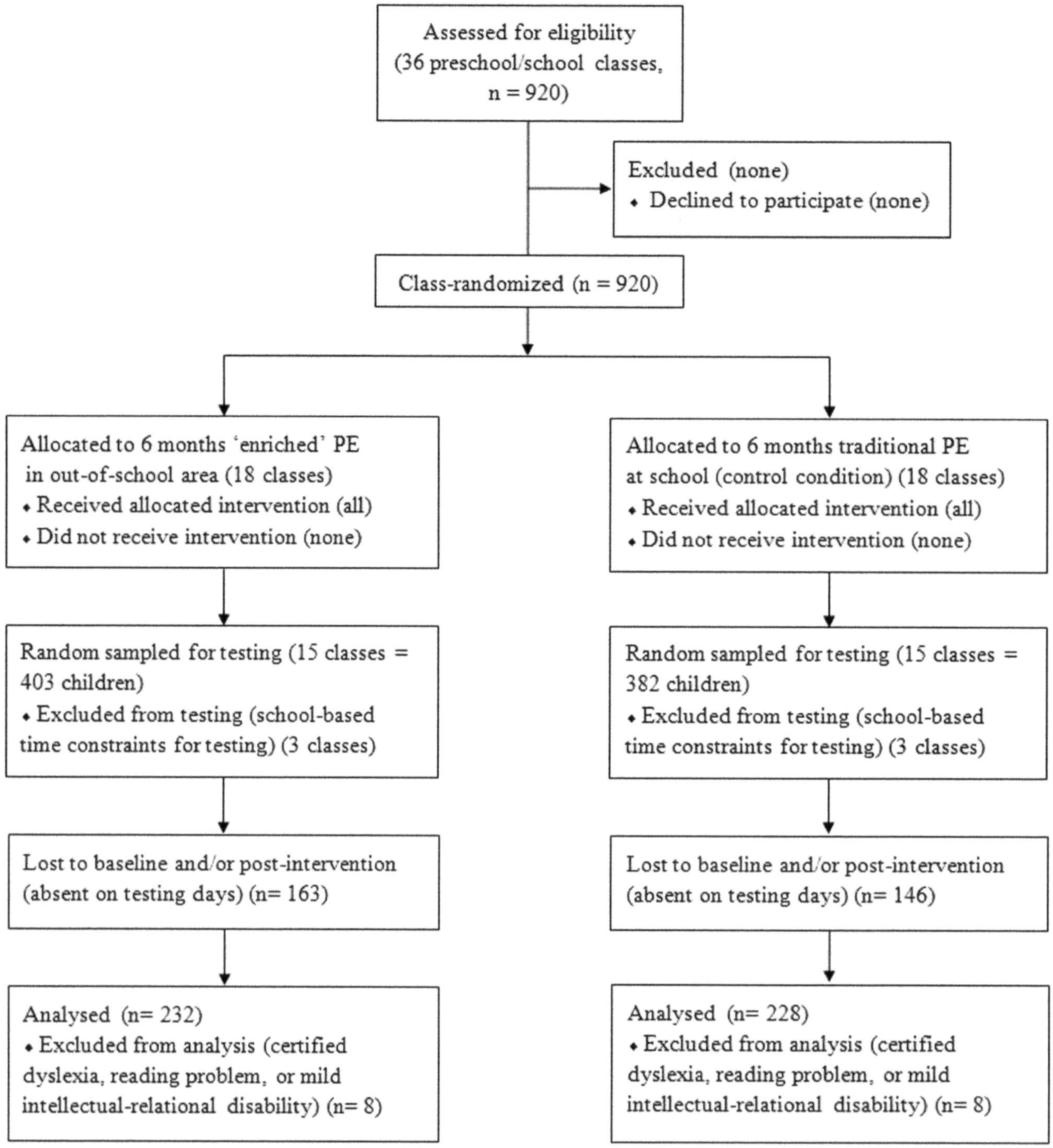

FIGURE 1 | Study flow diagram for the group-randomized trial.

the intervention program cooperatively during the curricular school time. Children were aware to be part of the intervention group, because the intervention was jointly led by an external PE specialist teacher and the classroom teacher in an out-of-school area rendered available by the municipality and equipped with sports facilities and managed by the corporate.

Both the generalists teaching in the control classes and those teaching in the intervention classes together with the PE specialists taught PE according to the age-related PE goals defined in the Italian curriculum for kindergarten and primary school, mainly focused on motor and social skills development (Ministry of Education, Universities and Research (MIUR), 2013). To ensure ecological validity of the control condition, the generalists teaching in the control classes did not receive any particular instruction by the researchers. Instead, those teaching in the experimental classes underwent teacher training together with the specialists once a month for 4 h to prepare the forthcoming teaching module, analyze teaching behaviors of the previous module and address interdisciplinary issues. To this aim, in all classes participating to the intervention, one lesson was videotaped for use as teacher training material.

There were four teaching modules, each lasting 6 weeks, with a total amount of 24 intervention hours. From a holistic view on education though movement based on the assumption that PE is critical to educating the whole child (National Association for Sport and Physical Education, 2011), all modules jointly pursued following improvement goals: physical fitness, motor coordination, cognition, life skills (Pesce et al., 2015). The modules were differentiated in that each of them addressed specific aspects of fitness, coordination, cognition and life skills through age-appropriate PA games. As an example in the first module, the focus was on the cardiovascular component of physical fitness, the perceptual-motor adaptation component of coordinative ability, the cognitive flexibility component of executive cognitive function and the goal setting component of life skills. Typical PA games that may jointly challenge these components are tag games. While any type of tag games involves moderate-to-vigorous running intensities that challenge the cardiovascular system and changes in running direction and speed according to changes in the environment that challenge perceptual-motor adaptation, the employed tag games were altered to enhance the demands on cognitive flexibility and goal setting. To stimulate cognitive flexibility, fixed roles for taggers and non-taggers where substituted by dual roles: in a 'rock, paper and scissors game'-like fashion, children (e.g., rock-children) had to tag some mates (e.g., scissors-children), while avoiding to be tagged by other mates (e.g., paper-children) (Tomporowski et al., 2015b).

To generate mental engagement and specifically stimulate executive function and motor coordination, PA games emphasized variability of practice (Pesce et al., in press) and contextual interference as applied in motor skill learning to deliberately keep children on the learning curve (Tomporowski et al., 2010). To ensure that the PA games were specifically tailored to challenge core executive functions, they were created based on instructional principles of executive tasks used in cognitive developmental research (Huizinga et al., 2006; Garon et al., 2008). According to the claim that interventions aiding executive functions work best when increasingly demanding and emotionally loaded (Diamond and Lee, 2011), we employed games characterized by age-appropriate variations in task complexity and emotionally engaging social interactions. Also, open-ended tasks were employed in which only the starting point, the rule(s) and the task goal were indicated and children were encouraged to find many possible solutions to perform it. This type of games challenges motor creativity that seems to rely on inhibitory efficiency (Scibinetti et al., 2011).

In sum, the PA games employed in this intervention had characteristics of deliberate play (Côté et al., 2007) and deliberate preparation (MacNamara et al., 2015). Cognitive teaching strategies and enjoyable problem solving conditions targeted to promote exploration and participation (typical for deliberate play) were developed and constrained in ways, exemplified above, that ensured the systematic stimulation of different facets of motor and life skill competence (typical for deliberate preparation). Cognitively challenging task demands were not only an issue of PE content, but also of delivery. In fact, they were generated employing a constraints-led approach to motor problem solving in which children alternately searched for 'the' optimal solution, or for a wider range of pertinent solutions, alternating repetition and change, stabilization and destabilization of movement patterns (Renshaw et al., 2010; Pesce et al., in press).

In the attempt to 'quantify' the qualitative characteristics of teaching and estimate their fit with the approach described above, stratified random sampling was performed to select four intervention and four control classes balanced as to preschool/school levels that were videotaped during a PE session for analysis of teaching behaviors. The qualitative intervention features were categorized as behavioral categories of teaching strategies (Rink, 2006) (**Table 1**) by two independent raters, experienced in video-analysis and categorization of teaching behaviors. The outcomes of the categorization, quantified as percentage (%) of events for time unit (20 s) during PE, were submitted to reliability computation. A satisfactory intra- and inter-observer agreement, indicated by a percentage of agreement [Agreements/(Agreements + Disagreements) × 100] ≥ 0.80, was reached.

TABLE 1 | Category definitions for teaching strategies (Rink, 2006).

Teaching strategies	
Interactive teaching	Teaching strategy most commonly used in PE. The instructional process is controlled by teacher who is responsible for the selection and progression of the content, for task communication (usually to an entire group), feedback and evaluation.
Peer teaching	Instructional strategy according to which some teacher's responsibilities are transferred to the student. The teacher usually maintains responsibility for content selection and progression, but uses one student to show or 'teach' a skill to another and to provide reciprocal feedback and evaluation.
Cognitive strategies	Group of teaching strategies designed to engage the learner cognitively in the content by producing solutions rather than reproducing any movement pattern they have been shown by teacher. This is an umbrella term for problem solving, guided and divergent discovery, and teaching through questions.
Cooperative learning	Teaching strategy according to which the goal to be achieved is meaningful and the task requires team work to be fulfilled, with process and product of the cooperative learning experience being evident to the learners.

Since the aim of the present study was to evaluate whether 'enriching' PE quality without enhancing its quantity would lead to joint coordinative and cognitive benefits, we needed to control for potential covariation of PA type and intensity. Thus, physical exercise intensity was indirectly monitored during 20 PE lessons of 10 experimental and 10 control, stratified for school grades, classes by recording heart rate (HR) with HR monitors (Polar S610i). According to the available amount of HR monitors, data were recorded on a total subsample of 127 children, similarly distributed among school grades and between intervention and control classes ($n = 67$ vs. 60, respectively). Mean HR and percentage of time spent in moderate or vigorous PA were calculated on the available subsample of HR data. The time spent in moderate or vigorous PA was operationalized as $140 \geq HR \geq 159$ and $HR \geq 160$ bpm, respectively (Wang et al., 2005).

Instruments and Procedures

Prior to the intervention, children's body height and weight and PA level were measured objectively and their outdoor play was estimated by means of a questionnaire completed by parents. Following familiarization to tests protocols, participants were assessed by trained experimenters at baseline and after the 6 months intervention period. Pre-post intervention assessments included a test of motor developmental level (Movement Assessment Battery for Children) administered to all children and tests of cognitive efficiency administered to two subsamples. Half of the children performed a test of working memory (Random Number Generation task, RNG) and half performed a test of attention (belonging to the Cognitive Assessment System, CAS). Cognitive testing was not preceded by PA lessons to avoid acute exercise effects. The same procedures and schedule were applied for pre- and post-intervention testing, maintaining the same order and time for test administration (always in the morning).

Weight Status and Spontaneous Outdoor Play Assessment

Children's body height and mass were measured for BMI (kg/m2) calculation. Age-referenced cut-off values of BMI were used to identify overweight and lean children (Cole et al., 2000). The percentage of children classified as overweight was similar in the sample of children initially random sampled for testing (25,6%) and in the final sample used for analysis (27,4%).

Children's spontaneous play habits in outdoors environments were estimated by means of the Children's Outdoor Play assessment questionnaire (Veitch et al., 2009). It consists of eight items for weekdays and eight for weekend. Parents were requested to report the number of days their child spent playing in locations as yard at home, friend's/neighbor's yard, own street/court/footpath, park/playground in out-of-school hours on weekdays and weekend days during a typical week. Weekday responses were based on a five-point scale ranging from never/rarely to 5 days per week, and weekend day responses were on a six-point scale ranging from never/rarely to every Saturday and Sunday. Parents were asked to count only the days where their child spent at least 10 min in a specific location, considering 10 min an appropriate minimum time span. The validation of the Italian version is described in the Preliminary analyses section.

Recently, it has been recommended to use parental-reports of PA only as context-specific measures, since they seem not useful as a proxy for children's general PA levels (Verbestel et al., 2015). Since for all children of all schools enrolled, a playground was rendered accessible on Sundays by the corporate for playing outdoor with their parents, to properly draw conclusions limitedly to the context-specific play behavior, only scores of outdoor play at weekend were used for main analyses.

Motor Coordination Assessment

To assess children's motor coordination performance, the Italian version of the Movement Assessment Battery for Children (M-ABC) developed by Henderson and Sudgen (1992) was used. The more recent version of the (M-ABC-2, Schulz et al., 2011) could not be used because at the pre-test time (October 2013) the M-ABC-2 still was not available in the Italian version. This test evaluates movement competence providing objective quantitative data on both gross motor and fine motor coordination of children aged from 4 to 12 years with eight tasks differentiated in four age-related difficulty levels. The M-ABC has been proved to be a valid and reliable research and diagnostic tool that covers the entire domain of motor ability and is used to identify motor problems and DCD (Croce et al., 2001). The tasks are grouped under three subheadings: manual dexterity (three tasks), ball skills (aiming and catching, two tasks), and static and dynamic balance (one and two tasks, respectively).

Manual dexterity

The first task is 'posting coins' (5–6 year-old), 'placing pegs' (7–8 year-old), or 'shifting pegs by rows' (9–10 year-old). The child must drop coins through the slot in a bank box, or place 12 plastic pegs in all holes on a board, or move pegs from a given row to another, respectively, one at a time as quickly as possible. The second task is 'threading beads' (5–6 year-old), 'threading lace' (7–8 year-old), or 'threading nuts on bolt' (9–10 year-old). The child must thread beads through a lace, or thread a lace back and forth through the holes in a lacing board, or screw nuts down a bolt, respectively, one at a time as quickly as possible. In both the first and second tasks, the examiner measures the seconds taken to complete each task. The third task is 'bicycle trail' (5–6 year-old), or 'flower trail' (7–10 year-old). The child must draw with the preferred hand one continuous line following the bicycle or flower trail on a record form without crossing its boundaries. The examiner records the number of errors, i.e., the number of times the drawn lines moves outside a boundary.

Ball (aiming and catching) skills

The first task is 'catching bean bag' (5–6 year-old), 'one-hand bounce and catch' (7–8 year-old), or 'two-hand catch' (9–10 year-old). The child must catch a bean bag tossed by the experimenter, or bounce a tennis ball on the floor and catch it with the same hand, or throw a tennis ball at the wall form behind a marked line and catch it at the return with both hands, respectively. The second task is 'rolling ball into goal' (5–6 year-old), or 'throwing bean bag into box' (7–10 year-old). The child must roll a tennis ball along the floor between two stands to score a 'goal,' or throw a bean bag into a target box on the floor form behind a marked line. In both types of tasks, the examiner records the number of correctly executed trials (successful catches and throws) out of 10 attempts.

Static and dynamic balance

The task evaluating static balance is 'one-leg balance' (5–6 year-old), 'stork balance' (7–8 year-old), or 'one-board balance' (9–10 year-old). The child must stand on one leg, with the arms held at the sides, or stand on a foot, place the sole of the other foot against the side of the supporting knee and the hands on the hips, or balance on one foot on a balance board, respectively. The examiner records the number of seconds up to 20 the child maintains balance. The second task is 'jumping over cord' (5–6 year-old), 'jumping in squares' (7–8 year-old), or 'hopping in squares' (9–10 year-old). The child must jump over the cord from a stationary position, or make five continuous jumps forward from a starting square to further five squares, or make five continuous hops forward from square to square on one foot, respectively. The examiner records if the child performs a successful jump ('jumping over cord') or the number of correct consecutive jumps/hops completed over five without performance errors ('jumping or hopping in squares'). The third task is 'walking heels raised' (5–6 year-old), 'heel-to-toe walking' (7–8 year-old), or 'ball balance' (9–10 year-old). The child must walk along a line with heels raised without stepping off the line, or placing the heel of one foot against the toe of the other, or walk around the outside of two stands and return to the starting point while steadying a board with a ball in the middle of it, respectively. The examiner records the number of steps performed by the child without leaving space between toe and heel or stepping off the line.

Data coding and scoring

For each of the three subheadings of manual dexterity, ball (aiming and catching) skills, and static and dynamic balance, the data were transformed into scores of impairment of motor function according to age-related normative data (Henderson and Sudgen, 1992). Each impairment score indicates the extent to which a child falls below the level of his/her age peers, while it does not differentiate between children who perform above this level. Test–retest reliability data were not collected, as high reliability results are available for children across all age groups considered in this study (Henderson and Sudgen, 1992; Croce et al., 2001).

Assessment of Executive Cognitive Function and Attention

Inhibition and working memory updating

To assess two core executive functions (inhibition and working memory updating), children individually performed the RNG task (Towse and Neil, 1998), lasting about 10 min, which has been proven feasible also with children 5 year-old and over (Towse and Mclachlan, 1999). They were told that the RNG is a game involving numbers and were instructed to verbally generate a random sequence of numbers between 1 and 10 to each beat of a 70-beat sequence with an inter-beat interval of 1.5 s. Prior to data collection by tape recording, participants performed a familiarization trial of 70 numbers and could ask questions concerning the test. Both the omission of a number generation in correspondence of one tone and the production of numbers lower than 1 (0) or higher than 10 (11, 12 etc.) were considered errors and discarded. If errors exceeded a predefined maximum threshold of five, the entire block was repeated.

The randomness of the sequence of numbers was measured by means of 18 different indices described by Towse and Neil (1998). Among those, five indices were selected as they reflect two components of executive function (Miyake et al., 2000): the ability to inhibit mental routines (turning point index [TPI], adjacency score [Adj], and runs score [Runs]) and the ability to update and manipulate information held in working memory (redundancy score [Red], and mean repetition gap [MeanRG]). A third index of working memory (coupon score [Coupon]), updating was excluded because its association to the other two indices (Red and MeanRG) was not confirmed in children (Crova et al., 2014).

The computation and meaning of these indices is extensively described in Audiffren et al. (2009). In short, the TPI is a ratio between the real frequency of turning points between ascending and descending series of numbers (e.g., the response change between the digits "2" and "5" in a hypothetical sequence "9, 7, 2, 5, 6, 8") generated by the participant and their theoretical frequency in random responses. The Adj measures the relative frequency of pairs of adjacent ascending or descending numbers (e.g., 7–8 or 4–3) as compared to the total number of response pairs produced by the participant. The Runs score is an index of variability of the number of digits in successive ascending or descending runs. The Red index reflects the unbalance of response alternative frequencies in a sequence that derives from a more frequent usage of given numbers than expected based on the theoretical frequency of each digit in random responses. The MeanRG is the mean number of responses given until each digit reoccurs calculated for all digits throughout the whole sequence (e.g., in the sequence "2, 8, 4, 6, 2, 9, 7, 8," the digits "2" and "8" reoccur with a mean gap equal to 4).

Turning point index, Adj and Runs were merged into an average index of inhibition, while Red and MeanRG into an average index of memory updating. High levels of TPI, but low values of Adj and Runs reflect a good ability to suppress the habitual tendency to count forward or backward, as well as high levels of MeanRG, but low levels of Red reflect a good ability to update information on already generated or still not generated digits held in working memory. Thus before averaging, all indices were z standardized and Adj, Runs, and Red were reversed (Crova et al., 2014).

Attention

To assess attention, the tasks belonging to a subscale of the CAS were used (Naglieri and Das, 1997, Italian version 2005). The CAS consists of 12 subtests that assess four aspects of cognition: Planning, Attention, Simultaneous and Successive processes (PASS theory) (Das et al., 1994). For the present study, because of school time constraints, participants only performed the Attention tasks, which is relevant for learning and sensitive to cognitively challenging PA games (Pesce et al., 2013a). We did not collect test-retest reliability data, since acceptable to good reliability data are available for children of the age considered in this study (Naglieri and Das, 1997). The Attention scale is composed of three subtests that require the child to use focal attention to detect target stimuli and avoid distractions. The raw score for each subtest is converted to an age-based standard score and summed to obtain a total scale value.

The first subtest, Expressive Attention, is a Stroop-like test composed of three items that measures attention selectivity and interference control under time pressure. The first and the second items are without interference condition, while the third is with interference. There are two age-specific sets of items. For example, in the version for children 8 years and older, the non-interference conditions are reading color words (Blue, Yellow, Green, and Red) all written in dark ink and naming the colors of a series of rectangles (printed in blue, yellow, green, and red). In the interference condition, the words Blue, Yellow, Green, and Red are printed in a different color ink than the colors the words name and the child is instructed to name the color ink the word is printed in, rather than to read the word. Only this last item is used as the measure of attention.

The second subtest, Number Detection, measures selectiveness and capacity to resist distraction under time pressure. It is comprised of pages of numbers where the child must underline the correct numbers among a large quantity of distracters in different formats. For example, the child must find a particular stimulus (the numbers 1, 2, and 3 printed in an open font) on a page containing many distracters (the same numbers printed in a different font style). The raw score is the ratio of the accuracy (total number correct minus the number of false detections) and the time to completion summed across the items.

The third subtest, Receptive Attention, is a two-page subtest that measures the ability to focus and then shift attention between different stimulus dimensions under time pressure. On the first page, children must identify and underline pairs of target letters that are physically identical (e.g., TT but not Tt), whereas on the second, pairs of letters that have the same name (e.g., Aa not Ba) are targets to be underlined. For all subtests, the raw score is the ratio of the accuracy (total number correct in the first subtest and total number correct minus the number of false detections in the second and third subtests) and time to completion summed across items/pages.

PRELIMINARY ANALYSES

Prior to main analyses, (1) the Italian version of the children's Outdoor Play assessment questionnaire was validated; (2) the quantitative and qualitative characteristics of PE lessons, as well as the enjoyment perceived by children in the intervention and control classes were contrasted to control for potential covariates of the qualitative characteristics of PE lessons. Specifically, it was controlled for potentially higher exercise intensity due to the expertise of PE specialist teachers and higher enjoyment due to the presence of the specialist teacher and the novelty of the out-of-school area and facilities that might explain eventual differential motor and cognitive outcomes in the intervention and control classes.

Validation of the Outdoor Play Assessment Questionnaire

The children's outdoor play assessment questionnaire (Veitch et al., 2009) was translated and back-translated to ensure adequacy of translation. Prior to the administration to the parents of the children who participated in the present study, the questionnaire was administered to a further sample of 71 parents twice, one week apart to verify its test–retest reliability, internal consistency, and criterion-based validity. Test–retest reliability was acceptable (Cronbach's $\alpha = 0.79$) only after removing the eighth item (play in an unspecified location). Internal consistency, as assessed by ICC computation, was at least moderate (ICC = 0.58–0.79) for all items. The criterion-based validation was performed on the base of the information delivered by a 7-day diary, where parents were asked to indicate on each of the nominated 7 days whether their child had played in specified outdoor locations (the same as in the likert-scale questionnaire) in after-school hours for at least 10 min. Kappa statistic (κ) and percent agreement between responses were used to assess validity. Kappa values for each specified outdoor location were moderate (range: 0.408–0.574).

Quantitative and Qualitative Analysis of Physical Education Lessons

The type of teaching strategies and the intensity of physical exercise during the recorded PE lessons are reported on **Table 2** for comparison between intervention and control classes. The main difference was that in generalist-led traditional PE lessons, interactive teaching was prioritized, whereas in the lessons led by specialists in cooperation with generalist classroom teachers, cognitive teaching strategies as problem solving and teaching through questions prevailed, representing more than half of the total teaching time. In general, in the intervention classes, there

TABLE 2 | Teaching styles (mean % of events for 20-s time unit), physical exercise intensity (mean heart rate and percentage of time spent in moderate or vigorous physical activity) and perceived enjoyment during representative PE lesson types: traditional, generalist-led and enriched, specialist-led.

	Traditional generalist-led (Control)	Enriched specialist-led (Intervention)
Teaching strategies	**% Events**	**% Events**
Interactive	87.7	25.3
Peer teaching	5.7	11.3
Cognitive	5.2	54.2
Cooperative	1.4	9.2
Exercise intensity		
Mean HR (bpm ± SD)	132.2 (±23.5)	131.9 (±17.4)
PE time spent in moderate PA (% ± SD)	22.5 (±12.1)	25.9 (±12.4)
PE time spent in vigorous PA (% ± SD)	16.7 (±15.5)	22.2 (±17.4)

was a more differentiated use of teaching strategies, while in the control classes the use of teaching strategies different from the interactive was negligible.

As regards exercise intensity, pairwise comparisons (t-tests) for independent samples did not yield significant differences between the intervention and the control group in mean HR, $t(125) = 0.18$, $p = 0.855$ and % time spent in moderate PA, $t(125) = 1.56$, $p = 0.120$, or in vigorous PA, $t(125) = 1.88$, $p = 0.062$ (**Table 2**).

RESULTS

Analysis of Intervention Effects

The statistical analyses that follow were performed with IBM SPSS statistics 23. We (i) tested for baseline differences in all outcome and moderator variables that might influence the intervention outcomes; (ii) analyzed the effects of the traditional vs. enriched PE intervention. Descriptive statistics are reported in **Table 3**.

TABLE 3 | Baseline and post-intervention level (mean ± SD) of motor coordination (for the total sample, $n = 460$), executive function and attention variables (two halves of the sample, $n = 230$, respectively) of 5–10 year-old children assigned to traditional or enriched PE lessons, led by the generalist teacher (G-led) or PE specialist teacher (S-led) in cooperation with the generalist.

		Traditional PE (G-led)	Enriched PE (S-led)
Manual dexterity			
(impairment score)	*pre*	5.9 ± 3.3	6.0 ± 3.5
(improvement ↓)	*post*	5.0 ± 3.6***	3.7 ± 3.1
Ball (aiming/catching) skills			
(impairment score)	*pre*	3.2 ± 2.9	3.0 ± 2.7
(improvement ↓)	*post*	1.7 ± 2.2***	1.0 ± 2.8
Static/dynamic balance			
(impairment score)	*pre*	4.2 ± 3.9**	5.3 ± 4.0
(improvement ↓)	*post*	2.6 ± 3.2***	1.7 ± 2.7
Inhibition			
(std. total score)	*pre*	−0.08 ± 2.5	−0.34 ± 2.3
(improvement ↑)	*post*	−0.60 ± 2.3*	1.11 ± 1.6
Working memory updating			
(std. total score)	*pre*	−0.07 ± 1.8	0.29 ± 1.8
(improvement ↑)	*post*	−0.06 ± 0.7	0.10 ± 0.6
Attention			
(scale sum score)	*pre*	25.1 ± 7.6	23.6 ± 7.6
(improvement ↑)	*post*	33.0 ± 8.0	30.0 ± 8.3
Expressive attention			
(subscale score)	*pre*	8.9 ± 3.2	8.3 ± 3.3
(improvement ↑)	*post*	11.3 ± 3.7	10.2 ± 3.5
Number detection			
(subscale score)	*pre*	7.7 ± 3.1	7.4 ± 3.0
(improvement ↑)	*post*	10.4 ± 2.9	10.2 ± 2.8
Receptive attention			
(subscale score)	*pre*	8.6 ± 3.2	7.9 ± 3.2
(improvement ↑)	*post*	11.2 ± 3.3	10.6 ± 3.5

*$p < 0.05$; **$p < 0.01$; ***$p < 0.001$.

(i) Pre-intervention impairment scores for manual dexterity, ball (aiming and catching) skills and static/dynamic balance (measured in the whole sample, $n = 460$), as well as average indices of inhibition and working memory updating and sum score for attention (measured in either of two sample halves) were submitted to multivariate analysis of variance (MANOVA) and subsequent ANOVAs. PE intervention (traditional vs. enriched) was the between-subjects factor. The MANOVA performed on motor coordination data showed a significant difference between groups at pre-test [Wilks $\lambda = 0.97$, $F(5,454) = 2.68$, $p = 0.021$, $\eta_p^2 = 0.03$]. ANOVAs revealed that this difference was significant only for static/dynamic balance [$F(1,458) = 9.05$, $p = 0.003$, $\eta_p^2 = 0.02$], with lower impairment score for the traditional PE group. The MANOVA performed on executive function indices (inhibition, working memory updating) and on individual attention subscales and sum score did not yield any significant difference between traditional and enriched PE types ($p_s > 0.40$). Also, neither tested moderators showed significant baseline differences between intervention and control classes (BMI: 17.2 ± 2.7 vs. 16.9 ± 2.6; outdoor play at weekend: 19.2 ± 6.3 vs. 19.6 ± 6.4, respectively).

(ii) After checking for potential baseline differences, we run the analysis of intervention effects. A general linear model was applied to post-intervention measures of the same motor and cognitive development variables, adding their counterpart baseline measures and age as covariates, with PE intervention (traditional vs. enriched) as main factor and gender, weight status (lean vs. overweight) and spontaneous outdoor play (low vs. high) as potential moderators of intervention effects. The nested model that is usually adopted for cluster-randomized data was deemed unsuitable for the present data set. Schools could not be nested within PE intervention groups because both intervention and control classes were stratified-random sampled in each participating school. Nesting children within classes would render the study underpowered because the average number of children tested in each of the 30 classes was relatively low (15) and above all unbalanced among classes.

Children assigned to the 'enriched' intervention showed more pronounced improvements (i.e., larger reduction of the impairment score) in all motor coordination assessments (**Table 3**): manual dexterity [$F(1,442) = 13.28$, $p < 0.001$, $\eta_p^2 = 0.03$], ball skills [$F(1,442) = 23.57$, $p < 0.001$, $\eta_p^2 = 0.05$], static/dynamic balance [$F(1,442) = 15.41$, $p < 0.001$, $\eta_p^2 = 0.03$]. Moreover, as regards ball skills, there were significant interactions of intervention type with weight status [$F(1,442) = 11.65$, $p = 0.001$, $\eta_p^2 = 0.03$] and outdoor play at weekend [$F(1,442) = 8.07$, $p = 0.005$, $\eta_p^2 = 0.02$]. *Post hoc* analysis of the interactions (t-tests, adjusted p for six comparisons 0.008) showed that the effect of intervention type on ball skills was independently moderated by weight status and outdoor play in an amplifying manner. Pre-post differences were more pronounced and the advantage of the enriched PE group in ball skills at post-test was significant when children were overweight (**Figure 2**, $p = 0.006$) and, regardless of weight status, when they were involved in outdoor play at a medium-to-high level during weekend days (**Figure 3**, $p < 0.001$). Among executive function and attention variables, only inhibition showed a differential effect of intervention type [$F(1,220) = 5.55$, $p = 0.019$, $\eta_p^2 = 0.03$], with higher post-intervention values for the enriched intervention than the traditional PE type. No main effect for gender emerged and gender didn't either moderate any of the differential effects of enriched and traditional PE. Analogous intervention effects on the same motor coordination and inhibition variables were obtained applying the change score method that is using pre-post delta scores.

Analysis of Mediating Mechanisms

The statistical analyses that follow were performed with PROCESS macro for SPSS. Cognitive performance (i.e., inhibition) was differentially affected by PE intervention type. Thus, it was entered into multiple mediation analysis (Hayes, 2013) to evaluate whether and to what extent the motor

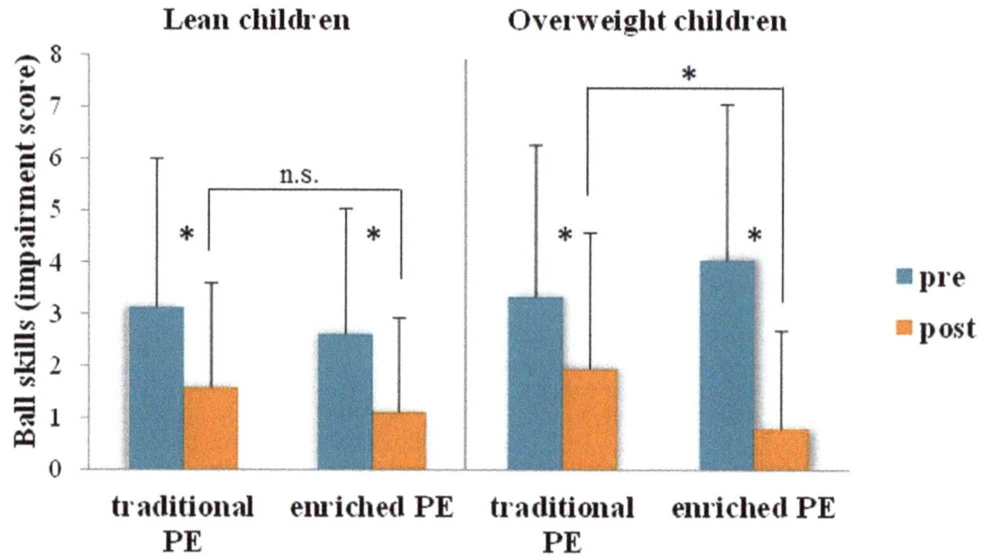

FIGURE 2 | Ball skills (impairment score – the lower, the better, ±SD) before and after traditional or enriched PE types as a function of children's weight status. *$p < 0.008$; n.s., non-significant.

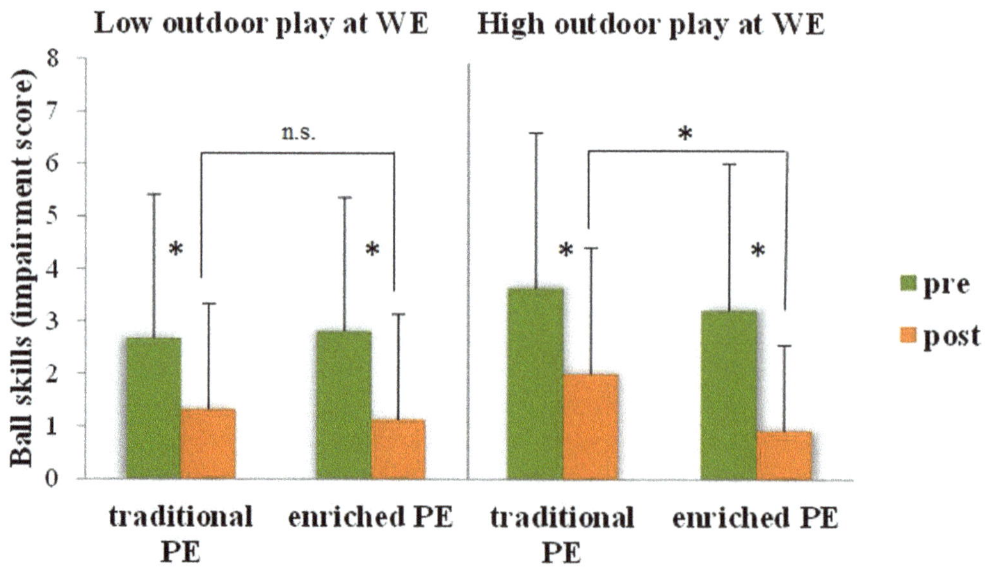

FIGURE 3 | Ball skills (impairment score – the lower, the better, ±SD) before and after traditional or enriched PE types as a function of children's spontaneous outdoor play habits at weekend. *$p < 0.008$; n.s., non-significant.

coordination outcomes of PE enrichment may be responsible for cognitive performance outcomes. In the case of ball skills, which were affected by the enriched PE intervention type in a moderated manner, a moderated mediation model was also applied.

Multiple Mediation

To test for mediation, regression analyses were performed on post-intervention data to assess the effects of:

(1) the independent variable (X: PE intervention type) on the dependent variable (Y: inhibition);
(2) the independent variable (X: PE intervention type) on each mediator (M: manual dexterity, ball skills, static/dynamic balance);
(3) the independent variable (X) and the potential mediators (Ms) on the dependent variable (Y).

The potential mediators were entered simultaneously to include the covariances among them and the independent variable in the regression equation. The parallel multiple mediator model allowed estimating if introducing all potential motor developmental mediators reduced the direct effect of the PE intervention on the efficiency of the inhibitory function (i.e., total indirect effect of X on Y through Ms).

Then, bootstrapping was applied to empirically estimate the sampling distribution of the indirect effect and generate a bootstrap confidence interval (95% CI) based on 10,000 bootstrap samples for bias corrected bootstrap CIs. This CI was used as a form of hypothesis test to estimate if the size of the indirect effect of each individual mediator, as well as the difference between the indirect effects of the mediators were different from zero (Hayes, 2013).

Significant results of the multiple mediation analysis are reported in **Figure 4**. The post-intervention improvement in ball skills, but not that in manual dexterity or static/dynamic balance, was found to mediate the beneficial effect of the enriched PE intervention on inhibitory function. This is indicated by the bootstrapping output: Only in the case of the ball skills variable, the 95% CI of bootstrap estimates of the indirect effect did not include the zero value (lower bound 0.02, upper bound 0.36). The bootstrap CI for the pairwise comparisons between the indirect effects of the three tested mediators yielded estimates of effect size differences statistically different from zero for the contrast Manual dexterity minus Ball skills (lower bound −0.43, upper bound −0.03), confirming the larger effect of Ball skills. The same mediation model was applied to pre-intervention data and to pre–post delta scores (absolute values and delta magnitude expressed in standard deviation units), but did not yield any significant result.

Moderated Mediation

Ball skills were the only significant movement-related mediator of cognitive outcomes of the intervention. In addition, the effect of the intervention on ball skills was moderated by weight status and outdoor play. Thus, a moderated mediation with a conditional indirect effect was also tested (Hayes, 2013). Specifically, it was estimated whether the mediating role of ball skills on the relationship between intervention type and inhibition outcomes was moderated by the fact that children were lean/overweight, or more/less used to playing outdoor at weekend.

Spontaneous outdoor play, but not weight status, resulted to be a significant moderator of the mediated path (**Figure 5**). The post-intervention outcome in ball skills found for the enriched PE intervention mediated the inhibition outcome. However, this mediation occurred only when the enriched intervention was

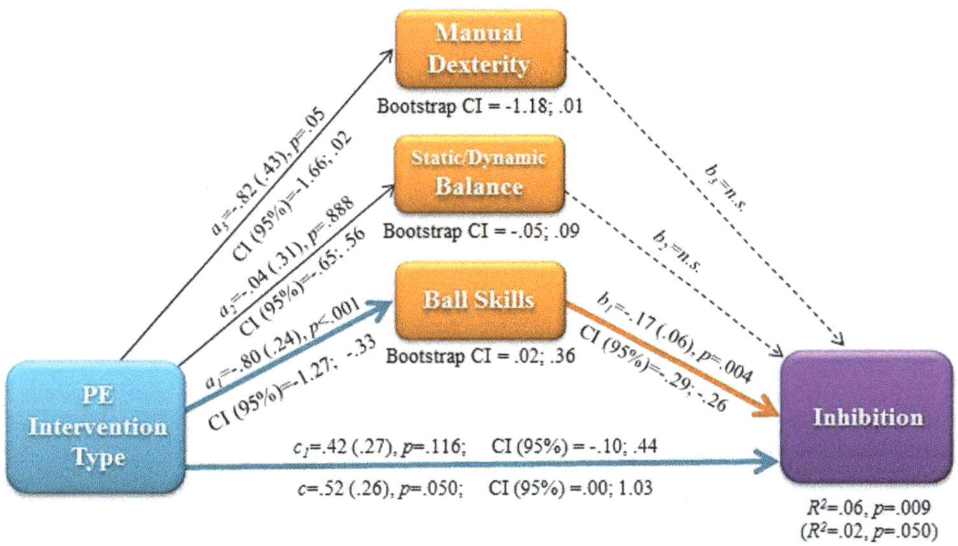

FIGURE 4 | Multiple mediation model: effects of PE intervention type on post-intervention inhibitory efficiency mediated by post-intervention level of ball (aiming and catching) skills. a, b, c: regression coefficients with (SE), p and CI (95%) values. c: total effect; $a_1 * b_1$, $a_2 * b_2$, $a_3 * b_3$: indirect effects; c1: direct effect after accounting for mediators. R^2 values with/without mediators (in parentheses) and bootstrap CI (95%) for indirect effects are also reported.

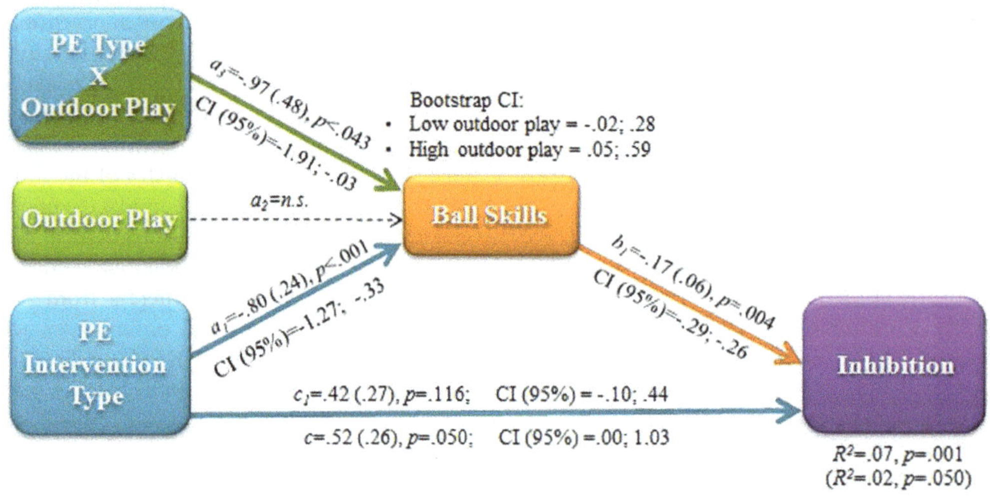

FIGURE 5 | Statistical model of moderated mediation: effects of PE intervention type on post-intervention inhibitory efficiency mediated by post-intervention level of ball (aiming and catching) skills. a, b, c: regression coefficients with (SE), p and CI (95%) values. c: total effect; c_1: direct effect after accounting for the conditional indirect effect of ball skills moderated by outdoor play. R^2 values with/without mediators (in parentheses) and bootstrap CI (95%) for indirect effects at low vs. high levels of the moderator are also reported.

paralleled by a relatively high level of outdoor play. This is indicated by the bootstrap 95% CI of the indirect effect not including the zero value only for high outdoor play and by the outcome of the test of equality of the conditional indirect effect in the two groups (lower bound −02, upper bound 0.54).

DISCUSSION

The present study aimed to further our understanding of the complex relationship between motor and cognitive development. It addressed the question of whether PA experiences centered on variability of practice (Pesce et al., in press) that join coordinative and cognitive challenges in a playful way may act as environmental enrichment that benefits children's higher-level cognition, the executive, and whether cognitive benefits are mediated by the motor coordination outcomes of the enrichment. It was also examined whether the lifestyle factors of outdoor play habits and weight status moderate the effects of the enriched PA intervention. In sum, the findings showed that enrichment in PE elicited small-size, but wide-ranging improvements of gross motor and fine motor skills and selective improvement of a core executive function—inhibitory processing (**Table 3**). The improvement of object control (aiming and catching) skills was also sensitive to lifestyle factors. The beneficial effect of participating to the enriched PE intervention compared to traditional PE was more pronounced for children, who also were habitual outdoor players (**Figure 3**). Spontaneous outdoor play habits appear to offer the natural ground for the stimulation by deliberate play to take root in children's mind, since the joint effect of outdoor and deliberate play in PE on object control skills resulted to mediate the effect on inhibitory efficiency (**Figure 5**).

Enriched Physical Activity as a Unique Means to Promote Motor and Cognitive Development

In several countries (as Italy in the present study), legislation for preschool and primary school levels is not supportive of sufficient amounts of PE that remains far below the minimum threshold to increase children's fitness level (Strong et al., 2005). That is why the target of school PE in such countries should be creating prerequisites for practice of and lifelong adherence to PA in out-of-school settings and for development and learning in motor and cognitive domains. The renewed attention to the link between motor and cognitive development has been paralleled by a shift, in exercise and cognition research, from the quantitative view on dose-response relations to a qualitative view on coordinative and cognitive movement task demands that may impact cognition (Best, 2010; Pesce, 2012). This has prompted researchers to create PA intervention programs in PE that stimulate children's executive functions and provide evidence on the beneficial 'side effects' of thoughtful PA experiences on the developing brain (Diamond, 2015; Diamond and Ling, 2015; Tomporowski et al., 2015a; Vazou et al., in press). Our study supports the suitability of age-appropriate, thoughtful PA games that exploit principles of variability of practice and deliberate play and preparation to promote motor and cognitive development jointly (Tomporowski et al., 2015b; Pesce et al., in press).

The broad range of intervention effects on different facets of motor coordination skills (manual dexterity, ball skills, balance) supports the view that variability of practice may act as a form of enrichment that broadly affects motor coordination (Pesce et al., 2013b). This outcome may also depend on the fact that our games joined characteristics of deliberate play, emphasizing exploration, playfulness and fun (Côté et al.,

2007), and features of deliberate preparation, supporting and facilitating the acquisition of fundamental motor and non-motor skills needed for proactive participation and learning success (MacNamara et al., 2015). In other words, the play experiences were well- and not ill-defined, as variability of practice and problem solving were constrained in ways that directed exploration to match the different objectives planned for the sequential teaching modules. Intriguing commonalities with the outcomes of other large-scale studies employing a well-defined intervention program regard the improvement of motor skills (Piek et al., 2013) and the reduction of hyperactive and inattentive behaviors that rely on inhibitory efficiency (Piek et al., 2015). Piek et al.'s (2010) "Animal fun" program, centered on deliberate play, incorporated variability of practice and task complexity and was structured in sequential modules specifically targeting all gross-motor and fine-motor skills in a playful social interaction context. Playfulness that is reported to be a positive determinant of children's motor skills (Iivonen and Sääkslahti, 2014) is naturally linked to enjoyment, which is considered relevant also for reaping cognitive benefits from PA (Diamond and Ling, 2015; Pesce and Ben-Soussan, 2016), as demonstrated with children in an ecological learning context (Vazou and Smiley-Oyen, 2014).

We found the enriched PE program beneficial for the inhibitory component of cognitive executive function, but not for working memory updating or attention, suggesting differential associations between specific aspects of motor competence and specific executive processes. Previous research had shown that children's ability to overcome interference or suppress mental routines may benefit from PE experiences that have inherent cognitive and social interaction demands (Crova et al., 2014; van der Niet et al., 2016). In those studies, however, PE had been enhanced in both quantity and quality. The present study isolated the effects of the qualitative component without altering the low dose of PE prescribed by the country legislation. One of the few studies tailored to disentangle spurious effects of aerobic exercise and cognitive challenges by movement found different effects compared to the present study and particularly no effects on inhibitory processes (Schmidt et al., 2015). This inconsistency, probably due to the team sport-based characteristics of Schmidt et al.'s intervention, suggests that the type of cognitive outcomes may depend on the type of coordinative and cognitive demands of the PA tasks. From a developmental perspective, this inconsistency may be related to the fact that different executive functions 'come online' at different time points along child development, with inhibition being the first to be fully developed and therefore more prone to changes in the early stages of cognitive development (Best and Miller, 2010).

The absence of differential intervention effects on attention as measured with the attention scale of the CAS is in line with the outcomes of some studies in which the quantity of PA had been manipulated (Davis et al., 2011; Fisher et al., 2011), but not other studies. Pesce et al. (2013a), for example, found that cognitively challenging PE benefited children's attention and that the benefits on different aspects of attention depended on children's motor developmental status. Future research is needed to ascertain the role of individual characteristics as moderators of the exercise-attention relation. The absence of enhanced PA effects on children's attention assessed with the CAS is also at odds with neuroscientific evidence of the beneficial effects of PA and fitness on task performances requiring executive attention (Pesce and Ben-Soussan, 2016). The lack of convergent findings calls for further research conducted with a broader set of executive and non-executive attention measures to distinguish between spurious and truly executive attention outcomes. The absence of effects on children's ability to manipulate information in working memory suggests that the central executive component of working memory may not be sensitive to cognitive stimulation by movement in preadolescent children (Crova et al., 2014). Rather, it seems related to the fitness outcomes of larger amounts of PA (Marchetti et al., 2015), as consistently found for hippocampal-dependent associative memory (Khan and Hillman, 2014).

Cognitive Outcomes of Enriched Physical Activity as a 'Side Effect' of Motor Competence

The novel and most interesting result is the unique causal relation linking the intervention outcomes on object control skills and inhibitory function (**Figure 4**). To our knowledge, no study has evaluated whether cognitive benefits obtained with cognitively enriched PA games are merely paralleled, or mediated by positive outcomes in motor coordination. We found evidence of mediation, supporting the hypothesis that beyond the direct cognitive stimulation via physical movement, there may be an indirect causal pathway that links the exposure to enriched PA to motor coordination outcomes that turn into more efficient executive function.

Although the enriched PE caused significantly larger gains in motor coordination and inhibition efficiency than the traditional PE, the extent to which inhibition improved was not explained by gains in motor coordination, as indicated by the absence of a mediation path between delta scores of motor skills and inhibitory function. In the ecological school context, several factors may have influenced children's baseline inhibitory performance and its changes over time, impeding to see a significant relationship between intervention-related gains in inhibitory efficiency and motor skills. However, a mediating mechanism was found to link motor (object control) skill and inhibitory performance after the intervention, but not before it. Thus, whatever the size of the motor skill and executive function gains, the enriched PE seems to "align" specific aspects of cognitive performance to specific motor skill competence.

The linkage between motor skills and inhibitory control has been also evidenced by cross-sectional studies (Haapala et al., 2014). The present finding adds a causal direction to this linkage and highlights the specificity in the type of motor skills involved. This specificity is also supported by cross-sectional evidence, suggesting some association of object control skills with executive inhibitory function, but not with attention (van der Fels et al., 2015). However, the interpretation of this relationship is tentative as inhibition is multifaceted in nature; different aspects of response inhibition (inhibition of prepotent responses, of mental routines, and interference control) might differently relate to motor control (Livesey et al., 2006). For instance, Castelli et al. (2006) found an association between the interference control aspect of inhibitory function and object control skills as assessed with sport-like ball skills. Our mediational results suggest the existence of shared mechanisms underpinning such relationship. Although consistent evidence of association between object control skills and working memory is reported (van der Fels et al., 2015), our enriched PA intervention failed to impact the central executive of working memory as assessed by the RNG task.

Based on our findings, we contend that the development of object control skill competence is not only a primary underlying mechanism that promotes long-lasting engagement in PA (Barnett et al., 2009; Robinson et al., 2015 for a review), but also a mechanism that partially explains why enriched PA benefits executive function. We hypothesize that executive inhibitory control is involved in and therefore challenged by the intentional control and environmental interaction needed to perform aiming and catching tasks. Promoting the development of ball skills has been shown beneficial to executive processes as planning, that relies on inhibitory efficiency (Westendorp et al., 2014), thus confirming the relevance of visuomotor adaptation experiences for recruiting prefrontal regions that support inhibition (Gentili et al., 2013). Trends in cognitive neurosciences that view cognition as subserving action and being grounded in sensorimotor interaction (Engel et al., 2013; Ben-Soussan et al., 2015a) are inspiring novel research on motor learning in ecological PA and sport settings as a means for cognitive training (Moreau and Conway, 2014) also for children in the school setting (Venditti et al., 2015). Our deliberate play and preparation approach centered on variability of practice (Pesce et al., in press) belongs to this emerging line of research.

It is also to consider that there were a large amount of teacher training and a consequently different use of teaching strategies by teachers of intervention and control classes (**Table 2**). Thus, the cognitive challenges that we assume responsible for the intervention outcomes were the resultant of interrelated content (coordinatively and cognitively engaging PA games) and delivery (cognitive teaching strategies as problem solving, guided and divergent discovery). Our PA games emphasized the roundtrip between repetition and change, between stability and flexibility, providing problem-solving opportunities and boundaries of exploration, manipulating key constraints on learners according to a constraints-led approach to motor learning that fits with the principles of deliberate play and preparation (Renshaw et al., 2010; Pesce et al., in press). In sum, a key feature of our multicomponent, holistic approach to motor and cognitive development promotion centered on deliberate play is the inextricability of cognitive task complexity and teaching strategies to generate complexity in a playful way.

The Converging Role of Environmental Enrichment and Lifestyle Factors

A further novelty of the study is the finding that educational intervention and lifestyle factors interactively contribute to determine object control competence and that this interaction also explains the mediated effect of PA enrichment on inhibitory efficiency. An intriguing study showed that a structured PA intervention at school was more beneficial for enhancing cognition than free play activities (Fredericks et al., 2006). However, the authors examined the effects of spontaneous play and structured PA practice independently from each other in two intervention arms. Instead, we tailored the intervention to promote converging effects of spontaneous (outdoor) and deliberate (intervention) play practice and found that spontaneous play at outdoor locations seems to amplify the benefits of the enriched PE intervention on ball skills (**Figure 3**). In fact, we designed PA games centered on deliberate play, which is activity done for its own sake, and deliberate practice, which is child-appropriate wide-ranging promotion of fundamental skills development. Both are characterized by flexibility and enjoyment and targeted to bridge spontaneous and deliberate practice (Côté et al., 2007; MacNamara et al., 2015). In this way, we attempted to generate continuity between spontaneous play and deliberate play activities in the enriched PE context. We did so based on the assumption that if strongly structured PA tasks were employed in the intervention, we would reduce both the feasibility of such experiences to be transferred to a spontaneous play context and the cognitive engagement needed to deal with open–ended, discovery learning tasks. The outcome of the moderated mediation model (**Figure 5**) suggests that the value added by spontaneous play extends from the motor to the cognitive domain.

The fact that the intervention effect on object control skills was largest for overweight children highlights how an enriched PA environment may provide equal development opportunities to children who are at risk of developing motor and cognitive disadvantage (D'Hondt et al., 2013; Krombholz, 2013; Reinert et al., 2013). In contrast to what expected based on previous evidence (Crova et al., 2014), the observed benefit of PA enrichment for overweight children emerged in the motor, but not in the cognitive domain and did not moderate the mediational path linking the PE intervention to its cognitive outcome through motor competence outcome. However, given the predictive value of object control competence for PA levels later in life (Robinson et al., 2015), playing enriched PA games may represent a means to promote positive developmental trajectories of health also for overweight children. This is in line with the increasing attention, at academic, as well as at policy level, for the value of play as a health factor (Alexander et al., 2014), contributing to the prevention of Exercise Deficit Disorder ("Play now or pay later," Faigenbaum and Myer, 2012, p. 196).

Limitations

The study has limitations to be addressed. Neither children, nor teachers could be blinded. Therefore, the intervention outcomes might be biased by a Hawthorne effect that is the tendency to a higher engagement if being involved in an experimental intervention. Particularly, a higher engagement by children must be taken into account because the deliberate play intervention emphasized variability of practice and was performed in an out-of-school area equipped with sports facilities. The felt novelty and diversity probably caused a higher enjoyment and motivation (Sylvester et al., 2014) that may have contributed to the motor and cognitive benefits of the enriched PE intervention. However, it is difficult and beyond the scope of this holistic approach to children's motor and cognitive development promotion to disentangle enjoyment effects from those of variability used as a means of embodied cognitive training (Pesce et al., in press), since bodily motion, emotion and cognition are strictly intertwined (Diamond and Ling, 2015; Pesce and Ben-Soussan, 2016).

A further limitation is that the amount of explained variance both in the analysis of intervention effects and in the mediation model was small and the direct effect of PA intervention on inhibition remained significant after accounting for the meaningful indirect effect by the ball skills gain. This suggests that enriched PA has only a small, though significant positive impact on cognitive functioning and multiple factors beyond motor coordination may mediate this benefit. However, the high reach and adoption and the broad range of outcomes counterbalances the low effect size of significant outcomes. Finally, the parental report of outdoor play is not an optimal indicator of children's physically active play activity (Verbestel et al., 2015). It is possible that the lack of measures that encompass a wide range of children's movements has made it difficult to show the convergent relation between motor skills and PA on cognitive development (Laukkanen et al., 2014). Finally, the large amount of missing data and the restrictive strategy used may have limited the statistical power of the study. However, given the large sample size and the absence of drop-out from participation, the reason of missing at testing days is primarily attributable to the need to find an adequate trade-off setpoint between research and school organizational needs.

Outlook and Future Directions

The unique characteristic of the present interventional study was its multicomponent nature. It incorporated various elements from different types of training programs into PA games. Those elements, such as cognitive and social stimulation embedded into enjoyable activities, have been proven suitable to aid executive function in children (Diamond and Lee, 2011). This enriched PA interventions implemented in natural school environment showed how cognitively challenging games during school PE lessons may support executive functions without decreasing PA intensity. The present intervention is inspired by the idea to employ deliberate play and preparation activities that can bridge spontaneous play and deliberate practice along the continuum of PA modalities (Côté et al., 2007; MacNamara et al., 2015). Moreover, it follows the call to ground synergistic commitments for PA promotion for children on the provision of their right to play (Leone et al., 2015) that has been repeatedly acknowledged by authoritative institutions (United Nations, 2013). Considering the emerging public health position on the role of "Playing for health" (Alexander et al., 2014, p. 155), future directions of applied research at the intersection of prevention science, developmental psychology, and cognitive neuroscience (Bryck and Fisher, 2012) should add quality PA into the equation.

AUTHOR CONTRIBUTIONS

CP: Main role in the conception and design of the work, data analysis and interpretation, drafting of the work, final approval of the version to be published and agreement to be accountable for all aspects of the work. IM: Data acquisition and analysis with relevant role in data acquisition coordination, drafting of the work, final approval of the version to be published and agreement to be accountable for all aspects of the work. RM: conception and design of the work with relevant role in project coordination, data interpretation, critical revision of the work for important intellectual content, final approval of the version to be published and agreement to be accountable for all aspects of the work. SV: Data interpretation, drafting and critical revision of the work for important intellectual content with specific contribution as regards the mechanisms of cognitive stimulation by designed PA, final approval of the version to be published and agreement to be accountable for all aspects of the work. AS: Data interpretation, drafting of the work with specific contribution as regards motor developmental contents, final approval of the version to be published and agreement to be accountable for all aspects of the work. PDT: data interpretation, critical revision of the work for important intellectual content with specific contribution as regards the chronic exercise-cognition relationship in children, final approval of the version to be published and agreement to be accountable for all aspects of the work.

FUNDING

This research was granted by the Ferrero Group as a part of its Corporate Social Responsibility initiatives to promote active lifestyles among young people.

ACKNOWLEDGMENTS

We thank the children, their school teachers and principals, the PE specialist teachers and their coordinator Davide Tibaldi, the provincial and regional PE coordinators Anna Motta and Marcello Strizzi, the representative of the local office of the Olympic Committee Loretta Fabiani for their valuable contribution to the planning, implementation and organization. Also, we wish to thank the managers or coordinators of this project within the Kinder + Sport Corporate Social Responsibility initiatives Alessandro Nervegna, Carlo Bresciano, Gianpiero Vietto, Mario Ciravegna, Alessandro Aimi, Alejandro Huertado for trusting us and our translational approach to whole child development promotion through PA. Moreover, we wish to thank the two Reviewers for the deep attention devoted to our work and the very detailed and useful comments, which helped significantly enhance the quality of our paper.

REFERENCES

Alexander, S. A., Frohlich, K. L., and Fusco, C. (2014). Playing for health? Revisiting health promotion to examine the emerging public health position on children's play. *Health Promot. Int.* 29, 155–164. doi: 10.1093/heapro/das042

Audiffren, M., Tomporowski, P. D., and Zagrodnik, J. (2009). Acute aerobic exercise and information processing: modulation of executive control in a Random Number Generation task. *Acta Psychol. (Amst)* 132, 85–95. doi: 10.1016/j.actpsy.2009.06.008

Barnett, S. M., and Ceci, S. J. (2002). When and where do we apply what we learn? A taxonomy for far transfer. *Psychol. Bull.* 128, 612–637.

Barnett, L. M., Van Beurden, E., Morgan, P. J., Brooks, L. O., and Beard, J. R. (2008). Does childhood motor skill proficiency predict adolescent fitness? *Med. Sci. Sports Exerc.* 40, 2137–2144. doi: 10.1249/MSS.0b013e31818160d3

Barnett, L. M., van Beurden, E., Morgan, P. J., Brooks, L. O., and Beard, J. R. (2009). Childhood motor skill proficiency as a predictor of adolescent physical activity. *J. Adolesc. Health* 2, 252–259. doi: 10.1016/j.jadohealth.2008.07.004

Bart, O., Hajami, D., and Bar-Haim, Y. (2007). Predicting school adjustment from motor abilities in kindergarten. *Infant Child Dev.* 16, 597–615. doi: 10.1002/icd.514

Ben-Soussan, T. D., Berkovich-Ohana, A., Piervincenzi, C., Glicksohn, J., and Carducci, F. (2015a). Embodied cognitive flexibility and neuroplasticity following Quadrato Motor Training. *Front. Psychol.* 6:1021. doi: 10.3389/fpsyg.2015.01021

Ben-Soussan, T. D., Glicksohn, J., and Berkovich-Ohana, A. (2015b). From cerebellar activation and connectivity to cognition: a review of the quadrato motor training. *Biomed Res. Int.* 2015, 954901. doi: 10.1155/2015/954901

Best, J., and Miller, P. H. (2010). A developmental perspective on executive function. *Child Dev.* 81, 1641–1660. doi: 10.1111/j.1467-8624.2010.01499.x

Best, J. R. (2010). Effects of physical activity on children's executive function: contributions of experimental research on aerobic exercise. *Dev. Rev.* 30, 331–351. doi: 10.1016/j.dr.2010.08.001

Bryck, R. L., and Fisher, P. A. (2012). Training the brain: practical applications of neural plasticity from the intersection of cognitive neuroscience, developmental psychology, and prevention science. *Am. Psychol.* 67, 87–100. doi: 10.1037/a0024657

Castelli, D., Erwin, H., Buck, S., and Hillman, C. (2006). Relationship between motor skill competency and cognitive processes in children. *Res. Q. Exerc. Sport* 77, A51–A52.

Chang, Y.-K., Tsai, Y.-J., Chen, T.-T., and Hung, T.-M. (2013). The impacts of coordinative exercise on executive function in kindergarten children: an ERP study. *Exp. Brain Res.* 225, 187–196. doi: 10.1007/s00221-012-3360-9

Cole, T. J., Bellizzi, M. C., Flegal, K. M., and Dietz, W. H. (2000). Establishing a standard definition for child overweight and obesity worldwide: international survey. *Br. Med. J.* 120, 1240–1243. doi: 10.1136/bmj.320.7244.1240

Côté, J., Baker, J., and Abernethy, B. (2007). "Play and practice in the development of sport expertise," in *Handbook of Sport Psychology*, eds G. Tenenbaum and R. C. Eklund (Hoboken, NJ: John Wiley & Sons), 184–202.

Côté, J., and Hancock, D. J. (2016). Evidence-based policies for youth sport programmes. *Int. J. Sport Policy Polit.* 8, 51–65. doi: 10.1080/19406940.2014.919338

Croce, R. V., Horvat, M., and McCarthy, E. (2001). Reliability and concurrent validity of the movement assessment battery for children. *Percept. Mot. Skills* 93, 275–280. doi: 10.2466/pms.2001.93.1.275

Crova, C., Struzzolino, I., Marchetti, R., Masci, I., Vannozzi, G., Forte, R., et al. (2014). Benefits of cognitively challenging physical activity in overweight children. *J. Sports Sci.* 32, 201–211. doi: 10.1080/02640414.2013.828849

Das, J. P., Naglieri, J. A., and Kirby, J. R. (1994). *Assessment of Cognitive Processes: The PASS Theory of Intelligence.* Needham Heights, MA: Allyn and Bacon.

Davis, C. L., Tomporowski, P. D., McDowell, J. E., Austin, B. P., Miller, P. H., Yanasak, N. E., et al. (2011). Exercise improves executive function and achievement and alters brain activation in overweight children: a randomized, controlled trial. *Health Psychol.* 30, 91–98. doi: 10.1037/a00 21766

D'Hondt, E., Deforche, B., Gentier, I., De Bourdeaudhuij, I., Vaeyens, R., Philippaerts, R., et al. (2013). A longitudinal analysis of gross motor coordination in overweight and obese children versus normal-weight peers. *Int. J. Obes.* 37, 61–67. doi: 10.1038/ijo.2012.55

Diamond, A. (2000). Close interrelation of motor development and cognitive development and of the cerebellum and prefrontal cortex. *Child Dev.* 71, 44–56. doi: 10.1111/1467-8624.00117

Diamond, A. (2015). Effects of physical exercise on executive functions: going beyond simply moving to moving with thought. *Ann. Sports Med. Res.* 2, 1011.

Diamond, A., and Lee, K. (2011). Interventions shown to aid executive function development in children 4 to 12 years old. *Science* 333, 954–969. doi: 10.1126/science.1204529

Diamond, A., and Ling, D. (2015). Conclusions about interventions, programs, and approaches for improving executive functions that appear justified and those that, despite much hype, do not. *Dev. Cogn. Neurosci.* doi: 10.1016/j.dcn.2015.11.005 [Epub ahead of print].

Engel, A. K., Maye, A., Kurthen, M., and König, P. (2013). Where's the action? The pragmatic turn in cognitive science. *Trends Cogn. Sci.* 17, 202–209. doi: 10.1016/j.tics.2013.03.006

Etnier, J. L., and Chang, Y. K. (2009). The effect of physical activity on executive function: a brief commentary on definitions, measurement issues, and the current state of the literature. *J. Sport Exerc. Psychol.* 31, 469–483.

Faigenbaum, A. D., and Myer, G. D. (2012). Exercise deficit disorder in youth: play now or pay later. *Curr. Sports Med. Rep.* 11, 196–200. doi: 10.1249/JSR.0b013e31825da961

Fisher, A., Boyle, J. M. E., Paton, J. Y., Tomporowski, P., Watson, C., McColl, J. H., et al. (2011). Effects of a physical education intervention on cognitive function in young children: randomized controlled pilot study. *BMC Pediatr.* 11:97. doi: 10.1186/1471-2431-11-97

Fjortoft, I. (2004). Landscape as playscape: the effects of natural environments on children's play and motor development. *Child Youth Environ.* 14, 21–44.

Fredericks, C. R., Kokot, J. K., and Krog, S. (2006). Using a developmental movement programme to enhance academic skills in grade 1 learners. *S. Afr. J. Res. Sport Phys. Educ. Recreat.* 28, 29–42.

Garon, N., Bryson, S., and Smith, I. M. (2008). Executive function in preschoolers: a review using an integrative framework. *Psychol. Bull.* 134, 31–60. doi: 10.1037/0033-2909.134.1.31

Gentili, R. J., Shewokis, P. A., Ayaz, H., and Contreras-Vidal, J. L. (2013). Functional near-infrared spectroscopy-based correlates of prefrontal cortical dynamics during a cognitive-motor executive adaptation task. *Front. Hum. Neurosci.* 7:277. doi: 10.3389/fnhum.2013.00277

Giblin, S., Collins, D., MacNamara, Á, and Kiely, J. (2014). "Deliberate preparation" as an evidence-based focus for primary physical education. *Quest* 66, 385–395. doi: 10.1080/00336297.2014.944716

Haapala, E. A., Poikkeus, A. M., Tompuri, T., Kukkonen-Harjula, K., Leppänen, P. H. T., Lindi, V., et al. (2014). Associations of motor and cardiovascular performance with academic skills in children. *Med. Sci. Sport Exerc.* 46, 1016–1024. doi: 10.1249/MSS.0000000000000186

Hayes, A. F. (2013). *Introduction to Mediation, Moderation, and Conditional Process Analysis. A Regression-Based Approach.* New York, NY: Guilford Press.

Henderson, S. E., and Sudgen, D. A. (1992). *Movement Assessment Battery for Children.* London: The Psychological Corporation. *Movement ABC—Batteria per la Valutazione Motoria del Bambino, 2000,* Italian Version, eds E. U. Mercuri and E. L. Mercuri (Firenze: Giunti O.S).

Hillman, C. H., Pontifex, M. B., Castelli, D. M., Khan, N. A., Raine, N. B., Scudder, M. R., et al. (2014). Effects of the FITKids randomized controlled trial on executive control and brain function. *Pediatrics* 134, 1062–1071. doi: 10.1542/peds.2013-3219

Huizinga, M., Dolan, C. V., and van der Molen, M. W. (2006). Age-related change in executive function: developmental trends and a latent variable analysis. *Neuropsychologia* 44, 2017–2036. doi: 10.1016/j.neuropsychologia.2006.01.010

Iivonen, S., and Sääkslahti, A. K. (2014). Preschool children's fundamental motor skills: a review of significant determinants. *Early Child Dev. Care* 184, 1107–1126. doi: 10.1080/03004430.2013.837897

Khan, N. A., and Hillman, C. H. (2014). The relation of childhood physical activity and aerobic fitness to brain function and cognition: a review. *Pediatr. Exerc. Sci.* 26, 138–146. doi: 10.1123/pes.2013-0125

Koziol, L. F., Budding, D. E., and Chidekel, D. (2011). From movement to thought: executive function, embodied cognition, and the cerebellum. *Cerebellum* 11, 505–525. doi: 10.1007/s12311-011-0321-y

Krombholz, H. (2013). Motor and cognitive performance of overweight preschool children. *Percept. Mot. Skills* 116, 40–57. doi: 10.2466/22.25.PMS.116.1.40-57

Laukkanen, A., Pesola, A., Havu, M., Sääkslahti, A., and Finni, T. (2014). Relationship between habitual physical activity and gross motor skills is multifaceted in 5- to 8-years-old children. *Scand. J. Med. Sci. Sports* 24, 102–110. doi: 10.1111/sms.12116

Leone, L., Ling, T., Baldassarre, L., Barnett, L., Capranica, L., and Pesce, C. (2015). Corporate responsibility for childhood physical activity promotion in the UK. *Health Promot. Int.* doi: 10.1093/heapro/dav051 [Epub ahead of print].

Livesey, D., Keen, J., Rouse, J., and White, F. (2006). The relationship between measures of executive function, motor performance and externalising behaviour in 5- and 6-year-old children. *Hum. Mov. Sci.* 25, 50–64. doi: 10.1016/j.humov.2005.10.008

Lopes, L., Santos, R., Pereira, B., and Lopes, V. (2013). Associations between gross motor coordination and academic achievement in elementary school children. *Hum. Mov. Sci.* 32, 9–20. doi: 10.1016/j.humov.2012.05.005

MacNamara, Á, Collins, D., and Giblin, S. (2015). Just let them play? Deliberate preparation as the most appropriate foundation for lifelong physical activity. *Front. Psychol.* 6:1548. doi: 10.3389/fpsyg.2015.01548

Marchetti, R., Forte, R., Borzacchini, M., Vazou, S., Tomporowski, P. D., and Pesce, C. (2015). Physical and motor fitness, sport skills and executive function in adolescents: a moderated prediction model. *Psychology* 6, 1915–1929. doi: 10.4236/psych.2015.614189

Mavilidi, M. F., Okely, A. D., Chandler, P., Cliff, D. P., and Paas, F. (2015). Effects of integrated physical exercises and gestures on preschool children's foreign language vocabulary learning. *Educ. Psychol. Rev.* 27, 413–426. doi: 10.1007/s10648-015-9337-z

Ministry of Education, Universities and Research (MIUR) (2013). Indicazioni nazionali per il curricolo della scuola dell'infanzia e del primo ciclo d'istruzione [National indications for the K-8 school curriculum]. *Gaz. Ufficiale Repubblica Ital.* 154, 30, 1–77.

Miyake, A., Friedman, N. P., Emerson, M. J., Witzki, A. H., Howerter, A., and Wager, T. D. (2000). The unity and diversity of executive functions and their contributions to complex 'frontal lobe' tasks: a latent variable analysis. *Cogn. Psychol.* 41, 49–100. doi: 10.1006/cogp.1999.0734

Moreau, D., and Conway, A. R. A. (2014). The case for an ecological approach to cognitive training. *Trends Cogn. Sci.* 18, 334–336. doi: 10.1016/j.tics.2014.03.009

Naglieri, J. A., and Das, J. P. (1997). *Cognitive Assessment System.* Itaca, IL: Riverside Publishing. *CAS Das-Naglieri Cognitive Assessment System – Una Misura dell'intelligenza Basata sul Modello dei Processi Cognitivi PASS, 2005,* Italian Version, ed. S. Taddei (Firenze: Giunti O.S).

National Association for Sport and Physical Education (2011). *Physical Education is Critical to Educating the Whole Child [Position Statement].* Reston, VA: Author.

Niederer, I., Kriemler, S., Gut, J., Hartmann, T., Schindler, C., Barral, J., et al. (2011). Relationship of aerobic fitness and motor skills with memory and attention in preschoolers (Ballabeina): a cross-sectional and longitudinal study. *BMC Pediatr.* 11:34. doi: 10.1186/1471-2431-11-34

Pellegrini, A. D., and Smith, P. K. (1998). Physical activity play: the nature and function of a neglected aspect of play. *Child Dev.* 69, 577–598. doi: 10.1111/j.1467-8624.1998.tb06226.x

Pesce, C. (2012). Shifting the focus from quantitative to qualitative exercise characteristics in exercise and cognition research. *J. Sport Exerc. Psychol.* 34, 766–786.

Pesce, C., and Ben-Soussan, T. D. (2016). "'Cogito ergo sum' or 'ambulo ergo sum'? New perspectives in developmental exercise and cognition research," in *Exercise-Cognition Interaction: Neuroscience Perspectives*, ed. T. McMorris (London: Elsevier), 251–282.

Pesce, C., Croce, R., Ben-Soussan, T. D., Vazou, S., McCullick, B., Tomporowski, P., et al. (in press). Variability of practice as an interface between motor and cognitive development promotion. *Int. J. Sport Exerc. Psychol.*

Pesce, C., Crova, C., Marchetti, M., Struzzolino, I., Masci, I., Vannozzi, G., et al. (2013a). Searching for cognitively optimal challenge point in physical activity for children with typical and atypical motor development. *Ment. Health Phys. Act.* 6, 172–180. doi: 10.1016/j.mhpa.2013.07.001

Pesce, C., Faigenbaum, A., Crova, C., Marchetti, R., and Bellucci, M. (2013b). Benefits of multi-sports physical education in the elementary school context. *Health Educ. J.* 72, 326–336. doi: 10.1177/0017896912444176

Pesce, C., Marchetti, R., Motta, A., and Bellucci, M. (2015). *Joy of Moving. MoviMenti con ImmaginAzione. Giocare con la Variabilità per Promuovere lo Sviluppo Motorio, Cognitivo e del Cittadino. [Joy of Moving. MindMovers & ImmaginAction – Playing with Variability to Promote Motor, Cognitive and Citizenship Development].* Perugia: Calzetti-Mariucci.

Piek, J. P., Bradbury, G. S., Elsley, S. C., and Tate, L. (2008a). Motor coordination and social-emotional behaviour in preschool-aged children. *Int. J. Disabil. Dev. Educ.* 55, 143–151. doi: 10.1080/10349120802033592

Piek, J. P., Dawson, L., Smith, L. M., and Gasson, N. (2008b). The role of early fine and gross motor development on later motor and cognitive ability. *Hum. Mov. Sci.* 27, 668–681. doi: 10.1016/j.humov.2007.11.002

Piek, J. P., Kane, R., Rigoli, D., McLaren, S., Roberts, C. M., Rooney, R., et al. (2015). Does the Animal Fun program improve social-emotional and behavioural outcomes in children aged 4-6 years? *Hum. Mov. Sci.* 43, 155–163. doi: 10.1016/j.humov.2015.08.004

Piek, J. P., McLaren, S., Kane, R., Jensen, L., Dender, A., Roberts, C., et al. (2013). Does the Animal Fun program improve motor performance in children aged 4-6 years? *Hum. Mov. Sci.* 32, 1086–1096. doi: 10.1016/j.humov.2012.08.004

Piek, J. P., Straker, L. M., Jensen, L., Dender, A., Barrett, N. C., McLaren, S., et al. (2010). Rationale, design and methods for a randomized and controlled trial to evaluate "Animal Fun" – a program designed to enhance physical and mental health in young children. *BMC Pediatr.* 10:78. doi: 10.1186/1471-2431-10-78

Reed, J. A., Maslow, A. L., Long, S., and Hughey, M. (2013). Examining the impact of 45 minutes of daily physical education on cognitive ability, fitness performance, and body composition of African American youth. *J. Phys. Act. Health* 10, 185–197.

Reinert, K. R. S., Po'e, E. K., and Barkin, S. L. (2013). The relationship between executive function and obesity in children and adolescents: a systematic literature review. *J. Obes.* 2013, 820956. doi: 10.1155/2013/820956

Renshaw, I., Chow, J. Y., Davids, K., and Hammond, J. (2010). A constraints-led perspective to understanding skill acquisition and game play: a basis for integration of motor learning theory and physical education praxis? *Phys. Educ. Sport Pedagogy* 15, 117–137. doi: 10.1080/17408980902791586

Rigoli, D., Piek, J. P., Kane, R., and Oosterlaan, J. (2012a). An examination of the relationship between motor coordination and executive functions in adolescents. *Dev. Med. Child Neurol.* 54, 1025–1031. doi: 10.1111/j.1469-8749.2012.04403

Rigoli, D., Piek, J. P., Kane, R., and Oosterlaan, J. (2012b). Motor coordination, working memory, and academic achievement in a normative adolescent sample: testing a mediation model. *Arch. Clin. Neuropsychol.* 27, 766–780. doi: 10.1093/arclin/acs061

Rink, J. E. (2006). *Teaching Physical Education for Learning*, 5th Edn. Boston, MA: McGraw Hill.

Robinson, L. E., Stodden, D. F., Barnett, L. M., Lopes, V. P., Logan, S. W., Rodrigues, L. P., et al. (2015). Motor competence and its effect on positive developmental trajectories of health. *Sports Med.* 45, 1273–1284. doi: 10.1007/s40279-015-0351-6

Roebers, C. M., Röthlisberger, M., Neuenschwander, R., Cimeli, P., Michel, E., and Jäger, K. (2014). The relation between cognitive and motor performance and their relevance for children's transition to school: a latent variable approach. *Hum. Mov. Sci.* 33, 284–297. doi: 10.1016/j.humov.2013.08.011

Roth, K., Ruf, K., Obinger, M., Mauer, S., Ahnert, J., Schneider, W., et al. (2010). Is there a secular decline in motor skills in preschool children? *Scand. J. Med. Sci. Sports* 20, 670–678. doi: 10.1111/j.1600-0838.2009.00982.x

Runhaar, J., Collard, D. C., Singh, A., Kemper, H. C., van Mechelen, W., and Chinapaw, M. (2010). Motor fitness in Dutch youth: differences over a 26-year period (1980-2006). *J. Sci. Med. Sport* 13, 323–328. doi: 10.1016/j.jsams.2009.04.006

Schmidt, M., Jäger, K., Egger, F., Roebers, C. M., and Conzelmann, A. (2015). Cognitively engaging chronic physical activity, but not aerobic exercise, affects executive functions in primary school children: a group-randomized controlled trial. *J. Sport Exerc. Psychol.* 37, 575–591. doi: 10.1123/jsep.2015-0069

Schulz, J., Henderson, S. E., Sugden, D. A., and Barnett, A. L. (2011). Structural validity of the movement ABC-2 test: factor structure comparisons across three age groups. *Res. Dev. Disabil.* 32, 1361–1369. doi: 10.1016/j.ridd.2011.01.032

Scibinetti, P., Tocci, N., and Pesce, C. (2011). Motor creativity and creative thinking in children: the diverging role of inhibition. *Creat. Res. J.* 23, 262–272. doi: 10.1080/10400419.2011.595993

Serrien, D. J., Ivry, R. B., and Swinnen, S. P. (2007). The missing link between action and cognition. *Prog. Neurobiol.* 82, 95–107. doi: 10.1016/j.pneurobio.2007.02.003

Skinner, R. A., and Piek, J. P. (2001). Psychosocial implications of poor motor coordination in children and adolescents. *Hum. Mov. Sci.* 20, 73–94. doi: 10.1016/S0167-9457(01)00029-X

Stodden, D., Goodway, J., Langendorfer, S., Robertson, M., Rudisill, M., and Garcia, C. (2008). A developmental perspective on the role of motor skill competence in physical activity: an emergent relationship. *Quest* 60, 290–306. doi: 10.1080/00336297.2008.10483582

Strong, W. B., Malina, R. B., Blimkie, C. J. R., Daniels, S. R., Dishma, R. K., Gutin, B., et al. (2005). Evidence based physical activity for school-age youth. *J. Pediatr.* 146, 732–737. doi: 10.1016/j.jpeds.2005.01.055

Sylvester, B. D., Standage, M., Ark, T. K., Sweet, S. N., Crocker, P. R., Zumbo, B. D., et al. (2014). Is variety a spice of (an active) life? Perceived variety, exercise behavior, and the mediating role of autonomous motivation. *J. Sport Exerc. Psychol.* 36, 516–527. doi: 10.1123/jsep.2014-0102

Telama, R. (2009). Tracking of physical activity from childhood to adulthood: a review. *Obes. Facts* 2, 187–195. doi: 10.1159/000222244

Tomkinson, G. R., and Olds, T. S. (2007). Secular changes in pediatric aerobic fitness test performance: the global picture. *Med. Sport Sci.* 50, 46–66. doi: 10.1159/000101075

Tomporowski, P. D., Lambourne, K., and Okumura, M. S. (2011). Physical activity interventions and children's mental function: an introduction and overview. *Prev. Med.* 52, 3–9. doi: 10.1016/j.ypmed.2011.01.028

Tomporowski, P. D., McCullick, B. A., and Horvat, M. (2010). *Role of Contextual Interference and Mental Engagement on Learning.* New York, NY: Nova Science Publishers.

Tomporowski, P. D., McCullick, B., Pendelton, D. M., and Pesce, C. (2015a). Exercise and children's cognition: the role of exercise characteristics and a place for metacognition. *J. Sport Health Sci.* 4, 47–55. doi: 10.1016/j.jshs.2014.09.003

Tomporowski, P. D., McCullick, B., and Pesce, C. (2015b). *Enhancing Children's Cognition with Physical Activity Games.* Champaign, IL: Human Kinetics.

Towse, J. N., and Mclachlan, A. (1999). An exploration of random generation among children. *Br. J. Dev. Psychol.* 17, 363–380. doi: 10.1348/026151099165348

Towse, J. N., and Neil, D. (1998). Analyzing human number generation behavior: a review of methods used and a computer program for describing performance. *Behav. Res. Methods Instrum. Comput.* 30, 583–591. doi: 10.3758/BF03209475

Tucker, P. (2008). The physical activity levels of preschool-aged children: a systematic review. *Early Child. Res. Q.* 23, 547–558. doi: 10.1016/j.ecresq.2008.08.005

United Nations (2013). *Committee on the Rights of the Child, General Comment No. 17. The Right of the Child to Rest, Leisure, Play, Recreational Activities, Cultural Life and the Arts (Article 31), CRC/C/GC/17, 18 March.* Available at: http://www2.ohchr.org/english/bodies/crc/docs/GC/CRC-C-GC-17_en.doc

van der Fels, I. M. J., Te Wierike, S. C. M., Hartman, E., Elferink-Gemser, M. T., Smith, J., and Visscher, C. (2015). The relationship between motor skills and cognitive skills in 4–16year old typically developing children: a systematic review. *J. Sci. Med. Sport* 18, 697–703. doi: 10.1016/j.jsams.2014.09.007

van der Niet, A. G., Smith, J., Oosterlaan, J., Scherder, E. J. A., Hartman, E., and Visscher, C. (2016). Effects of a cognitively demanding aerobic intervention during recess on children's physical fitness and executive functioning. *Pediatr. Exerc. Sci.* 28, 64–70. doi: 10.1123/pes.2015-0084

Vandorpe, B., Vandendriessche, J., Lefevre, J., Pio, J., Vaeyens, R., Matthys, S., et al. (2011). The KörperkoordinationsTest für Kinder: reference values and suitability for 6–12-year-old children in Flanders. *Scand. J. Med. Sci. Sports* 21, 378–388. doi: 10.1111/j.1600-0838.2009.01067.x

Vazou, S., Pesce, C., Lakes, K., and Smiley-Owen, A. (in press). More than one road leads to Rome: a narrative review and meta-analysis of physical activity intervention effects on children's cognition. *Int. J. Sport Exerc. Psychol.*

Vazou, S., and Smiley-Oyen, A. (2014). Moving and academic learning are not antagonists: acute effects on executive function and enjoyment. *J. Sport Exerc. Psychol.* 36, 474–485. doi: 10.1123/jsep.2014-0035

Veitch, J., Salmon, J., and Ball, K. (2009). The validity and reliability of an instrument to assess children's outdoor play in various locations. *J. Sci. Med. Sport* 12, 579–582. doi: 10.1016/j.jsams.2008.09.001

Venditti, S., Verdone, L., Pesce, C., Tocci, N., Caserta, M., and Ben-Soussan, T. D. (2015). Creating well-being: increased creativity and proNGF decrease following Quadrato Motor Training. *Biomed Res. Int.* 2015, 275062. doi: 10.1155/2015/275062

Verbestel, V., De Henauw, S., Bammann, K., Barba, G., Hadjigeorgiou, C., Eiben, G., et al. (2015). Are context-specific measures of parental-reported physical activity and sedentary behaviour associated with accelerometer data in 2-9-year-old European children? *Public Health Nutr.* 18, 860–868. doi: 10.1017/S136898001400086x

Wang, G. Y., Pereira, B., and Mota, J. (2005). Indoor physical education measured by heart rate monitor: a case study in Portugal. *J. Sports Med. Phys. Fitness* 45, 171–177.

Westendorp, M., Houwen, S., Hartman, E., Mombarg, R., Smith, J., and Visscher, C. (2014). Effect of a ball skill intervention on children's ball skills and cognitive functions. *Med. Sci. Sports Exerc.* 46, 414–422. doi: 10.1249/MSS.0b013e3182a532b3

Conflict of Interest Statement: The authors declare that the research was conducted in the absence of any commercial or financial relationships that could be construed as a potential conflict of interest.

Financial support from the Ferrero Group within the Kinder+Sport pillar of its Corporate Social Responsibility initiatives was received for the research project the submitted work belongs to. However, the funders had no role in the collection, analysis and interpretation of data; in the writing of the report; and in the decision to submit the article for publication.

Permissions

All chapters in this book were first published in MSTFRPSCD, by Frontiers Media SA; hereby published with permission under the Creative Commons Attribution License or equivalent. Every chapter published in this book has been scrutinized by our experts. Their significance has been extensively debated. The topics covered herein carry significant findings which will fuel the growth of the discipline. They may even be implemented as practical applications or may be referred to as a beginning point for another development.

The contributors of this book come from diverse backgrounds, making this book a truly international effort. This book will bring forth new frontiers with its revolutionizing research information and detailed analysis of the nascent developments around the world.

We would like to thank all the contributing authors for lending their expertise to make the book truly unique. They have played a crucial role in the development of this book. Without their invaluable contributions this book wouldn't have been possible. They have made vital efforts to compile up to date information on the varied aspects of this subject to make this book a valuable addition to the collection of many professionals and students.

This book was conceptualized with the vision of imparting up-to-date information and advanced data in this field. To ensure the same, a matchless editorial board was set up. Every individual on the board went through rigorous rounds of assessment to prove their worth. After which they invested a large part of their time researching and compiling the most relevant data for our readers.

The editorial board has been involved in producing this book since its inception. They have spent rigorous hours researching and exploring the diverse topics which have resulted in the successful publishing of this book. They have passed on their knowledge of decades through this book. To expedite this challenging task, the publisher supported the team at every step. A small team of assistant editors was also appointed to further simplify the editing procedure and attain best results for the readers.

Apart from the editorial board, the designing team has also invested a significant amount of their time in understanding the subject and creating the most relevant covers. They scrutinized every image to scout for the most suitable representation of the subject and create an appropriate cover for the book.

The publishing team has been an ardent support to the editorial, designing and production team. Their endless efforts to recruit the best for this project, has resulted in the accomplishment of this book. They are a veteran in the field of academics and their pool of knowledge is as vast as their experience in printing. Their expertise and guidance has proved useful at every step. Their uncompromising quality standards have made this book an exceptional effort. Their encouragement from time to time has been an inspiration for everyone.

The publisher and the editorial board hope that this book will prove to be a valuable piece of knowledge for researchers, students, practitioners and scholars across the globe.

List of Contributors

Giulia Piallini, Stefania Brunoro, Chiara Fenocchio, Costanza Marini and Alessandra Simonelli
Department of Developmental Psychology and Socialization, University of Padua, Padua, Italy

Struttura Complessa Tutela
Salute Bambini Adolescenti Donne Famiglia, Azienda Sanitaria Universitaria Integrata di Trieste, Trieste, Italy

George F. Michel and Julie M. Campbell
Department of Psychology, The University of North Carolina at Greensboro, Greensboro, NC, USA

Emily C. Marcinowski
Department of Physical Therapy, Virginia Commonwealth University, Richmond, VA, USA

Eliza L. Nelson
Department of Psychology, Florida International University, Miami, FL, USA

Iryna Babik
Department of Physical Therapy, University of Delaware, Newark, NJ, USA

Sandy L. Gonzalez, Bethany C. Reeb-Sutherland and Eliza L. Nelson
Department of Psychology, Florida International University, Miami, FL, USA

Christa Einspieler
Research Unit iDN - interdisciplinary Developmental Neuroscience, Institute of Physiology, Center for Physiological Medicine, Medical University of Graz, Graz, Austria

Arend F. Bos
Division of Neonatology, Department of Pediatrics, Beatrix Children's Hospital, University Medical Center, University of Groningen, Groningen, Netherlands

Melissa E. Libertus
Department of Psychology, Learning Research Development Center, University of Pittsburgh, Pittsburgh, PA, USA

Peter B. Marschik
Research Unit iDN - interdisciplinary Developmental Neuroscience, Institute of Physiology, Center for Physiological Medicine, Medical University of Graz, Austria
Center of Neurodevelopmental Disorders, Department of Women's Children's Health, Karolinska Institutet, Stockholm, Sweden

Markus Krüger
Entwicklungspsychologie und Pädagogische Psychologie, Institut für Psychologie, Ernst-Moritz-Arndt-Universität Greifswald, Greifswald, Germany

Georg Jahn
Institute for Multimedia and Interactive Systems, University of Lübeck, Lübeck, Germany

Eric A. Walle
Psychological Sciences, University of California, Merced, Merced, CA, USA

Annarita Contaldo, Antonio Narzisi and Filippo Muratori
Department of Developmental Neuroscience, IRCCS Stella Maris, Calambrone, Italy

Costanza Colombi
Department of Psychiatry, University of Michigan, Ann Arbor, MI, USA

Vincent O. Mancini, Daniela Rigoli, Lynne D. Roberts and Jan P. Piek
School of Psychology and Speech Pathology, Curtin University, Perth, WA, Australia

John Cairney
Department of Family Medicine, McMaster University, Hamilton, ON, Canada

Ora Oudgenoeg-Paz, M(Chiel). J. M. Volman and Paul P. M. Leseman
Department of Child, Family and Education Studies, Utrecht University, Utrecht, Netherlands

Sarah E. Wiesen and Amy Work Needham
Infant Learning Lab, Department of Psychology and Human Development, Peabody College, Vanderbilt University, Nashville, TN, USA

Rachel M. Watkins
Auditory Development Lab, Department of Hearing and Speech Sciences, Vanderbilt University, Nashville, TN, USA

Tanya St. John and Annette M. Estes
Speech and Hearing Sciences, University of Washington, Seattle, WA, USA
UW Autism Center, Center on Human Development and Disability, University of Washington, Seattle, WA, USA

Stephen R. Dager
UW Autism Center, Center on Human Development and Disability, University of Washington, Seattle, WA, USA
Department of Radiology, University of Washington, Seattle, WA, USA

Penelope Kostopoulos
McConnell Brain Imaging Centre, Montreal Neurological Institute, Montreal, CA, USA

Jason J. Wolff
Department of Educational Psychology, University of Minnesota, Minneapolis, MN, USA

Juhi Pandey, Sarah J. Paterson and Robert T. Schultz
Department of Pediatrics, The Center for Autism Research, Children's Hospital of Philadelphia, University of Pennsylvania, Philadelphia, PA, USA

Jed T. Elison
Institute of Child Development, University of Minnesota, Minneapolis, MN, USA

Kelly Botteron
Department of Psychiatry, Washington University School of Medicine, Saint Louis, MO, USA

Heather Hazlett and Joseph Piven
Carolina Institute for Developmental Disabilities, Chapel Hill, NC, USA
Department of Psychiatry, University of North Carolina, Chapel Hill, NC

Priska Hagmann-von Arx, Olivia Manicolo and Alexander Grob
Department of Psychology, University of Basel, Basel, Switzerland

Sakari Lemola
Department of Psychology, University of Warwick, Coventry, UK

Nicola J. Pitchford, Chiara Papini, Laura A. Outhwaite and Anthea Gulliford
School of Psychology, University of Nottingham, Nottingham, UK

Andrea Frick
Department of Psychology, University of Bern, Bern, Switzerland
Department of Psychology, University of Fribourg, Fribourg, Switzerland

Wenke Möhring
Department of Psychology, University of Fribourg, Fribourg, Switzerland
Department of Psychology, Temple University, Philadelphia, PA, USA

Lorcan Kenny
Centre for Research in Autism and Education (CRAE), University College London, Institute of Education, London, UK
School of Psychology, The University of Nottingham, Nottingham, UK

Elisabeth Hill
Department of Psychology, Goldsmiths, University of London, London, UK

Antonia F. de C. Hamilton
School of Psychology, The University of Nottingham, Nottingham, UK
Institute of Cognitive Neuroscience, University College London, London, UK

Lisette De Jonge-Hoekstra, Paul Van Geert and Ralf F. A. Cox
Department of Developmental Psychology, Behavioural and Social Sciences, University of Groningen, Groningen, Netherlands

Steffie Van der Steen
Department of Special Needs Education and Youth Care, Behavioural and Social Sciences, University of Groningen, Groningen, Netherlands

Valentina Focaroli and Flavio Keller
Laboratory of Developmental Neuroscience, Università Campus Biomedico di Roma, Rome, Italy

Fabrizio Taffoni
Laboratory of Biomedical Robotics and Biomicrosystems, Università Campus Biomedico di Roma, Rome, Italy

Shelby M. Parsons and Jana M. Iverson
Department of Psychology, University of Pittsburgh, Pittsburgh, PA, USA

Rebecca J. Landa and Joshua L. Haworth
Center for Autism and Related Disorders, Kennedy Krieger Institute, Baltimore, MD, USA
Department of Psychiatry and Behavioral Sciences, Johns Hopkins University School of Medicine, Baltimore, MD, USA

Mary Beth Nebel
Center for Neurodevelopmental and Imaging Research, Kennedy Krieger Institute, Baltimore, MD, USA
Department of Neurology, Johns Hopkins University School of Medicine, Baltimore, MD, USA

Shannon Ross-Sheehy
Department of Psycology, University Tennessee Knoxville, TN, USA

Sammy Perone
Institute of Child Development, University of Minnesota, Minopoli, MN, USA

Shaun P. Vecera
Department of Psychology, The University of Lowa, Lowa City, IA, USA

Lisa M. Oakes
Department of Psychology, University of California, Davis, Davis, CA, USA

Brody Heritage
School of Psychology and Exercise Science, Murdoch University, Perth, WA, Australia

Caterina Pesce, Ilaria Masci and Rosalba Marchetti
Department of Movement, Human and Health Sciences, Italian University Sport and Movement "Foro Italico", Rome, Italy

Spyridoula Vazou
Department of Kinesiology, Iowa State University, Ames, IA, USA

Marina Biancotto and Stefania Zoia
Department of Developmental Psychology and Socialization, University of Padua, Padua, Italy
Struttura Complessa Tutela Salute Bambini Adolescenti Donne Famiglia, Azienda Sanitaria Universitaria Integrata di Trieste, Trieste, Italy

Phillip D. Tomporowski
Department of Kinesiology, University of Georgia, Athens, GA, USA

Arja Sääkslahti
Department Of Sport Sciences, University Of Jyväskylä, Jyväskylä, Finland

Index

CPSIA information can be obtained
at www.ICGtesting.com
Printed in the USA
LVHW060853030122
707669LV00002B/116

9 781639 891030